Macro-Modelling for the Eleventh Five Year Plan of India

Macro-Modelling for the Eleventh Five Year Plan of India

PLANNING COMMISSION
GOVERNMENT OF INDIA
NEW DELHI

Edited by
Kirit S. Parikh

Published by

ACADEMIC FOUNDATION
NEW DELHI

First Published in 2009 by
Academic Foundation
4772-73 / 23 Bharat Ram Road, (23 Ansari Road), Darya Ganj, New Delhi - 110 002 (India).
Phones : 23245001 / 02 / 03 / 04. Fax : +91-11-23245005. E-mail : academic@vsnl.com
www.academicfoundation.com

on behalf of

Planning Commission,
Government of India,
New Delhi.

Macro-Modelling for the Eleventh Five Year Plan of India
ISBN 13: 9788171887736
ISBN 10: 8171887732

Designed and typeset by Italics India, New Delhi
Printed and bound in India.

Contents

List of Tables and Figures

Tables

Figures

एम. एस. आहलुवालिया
MONTEK SINGH AHLUWALIA

उपाध्यक्ष
योजना आयोग
भारत
DEPUTY CHAIRMAN
PLANNING COMMISSION
INDIA

Foreword

Model Building has been an integral part of the Plan formulation in India ever since the earlier Five Year Plans when the works of Sir Roy Harrod and Evsey Domar and the parallel work of Feldman and Mahalanobis were used to determine the growth rate that could be achieved in the Plan given the savings rate and investment rates in the economy and the incremental capital output ratio.

Over the years, the models used in formulating the Plan attained greater degree of sophistication and disaggregation and a large number of models were developed, both within the Planning Commission and outside, that were used for fixing growth rates at aggregate and sectoral levels, as well as investment requirement and its sectoral allocations. The principal constraints that the Indian economy faced at that time were 'savings constraints' and 'foreign exchange constraints' and nearly all the plan models incorporated these.

The transition of the Indian economy from a 'planned' economy to a more 'market-based economy', and one more integrated with the rest of the world, has seen the role of planning undergoing a change both in terms of priorities as well as instruments. With the growth of a fairly sophisticated private sector with demonstrable entrepreneurial capacity it is felt that government need not try to produce products that can be produced just as well by the market, instead it should devote its scarce resources to providing public goods including especially educational and health services and programmes for social inclusion. Infrastructure development is another priority area since lack of infrastructure is a crucial constraint on the growth of the economy. The role of the government in infrastructure development is obviously critical. The shift to a more open market economy has also created the need to expand modelling capacity to reflect the features of openness including the macroeconomic implications of openness.

For all these reasons, the modelling framework needed to undergo a change from being more deterministic and disaggregated to bring more aggregative and indicative.

During the Eleventh Plan, the Planning Commission decided to rely not only on the traditional 'in-house' model but also to work with models built by various research institutes engaged in macro-modelling on what they have to say on the prospects of the Eleventh Plan. Dr. Kirit S. Parikh, Member in-charge of Perspective Planning has enlisted the support of some of the best research institutions in the country in the business of macro-modelling *viz.*, the

योजना भवन, संसद मार्ग, नई दिल्ली – 110001 दूरभाष : 23096677, 23096688 फैक्स : 23096699
Yojana Bhawan, Parliament Street, New Delhi : 110001 Phones: 23096677, 23096688 Fax : 23096699
E-mail : dch@yojana.nic.in

National Council for Applied Economic Research (NCAER), New Delhi, Institute of Economic Growth (IEG), Delhi, Indira Gandhi Institute of Development Research (IGIDR), Mumbai and Indian Statistical Institute (ISI), Bangalore.

This volume contains essays by the relevant model builders reporting on the various models used in the course of formulating the Eleventh Plan. An overview paper by Dr. Parikh is presented as Chapter 1.

I hope that publication of this book will bring greater awareness of the issues faced and the approaches taken by the Planning Commission.

(Montek Singh Ahluwalia)

डॉ. किरीट एस. परीख
Dr. Kirit Parikh

सदस्य
योजना आयोग
योजना भवन
नई दिल्ली–110 001
MEMBER
PLANNING COMMISSION
YOJANA BHAWAN
NEW DELHI-110 001

Preface

The emphasis of planning has changed from detailed sectoral allocation to policies and strategies of growth that respect macroeconomic balances and stability.

Any policy analysis or exploration of alternative strategies requires answering an 'if... then...' question. This is answered using a model, whether it is a mental model or a formal one. While mental models formed from experience can integrate intuitively many vaguely defined objectives and constraints, formal models have the advantage of consistency and transparency of assumptions. They also help in improving one's mental model.

Formal models provide insight into inter-relationships between different actors and sectors of the economy. Based on such models it is often possible to creatively design scenarios that can throw light on a variety of issues. Planning Commission has always used models to guide its work.

The Planning Commission during the Eleventh Plan made a significant departure from the past practice. Instead of relying on a single in-house model it was decided to request some of the reputed institutes in the field of economic model building to carry out modelling exercises that could be used not only for the purpose of plan formulation but also could answer some of the questions that arise from time to time such as the impact of rising oil prices on the performance of Indian economy, the impact of global meltdown, etc. (please see Chapter 1 for details). Periodic meetings were held where the results from different models on the same issues were discussed.

The objectives behind outsourcing and setting up of a "modelling forum" were many: (i) A model necessarily is based on certain assumptions and perceptions, which may not accurately reflect reality. Reliance on a number of different models brings a variety of perspectives on the issue to get a better understanding. (ii) To stimulate modelling activities and capacity building in academic and research institutions as the modellers would feel involved in policy formulation. (iii) A set of competing models would provide incentives to update and innovate to keep the models state-of-the-art. The institutes that have worked in close coordination with the Planning Commission are the National Council of Applied Economic Research (NCAER), New Delhi, Institute of Economic Growth (IEG), Delhi, Indira Gandhi Institute of Development Research (IGIDR), Mumbai and Indian Statistical Institute (ISI), Bangalore. The contribution of these institutes are given in Chapter 2 to 6 and the salient features of each of these models and results of some of the issues are discussed in Chapter 1.

दूरभाष :+91-11-23096568 टेलीफैक्स : +91-11-23096569
Telephone: +91-11-23096568 Telefax : +91-11-23096568, e-mail: kirit.parikh@nic.in

A series of meetings were held in the Planning Commission between the authors of various Chapters, Members of Planning Commission and number of experts. These discussions helped sharpen the analysis.

A number of persons have contributed to make this venture a success. First of all, I would like to thank Deputy Chairman of Planning Commission, Shri Montek Singh Ahluwalia, who constantly enquired about the progress throughout the period when the work was going on and took active part in the discussions of the results. I also thank various Members of the Planning Commission, as well as other experts who participated in the discussions. Special thanks are due to the participating authors Sabyasachi Kar and Basanta K. Pradhan of Institute of Economic Growth (IEG), Delhi, Shashank Bhide and Purna Chandra Parida of National Council of Applied Economic Research (NCAER), New Delhi, A. Ganesh Kumar of Indira Gandhi Institute of Development Research (IGIDR), Mumbai, Manoj Panda of Centre for Economic and Social Studies (CESS), Hyderabad, N.S.S. Narayana of the Indian Statistical Institute (ISI), Bangalore and Probal P. Ghosh of Integrated Research for Action and Development (IRADe), New Delhi. I would also like to thank the officers of the Perspective Planning Division of Planning Commission not only for contributing Chapters to this volume but also coordinating the work. I would like to record my appreciation of the work done by Shri Sanjay Vasnik who typed the manuscript and carried out umpteen revisions in them from time to time without showing a sign of fatigue.

Last but not the least I would like to thank our publishers Academic Foundation for bringing out this document in time.

(Kirit S. Parikh)

CHAPTER 1

Background, Approach and Overview

Kirit S. Parikh

1.1 Introduction: The Changed Context and Role of Planning

Planning was introduced in the country because of a number of reasons:

(i) In a country with large disparity of incomes and wealth, a competitive market would not lead to a socially desirable outcome.

(ii) Scarce investible resource and foreign exchange should be directed in socially desirable activities, which required government activism.

(iii) Development of infrastructure involved long gestation and required technology and large investments which the private sector was not capable of undertaking.

(iv) The diversity of the country required a regionally balanced development.

Once the need for activist government policies was recognised looking at the global experience of the previous 30 years we decided in 1950 to follow a path of centrally planned mixed economy.

(i) The Soviet Union had progressed from a peasant economy to an industrialised global power in 30 years using central planning.

(ii) During the years of Second World War both the United States and United Kingdom had used price controls effectively.

(iii) The world trade had hardly grown over 30 years and an export-led growth seemed unlikely.

Recognising that India had millions of small farmers and a large number of entrepreneurs engaged in small businesses, a mixed economy model was chosen keeping agriculture in private hands and giving scope for private industrial enterprises albeit under government direction.

The specific instruments of policy used were as follows:

(i) Given the scarcity of investible goods and export pessimism (as exports were considered unlikely to grow without loss of terms of trade for a large country) investments and foreign exchange had to be allocated to different uses.

(ii) A balanced growth was required as trade could not be relied upon to balance sectoral mismatches. This required that sectoral targets were set in a balanced manner by the Planning Commission and investment and import allocations had to be consistent with the targets.

(iii) To ensure regional balance, location of industries and infrastructure had to be controlled.

(iv) To prevent further worsening of disparities of income and wealth and to redress it, role of public sector had to grow and reach commanding heights.

(v) To promote domestic industrial development, high level of protection was provided against imports.

This broad strategy delivered on many counts, steady economic growth was realised, poverty was reduced, a diversified industrial economy developed, growth was regionally more balanced than it would have been otherwise. All this was attained in a democracy with adult franchise in a country with many languages, religions, castes and creeds. In a sense this was a remarkable historically unprecedented achievement.

Yet there were problems. Our growth paled in comparison with what was achieved by many East Asian countries—including a large country like China. Our industry, though diversified, was high cost and not always internationally competitive. Our public sector generated much less surplus than was anticipated, gave a very low rate of return and many of them made losses. World trade had boomed and our export pessimism proved to be uncalled for. The resilience of the economy to withstand shocks was insufficient.

This led to the reforms which were given a big thrust in 1991. At one go, industries were freed to decide what to produce, how much to produce, where to produce and how to (using what technology) produce, all of which were controlled till then. Import quotas were done away with and tariffs reduced which have over the years come down almost to international levels.

Given this liberalisation and deregulation what is the need and role of planning?

As long as disparities in income, endowments and wealth persist, access to public goods and services is uneven and infrastructure paucity is there, we need active government policy. We need planning.

We don't need to set industry specific targets. We don't need to worry about consistency and sectoral balance at least for the production of tradable goods as trade can take care of surpluses and shortages. However, non-tradables such as infrastructure and services need to be planned. Also, provision of public goods and services and various poverty programmes have to be planned for one needs to decide how much to spend on these different activities.

We also need to ensure macro balance and consistency among growth targets, savings, investment, current account balance and public expenditures and incomes. Policies required to obtain this consistency have to be practical. Thus, compared to old fashioned planning that concentrated on allocative efficiency across different sectors, planning today is much more concerned with programmes, macro consistency and policy to realise the goals.

1.2 The Broad Strategy of the 11th Plan

In the last two years of the 10th Plan period, Indian economy accelerated and GDP at factor cost grew at 9.5 per cent and 9.8 per cent. A rapid growth for the 11th Plan seemed realisable. Also, it was clear that the benefits of growth did not reach all segments of the society and all regions in any equitable manner. An inclusive growth that reduces disparities and bridges divides across classes and regions is needed and is of course desirable, but rapid growth makes it attainable too. Thus, the 11th Plan's goal is to have "Faster and More Inclusive Growth".

The Indian economy is much more open today and is globalised to an extent unimagined in the 1980s. India's exports have been growing rapidly and foreign exchange reserves have exceeded all our expectations and were $199.2 billion in March 2007 and $309.7 billion in March 2008, amounting to 15 months of imports. A comfortable situation of foreign exchange reserves provides a cushion against shocks from the international market, makes the economy more resilient and thus faster growth can be attempted without a fear of falling flat on one's face. Nonetheless an open economy has to be more concerned about the global situation. Exports get affected by growth of the global economy. While transient fluctuations can be dealt with using the reserves, long-term trends have to be factored in our strategy of development.

Oil prices pose a particular threat. We must depend on imports of oil for 70 per cent of our consumption. Oil prices have been extremely volatile and there is a growing concern that oil is running out, that global demand for oil is growing rapidly and that oil production will reach its peak in the next few years.

The target of faster growth should be attained in a sustainable manner. For growth that maintains its momentum and is stable, price stability has to be maintained. This calls for fiscal responsibility. Keeping this in mind the Parliament has passed the Fiscal Responsibility and Budget Management (FRBM) Act. The 11th Plan strategy has to respect the requirements of this act.

1.3 The Analytical Questions

For deciding specific targets for the 11th Plan we need to answer a number of questions covering different aspects:

(a) *Macroeconomic Consistency*: What growth rate is possible? What are the macroeconomic parameters of alternate growth paths? What are the savings and investment requirements? How much public saving is needed? What would be the broad sectoral composition? What would be trade levels and current account deficit? What are the implication of FRBM targets?

(b) *Oil Price Increase*: Seventy per cent of our oil consumption is based on imports. Thus, global oil price can have a significant impact on our economy. How does higher oil price affect growth and inflation?

(c) *Impact of Global Growth*: The economies of industrialised countries are expected to slow down. Now that Indian economy has become globalised it would be affected by this slow down. These concerns have become more acute in the first quarter of 2008 due to the sub-prime mortgage crisis in the world. It will lower our exports and that would affect growth. What would be the extent of such impacts? How does export growth affect growth of GDP?

(d) *Resources for Inclusive Growth*: Inclusive growth would require many specific programmes requiring substantial resources. Are needed resources available? What would be the impact on growth of these programmes? How would sectoral demands be affected? What would be the impact of infrastructure development, particularly in rural areas, on productivity, efficiency and growth?

1.4 The Approach

A variety of issues and questions needs to be explored. It is difficult to construct one model that can address all these issues equally satisfactorily. Different models can address different issues better. Also, model results depend on its structure, parameters and certain inevitable compromises. While the structure and parameter should describe the economy as it exists, it is often not easy to do so. Thus, a model involves compromises and the art of modelling lies in making simplifications that least affect the results of the issues of primary focus of the modeller.

We have, therefore, used a set of models developed by different modelling groups to address the same issues. This way we can be more confident if a set of models give similar results and lead to the same conclusion.

Using models by different groups of researches has another advantage. In this process, Planning Commission encourages development of independent policy analytical capability in the country.

The models used span the range of macro-modelling approaches used in the literature. A macro-model is based on an appropriate theoretical framework. The particular paradigm used, whether Walrasian, Keynesian or structuralist, depends on the modeller's choice. The equations represent the structure of the economy as also a number of behavioural equations based on established economic theory.

The paradigms that have guided modellers can be broadly categorised as follows:

(a) *Input-Output*: The Leontief input-output framework represents production of a good using inputs in fixed proportion. This helps in ensuring consistency across different sectors of the economy. Its further extension into linear programming multi-sectoral inter-temporal models into a typical planning model can guide in allocation across sectors, choice of techniques and even decisions on domestic production *versus* imports. Indian Planning models have used this extensively as described in Appendix 1.

(b) *Walrasian*: Named after Leon Walras, this too represents an economy by flows of commodities and financial flows and accounting identities that balance them. In the more modern version where these flows are balanced at the level of economic agents who are characterised by their optimising behaviour (e.g., producers maximise profit, consumers maximise utility subject to various constraints, etc.) we get a general equilibrium model.

(c) *Neoclassical*: Supply and demand react to prices and prices balance them. This applies to factors of production (labour, capital, land etc.) as well. There is always full employment at prevailing wage rate, which can be very low, no one who is willing to work is unemployed.

(d) *Keynesian*: Keynes recognised that there are wage rigidities, liquidity preference and consumption behaviour that can restrict aggregate demand to a level such that full capacity utilisation does not take place. An underemployed equilibrium or a trap, may result.

(e) *Structuralist*: This argues that there are more imperfections and rigidities than just wage rigidity. Markets are imperfect, countries face savings and foreign exchange constraints, the economy may not be fully monetised and quantitative adjustments may dominate over price adjustments.

(f) *Vector Auto Regression/Error Correction*: Promoted by Christopher Sims, Clive Granger, Robert Engle, etc., this approach opposes specifications with an underlying structural paradigm. It argues that one should let "data speak for themselves" and uses a framework in which all variables depend on lagged values of all variables. Simultaneous equations, estimation of the parameters from time series data, define the appropriate model which can be used for forecasting or analysis of responses to changes in different variables.

(g) *New Neoclassical*: Recent views emphasise microeconomic foundation of macroeconomics as also the importance of information, expectations and contracts. Macro-models today are difficult to classify in such neat boxes. They are much more eclectic and embody aspects of different paradigms. Thus, structural rigidities and imperfections are introduced in many models. Of course one would like to minimise them and let them emerge out of optimising behaviour of the agents.

(h) *Dynamic Stochastic General Equilibrium*: One important new front in macroeconomic modelling is DSGE (Dynamic Stochastic General Equilibrium). These models are macroeconomic (in the sense that general equilibrium is solved out). They contain forward looking and optimising economic agents. They are immune to the Lucas critique in that the parameters are deep, optimisation takes place, so that the models can be used for policy analysis. Important new innovations in econometrics have come together to make it possible to estimate the models through Bayesian MLE (Maximum Likelihood Estimators), combining parameter values from micro studies with the likelihood function that follows from the DSGE model. The most important applications of these models lie in analysing fiscal policy rules and monetary policy rules. There is relatively little work on DSGE models for emerging markets. Unfortunately, no DSGE model for India is available at present.

The models used span this broad range of approaches.

1.5 The Models

Six different models with different analytical approaches have been used. Their approaches and analytical orientations are briefly described below:

1.5.1 Perspective Planning Division's In-house Model (PPDIHM)

This model developed by the Perspective Planning Division of the Planning Commission is a macro-consistency planning model. It was updated by Arvinder S. Sachdeva and Probal P. Ghosh. Given certain growth objectives it works out the implications for various macro-variables. Thus, once we prescribe growth rates for GDP and agriculture it works out required growth rates of other sectors as well as needed savings, investment, etc. It is essentially a set of accounting equations. The parameters of the equations are econometrically estimated simultaneously for all equations from time series data.

1.5.2 A VAR/VEC Model from ISI, Bangalore

This model developed by N.S.S. Narayana and Probal P. Ghosh uses Vector Auto Regression/Vector Error Correction (VAR/VEC) procedure to estimate a system of equations.

The innovation is that the economy is split into different subsystems (agriculture, industry and services) and separate VAR/VEC models are estimated for each subsystem which are then pulled together to form a simulation model for the economy. This gets around the problem of inadequate degrees of freedom in estimation of the system at one go. The model also estimates the effects on private final consumption expenditure and household savings. Several macro variables such as real money supply, budget deficit, domestic oil price index, trade performance etc., besides rainfall index are incorporated into the model—thus facilitating policy analyses.

1.5.3 A General Equilibrium Model from IGIDR, Mumbai

This general equilibrium model has been developed by A. Ganesh Kumar and Manoj Panda. It is a model of an open economy with a large number of sectors and has endogenous income distribution. It is built around the social accounting matrix (SAM) of 2003-04. In each tradable sector, domestic goods and foreign goods are treated as imperfect substitutes of each other. It has the flexibility to permit market clearing or administratively fixed prices in any sector, and has a rich mix of policies which permits multiple price layers. It allows for segmented labour markets that cause wage rates to vary for different labour types. Income distribution across households depends upon factor prices and the endogenous levels of factor employment. A novel feature of this model is that it incorporates the National Rural Employment Guarantee Scheme (NREGS).

The model determines relative prices but does not, however, have money as a store of value. It is a static one, particularly suitable for assessing questions of allocative efficiency and distributive impacts of some of the policies for inclusive growth such as the NREGS.

1.5.4 An Econometric Model from IEG, Delhi

This is an econometric model with an eclectic approach developed by B.B. Bhattacharya and Sabyasachi Kar. It is Keynesian in outlook, but also combines neoclassical and structuralist elements. It has four blocks, production, fiscal, monetary and external. Equations are estimated from time series data often with lagged dependant variables. This facilitates characterisation of dynamic aspects such as adaptive expectations. The use of an extended time series data for the estimation of the model allows it to capture the long run behaviour of the economy. Simultaneously, keeping in mind the current changes in the economy following the reforms, the model explicitly incorporates a market-oriented structure for the post-reform period. The strength of the model is that it has specifically incorporated the major channels through which domestic and global shocks have an impact on the Indian economy. This enables the model to analyse the effect of events like a hike in the international petroleum prices, global trade slowdown or a rainfall shortfall on the growth rate, the inflation rate and the macro balances of the economy.

1.5.5 Macro-Econometric Model of NCAER, New Delhi

It is a system of equations that describe production, demand and pricing of major sectors of the economy inter-linked with each other mainly through relative prices—under a common fiscal, monetary and trade environment. The strength of the model is explicit incorporation of sources of productivity growth. Thus, the impact of infrastructure development, faster growth of agriculture and rising FDI can be assessed. The model has endogenously determined interest rate but an exogenously specified exchange rate. Model is estimated using Ordinary Least Squares (OLS) correcting for autocorrelation whenever needed.

Detailed descriptions with full technical details are given in subsequent chapters. However, this brief description have hinted at the specific strengths of different models. Scenarios have been developed by each of these models addressing the questions posed in Section 1.3. In the following sections we compare the results of the scenarios to get insights on the questions posed.

1.6 Macroeconomic Consistency

The first set of questions relate to macroeconomic dimension of the Plan. What growth rates are feasible and what do they imply for various other macroeconomic variables?

Table 1.1 summarises the results of the scenarios that come closest to 9 per cent growth rate of GDP. The 11th Plan targets also shown in Table 1.1 are within the range of projections made by these models. Also, when compared to the actuals of 2006-07, they look quite attainable. For example, the average savings ratio in the 11th Plan is targeted to be 34.8 per cent, which was already achieved during 2006-07. Similarly the investment ratio during 2006-07 was 35.9 per cent and required for the 11th Plan targets is 36.7 per cent. A growth rate of private final consumption expenditure of 7 per cent or more is indicated by all the models. The targeted export growth rate is 20 per cent compared to the 2006-07 growth rates of 21.8 per cent. As can be seen from Table 1.1, the expected growth rate in the 11th Plan varies from 8.41 per cent to 9.34 per cent. Similar variations are there in the sectoral growth rates. The variations in the

Table 1.1: Macroeconomic Projections for the 11th Plan Period 2007-08 to 2011-12

Sl. No.	Variables	2006-07	PPD	ISI	IEG#	NCAER#	Range	11th Plan Targets
1.	Total GDP Growth Rate	9.8	9.0	9.34	8.41	9.0	8.41 - 9.34	9.0
2.	Agriculture Growth Rate	4.0	4.0	3.05	3.41	2.7	2.4 – 4.0	4.0
3.	Industry Growth Rate	11.0	10-11	10.94	9.35	9.1	9.2 – 11	10-11
4.	Services Growth Rate	11.2	9-11	10.41	9.5	10.8	9 – 11	9-11
5.	Private Final Consumption Expenditure (PFCE) Growth Rate	6.4	7.1	7.0	9.3	8.0	7.0 to 9.3	7.1
6.	Savings Ratio	34.8	34.8	31.9	34.03	27.1	27.1 – 34.8	34.8
7.	Private Savings Ratio	31.6	30.3	30.95[+]			30.3	30.3
8.	Public Savings Ratio	3.2	4.5				4.5	4.5
9.	Investment Ratio	35.9	36.7	32.9	35.68	29.8	29.8 – 36.7	36.7
10.	Private Investment Ratio	28.1	28.7	NA	29.68	NA	28.7 – 29.68	28.7
11.	Public Investment Ratio	7.8	8.0	NA	6.0	NA	6.0 – 8.0	8.0
12.	Private Consumption Ratio					57.2		
13.	Public Borrowings		3.5	NA	NA	NA	3.5	
14.	Fiscal Deficit	6.2	6	0.5*	6.31	2.1	0.5 – 6.6	6
15.	Exports Growth rate	21.8	20	15.1	21.0	21.9	14.7– 21.0	20
16.	Imports Growth rate	21.8	23	13.50	25.18	23.3	13.5 – 25.18	23
17.	Current Account Balance	1.1	-1.9	-1.0	-1.65	-2.7	-2.7 to -1.0	-1.9
	Crude Oil prices		2006=67 $/barell & 10% increase each year	US $ 27 per bbl in 2003	2006=67$/barell 2007=80$/barell 2008=90$barell 60$ thereafter	82$ in 2007-08 and continues at that level		

Note: Rates are in per cent per year and ratios are ratio to GDP.

Savings rate calculated as investment rate + current account balance.

* Figure refers to average Budget deficit for the period 2007-08 to 2011-12 and for Centre only.

[+] 100 (household savings + corporate savings)/GDPMP, where GDPMP = GDP at market prices=1.09 (GDP at factor prices).

growth rate of agriculture sector are noteworthy. The investment ratio of NCAER is on the lower side, mainly because of the productivity effects of infrastructure developed and FDI inflows.

1.7 Oil Price Volatility

Price of crude oil has been very volatile in the international market. Since imports meet more than 70 per cent of our domestic needs, scenarios were developed to assess the impact of change in crude oil price on the economy.

Table 1.3 summarises these results. The oil price assumptions vary from model to model and these are described in Table 1.2. The numbers in Table 1.3 show the change from the value in the corresponding reference run.

The degree of price shock varies from model to model. In the ISI model the impact is mainly captured by domestic price of petroleum products, wherein domestic petroleum product price index increases gradually and doubles by 2011-12, a reduction in GDP growth rate of 0.92 percentage points is indicated (Scenario 16 and Table 3.25 of Chapter 3). The NCAER model scenario with a smaller price increase (from $82 to $100) shows a GDP decrease of only 0.2 percentage points, whereas IEG scenario with a higher price increase shows a decrease in GDP growth rate of 0.52 percentage point.

The impact of oil price shock is also examined by the static general equilibrium model of IGIDR. Though the model is calibrated to the year 2003-04, one can assess the impact of oil price change by comparing the results with that of a reference run. When crude price increases by 70 per cent and petroleum products prices increase by 50 per cent and only 10 per cent of price increase is passed through to consumers, the GDP falls by 0.4 percentage points and investment falls by 10.9 per cent. This implies that GDP growth rate in the subsequent year would fall by around 1 percentage point.

The models thus show an adverse impact of oil price increase on GDP growth rate of around 0.5 to 1 percentage point and private final consumption expenditure of 0 to 1 per cent related to the decrease in the GDP growth rate.

The impact of policy measures to counter the effect of oil price increase is also shown by the scenarios described in the chapters of different models. When public investment rate is increased by 0.4 percentage points, the IEG model shows that the decrease in growth rate due to oil price rise is almost fully neutralised. The NCAER model has explored alternative pricing and financing mechanisms which show that partial pass through of price along with oil bonds is the preferred strategy as it has least loss of GDP growth rate.

The ISI model shows that even with higher oil prices, with increase in exports and an increase in real budget deficit (Scenario 18 and Table 3.25 of Chapter 3), the GDP growth rate can even exceed that of reference run by 1 percentage point with increase in growth rates of agriculture and industry by 2.1 and 3.9 percentage points respectively over the reference run.

Table 1.2: Oil Price Shock Scenarios Assumptions

Sl. No.	Alternative Scenarios	ISI	IEG	NCAER
1.	Reference Run	US $30.8 per barrel. Domestic price remains same as in 2002-03.	US $67 in 2006-07 for Indian Basket.	Base price of 2002-06 (A little over $42/bbl) and price of US $82 per bbl for 2007-08.
2.	Oil Price Shock	Domestic prices actual up to 2005-06, and gradual increases every year: by 5 per cent in 2006-07 upto 20 per cent in 2011-12 becoming twice the 2005-06 value.	US $67 in 2006-07, $ 80 in 2007-08, $100 in 2008-09 and remains same thereafter.	US $100 in 2007-08 to 2011-12 for Indian Basket.

Table 1.3: Impact of Oil Price Shock on Macroeconometric Indicators 2007-08 to 2011-12

Sl. No	Alternative Scenarios	ISI	IEG	NCAER
1.	Total GDP Growth Rate	-0.92	-0.52	-0.2
2.	Agriculture Growth Rate	-0.75	-0.27	
3.	Industry Growth Rate	-1.04	-0.31	
4.	Services Growth Rate	-0.92	-0.70	
5.	PFCE Growth Rate	-1.0	-0.15	0.0
6.	Savings Ratio		-1.15	-0.5
7.	Investment Ratio		3.82	-0.7
8.	Private Investment Ratio		3.82	
9.	Public Investment Ratio			
10.	Private Consumption Ratio			2.4
11.	Public Borrowings			
12.	Fiscal Deficit	0.05*	0.0	-0.4
13.	Exports Growth Rate	0.0		0.7
14.	Imports Growth Rate	0.0		-0.5
15.	Current Account Balance	0.0	-4.45	0.2

Note: 1. Changes in growth rates are in percentage points from the corresponding reference run, others are changes in ratios.

2. All the above scenarios assume full pass through of world oil price to consumers.

3. ISI scenario is no. 16 of Chapter 3, IEG Scenario is no. 3 of Chapter 5 and NCAER Scenario (Table 6.5, Full Price Pass Through) of Chapter 6.

* Centre only

These scenarios show that oil price increase, which subsequently have reversed, can have adverse impact on the GDP growth rate but that appropriate policy response can moderate the impact.

1.8 Impact of Global Slowdown

When this volume was being finalised, one of concerns was the impact of possible slow down of global economy. Model scenarios explored this issue.

Global slow down is modelled by reduction in export growth rates by ISI and IEG models, whereas the NCAER model uses slowdown in the growth rate of the global economy as an exogenous variable which in turn affects exports. Being essentially a plan model, the scenarios developed by PPD did not show significant impact of global slowdown on macroeconomic parameters and hence not reported. The specifications of the scenarios are given in Table 1.4. The results shown in Table 1.5 shows two scenarios. The 2nd scenario considers greater slowdown in global economy or includes some additional contagion effects such as fall in business confidence index and consequent reduction in investments. The NCAER scenarios show reduction of 0.7 to 1.1 percentage point in growth rate.

IEG Scenario I with a fall in export growth rates show a reduction of 0.9 percentage point in growth rate. A change in investment function to reflect change in business confidence shows a fall of 1.8 percentage point.

The ISI model also finds a fall by 0.9 percentage points in the GDP growth rate due to lower export growth rates. ISI Scenario II has considered in addition, increased oil price and higher invisible imports, which can be interpreted also as fall in external inflows, the growth rate falls by 1.8 percentage points.

All the model scenarios show decrease in the growth rate of private final consumption expenditure which, though somewhat smaller, correspond to the fall in the GDP growth rate.

Table 1.4: Global Slowdown Impact—Scenario Assumptions

Sl. No.	Alternative Scenarios	ISI	IEG	NCAER
1.	Base Run	Growth of Agri. and Non Agri. exports 10%.	Exports growth rate 23% during Plan.	Growth rate of world GDP (real)—5% in 2008-09 and 2009-10 and remains at same level afterwards.
2.	Alternative Scenario	*Scenario I:* Slowdown in agricultural exports growth to 6% p.a. during 2005-06–2007-08, and 4% p.a. from 2008-09 to 2011-12. Non-agricultural exports growth declines from 10% p.a. to 6% p.a. during 2008-09 to 2011-12.	*Scenario I:* Exports growth rate falls to 10% in 2008-09 and 2009-10 and 15% in 2010-11 and 2011-12.	*Scenario I:* Growth rate of world GDP (real) 3.7% in 2008-09 and 2.2% in 2009-10 with decline in private GCF and PFCE.
		Scenario II: Scenario I along with growth of invisible imports increasing to 23% and crude oil price rising to US $ 75 and 83 in 2007-08 and 2008-09.	*Scenario II:* Scenario I along with changes in investment function.	*Scenario II:* Same world GDP growth as in Scenario I, but greater decline in private GCF and PFCE.

Table 1.5: Impact of Global Slowdown on Macroeconomic Indicators 2007-08 to 2011-12

Sl. No.	Alternative Scenarios	ISI#		IEG@		NCAER^	
		I	II	I	II	I	II
1.	Total GDP Growth Rate	-0.9	-1.8	-0.9	-1.8	-0.7	-1.1
2.	Agriculture Growth Rate	-2.4	-1.3	-0.2	-0.4	0.3	0.3
3.	Industry Growth Rate	-2.3	-3.7	-0.4	-1.5	-1.0	-1.1
4.	Services Growth Rate	0.2	-1.1	-1.3	-2.4	-0.7	-1.4
5.	PFCE Growth Rate	-0.3	-1.5	-0.7	-1.6	-0.8	-0.9
6.	Savings Ratio	0.0	0.0	-0.9	-1.9		
7.	Investment Ratio	-0.1	-0.1	0.8	-2.1		
8.	Private Investment Ratio			0.8	-2.1		
9.	Public Investment Ratio			0.0	0.0		
10.	Private Consumption Ratio					2.6	2.8
11.	Public Borrowings						
12.	Fiscal Deficit	0.0*	Neg.	0.0	0.0	-0.1	-0.3
13.	Exports Growth Rate	-1.3	-1.3	-6.8	-6.8	-3.0	-3.0
14.	Imports Growth Rate	0.0	2.3	-5.0	-5.3	-0.7	-1.4
15.	Current Account Balance	0.1	0.1	-1.8	0.2	-1.9	-1.2

Notes: # I. Pertains to Scenario 19 in ISI model. II. Pertains to Scenario 22 of ISI model, Chapter 3.

@ IEG model—Scenario I is Trade Shock (Table 5.7) and Scenario II is Trade Shock with domestic investment shock (Table 5.8) and the deviations are *vis-à-vis* Table 5.3 of IEG paper, Chapter 5.

^ NCAER model—base run with GDP 9.0 per cent. Scenario I corresponds to simulation 1 and Scenario II corresponds to simulation 3 of NCAER paper Table 6.9, Chapter 6.

* Centre only

The impact of fall in exports and reduced foreign capital inflows were also explored by IGIDR's static general equilibrium model. In the model, labour mobility was restricted within sectors of a group such as agriculture, organised manufacture, small-scale industries, services, etc. A 10 per cent reduction in dollar value of exports led to a fall of 3.3 per cent in GDP. When in addition to export fall, foreign inflows decline by some 30 per cent, GDP falls by 5.1 per cent. Real income losses for households following these two external shocks range between 4.4 per cent and 5.7 per cent, with the urban households suffering slightly higher losses than their rural counterparts (see Figure 1.1). Also shown in the figure is the impact of counter measures including expansion of National Rural Employment Guarantee (NREG) programme. These measures show that much of the adverse impact on the rural poor can be reversed by effective implementation of NREG programme. In this static general equilibrium model, all impacts are worked out within the year and the impact can be expected to be somewhat larger.

Figure 1.1: Real Income Losses across Households following Global Slowdown

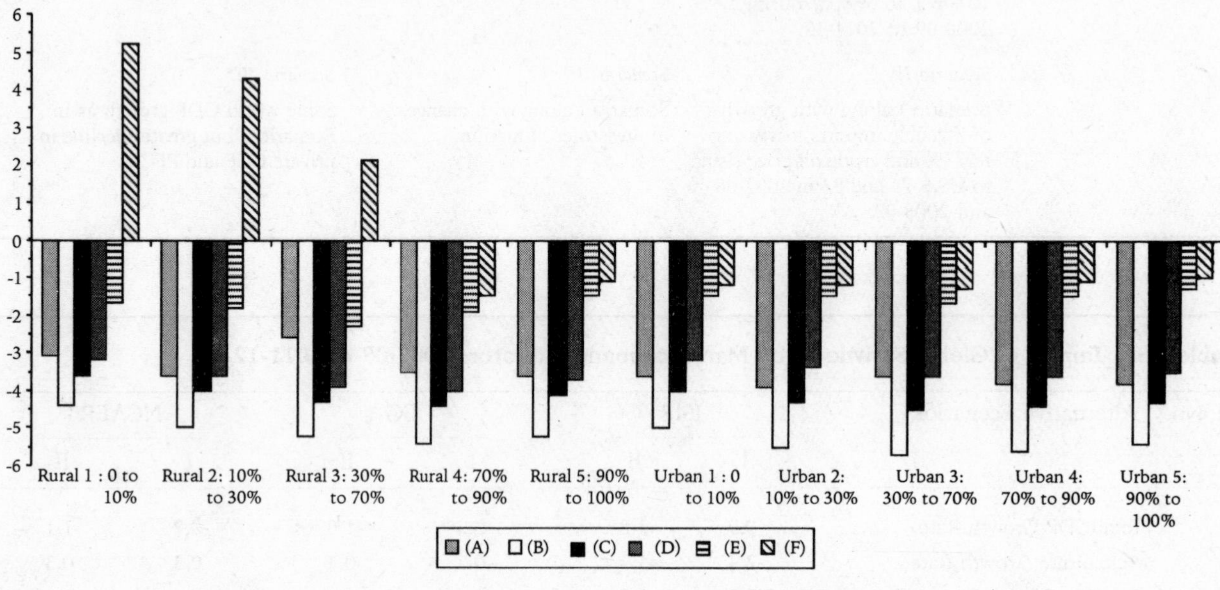

Scenarios: (A) = Exports fall; (B) = (A) + Inflows fall; (C) = (B) + Global oil price fall; (D) = (C) + Govt cons rise; (E) = (D) + Indirect tax cut; (F) = (E) + NREGS

These scenarios thus indicate that India would be affected by the global slowdown and its growth rate for 2009-10 may come down significantly.

1.9 Impact of Mitigation Measures

There is large uncertainty about the global economic situation and IMF is updating its forecasts almost every month. Thus before a scenario run is made, it almost seems to be obsolete. How the global meltdown will progress, how long will it last, what kind of recovery will it be, will it be a V-shaped, a U-shaped or even an L-shaped, one is not clear. The models simulations provide some feel for its impact on the Indian economy and the possible effectiveness of measures to counter it. The scenarios of previous section involve no mitigating counter measures by the government. The government has in fact taken stimulus measures to mitigate the impact of global slowdown. In order to asses the impact of various measures we use the model scenarios to work out impact factors on growth.

The different models provide ranges of these impacts which are summarised in Table 1.6. Since the concern is about what will happen in 2009-10, the impact factors refer to growth rate in 2009-10.

Table 1.6: Impact Multipliers of Shocks and Stimulus Measures on the GDP Growth Rate for 2009-10

Sl. No.	Shock or Policy Measures	% Change	Impact on GDP of 2009-10 (percentage point)
1.	Private Investment	1% of GDP—decrease	-0.17, -0.35
2.	Public Investment	1% of GDP—increase	0.5
	- In agriculture		1.2
	- In industry		0.3
	- In service		1.1
3.	Monetary Stimulus (lower interest rates, PLR etc.)	1% of GDP	0.2, 0.4
4.	Crude Oil Price (partial pass through)	30% decrease in domestic price	0.3
5.	Exports Volume	10% fall	-1.5
6.	Foreign Inflows (including remittances)	30% decline	-1.8*
7.	Government Consumption	1% of GDP—increase	0.5*, 0.8
8.	Indirect Tax Cut	1% of GDP	0.8*, 1.1
9.	NREGs Full Coverage	1% of GDP—increase	0.35*, 0.5*
10.	Public Investment in Construction Financed Through Inflows or Reserve Depletion	1% of GDP—increase	0.6, 2.2*

Note: * From a general equilibrium model in which it is assumed that the adjustments to the new equilibrium are completed in one year. Thus, the impacts may be overstated as in reality this may not be the case.

These impact factors show that the government has a number of policy instruments which can mitigate to some extent the impact of global slowdown. With an appropriate mix of stimulus measures, from the vantage point of April 2009, it seems that the economy can have a growth rate exceeding fairly high growth even in 2009-10.

1.10 Concluding Comments

The various model scenarios presented here show that the direction of impacts are similar even though the structure and philosophy of the models are different. While the magnitude of the impacts vary from model to model, they are by and large reasonably similar, particularly where one considers the difficulties involved in comparing scenarios of different models. Nonetheless the models provide deeper understanding on the working of the economy and possible impacts of policy measures. The results also suggest the need to use a variety of models for planning and policy analysis.

CHAPTER 2

A Macro Consistency Planning Model*

Arvinder S. Sachdeva and Probal P. Ghosh

2.1 Background

Accelerating the growth rate of the economy is central to the attainment of a number of objectives that the planners have set over the last five decades. There is by now enough evidence to show that rapid growth has poverty reducing effects especially when it is complemented with policies that are sensitive to the needs of the poor. Accelerated growth also helps in realising the objectives of increasing employment. However, the linkage between growth, employment and poverty reduction depends crucially upon the sectoral pattern of growth and on the degree to which the disadvantaged segments of the population and the backward regions of the country are successfully integrated into the wider development process. Agricultural growth plays a crucial role in reducing poverty and promoting inclusive growth.

The total volume of investible resources or total savings available in the economy is determined both by the level of domestic savings and by the inflow of foreign savings. Domestic savings originate from three principal sectors, namely: (a) the Government, including the public sector; (b) the private corporate sector; and (c) households. The inflow of foreign savings is the current account deficit and can be financed either in the form of debt, both public and private, or foreign investment, both direct and portfolio.

Since its inception, the planning methodology in India has been based on the assumption that the economy is savings constrained, though to a lesser degree in the last few years. In other words, it is assumed that the demand for investible resources generally exceeds the supply from domestic sources, and hence the total level of investment is determined largely and almost uniquely by the available level of savings.

There are three principal constraints to acceleration of growth in India. These are: (a) availability of savings for investible resources, (b) availability of resources to the Government, both Centre and State, for meeting the development objectives; and (c) adequate availability of infrastructure for supporting high level of capacity utilisaton. These constraints are not entirely independent of each other and tend to act in an inter-dependent manner. In order to examine the implications of alternative growth scenarios, a model has been developed which can take account of at least some of the constraints discussed above in a fairly transparent manner. The only constraint which is handled less than satisfactorily is the infrastructural constraint, which is handled by certain assumptions regarding efficiency.

The model has been developed with the specific purpose of examining the implications of target growth rate for the economy.

---

* The current chapter is a revised version of the models that were used in the Ninth and the Tenth Plans. Dr. Pronab Sen, Dr. Mohan Chutani, S.V. Ramanamurthy, Archana Mathur and Sibani Swain and the first author of this Chapter were involved in the development of those models.

Arvinder S. Sachdeva, Planning Commission and Probal P. Ghosh, Integrated Research for Action and Development (IRADe).

2.2 The Model

The main target variables contained in the model are: (a) the rate of growth on GDP and that of sectors; (b) the current account deficit as a percentage of GDP; (c) government borrowings as a percentage of GDP. The model starts with an exogenously specified target growth rate of GDP at factor cost. This is broken up into sectoral growth rates on the basis of sectoral consistency ratios. The investment requirements for attaining the target growth rate are computed on the basis of the sector specific average capital output ratios (ACOR) of these sectors.

$$I_{it} = (Y_{it} - Y_{it-1}) * v_i \quad (1)$$

and $$I_t = \Sigma I_{it} \quad (2)$$

where v_i = average capital value added ratio of sector i

I_{it} = investment in sector i in the year t

Y_{it} = value added in sector i in the year t

These sectoral ACORs are estimated using past data.

Aggregate and sectoral private investment [I_t (Pvt), I_{it} (Pvt)] are estimated on the basis of investment demand functions which are primarily explained by the accelerator principle and the credit availability to the private sector. Public investment [I_t(Pub)] is assumed to bridge the gap between the required investment as given by equation (2) and investment forthcoming from the private sector as derived from equation (33). It is, therefore, a residual.

GDP at market prices (GDPmp) is estimated as a function of GDP at factor cost (GDPfc) and is projected accordingly.

$$GDPmp = p(1) + p(2) * GDPfc \quad (3)$$

Since the difference between the two estimates of GDP is the estimated behaviour of net indirect taxes (NIT) (i.e., indirect taxes less subsidies), this formulation implicitly assumes that the trend behaviour of net indirect taxes will continue.

$$NIT = GDP_{mp} - GDP_{fc} \quad (4)$$

Net factor income from abroad (NFI) and other current transfers (OCT) are estimated as a function of world GDP, lagged dependent variable with a dummy for the post-reforms period. These are added to GDP at market prices to obtain the national disposable income (NDI).

$$NFI= p(3) + p(4).NFI(-1) + p(5).WGDP + c(6).L91 \quad (5)$$

$$OCT= p(7) + p(8).OCT(-1) + p(9).WGDP \quad (6)$$

$$NDI = GDPmp + NFI + OCT \quad (7)$$

$WGDP_t$ = growth rate of World GDP ....*

Direct taxes (DIRTAX) are the sum of household taxes (HHT_t), corporate taxes (CT_t) and miscellaneous taxes (MT_t), each of which is a constant fraction of GDP at market prices

$$DIRTAX=HHT_t+CT_t+MT_t \quad (8)$$

a. $HHT=h.GDPMP_t$ .... *

b. $CT_t=c.GDPMP_t$ ....*

c. $MT_t=m.GDPMP_t$ ....*

Total taxes (TAX_t) are the sum of direct taxes and net indirect taxes

$$TAX_t = NIT_t + DIRTAX_t \quad (9)$$

Private disposable income (PDI) is an identity reflecting the difference between national disposable income (NDI) and total tax i.e., the difference between equation (7) and equation (9).

$$PDIt = NDI_t - TAX_t \quad (10)$$

Private consumption [PC] is estimated as a function of private disposable income

$$PC_t = p(10) + p(11) * PDI_t \quad (11)$$

Total revenue is a function of total tax collection

$$TR_t = p(12) + p(13).TAX_t \quad (12)$$

Budget deficit is taken to be certain proportion of GDP at market prices (GDPMP)

$$BD_t = b.GDPMP_t ....*$$

Total government expenditure is the sum of total revenue and budget deficit

$$TE_t = BD_t + TR_t \quad (13)$$

Government consumption [GC], is a function of total government expenditure.

$$GC_t = p(14) + p(15).TE_t \quad (14)$$

Total consumption, that is the sum of private and public consumption, as derived in equations (13) and (14), is deducted from national disposable income to yield total gross domestic savings (S).

$$S_t = NDI - [PC_t + GC_t] \quad (15)$$

The difference between total domestic savings and private savings (which is the difference between PDI and PC) yields public savings [PUBS], i.e.,

$$PVTS_t = PDI_t - PC_t \quad (16)$$

and $$PUBS_t = S_t - PVTS_t \quad (17)$$

In the balance of payments block, exports of goods are estimated by relating it to domestic GDP, world GDP and non-agricultural imports. While domestic GDP and non-agricultural imports represent the supply side, world GDP acts on the demand side. Non-agriculture imports comprise mainly intermediate goods and capital goods (machinery and equipment) that go as input for production and exports. The export propensities of these sectors are assumed to be influenced by policy factors not explicitly captured in the model *viz.*, tariff rates, exchange rates, etc.

$$EXPT_t = p(16)GDPMP_t + p(17) * WGDP_t + p(18) * NAGIMP_t \quad (18)$$

$EXPT_t$ = Real merchandise exports,

Merchandise imports comprise three broad categories *viz.*, agriculture imports, non-agriculture imports and petroleum imports. Agriculture imports are generally treated in most cases as residual as such goods are imported to meet shortfall in domestic production as and when such shortfalls occur. Hence, they have been modelled as univariate forecast instead of making it a function of policy variables. Petroleum imports include both crude petroleum and petroleum products. These are a function of GDP of the non-agriculture sector (the major user of these products) and its own lagged value to reflect the minimum requirement. Non-agriculture imports comprise mainly intermediate goods and capital goods (machinery and equipment) that go as input for production and exports.

$$AGIMP_t = p(19) + p(20) * AGIMP_{t-1} \quad (19)$$

$$PETIMP_t = p(21) + p(22) * NAGDP_t + p(23) * PETIMP_{t-1} \quad (20)$$

$AGIMP_t$ = Real agriculture imports.

$PETIMP_t$ = Real petroleum imports.

$NAGIMP_t$ = Real non-agriculture imports. (based on exogenous growth rate of real non-agriculture imports.

The exports of invisibles are a function of services sector value-added, world GDP and imports of invisibles in the last year. While the service sector GDP and the imports of invisibles represent the supply side, the world GDP represents the demand side.

$$INVEXP_t = p(24) + p(25) * SGDP_t + p(26) * WGDP_t + p(27) * INVIMP_{t-1} \quad (21)$$

$INVEXP_t$ = Real invisible exports

$SGDP_t$ = Services GDP

$INVIMP_t$ = Real invisible imports

The imports of invisibles are a function of services sector GDP, world GDP and exports of invisibles. While the service sector GDP and the exports of invisibles represent the demand side, the world GDP represents the supply side. The imports of invisibles are expected to vary positively with exports of invisibles, as the higher imports of invisible are expected to be financed by higher earnings on account of invisible exports.

$$INVIMP_t = p(28) * SGDP_{t-1} + p(29) * WGDP_t + p(30) * INVEXP_t \quad (22)$$

$INVIMP_t$ = Real invisible imports

The investment requirement for the plan has been worked out using the Average Capital Output Ratio (ACOR) for three major sectors *viz.*, agriculture, industry and services. The ACOR represents the technical relationship between output and level of capital stock. $ACOR_{it}$ in each sector i has been made a function of different demand and supply side variables. Thus, given the values of demand and supply side factors and hence given the state of the economy for each year, the ACOR's are calculated and from the ACOR's the required capital stock to attain a given level of output.

The agricultural ACOR is specified as a technical relationship with the proportion of area under HYV ($HYVPRP_t$) at time t, rainfall ($RFINDEX_t$) at time t and agricultural GDP ($AGDP_t$) at time t. The proportion of area under HYV is also made a function of proportion of area under fertiliser and proportion of area under irrigation.

$$HYVPRP_t = p(31) * IRGPRP_t + p(32) * FRTPRP_t \quad (23)$$

$$AACOR_t = p(33) + c(34) * HYVPRP_t + p(35) * RFINDEX_t + p(36) * AGDP_{t-1} \quad (24)$$

$AACOR_t$ = Agricultural ACOR

$HYVPRP_t$ = Proportion of HYV to Gross Cropped Area

$RFINDEX_t$ = Rainfall index for all India

AGDPt = Value added of agriculture sector

The industrial ACOR is specified as a function of supply side factors such as real non-agriculture imports ($NAGIMP_t$), oil price index ($WPIOIL_t$) and agricultural GDP (AGDP) and demand side factors such as Government consumption (GCON). The impact of liberalisation on industrial sectors efficiency is also allowed for through the dummy variable $L93_t$.

$$IACOR_t = p(37) + p(38) * NAGIMP_{t-1} + p(39) * WPIOIL_{t-1} + p(40) * GCON_t + p(41) * AGDP_t + p(42) * L93_t \quad (25)$$

$IACOR_t$ = Industrial ACOR,

$NAGIMP_t$ = Non-agricultural imports,

$WPIOIL_t$ = Wholesale price index of fuel prices,

$GCON_t$ = Government consumption,

$L93_t$ = Level shift at 1993

p = Growth rate of oil price index ($WPIOIL_t$) ....*

The services ACOR is specified as a function of only demand side factors such as real non-services GDP ($NSGDP_t = AGDP_t + IGDP_t$) which is the total of agricultural and industrial GDP, trade balance on merchandise goods and real invisible exports ($INVEXP_t$). The services sector had been growing much before economic liberalisation reforms. In fact it is a known fact that much of the reforms for the services sector had been initiated in the eighties decade itself. Hence, for the services ACOR it was the level shift dummy from the year 1985 that became significant instead of 1991 or 1993.

$$SACOR_t = p(43) + p(44) * NSGDP_t + p(45) * TB_{t-1} + p(46) * INVEXP_{t-1} + p(47) * L85_t \quad (26)$$

$SACOR_t$ = Services $ACOR_t$

$NSGDP_t$ = Non-services GDP

TB_t = Trade balance in merchandise goods

$INVEXP_t$ = Invisible exports

$L85_t$ = Level shift dummy from 1985

Given the $ACOR_{it}$ ($ACOR_{it}$ is calcuted using net capital stock) the gross capital stock is calculated from the relation

$$K_{it} = ACOR_{it} * GDPFC_{it} + \delta_{it} * K_{it-1} \quad (27)$$

Thus, investment in the ith sector at time t I_{it} is given by

$$I_{it} = K_{it} - K_{it-1} \quad (28)$$

Total investment requirement in the economy is then obtained as

$$I_t = \Sigma I_{it} \text{ for i = agriculture, industry and services} \quad (29)$$

Foreign savings or the current account deficit (CAD) is obtained as the difference between total investment and total domestic savings in order to ensure savings-investment balance.

$$CAD_t = I_t - S_t \quad (30)$$

Private corporate savings is specified as a function of value added in the non-agriculture (Industry + Services) sector ($NAGDP_t = IGDP_t + SGDP_t$) and corporate taxes ($CT_t$)

$$PCS_t = p(48) + p(49).NAGDP_t + p(50).CT_t \quad (31)$$

Household savings (HHS_t) is the difference of private savings ($PVTS_t$) and private corporate savings (PCS_t)

$$HHS_t = PVTS_t - PCS_t \quad (32)$$

Private investment ($PVTI_t$) is estimated as a function of domestic private corporate savings, foreign savings (CAD_t) and public investment. The latter variable is to reflect the crowding in/crowding out effect

$$PVTI_t = p(51) + p(52).PCS_t + p(53).CAD_{t-1} + p(54).PUBI_{t-1} \quad (33)$$

Public investment ($PUBI_t$) is the difference of total investment and private investment

$$PUBI_t = I_t - PVTI_t \quad (34)$$

Gross fixed investment is obtained as a fixed proportion of total investment.

$$GFI_t = a.I_t \quad (35)$$

Change in stocks at time t is obtained from the relation

$$CHST_t = I_t - GFI_t \quad (36)$$

Public borrowing ($PUBB_t$) is the difference between public investment and public savings

$$PUBB_t = PUBI_t - PUBS_t$$

In the model, variables are interrelated through various equations. The controlling parameters in the model are the ones marked by * *viz.*, direct tax rates (h,c,m), world GDP growth rate (wg), budget deficit as a proportion of GDPMP (b), growth rate of oil price index (p) and growth rate of real non-agriculture imports (g).

2.3 Model Estimated Equations

$D(GDPMP_t,2) = c(1)*D(GDPFC_t,2) + C(2)*D(GDPFC_{t-1},2)$

$GDPMP_t$, $GDPFC_t$, are GDP at market prices and factor cost respectively.

$D(NFI_t) = c(3)*D(NFI_{t-1})+c(4)*D(WGDP_t)+c(61)*I91_t$

NFI_t = net factor income, $WGDP_t$ = world GDP, $I91_t$ = level dummy at 1991

$D(OCT_t) = c(5)*D(OCT_{t-1})+c(6)*D(WGDP_t)$

OCT_t = other current transfers from the rest of the world, $WGDP_t$ = world GDP

$D(PVTCON_t) = c(7)+c(8)*D(PDI_t)$

$PVTCON_t$ = Private consumtion expenditure, PDI_t = Personal disposable income

$D(TREV_t) = c(10)*D(TAX_t)$

$TREV_t$ = Total revenue income of the government Centre and states combined, TAX_t = Total tax collections of the government

$D(GCON_t) = c(12)*D(TEXP_t)$

$GCON_t$ = Government consumption expenditure, $TEXP_t$ = Total expenditure of government Centre and states combined

$D(AACOR_t) = c(13) + c(14)*D(HYVPRP_t) + c(15)*RFINDEX_t + c(16)*D(AGDP_{t-1})$

$AACOR_t$ =Agricultural ACOR, $HYVPRP_t$ = Proportion of HYV to Gross cropped area, $RFINDEX_t$ = rainfall index for all India, AGDPt = Agricultural GDP

$D(IACOR_t) = c(17) + c(18)*D(NAGIMP_{t-1}) + c(19)*D(WPIOIL_{t-1},2) + c(20)*L93_t + c(21)*D(GCON_t) + c(22)*D(AGDP_t)$

$IACOR_t$ = Industrial ACOR, $NAGIMP_t$= Non-agricultural imports, $WPIOIL_t$ = Wholesale price index of fuel prices, $GCON_t$ = Government consumption, $L93_t$ = level shift at 1993

$D(SACOR_t) = c(23) + c(24)*D(NSGDP_t)+ c(25)*D(TB_{t-1})+ c(26)*D(INVEXP_{t-1})+c(27)*D(L85_t)$

$SACOR_t$ = Services $ACOR_t$, $NSGDP_t$ = Non-services GDP, TB_t = Trade balance, $INVEXP_t$ = Invisible exports, $L85_t$ = level shift dummy from 1985

$D(PCS_t) = c(28)*D(NAGDP_t,2) + c(29)*D(CT_t)$

PCS_t = Private corporate savings, $NAGDP_t$ = Non-agricultural GDP, CT_t = Corporate taxes

$D(PVTI_t) = c(31)*D(PCS_t) + c(32)*D(CAD_{t-1})$

$PVTI_t$ = Private investment, CAD_t = Current account deficit

$D(EXPT_t) = c(37)*D(GDPMP_{t-1},2) + c(38)*D(WGDP_t) + c(39)*D(NAGIMP_t)$

$EXPT_t$ = Real merchandise exports,

$D(INVEXP_t) = c(40)+ c(41)*D(SGDP_t,2) + c(42)*D(WGDP_t) + c(43)*D(INVIMP_{t-1})$

$INVEXP_t$ = Real invisible exports, $SGDP_t$ = Services GDP, $INVIMP_t$ = Real invisible imports

$D(INVIMP_t) = c(45)*D(SGDP_{t-1},2) + c(46)*D(WGDP_t) + c(47)*D(INVEXP_t)$

$D(PETIMP_t) = c(50)*D(NAGDP_t,2) + c(51)*D(PETIMP_{t-1})$

$PETIMP_t$ = Real petroleum imports

Estimated Coefficients

	Coefficient	t-Statistic	Prob.
C(1)	1.07	29.36	0.0000
C(2)	0.07	1.96	0.0507
C(3)	0.20	2.14	0.0328
C(4)	-1.83	-4.49	0.0000
C(61)	1598.59	3.16	0.0017
C(5)	-0.32	-3.43	0.0007
C(6)	5.23	3.92	0.0001
C(7)	4132.10	2.09	0.0370
C(8)	0.57	32.71	0.0000
C(10)	1.35	23.84	0.0000
C(12)	0.40	8.87	0.0000
C(13)	0.78	3.47	0.0006
C(14)	-3.20	-2.73	0.0065
C(15)	-0.01	-3.37	0.0008
C(16)	0.00	4.32	0.0000
C(17)	0.08	3.85	0.0001
C(18)	0.00	-2.58	0.0102
C(19)	0.01	2.52	0.0121
C(20)	-0.14	-4.51	0.0000
C(21)	0.00	3.87	0.0001
C(22)	0.00	-2.38	0.0178
C(23)	-0.06	-6.17	0.0000
C(24)	0.00	-2.49	0.0130
C(25)	0.00	4.64	0.0000
C(26)	0.00	4.86	0.0000
C(27)	-0.08	-2.25	0.0250
C(28)	0.24	3.47	0.0006
C(29)	2.34	10.91	0.0000
C(31)	2.25	12.06	0.0000
C(32)	-0.34	-3.78	0.0002
C(37)	0.10	4.83	0.0000
C(38)	7.40	4.30	0.0000
C(39)	0.48	10.36	0.0000
C(40)	-10143.50	-2.48	0.0135
C(41)	0.54	4.09	0.0001
C(42)	19.29	4.37	0.0000
C(43)	0.80	5.03	0.0000
C(45)	0.14	2.12	0.0348
C(46)	3.01	1.90	0.0585
C(47)	0.40	8.98	0.0000
C(50)	0.17	2.76	0.0060
C(51)	0.62	8.15	0.0000

Data for estimations have been taken mainly from NAS and converted to 2006-07 prices using appropriate deflators. The equations have been estimated simultaneously using Zellner's SURE methodology.

Model Estimated Equations

$$D(GDPMP_t,2) = 1.07*D(GDPFC_t,2) + 0.07*D(GDPFC_{t-1},2)$$
(29.36) (1.96)

$$D(NFI_t) = 0.20*D(NFI_{t-1}) - 1.83*D(WGDP_t) + 1598.59*I91_t$$
(2.14) (-4.49) (3.16)

$$D(OCT_t) = -0.32*D(OCT_{t-1}) + 5.23*D(WGDP_t)$$
(-3.43) (3.92)

$$D(PVTCON_t) = 4132.10 + 0.57*D(PDI_t)$$
(2.09) (32.71)

$$D(TREV_t) = 1.35*D(TAX_t)$$
(23.84)

$$D(GCON_t) = 0.40*D(TEXP_t)$$
(8.87)

$$D(AACOR_t) = 0.78 - 3.20*D(HYVPRP_t) - 0.01*RFINDEX_t + 0.0000023*D(AGDP_{t-1})$$
(3.47) (-2.73) (-3.37) (4.32)

$$D(IACOR_t) = 0.08 + -0.0000023*D(NAGIMP_{t-1}) + 0.01*D(WPIOIL_{t-1},2) - 0.14*L93_t + 0.000006*D(GCON_t) + -0.000002*D(AGDP_t)$$
(3.85) (-2.58) (2.52) (-4.51) (3.87) (-2.38)

$$D(SACOR_t) = -0.065 - 0.0000006*D(NSGDP_t) + 0.0000021*D(TB_{t-1}) + 0.0000028*D(INVEXP_{t-1}) - 0.0843812*D(L85_t)$$
(-6.17) (-2.49) (4.64) (4.86) (-2.25)

$$D(PCS_t) = 0.24*D(NAGDP_t,2) + 2.34*D(CT_t)$$
(3.47) (10.91)

$$D(PVTI_t) = 2.25*D(PCS_t) + -0.34*D(CAD_{t-1})$$
(12.06) (-3.78)

$$D(EXPT_t) = 0.10*D(GDPMP_{t-1},2) + 7.40*D(WGDP_t) + 0.48*D(NAGIMP_t)$$
(4.83) (4.30) (10.36)

$$D(INVEXP_t) = -10143.50 + 0.54*D(SGDP_t,2) + 19.29*D(WGDP_t) + 0.80*D(INVIMP_{t-1})$$
(-2.48) (4.09) (4.37) (5.03)

$$D(INVIMP_t) = 0.14*D(SGDP_{t-1},2) + 3.01*D(WGDP_t) + 0.40*D(INVEXP_t)$$
(2.12) (1.90) (8.98)

$$D(PETIMP_t) = 0.17*D(NAGDP_t,2) + 0.62*D(PETIMP_{t-1})$$
(2.76) (8.15)

2.4 Policy Results

The focus of the model is to estimate the sectoral growth rates consistent with the overall growth rate of the economy and given the fact that agriculture sector is targeted to grow at 4 per cent per annum during the Plan period. Range of growth rates of different sectors is given in Table 2.1 which corresponds to 9 per cent aggregate growth and 4 per cent growth of agriculture.

Table 2.1: Alternative Growth Rates for Different Sectors in XI Plan

(% per annum)

Agriculture	4.0
Industry	9.0-11.0
Services	9.0-11.0
GDP at Factor cost	9.0
Private Final Consumption Expenditure	7.1

The average savings rate, investment rate and current account balance for the plan are given in Table 2.2.

Table 2.2: Private Consumption, Savings, Investment Rates and Current Account Balance in XI Plan (% of GDP at Market Prices)

Private Final Consumption Expenditure	55.8
Savings Rate	34.8
Investment Rate	36.7
Current Account balance	1.9

Some of the alternative policy results have been discussed in Chapter 1.

Chapter 3

Macroeconomic Simulations based on VEC Models

N.S.S. Narayana and Probal P. Ghosh*

3.1 Introduction

The Indian government vigorously pursues various economic policies to push up the economic growth with a hope to attain a status of 'developed country' at the earliest. Major economic reforms have been initiated in 1991, which have led to improved economic environment for growth. Apart from the effects of the Government policies, the economy also experiences shocks from external sources. In this paper, a macroeconomic simulation model has been developed for the Indian economy, based on four VEC/VAR component-models estimated separately. This paper is concerned with the likely production performance, investments, price effects and households' savings and disaggregated consumption patterns during the 11th Five Year Plan period (FYP). In the next section scope of our models is presented. Later, the four VEC models, long-run equilibrium relations and error correction mechanisms are presented. After diagnosing the estimated models, a reference run is presented. Then policy analyses are taken up. The last section presents concluding remarks.

3.2 Scope of the Models

The simulation model has four components. Three of them are production components dealing with agriculture, industry and services (including public administration) sectors, modelled separately. These three components pooled together cover broadly the production structure of the entire economy. The fourth component models households' aggregate private final consumption expenditure (PFCE—later to be disaggregated into eight commodity groups), their savings in financial assets (HFS) and physical assets (HPS). For each sectoral production component, a vector error correction (VEC) model has been estimated with the corresponding GDP, investment (GCF—gross capital formation) and prices (PDFL—price deflator) as three endogenous variables. For the consumption component, another VEC model has been estimated with PFCE, HFS and HPS as three endogenous variables. That means, mutual dependence among the endogenous variables in each of the four VEC models is characterised as a long-run

---

* The authors thank Kirit S. Parikh for many helpful suggestions. The formers alone are responsible for any errors of omission and commission. This paper is basically a revised and extended version of our earlier paper Narayana and Ghosh (2005), with a consumption component included now. Therefore, discussion of the production components in this paper is drawn from the earlier one, though some details covered earlier have been omitted now.

N.S.S. Narayana, Indian Statistical Institute (ISI) and Probal P. Ghosh, Integrated Research for Action and Development (IRADe).

equilibrium relation (LRE) with corresponding error correction existing. Each of these endogenous variables could also be influenced by some predetermined and exogenous variables as follows:

(RF)	rainfall
(RM3)	real money supply
(WPF)	fuel price index
(RBR)	real bank rate
(RBD)	real budget deficit
(PCSS)	corporate savings
(NETPETIMP)	real net petroleum imports
(AGEXP)	real agricultural exports
(AGIMP)	real agricultural imports
(NAGEXP)	real non-agricultural exports
(NAGIMP)	real non-agricultural imports
(NETNAGEXP=NAGEXP-NAGIMP)	real net non-agricultural exports
(RINVEXP)	real invisibles exports
(RINVIMP)	real invisibles imports
(NETRINVEXP=RINVEXP-RINVIMP)	real net invisibles exports

Basic data are presented in Tables A-3.1 (a to i) in Appendix A-3.1.

These exogenous variables are mostly common for all the sectors. Past-periods' values of the endogenous variables (GDP_{t-1}, GCF_{t-1}. etc.) in any model are predetermined variables and their presence in the equations accounts for inter-sectoral influences. The paper also takes into account if any permanent shift has occurred in the LREs due to the economic reforms initiated in the year 1991. Towards this two trend variables TR81 and TR91, and a level-shift variable L91 are also considered for incorporation into the LREs of the models.

Henceforth, we adopt a notation as follows:

$D(X_t) = (X_t - X_{t-1})$ and $D^2(X_t) = D(D(X_t)) = (X_t - X_{t-1}) - (X_{t-1} - X_{t-2})$

AGDP/IGDP/SGDP:	GDP of agriculture/industry/services sectors
AGCF/IGCF/SGCF:	Investment in agriculture/industry/services sectors
APDFL/IPDFL/SPDFL:	Price deflator of agriculture/industry/services sectors
TGDP/TGCF/TPDFL:	GDP/gross capital formation i.e., investment/price deflator over all the sectors put together
PFCE:	Households' aggregate private final consumption expenditure at 1993-94 prices
HFS/HPS:	Households' savings in financial assets/ Households' savings in physical assets
FMMB:	Expenditure on food & beverages
CLR:	Expenditure on clothing & footwear
FLP:	Expenditure on fuel, electricity, water & rent
OT:	Expenditure on furniture, furnishings, transport etc. (or all others)
ED:	Expenditure on education
CO:	Expenditure on communication

MI:	Miscellaneous expenditure
MD:	Medical expenditure
CRL:	Cereals and bread
PUL:	Pulses
MIL:	Milk and milk products
OF:	All other foods

The GDPs, GCFs, PFCE, HFS, HPS and all the expenditure variables are at constant prices (base year, 1993-94). The price deflators are price indexes with base 1993-94. The data that we have are only for the years 1953 to 2003 (see Appendix A-3.1). The time-series data on commodity expenditures are even less: only from 1961 to 2003. Setting up a large VEC model (instead of sub-models as mentioned above) with long lag structures is not possible with this data. For this reason the problem has been split into estimating 4 separate VEC models: one each for agriculture, industry, services and households instead of estimating one big model with all the variables together.

First, all the variables were tested for their order of integration. Test results are given in Table 3.1.

Table 3.1: Unit Root Tests

Variable	ADF	SP		KPSS		Saikkonen & Luetkepohl		
		Rho test	Tau test	Level stationarity	Trend stationarity	Impulse	Shift	Exponential
AGDP	I(1)	I(1)	I(1)	I(1)	I(1)	I(2)	I(2)	I(2)
AGCF	I(1)	I(1)	I(1)	I(1)	I(0)	I(1)	I(1)	I(1)
APDFL	I(2)	I(2)	I(2)	I(2)	I(1)	I(2)	I(2)	I(2)
IGDP	I(1)	I(1)	I(1)	I(2) / (1)	I(2) / (1)	I(2)	I(2)	I(2)
IGCF	I(1)	I(1)	I(1)	I(1)	I(1)	I(2)	I(2)	I(2)
IPDFL	I(2)	I(1)	I(1)	I(2)	I(1)	I(2)	I(2)	I(2)
SGDP	I(2)	I(2)	I(2)	I(2)	I(2)	I(2)	I(3)	I(2)
SGCF	I(1)	I(1)	I(1)	I(1)	I(1)	I(2)	I(2)	I(2)
SPDFL	I(2)	I(2)	I(2)	I(2)	I(2)	I(3)	I(3)	I(2)
PFCE	I(2)	I(1)	I(1)	I(2)	I(2)	I(3)	I(2)	I(2)
HFS	I(1)	I(1)	I(1)	I(2)	I(1)	I(2)	I(2)	I(2)
HPS	I(1)	I(1)	I(1)	I(2)/I(1)	I(1)	I(3)	I(2)	I(1)
RI	I(0)	I(0)	I(0)	I(0)	I(0)	I(1)	I(1)	I(1)
WPF	I(2)	I(1)	I(1)	I(2)	I(2)	I(2)	I(2)	I(2)
RM3	I(2)	I(2)	I(2)	I(2)	I(2)	I(3)	I(3)	I(2)
RBD	I(0)	I(0)	I(0)	I(0)	I(0)	I(1)	I(1)	I(1)
RBR	I(0)	I(0)	I(0)	I(0)	I(0)	I(1)	I(1)	I(1)
RTB	I(1)	I(1)	I(1)	I(1)	I(0)	I(2)	I(1)	I(2)
PCSS	I(1)	I(1)	I(1)	I(1)	I(1)	I(2)	I(2)	I(1)
AGEXP	I(1)	I(1)	I(1)	I(1)	I(1)	I(2)	I(2)	I(1)
AGIMP	I(1)	I(1)	I(1)	I(0)	I(0)	I(1)	I(1)	I(1)
NAGEXP	I(2)	I(2)/I(1)	I(1)	I(1)	I(1)	I(2)	I(2)	I(2)
NAGIMP	I(1)	I(1)	I(1)	I(2)/I(1)	I(1)	I(2)	I(2)	I(2)
NETNAGEXP	I(0)	I(1)	I(1)	I(0)	I(0)	I(0)	I(0)	I(0)
NETPETIMP	I(2)/I(1)	I(1)	I(1)	I(1)	I(1)	I(2)	I(2)	I(2)
RINVEXP	I(2)/I(1)	I(1)	I(1)	I(2)/I(1)	I(2)/I(1)	I(3)	I(2)	I(2)
RINVIMP	I(2)/I(1)	I(1)	I(1)	I(2)/I(1)	I(1)	I(2)	I(2)	I(2)
NETRINVEXP	I(2)	I(1)	I(1)	I(1)	I(1)	I(2)	I(3)	I(3)

Note: ADF denotes the Augmented Dickey Fuller test, SP the Schimidt-Philips test, KPSS the Kwiatkowski-Philips Schimidt and Shin test. SP has two test statistics: Tau statistic and Rho statistic. KPSS tests are under two assumptions of stationarity: levels stationarity and trend stationarity.

Based on the test results given in Table 3.1 the following are considered as the orders of integration for the endogenous and exogenous variables.

Endogenous Variables:

I(2): APDFL of the agricultural sector, IGDP, IGCF and IPDFL of the industrial sector, and SGDP and SPDFL of the services sector and PFCE, HFS and HPS of the households.

I(1): AGDP and AGCF of the agricultural sector and the SGCF of the services.

Since only I(1) variables can be endogenous variables in a VEC model, the first differences of the I(2) variables (APDFL, IGDP, IGCF, IPDFL, SPDFL, SGDP, PFCE, HFS and HPS) are included in the co-integrating equation along with AGDP, AGCF, SGCF.

Exogenous Variables:

I(0): RF, RBR and RBD

I(1): AGEXP, AGIMP, NAGEXP, NAGIMP, RINVEXP, RINVIMP, NETRINVEXP, NETPETIMP and PCSS

I(2): RM3 and WPF.

3.3 VEC Methodology

The general form of the VEC model is as follows:

$$C_0\Delta Y_t = a[b'\eta']\begin{bmatrix} Y_{t-1} \\ T_{t-1} \end{bmatrix} + C_1\Delta Y_{t-1} + \ldots\ldots + C_p\Delta Y_{t-p} + d_0\, X_t + \ldots + d_q\, X_{t-q} + \delta\, Z_t + u_t$$

where Y_t is the vector of endogenous variables, C_0 is an identity matrix, a the vector of adjustment parameters, b the vector of cointegrating parameters, c_i are the short-run parameters of the lagged endogenous variables, d_i the short-run parameters of the exogenous and predetermined variables, T_t and Z_t are deterministic variables (and/or constant) with associated coefficients η and δ respectively. u_t is the vector of error terms.

See Appendix A-3.2 for technical details on estimation of the number of cointegrating vectors. In each of the VEC component models there exists only one cointegrating vector (CIV). As stated earlier, while building up the VEC models, we also account for the significant effects if any of the 1991 reforms on the LRE.[1] Towards this a level-shift variable (L91) and two trend variables (TR81 and TR91) are defined as follows:

$L91_t$ = 0 for $1953 \le t \le 1990$, and

= 1 for $t \ge 1991$;

$TR81_t$ = 0 for $1953 \le t \le 1980$, and

= (t-1980) for $t \ge 1981$;

$TR91_t$ = 0 for $1953 \le t \le 1990$, and

= (t-1990) for $t \ge 1991$;

where t represents year (time). $L91_t$ $TR81_t$ and $TR91_t$ figure in either T_t or Z_t in a model but not in both.

1. There is a lot of literature dealing with incorporation of deterministic trends into CIVs. See Luetkepohl and Kratzig (2004), Hungnes (2004), Philips and Catherine (2000), Hendry and Mizon (2001) etc.

3.4 Model Estimations

Now the specifics. In the equations below, l stands for lag structure (l=0,1,2) and the summation Σ is over l. a1, a2 and a3 are the adjustment parameters, b_1, b_2, η_1 and η_2 are the parameters in the CIV. $c1_{il}$, $c2_{il}$ and $c3_{il}$ are the short-run parameters associated with the lagged endogenous variables, and $d1_{il}$, $d2_{il}$ and $d3_{il}$ are the short-run parameters associated with the exogenous and predetermined variables.

3.4.1 Agriculture

AGDP, AGCF, D(APDFL), L91 and TR91 are the variables appearing in the cointegrating vector. Lagged D^2(IGDP) and D^2(IPDFL) are the predetermined variables (estimated in the industry sub-model). The postulated VEC model with a lag structure of 2 periods is as follows [estimation results in Table 3.2(a)]:

$$\begin{aligned} D(AGDP_t) = {} & a1[AGDP_{t-1} - b_1 AGCF_{t-1} - b_2 D(APDFL_{t-1}) - \eta_1 L91_{t-1} - \eta_2 TR91_{t-1}] \\ & + \Sigma\, c1_{1l}.D(AGDP)_{t-l} + \Sigma\, c1_{2l}.D(AGCF)_{t-l} + \Sigma\, c1_{3l}.D^2(APDFL)_{t-l} \\ & + d1_1.RI_t + d1_2.D^2(WPF)_{t-1} + \Sigma\, d1_{3l}.RBD_{t-l} + \Sigma\, d1_{4l}.D(NAGEXP)_{t-l} \\ & + \Sigma\, d1_{5l}.D(NAGIMP)_{t-l} + \Sigma\, d1_{6l}.D(AGEXP)_{t-l} + \Sigma\, d1_{7l}.D^2(IGDP)_{t-l} \\ & + \Sigma\, d1_{8l}.D^2(IPDFL)_{t-l} + constant + u_{1t} \end{aligned} \qquad (1)$$

$$\begin{aligned} D(AGCF_t) = {} & a2[AGDP_{t-1} - b_1 AGCF_{t-1} - b_2 D(APDFL_{t-1}) - \eta_1 L91_{t-1} - \eta_2 TR91_{t-1}] \\ & + \Sigma\, c2_{1l}.D(AGDP)_{t-l} + \Sigma\, c2_{2l}.D(AGCF)_{t-l} + \Sigma\, c2_{3l}.D^2(APDFL)_{t-l} \\ & + d2_1.RI_t + d2_2.D^2(WPF)_{t-1} + \Sigma\, d2_{3l}.RBD_{t-l} + \Sigma\, d2_{4l}.D(NAGEXP)_{t-l} \\ & + \Sigma\, d2_{5l}.D(NAGIMP)_{t-l} + \Sigma\, d2_{6l}.D(AGEXP)_{t-l} + \Sigma\, d2_{7l}.D^2(IGDP)_{t-l} \\ & + \Sigma\, d2_{8l}.D^2(IPDFL)_{t-l} + constant + u_{2t} \end{aligned} \qquad (2)$$

$$\begin{aligned} D^2(APDFL_t) = {} & a3[AGDP_{t-1} - b_1 AGCF_{t-1} - b_2 D(APDFL_{t-1}) - \eta_1 L91_{t-1} - \eta_2 TR91_{t-1}] \\ & + \Sigma\, c3_{1l}.D(AGDP)_{t-l} + \Sigma\, c3_{2l}.D(AGCF)_{t-l} + \Sigma\, c3_{3l}.D^2(APDFL)_{t-l} \\ & + d3_1.RI_t + d3_2.D^2(WPF)_{t-1} + \Sigma\, d3_{3l}.RBD_{t-l} + \Sigma\, d3_{4l}.D(NAGEXP)_{t-l} \\ & + \Sigma\, d3_{5l}.D(NAGIMP)_{t-l} + \Sigma\, d3_{6l}.D(AGEXP)_{t-l} + \Sigma\, d3_{7l}.D^2(IGDP)_{t-l} \\ & + \Sigma\, d3_{8l}.D^2(IPDFL)_{t-l} + constant + u_{3t} \end{aligned} \qquad (3)$$

3.4.2 Industry

D(IGDP), D(IGCF), D(IPDFL) and TR91 are the variables appearing in the co-integrating vector. D(AGDP) and lagged D^2(APDFL) are the predetermined variables (estimated in the agriculture sub-model). PCSS is one of the several exogenous variables here (see Figure 3.1). The postulated VEC model with a lag structure of one period is as follows [estimation results in Table 3.2(b)]:

$$\begin{aligned} D^2(IGDP_t) = {} & a1[D(IGDP_{t-1} - b_1 D(IGCF_{t-1}) - b_2 D(IPDFL_{t-1}) - \eta_1 TR91_{t-1}] \\ & + \Sigma\, c1_{1l}.D^2(IGDP)_{t-l} + \Sigma\, c1_{2l}.D^2(IGCF)_{t-l} + \Sigma\, c1_{3l}.D^2(IPDFL)_{t-l} \\ & + \Sigma\, d1_{1l}.D^2(WPF)_{t-l} + \Sigma\, d1_{2l}.D^2(RM3)_{t-l} + d1_3.D(PCSS)_t + \\ & + d1_4.D(NAGEXP)_t + d1_5.D(NETPETIMP)_t + \Sigma\, d1_{6l}.RBR_{t-l} + \Sigma\, d1_{7l}.RBD_{t-l} \\ & + d1_8.D(AGDP)_t + \Sigma\, d1_{9l}.D^2(APDFL)_{t-l} + \delta 1_1.L91_{t-l} + u_{1t} \end{aligned} \qquad (4)$$

$$\begin{aligned} D^2(IGCF_t) = {} & a2[D(IGDP_{t-1} - b_1 D(IGCF_{t-1}) - b_2 D(IPDFL_{t-1}) - \eta_1 TR91_{t-1}] \\ & + \Sigma\, c2_{1l}.D^2(IGDP)_{t-l} + \Sigma\, c2_{2l}.D^2(IGCF)_{t-l} + \Sigma\, c2_{3l}.D^2(IPDFL)_{t-l} \\ & + \Sigma\, d2_{1l}.D^2(WPF)_{t-l} + \Sigma\, d2_{2l}.D^2(RM3)_{t-l} + d2_3.D(PCSS)_t + \\ & + d2_4.D(NAGEXP)_t + d2_5.D(NETPETIMP)_t + \Sigma\, d2_{6l}.RBR_{t-l} + \Sigma\, d2_{7l}.RBD_{t-l} \\ & + d2_8.D(AGDP)_t + \Sigma\, d2_{9l}.D^2(APDFL)_{t-l} + \delta 2_1.L91_{t-l} + u_{2t} \end{aligned} \qquad (5)$$

$$\begin{aligned} D^2(IPDFL_t) = {} & a3[D(IGDP_{t-1} - b_1D(IGCF_{t-1}) - b_2D(IPDFL_{t-1}) - \eta_1 TR91_{t-1}] \\ & + \Sigma\, c3_{1l}.D^2(IGDP)_{t-1} + \Sigma\, c3_{2l}.D^2(IGCF)_{t-1} + \Sigma\, c3_{3l}.D^2(IPDFL)_{t-1} \\ & + \Sigma\, d3_{1l}.D^2(WPF)_{t-1} + \Sigma\, d3_{2l}.D^2(RM3)_{t-1} + d3_3.D(PCSS)_t + \\ & + d3_4.D(NAGEXP)_t + d3_5.D(NETPETIMP)_t + \Sigma\, d3_{6l}.RBR_{t-1} + \Sigma\, d3_{7l}.RBD_{t-1} \\ & + d3_8.D(AGDP)_t + \Sigma\, d3_{9l}.D^2(APDFL)_{t-1} + \delta 3_1.L91_{t-1} + u_{3t} \end{aligned} \quad (6)$$

3.4.3 Services

D(SGDP), SGCF and D(SPDFL) are the variables appearing in the cointegrating vector. D^2(NSGDP), D^2(IGCF) and D^2(IPDFL) are the predetermined variables (estimated in the sub-models of the industry and agriculture sectors). The postulated VEC model with a lag structure of 2 periods is as follows [estimation results in Table 3.2(c)]:

$$\begin{aligned} D^2(SGDP_t) = {} & a1[D(SGDP_{t-1} - b_1SGCFt_{t-1} - b_2D(SPDFL_{t-1})] \\ & + \Sigma\, c1_{1l}.D^2(SGDP)_{t-1} + \Sigma\, c1_{2l}.D(SGCF)_{t-1} + \Sigma\, c1_{3l}.D^2(SPDFL)_{t-1} \\ & + \Sigma\, d1_{1l}.D^2(WPF)_{t-1} + \Sigma\, d1_{2l}.D^2(RM3)_{t-1} + \Sigma\, d1_{3l}.D(RINVEXP)_{t-1} + \Sigma\, d1_{4l}.D(RINVIMP)_{t-1} \\ & + d1_5.D^2(NSGDP)_t + d1_6.D^2(IGCF)_t + \Sigma\, d1_{7l}.D^2(IPDFL)_{t-1} + d1_8.RBD_{t-1} + d1_9.RBR_t \\ & + d1_{10}.NETNAGEXP_t + \delta 1_1.TR81_t + constant + u_{1t} \end{aligned} \quad (7)$$

$$\begin{aligned} D(SGCF_t) = {} & a2[D(SGDP_{t-1} - b_1SGCFt_{t-1} - b_2D(SPDFL_{t-1})] \\ & + \Sigma\, c2_{1l}.D^2(SGDP)_{t-1} + \Sigma\, c2_{2l}.D(SGCF)_{t-1} + \Sigma\, c2_{3l}.D^2(SPDFL)_{t-1} \\ & + \Sigma\, d2_{1l}.D^2(WPF)_{t-1} + \Sigma\, d2_{2l}.D^2(RM3)_{t-1} + \Sigma\, d2_{3l}.D(RINVEXP)_{t-1} + \Sigma\, d2_{4l}.D(RINVIMP)_{t-1} \\ & + d2_5.D^2(NSGDP)_t + d2_6.D^2(IGCF)_t + \Sigma\, d2_{7l}.D^2(IPDFL)_{t-1} + d2_8.RBD_{t-1} + d2_9.RBR_t \\ & + d2_{10}.NETNAGEXP_t + \delta 2_1.TR81_t + constant + u_{2t} \end{aligned} \quad (8)$$

$$\begin{aligned} D^2(SPDFL_t) = {} & a3[D(SGDP_{t-1} - b_1SGCFt_{t-1} - b_2D(SPDFL_{t-1})] \\ & + \Sigma\, c3_{1l}.D^2(SGDP)_{t-1} + \Sigma\, c3_{2l}.D(SGCF)_{t-1} + \Sigma\, c3_{3l}.D^2(SPDFL)_{t-1} \\ & + \Sigma\, d3_{1l}.D^2(WPF)_{t-1} + \Sigma\, d3_{2l}.D^2(RM3)_{t-1} + \Sigma\, d3_{3l}.D(RINVEXP)_{t-1} + \Sigma\, d3_{4l}.D(RINVIMP)_{t-1} \\ & + d3_5.D^2(NSGDP)_t + d3_6.D^2(IGCF)_t + \Sigma\, d3_{7l}.D^2(IPDFL)_{t-1} + d3_8.RBD_t + d3_9.RBR_t \\ & + d3_{10}.NETNAGEXP_t + \delta 3_1.TR81_t + constant + u_{3t} \end{aligned} \quad (9)$$

where $NSGDP_t = AGDP_t + IGDP_t$ = Non-services GDP is I(2).

3.4.4 Households

D(PFCE), D(HFS) and D(HPS) are the variables appearing in the cointegrating vector. D(AGDP) and D^2(NAGDP) are the predetermined variables (estimated in the sub-models of the agriculture, industry and services sectors). The postulated VEC model with a lag structure of 2 periods is as follows [estimation results in Table 3.2(d)]:

$$\begin{aligned} D^2(PFCE_t) = {} & a1[D(PFCE_{t-1}) - b_1D(HFS_{t-1} - b_2D(HPS_{t-1})] \\ & + \Sigma\, c1_{1l}.D^2(PFCE)_{t-1} + \Sigma\, c1_{2l}.D^2(HFS)_{t-1} + \Sigma\, c1_{3l}.D^2(HPS)_{t-1} \\ & + \Sigma\, d1_{1l}.D^2(RM3)_{t-1} + d1_2.D(NETRINVEXP)_t + \Sigma\, d1_{3l}D(NAGIMP_{t-1}) + \Sigma\, d1_{4l}RBR_{t-1} \\ & + \Sigma\, d1_{5l}.D^2(WPF)_{t-1} + d1_{6l}.D(NAGEXP_t) + \Sigma\, d1_{7l}D(AGDP_{t-1}) + \Sigma\, d1_{8l}.D^2(NAGDP_{t-1}) \\ & + \Sigma\, d1_{9l}D(AGEXP_{t-1}) + constant + u_{1t} \end{aligned} \quad (10)$$

$$\begin{aligned} D^2(HFS_t) = {} & a2[D(PFCE_{t-1}) - b_1 D(HFS_{t-1}) - b_2 D(HPS_{t-1})] \\ & + \Sigma\, c2_{1l}.D^2(PFCE)_{t-l} + \Sigma\, c2_{2l}.D^2(HFS)_{t-l} + \Sigma\, c2_{3l}.D^2(HPS)_{t-l} \\ & + \Sigma\, d2_{1l}.D^2(RM3)_{t-l} + d2_2.D(NETRINVEXP)_t + \Sigma\, d2_{3l} D(NAGIMP_{t-l}) + \Sigma\, d2_{4l} RBR_{t-l} \\ & + \Sigma\, d2_{5l}.D^2(WPF)_{t-l} + d2_{6l}.D(NAGEXP_t) + \Sigma\, d2_{7l} D(AGDP_{t-l}) + \Sigma\, d2_{8l} D^2(NAGDP_{t-l}) \\ & + \Sigma\, d2_{9l} D(AGEXP_{t-1}) + constant + u_{2t} \end{aligned} \tag{11}$$

$$\begin{aligned} D^2(HPS_t) = {} & a3[D(PFCE_{t-1}) - b_1 D(HFS_{t-1}) - b_2 D(HPS_{t-1})] \\ & + \Sigma\, c3_{1l}.D^2(PFCE)_{t-l} + \Sigma\, c3_{2l}.D^2(HFS)_{t-l} + \Sigma\, c3_{3l}.D^2(HPS)_{t-l} \\ & + \Sigma\, d3_{1l}.D^2(RM3)_{t-l} + d3_2.D(NETRINVEXP)_t + \Sigma\, d3_{3l} D(NAGIMP_{t-l}) + \Sigma\, d3_{4l} RBR_{t-l} \\ & + \Sigma\, d3_{5l}.D^2(WPF)_{t-l} + d3_{6l}.D(NAGEXP_t) + \Sigma\, d3_{7l} D(AGDP_{t-l}) + \Sigma\, d3_{8l} D^2(NAGDP_{t-l}) \\ & + \Sigma\, d3_{9l} D(AGEXP_{t-1}) + constant + u_{3t} \end{aligned} \tag{12}$$

where $NAGDP_t = IGDP_t + SGDP_t$ = Non-agricultural GDP is I(2).

The results of the estimations, using the J-Multi software, are presented in Tables 3.2(a), 3.2(b), 3.2(c) and 3.2(d). For the lags and the number of cointegrating rank, the stability of the estimated models has been checked and the residual auto-correlations checked. Since the stability conditions are met and residuals are free from auto-correlations, the estimated models are considered to be satisfactory and reliable for forecasting purposes. More on these issues follows later under diagnostics.

Table 3.2(a): Agriculture: VEC Model Estimation Results

CIV_t	$AGDP_t$	$AGCF_t$	$D(APDFL_t)$	$L91_t$	$TR91_t$				
Coef	1.00	-3.5491	-1311004.3222	57159.176	-9680.4531				
t-statistics		-2.867	-4.557	2.414	-4.321				
$D(AGDP_t)$	$D(AGDP_{t-1})$	$D(AGDP_{t-2})$	$D(AGCF_{t-1})$	$D(AGCF_{t-2})$	$D^2(APDFL_{t-1})$	$D^2(APDFL_{t-2})$	CONST	CIV_{t-1}	RI_t
Coef	–0.1795	–0.0774	–0.8292	0.8772	–48712.5311	–56095.3052	–24600.715	–0.1202	371.5429
t-statistics	-1.71	-0.788	-1.417	1.174	-1.144	-1.373	-3.523	-3.457	6.158
	$D^2(WPFL_{t-1})$	RBD_{t-1}	$D(NAGEXP_{t-1})$	$D(NAGIMP_{t-1})$	$D(AGEXP_{t-1})$	$D^2(IGDP_{t-1})$	$D^2(IPDFL_{t-1})$	$D^2(IPDFL_{t-2})$	
Coef	– 416.3183	0.5712	0.6894	–1.3609	0.7594	0.9488	254609.5648	81355.4223	
t-statistics	-2.714	4.262	2.704	-4.591	0.952	4.348	3.801	1.298	
$D(AGCF_t)$	$D(AGDP_{t-1})$	$D(AGDP_{t-2})$	$D(AGCF_{t-1})$	$D(AGCF_{t-2})$	$D^2(APDFL_{t-1})$	$D^2(APDFL_{t-2})$	CONST	CIV_{t-1}	RI_t
Coef	–0.0104	0.0090	–0.5629	–0.0766	8834.9930	23392.4231	–1595.340	0.0178	11.0565
t-statistics	-0.473	0.435	- 4.567	-0.487	0.985	2.719	-1.085	2.434	0.870
	$D^2(WPFL_{t-1})$	RBD_{t-1}	$D(NAGEXP_{t-1})$	$D(NAGIMP_{t-1})$	$D(AGEXP_{t-1})$	$D^2(IGDP_{t-1})$	$D^2(IPDFL_{t-1})$	$D^2(IPDFL_{t-2})$	
Coef	–73.8772	–0.0853	0.0323	0.1095	0.3275	–0.0431	–51341.4662	–39172.1448	
t-statistics	-2.287	-3.020	0.601	1.753	1.950	-0.939	-3.639	-2.967	
$D^2(APDFL_t)$	$D(AGDP_{t-1})$	$D(AGDP_{t-2})$	$D(AGCF_{t-1})$	$D(AGCF_{t-2})$	$D^2(APDFL_{t-1})$	$D^2(APDFL_{t-2})$	CONST	CIV_{t-1}	RI_t
Coef	–5.86E-07	–9.57E-07	7.52E-06	–5.79E-07	– 0.0147	– 0.132	–0.0339	6.37E-07	–1.78E-04
t-statistics	-2.071	-3.617	4.771	-0.288	-0.128	-1.197	-1.803	6.798	-1.096
	$D^2(WPFL_{t-1})$	RBD_{t-1}	$D(NAGEXP_{t-1})$	$D(NAGIMP_{t-1})$	$D(AGEXP_{t-1})$	$D^2(IGDP_{t-1})$	$D^2(IPDFL_{t-1})$	$D^2(IPDFL_{t-2})$	
Coef	9.69E-04	9.43E-07	–1.52E-06	1.51E-06	4.11E-06	4.91E-07	–0.0682	–0.285	
t-statistics	2.346	2.612	-2.222	1.893	1.915	0.836	-0.378	-1.688	

No. of observations: 43; Degrees of freedom: 13; CIV=Cointegration Vector.

Table 3.2(b): Industry: VEC Model Estimation Results

CIV_t	$D(IGDP_t)$	$D(IGCF_t)$	$D(IPDFL_t)$	$TR91_t$				
Coef	1.00	-0.5851	-158848.3909	-2149.3102				
t-statistics		-8.501	-5.921	-6.916				
$D^2(IGDP_t)$	$D^2(IGDP_{t-1})$	$D^2(IGCF_{t-1})$	$D^2(IPDFL_{t-1})$	CIV_{t-1}	$L91_{t-1}$	$D^2(WPF_{t-1})$	$D^2(RM3_{t-1})$	$D(PCSS_t)$
Coef	– 0.1774	– 0.0654	– 4808.7767	– 0.364	– 11186.7809	– 194.7879	0.2042	0.2453
t-statistics	-1.319	-1.867	-0.124	-3.898	-4.668	-2.269	4.243	1.121
	$D(NAGEXP_t)$	$D(NETPETIMP_t)$	RBR_{t-1}	RBD_{t-1}	RBD_{t-2}	$D(AGDP_t)$	$D^2(APDFL_{t-1})$	
Coef	0.9788	– 0.4969	– 160.2381	– 0.1049	– 0.0869	0.1589	52443.6835	
t-statistics	5.361	-3.115	-1.176	-1.896	-1.327	3.140	2.290	
$D^2(IGCF_t)$	$D^2(IGDP_{t-1})$	$D^2(IGCF_{t-1})$	$D^2(IPDFL_{t-1})$	CIV_{t-1}	$L91_{t-1}$	$D^2(WPF_{t-1})$	$D^2(RM3_{t-1})$	$D(PCSS_t)$
Coef	– 0.5928	0.0657	117665.6722	1.7303	24319.1195	– 330.6235	0.6124	2.2193
t-statistics	-1.105	0.470	0.762	4.646	2.544	-0.965	3.190	2.542
	$D(NAGEXP_t)$	$D(NETPETIMP_t)$	RBR_{t-1}	RBD_{t-1}	RBD_{t-2}	$D(AGDP_t)$	$D^2(APDFL_{t-1})$	
Coef	0.7100	– 1.0958	– 1313.9845	– 0.3814	0.0127	0.0965	138071.2371	
t-statistics	0.975	-1.722	-2.418	-1.728	0.048	0.478	1.512	
$D^2(IPDFL_t)$	$D^2(IGDP_{t-1})$	$D^2(IGCF_{t-1})$	$D^2(IPDFL_{t-1})$	CIV_{t-1}	$L91_{t-1}$	$D^2(WPF_{t-1})$	$D^2(RM3_{t-1})$	$D(PCSS_t)$
Coef	– 1.27E-06	3.8E-07	– 0.498	7.35E-07	0.00113	6.22E-04	4.07E-07	1.73E-06
t-statistics	-2.876	3.305	-3.921	2.401	0.144	2.207	2.578	2.415
	$D(NAGEXP_t)$	$D(NETPETIMP_t)$	RBR_{t-1}	RBD_{t-1}	RBD_{t-2}	$D(AGDP_t)$	$D^2(APDFL_{t-1})$	
Coef	8.47E-07	– 6.54E-07	– 4.25E-04	7.14E-07	– 6.26E-07	– 1.61E-07	0.261	
t-statistics	1.415	-1.250	-0.951	3.936	-2.914	-0.971	3.474	

No. of observations: 43; Degrees of freedom: 13; CIV=Cointegration Vector.

Table 3.2(c): Services: VEC Model Estimation Results

CIV_t	$D(SGDP_t)$	$SGCF_t$	$D(SPDFL_t)$							
Coef	1.00	-0.51882	154343.4241							
t-statistics		-5.016	2.845							
$D^2(SGDP_t)$	$D^2(SGDP_{t-1})$	$D^2(SGDP_{t-2})$	$D(SGCF_{t-1})$	$D(SGCF_{t-2})$	$D^2(SPDFL_{t-1})$	$D^2(SPDFL_{t-2})$	CONST	CIV_{t-1}	$TR81_t$	$D^2(WPF_{t-1})$
Coef	–0.1171	0.2463	–0.0995	–0.2582	55268.0357	11833.3208	–5226.6476	–0.7901	225.9592	–179.4704
t-statistics	-0.779	2.341	-1.139	-2.662	1.578	0.414	-5.199	-5.090	2.691	-2.829
	$D^2(RM3_t)$	$D^2(RM3_{t-1})$	$D(RINVEXP_{t-1})$	$D(RINVIMP_{t-1})$	$D^2(NSGDP_t)$	$D^2(IGCF_t)$	$D^2(IPDFL_t)$	$D^2(IPDFL_{t-1})$	RBD_t	RBR_t
Coef	0.1065	0.1132	0.4217	–0.6067	–0.0202	0.0341	–119409.2790	93257.4899	–0.0648	79.2295
t-statistics	2.333	2.540	4.407	-2.891	-1.369	1.961	-4.032	2.814	-1.134	0.987
	$NETNAGEXP_t$									
Coef	–0.2297									
t-statistics	-4.073									
$D(SGCF_t)$	$D^2(SGDP_{t-1})$	$D^2(SGDP_{t-2})$	$D(SGCF_{t-1})$	$D(SGCF_{t-2})$	$D^2(SPDFL_{t-1})$	$D^2(SPDFL_{t-2})$	CONST	CIV_{t-1}	$TR81_t$	$D^2(WPF_{t-1})$
Coef	–0.1339	0.5459	0.4816	0.1519	–44213.3754	56283.8311	3817.9199	0.6562	–457.7458	–340.6785
t-statistics	-0.524	3.051	3.241	0.921	-0.742	1.158	2.233	2.486	-3.206	-3.158
	$D^2(RM3_t)$	$D^2(RM3_{t-1})$	$D(RINVEXP_{t-1})$	$D(RINVIMP_{t-1})$	$D^2(NSGDP_t)$	$D^2(IGCF_t)$	$D^2(IPDFL_t)$	$D^2(IPDFL_{t-1})$	RBD_t	RBR_t
Coef	0.4185	0.064	–0.1445	1.273	0.0571	0.2179	169268.9807	99697.2861	0.2162	–176.435
t-statistics	5.392	0.844	-0.888	3.568	2.275	7.372	3.361	1.769	2.225	-1.292
	$NETNAGEXP_t$									
Coef	0.1911									
t-statistics	1.993									

...contd...

...contd...

$D^2(SPDFL_t)$	$D^2(SGDP_{t-1})$	$D^2(SGDP_{t-2})$	$D(SGCF_{t-1})$	$D(SGCF_{t-2})$	$D^2(SPDFL_{t-1})$	$D^2(SPDFL_{t-2})$	CONST	CIV_{t-1}	$TR81_t$	$D^2(WPF_{t-1})$
Coef	2.28E-06	1.04E-06	– 7.54E-07	– 6.09E-07	– 0.419	– 0.0813	– 0.00458	– 1.06E-06	4.61E-4	6.93E-04
t-statistics	5.431	3.535	-3.086	-2.248	-4.281	-1.017	-1.630	-2.451	1.966	3.907
	$D^2(RM3_t)$	$D^2(RM3_{t-1})$	$D(RINVEXP_{t-1})$	$D(RINVIMP_{t-1})$	$D^2(NSGDP_t)$	$D^2(IGCF_t)$	$D^2(IPDFL_t)$	$D^2(IPDFL_{t-1})$	RBD_t	RBR_t
Coef	– 5.94E-07	– 5.68E-07	– 7.00E-07	1.57E-06	4.45E-09	1.54E-07	0.387	0.242	– 1.80E-07	– 4.46E-4
t-statistics	-4.658	-4.563	-2.619	2.683	0.108	3.180	4.676	2.612	-1.128	-1.985
	$NETNAGEXP_t$									
Coef	– 5.66E-8									
t-statistics	-0.359									

No. of observations included: 45; Degrees of freedom: 15; CIV=Cointegration Vector.

Table 3.2(d): Consumption: VEC Model Estimation Results

CIV_t	$D(PFCE_t)$	$D(HFS_t)$	$D(HPS_t)$
Coef	1.00	-3.0838	-0.7632
t-statistics		-7.099	-2.761

$D^2(PFCE_t)$	$D^2(PFCE_{t-1})$	$D^2(PFCE_{t-2})$	$D^2(HFS_{t-1})$	$D^2(HFS_{t-2})$	$D^2(HPS_{t-1})$	$D^2(HPS_{t-2})$	CONST	CIV_{t-1}	$D^2(RM3_{t-1})$	
Coef	– 0.4279	– 0.1646	– 0.6255	– 0.3422	– 0.0128	0.0063	– 150.5647	– 0.3137	– 0.0635	
t-statistics	-3.260	-1.828	-3.228	-2.534	-0.118	0.078	-0.174	-3.533	-0.640	
	D(NETRINV EXP $_t$)	D(NAG IMP $_{t-1}$)	RBR_{t-1}	$D^2(WPF_{t-1})$	D(NAG EXP $_t$)	$D(AGDP_t)$	D^2(NA GDP $_t$)	D^2(NA GDP $_{t-1}$)	$D(AGDP_{t-1})$	D(AG EXP $_{t-1}$)
Coef	0.0195	0.5195	235.9115	-3.2347	– 0.6929	0.6845	0.4093	0.1495	– 0.0840	– 1.0549
t-statistics	0.089	2.916	1.178	-0.026	-4.167	7.985	3.717	0.931	-0.686	-1.085
$D^2(HFS_t)$	$D^2(PFCE_{t-1})$	$D^2(PFCE_{t-2})$	$D^2(HFS_{t-1})$	$D^2(HFS_{t-2})$	$D^2(HPS_{t-1})$	$D^2(HPS_{t-2})$	CONST	CIV_{t-1}	$D^2(RM3_{t-1})$	
Coef	– 0.9084	– 0.4840	0.6116	0.1543	0.4766	0.3240	–3356.8695	0.6483	– 0.1219	
t-statistics	-5.584	-4.336	2.545	0.922	3.557	3.231	-3.134	5.889	-0.992	
	D(NETRINV EXP $_t$)	D(NAG IMP $_{t-1}$)	RBR_{t-1}	$D^2(WPF_{t-1})$	D(NAG EXP $_t$)	$D(AGDP_t)$	D(NA GDP $_t$)	D(NA GDP $_{t-1}$)	$D(AGDP_{t-1})$	D(AG EXP $_{t-1}$)
Coef	0.5779	– 0.4368	– 119.8926	157.7492	0.1083	0.0108	– 0.0513	0.6349	0.2890	1.1008
t-statistics	2.127	-1.977	-0.483	1.010	0.525	0.101	-0.376	3.191	1.903	0.914
$D^2(HPS_t)$	$D^2(PFCE_{t-1})$	$D^2(PFCE_{t-2})$	$D^2(HFS_{t-1})$	$D^2(HFS_{t-2})$	$D^2(HPS_{t-1})$	$D^2(HPS_{t-2})$	CONST	CIV_{t-1}	$D^2(RM3_{t-1})$	
Coef	0.4120	0.2020	0.5645	0.4248	– 0.4147	– 0.0806	123.5840	0.2019	0.7818	
t-statistics	3.348	2.392	3.106	3.355	-4.092	-1.063	0.153	2.425	8.410	
	D(NETRINV EXP $_t$)	D(NAG IMP $_{t-1}$)	RBR_{t-1}	$D^2(WPF_{t-1})$	D(NAG EXP $_t$)	$D(AGDP_t)$	D(NA GDP $_t$)	D(NA GDP $_{t-1}$)	$D(AGDP_{t-1})$	D(AG EXP $_{t-1}$)
Coef	– 0.6646	0.1003	– 546.1539	– 759.3496	0.5570	0.0770	0.4304	– 0.6838	– 0.6686	1.7447
t-statistics	-3.233	0.600	-2.909	-6.429	3.573	0.958	4.168	-4.543	-5.823	1.915

No. of observations included: 45; Degrees of freedom: 15; CIV=Cointegration Vector.

3.4.5 Commodity-wise Consumption Expenditures

In the households' sub-model above, the aggregate (over all commodities and over all households) private final consumption expenditure (PFCE) was estimated. Next step is to disaggregate the estimated PFCE into commodity-wise consumptions.

Usually knowing the total consumption expenditure and commodity-wise prices, commodity-wise disaggregations are modelled as a complete demand system such as Linear Expenditure System (LES) etc. Such complete demand systems are generally estimated using the available large-scale cross-sectional data. For India, such data are provided by the consumer expenditure surveys conducted by the National Samples Survey Organisation, but these data are not available for all the years continuously. Hence, these data are only of limited use for our purpose here. Besides, all the basic data that have been used in estimating the above four components are from the National Accounts Statistics (NAS) provided by the Central Statistical

Organisation (CSO). The NAS data provide commodity-wise consumption data for all the years continuously (year 1961 onwards)—but these data are not cross-sectional. They represent aggregation over all households in the country and hence with only one observation per year for different commodity groups. We have decided to use the NAS' commodity-wise time-series data (with necessary re-aggregation) for estimating a LES-type disaggregation system to split the PFCE into different commodity groups.[2] Appendix A-3.3 (with equations 13 to 30) gives the technical details of our estimations.

For disaggregating the PFCE into commodity groups two alternative groupings are made as follows:

Group A:

(i)	(FMMB)	Food, beverages etc.
(ii)	(CLR)	Clothing etc.
(iii)	(FLP)	Fuel etc.
(iv)	(OT)	Transport, Furnishings etc.
(v)	(ED)	Education
(vi)	(CO)	Communication
(vii)	(MI)	Miscellaneous
(viii)	(MD)	Medical expenditure
(viii)	(MD)	Medical expenditure

Table A-3.3(a) (in Appendix A-3.3) presents the corresponding LES estimated as Zellner's Seemingly Unrelated Equations System.

Group B:

(i)	(CRL)	Cereals and bread
(ii)	(PUL)	Pulses
(iii)	(MIL)	Milk and milk products
(iv)	(OF)	All other foods
(v)	(CLR)	Clothing etc.
(vi)	(FLP)	Fuel etc.
(vii)	(CO)	Communication
(viii)	(OT)	All Others

Table A-3.3(b) (in Appendix A-3.3) presents the corresponding estimated LES.

(i), (ii), (iii) and (iv) in group B would add up to (i) in group A.

(iv), (v), (vii) and (viii) in group A would add up to (viii) in group B.

Tables A-3.1(f) and A-3.1(g) (in Appendix A-3.1) present the data.

3.5 Estimation Results

3.5.1 Long-run Equilibrium (LRE) Relations

The estimated LREs (otherwise CIVs), where all the coefficients are significant in all the four VEC models [Tables 3.2(a-d)] are:

Agriculture:

$$AGDP_t = 3.5491*AGCF_t + 1311004.3221*D(APDFL_t) - 57159.176*L91_t + 9680.4531*TR91_t \quad (31)$$

2. Had the NSSO data been used by us, the controversial issue of mismatch between the consumption data of NAS and NSSO would arise.

Industry:

$$D(IGDP_t) = 0.5851*D(IGCF_t) + 158848.3909*D(IPDFL_t) + 2149.3102*TR91_t \quad (32)$$

Services:

$$D(SGDP_t) = 0.51882*SGCF_t - 154343.4241*D(SPDFL_t) \quad (33)$$

Households:

$$D(PFCE_t) = 3.0838*D(HFS_t) + 0.7632*D(HPS_t) \quad (34)$$

In agriculture and industry the respective GDPs have positive responses to prices and investments in the long-run. In the case of services, SGDP has positive relation to the rising SGCF but negative relation with prices. Within the cointegrating relations, the TR91 variable is significant both for agriculture and industry, but not for services. The L91 variable turned out significant only in agriculture (with a negative sign). The results imply that the reform effects on agriculture GDP were negative in the beginning and only later on turned out positive (57159.18/9680.45=5.90, i.e., 6 years approximately; thus from 1996-97 onwards positive). In agriculture and industry the significance of the TR91 variable indicates that the 1991 reforms caused a trend shift in the corresponding cointegrating relations. The L91 variable though turned out insignificant (hence dropped) in the industry's cointegrating relation, it is significant however with a lag (i.e. $L91_{t-1}$) in the VAR part of the industry model showing short-run negative effect on IGDP and positive effect on IGCF and insignificant effect on IPDFL. Neither TR91 nor L91 variable turned out significant within the cointegrating relation of the services sector. Services sector is however known to have been doing quite well because some of the reforms that the sector needed were initiated during the 1980s itself (TR81 variable in the VAR part shows positive significant affects on the SGDP and SPDFL). The 1991-reforms did not lead to any significant affect on the basic long-run relation that prevails between the GDP, investment and prices within the services sector. Similar result holds true for the households also: neither L91, nor TR81, nor TR91 turned out to be significant in the long-run relation between the consumption expenditure and the savings in the form of financial and physical assets.

It is possible to give economic interpretation to the long-run cointegrated relations. However, this depends on which variable is normalised. For example consider the LREs of the agricultural and industrial sectors.

$$AGDP_t = 3.5491*AGCF_t+1311004.3221*D(APDFL_t) - 57159.176*L91_t + 9680.4531*TR91_t \quad (31)$$

$$D(IGDP_t) = 0.5851*D(IGCF_t) + 158848.3909*D(IPDFL_t) + 2149.3102*TR91_t \quad (32)$$

As the investments and/or prices go up the GDPs go up. Thus, it could be treated as an aggregate supply response of the agricultural and industrial GDPs to the corresponding prices and investment. Now consider the services sector's LRE.

$$D(SGDP_t) = 0.51882*SGCF_t - 154343.4241*D(SPDFL_t) \quad (33)$$

Here the SGDP is negatively related to the services prices and positively to the investment. Could this be supply or demand equation? For example, when this equation is normalised with respect to prices and the model is re-estimated, the following LRE is obtained:

$$D(SPDFL_t) = 0.00000336*SGCF_t - 0.00000648*D(SGDP_t) \quad (33')$$

The parameter estimates of all the other variables (except for the adjustment parameter) are same as with the former GDP-normalised model (i.e., equations 7 to 9) model. But now equation (33') can be interpreted as, prices would fall with increasing GDP. For the households sector the corresponding LRE indicates that the aggregate consumption and the total (financial + physical) savings balance each other moving in the same direction. That implies that in India growth in households' savings (consumptions) is not at the expense of cutting down their consumption (savings) level. However, there could be a trade off between the forms of (financial or physical) savings given the consumption level.

3.5.2 Error Corrections and Adjustments

The signs and p-values of the adjustment parameters (a1, a2, a3 and a4) in the equations (1 to 12) of the four sectors are as follows [see Tables 3.2(a), 3.2(b), 3.2(c) and 3.2(d)]:

	D(AGDP)	D(AGCF)	D^2(APDFL)
Agriculture:	-ve & Significant(0.00)	+ve & Significant(0.021)	+ve & Significant(0.00)
	D^2(IGDP)	D^2(IGCF)	D^2(IPDFL)
Industry:	-ve & Significant(0.015)	+ve & Significant(0.00)	+ve & Significant(0.004)
	D^2(SGDP)	D(SGCF)	D^2(SPDFL)
Services:	-ve & Significant(0.00)	+ve & Significant(0.014)	-ve & Significant(0.00)
	D^2(PFCE)	D^2(HFS)	D^2(HPS)
Households:	-ve & Significant(0.00)	+ve & Significant(0.00)	+ve & Significant(0.025)

This constitutes an important result. The error correction mechanisms work as follows. The GDPs, investments and prices together react to any deviations from the long-run equilibrium path and adjust themselves to return to the equilibrium path. In the case of services, for example, when either the SGDP and/or SPDFL rise too high relative to the SGCF the disturbed long-run equilibrium path gets restored by a fall in the D^2(SGDP) and/or D^2(SPDFL) and a rise in the D(SGCF). Note that the adjustment parameters are all significant, and negative for D^2(SGDP) and D^2(SPDFL) but positive for D(SGCF). In the case of agriculture, any positive deviations from the equilibrium path cause the D(AGDP) to fall and the D(AGCF) and D^2(APDFL) to rise. All the adjustment parameters are significant, and negative for the D(AGDP) and positive for the D(AGCF) and D^2(APDFL). The situation is exactly similar in the case of industry also. Recall that actually different unit root tests indicated different orders of integration (Table 3.1). So when the industry model was estimated treating IGDP and IGCF as I(1) not only the signs of the co-integrating parameters were wrong, but also some of the adjustment coefficients turned out insignificant. Under the circumstances, one way out could have been the Bounds Testing Approach suggested by Pesaran, Shin and Smith (2001) which tests for existence of level relationships between the variables when the orders of integration are not known whether they are I(0) or I(1). Here in our case they are certainly not I(0). The uncertainty is, are they I(1) or I(2)? Only when they were treated as I(2) as in equations 4, 5 and 6, the results turned out satisfactory and also the signs of all the adjustment parameters turned out sensible. This demonstrates that misidentification of the order of integration could lead to wrong signs of the adjustment parameters. In the case of households, whenever the PFCE rises above the long-run equilibrium level, the error correction brings it down (adjustment parameter negative) and pushes up both the forms of savings (adjustment parameters positive).

3.6 Diagnostics

The estimated VEC models have been diagnosed with respect to the issues such as multicollinearity, stationarity of the LREs, auto-correlations, stability of the estimated parameters and stability of the models. Appendix A-3.4 and Tables A-3.4(a) and A-3.4(b) therein give the technical details associated in this regard.

3.7 Simulation Model

In general, policy analysis in the case of VEC/VAR models is done through impulse response functions (IRF). The IRF procedure rests on analysing the impact of an innovation in one of the endogenous (but not exogenous) variables on the other endogenous variables—usually done through the Vector Moving Average (VMA) representation based on the crucial feature that the endogenous variables and 'error terms' are correlated. Here our interest is not only in assessing the impacts on some endogenous variables due to innovations in some other endogenous variables (as in the IRF analysis), but also assessing the impacts due to changes in exogenous variables. Our interest is to analyse, for example, the impact of a drastic change in the fuel prices or money supply or budget deficit etc., or the impact of inadequate rainfall (and so on), on GDPs, GCFs, price levels and consumption patterns.

IRF analysis is useful to analyse the effects of unpredictable structural shocks within the endogenous variables. This is not applicable to analyse the effects of changes in the exogenous variables on endogenous variables. Luetkepohl and Kratzig (2004: 161) say " ....exogenous variables if they are under the control of some policy maker, may not react to stochastic shocks of the system......". We believe, the specified levels of exogenous variables under the planners' control are uncorrelated with any error terms. Keeping this in mind, our simulation analysis based on the above estimated VEC models has been done as follows.

The simulation model involves pooling the above VEC models in a particular sequence. For each time period (year), simulate first the agriculture model with already known values of the predetermined variables and pre-specified levels of the exogenous variables such as RM3, NAGEXP, NAGIMP, RBR etc. Collect the forecast values of the AGDP, AGCF and APDFL. Then simulate the industry model using the forecasts of the agriculture model as predetermined variables along with other pre-specified exogenous variables. This gives forecasts of the IGDP, IGCF and IPDFL. Now simulate the services model using the forecasts of the agriculture and industry models as predetermined variables along with other pre-specified exogenous variables. This gives forecasts of the SGDP, SGCF and SPDFL. Using these forecasts of the sectoral GDPs and price deflators, and the given levels of exogenous variables, forecasts of the PFCE, HFS and HPS are simulated. Using the PFCE, the estimated equations (30) and (28) (in Appendix A-3.3) give us the commodity-wise consumption expenditures at 1993-94 prices for each i (i=1,8). Now move on to the next period simulation where the current period forecasts of the GDPs, GCFs and PDFLs of the three sectors would be used as one-period lagged (hence predetermined) values. Since for each period, only the forecast values (and not actual data) of the previous periods are used, this is dynamic simulation.

3.8 Dynamic Simulation within the Sample Period

While simulating the model, static simulations have been restricted to the period up to 1994. From 1995 to 2003 dynamic simulations have been made using actual data only for the exogenous variables, but not for the predetermined and endogenous variables for which the forecasts already made have been used. If the model generated forecasts of the endogenous variables for the period 1995-2003 (9 years) could come close to the actual data, the model could be treated as reliable for forecasting for the future (2004-2012).[3] See Tables 3.3 (a to d). The dynamic forecasting performance of the models for 1995 to 2003 can be assessed by the details given in Table 3.4.

There are 12 endogenous variables, each forecasted for 9 years period; i.e. total 108 different forecasts could be compared with the corresponding actual data. Table 3.4 shows that 53 per cent (57 out of 108) forecasts come within 3 per cent accuracy. 79 per cent forecasts fall within 6 per cent deviation, and 93 per cent forecasts fall within 10 per cent deviation.

3. Some studies follow a different procedure. They generally omit 3 to 4 years' data towards the end of the sample while estimating the models; and then forecasts made for the omitted period are compared for their closeness with the actual data. This procedure is fine if only there are not any major structural breaks in the omitted period and enough data are available. We have not omitted any observations during estimation since already severe data shortage problems exist, and there would not have been enough degrees of freedom if some data are to be omitted during estimation.

Table 3.3(a): Actual Data and Reference Run Forecasts [CAGR: Compound Annual Growth Rate between 2005 (Forecast) and 2012 (Forecast)]

Sector: Year	Total TGDP (Forecast)	Total TGDP (Actual)	Total TGCF (Forecast)	Total TGCF (Actual)	Total TPDFL (Forecast)	Total TPDFL (Actual)	Services SGDP (Forecast)	Services SGDP (Actual)	Services SGCF (Forecast)	Services SGCF (Actual)	Services SPDFL (Forecast)	Services SPDFL (Actual)
1995	844032	838031	224132	229879	1.0877	1.0943	359891	357890	89777	95360	1.0843	1.0890
1996	886454	899563	278004	284557	1.1957	1.1931	389821	395312	94676	94300	1.1956	1.1849
1997	959769	970083	243904	248631	1.2778	1.2819	426924	423774	86064	84785	1.2694	1.2738
1998	984455	1016594	253058	256551	1.3858	1.3675	450571	465423	97502	89591	1.3668	1.3420
1999	1082085	1082748	233588	243697	1.4682	1.4760	512476	504307	89699	87045	1.4335	1.4517
2000	1104583	1148368	267946	267284	1.5624	1.5342	535877	555049	106827	102988	1.5541	1.5211
2001	1196399	1198592	255307	254853	1.6123	1.5877	594975	585535	120598	110977	1.5927	1.5853
2002	1249910	1267833	241144	253230	1.7042	1.6492	615203	625090	117745	118164	1.7082	1.6512
2003	1318279	1318321	250445	270825	1.7520	1.7063	677743	669719	122822	115732	1.7466	1.7038
2004	1397763	0	254128	0	1.8409	0	720495	0	119383	0	1.8533	0
2005	1529447	0	282111	0	1.8886	0	794506	0	136306	0	1.8929	0
2006	1631959	0	335649	0	1.9582	0	855094	0	156097	0	1.9708	0
2007	1767680	0	401217	0	2.0072	0	934357	0	189072	0	2.0105	0
2008	1920535	0	456488	0	2.0526	0	1018310	0	207102	0	2.0472	0
2009	2090250	0	529954	0	2.0985	0	1119865	0	233652	0	2.0811	0
2010	2285800	0	609621	0	2.1487	0	1238310	0	260159	0	2.1197	0
2011	2510862	0	706410	0	2.1981	0	1374829	0	299350	0	2.1545	0
2012	2763078	0	815492	0	2.2416	0	1533055	0	345792	0	2.1763	0
CAGR:	8.82%		16.37%		2.48%		9.85%		14.22%		2.01%	

Sector: Year	Industry IGDP (Forecast)	Industry IGDP (Actual)	Industry IGCF (Forecast)	Industry IGCF (Actual)	Industry IPDFL (Forecast)	Industry IPDFL (Actual)	Agriculture AGDP (Forecast)	Agriculture AGDP (Actual)	Agriculture AGCF (Forecast)	Agriculture AGCF (Actual)	Agriculture APDFL (Forecast)	Agriculture APDFL (Actual)
1995	222100	226051	118114	117734	1.0886	1.0995	262041	254090	16241	16785	1.0917	1.0971
1996	243280	252359	164305	172568	1.2129	1.1958	253353	251892	19023	17689	1.1792	1.2033
1997	258052	270218	139540	145520	1.2591	1.2625	274794	276091	18301	18326	1.3084	1.3134
1998	266879	281788	135559	148666	1.3912	1.3433	267004	269383	19996	18294	1.4124	1.4366
1999	276706	292347	127201	139182	1.4436	1.4488	292903	286094	16688	17470	1.5524	1.5467
2000	290384	306336	140071	144272	1.5379	1.4872	278321	286983	21049	20024	1.6040	1.6097
2001	311643	326391	115180	124298	1.5974	1.5512	289781	286666	19530	19578	1.6686	1.6342
2002	325417	337480	105505	114608	1.6688	1.5909	309290	305263	17894	20458	1.7337	1.7097
2003	348113	359216	104393	133226	1.7383	1.6662	292424	289386	23231	21867	1.7807	1.7620
2004	377258	0	111287	0	1.8024	0	300010	0	23458	0	1.8593	0
2005	415326	0	120058	0	1.8560	0	319615	0	25747	0	1.9205	0
2006	456078	0	151670	0	1.9191	0	320787	0	27882	0	1.9799	0
2007	504592	0	183558	0	1.9860	0	328731	0	28587	0	2.0303	0
2008	560601	0	219613	0	2.0479	0	341623	0	29773	0	2.0765	0
2009	622012	0	264688	0	2.1172	0	348372	0	31613	0	2.1213	0
2010	690480	0	316330	0	2.1921	0	357011	0	33133	0	2.1655	0
2011	766280	0	372673	0	2.2718	0	369752	0	34387	0	2.2072	0
2012	848090	0	433601	0	2.3581	0	381933	0	36098	0	2.2451	0
CAGR:	10.74%		20.14%		3.48%		2.58%		4.95%		2.26%	

Table 3.3(b): Actual Data and Reference Run Forecasts [CAGR: Compound Annual Growth Rate between 2005 (Forecast) and 2012 (Forecast)]

Sector: Year	Consumption PFCE(Forecast)	Consumption PFCE(Actual)	Saving HFS(Forecast)	Saving HFS(Actual)	Saving HPS(Forecast)	Saving HPS(Actual)
1995	607759	601481	106377	110329	72896	71850
1996	632494	638938	96918	88608	87243	92549
1997	685560	689566	119146	110509	73523	71450
1998	696374	707285	126925	107336	72776	88968
1999	761798	752440	114694	122186	106669	99225
2000	783879	797653	157165	134103	93473	129486
2001	824825	819637	138162	140280	146675	148325
2002	863022	867139	188644	154831	114677	161183
2003	900412	891419	155657	148763	162356	187235
2004	938312	0	195449	0	162579	0
2005	1008409	0	208880	0	205224	0
2006	1050022	0	227144	0	233049	0
2007	1123375	0	238888	0	268829	0
2008	1195937	0	267935	0	299512	0
2009	1273671	0	291446	0	334873	0
2010	1362419	0	331432	0	363769	0
2011	1466356	0	371314	0	385305	0
2012	1578327	0	415796	0	401086	0
CAGR:	6.61 %		10.33 %		10.05 %	

Table 3.3(c): Actual Data and Reference Run Forecasts [CAGR: Compound Annual Growth Rate between 2005 (Forecast) and 2012 (Forecast)]

	FMMB		CLR		FLP		OT	
Year	FORECAST	ACTUAL	FORECAST	ACTUAL	FORECAST	ACTUAL	FORECAST	ACTUAL
1995	327527	325436	84167	82372	22946	22494	93743	94250
1996	334564	340124	86429	85755	23918	23333	100400	103530
1997	359145	369285	89630	89232	26071	24379	112015	112464
1998	354819	363253	91905	93964	26367	27396	117563	118971
1999	387337	393468	95555	91245	28883	28495	131022	125798
2000	387644	400587	98415	98269	29707	30284	139412	134436
2001	401273	387447	101440	100180	30907	31529	148625	150407
2002	413824	413672	104525	101278	32178	31892	158064	158755
2003	422572	404034	107443	107267	33168	33765	166404	169013
2004	434579	0	110421	0	34306	0	175044	0
2005	464608	0	114443	0	36972	0	189868	0
2006	472331	0	117984	0	38461	0	201683	0
2007	500642	0	122320	0	41133	0	218187	0
2008	523907	0	126952	0	43888	0	236341	0
2009	548185	0	131856	0	46761	0	256000	C
2010	576891	0	137203	0	50042	0	278192	0
2011	611485	0	143198	0	53973	0	304129	0
2012	646684	0	149699	0	58223	0	332920	0
CAGR:	4.84		3.91		6.70		8.35	

contd...

contd...

	ED		CO		MI		MD	
Year	FORECAST	ACTUAL	FORECAST	ACTUAL	FORECAST	ACTUAL	FORECAST	ACTUAL
1995	10807	10244	5118	4964	41811	39951	21641	21770
1996	11458	11101	6091	5866	45762	44997	23871	24232
1997	12340	12020	7195	6887	52505	48421	26659	26878
1998	12942	13526	8445	7861	55017	52501	29316	29813
1999	13913	14605	9861	9374	62495	56376	32732	33079
2000	14661	16303	11465	11322	66438	69370	36139	37082
2001	15445	17518	16377	16208	70899	75135	39860	41213
2002	16240	17192	18848	19194	75468	78948	43876	45805
2003	16983	16914	26430	26730	79313	82765	48099	50931
2004	17736	0	30237	0	83376	0	52614	0
2005	18788	0	34551	0	91323	0	57857	0
2006	19722	0	39438	0	97106	0	63298	0
2007	20892	0	44975	0	105790	0	69437	0
2008	22171	0	51248	0	115273	0	76156	0
2009	23554	0	58355	0	125474	0	83487	0
2010	25092	0	66408	0	137053	0	91538	0
2011	26850	0	75531	0	150733	0	100458	0
2012	28796	0	85866	0	165875	0	110265	0
CAGR:	6.29		13.89		8.90		9.65	

Table 3.3(d): Actual Data and Reference Run Forecasts [CAGR: Compound Annual Growth Rate between 2005 (Forecast) and 2012 (Forecast)]

	CRL		PUL		MIL		OF	
Year	FORECAST	ACTUAL	FORECAST	ACTUAL	FORECAST	ACTUAL	FORECAST	ACTUAL
1995	81148	82525	11902	12707	51068	48790	185792	181414
1996	83165	84123	12010	11364	53526	54491	189193	190146
1997	85473	91119	12158	13045	56060	58634	209751	206487
1998	87895	82564	12313	11887	58668	62189	200215	206613
1999	90392	87535	12470	13398	61353	64371	228430	228164
2000	92957	88637	12628	11620	64112	71406	223238	228924
2001	79186	76194	10443	9418	66948	64528	242918	237307
2002	94817	90739	12481	11712	69858	67166	238092	244055
2003	73980	74246	9593	9698	72844	68067	258581	252023
2004	98151	0	12566	0	75905	0	246807	0
2005	105555	0	13278	0	79042	0	271572	0
2006	109466	0	13545	0	82254	0	275004	0
2007	112691	0	13724	0	85542	0	298895	0
2008	115822	0	13886	0	88905	0	316610	0
2009	118984	0	14044	0	92344	0	334493	0
2010	122205	0	14201	0	95858	0	356194	0
2011	125490	0	14359	0	99447	0	383151	0
2012	128840	0	14516	0	103112	0	409815	0
CAGR:	2.89		1.28		3.87		6.05	

contd...

contd...

Year	CLR FORECAST	CLR ACTUAL	FLP FORECAST	FLP ACTUAL	CO FORECAST	CO ACTUAL	OT FORECAST	OT ACTUAL
1995	83966	82372	22717	22494	5075	4964	166091	166215
1996	86008	85755	23578	23333	6008	5866	179007	183860
1997	89514	89232	25915	24379	7074	6887	199615	199783
1998	91362	93964	25980	27396	8292	7861	211648	214811
1999	95412	91245	28690	28495	9684	9374	235367	229858
2000	98013	98269	29369	30284	11274	11322	252288	257191
2001	101822	100180	31530	31529	16063	16208	275916	284273
2002	104291	101278	31978	31892	18563	19194	292943	300700
2003	108082	107267	34107	33765	26154	26730	317071	319623
2004	109926	0	33848	0	30092	0	331017	0
2005	113669	0	36057	0	34592	0	354643	0
2006	116822	0	37349	0	39733	0	375848	0
2007	121378	0	40228	0	45608	0	405310	0
2008	126343	0	43265	0	52319	0	438786	0
2009	131601	0	46397	0	59988	0	475819	0
2010	137396	0	49955	0	68750	0	517859	0
2011	144019	0	54242	0	78761	0	566888	0
2012	151178	0	58856	0	90199	0	621811	0
CAGR:	4.16		7.25		14.67		8.35	

Table 3.4: Number of Cases with Per cent Deviations of the Forecasts from Actual Data

	≤ 3.0%	3% - 6%	6% - 10%	≥ 10%
Productions:				
AGDP	7	2	0	0
AGCF	2	3	3	1
APDFL	9	0	0	0
IGDP	1	8	0	0
IGCF	2	2	4	1
IPDFL	5	4	0	0
SGDP	7	2	0	0
SGCF	3	3	3	0
SPDFL	8	1	0	0
Total	44 (54%)	25 (85%)	10 (98%)	2 (100%) = 81
Households:				
PFCE	9	0	0	0
HFS	1	2	4	2
HPS	3	1	1	4
Total	13 (48%)	3 (59%)	5 (78%)	6 (100%) = 27

contd...

...contd...

	≤ 3.0%	3% - 6%	6% - 10%	≥ 10%
Commodity Expenditures:				
GROUP A				
FMMB	6	3	0	0
CLR	7	2	0	0
FLP	7	1	1	0
OT	6	3	0	0
ED	2	5	0	2
CO	4	4	1	0
MI	1	6	1	1
MD	6	3	0	0
Total	39 (54%)	27 (92%)	3 (96%)	3 (100%) = 72
GROUP B				
CRL	3	4	2	0
PUL	1	2	5	1
MIL	1	6	1	1
OF	8	1	0	0
CLR	9	0	0	0
FLP	6	2	1	0
CO	6	3	0	0
OT	9	0	0	0
Total	43 (60%)	18 (85%)	9 (97%)	2 (100%) = 72

For commodity expenditures (either Group A or Group B), there are 8 endogenous variables each forecasted for 9 years period; i.e., total 72 different forecasts could be compared with the corresponding actual data. Table 3.4 shows that for Group A 92 per cent, and for Group B 85 per cent of the forecasts fall within 6 per cent accuracy.

The forecasts corresponding to the AGCF, IGCF and SGCF (and also for pulses) are somewhat unsatisfactory. Actually the years 1996 to 1999 seem to be really outliers for both IGCF and SGCF as well as for HPS, where a rising trend suddenly changed direction in these cases. The actual data (Rs. Crores[4]) for the IGCF, SGCF, AGCF, HPS and PUL may be noted:

	1994	1995	1996	1997	1998	1999	2000	2001	2002	2003
IGCF:	90735	117734	172568	145520	148666	139182	142754	124298	114608	133226
SGCF:	75149	95360	94300	84785	89591	87045	102988	110977	118164	115732
AFCF:	15249	16785	17689	18326	18294	17470	20024	19578	20458	21867
HPS:	63572	71850	92549	71450	88968	99225	129486	148325	161183	187235
PUL:	11994	12707	11364	13045	11887	13398	11620	9418	11712	9698

The ups and downs in the SGCF data are almost similar to the IGCF data. In general, in India the investment data particularly in the mid-1990s show drastic ups and downs causing much difficulty in modelling. Despite these hurdles, the static (1958 to 1994) and the dynamic (1995 to 2003) simulation results in general look quite satisfactory. Forecasting for future, and policy impacts are taken up in the next sections.

4. A crore = 10 millions = 100 lakhs.

3.9 Reference Run

3.9.1 Specifications

To quantify any policy impacts, first a reference run (RefRun—henceforth) is to be arrived at. Since this involves certain specifications for the exogenous variables for the period 2004-2012, the figures under the RefRun are not the conventional forecasts of the economy in the usual sense. They are only benchmarks for the policy runs to be compared with. Based on the past data of the exogenous variables for the period 1990 to 2003 [see Tables A-3.1(a to i) in Appendix A-3.1], specifications for the reference run have been arrived at as follows:

Rainfall (RF): Year 2003 would have actual rainfall and all the other years would have normal rainfall.

Fuel price index (WPF): Between the years 1990 and 1991, the fuel price rose nearly by 28 per cent; and between 1995 and 1996, it fell down marginally. The median value of year-to-year growth rates was more than 10 per cent. However, for the reference run, year 2003 would have actual price, and in the later years the same price would continue. This of course is quite an optimistic assumption.

Real money supply (RM3): [$RM3_t/GDP_t$] which was about 52 per cent in 1991 rose gradually to 76 per cent in the year 2003. This movement indicates that [$RM3_t/GDP_t$] is very likely to go up in the future periods too. RM3 grew by 4.1 per cent between 1990 and 1991 (minimum observed) and 12.9 per cent (maximum) between 2000 and 2001. For the period 1997 to 2003, annual growth rate has been mostly around 10 per cent. The reference run specification for RM3 is kept at 11 per cent growth a year for the period 2004 to 2011.

Real bank rate (RBR): The pre-reforms period was a regime of administered interest rates. From 1993 onwards, they are mostly market determined. This paper considers the bank rate as a surrogate for the interest rate structure (call money rate, treasury bill rate and commercial paper rate etc.). Real bank rate is defined as nominal bank rate minus inflation [$100.0*(TPDFL_t-TPDFL_{t-1})/TPDFL_{t-1}$; where TPDFL: Total GDP deflator.]. The RBR was negative in 1991 and 1992. The maximum was 4.56 per cent in 1997, while the median value was 2.71 per cent. The specified RBR in the reference run is 2.78 per cent for 2003 (actual value) and 0 per cent for all the later years up to 2012—that is, nominal bank rate is equal to inflation.

Real budget deficit (RBD): Since data on fiscal deficit are not available for all the years, 1951 to 2003, RBD was used as a surrogate variable in this paper. Real budget deficit is defined as nominal budget deficit divided by the GDP deflator [$TGDP_{\text{current prices}}/TGDP_{\text{1993-94 prices}}$]. RBD was, though negative in some years, generally positive. [RBD_t/GDP_t] was at maximum at 4.5 per cent in 1998, while the median value was 1.12 per cent. Either in this ratio or in annual growth rate, the RBD data however do not show any regular pattern. In the reference run, RBD is specified to grow at 20 per cent every year from 2004 onwards.

Real trade: In India, imports have always been more than the exports. Thus, trade balance has always been negative. In our model agricultural exports (AGEXP), non-agriculture exports & imports (NAGEXP and NAGIMP respectively), net petroleum imports (NETPETIMP), and exports & imports of invisibles including software (RINVEXP and RINVIMP respectively) have been distinguished, all in real terms. The pattern of the past data, and specifications for the reference run are as follows [also see Table A-3.1(e) in Appendix A-3.1]:

Annual Growth Rate (%) of the Variable	1991-2003				2002-2003		2003-2004		2004-05 to 2011-12 in the RefRun
	Average	Median	Minimum	Maximum	Actual	Specified	Actual	Specified	Specified
AGEXP	8.62	8.50	-7.91	40.62	10.74	10.74	3.51	10.00	10.00
NAGEXP	10.82	13.46	-1.54	20.55	18.14	18.14	11.96	11.00	10.00
NAGIMP	8.73	10.07	-11.11	27.57	13.48	13.48	21.59	10.00	9.50
NETPETIMP	17.12	11.66	-19.77	97.46	23.48	23.48	4.06	10.00	21.00
RINVEXP	15.92	14.60	-2.90	53.82	11.14	11.00	17.53	17.00	19.00
RINVIMP	12.10	9.22	-9.68	33.27	11.41	11.00	-4.80	-5.00	13.00

Private corporate savings (PCSS): Table A-3.1(b) shows that the ratio ($PCSS_t$/Non-agricultural GDP_{t-1}) varied between 4.4 per cent and 8.4 per cent during the 1990s. The data show a clear rising trend over time with a median value of 5.9 per cent for the period 1990-2003. In the reference run, the ratio was rather conservatively specified to be at 5 per cent for the years 2005 to 2012.

Thus, our reference run specifications, more or less, conform to a kind of "business as usual" except for the two quite optimistic assumptions that there would not be any hike in fuel prices and a normal rainfall would prevail in all the years, 2005 to 2012. The simulations have been made up to the year 2012. See Tables A-3.3(a to d) above. We report below cumulative annual growth rates (C.A.G.R) computed for two alternative durations—one for the period 2003 to 2012 (using the actual data for the year 2003 and forecast values for the year 2012), and the other for the period 2005 to 2012 (using the forecast values for the years 2005 and 2012).

3.9.2 Production Forecasts

The reference run subject to normal rainfall, no fuel price hike etc., indicates that overall the Indian economy can grow at about 8.82 per cent rate p.a. during 2005-2012; see Table 3.5. This constitutes agricultural growth at 2.58 per cent, services growth at 9.85 per cent and industry growth faster than the former two at 10.74 per cent rate. Industrial investment and industry prices grow faster than those of services and agriculture prices. In a way it seems, agriculture may continue to get low priority in terms of investment and thus unable to show impressive growth performance. Aggregate household consumption may grow at the rate of 6.61 per cent, financial savings at 10.33 per cent and physical assets at 10.05 per cent p.a.

Table 3.5: Compound Annual Growth Rates (CAGR %) under the RefRun

	2003 (actual) to 2012 (forecast)			2005 (forecast) to 2012 (forecast)		
	GDP	GCF	PDFL	GDP	GCF	PDFL
Agriculture:	3.13	5.73	2.73	2.58	4.95	2.26
Industry:	10.02	14.01	3.93	10.74	20.14	3.48
Services:	9.64	12.93	2.76	9.85	14.22	2.01
Total:	8.57	13.03	3.08	8.82	16.37	2.48
	PFCE	HFS	HPS	PFCE	HFS	HPS
Households:	6.55	12.10	8.83	6.61	10.33	10.05

Table 3.6: Compound Annual Growth Rates (CAGR) (%)—Past and Future

	1951-1960	1960-1970	1970-1980	1980-1990	1990-2003	2003 (actual) - 2012 (forecast)*	2005 (forecast) - 2012 (forecast)*
GDP	3.53	3.89	2.79	5.83	5.51	8.57	8.82
AGDP	2.62	2.28	0.96	4.27	2.34	3.13	2.58
IGDP	5.68	6.43	3.62	6.78	5.69	10.02	10.74
SGDP	4.08	4.88	4.45	6.63	7.33	9.64	9.85
GCF	7.1	5.43	5.55	5.52	4.16	13.03	16.37
AGCF	0.48	8.44	6.89	-2.54	3.82	5.73	4.95
IGCF	11.21	7.92	5.81	6.16	3.92	14.01	20.14
SGCF	6.87	2.16	4.56	7.59	4.51	12.93	14.22
PDFL	1.39	6.2	7.56	8.61	7.49	3.08	2.48
APDFL	0.54	7.66	6.84	8.4	8.12	2.73	2.26
IPDFL	1.9	4.99	9.11	8.59	7.02	3.93	3.48
SPDFL	2.41	4.75	7.47	8.72	7.37	2.76	2.01
HFS	22.40	1.50	12.33	10.54	7.67	12.10	10.33
HPS	3.76	8.30	3.83	7.24	7.47	8.83	10.05
PFCE	3.66	3.16	2.77	4.67	4.50	6.55	6.61

Note: *: The forecasts assume normal rainfall and no hike in fuel prices. GCF = AGCF+IGCF+SGCF does not include the component of adjustments for errors of omissions & commissions.

The total GDP is the sum of the sectoral (agriculture + industry + services) GDPs obtained from the respective models. The total GCF is merely the sum of the sectoral GCFs. This total is not equal to the total gross capital formation adjusted for errors & omissions, or "difference" as reported in the National Accounts Statistics. More discussion follows on this later (Section 3.9.7). The total price index (TPDFL) is the weighted sum of the sectoral prices, the weights being the shares of the different sectors in the total GDP. Juxtaposing these forecasts along with the C.A.G.R's of the actual data of the previous periods, Table 3.6 presents a comparative picture emerging between the past and the future.

3.9.3 Forecasts of Commodity Groups-wise Expenditures

The projected commodity groups-wise expenditures at 1993-94 prices corresponding to the above projections of the GDPs and the PFCE are reported in Tables 3.3(c) and 3.3(d). The commodity-wise projections are as follows:

Table 3.7: CAGRs (%) under the RefRun—Commodity-wise Consumptions

	2002 (actual) to 2012 (forecast)	2005 (forecast) to 2012 (forecast)		2002 (actual) to 2012 (forecast)	2005 (forecast) to 2012 (forecast)
GROUP A:			**GROUP B:**		
FMMB:	4.57	4.84	CRL:	3.57	2.89
CLR:	3.98	3.91	PUL:	2.17	1.28
FLP:	6.20	6.70	MIL:	4.38	3.87
OT:	7.69	8.35	OF:	5.32	6.05
ED:	5.29	6.29	CLR:	4.09	4.16
CO:	16.16	13.89	FLP:	6.32	7.25
MI:	7.71	8.90	CO:	16.74	14.67
MD:	9.18	9.65	OT:	7.54	8.35
TOTAL PFCE:	6.17	6.61	TOTAL PFCE:	6.17	6.61

Juxtaposing these forecasts along with the C.A.G.R's of the actual data of the previous periods, Table 3.8 presents a comparative picture emerging between the past and the future.

The aggregate consumption expenditure (PFCE) has grown at a rate more than 4.5 per cent between 1980 and 2003. The projections for 2005 to 2012 (covering the 11th FYP) indicate that this growth rate may go beyond 6.5 per cent. This is consistent with the expected increase in the GDPs' growth rates during the same period.

Table 3.8: Compound Annual Growth Rates (CAGR) (%) – Past and Future

	1951-1960	1960-1970	1970-1980	1980-1990	1990-2003	2002 (actual) - 2012 (forecast)*	2005 (forecast) - 2012 (forecast)*
PFCE	3.66	3.16	2.77	4.67	4.50	6.17	6.61
GROUP A		1961-1971	1971-1981	1981-1991	1991-2002	2002 (actual) - 2012 (forecast)*	2005 (forecast) - 2012 (forecast)*
FMMB	NA	2.84	2.83	3.31	3.19	4.57	4.84
CLR	NA	2.69	4.55	4.11	2.46	3.98	3.91
FLP	NA	2.68	3.12	3.30	4.58	6.20	6.70
OT	NA	5.18	4.37	8.96	7.30	7.69	8.35
ED	NA	8.65	3.69	5.48	5.46	5.29	6.29
CO	NA	13.26	5.91	6.08	17.52	16.16	13.89
MI	NA	1.92	4.08	6.55	8.80	7.71	8.90
MD	NA	7.54	5.71	2.14	8.61	9.18	9.65

contd...

contd...

GROUP B		1961-1971	1971-1981	1981-1991	1991-2002	2002 (actual)-2012 (forecast)*	2005 (forecast)-2012 (forecast)*
CRL	NA	2.81	1.88	3.15	1.21	3.57	2.89
PUL	NA	-0.74	1.92	2.89	-0.84	2.17	1.28
MIL	NA	1.16	6.19	4.86	4.66	4.38	3.87
OF	NA	3.56	2.80	3.06	3.91	5.32	6.05
CLR	NA	2.69	4.55	4.11	2.46	4.09	4.16
FLP	NA	2.68	3.12	3.30	4.58	6.32	7.25
CO	NA	13.26	5.91	6.08	17.52	16.74	14.67
OT	NA	4.87	4.51	6.87	7.74	7.54	8.35

Note: *: The forecasts assume normal rainfall and no hike in fuel prices.

Group A:

(i) (FMMB) Food, beverages etc.
(ii) (CLR) Clothing etc.
(iii) (FLP) Fuel etc.
(iv) (OT) Transport, furnishings etc.
(v) (ED) Education
(vi) (CO) Communication
(vii) (MI) Miscellaneous
(viii) (MD) Medical expenditure

Group B:

(i) (CRL) Cereals and bread
(ii) (PUL) Pulses
(iii) (MIL) Milk and milk products
(iv) (OF) All other foods
(v) (CLR) Clothing etc.
(vi) (FLP) Fuel etc.
(vii) (CO) Communication
(viii) (OT) All Others

(i), (ii), (iii) and (iv) in group B would add up to (i) in group A.

(iv), (v), (vii) and (viii) in group A would add up to (viii) in group B.

3.9.4 Food Items

The expenditure on total food under group A (cereals, pulses, beverages, meat, milk products and other food items together as FMMB) may grow at 4.57 per cent between 2002 and 2012 (or at 4.84 per cent between 2005 and 2012) compared to 3 and odd per cent observed for the period 1981 to 2002.[5] If the food is disaggregated into cereals (CRL), pulses (PUL), milk & milk products (MIL) and all other foods (OF) as in group B, some interesting patterns can be seen.

---

5. The growth rates of expenditures are presented with reference to 2002 (actual) since the years and 2001 and 2003 seem to be outliers. See Tables A-3.1(f) and A-3.1(g).

First, the (1961 to 2003) average percentages of these four items within the total food come to 27.11, 4.50, 12.46 and 55.33. The corresponding projected growth rates (in group B) for 2002-2012 are 3.57 per cent, 2.17 per cent, 4.38 per cent and 5.32 per cent. Using the proportions as weights, the weighted average growth rate of these four items comes to 4.59 per cent. Instead, if the simulated growth rates for 2005-2012 (i.e., 2.89 per cent, 1.28 per cent, 3.87 per cent and 6.05 per cent) are considered, the corresponding weighted average growth rate comes to 4.67 per cent. These figures are quite close to the 4.57 per cent and 4.84 per cent as projected in the group A exercise. This in a way implies the stability and reliability of the estimates and hence the projections.

Second, observe the growth rates of the four items for the decades 1981-1991 and 1991-2002 (Table 3.8). For cereals, the decadal growth rate has fallen from 3.15 per cent in 1981-1991 to 1.21 per cent in 1991-2002. The projections for 2012 indicate that cereals consumption growth rate may return to growing at nearly 3.0 per cent if not more. For pulses the growth rate actually has fallen down from 2.89 per cent in 1981-1991 to –0.84 per cent in 1991-2002 (i.e., pulses consumption has fallen down in absolute terms). Here also, the projections indicate that the pulses consumption may increase and the growth rate may pick up. Milk consumption has been more or less stable growing at more than 4.6 per cent since 1981. The future growth rate may also be approximately the same. However, there is a minor downward trend noticeable here. More interesting to note is the growth rate in the other foods category, which includes the non-vegetarian food, beverages, intoxicants etc. The growth rate here has been historically going up since 1971. It has been nearly 4.0 per cent between 1991-2002. The projections indicate that this growth may even further increase going up to 5.3 per cent if not more. This points out the trend in increased non-vegetarianism. To sum up, the projections indicate that in future: (a) for cereals and pulses consumption, the growth rates may increase reverting back to the pattern of the 1981-1991 period; (b) milk consumption would be growing at the same level as in the past; and (c) demand for non-vegetarian food may increase substantially.

To understand better the food demand situation presented above, the projected expenditures on cereals and pulses (Group B) have been converted into quantity terms. Table 3.9 gives the details of the necessary computations involved. Observe the data of cereals and pulses production levels in years 2002 and 2005. These levels may be adjusted for net exports and change in public stocks. The resulting figure must have been for the domestic demand (including private stocks). Applying the projected expenditure growth rates of cereals and pulses (Table 3.8) to this figure, the minimum required production levels may be obtained.

According to the calculations in Table 3.9, the demand for cereals by 2012 can be somewhere between 220 to 268 million tonnes (mlt). There is quite a difference between these two estimates. The latter estimate (268 mlt) is however based on the unusually high data figure for the year 2001-02 (i.e. 199.48 mlt) and hence quite unlikely. In fact, both years 2000-01 and 2002-03 are unusually low production years due to bad rainfall. Though 2001-02 is not a bad rainfall year, however the production level seems to be unusually high.

The following are the relevant data:

Year:	1998-99	1999-2000	2000-01	2001-02	2002-03	2003-04
Rainfall Index:	115.5	103.0	89.5	97.9	81.8	115.3
Cereals Production (mlt):	188.7	196.4	185.7	199.5	163.7	198.3
Pulses Production (mlt):	14.9	13.4	11.1	13.4	11.1	14.9

Therefore, of the two estimates, i.e. 220 and 268 mlt, the most likely and reasonable estimate seems to be the former one, 220 mlt. The corresponding estimates for pulses are 15 to 19 mlt. Though there is not much to choose between these two estimates, still for the same reasons as in the case of cereals, the reasonable estimate for demand for pulses by 2012 seems to be 15 mlt. Additional demands if any for further changes in the public buffer stocks and for exports have to be added up to these figures.

Table 3.9: Computation of Minimum Production Levels Required to Meet Domestic Food Demand

Year	Cereals					Pulses					Foodgrain Stocks (Mainly Rice and Wheat)
	GSA ('000 ha)	Production ('000 tonnes)	Yield (kg/ha)	Export ('000 tonnes)	Import ('000 tonnes)	GSA ('000 ha)	Production ('000 tonnes)	Yield (kg/ha)	Export ('000 tonnes)	Import ('000 tonnes)	
1990-91	103173	162130	1571	652	129	24662	14260	578	15	1274	NA
1991-92	99329	156360	1574	1351	12	22543	12020	533	26	313	12170
1992-93	100788	166660	1654	634	1466	22360	12820	573	34	383	14017
1993-94	100504	170950	1701	893	317	22250	13310	598	44	628	21935
1994-95	100832	177460	1760	1062	8	23028	14038	610	51	554	27716
1995-96	98732	168110	1703	5575	8	22283	12310	552	61	486	20822
1996-97	101134	185190	1831	3729	613	23194	14460	620	55	655	16410
1997-98	100976	179290	1776	2403	1486	22870	12970	570	171	1008	18122
1998-99	101666	188700	1856	4975	1812	23501	14907	634	104	564	21820
1999-00	101869	196390	1928	1906	1606	21190	13410	633	192	253	28906
2000-01	100700	185739	1840	2393	47	20348	11070	544	244	351	44695
2001-02	100256	199480	1990	4995	6	21656	13370	620	162	2232	50951
2002-03	91450	163650	1789	8835	2	20050	11130	555	na	na	32802
2003-04	99990	198280	1983	8109	2	23440	14910	636	na	na	20000
2004-05		185230		7965	7		13130		na	na	17407

Cereals:

(i) In 2001-02 (Production level = 199.5 million tonnes) - (net exports= 5 mlt) - (change in stocks=51-45=6 mlt) =188.5 mlt.

Projected growth rate of cereals consumption expenditure between 2001-02 to 2011-12 = 3.57% p.a . (Table 3.8).

((188.5)*((1.0357) ^ 10)) = 267.7 million tonnes.

(ii) In 2004-05 (Production level = 185.23 million tonnes) - (net exports= 8mlt) - (change in stocks=17.5-20=-2.5 mlt) = 179.7 mlt.

Projected growth rate of cereals consumption expenditure between 2004-05 to 2011-12 = 2.89% p.a . (Table 3.8).

((179.7)*((1.0289) ^ (7))) = 219.4 million tonnes.

Pulses:

(i) In 2001-02 (Production level = 13.4 million tonnes) - (net exports= 2.1 mlt) =15.5 mlt.

Projected growth rate of pulses consumption expenditure between 2001-02 to 2011-12 = 2.17% p.a . (Table 3.8).

((15.5)*((1.0217) ^ 10)) = 19.2 million tonnes

(ii) In 2004-05 (Production level = 13.13 million tonnes) - (net exports= 0.5 mlt, say) = 13.63 mlt.

Projected growth rate of pulses consumption expenditure between 2004-05 to 2011-12 = 1.28% p.a . (Table 3.8).

((13.6)*((1.0128) ^ (7))) = 14.9 million tonnes.

Cereals: 220 to 268 mlt by 2012 and **Pulses: 15** to 19 mlt by 2012

We may need to provide an explanation/justification for our projected CAGR of 2.89 per cent for cereals (CRL), compared to what had been in the past.

Let us look at the annual growth rates of cereals consumption expenditure (according to the NAS data, Rs. crores at 1993-94 prices) (Table 3.10):

Table 3.10: NAS Data on Cereals Expenditure

Year	Cereals Expenditure (Rs. crores)	Annual Growth Rate (%)	Compound Annual Growth Rate (%) (1990-91–2001-02)
1989-90:	72672		
1990-91:	79454	9.33	
1991-92:	80874	1.79	
1992-93:	74262	-8.18	
1993-94:	80267	8.09	
1994-95:	82525	2.81	
1995-96:	84123	1.94	
1996-97:	91119	8.32	
1997-98:	82564	-9.39	
1998-99:	87535	6.02	
1999-00:	88637	1.26	
2000-01:	76194	-14.04	
2001-02:	90739	19.09	1.21

We do not think there is any particular sanctity associated with the compound annual growth rate observed between 1990-91 and 2001-02, which is about 1.21 per cent p.a. This anyway depends only on the end-points, i.e., levels in 1990-91 and 2001-02. This does not take into account what happened during the intermediate years. Table 3.10 also shows the annual growth rates for the cereals-expenditure data. The annual growth rates have actually been fluctuating. They range anywhere between +19.09 per cent to –14.04 per cent. The median of the above series of annual growth rates actually turns out to be 2.38 per cent and the average is 2.25 per cent. So the projected compound annual growth rate of mere 2.89 per cent during the 11th FYP may not be unreliable!

Besides, the growth rate of the total private final consumption expenditure also will be higher during the 11th FYP, than in the past. Assume that such rise in the growth rate occurs more significantly for poorer sections of the population (indeed it should be so in an "inclusive growth" pattern). Obviously this has its own impact in raising the growth rate of the cereals expenditure.

3.9.5 Rice, Wheat and Coarse Cereals

The above forecasts of cereals include rice, wheat and coarse cereals all put together. One may be interested to know what would be their individual forecasts, particularly for rice and wheat. Unfortunately, the National Accounts and Statistics do not provide separate data on the private final consumption expenditure for rice and wheat; and hence they could not be explicitly brought under the above LES exercise. For estimating their demands and productions we follow a different procedure as follows. We have data for rice, wheat, coarse cereals and pulses on their gross productions, import and export levels and public stocks. Their gross availability (gross production + net imports – change in public stocks) must have been the total domestic demand that includes human consumption, seed, feed, wastage and private stocks held if any. Such time-series have been computed from these data, and presented in Table A-3.1(h). The plots for gross production and gross availability are shown in Figure 3.3(a and b). Pure time-series models have been fitted to these data—both for gross productions and gross availability. Certainly the rice and pulses data are not deterministic trends. Though the wheat data appear to be deterministic trends, they too turned out to be not so. Thus, all of them have to be modelled as stochastic trends. Results of the estimated models have been reported in Tables 3.11(a) and 3.11(b). These estimated models appear to be quite reasonable with significant coefficients, free of auto-correlations and are stationary with stability conditions satisfied. Using them, the forecasts for the 11th FYP have been made.

Table 3.12 provides year-wise forecasts both within the sample and post sample periods. Table 3.13 provides the estimates of demand, production and the gap between them for rice, wheat, other cereals and pulses, based on the time-series analysis. Table 3.14 provides a comparison between the VEC-model based estimates and the time-series based estimates of demand for total cereals and pulses.

Table 3.11(a): Time-series Analysis Estimation Results

Rice Availability

Dependent Variable: D(RAV)			Sample (adjusted): 1954 2003
Variable	Coefficient		t-Statistic
C	1214.4836		4.12
D(P03)	-9234.9478		-1.94
AR(1)	-0.7878		-5.57
AR(2)	-0.3892		-2.70
Akaike info criterion	19.73	Schwarz criterion	19.89
Inverted AR Roots	-.39+.48i	-.39-.48i	

Rice Production

Dependent Variable: D(RPR)			Sample (adjusted): 1954 2006
Variable	Coefficient		t-Statistic
C	1219.9088		4.07
D(P03)	-17131.7625		-4.24
AR(1)	-0.6766		-4.96
AR(2)	-0.3899		-2.90
Akaike info criterion	19.74	Schwarz criterion	19.88
Inverted AR Roots	-.34+.52i	-.34-.52i	

Wheat Availability

Dependent Variable: D(WAV)			Sample (adjusted): 1954 2003
Variable	Coefficient		t-Statistic
C	1171.0616		5.54
D(P97)	8194.0764		3.55
AR(1)	-0.4046		-3.04
AR(2)	-0.5544		-4.08
Akaike info criterion	18.88	Schwarz criterion	19.03
Inverted AR Roots	-.20-.72i	-.20+.72i	

Wheat Production

Dependent Variable: D(WPR)			Sample (adjusted): 1953 2006
Variable	Coefficient		t-Statistic
C	1265.0242		5.04
D(P00)	6467.1851		2.90
P03	-5596.6223		-2.28
AR(1)	-0.4710		-3.70
Akaike info criterion	18.69	Schwarz criterion	18.84
Inverted AR Roots	-0.47		

Table 3.11(b): Time-series Analysis Estimation Results (Continued)

Other Cereals Availability

Dependent Variable: D(OCAV)		Sample (adjusted): 1952 2003	
Variable	Coefficient		t-Statistic
C	202.2877		3.26
MA(1)	-0.9403		-11.22
Akaike info criterion	18.88	Schwarz criterion	18.95
Inverted MA Roots	0.94		

Other Cereals Production

Dependent Variable: D(OCPR)		Sample (adjusted): 1952 2003	
Variable	Coefficient		t-Statistic
C	221.5358		4.09
MA(1)	-0.9242		-12.16
Akaike info criterion	18.69	Schwarz criterion	18.77
Inverted MA Roots	0.92		

Pulses Availablility

Dependent Variable: D(PUAV)		Sample (adjusted): 1952 2003	
Variable	Coefficient		t-Statistic
C	63.9799		2.24
MA(1)	-0.8694		-12.66
Akaike info criterion	17.28	Schwarz criterion	17.35
Inverted MA Roots	0.87		

Pulses Production

Dependent Variable: D(PUPR)		Sample (adjusted): 1954 2006	
Variable	Coefficient		t-Statistic
C	-2938.1166		-4.18
RF	30.6100		4.46
D(PUPR(-1))	-1.0422		-14.49
D(PUPR(-2))	-0.6948		-8.68
MA(1)	0.1925		2.60
MA(3)	-0.8804		-1100.84
R-squared	0.6332	Adjusted R-squared	0.5942
Akaike info criterion	16.99	Schwarz criterion	17.21
S.E. of regression	1121.62	Durbin-Watson stat	1.70
F-statistic	16.23	Prob(F-statistic)	0.000000
Inverted MA Roots	0.9	-.55-.83i	-.55+.83i

Note: RAV & RPR: Rice availability & production. WAV & WPR: Wheat availability & production.
OCAV & OCPR: Coarse Cereals availability & production.
TCAV & TCPR: Total Cereals availability & production (Rice + Wheat + Coarse Cereals)
PUAV & PUPR: Pulses availability & production. $D(X)=X_t-X_{t-1}$

Table 3.12: Forecasting Performance of Time-series Models

Year	RAV Actual	RAVF Forecast	WAV Actual	WAVF Forecast	OCAV Actual	OCAVF Forecast	TCAV Actual	TCAVF Forecast	PUAV Actual	PUAVF Forecast
1995	83150	75458	65344	59652	30390	31746	178884	166855	14117	13380
1996	76100	75681	68012	59904	28965	31948	173077	167533	12792	13444
1997	81176	77686	71134	68371	34086	32150	186396	178208	14774	13508
1998	77794	78664	62115	62366	30384	32353	170293	173382	13316	13572
1999	80506	79757	67635	63596	31541	32555	179682	175908	15152	13636
2000	82060	81159	67709	64827	30478	32757	180247	178744	13379	13700
2001	75987	82273	60584	66058	31078	32960	167648	181290	11176	13764
2002	89411	83494	65592	67288	33370	33162	188372	183944	15441	13828
2003	74608	75508	72811	68519	26070	33364	173489	177391	12594	13892
2004		85928		69750		33566		189244		13956
2005		87152		70981		33769		191901		14020
2006		88370		72211		33971		194552		14084
2007		89578		73442		34173		197193		14148
2008		90796		74673		34376		199845		14212
2009		92010		75903		34578		202492		14276
2010		93224		77134		34780		205138		14340
2011		94439		78365		34982		207786		14404
2012		95653		79596		35185		210434		14468

Year	RPR Actual	RPRF Forecast	WPR Actual	WPRF Forecast	OCPR Actual	OCPRF Forecast	TCPR Actual	TCPRF Forecast	PUPR Actual	PUPRF Forecast
1995	81157	78498	65469	60462	30350	31896	176976	170856	14038	12973
1996	76975	79340	62097	62030	29033	32117	168105	173487	12310	12839
1997	81737	81993	69350	63152	34105	32339	185192	177484	14460	12954
1998	82535	82390	66345	64485	30399	32560	179279	179435	12970	13446
1999	86077	83608	71288	65718	31335	32782	188700	182107	14907	13450
2000	89680	85150	76370	73465	30340	33003	196390	191618	13410	13319
2001	84980	86153	69681	68256	31078	33225	185739	187634	11070	13254
2002	93340	87394	72770	69524	33370	33446	199480	190365	13370	13471
2003	71820	71552	65760	65191	26070	33668	163650	170411	11130	12857
2004	88530	89848	72150	66457	37600	33889	198280	190195	14910	13937
2005	83130	91079	68640	67721	33460	34111	185230	192911	13130	13361
2006	91040	92313	69480	68987	34670	34332	195190	195632	13110	13334
2007		93519		70252		34554		198325		13885
2008		94743		71517		34776		201035		13452
2009		95966		72782		34997		203744		13643
2010		97182		74047		35219		206447		13868
2011		98403		75312		35440		209155		13624
2012		99624		76577		35662		211862		13845

Note: RAV & RPR: Rice availability & production. WAV & WPR: Wheat availability & production.

OCAV & OCPR: Coarse Cereals availability & production.

TCAV & TCPR: Total Cereals availability & production (Rice + Wheat + Coarse Cereals)

PUAV & PUPR: Pulses availability & production.

Table 3.13: Projections based on Time-series Analysis Models

			Rice (Gap=RPRF-RAVF)				
Year:	2005-06	2006-07	2007-08	2008-09	2009-11	2010-11	2011-12
Demand:	88.37	89.58	90.80	92.01	93.22	94.44	95.65
Production:	92.31	93.52	94.74	95.97	97.18	98.40	99.62
Gap:	3.94	3.94	3.94	3.96	3.96	3.96	3.97
			Wheat (Gap=WPRF-WAVF)				
Year:	2005-06	2006-07	2007-08	2008-09	2009-11	2010-11	2011-12
Demand:	72.21	73.44	74.67	75.90	77.13	78.36	79.60
Production:	68.99	70.25	71.52	72.78	74.05	75.31	76.58
Gap:	-3.22	-3.19	-3.15	-3.12	-3.08	-3.05	-3.02
			Coarse Cereals (Gap=OCPRF-OCAVF)				
Year:	2005-06	2006-07	2007-08	2008-09	2009-11	2010-11	2011-12
Demand:	33.97	34.17	34.38	34.58	34.78	34.98	35.18
Production:	34.33	34.55	34.78	35.00	35.22	35.44	35.66
Gap:	0.36	0.38	0.40	0.42	0.44	0.46	0.48
			Total Cereals (Rice + Wheat + Coarse Cereals) (Gap=TCPRF-TCAVF)				
Year:	2005-06	2006-07	2007-08	2008-09	2009-11	2010-11	2011-12
Demand:	194.55	197.19	199.84	202.49	205.14	207.79	210.43
Production:	195.63	198.32	201.04	203.74	206.45	209.16	211.86
Gap:	1.08	1.13	1.20	1.25	1.31	1.37	1.43
			Total Pulses (Gap=PUPRF-PUAVF)				
Year:	2005-06	2006-07	2007-08	2008-09	2009-11	2010-11	2011-12
Demand:	14.08	14.15	14.21	14.28	14.34	14.40	14.47
Production:	13.33	13.89	13.45	13.64	13.87	13.62	13.84
Gap:	-0.75	-0.26	0.76	-0.64	-0.47	-0.78	-0.63

Let us juxtapose these time-series analysis based estimates with the earlier VEC-models based LES estimates for the year 2011-12.

Table 3.14: Comparative Estimates of VEC-based LES and Time-series Analysis

	Year 2011-12			
	VEC-Models based LES estimate (mlt)	Time-series Analysis based estimate (mlt)		
	Demand (#)	Demand	Production	Gap
Total Cereals:	219.4	210.4	211.8	1.4
Rice:	NA	95.7	99.6	4.0
Wheat:	NA	79.6	76.6	-3.0
Coarse Cereals:	NA	35.2	35.7	0.5
Total Pulses:	14.9	14.5	13.8	-0.7

Note: #: VEC-model based LES does not involve forecasting the production figures for total cereals and total pulses.
(mlt): million tonnes.

Let us note the implications of the "Gaps" presented above in Table 3.13.

Demand = Gross Availability = Gross Production + Net Imports – Change in Stocks in a give year (t).

Change in Stocks = Net additions to stocks in the current year

=(Stocks of the current year – Stocks of the previous year).

Gap (G_t) = Gross Production – Demand = -Net Imports (I_t) + Change in Stocks in a give year (ΔS_t).

= Net Exports (E_t) + $\Delta S_t \lesseqgtr 0$.

Case A: Excess Supply: $G_t = E_t + \Delta S_t > 0$.,

(i) E_t and ΔS_t could both be > 0, implying possibility for some exports and some additions to stocks.

(ii) if $E_t < 0$, then $\Delta S_t > 0$, implying though there is no domestic shortage, imports are made only to build up stocks.

(iii) if $\Delta S_t < 0$, then $E_t > 0$, implying some stocks have been released only to export.

Case B: Excess Demand: $G_t = E_t + \Delta S_t < 0$.,

(iv) E_t and ΔS_t could both be < 0, implying possibility for some imports and some depletion of stocks.

(v) if $E_t < 0$ and $\Delta S_t > 0$, implying imports are made part of which are also used for building up stocks in addition to meeting the excess domestic demand.

(vi) if $\Delta S_t < 0$ and $E_t > 0$, implying stocks have been released part of which are used for exporting in addition to meeting the excess domestic demand.

For the year 2011-12, in the case of total cereals, the VEC-based LES model (VBM) indicates a necessity of imports in future by about 7 to 8 million tonnes (mlt), where as the time-series models (TSM) indicate more or less self-sufficiency. The demand estimates differ between these two procedures only marginally, 219 mlt under the VBM *versus* 210 mlt under the TSM. The TSM indicate that a shortfall in wheat domestic production could be major concern in future. For wheat, it may become necessary to either import or deplete the previously built-up stocks or both. In the case of rice, either exports can be made or further stocks can be built up. In the case of coarse cereals, the domestic demand and the productions more or less evenly balance. In the case of demand for total pulses, there is a remarkable consistency between the VBM and TSM forecasts—both of them yield almost the same estimates (14.9 mlt under the VBM and 14.5 mlt under the TSM), though these two approaches are totally independent of each other! Both of them indicate the necessity of importing them by about a million tonne.

Definitely, projections based on rigorous studies of farmers' crop-wise acreage allocation decisions and crop-yield responses would be much more insightful. Such studies would also indicate to the planners with regard to what can (and should) be done with regard to agricultural infrastructure such as irrigation, fertilisers and HYV adoptions and policy responses (including due to prices)—if the agricultural production has to break the past trends and achieve vigorous growth beyond 4 to 5 per cent in future.

3.9.6 Non-food Items

We discuss only the VEC-models based results here. See Table 3.8 above. The expenditure on all others under group B (OT—medicals, miscellaneous, education and others) may grow at 8.35 per cent between 2005 and 2012 compared to 6.87 per cent and 7.74 per cent observed for the period 1981-1991 and 1991-2002 respectively. This expenditure is disaggregated into others, education, miscellaneous and medicals in group A.

The (1961 to 2003) average percentages of these four items within the all others category come to 49.44, 7.39, 25.39 and 17.77. The corresponding projected (for 2005-2012) growth rates (in group A) are 8.35 per cent, 6.29 per cent, 8.9 per cent and 9.65 per cent. Using these proportions as weights, the weighted average growth rate of these four items would come to 8.57 per cent. This almost corresponds to the 8.35 per cent as projected in the group B exercise. This again in a way implies the stability and reliability of the estimates and hence the projections. Both, the expenditure on education and the medical expenditure (perhaps due to increased non-vegetarianism and fast food!) may rise compared to what had been since 1981.

Expenditure on fuel, electricity, water and rent: Both group A and group B exercises indicate that this expenditure may grow at around 7.0 per cent (6.7 per cent in group A and 7.25 per cent in group B). This expenditure had been growing only around 4.5 per cent during 1991-2002, which itself was quite a rise over the still previous decades. This implies that rise in demand for fuel, electricity and water would be quite substantial in future.

Expenditure on clothing and footwear: Both group A and group B exercises indicate that this expenditure may grow at around 4.0 per cent (3.91 per cent in group A and 4.16 per cent in group B). This expenditure grew at more than 4 per cent between 1971 and 1991, but fell down to less than 2.5 per cent during 1991-2002. The fall down is somewhat surprising, because there are no substitutes available for clothing and footwear! The projections indicate that the consumption growth rate would revert back to the higher growth rates of the seventies and eighties.

Expenditure on communications: Both group A and group B exercises indicate that this expenditure may grow at around 15.0 per cent (13.89 per cent in group A and 14.67 per cent in group B). This expenditure had grown enormously between 1991-2002 (more than 17.5 per cent) compared to the previous periods (around 6 per cent). Basically the projections indicate that this rising trend would somewhat be stabilised in future.

3.9.7 Total Investment, Net Capital Inflow and Foreign Investment

This section presents the implicit forecasts on net capital inflows and estimated foreign investment up to 2012. Earlier it was mentioned that the sum of the sectoral investments (henceforth, TGCF) in our model is not equal to the total gross capital formation adjusted for errors & omissions (henceforth, GCFAEC) as reported in the National Accounts Statistics. The National Accounts Statistics (NAS) presents the data on GCFAEC in three ways.

1) First Method:

Gross Capital Formation adjusted for errors & commissions (GCFAEC) = Total Gross Domestic Savings (GDS) + Net Capital Inflow (NCI). This NCI is the surplus on current account transactions within the balance of payments; and does not include capital transfers to general government etc. Nor does it include foreign investment. Foreign investment comes under the capital account of the balance of payments accounts, as follows:

Total Capital Account = Foreign Investment + Loans + Banking Capital + Rupee Debt Service + Other Capital + Errors & Omissions, where, Foreign Investment = That in India (Direct + Portfolio) + Abroad.

2) Second Method:

Total Capital Formation by Industry of Use (TCFIU) = Sum of the Gross Capital Formations in 9 industries of use. These 9 industries of use are (Agricultural sectors + Industrial sectors + Services sectors). In other words, the TGCF in our model is the same as TCFIU. However this total (i.e., TCFIU) is not equal to the GCFAEC presented in the first method. There is always a difference, which is simply reported in the NAS as "Difference".

3) Third Method:

Gross Capital Formation adjusted for errors & commissions (GCFAEC) = Gross Fixed Capital Formation in Construction (public & private) and Machinery & Equipment (public & private) + Change in Stocks + Errors & Omissions. For the discussion below, this third method is irrelevant. We shall keep it aside.

Our procedure to provide the implicit estimates of foreign investments and net capital inflows is as follows:

Define, Total real foreign direct investment (RFDI) = real foreign direct investment in (India + abroad)
Total reai foreign portfolio investment (RPI) = real foreign portfolio investment in (India+ abroad)
INTDIFF= Interest differential = US' Federal Bank's real discount rate – RBI's real bank rate.

Step 1: We regress RFDI as a function of TGDP, and RPI as a function of TGDP and INTDIFF. Using these regressions and the model forecasts of the TGDP (and exogenously specified INTDIFF for future) the forecasts of the RFDI and RPI have been obtained.

Step 2: Next we regress real net capital inflows (RNCI) as a function of RFDI and RPI. Using this regression result and the forecasts of the RFDI and RPI obtained in step 1, RNCI forecasts for the future have been obtained.

Our estimations are based on the data from 1991-92 to 2003-04. Data from 1999 to 2004 are reported in Table A-3.1(i). The regression results and computation details are given in Tables 3.15 and 3.16 respectively. Data problems are quite serious, a discussion of which is however avoided here. For example, interpretation of negative foreign investments abroad by Indians does not seem to be straightforward.

Step 3: In our model, only corporate savings, and households' financial and physical savings are explicitly available; public savings are not worked out. Therefore, using the figure of the average savings rate (34.8%) given by the Planning Commission's document, 11th Five Year Plan Approach, we work out the total gross domestic savings (since the total GDPs are anyway forecasted in our model). Thus, GDS (gross domestic savings) estimates could also be made, and then the sum of the GDS estimates and the RNCI (step 2) estimates at an interest rate (%) differential (INTDIFF) of -0.3811 would give the estimates of GCFAEC as follows:

Estimates of Real Net Capital Inflow and Total Gross Capital Formation

Year	TGDP	GDS	RFDI	RPI	INTDIFF	RNCI	RNCI/TGDP (%)	GCFAEC
2006-07	1767680	615153	12316	16374	-0.3811	17028	0.96	632181
2007-08	1920535	668346	13064	11599	-0.3811	15254	0.79	683600
2008-09	2090250	727407	13857	11518	-0.3811	18673	0.89	746080
2009-10	2285800	795458	14730	14184	-0.3811	25249	1.10	820707
2010-11	2510861	873780	15694	15275	-0.3811	30560	1.22	904340
2011-12	2763078	961551	16733	14576	-0.3811	34399	1.24	995950

Note: TGDP, GDS, RFDI, RPI, RNCI and GCFAEC: all in Rs. crores (1993-94 prices). See Table A-3.1(i).

The INTDIFF value -0.3811 assumed above is the forecast given by the trend fitted to the data (see 3rd regression in Table 3.15). Looking at actual data and the fluctuations over time [Table A-3.1(i)], this forecast does not however seem to be appropriate. Therefore, the estimates of real net capital inflow were computed for different assumptions of INTDIFF. The results are shown in Table 3.16. Past data [Table A-3.1(i)] shows that this percentage was fluctuating between negatives and positives. Our estimates here show that according to the economic environment characterised under the RefRun it would only be positive over the years 2007 to 2012 varying between 0.73 and 1.32 depending on the interest rate differential. Were the economic environment to be something else obviously the figures would be different. See Section 10.6 below for analysis under such a different scenario. Also see, the Planning Commission (Government of India's) report (2002) on foreign investment for causes and reasons for low FDI inflows into India.

Table 3.15: Estimations of Foreign Investments and Net Capital Inflows

1. Dependent Variable: LOG(RFDI)	Sample(adjusted): 1992-2004			
Variable	Coefficient	Std. Error	t-Statistic	Prob.
LOG(GDPCON)	0.655932	0.027579	23.78373	0.0000
AR(1)	0.731115	0.072398	10.09854	0.0000
R-squared: 0.9226	Adjusted R-squared: 0.9155,		Inverted AR Roots: .73	

contd...

...contd...

2. Dependent Variable: RPI	Sample(adjusted): 1993-2004			
Variable	Coefficient	Std. Error	t-Statistic	Prob.
C	6175.933	478.6104	12.90388	0.0000
D(GDPCON,2)	0.297055	0.078498	3.784239	0.0054
INTDIFF	-874.4040	454.0392	-1.925834	0.0903
MA(1)	-0.989878	0.000266	-3726.878	0.0000
R-squared: 0.8388	Adjusted R-squared: 0.7784,		Inverted MA Roots: .99	
3. Dependent Variable: INTDIFF	Sample: 1991-2006			
Variable	Coefficient	Std. Error	t-Statistic	Prob.
C	-0.381065	0.746636	-0.510376	0.6177
MA(1)	0.502175	0.232657	2.158433	0.0487
R-squared: 0.1967	Adjusted R-squared: 0.1394,		Inverted MA Roots: -.50	
4. Dependent Variable: RNCI	Sample(adjusted): 1993-2004			
Variable	Coefficient	Std. Error	t-Statistic	Prob.
C	-55600.70	15011.86	-3.703785	0.0100
RFDI	0.989681	0.397567	2.489343	0.0472
RFDI(-1)	3.696694	0.556194	6.646406	0.0006
RPI	1.055702	0.183073	5.766551	0.0012
AR(1)	0.696047	0.141521	4.918340	0.0027
MA(2)	2.029966	0.985030	2.060817	0.0850

Note: R-squared: 0.9899 Adjusted R-squared: 0.9815, Inverted AR Roots: .70

Table 3.16: Implicit Forecasts of Real Net Capital Inflow at 1993-94 Prices for the Reference Run at Different Interest Rate Differentials (See Table 3.15 for the Estimated Regressions, and Table A-3.1(i) for Explanations)

REFRUN

Year	TGDP (RefRun)	GDS= TGDP*AVSR	TCFIU= TGCF (RefRun)	Real Foreign Direct Investment in India & Abroad (RFDI)	INTDIFF	Real Foreign Portfolio Investment in India & Abroad (RPI)	Real Net Capital Inflow (RNCI)	RNCI/ TGDP (%)	GCFAEC = GCF with all adjustments
2007	1767680	615153	401217	12316	- 2.50	18227	18984	1.07	634136
2008	1920535	668346	456487	13064	- 2.50	13451	17210	0.90	685556
2009	2090250	727407	529953	13857	- 2.50	13371	20629	0.99	748036
2010	2285800	795458	609621	14730	- 2.50	16037	27205	1.19	822664
2011	2510861	873780	706410	15694	- 2.50	17127	32516	1.30	906296
2012	2763078	961551	815492	16733	- 2.50	16429	36355	1.32	997906

Year	TGDP (RefRun)	GDS= TGDP*AVSR	TCFIU= TGCF (RefRun)	Real Foreign Direct Investment in India & Abroad (RFDI)	INTDIFF	Real Foreign Portfolio Investment in India & Abroad (RPI)	Real Net Capital Inflow (RNCI)	RNCI/ TGDP (%)	GCFAEC = GCF with all adjustments
2007	1767680	615153	401217	12316	- 0.3811	16374	17028	0.96	632181
2008	1920535	668346	456487	13064	- 0.3811	11599	15254	0.79	683600
2009	2090250	727407	529953	13857	- 0.3811	11518	18673	0.89	746080
2010	2285800	795458	609621	14730	- 0.3811	14184	25249	1.10	820707
2011	2510861	873780	706410	15694	- 0.3811	15275	30560	1.22	904340
2012	2763078	961551	815492	16733	- 0.3811	14576	34399	1.24	995950

contd...

...contd...

Year	TGDP (RefRun)	GDS= TGDP*AVSR	TCFIU= TGCF (RefRun)	Real Foreign Direct Investment in India & Abroad (RFDI)	INTDIFF	Real Foreign Portfolio Investment in India & Abroad (RPI)	Real Net Capital Inflow (RNCI)	RNCI/ TGDP (%)	GCFAEC = GCF with all adjustments
2007	1767680	615153	401217	12316	0.	16041	16676	0.94	631828
2008	1920535	668346	456487	13064	0.	11265	14902	0.78	683249
2009	2090250	727407	529953	13857	0.	11185	18321	0.88	745728
2010	2285800	795458	609621	14730	0.	13851	24898	1.09	820356
2011	2510861	873780	706410	15694	0.	14941	30208	1.20	903988
2012	2763078	961551	815492	16733	0.	14243	34047	1.23	995598

Year	TGDP (RefRun)	GDS= TGDP*AVSR	TCFIU= TGCF (RefRun)	Real Foreign Direct Investment in India & Abroad (RFDI)	INTDIFF	Real Foreign Portfolio Investment in India & Abroad (RPI)	Real Net Capital Inflow (RNCI)	RNCI/ TGDP (%)	GCFAEC = GCF with all adjustments
2007	1767680	615153	401217	12316	1.0	15166	15753	0.89	630905
2008	1920535	668346	456487	13064	1.0	10391	13979	0.73	682325
2009	2090250	727407	529953	13857	1.0	10310	17398	0.83	744805
2010	2285800	795458	609621	14730	1.0	12977	23975	1.05	819433
2011	2510861	873780	706410	15694	1.0	14067	29285	1.17	903065
2012	2763078	961551	815492	16733	1.0	13369	33124	1.20	994675

3.10 Policy Simulations

A few policy/counter-factual scenarios are now postulated within the scope of the above estimated VECMs. This basically involves changing the exogenous specifications of the reference run (RefRun), based on the past trends (see Tables A-3.1). A change in policy specification is effected from the year 2005 and the economic impacts for the period 2005-2012 are simulated. We draw attention to an aspect in this connection. In reality there can be a lot more to policy making than the broad level at which we talk in this paper. For example, a policy that influences the corporate savings may itself involve several sub-policies with regard to several taxes and subsidies, which are not dealt with here. With this caution we now present some policy runs categorised as different issues: corporate savings, international trade, budget deficit and oil imports and fuel prices. Our discussion is mostly in terms of changes in the compound annual growth rates (CAGR) of various endogenous variables between 2004-05 and 2011-12, compared to the RefRun.

3.10.1 Rise in Private Corporate Savings

3.10.1.1 Scenario 2 (Corporate Savings Increase)

In the reference run (RefRun) private corporate savings (PCSS) were specified to be at 5 per cent of the total non-agricultural GDP in the previous time-period. In scenario 2 (see Table 3.17) this ratio increases to 7.5 per cent. Consequent rise in the PCSS leads to around 1 per cent higher growth rate in Total GDP (TGDP—from 8.82 per cent to 9.91 per cent), constituting 0.85 per cent rise in the growth rate of agricultural GDP (AGDP—from 2.58 per cent to 3.43 per cent), 2.5 per cent rise in industrial GDP (IGDP—from 10.74 per cent to 13.24 per cent) and 0.34 per cent rise in services GDP (SGDP—from 9.85 per cent to 10.19 per cent). These rising incomes also increase the growth rate of private final consumption expenditure (PFCE—from 6.61 per cent to 7.48 per cent) by 0.87 per cent. Growth rate of total gross capital formation (TGCF) too rises by 5.46 per cent (from 16.37 per cent to 21.83 per cent)—this rise is mostly contributed by 8.89 per cent rise in the growth rate of industrial GCF (IGCF—from 20.14 per cent to 29.03 per cent), followed by 1.32 per cent rise in the growth rate of the services GCF

(SGCF—from 14.22 per cent to 15.54 per cent). Growth in agricultural GCF (AGCF—from 4.95 per cent to 4.30 per cent) however decreases. Rise in the PCSS has some indirect effect on the agricultural GCF through prices. Growth rate of total price index (TPDFL—from 2.48 per cent to 3.48 per cent) increases by 1 per cent compared to the RefRun. This rise in TPDFL growth rate comes through 1.31 per cent rise in industrial prices (IPDFL) growth rate, 0.23 per cent rise in agricultural prices index (APDFL) growth rate, and 0.93 per cent rise in services prices index (SPDFL) growth rate. Since most of the private corporate savings (PCSS) in India go to industry and services, their investments get a direct fillip due to rise in PCSS. Agriculture is only indirectly affected. Rise in agricultural incomes should in principle lead to rise in investment (AGCF) but rise in industrial prices offsets this gain. Industrial prices (IPDFL) rise faster than agricultural prices (APDFL), thus making investment goods costlier leading to a fall in AGCF growth rate. With higher GDPs particularly in the industry and services, household savings (investments) in the form of financial assets (HFS) grow faster as they give higher returns on account of rising corporate incomes. The results show that a rise in PCSS leads to a marginal fall in the growth rate of household savings in the form of physical assets (HPS). Basically the results indicate that in a situation of growing corporate sector, households' preferences shift more towards savings in financial assets than in physical assets.

Table 3.17: Scenario 2: Simulated CAGRs (%) for 2004-05 to 2011-12

Variable Specifications	RefRrun PCSS/NAGDP$_{t-1}$ @ 5%	Scenario 2 PCSS/NAGDP$_{t-1}$ @ 7.5% from 2005-06
TGDP	8.82	9.91
TGCF	16.37	21.83
TPDFL	2.48	3.48
AGDP	2.58	3.43
AGCF	4.95	4.30
APDFL	2.26	2.49
IGDP	10.74	13.24
IGCF	20.14	29.03
IPDFL	3.48	4.79
SGDP	9.85	10.19
SGCF	14.22	15.54
SPDFL	2.01	2.94
PFCE	6.61	7.48
HFS	10.33	11.47
HPS	10.05	9.92

Reference Run Specifications: Rainfall normal, No rise in fuel price, RM3 grows @ 11% p.a., RBR grows @ 0% p.a., RBD grows @20% p.a. PCSS/NAGDP$_{t-1}$ @ 5%, AGEXP grows @ 10% p.a., NAGEXP grows @ 10% p.a., NAGIMP grows @ 9.5% p.a., NETPETIMP grows @ 21% p.a., RINVEXP grows @ 19% p.a., RINVIMP grows @ 13% p.a.

3.10.2 International Trade

In our model agricultural, non-agricultural and invisibles' exports and imports were distinguished. Thus, the effects of changes in the growth rates of these exports and imports were analysed separately (see Table 3.18).

3.10.2.1 Scenario 3 (Agriculture Exports' Growth Decreases)

In the RefRun agricultural exports were specified to grow at 10 per cent p.a. In scenario 3, this growth rate is reduced to 6 per cent p.a. This leads to a slight decrease in the growth rate of total GDP,

Table 3.18: Scenarios 3-10: Simulated CAGRs (%) for 2004-05 to 2011-12

Specifications under Reference Run (RefRun)		AGEXP @ 10%	NAGEXP @ 10%	RINVEXP @ 19%	RINVIMP @ 13%	NAGEXP @ 10%, NAGIMP @ 9.5%	AGEXP @ 10%, NAGEXP @ 10%	Actual Data of all Exogenous Variables Up to 2004, AGEXP @ 10% NAGEXP @ 10%	RINVEXP @ 19%, RINVIMP @ 13%
Modified Specifications under Scenario		AGEXP @ 6% from 2005-06	NAGEXP @ 13% from 2005-06	RINVEXP @ 21% from 2005-06	RINVIMP @ 16% from 2005-06	NAGEXP @ 15%, NAGIMP @ 14% from 2005-06	AGEXP @ 6%, NAGEXP @ 12.5% from 2005-06	AGEXP @ 15% NAGEXP @ 8% from 2005-06	RINVEXP @ 25%, RINVIMP @ 23% from 2005-06
Variable	RefRun	Scenario 3	Scenario 4	Scenario 5	Scenario 6	Scenario 7	Scenario 8	Scenario 9	Scenario 10
TGDP	8.82	8.74	9.86	8.99	8.78	10.54	9.60	8.28	9.20
TGCF	16.37	16.18	21.16	16.52	16.92	23.58	20.24	13.12	18.83
TPDFL	2.48	2.43	2.81	2.27	2.78	3.31	2.71	2.34	2.96
AGDP	2.58	2.23	4.34	2.59	2.57	3.70	3.73	2.00	2.60
AGCF	4.95	4.33	5.15	4.93	4.95	6.13	4.50	5.75	4.92
APDFL	2.26	1.99	1.99	2.26	2.26	2.32	1.77	2.8	2.25
IGDP	10.74	10.65	13.62	10.75	10.73	15.29	13.07	8.89	10.76
IGCF	20.14	19.85	27.54	20.24	20.10	31.17	26.21	14.34	20.31
IPDFL	3.48	3.47	3.98	3.49	3.47	4.54	3.88	3.19	3.50
SGDP	9.85	9.84	9.59	10.14	9.78	9.99	9.62	10.01	10.52
SGCF	14.22	14.18	16.02	14.44	15.50	16.66	15.67	13.16	19.34
SPDFL	2.01	2.00	2.31	1.64	2.57	2.75	2.25	1.84	2.89
PFCE	6.61	6.55	7.02	6.76	6.56	7.33	6.89	6.44	6.91
HFS	10.33	10.14	11.13	11.80	9.55	10.64	10.81	10.15	12.19
HPS	10.05	9.23	11.41	6.00	12.00	14.53	10.40	10.42	5.73

Reference Run Specifications: Rainfall normal, No rise in fuel price, RM3 grows @ 11% p.a., RBR grows @ 0% p.a., RBD grows @20% p.a. PCSS/NAGDP$_{t-1}$ @ 5%, AGEXP grows @ 10% p.a., NAGEXP grows @ 10% p.a., NAGIMP grows @ 9.5% p.a., NETPETIMP grows @ 21% p.a., RINVEXP grows @ 19% p.a., RINVIMP grows @ 13% p.a.

(TGDP—from 8.82 per cent to 8.74 per cent p.a.). The fall in the growth rate of agriculture GDP by about 0.35 per cent (AGDP—from 2.58 per cent to 2.23 per cent) is more substantial, than the fall in the growth rates of industrial and services GDPs (IGDP and SGDP—by about 0.09 per cent and 0.01 per cent respectively). Lower growth in incomes in all the sectors (GDPs) leads to lower growth rate of private consumption expenditure (PFCE decreases marginally by -0.06 per cent). Sectoral price movement is analogous to the movement in the corresponding GDPs. Though the growth rate in the total price deflator (TPDFL) decreases only by –0.05 per cent, the fall (by about 0.27 per cent p.a.) in the growth rate of agricultural prices (APDFL—from 2.26 per cent to 1.99 per cent) is more substantial. Industrial and services prices are hardly affected. This implies a fall in relative prices of agricultural goods. Investment growth in agriculture is negatively affected (AGCF growth rate falls by 0.62 per cent from 4.95 per cent to 4.33 per cent p.a.), and so are the investments in industry and services too. IGCF and SGCF growth rates also fall by 0.29 per cent and 0.04 per cent. Overall the effect of a fall in the agricultural exports growth is substantial on the agricultural incomes and investment, and industrial investment, but is only marginal on the services sector. Lower growth in agriculture and industry incomes lead to fall in the growth of household savings.

3.10.2.2 Scenario 4 (Non-agriculture Exports' Growth Increases)

In the RefRun non-agricultural exports were specified to grow at 10 per cent p.a. In scenario 4, this growth rate is increased to 13 per cent p.a. Consequently growth rate in total GDP increases by 1.04 per cent p.a. (TGDP—from 8.82 per cent to 9.86 per cent). This increase comes mostly from industry (IGDP rises by 2.88 per cent—from 10.74 per cent to 13.62 per cent p.a.) and agriculture (AGDP rises by 1.76 per cent from 2.58 per cent to 4.34 per cent p.a.). The substantial positive effect on the agriculture sector due to increased growth in non-agricultural exports is worth noticing. However, services' GDP decreases though only marginally (SGDP—from 9.85 per cent to 9.59 per cent). Growth rates of industry and services prices rise (IPDFL by 0.5 per cent from 3.48 per cent to 3.98 per cent, and SPDFL by 0.3 per cent from 2.01 per cent to 2.31 per cent p.a.), but agricultural prices' growth falls (APDFL by 0.27 per cent from 2.26 per cent to 1.99 per cent). Overall, TPDFL increases by 0.33 per cent p.a. All sectoral investments rise. Agricultural investment rises by 0.2 per cent p.a. (AGCF from 4.95 per cent to 5.15 per cent), industrial investment by 7.4 per cent p.a. (IGCF from 20.14 per cent to 27.54 per cent) and services investment by 1.8 per cent p.a. (SGCF from 14.22 per cent to 16.02 per cent despite a marginal fall in the growth of SGDP!). Rising incomes in agriculture and industry lead to higher growth not only in consumption expenditure (PFCE) but also in financial savings (HFS) and savings in physical assets (HPS).

3.10.2.3 Scenario 5 (Invisibles' Exports Growth Increases)

In the RefRun, real invisibles' exports (RINVEXP) were specified to grow at 19 per cent p.a. In scenario 5, this growth rate is increased to 21 per cent p.a. Consequently, though the impact on incomes, investments and prices in agriculture and industry is hardly any, total GDP however increases by 0.17 per cent p.a. (TGDP from 8.82 per cent to 8.99 per cent) brought through a rise in the growth rate of services GDP. Growth rate of SGDP goes up by 0.29 per cent p.a. (from 9.85 per cent to 10.14 per cent). Growth rate of PFCE rises by 0.15 per cent p.a. Growth rate of total prices index (TPDFL) decreases by 0.21 per cent p.a. due to 0.37 per cent p.a. fall in services prices' growth rate (SPDFL—from 2.01 per cent to 1.64 per cent). Growth rate of total investment increases by 0.15 per cent p.a. (TGCF—from 16.37 per cent to 16.52 per cent), which basically reflects the 0.22 per cent p.a. increase in the services' sector investment (SGCF—from 14.22 per cent to 14.44 per cent). While there is a rise in the growth rate of consumption expenditure (PFCE growth rises by 0.15 per cent p.a.), in the case of household savings there is strong tilt favouring financial assets (HFS growth rate increases by 1.47 per cent p.a. from 10.33 per cent to 11.80 per cent) against physical assets (HPS growth rate decreases by 4.5 per cent p.a. from 10.05 per cent to 6.00 per cent). This is puzzling!

3.10.2.4 Scenario 6 (Invisibles' Imports Growth Increases)

In the RefRun, real invisibles' imports (RINVIMP) were specified to grow at 13 per cent p.a. In scenario 6, this growth rate is increased to 16 per cent p.a. The impact of a rise in the growth rate of RINVIMP is only marginal on agriculture and industry. The major impact is only on the services sector. Growth rate of the investment in the sector, SGCF increases by 1.28 per cent (from 14.22 per cent to 15.50 per cent p.a.), and of prices SPDFL increases by 0.56 per cent (from 2.01 per cent to 2.57 per cent p.a.). Thus, a rise in the growth rate of either imports or exports of invisibles seems to increase investment in services for different reasons (see scenario 5).

The scenarios 3 to 6 have analysed the impacts of the exports/imports of agriculture, non-agriculture and invisibles in isolation. Scenarios 7 to 10 would look at the impacts of combinations of these trade patterns.

3.10.2.5 Scenario 7 (Both Exports and Imports of Non-agriculture Increase)

In the RefRun non-agriculture exports were specified to grow at 10 per cent p.a. and non-agriculture imports to grow at 9.5 per cent. In scenario 7, these growth rates are increased to 15 per cent p.a. and 14 per cent respectively. The impact on the sectoral GDPs is positive, with those on the agriculture and industry being quite substantial. AGDP growth rate goes up by 1.12 per cent (from 2.58 per cent to 3.70

per cent p.a.) and that of IGDP by 4.55 per cent (from 10.74 per cent to 15.29 per cent p.a.), though that of SGDP goes up only by 0.14 per cent (from 9.85 per cent to 9.99 per cent p.a.). Similar is the situation with the corresponding investments: AGCF growth rate goes up by 1.18 per cent (from 4.95 per cent to 6.13 per cent p.a.), IGCF growth rate by 11.03 per cent (from 20.14 per cent to 31.17 per cent p.a.) and also that of SGCF by 2.44 per cent (from 14.22 per cent to 16.66 per cent p.a.). Compared to the rises in the GDPs and investments, the rises in the growth rates of the prices are rather modest: growth rate of APDFL rises by 0.06 per cent (from 2.26 per cent to 3.32 per cent p.a.), that of IPDFL by 1.06 per cent (from 3.48 per cent to 4.54 per cent p.a.) and that of SPDFL by 0.74 per cent (from 2.01 per cent to 2.75 per cent p.a.). Growth rate of consumption expenditure rises by 0.72 per cent from 6.61 per cent to 7.33 per cent p.a. Though the rise in the growth rate of savings in the financial assets (HFS) is only marginal (0.31 per cent) p.a., the rise in the savings in terms of physical assets is about 4.5 per cent (from 10.05 per cent to 14.53 per cent p.a.).

3.10.2.6 Scenario 8 (Agriculture Exports' Growth Decreases while Non-agriculture Exports Increases)

In the RefRun both agriculture and non-agriculture exports were specified to grow at 10 per cent p.a. In scenario 8, agriculture exports are specified to grow only at 6 per cent, but non-agriculture exports grow at an increased rate of 12.5 per cent p.a. Recall that in scenario 3 a fall in the agriculture exports growth rate reflected as substantial negative impact on the agriculture GDP and investment (AGDP and AGCF), and in scenario 4, a rise in the growth rate of non-agriculture exports reflected as substantial positive impact on GDPs and investments in both agriculture and industry. The present scenario 8 being a combination of the earlier scenarios 3 and 4, the results obviously showed up accordingly. The positive impacts of a mere 2.5 per cent p.a. (from 10 per cent to 12.5 per cent) rise in the non-agriculture exports growth rate could more than compensate the negative impacts of a 4 per cent p.a. (from 10 per cent to 6 per cent) fall in the agriculture exports.

3.10.2.7 Scenario 9 (Agriculture Exports' Growth Increases while Non-agriculture Exports Decreases)

In the RefRun both agriculture and non-agriculture exports were specified to grow at 10 per cent p.a. In scenario 9, agriculture exports are specified to grow at 15 per cent, but non-agriculture exports grow only at a rate of 8 per cent p.a. Basically this scenario inquires whether a 5 per cent rise in the annual agricultural export growth rate can compensate a 2 per cent fall in the annual non-agricultural export growth rate. The answer is broadly in the negative. Growth rates of both agriculture and industry GDPs (AGDP and IGDP) fall. Though investment growth rate in agriculture shows slight improvement, but the growth rates of investments in industry and services fall substantially. This is in contrast to the results under scenario 8 where rising non-agricultural exports growth rate could compensate for the negative impacts of a fall in the agricultural exports growth rate.

3.10.2.8 Scenario 10 (Growth Rates of Exports and Imports of Invisibles Increase)

In the RefRun exports of invisibles grow at @ 19 per cent and corresponding imports grow at 13 per cent p.a. In scenario 10, these are specified to grow at 25 per cent and 23 per cent p.a. respectively. The impact on agriculture and industry is hardly any compared to the RefRun. The services GDP growth rate increases by 0.67 per cent p.a. (SGDP—from 9.85 per cent to 10.52 per cent p.a.), and corresponding price index growth rate goes up by 0.88 per cent p.a.(SPDFL—from 2.01 per cent to 2.89 per cent). However, the impact on the growth rate of services investment is more predominant, it goes up by 5.12 per cent p.a. (SGCF—from 14.22 per cent to 19.34 per cent). Since the total GDP increase by 0.38 per cent p.a. (TGDP—from 8.82 per cent to 9.20 per cent), the consumption expenditure growth rate also correspondingly increases by 0.30 per cent p.a. (PFCE—from 6.61 per cent to 6.91 per cent). However, there is substantial reorientation in the trend of household savings. The growth rate of financial savings goes up by 1.86 per cent p.a. (HFS—from 10.33 per cent to 12.19 per cent) but that of the physical assets decreases by 4.32 per cent p.a. (HPS—from 10.05 per cent to 5.73 per cent).

Summary: The net result of fall in agricultural exports' growth rate is that it reduces the farm incomes due to lower agriculture prices brought about by more domestic supply. The lower farm incomes further lead to fall in agricultural investment also. Though the effects on industry and service sectors are only marginal, however these two sectors too only experience negative impacts. It may be noted that after 1997, India's annual growth rate of agricultural exports in real terms rarely exceeded 10 per cent.

Contrarily, a rise in the growth rate of non-agricultural exports has substantial positive impacts on both agriculture and industry sectors. The estimation results (Tables 3.2 (a to c)] clearly indicate that rising NAGEXP leads to rise in both AGDP and NAGDP. Besides AGDP and IGDP have mutually reinforcing positive impacts, one on the other. Thus, though the agricultural prices in scenario 4 also are lower (as in scenario 3) compared to the RefRun, however that did not lead to lower farm incomes due to a rise in the AGDP brought through the rise in the industry GDP. In other words, when agricultural exports' growth rate falls, it could lead to a glut in the domestic agricultural markets, which even the industry cannot absorb, thus leading to fall in the agricultural prices, farm incomes and investment; whereas when non-agricultural exports' growth rate increases it not only leads to more of industrial production (IGDP) but also ensures that consequent rise in the AGDP growth rate compensates the farm incomes for the lower prices. Thus in the latter case, investments in the two sectors actually gain substantially.

Scenario 7 reflects on the benefits of liberalisation of trade in non-agricultural sectors. A rise in both the imports and exports of non-agricultural goods pushes up the incomes and industrial GDPs quite substantially. And the increasing demand for the agricultural goods by the industry pushes up agricultural prices also. Thus, the relative price of industrial goods with regard to agricultural goods is lower here (compared to scenario 4) pushing up the agricultural investment also.

In reality it may so happen that agricultural exports growth rate may go up or down simultaneously with a rise or fall in the growth rate of exports of non-agricultural goods. During the years 1998 to 2000, agricultural exports were continuously falling while it is reverse process for the non-agricultural goods. In 2002, both agricultural and non-agricultural exports fell compared to 2001. In the distant past there were times when agricultural exports increased while non-agricultural exports decreased, compared to the previous period. Scenarios 8 and 9 illustrate the effects of such phenomena. Scenario 8 is basically a mixture of scenarios 3 (fall in agricultural exports growth rate leads to lower agricultural prices, incomes and investment) and 4 (a rise in non-agricultural exports growth rate leads to higher incomes and investments in both agriculture and industry). Obviously the results under scenario 8 would be a net outcome of the negative impacts of scenario 3 and positive impacts of scenario 4. However, there is an interesting point to note here. Earlier in scenario 4 we agued that though the growth rate of the APDFL is lower (than in the RefRun) agricultural investment growth rate increased due to increased farm incomes. Now in scenario 8 too, farm incomes are higher and prices are lower (than in the RefRun). Yet, AGCF growth rate is lower here—because the relative price of investment goods is higher here compared to that in the RefRun and scenario 4. The results indicate that if keeping up the agricultural exports growth rate is quite difficult, at least non-agricultural exports growth rate should be pushed up. Though such a strategy may make investment goods costlier, however keeping up the non-agricultural exports growth rate is quite important. For example, one may ask, what may happen if at all agricultural exports growth rate is reasonably pushed up, but not that of non-agricultural goods? Scenario 9 attempts to answer this. First, non-agricultural GDP and consequently agricultural GDP growth rates fall down. Second, growth rate of agricultural prices increases due to less supply domestically; consequently relatively cheaper investment goods lead to more agricultural investment. However, non-agricultural investment growth rate falls down substantially. Overall such a scenario seems to be bad thing to happen. The essence of the above scenarios is that the growth pattern of agricultural and non-agricultural trade should be such that farm incomes are protected, simultaneously keeping investment goods not costly. The following table may illustrate the point (also see Appendix A-3.5).

Scenario	IPDFL_Grt	APDFL_Grt	IPDFL_Grt/APDF_Grt	AGDP_Grt	AGCF_Grt
S9	3.19	2.8	1.1393	2.00	5.75
S6	3.47	2.26	1.5354	2.57	4.95
RefRun	3.48	2.26	1.5398	2.58	4.95
S5	3.49	2.26	1.5442	2.59	4.93
S10	3.49	2.25	1.5556	2.6	4.92
S3	3.47	1.99	1.7437	2.23	4.33
S7	4.54	2.32	1.9569	3.7	6.13
S4	3.98	1.99	2.0000	4.34	5.15
S8	3.88	1.77	2.1921	4.34	4.5

Grt: CAGR

As the relative growth rate of the IPDFL with respect to APDFL kept increasing over the scenarios above, the growth rate of AGCF kept falling down. However, in scenarios 7 and 4 the substantially higher AGDP growth rate pushed up the AGCF growth rate. But in scenario 8, even that high AGDP growth rate could not sustain the AGCF growth rate since the investment goods became 'too costly'.

The growth pattern of invisibles, imports or exports, seem to have only marginal effects on agriculture and industry.

3.10.3 Budget Deficit

Movements in the real budget deficit data are quite erratic with no clear trends at all [see Table A-3.1(b)]. It is quite difficult to specify a likely pattern for the future.

3.10.3.1 Scenario 11 (Budget Deficit as a Fixed Proportion of the GDP$_{t-1}$):

Instead of specifying that the real budget deficit would grow 20 per cent p.a. as in the RefRun, it is exogenously fixed in scenario 11 at actual levels till the year 2005-06, and as 1.17 per cent of the previous year's total GDP from the year 2006-07. This figure is the median value observed for the data of 1990-2003.

Year	Real Budget Deficit in the RefRun @ 20% p.a. (Rs.crores)	Real Budget Deficit in scenario 11 as 1.17% of GDP$_{t-1}$ (Rs.crores)	(iii)/(ii)	Real Budget Deficit in scenario 17 (later) as 2.0% of GDP$_{t-1}$. (Rs.crores)	(v)/(ii)
(i)	(ii)	(iii)	(iv)	(v)	(vi)
2000	-10718	-10718	1.00	-10718	1.00
2001	1990	1990	1.00	1990	1.00
2002	4964	4964	1.00	4964	1.00
2003	3326	3250	0.98	3250	0.98
2004	3991	15424	3.86	15424	3.86
2005	4789	12831	2.68	12831	2.68
2006	5747	460	0.08	467	0.08
2007	6897	19174	2.78	33935	4.92
2008	8276	20618	2.49	37388	4.52
2009	9931	22486	2.26	41483	4.18
2010	11918	24512	2.06	44779	3.76
2011	14301	26811	1.87	50953	3.56
2012	17161	29373	1.71	56564	3.30

At 1.17 per cent of the GDP_{t-1} this specification amounts to massive increase in the real budget deficit; obviously the increase would be even more at 2 per cent of the GDP_{t-1} (as in some later scenarios). The extent of increase in the real budget deficit due to modifications in the specification(s) can be gauged above.

Possibly such massive increases in the budget deficit would be beyond the disciplinary principles specified by the Fiscal Responsibility and Budget Management Act, 2003 (see Government of India (2003)).

See Table 3.19 for the scenario 11 results. Such a change leads to a 0.72 per cent rise in the growth rate of the agriculture GDP (AGDP—from 2.58 per cent to 3.3 per cent p.a.), and to a 0.6 per cent rise in the growth rate of the corresponding price index (APDFL by 0.6 per cent p.a. from 2.26 per cent to 2.86 per cent). AGCF growth rate however falls down by 0.86 per cent p.a. from 4.95 per cent to 4.09 per cent. In the case of industry there is a negative impact both on the corresponding GDP and investment, but positive impact on the price index—growth rate of IGDP falls by 0.65 per cent p.a. from 10.74 per cent to 10.09 per cent, that of IGCF by 2.62 per cent p.a. from 20.14 per cent to 17.52 per cent, and that of IPDFL rises by 0.38 per cent p.a. from 3.48 per cent to 3.86 per cent. However, in the case of services the growth rates of the corresponding GDP, investment and price index, all increase—but only marginally. The consumption expenditure growth rate goes up marginally by 0.23 per cent p.a. (PFCE—from 6.61 per cent to 6.84 per cent). While the rise in the growth rate of household savings in financial assets (HFS) is only 0.48 per cent p.a., growth rate of savings in physical assets (HPS) however falls by 0.68 per cent p.a. from 10.05 per cent to 9.37 per cent. Thus, in general rising real budget deficit leads to price increases in all the sectors, it may only help the agriculture GDP but harm the industry.

Table 3.19: Scenario 11: Simulated CAGRs (%) for 2004-05 to 2011-12

Variable Specifications	RefRun Actual data of all exogenous variables up to 2004	Scenario 11 RBD is at actual levels up to 2005-06, later @ 1.17% of GDP_{t-1}; all others are as in the RefRun
TGDP	8.82	8.79
TGCF	16.37	15.07
TPDFL	2.48	2.68
AGDP	2.58	3.30
AGCF	4.95	4.09
APDFL	2.26	2.86
IGDP	10.74	10.09
IGCF	20.14	17.52
IPDFL	3.48	3.86
SGDP	9.85	9.99
SGCF	14.22	14.44
SPDFL	2.01	2.04
PFCE	6.61	6.84
HFS	10.33	10.81
HPS	10.05	9.37

Reference Run Specifications: Rainfall normal, No rise in fuel price, RM3 grows @ 11% p.a., RBR grows @ 0% p.a., RBD grows @20% p.a. PCSS/$NAGDP_{t-1}$ @ 5%, AGEXP grows @ 10% p.a., NAGEXP grows @ 10% p.a., NAGIMP grows @ 9.5% p.a., NETPETIMP grows @ 21% p.a., RINVEXP grows @ 19% p.a., RINVIMP grows @ 13% p.a.

3.10.4 Oil Imports and Prices

This section explores the impacts of changes in petroleum imports and fuel prices. See Table 3.20.

Table 3.20: Scenarios 12-16: Simulated CAGRs (%) for 2004-05 to 2011-12

Specifications under Reference Run (RefRun)		NETPETIMP @ 21%	No rise in fuel price	Fuel price actual data up to 2003; No rise later	Fuel price actual data up to 2003; No rise later	Fuel price actual data up to 2003; No rise later
Modified Specifications under Scenario		NETPETIMP @ 17% from 2005-06	10% rise in fuel price from 2003-04 onwards	Fuel price actual data up to 2006 and 10% rise p.a. in later years	Fuel price actual data up to 2006 and 25%, 20% and 15% rise in 2007, 2008 and 2009; and 5% rise p.a. inlater years	Fuel price actual data up to 2006 and gradually rises: 5% in 2007 to 20% in 2012
Variable	RefRun	Scenario 12	Scenario 13	Scenario 14	Scenario 15	Scenario 16
TGDP	8.82	9.31	8.27	8.01	7.72	7.84
TGCF	16.37	18.90	14.17	13.01	11.71	12.07
TPDFL	2.48	2.70	2.92	3.06	3.16	3.29
AGDP	2.58	3.08	2.48	2.42	2.47	1.91
AGCF	4.95	4.65	4.55	4.29	5.06	2.71
APDFL	2.26	2.32	2.29	2.32	2.30	2.51
IGDP	10.74	11.94	10.00	9.67	9.24	9.50
IGCF	20.14	24.32	15.99	13.77	10.31	12.91
IPDFL	3.48	3.73	4.07	4.28	4.43	4.46
SGDP	9.85	9.93	9.24	8.96	8.65	8.88
SGCF	14.22	14.94	13.91	13.63	13.81	12.68
SPDFL	2.01	2.23	2.48	2.61	2.72	2.87
PFCE	6.61	7.00	5.93	5.66	5.28	5.50
HFS	10.33	10.77	10.14	10.17	10.42	10.34
HPS	10.05	10.23	5.76	3.17	0.26	0.41

Reference Run Specifications: Rainfall normal, No rise in fuel price, RM3 grows @ 11% p.a., RBR grows @ 0% p.a., RBD grows @20% p.a. PCSS/NAGDP$_{t-1}$ @ 5%, AGEXP grows @ 10% p.a., NAGEXP grows @ 10% p.a., NAGIMP grows @ 9.5% p.a., NETPETIMP grows @ 21% p.a., RINVEXP grows @ 19% p.a., RINVIMP grows @ 13% p.a.

For data on international prices and domestic fuel price index see Table 3.21. It may be noted that the movements in domestic fuel price index need not reflect the movements in the world oil price. When it is said below 'fuel prices rise or fall', what is meant is that the domestic fuel price index rises or falls. Only to provide an idea of what is simultaneously happening in the world oil market, the world oil price (in $) is occasionally mentioned.

3.10.4.1 Scenario 12 (Petroleum Imports Growth Rate Decreases)

Table A-3.1(e) presents data on net petroleum imports (NETPETIMP) of India at constant prices. Since the 1990s, though net petroleum imports have only occasionally gone down compared to the previous year, in most of the years they have risen by substantial proportions. In the RefRun, net petroleum imports were specified to grow at 21 per cent p.a. with no rise in fuel prices over the years. In scenario 12 the NETPETIMP is specified to grow at only at 17 per cent p.a. The resources thus saved result in increasing the growth rate of investment particularly in industry—IGCF growth rate increases by 4.18 per cent p.a. from 20.14 per cent to 24.32 per cent. Consequently, industrial GDP increases, IGDP growth rate increases by 1.2 per cent p.a. from 10.74 per cent (RefRun) to 11.94 per cent; and agricultural GDP (AGDP) growth rate increases by 0.5 per cent from 2.58 per cent (RefRun) to 3.08 per cent. The impact on the growth rates of other variables is only marginal (mostly less than 0.5 per cent p.a.).

3.10.4.2 Scenario 13 (Fuel Prices Rise)

Fuel prices enter as important explanatory variables in all the models estimated. In the RefRun fuel prices remain unchanged from the year 2002-03 (around $27 to $31 per barrel in 2003), which is somewhat unrealistic. In scenario 13 fuel (oil) prices are specified to go up at 10 per cent p.a. from the year 2003-04. This yearly rise shows up negative impacts on almost all the variables. Industrial investment growth rate falls by 4.15 per cent p.a. (IGCF—from 20.14 per cent to 15.99 per cent), industry GDP growth rate by 0.74 per cent p.a. (IGDP—from 10.74 per cent to 10.0 per cent), and industry prices growth rate goes up by 0.59 per cent p.a. (IPDFL—from 3.48 per cent to 4.07 per cent). The corresponding figures in the case of services growth are 0.31 per cent p.a. fall (SGCF—from 14.22 per cent to 13.91 per cent), 0.61 per cent p.a. fall (SGDP—from 9.85 per cent to 9.24 per cent) and 0.47 per cent p.a. rise (SPDFL—from 2.01 per cent to 2.48 per cent). Similarly the corresponding figures in the case of agriculture growth are 0.4 per cent p.a. fall (AGCF—from 4.95 per cent to 4.55 per cent), 0.10 per cent p.a. fall (AGDP—from 2.58 per cent to 2.48 per cent), and 0.03 per cent rise (APDFL—from2.26 per cent to 2.29 per cent). Thus, the rise in the oil prices causes fall in the growth rates of investments and GDPs and rise in the prices all over the economy—with industry being the worst sufferer. Further, it causes a dent in the growth of consumption expenditure—PFCE growth rate falls down by 0.68 per cent p.a. (from 6.61 per cent to 5.93 per cent). Though household savings in financial assets (HFS) is hardly affected, the 4.29 per cent p.a. fall in the growth rate of savings in physical assets is substantial (HPS—from 10.05 per cent to 5.76 per cent).

3.10.4.3 Scenario 14 (Fuel Prices Rise from 2008-09)

This is a minor variation of the earlier scenario 13. In the Refrun as well as in scenario 13 the actual fuel prices were specified only till 2002-03. In this scenario 14, the actual fuel prices were specified till 2005-06 ($56 per barrel in 2005-06), and for the years following from 2006-07 onwards the price is specified to grow at 10 per cent p.a. This specification further aggravates (compared to the scenario 13) the negative impacts on all the sectors, particularly on the investment in industry.

3.10.4.4 Scenario 15 (Fuel Prices Shoot up for 3 Consecutive Years and Later the Rise Becomes Modest)

Sometimes oil prices substantially rise in one or two years and later gradually fall; in other words it is a severe shock that occurs occasionally. That would cause serious disturbances in the economy taking several years to recover. This feature is incorporated in scenario 15, where the actual fuel prices were specified till 2005-06 as in scenario 14 ($56 per barrel in 2005-06), and in 2006-07, 2007-08 and 2008-09 fuel prices go up by 25 per cent, 20 per cent and 15 per cent respectively. In the later years the rise is only by 5 per cent p.a.

Table 3.21 below shows the year to year dynamics of the growth process, how the three sectors suffer in the years following the shock, and later how they recover. Compare the present results with respect to scenario 14. From 2006-07 onwards, fuel price is higher in scenario 15 than what it is in scenario 14. Initially in the year 2007-08, agriculture GDP (AGDP) experiences severe setback registering a growth rate of only 0.41 per cent (compound annual growth rate (CAGR) from 2004-05) compared to the CAGR of 2.82 per cent in Run 14. Similar is the situation of investment in agriculture (AGCF's CAGR is -1.42 per cent now compared to 4.13 per cent in scenario14). Agriculture prices go up though. In industry, IGDP's CAGR falls from 9.25 per cent (in scenario 14) to 8.25 per cent now, and investment, IGCF's CAGR falls from 10.23 per cent (scenario 14) to 4.9 per cent now. Industry prices too go up. The pattern is similar in the services sector also. However, by 2010-11, only the agriculture sector would recover; whereas the industry and services sectors would not even by 2011-12. SGCF would however recover only by 2011-12.

3.10.4.5 Scenario 16 (Fuel Prices Rise at an Increasing Per cent Every Year)

In scenario 16 the actual fuel prices were specified till 2005-06 as in scenarios 14 and 15 ($56 per barrel in 2005-06), and from 2006-07 onwards fuel prices go up at an increasing percentage every year. The increasing percentages specified by which fuel prices would go up are 5 per cent in 2006-07, 8 per cent in 2007-08, 12 per cent in 2008-09, 15 per cent in 2009-10, 18 per cent in 2010-11 and 20 per cent in 2011-12. This specification implies that, for the years 2007 to 2009, fuel price is lower in this scenario compared to scenario 14. In 2010, it is almost the same in both the scenarios, and in the later years this scenario would have higher fuel price than that in the scenario 14. Simulation results are presented in

Table 3.21: RefRun and Scenarios 14-16: Year to Year CAGRS from 2004-05 to 2011-12

	RefRun					Scenerio 14				Scenerio 15				Scenerio 16			
Agriculture	Fuel Price Index	World Oil Price pbl	AGDP	AGCF	APDFL	Fuel Price Index	AGDP	AGCF	APDFL	Fuel Price Index	AGDP	AGCF	APDFL	Fuel Price Index	AGDP	AGCF	APDFL
2006	237.97	30.79	0.37	8.29	3.09	370.69	-1.67	1.41	3.81	370.69	-1.67	1.41	3.81	370.69	-1.67	1.41	3.81
2007	237.97	30.79	1.42	5.37	2.82	407.76	0.96	0.34	3.16	463.36	0.96	0.34	3.16	389.22	0.96	0.34	3.16
2008	237.97	30.79	2.24	4.96	2.64	448.53	2.82	4.13	2.47	556.04	0.41	-1.42	3.34	420.36	3.60	5.86	2.17
2009	237.97	30.79	2.18	5.26	2.52	493.39	1.94	4.68	2.58	639.44	1.08	1.29	2.89	470.81	1.98	5.24	2.57
2010	237.97	30.79	2.24	5.17	2.43	542.73	1.92	4.62	2.51	671.41	1.85	2.20	2.70	541.43	1.56	4.46	2.58
2011	237.97	30.79	2.46	4.94	2.35	597.00	2.48	4.15	2.43	704.98	2.81	5.12	2.20	638.88	2.26	3.14	2.56
2012	237.97	30.79	2.58	4.95	2.26	656.70	2.42	4.29	2.32	740.23	2.47	5.06	2.30	766.66	1.91	2.71	2.51
Industry			IGDP	IGCF	IPDFL		IGDP	IGCF	IPDFL		IGDP	IGCF	IPDFL		IGDP	IGCF	IPDFL
2006	237.97	30.79	9.81	26.33	3.40	370.69	7.94	12.70	5.09	370.69	7.94	12.70	5.09	370.69	7.94	12.70	5.09
2007	237.97	30.79	10.22	23.65	3.44	407.76	8.52	8.45	4.82	463.36	8.52	8.45	4.83	389.22	8.52	8.45	4.83
2008	237.97	30.79	10.52	22.30	3.33	448.53	9.25	10.23	4.32	556.04	8.25	4.90	4.94	420.36	9.58	11.90	4.11
2009	237.97	30.79	10.62	21.85	3.35	493.39	9.31	11.92	4.21	639.44	8.50	5.32	5.01	470.81	9.48	13.44	4.00
2010	237.97	30.79	10.70	21.38	3.38	542.73	9.50	13.52	4.29	671.41	8.70	5.41	4.83	541.43	9.58	14.82	4.27
2011	237.97	30.79	10.75	20.78	3.43	597.00	9.64	13.59	4.24	704.98	9.16	8.77	4.59	638.88	9.63	13.73	4.29
2012	237.97	30.79	10.74	20.14	3.48	656.70	9.67	13.77	4.28	740.23	9.24	10.31	4.43	766.66	9.50	12.91	4.46
Services			SGDP	SGCF	SPDFL		SGDP	SGCF	SPDFL		SGDP	SGCF	SPDFL		SGDP	SGCF	SPDFL
2006	237.97	30.79	7.63	14.52	4.12	370.69	6.43	8.02	5.63	370.69	6.43	8.02	5.63	370.69	6.43	8.02	5.63
2007	237.97	30.79	8.44	17.78	3.06	407.76	7.35	12.25	4.36	463.36	7.35	12.25	4.36	389.22	7.35	12.25	4.36
2008	237.97	30.79	8.62	14.96	2.65	448.53	7.66	12.71	3.54	556.04	7.13	8.65	4.35	420.36	7.83	13.99	3.27
2009	237.97	30.79	8.96	14.42	2.40	493.39	7.97	13.13	3.22	639.44	7.45	10.45	3.95	470.81	8.10	13.64	3.06
2010	237.97	30.79	9.28	13.80	2.29	542.73	8.29	13.39	3.01	671.41	7.80	10.54	3.62	541.43	8.34	13.67	2.98
2011	237.97	30.79	9.57	14.01	2.18	597.00	8.67	13.38	2.77	704.98	8.24	13.33	3.08	638.88	8.70	12.86	2.83
2012	237.97	30.79	9.84	14.22	2.01	656.70	8.96	13.63	2.61	740.23	8.65	13.81	2.72	766.66	8.88	12.68	2.87
Total			TGDP	TGCF	TPDFL		TGDP	TGCF	TPDFL		TGDP	TGCF	TPDFL		TGDP	TGCF	TPDFL
2006	237.97	30.79	6.70	18.98	3.68	370.69	5.18	9.40	5.09	370.69	5.18	9.40	5.09	370.69	5.18	9.40	5.09
2007	237.97	30.79	7.51	19.26	3.09	407.76	6.39	9.61	4.24	463.36	6.39	9.62	4.24	389.22	6.39	9.61	4.24
2008	237.97	30.79	7.89	17.40	2.81	448.53	7.14	10.93	3.54	556.04	6.13	6.23	4.31	420.36	7.48	12.42	3.28
2009	237.97	30.79	8.12	17.07	2.67	493.39	7.19	11.92	3.37	639.44	6.53	7.58	4.05	470.81	7.32	12.86	3.22
2010	237.97	30.79	8.37	16.66	2.61	542.73	7.45	12.75	3.28	671.41	6.94	7.77	3.80	541.43	7.44	13.45	3.28
2011	237.97	30.79	8.61	16.53	2.56	597.00	7.82	12.77	3.14	704.98	7.50	10.83	3.37	638.88	7.80	12.51	3.21
2012	237.97	30.79	8.82	16.37	2.48	656.70	8.01	13.01	3.06	740.23	7.72	11.71	3.16	766.66	7.84	12.07	3.29
Data	1994-95	1995-96	1996-97	1997-98	1998-99	1999-2000	2000-01	2001-02	2002-03	2003-04	2004-05	2005-06	2006-07				
Fuel Price Index (India)	108.17	108.16	124.5	144.8	148.25	167.77	207.4	224.5	239.47	264.30	315.2	373.4					
World oil price ($/brl)									30.8		38.9	55.4	67.0				

Table 3.20 above. For the year to year dynamics see *Table 3.21*. Obviously the various GDPs and GCFs recorded higher (lower) CAGRs in the initial (later) years compared to those in scenario 14.

Summary: Though reduction in the net petroleum imports might help push up the industrial GDP and investment (IGDP and IGCF), it may also lead to higher prices for industrial goods, thus the agricultural investment growth rate is likely to go down. Rising oil price would severely harm the economy on all fronts in all the sectors: growth rates of GDPs' and investments substantially fall down while prices grow faster; and that of real consumption expenditure falls down too (Table 3.20). Agriculture sector's gains or losses seem to be though severe but somewhat indirectly passed on to it via the industry. While wild increases in the oil price, such as 25 per cent (or even higher) rise in one go, can severely derail the growth process, there is a possibility to recover the growth process in case the oil price satbilises in the later periods after such wild increase. Should such a thing happen (in deed it is right now happening; the world price of the 'crude' fell down to less than $40 per barrel after it shot up to more than $130 per barrel just a few months ago), all the sectors would recover with agriculture recovering faster than the others. It may also be noted that the growth rate of households' savings in physical assets (HPS) would suffer the most in the situation of rising oil prices.

3.10.5 Combination of Different Policies

Here we present two scenarios that combine different policies together. See Table 3.22.

Table 3.22: Scenarios 17-18: Simulated CAGRs (%) for 2004-05 to 2011-12

Specifications under Reference Run (RefRun)		Actual data of all exogenous variables up to 2004. RBD growth rate @ 20% p.a.AGEXP @ 10%, NAGEXP @ 10%, NAGIMP @ 9.5%, RINVIMP @ 13%,NETPETIMP @ 21%	Actual data of all exogenous variables up to 2004. No rise in fuel prices. NETPETIMP gr. rate @21%, NAGEXP @ 10%, RBD gr. rate @ 20%, PCSS/NAGDP$_{t-1}$ = 0.05
Modified Specifications under Scenario		Actual data of all exogenous variables up to 2006. RBD is @ 2% of GDP$_{t-1}$Annual growth rates of AGEXP @ 16%, NAGEXP @ 14%, NAGIMP @ 13%, RINVIMP @ 15%,NETPETIMP @ 31%	Fuel price actual data up to 2006 and gradually rises: from 5% in 2007 to 20% in 2012; RBD is @ 1.17% of GDP$_{t-1}$,In 2008 and 2009: [NETPETIMP gr. rate 15%, NAGEXP @ 20%, and PCSS/NAGDP$_{t-1}$ = 0.06]
Variable	**RefRun**	**Scenario 17**	**Scenario 18**
TGDP	8.82	10.25	9.21
TGCF	16.37	12.63	18.64
TPDFL	2.48	4.73	4.09
AGDP	2.58	2.87	4.28
AGCF	4.95	7.45	1.35
APDFL	2.26	4.05	3.21
IGDP	10.74	11.98	12.73
IGCF	20.14	8.77	24.56
IPDFL	3.48	5.13	5.61
SGDP	9.85	11.69	8.94
SGCF	14.22	17.49	15.08
SPDFL	2.01	4.61	3.36
PFCE	6.61	7.35	6.55
HFS	10.33	9.31	11.77
HPS	10.05	17.21	1.06

Reference Run Specifications: Rainfall normal, No rise in fuel price, RM3 grows @ 11% p.a., RBR grows @ 0% p.a., RBD grows @20% p.a. PCSS/NAGDP$_{t-1}$ @ 5%, AGEXP grows @ 10% p.a., NAGEXP grows @ 10% p.a., NAGIMP grows @ 9.5% p.a., NETPETIMP grows @ 21% p.a., RINVEXP grows @ 19% p.a., RINVIMP grows @ 13% p.a.

3.10.5.1 Scenario 17 (Actual Data of all Exogenous Variables up to 2005-06, and Several Other Changes in Specifications)

The RefRun specifications have been changed in this scenario as follows: The data of all exogenous variables were specified to be at actual levels up to 2005-06. From 2006-07 onwards, real budget deficit (RBD) is specified to be at 2.0 per cent of the previous year total GDP (instead of growing at 20 per cent p.a. as in the RefRun), net petroleum exports would grow at 31 per cent p.a. (instead of 21 per cent as in the RefRun), agricultural exports would grow at 16 per cent p.a. (instead of 10 per cent as in the RefRun), non-agricultural exports would grow at 14 per cent p.a. (instead of 10 per cent as in the RefRun), non-agricultural imports would grow at 13 per cent p.a. (instead of 9.5 per cent as in the RefRun) and real invisible imports would grow at 15 per cent p.a. (instead of 13 per cent as in the RefRun). Thus, this is a scenario reflecting some 'bad' things and some 'good' things happening. The results indicate that overall the economy could grow under such a regime at 10.25 per cent p.a. (TGDP) between 2004-05 and 2011-12, total investment (TGCF) at 12.63 per cent and prices at 4.73 per cent. Though, the agriculture (AGDP) may not show great difference between the RefRun and this scenario, industry (IGDP) would benefit by more than 1.2 per cent p.a. and services (SGDP) by more than 1.8 per cent p.a. The increased incomes would lead to increased consumption expenditure (PFCE) by 0.74 per cent p.a. (from 6.61 per cent to 7.35 per cent). Though there is a fall in the growth rate of financial savings (HFS—from 10.33 per cent p.a. to 9.31 per cent p.a.), the rise in the savings in physical assets is substantial (HPS growth rate rises by 7.16 per cent p.a. from 10.05 per cent to 17.21 per cent). Basically this scenario demonstrates that better trade performance can offset the negative impacts of increased petroleum imports.

3.10.5.2 Scenario 18 (Actual Data of Fuel Price up to 2005-06, and Several Other Changes in Specifications)

The RefRun specifications have been changed in this scenario as follows: The data of only fuel price index were specified to be at actual levels up to 2005-06. From 2006-07 onwards the fuel price goes up every year at an increasing percentage as in scenario 16. Further, from 2006-07 onwards, real budget deficit (RBD) is specified to be at 1.17 per cent of the previous year total GDP (instead of growing at 20 per cent p.a. as in the RefRun). Besides only for two years, *viz.*, in 2007-08 and 2008-09: (i) net petroleum imports would grow only by 15 per cent p.a. (instead of at 21 per cent as in the RefRun), (ii) non-agricultural exports would grow by 20 per cent p.a. (instead of at 10 per cent as in the RefRun), (iii) corporate savings as a proportion of the non-agricultural GDP would be 6 per cent (instead of 5 per cent as in the RefRun). From 2009-10 onwards, these three would return to the RefRun specifications. This scenario demonstrates the impact of somewhat unstable policies. Some 'tightening' for two years on the side of petroleum imports, and vigorous push on the side of non-agricultural exports and in corporate savings, helped industry (IGDP growth rate goes up from 10.74 per cent p.a. to 12.73 per cent, and investment IGCF from 20.14 per cent p.a. to 24.56 per cent), and agriculture GDP (AGDP) growth rate rises from 2.58 per cent to 4.28 per cent p.a. But the rise in the investment growth rate in services did not lead to corresponding rise in the corresponding GDP (SGDP growth rate falls from 9.85 per cent to 8.94 per cent, though SGCF growth rate rises from 14.22 per cent to 15.02 per cent p.a.). Price indexes growth rates increased in all the sectors. Household savings in physical assets (HPS) registered a CAGR of only 1.06 per cent p.a. between 2004-05 and 2011-12.

Summary: It is quite difficult to expect that net petroleum imports could be cut down substantially. In fact they may substantially go up as in scenario 17 (from 21 per cent p.a. to 31 per cent p.a.). The results suggest that in such a case, a vigorous promotion of trade and modified permissible levels of budget deficit might compensate for the negative impacts of the increased petroleum imports. However, prices would grow at far higher levels than in the RefRun.

Earlier (scenarios 15 and 16) we had seen that steep rise in oil price over the years with no reduction in later periods is the worst thing to happen—especially industry and agriculture are the worst affected. In such a case, even if only for two years the net petroleum imports could be reduced, and non-agricultural exports growth rate and corporate savings rate could be pushed up, and the permissible levels of the budget deficit could be modified, the agriculture and industry sectors could be made to perform better compared to the RefRun and scenarios 15 and 16 levels. Besides there would be some recovery in the final consumption expenditure growth rate, though the services sector would not yet recover.

3.10.6 Crisis Scenarios

The IMF and the World Bank view that the growth rates of world economic growth and world trade will come down drastically in the near future. They are already low in sevral advanced countries. Besides, the oil producing countries are meanwhile planning to reduce the level of oil production. Though such a 'global crisis' has several dimensions (banking, financial, economic, etc.), is the 'crisis' really global? If yes, in the context of our model it gets related to India's export performance, foreign capital inflows, ability to import adequate oil and oil prices. Agricultural and non-agricultural exports growth rates may fall, invisibles' imports growth rate may go up, petroleum imports may not come down, and even oil price may go up. However, one may ask—even if India's export performance is seriously affected by the 'global crisis', will it and when will it lead to a domestic 'crisis' in terms of GDP growth performance? Here we present eight likely scenarios (see Table 3.23) in view of the current 'global crisis'.

3.10.6.1 Scenario 19

In this scenario agricultural exports' growth rate is specified to come down from 10 per cent p.a. to 6 per cent p.a. in the years 2005-06 to 2007-08, and further fall down to only 4 per cent p.a. from 2008-09 to 2011-12. Non-agricultural exports' growth rate is specified to come down from 10 per cent p.a. to 6 per cent p.a. from 2008-09 to 2011-12. Under such a scenario, agricultural GDP growth rate would fall down drastically from 2.58 per cent (as in the RefRun) to mere 0.87 per cent p.a. In industry too, GDP and investment would experience fall in their growth rates.

3.10.6.2 Scenario 20

In this scenario not only the agricultural and non-agricultural exports' growth rates are specified to come down as in the scenario 19 above, but also the invisibles imports' growth rate to go up from 13 per cent p.a. to 23 per cent p.a. from 2008-09 onwards. Now the results indicate that, even the services GDP growth rate has negative impact, though only marginally.

3.10.6.3 Scenario 21

Further to the previous scenario 20, net petroleum imports' growth rate is specified to go up from 21 per cent (as in the RefRun) to 25 per cent p.a. from 2008-09. Under this scenario the total GDP growth rate would come down to 7.78 per cent p.a. compared to the RefRun. Agriculture would be severely affected, besides the industry. Obviously the consumption expenditure growth rate would also fall down.

3.10.6.4 Scenario 22

The world oil price rose by about 43 per cent between 2004-05 and 2005-06 and by another 20 per cent in the following year. In view of this phenomenon, further to the specifications as in scenario 20, now the domestic fuel price is also presumed to go up by 43 per cent (but) in 2006-07 and by 10 per cent p.a. in 2007-08 and 2008-09 respectively. Later it would stay at that level. Net petroleum imports would grow only at @ 21 per cent p.a. as in the RefRun. Under such specifications, agriculture would grow at 1.5 per cent p.a. but the industry and services would be severely affected. IGDP grows only 7.62 per cent p.a.; investment would be hard hit, with IGCF fluctuating and registering an unimaginably low CAGR of 2.17 per cent! Total GDP would grow only at 7.18 per cent p.a., total investment, TGCF, at 10.12 per cent. There would be a drastic fall in the growth rate of consumption expenditure, PFCE growth rate would come down from 6.61 per cent p.a. (as in the RefRun) to 5.19 per cent p.a. now. Obviously the savings grow at substantially lower rates compared to the RefRun.

Table 3.24 presents estimates of net capital inflows, foreign direct and portfolio investments under scenario 22 at various interest rate differentials. The effect on foreign direct investment seems to be marginal compared to the effect on foreign portfolio investment which turns out to be even negative for some years under this scenario. Earlier in Table 3.16 corresponding to the RefRun, real net capital inflows as a percentage of the total GDP came to be positive varying between 0.89 and 1.32. Under scenario 22 this picture has changed. Not only the percentage turned out negative for some years, but also the extent of variation over the years 2010 to 2012 increased (from -1.37 to 1.70) depending on the interest rate differential. In any case this variation is still much lower compared to the figures recorded in the past. See Table A-3.1(i). In 2003-04, real net capital inflows as a percentage of the total GDP was -2.14, and in 1999-2000 it was 1.37.

3.10.6.5 Scenario 23

Here specifications of the agricultural and non-agricultural exports' growth rates are as in scenario 19; the fuel price is specified to be as in scenario 22. Growth rates of net petroleum imports and invisible imports (21 per cent and 13 per cent respectively) are as in the RefRun. Thus this scenario is only a slight modification of the scenario 22—the difference is only with respect to the invisibles' imports. Obviously except in the case of the services sector, hardly any difference is seen in the results of the agriculture and industry. This feature is in conformity of the results seen earlier under the scenario 6.

3.10.6.6 Scenario 24

The only difference between the earlier scenario (23) and this scenario is that the growth rate of the agricultural exports (AGEXP) would only be 1 per cent p.a. from 2009. The growth rate of the non-agricultural exports (NAGEXP) would remain at 6 per cent p.a. The effects are of similar nature as are the differences between the RefRun and scenario 3 (section 10.2). Now the agricultural GDP's growth rate would come down to mere 1.38 per cent p.a. The growth rate of the consumption expenditure would fall to 5.32 per cent p.a.

Are there ways to avoid such drastic falls in the growth rates of domestic GDPs and investments in case India's trade performance is severely affected by the global crisis? Next two scenarios may provide some insights.

3.10.6.7 Scenario 25

In addition to the specifications under scenario 24 above, now the growth rate of real money supply (RM3) is specified to be 13 per cent p.a. instead of 11 per cent p.a. as in the RefRun. Such increase cheers up the economy, a little bit. Growth rates of all the sectoral GDPs would go up. Particularly the growth rate of industrial investment (IGCF) picks up substantially—from less than 2.34 per cent in scenarios 22 to 24, now to 8.25 per cent p.a. However, the industrial prices also grow at a higher rate now!

3.10.6.8 Scenario 26

In addition to the specifications under scenario 25 above, now the economy is also assumed to manage with a reduction in the growth rate of net petroleum imports—from 21 per cent (as in scenario 25) down to 18 per cent p.a. Recall the results seen earlier in section 10.4.1 (scenario 12) that such reduction if possible would help industrial GDP and investment, and agricultural GDP. The same feature prevails now—the growth rates of these variables would increase. Thus the AGDP would now grow at 2.02 per cent p.a. IGDP at 8.72 per cent, and IGCF at 10.65 per cent (instead of 1.78 per cent, 8.25 per cent and 7.65 per cent respectively as in scenario 25, and 1.38 per cent, 7.6 per cent and 2.15 per cent as in scenario 24).

Summary: To the extent that the current global crisis negatively affects the performance of the agricultural and non-agricultural exports, there can be serious threat to the prospects of the Indian economy. The problems would only aggravate if the oil prices also keep rising without any respite. Besides, there could be a reduction in the foreign direct investment approximately to an order of Rs.1000 crore to Rs.1200 crore a year (at 1993-94 prices). More severely affected is the foreign portfolio investment (compare Tables 3.16 and 3.24). However, there seem to be some ways and means in overcoming these negative effects by adopting appropriate monetary policies and managing the interest rates and inflation.

Table 3.23: Scenarios 19-26: Simulated CAGRs (%) for 2004-05 to 2011-12

Specifications under Reference Run (RefRun)		Actual data of all exogenous variables up to 2004. From 2005-06: AGEXP @ 10%, NAGEXP @ 10%	Actual data of all exogenous variables up to 2004. From 2005-06: AGEXP @ 10%, NAGEXP @ 10%, RINVIMP @ 13%	Actual data of all exogenous variables up to 2004. From 2005-06: AGEXP @ 10%, NAGEXP @ 10% , NETPETIMP @ 21%	Actual data of all exogenous variables up to 2004. From 2005-06: AGEXP @ 10%, NAGEXP @ 10%, RINVIMP @ 13%, Fuel price remains same.
Modified Specifications under Scenario		Actual data of all exogenous variables up to 2004. For 2006 to 2008: AGEXP @ 6%, NAGEXP @ 10%. Later AGEXP @ 4%, and NAGEXP @ 6%.	Actual data of all exogenous variables up to 2004. For 2006 to 2008: AGEXP @ 6%, NAGEXP @ 10%. Later AGEXP @ 4%, NAGEXP @ 6%, RINVIMP @ 23%	Actual data of all exogenous variables up to 2004. For 2006 to 2008: AGEXP @ 6%, NAGEXP @ 10%. Later AGEXP @ 4%, NAGEXP @ 6%, NETPETIMP @ 25%	Actual data of all exogenous variables up to 2004. For 2006 to 2008: AGEXP @ 6%, NAGEXP @ 10%. Later AGEXP @ 4%, NAGEXP @ 6%. RINVIMP @ 23%. Fuel price actual data up to 2006, 43% rise in 2007, and 10% rise for next two years.
Variable	**RefRun**	**Scenario 19**	**Scenario 20**	**Scenario 21**	**Scenario 22**
TGDP	8.82	8.16	8.03	7.78	7.18
TGCF	16.37	13.37	14.54	13.00	10.12
TPDFL	2.48	2.33	2.63	2.53	2.96
AGDP	2.58	0.87	0.86	0.50	1.50
AGCF	4.95	4.11	4.13	4.33	5.01
APDFL	2.26	2.18	2.18	2.17	2.15
IGDP	10.74	9.05	9.04	8.40	7.62
IGCF	20.14	15.35	15.27	12.18	2.17
IPDFL	3.48	3.24	3.23	3.10	3.91
SGDP	9.85	9.99	9.76	9.74	8.78
SGCF	14.22	12.91	15.37	14.91	15.62
SPDFL	2.01	1.95	2.46	2.37	2.73
PFCE	6.61	6.36	6.23	6.04	5.19
HFS	10.33	9.75	8.32	8.12	7.62
HPS	10.05	7.95	10.94	10.77	5.64

Reference Run Specifications: Rainfall normal, No rise in fuel price, RM3 grows @ 11% p.a., RBR grows @ 0% p.a., RBD grows @20% p.a. PCSS/NAGDP$_{t-1}$ @ 5%, AGEXP grows @ 10% p.a., NAGEXP grows @ 10% p.a., NAGIMP grows @ 9.5% p.a., NETPETIMP grows @ 21% p.a., RINVEXP grows @ 19% p.a., RINVIMP grows @ 13% p.a.

Table 3.23: Scenarios 19-26: Simulated CAGRs (%) for 2004-05 to 2011-12 (contd...)

Specifications under Reference Run (RefRun)		Actual data of all exogenous variables up to 2004. From 2005-06: AGEXP @ 10%, NAGEXP @ 10%, Fuel price remains same.	Actual data of all exogenous variables up to 2004. From 2005-06: AGEXP @ 10%, NAGEXP @ 10%. Fuel price remains same.	Actual data of all exogenous variables up to 2004. From 2005-06: AGEXP @ 10%, NAGEXP @ 10%. RM3 @11%. Fuel price remains same.	Actual data of all exogenous variables up to 2004. From 2005-06: AGEXP @ 10%, NAGEXP @ 10%. RM3 @ 11%. Fuel price remains same. NETPETIMP @ 21%.
Modified Specifications under Scenario		Actual data of all exogenous variables up to 2004. For 2006 to 2008: AGEXP @ 6%, NAGEXP @ 10%. Later AGEXP @ 4%, NAGEXP @ 6%. Fuel price actual data up to 2006, 43% rise in 2007, and 10% rise for next two years.	Actual data of all exogenous variables up to 2004. For 2006 to 2008: AGEXP @ 6%, NAGEXP @ 10%. Later AGEXP @ 1%, NAGEXP @ 6%. Fuel price actual data up to 2006, 43% rise in 2007, and 10% rise for next two years.	Actual data of all exogenous variables up to 2004. For 2006 to 2008: AGEXP @ 6%, NAGEXP @ 10%. Later AGEXP @ 1%, NAGEXP @ 6%. Fuel price actual data up to 2006, 43% rise in 2007, and 10% rise for next two years. RM3 @ 13% during 2009-12.	Actual data of all exogenous variables up to 2004. For 2006 to 2008: AGEXP @ 6%, NAGEXP @ 10%. Later AGEXP @ 1%, NAGEXP @ 6%. Fuel price actual data up to 2006, 43% rise in 2007, and 10% rise for next two years. RM3 @ 13% and NETPETIMP @ 18% during 2009-12.
Variable	**RefRun**	**Scenario 23**	**Scenario 24**	**Scenario 25**	**Scenario 26**
TGDP	8.82	7.32	7.30	7.82	8.00
TGCF	16.37	8.52	8.43	11.59	12.84
TPDFL	2.48	2.68	2.66	2.38	2.46
AGDP	2.58	1.51	1.38	1.78	2.02
AGCF	4.95	5.00	4.77	4.54	4.39
APDFL	2.26	2.15	2.06	2.04	2.05
IGDP	10.74	7.63	7.60	8.25	8.72
IGCF	20.14	2.34	2.15	7.65	10.65
IPDFL	3.48	3.92	3.91	4.07	4.16
SGDP	9.85	9.03	9.02	9.52	9.54
SGCF	14.22	13.04	13.01	15.35	15.67
SPDFL	2.01	2.23	2.23	1.65	1.71
PFCE	6.61	5.33	5.32	5.73	5.87
HFS	10.33	9.07	9.00	9.07	9.20
HPS	10.05	0.83	0.40	5.46	5.64

Reference Run Specifications: Rainfall normal, No rise in fuel price, RM3 grows @ 11% p.a., RBR grows @ 0% p.a., RBD grows @20% p.a. PCSS/$NAGDP_{t-1}$ @ 5%, AGEXP grows @ 10% p.a., NAGEXP grows @ 10% p.a., NAGIMP grows @ 9.5% p.a., NETPETIMP grows @ 21% p.a., RINVEXP grows @ 19% p.a., RINVIMP grows @ 13% p.a.

Table 3.24: Implicit Forecasts of Real Net Capital Inflow at 1993-94 Prices for the Scenario 22 at Different Interest Rate Differences
(See Table 3.15 for the Estimated Regressions, and Table A-3.1(i) for Explanations)

Year	TGDP (Scenario 22)	GDS= TGDP*AVSR	TCFIU= (Scenario 22)	Real Foreign Direct Investment in India & Abroad (RFDI)	INTDIFF	Real Foreign Portfolio Investment in India & Abroad (RPI)	Real Net Capital Inflow (RNCI)	RNCI/ TGDP (%)	GCFAEC = GCF with All Adjustments
2007	1705060	593361	316005	12028	- 2.50	20804	20607	1.21	613968
2008	1736952	604459	261474	12231	- 2.50	-17784	-17654	-1.02	586806
2009	1967264	684608	347455	13316	- 2.50	67304	73951	3.76	758559
2010	2066206	719040	334847	13786	- 2.50	-30662	-25027	-1.21	694013
2011	2226663	774879	498504	14505	- 2.50	26635	37886	1.70	812765
2012	2448870	852207	517043	15459	- 2.50	26705	41547	1.70	893754

Year	TGDP (Scenario 22)	GDS= TGDP*AVSR	TCFIU= (Scenario 22)	Real Foreign Direct Investment in India & Abroad (RFDI)	INTDIFF	Real Foreign Portfolio Investment in India & Abroad (RPI)	Real Net Capital Inflow (RNCI)	RNCI/ TGDP (%)	GCFAEC = GCF with All Adjustments
2007	1705060	593361	316005	12028	- 0.3811	18951	18651	1.09	612012
2008	1736952	604459	261474	12231	- 0.3811	-19636	-19610	-1.13	584850
2009	1967264	684608	347455	13316	- 0.3811	65451	71995	3.66	756603
2010	2066206	719040	334847	13786	- 0.3811	-32515	-26983	-1.31	692057
2011	2226663	774879	498504	14505	- 0.3811	24782	35930	1.61	810809
2012	2448870	852207	517043	15459	- 0.3811	24852	39591	1.62	891798

Year	TGDP (Scenario 22)	GDS= TGDP*AVSR	TCFIU= (Scenario 22)	Real Foreign Direct Investment in India & Abroad (RFDI)	INTDIFF	Real Foreign Portfolio Investment in India & Abroad (RPI)	Real Net Capital Inflow (RNCI)	RNCI/ TGDP (%)	GCFAEC = GCF with All Adjustments
2007	1705060	593361	316005	12028	0.	18618	18300	1.07	611660
2008	1736952	604459	261474	12231	0.	-19970	-19962	-1.15	584498
2009	1967264	684608	347455	13316	0.	65118	71644	3.64	756251
2010	2066206	719040	334847	13786	0.	-32848	-27335	-1.32	691705
2011	2226663	774879	498504	14505	0.	24449	35579	1.60	810457
2012	2448870	852207	517043	15459	0.	24519	39239	1.60	891446

Year	TGDP (Scenario 22)	GDS= TGDP*AVSR	TCFIU= (Scenario 22)	Real Foreign Direct Investment in India & Abroad (RFDI)	INTDIFF	Real Foreign Portfolio Investment in India & Abroad (RPI)	Real Net Capital Inflow (RNCI)	RNCI/ TGDP (%)	GCFAEC = GCF with All Adjustments
2007	1705060	593361	316005	12028	1.0	17743	17376	1.02	610737
2008	1736952	604459	261474	12231	1.0	-20844	-20885	-1.20	583575
2009	1967264	684608	347455	13316	1.0	64243	70720	3.59	755328
2010	2066206	719040	334847	13786	1.0	-33723	-28258	-1.37	690782
2011	2226663	774879	498504	14505	1.0	23575	34655	1.56	809534
2012	2448870	852207	517043	15459	1.0	23645	38316	1.56	890523

3.11 Conclusions

Table 3.25 presents the growth rates of the endogenous variables observed from the RefRun as well as all the scenarios, at one place. The table also presents the CAGRs worked out for the 11th FYP period (2006-07 to 2011-12).

One shortcoming in our paper, possibly along with many others known and unknown, is that the exogenous variables are treated as purely exogenous. But in reality there is a difference between exogeneity of rainfall and exogeneity of money supply, interest rates etc. In this paper money supply etc., are assumed to be completely under the policy makers' control, and hence have nothing to do with the error terms of the equations of the model—and therefore, they are also exogenous. This assumption may be questioned on reasonable grounds. In any case, correct identification of 'which variable is exogenous and which is endogenous' is not an easy task. There is no guarantee that the causality tests would provide a clear answer in such situations. For instance, even after conducting such tests one may not be sure whether money supply depends on output or output depends on money supply. Similar may be the situation between interest rates and inflation. Several of such dilemmas can be taken care under general equilibrium approach, where everything (except rainfall of course) depends on everything else. However, for computable general equilibrium analysis, not only data requirements are too many but also computational burden is too heavy and usually it is a time consuming effort. Besides, while the philosophy of general equilibrium is profoundly appreciable, the principles of 'cointegration' and the error correction under the VEC models are equally appealing.

There is a belief that time-series models are not that helpful for policy analysis. At least, not as much as structural equations models. However, VEC methodology provides a sort of reconcilement between pure time-series models and structural models. Thus, the VEC methodology seems to provide reasonable scope not only for forecasting purposes but also for analysing policy impacts. This paper has attempted to provide an illustration in that direction.

Table 3.25: Summary of the CAGRS (2005 to 2012, and 2007 to 2012)

Scenario		2005 to 2012	2007 to 2012	2005 to 2012	2007 to 2012	2005 to 2012	2007 to 2012			2005 to 2012	2007 to 2012	2005 to 2012	2007 to 2012	2005 to 2012	2007 to 2012
		GDP	GDP	GCF	GCF	PDFL	PDFL			PFCE	PFCE	HFS	HFS	HPS	HPS
RefRun	Agr	2.58	3.05	4.95	4.78	2.26	2.03								
RefRun	Ind	10.74	10.94	20.14	18.76	3.48	3.49								
RefRun	Srv	9.84	10.41	14.22	12.83	2.01	1.60								
RefRun	Total	8.82	9.34	16.37	15.24	2.48	2.23	RefRun	Hhld	6.61	7.04	10.33	11.72	10.05	8.33
S2	Agr	3.43	3.01	4.30	6.22	2.49	2.35								
S2	Ind	13.24	13.27	29.03	22.18	4.79	4.64								
S2	Srv	10.19	10.72	15.54	12.86	2.94	2.65								
S2	Total	9.91	10.21	21.83	17.93	3.48	3.31	S2	Hhld	7.48	7.73	11.48	13.31	9.92	7.03
S3	Agr	2.23	2.61	4.33	4.13	1.99	1.69								
S3	Ind	10.65	10.82	19.85	18.37	3.47	3.48								
S3	Srv	9.84	10.40	14.18	12.78	2.00	1.58								
S3	Total	8.74	9.24	16.18	14.99	2.43	2.17	S3	Hhld	6.55	6.95	10.14	11.54	9.23	7.34
S4	Agr	4.34	5.02	5.15	5.24	1.99	1.71								
S4	Ind	13.62	14.39	27.54	27.40	3.98	4.12								
S4	Srv	9.59	10.11	16.02	14.56	2.31	2.00								
S4	Total	9.86	10.57	21.16	20.81	2.81	2.69	S4	Hhld	7.02	7.55	11.13	12.58	11.41	9.56
S5	Agr	2.59	3.06	4.93	4.76	2.26	2.03								
S5	Ind	10.75	10.97	20.24	18.90	3.49	3.51								
S5	Srv	10.14	10.79	14.44	13.19	1.64	1.10								
S5	Total	8.99	9.57	16.52	15.47	2.28	1.96	S5	Hhld	6.76	7.24	11.80	13.44	6.00	3.24

contd...

...contd...

Scenario		2005 to 2012	2007 to 2012	2005 to 2012	2007 to 2012	2005 to 2012	2007 to 2012			2005 to 2012	2007 to 2012	2005 to 2012	2007 to 2012	2005 to 2012	2007 to 2012
		GDP	GDP	GCF	GCF	PDFL	PDFL			PFCE	PFCE	HFS	HFS	HPS	HPS
S6	Agr	2.57	3.04	4.95	4.78	2.26	2.03								
S6	Ind	10.73	10.93	20.10	18.70	3.47	3.49								
S6	Srv	9.78	10.35	15.50	14.25	2.57	2.33								
S6	Total	8.78	9.31	16.92	15.83	2.78	2.63	S6	Hhld	6.56	6.98	9.55	10.84	12.00	10.75
S7	Agr	3.70	4.30	6.13	6.22	2.32	2.11								
S7	Ind	15.29	16.38	31.17	31.45	4.54	4.85								
S7	Srv	9.99	10.63	16.66	15.37	2.75	2.57								
S7	Total	10.54	11.44	23.58	23.67	3.31	3.33	S7	Hhld	7.33	7.99	10.64	11.91	14.53	13.40
S8	Agr	3.73	4.28	4.50	4.52	1.76	1.43								
S8	Ind	13.07	13.72	26.21	25.83	3.88	4.00								
S8	Srv	9.62	10.15	15.67	14.21	2.25	1.92								
S8	Total	9.60	10.26	20.24	19.73	2.71	2.55	S8	Hhld	6.89	7.37	10.81	12.26	10.40	8.42
S9	Agr	1.99	2.52	5.75	5.51	2.80	2.72								
S9	Ind	8.89	8.76	14.34	11.86	3.19	3.13								
S9	Srv	10.01	10.59	13.16	11.86	1.84	1.36								
S9	Total	8.28	8.74	13.12	11.43	2.34	2.04	S9	Hhld	6.44	6.85	10.15	11.53	10.42	9.11
S10	Agr	2.60	3.07	4.92	4.74	2.25	2.03								
S10	Ind	10.76	10.97	20.31	19.00	3.50	3.53								
S10	Srv	10.52	11.38	19.34	18.97	2.89	2.77								
S10	Total	9.20	9.89	18.83	18.19	2.96	2.88	S10	Hhld	6.91	7.46	12.19	14.06	5.73	2.82
S11	Agr	3.30	4.40	4.09	2.43	2.86	2.89								
S11	Ind	10.09	10.23	17.52	15.59	3.86	3.91								
S11	Srv	9.99	10.61	14.44	13.29	2.04	1.59								
S11	Total	8.79	9.44	15.07	13.65	2.68	2.47	S11	Hhld	6.84	7.42	10.81	11.97	9.37	7.95
S12	Agr	3.08	3.67	4.65	4.45	2.32	2.11								
S12	Ind	11.94	12.46	24.32	23.61	3.73	3.81								
S12	Srv	9.93	10.53	14.94	13.61	2.22	1.87								
S12	Total	9.31	9.97	18.90	18.23	2.70	2.52	S12	Hhld	7.00	7.53	10.77	12.31	10.23	8.49
S13	Agr	2.48	2.56	4.55	4.50	2.29	2.14								
S13	Ind	10.00	10.16	15.99	15.95	4.07	4.13								
S13	Srv	9.24	9.74	13.91	13.07	2.48	2.07								
S13	Total	8.27	8.66	14.17	13.81	2.92	2.71	S13	Hhld	5.93	6.24	10.14	11.69	5.76	3.61
S14	Agr	2.42	3.02	4.29	5.92	2.32	1.98								
S14	Ind	9.67	10.13	13.77	15.98	4.28	4.06								
S14	Srv	8.96	9.62	13.63	14.18	2.61	1.92								
S14	Total	8.01	8.66	13.01	14.40	3.06	2.59	S14	Hhld	5.66	6.20	10.17	12.08	3.17	3.01
S15	Agr	2.47	3.08	5.06	7.01	2.30	1.95								
S15	Ind	9.24	9.53	10.31	11.06	4.43	4.27								
S15	Srv	8.65	9.18	13.81	14.44	2.72	2.07								
S15	Total	7.72	8.25	11.71	12.57	3.16	2.73	S15	Hhld	5.28	5.66	10.42	12.43	0.26	-1.03
S16	Agr	1.91	2.30	2.71	3.67	2.51	2.26								
S16	Ind	9.50	9.90	12.91	14.75	4.46	4.32								
S16	Srv	8.88	9.49	12.68	12.86	2.87	2.28								
S16	Total	7.84	8.42	12.07	13.07	3.29	2.91	S16	Hhld	5.50	5.97	10.34	12.32	0.41	-0.83
S17	Agr	2.87	4.48	7.45	8.62	4.05	3.89								
S17	Ind	11.98	10.13	8.77	10.78	5.13	4.98								
S17	Srv	11.69	12.53	17.49	17.26	4.61	4.75								
S17	Total	10.25	10.52	12.63	13.81	4.73	4.73	S17	Hhld	7.35	7.72	9.31	11.06	17.21	17.46
S18	Agr	4.28	5.17	1.35	2.38	3.20	3.09								
S18	Ind	12.73	14.82	24.56	35.82	5.61	5.78								
S18	Srv	8.94	9.53	15.08	16.07	3.36	3.00								
S18	Total	9.21	10.34	18.64	23.75	4.09	3.98	S18	Hhld	6.55	7.34	11.77	14.10	1.06	0.44

contd...

...contd...

Scenario		2005 to 2012	2007 to 2012	2005 to 2012	2007 to 2012	2005 to 2012	2007 to 2012			2005 to 2012	2007 to 2012	2005 to 2012	2007 to 2012	2005 to 2012	2007 to 2012
		GDP	GDP	GCF	GCF	PDFL	PDFL			PFCE	PFCE	HFS	HFS	HPS	HPS
S19	Agr	0.87	0.69	4.11	3.83	2.18	1.96								
S19	Ind	9.05	8.59	15.35	12.19	3.24	3.16								
S19	Srv	9.99	10.62	12.91	11.03	1.95	1.51								
S19	Total	8.16	8.43	13.37	11.13	2.33	2.04	S19	Hhld	6.36	6.68	9.75	10.98	7.95	5.58
S20	Agr	0.86	0.68	4.13	3.85	2.18	1.96								
S20	Ind	9.04	8.58	15.27	12.09	3.23	3.14								
S20	Srv	9.76	10.29	15.37	14.42	2.46	2.22								
S20	Total	8.03	8.25	14.54	12.73	2.63	2.45	S20	Hhld	6.23	6.50	8.32	8.97	10.94	9.71
S21	Agr	0.50	0.18	4.33	4.14	2.17	1.95								
S21	Ind	8.40	7.68	12.18	7.91	3.10	2.96								
S21	Srv	9.74	10.26	14.91	13.79	2.37	2.10								
S21	Total	7.78	7.90	13.00	10.62	2.53	2.31	S21	Hhld	6.04	6.23	8.12	8.69	10.77	9.46
S22	Agr	1.50	1.76	5.01	7.21	2.15	1.78								
S22	Ind	7.62	7.27	2.17	-0.23	3.91	3.54								
S22	Srv	8.78	9.36	15.62	17.01	2.73	2.09								
S22	Total	7.18	7.51	10.12	10.35	2.96	2.47	S22	Hhld	5.19	5.53	7.62	8.56	5.64	6.66
S23	Agr	1.51	1.77	5.00	7.19	2.15	1.78								
S23	Ind	7.63	7.28	2.34	0.00	3.92	3.55								
S23	Srv	9.03	9.70	13.04	13.36	2.23	1.40								
S23	Total	7.32	7.71	8.52	8.11	2.68	2.07	S23	Hhld	5.33	5.73	9.07	10.61	0.83	-0.08
S24	Agr	1.38	1.59	4.77	6.87	2.06	1.67								
S24	Ind	7.60	7.24	2.15	-0.25	3.91	3.54								
S24	Srv	9.02	9.70	13.01	13.32	2.23	1.39								
S24	Total	7.30	7.67	8.43	7.99	2.66	2.05	S24	Hhld	5.32	5.71	9.00	10.50	0.40	-0.67
S25	Agr	1.78	2.15	4.54	6.54	2.04	1.63								
S25	Ind	8.25	8.15	7.65	7.35	4.07	3.77								
S25	Srv	9.52	10.40	15.35	16.62	1.65	0.58								
S25	Total	7.82	8.41	11.59	12.41	2.38	1.66	S25	Hhld	5.73	6.29	9.07	10.61	5.46	6.40
S26	Agr	2.02	2.49	4.39	6.32	2.05	1.64								
S26	Ind	8.72	8.80	10.65	11.55	4.16	3.89								
S26	Srv	9.54	10.43	15.67	17.08	1.71	0.67								
S26	Total	8.00	8.66	12.84	14.18	2.46	1.76	S26	Hhld	5.87	6.48	9.20	10.79	5.64	6.66

Agr: Agriculture, Ind: Industry, Srv: Services, Total: Agr+Ind+Srv, Hhld: Households. RefRun: Reference Run. S2, S3 etc. are scenarios 2, 3 and so on.

References

Banerjee, A., J. Dolado, J.W. Galbraith and D.F. Hendry (1993). *Cointegration, Error-correction and the Econometric Analysis of Non-Stationary Data*. Oxford Univ. Press.

Canova, Fabio and Pina Joaquim Pires (1999). *Monetary Policy Misspecification in VAR Models*. Universitat Pompeu Fabra, Univeristy of Southampton and CEPR.

Govt. of India (2002). *Foreign Investment: India—Report of the Steering Group on Foreign Direct Investment*. New Delhi: Planning Commission.

———. (2003). *The FRBM Act and Associated Rules, in the Gazette of India, Extraordinary*. Ministry of Law and Justice (Legislative Department), New Delhi. No. 39 of 2003, 26 August.

Hendry, David F. and Grayham E. Mizon (2001). "Forecasting in the Presence of Structural Breaks and Policy Regime Shifts". *Economics Papers 2002-W12*. Economics Group, Nuffield College, Univ. of Oxford.

Hungnes, Havard (2004). *Identifying Structural Breaks in Cointegrated VAR Models*. June. (*http://folk.ssb.no/hhu*)

Luetkepohl, Helmut (1991). *Introduction to Multiple Time Series Analysis*. Springer Verlag.

Luetkepohl, Helmut and Markus Kratzig (2004). *Applied Time Series Econometrics*. Cambridge Univ. Press.

Narayana, N.S.S., Kirit S. Parikh and T.N.Srinivasan (1991). *Agriculture, Growth and Redistribution of Income—Policy Analysis with a General Equilibrium Model of India*; North Holland, Elsevier Scince Publishers. Indian edition: Allied Publishers.

Narayana, N.S.S. and Probal P. Ghosh (2005). "Macroeconomic Simulation Results for India based on VEC/VAR Models", *Indian Journal of Agricultural Economics* 60(4): 577-616, October-December.

Pesaran, M.H, Y. Shin and R.J. Smith (2001). "Bounds Testing Approaches to the Analysis of Level Relationships", *Journal of Applied Econometrics* 16: 289-326

Philips, Andrade and Catherine Bruneau (2000). *Cointegration with Structural Breaks: From the Single Equation Analysis to the Multivariate Approach with Application to US Money Demand*. January 2000 (*Andrade@u-paris10.fr, cbruneau@u-paris10.fr*)

Reinsel, C. Gregory (1993). *Elements of Multivariate Time Series Analysis*. Springer Verlag.

Saikkonen, P. and H. Luetkepohl (2000). "Testing for a Cointegrating Rank of a VAR Process with Structural Shifts", *Journal of Business & Economic Statistics* 18: 451-464.

Stock, James H. and Mark W. Watson (2001). "Vector Autoregressions", *Journal of Economic Perspectives* 15(4): 101-115, Fall.

Valadkhani, Abbas (2004). "History of Macroeconometric Modeling: Lessons from Past Experience", *Journal of Policy Modeling* 26: 265-281.

Figure 3.1: IGCF and PCSS

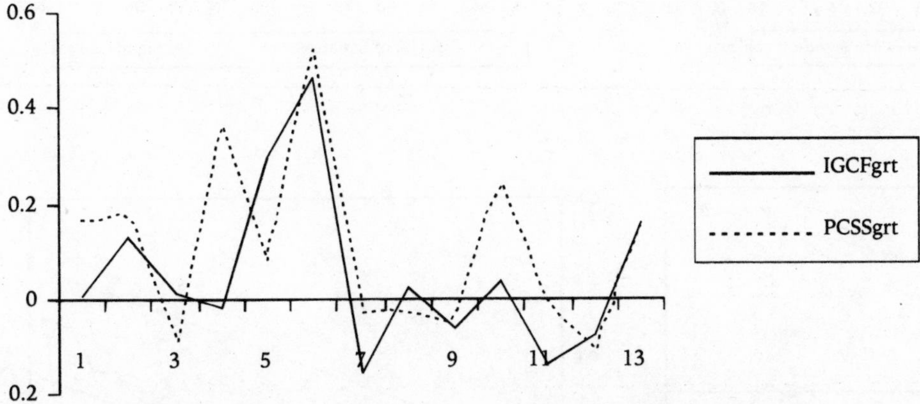

IGCFgrt and PCSSgrt are the annual growth rates from 1990-91 to 2002-03.

Figure 3.2(a): CUSUM and CUSUM-Squares

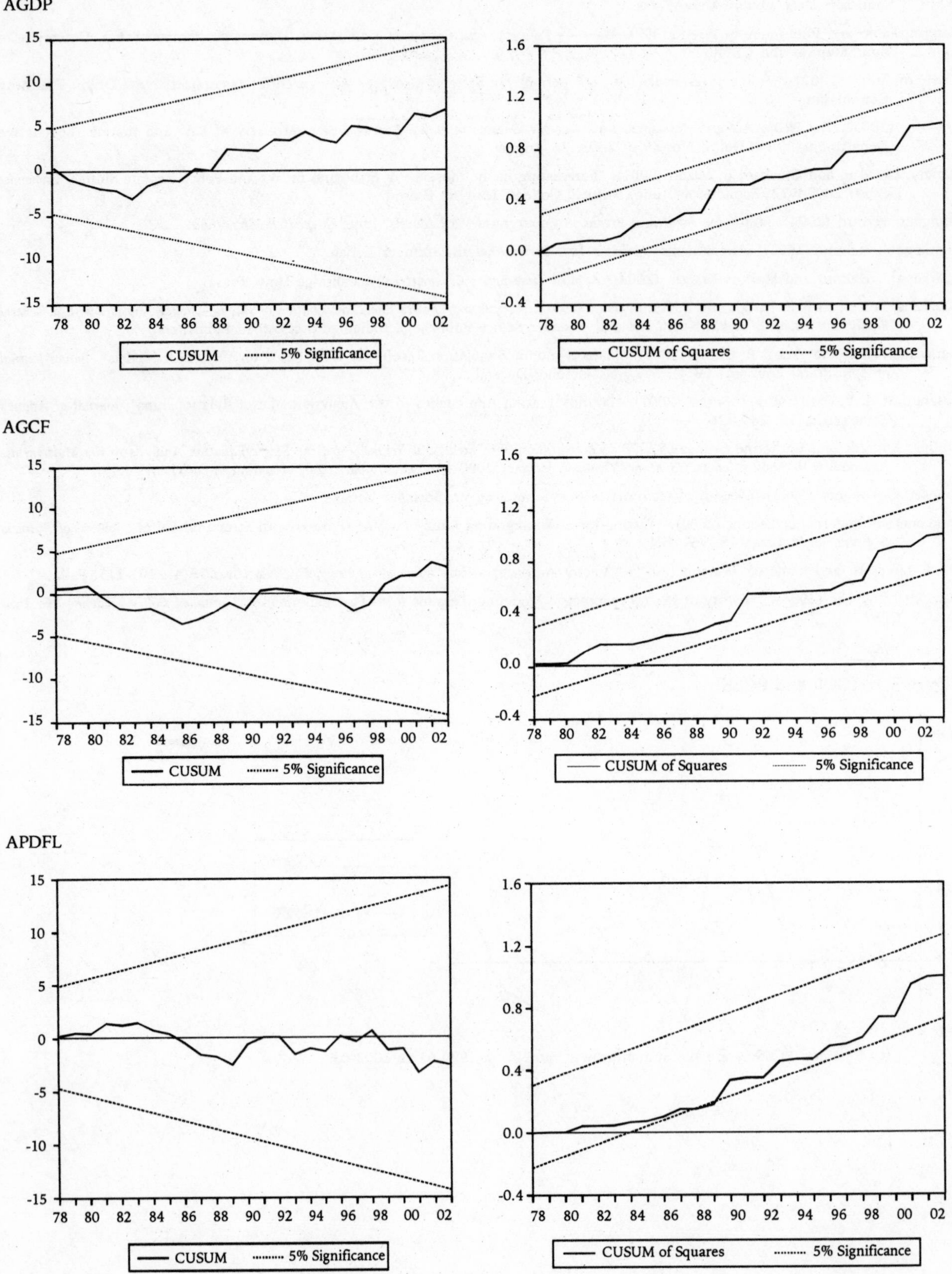

Figure 3.2(b): CUSUM and CUSUM-Squares

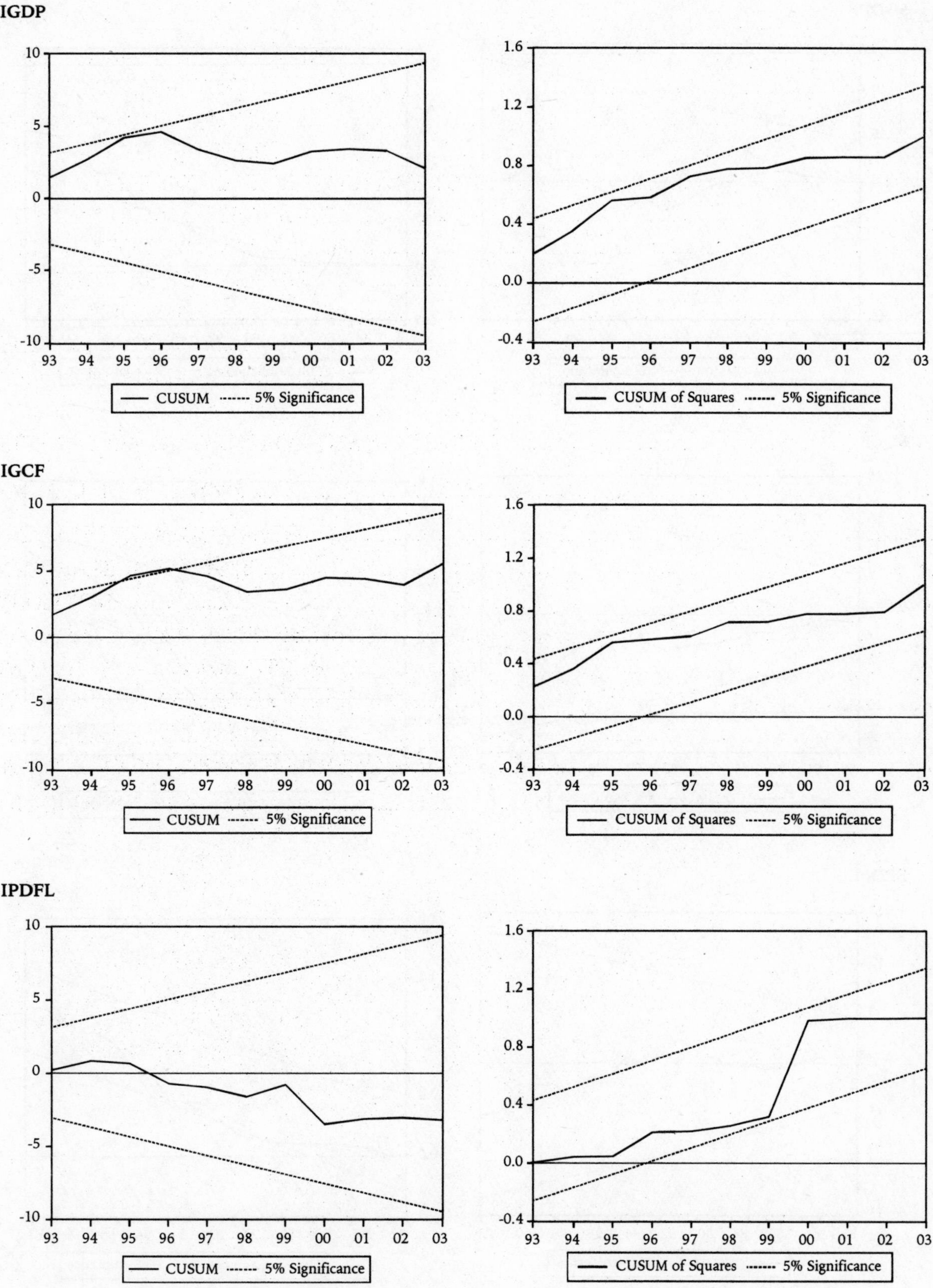

Figure 3.2(c): CUSUM and CUSUM-Squares

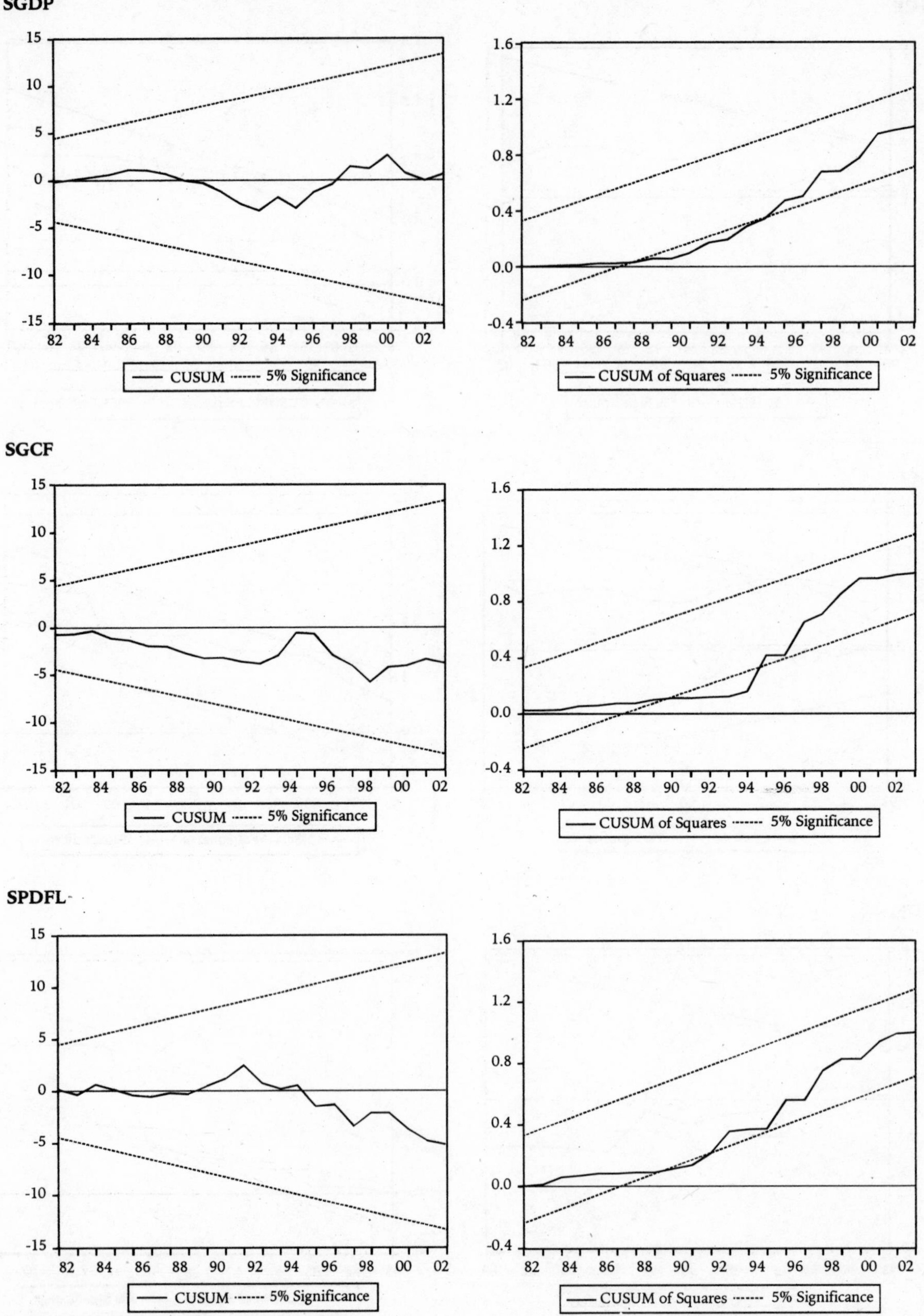

Figure 3.2(d): CUSUM and CUSUM-Squares

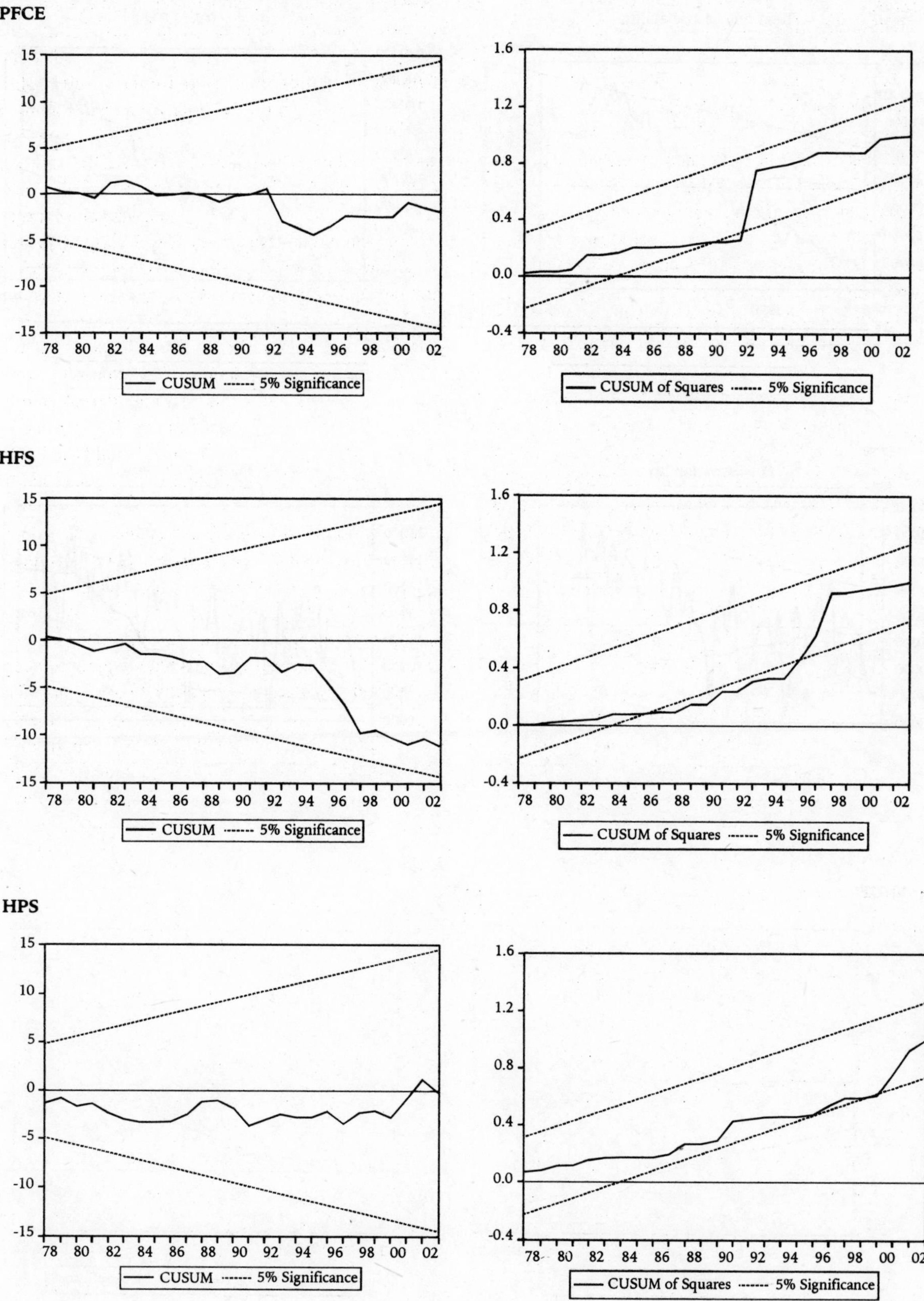

Figure 3.3(a): Plots of Availability and Productions ('000 tonnes)

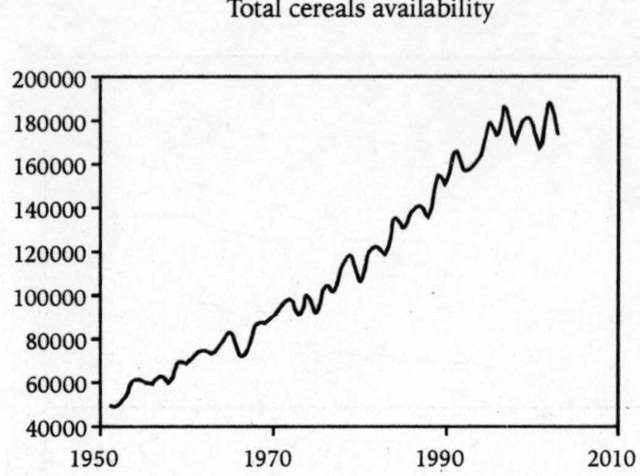

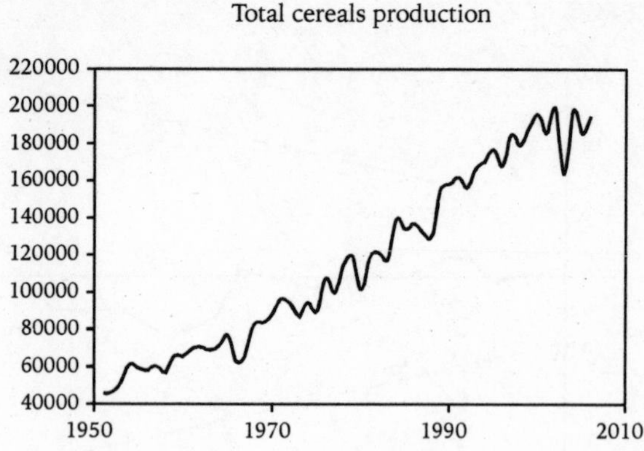

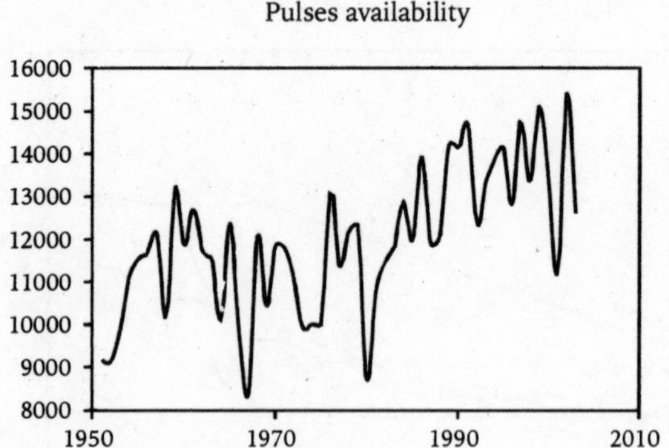

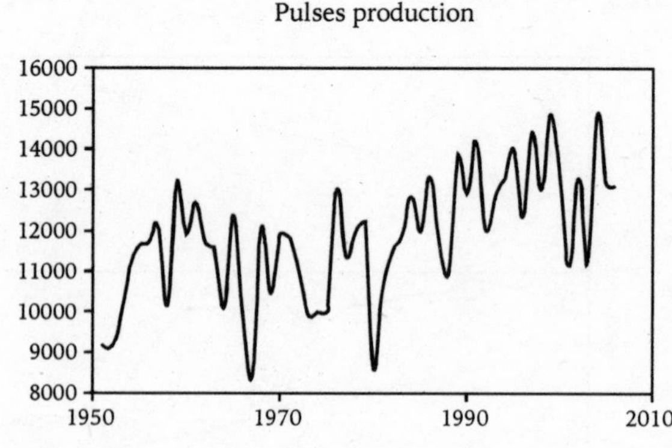

Figure 3.3(b): Plots of Availability and Productions ('000 tonnes)

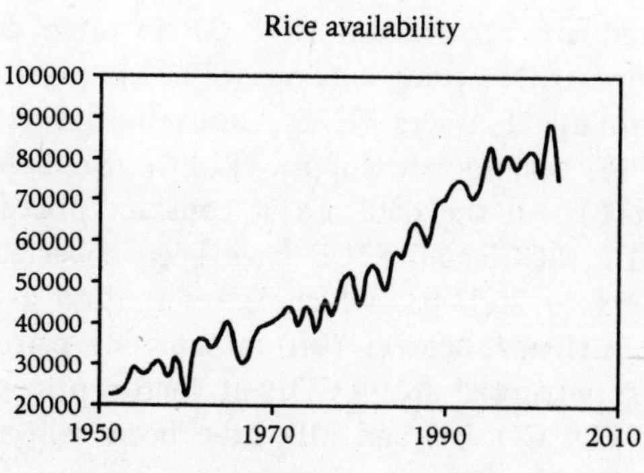

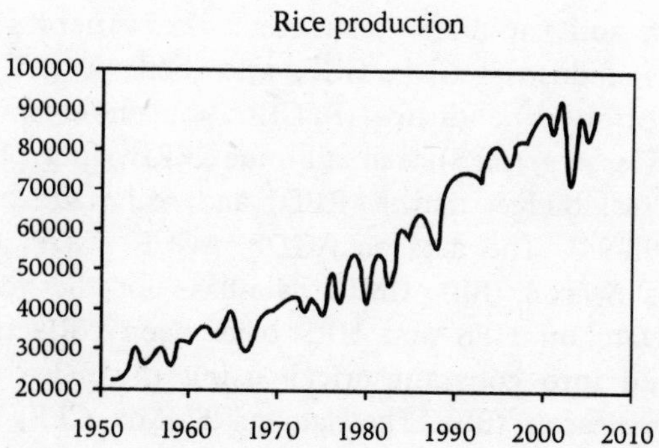

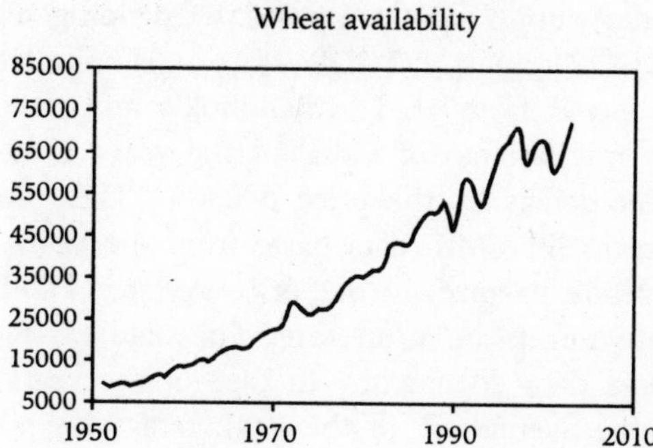

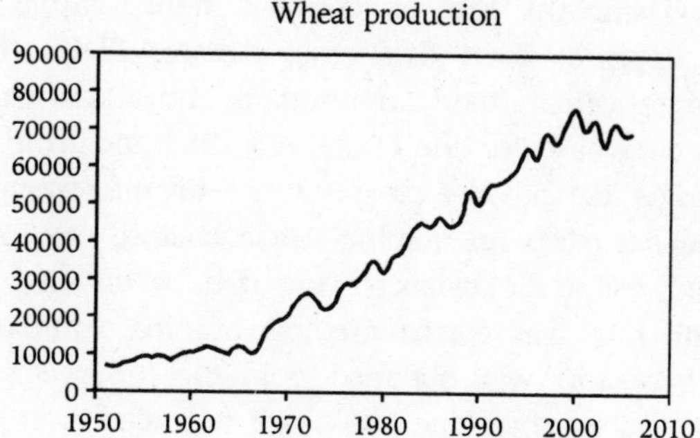

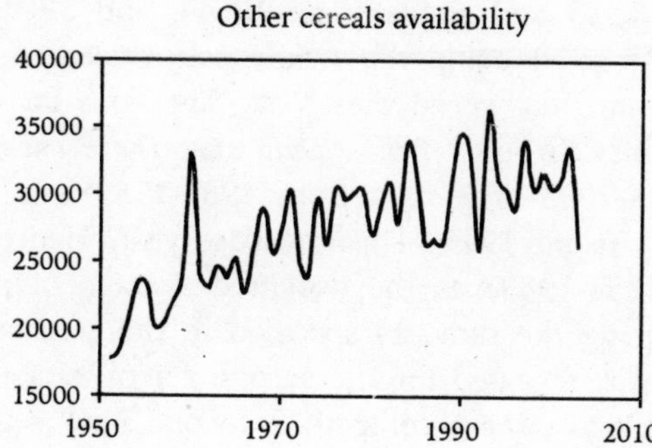

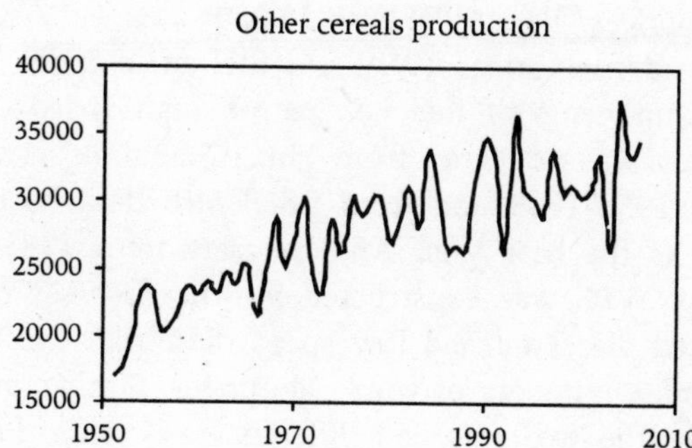

Appendix A-3.1

Data and variables considered: The variables considered are agricultural GDP, GCF, price deflator (APDFL), industrial GDP, GCF, price deflator (IPDFL), services GDP, price deflator (SPDFL), private final consumption expenditure (PFCE), household savings in financial assets (HFS), household savings in financial assets (HPS), rainfall Index (RI), fuel prices (WPF), real money supply (RM3), real bank rate (RBR), real budget deficit (RBD) and real trade balance (RTB). All the data are at constant prices (base year 1993-94). The data on AGDP, AGCF, IGDP, IGCF, SGDP, SGCF and PFCE have been collected from Business Beacon (BB), CMIE data-base for the years 1952-53 to 2002-03, which is referred to as 1953-2003. Data on HFS and HPS have been collected from Business Beacon (BB) at current prices and converted into constant prices using the price deflator constructed from GDP at factor prices from Business Beacon (BB). The data on FMMB, CLR, FLP, OT, ED, CO, MI and MD have been collected for the years 1961-2003 from Business Beacon (BB). The data on the other variables were computed using procedures as described now. Data on nominal money supply was collected from BB for the years 1971-2003 and for the years 1953-1970 from H.L. Chandhok's and the Policy Group's *Indian Ddata Base-The Economy*. Using the data on nominal money supply, real money supply was computed by dividing nominal money supply by total GDP price deflator PDFL ($PDFL=[(TGDP_{current\ prices}/TGDP_{1993\text{-}94\ prices})]$. Similarly for real budget deficit, data on nominal budget deficit were collected from H. L. Chandhok's and the Policy Group's data base for the year 1953-1989 and from the Economic Surveys of India for the years 1989-2003. Real budget deficit was computed by dividing nominal budget deficit by the price deflator PDFL. For real trade balance, data on nominal trade balance was collected from BB, CMIE data base, from the years 1953-2003 and real trade balance computed by dividing nominal trade balance by the price deflator PDFL. The real bank rate was constructed as nominal annual bank rate minus inflation rate. The data on nominal annual bank rate was obtained from the Reserve Bank of India data documents. In case of the years when there was more than one bank rate prevailed over the year, the average of all the bank rates was taken as the annual bank rate for that year. The inflation rate was computed as the percentage change in the price deflator PDFL i.e., inflation rate = $(PDFL_t - PDFL_{t-1})/ PDFL_{t-1}$. The sectoral price deflators APDFL, IPDFL and SPDFL were constructed respectively as the ratio of the corresponding sectoral GDPs at current and constant prices, i.e., APDFL = $(AGDP_{current\ prices}/AGDP_{1993\text{-}94\ prices})$ and similarly for IPDFL and SPDFL. In the case of fuel prices (WPF), a fuel price index was constructed using the whole sale prices of three major components of fuel i.e., petrol, high speed diesel oil and low speed diesel oil. The data on whole sale prices was collected from H.L. Chandhok's and the Policy Group's *Indian Data Base-The Economy* for the year 1953-1989 and from BB, CMIE data base for 1983-2003. The data from 1953-1989 was using 1970-71 as the base year. And the data from 1983-2003 was using 1993-94 as the base year. Hence as a first step, WPF was constructed for the first set of data (1953-1989) as the weighted average of petrol, high speed diesel oil and low speed diesel oil, the weights being the same as specified in the construction of the index numbers of wholesale prices. Similar procedure was repeated for the second set of data (1983-2003). As the two sets had different base years, in order to make them compatible to one base year i.e., 1993-94 the first data set was proportionally spliced with the second data set. Similarly in the case of the rainfall index (RI), data for actual rainfall was collected from BB, CMIE data base, for the year 1971-2003. The Rainfall index was computed using this data by dividing the series by the arithmetic average of the series from 1971 to 2003. Data for another similarly constructed rainfall index was taken from the AGRIM model (Narayana, Parikh and Srinivasan (1991)) for the years 1953-1970. Again the splicing technique was used to make the two series of the indexes compatible with each other.

Data on merchandise trade for 1971-2005 have been obtained from *RBI Handbook of Statistics* and for 1951-1971 from *Data on the Indian Economy* of Trade Development Authority (January 1972).

The classification of various commodities into agricultural, non-agricultural and petroleum is as explained below.

Exports

1951-1971

Agriculture

Fish and Fish preparations, Pulses, Fruits and Vegetable preparations, Sugar (including Molasses), Coffee, Tea, Spices, Oil cakes, Tobacco, Raw and manufactured, Hides & Skins, Raw, Tanned & Dressed, Raw Wool, Raw Cotton, Gums, Resins and Lacs, Oils Non-essential, Vegetable Oils essential.

Non-agriculture:

Kyanite Ore, Salt, Mica, Metalliferous Ores and Metal Scrap, Iron Ore and Concentrates, Manganese Ore, Coal and Coke, Chemicals and Allied products, Chemicals and Allied products, Vegetable Oils essential, Leather and Manufactures of Leather, Woolen Yarn and manufactures, Cotton Yarn and Manufactures, Coir Yarn and Manufactures, Art Silk Fabrics, Jute Yarn and Manufactures, Cement, Metals and Manufactures of Metals, Footwear.

1971-1987

Agriculture:

Fish and fish preparations, Cereals and cereal preparations, Fruits and vegetables consisting of Cashew kernels & Others, Coffee, Tea, Spices consisting of Black Pepper and Others, Feeding stuff for animals, Sugar and Honey, Others, Beverages and Tobacco consisting of unmanufactured Tobacco, and Others, Animal and vegetable oils and fats consisting of Fixed vegetable oils and fats and Others.

Non-agriculture:

Crude materials, inedible, except fuels like Hides, Raw Skins and Fur Skins, Wool and other animal hair, Cotton textile fibre and waste, Jute textile fibre and waste, Mica, Iron ore and concentrates Manganese ore, Lac, Others.

Chemicals including Chemical elements and compounds, Dyeing, tanning and colouring materials Medicinal and pharmaceutical products, Essential oils and perfume materials, Plastic materials, regenerated cellulose and artificial resins, Other chemicals,

Manufactured goods such as Leather and manufactures n.e.s. and dressed fur skins, Cotton manufactures excluding yarn and thread and clothing, Textile yarn and thread, Jute manufactures excluding twist and yarn, woolen carpets and rugs, Pearls, precious and semi-precious stones, Manufacture of metals n.e.s., Iron and steel, Non-ferrous metals, 10 Other machineries,

Machinery and transport equipment like Machinery, other than electric, Electrical machinery, apparatus and appliances and Transport equipment, Miscellaneous manufactured articles like Footwear, Clothing, Others and commodities and transactions not classified elsewhere.

Petroleum:

Mineral fuels, lubricants and related materials consisting of petroleum crude and partly refined, petroleum products and others.

1987-2005

Agriculture:

Agriculture and allied products like Tea, Coffee, Rice, Wheat, raw Cotton including waste, Tobacco, Cashew including cashew nut shell liquid, Spices, Oil meals, Fruits and vegetables, Processed fruits, juices, miscellaneous processed items, Marine products, Sugar and molasses, Meat and meat preparations and others.

Non-agriculture:

Leather and manufactures, Chemicals and Related products like Basic Chemicals, Pharmaceuticals & Cosmetics, Plastic and linoleum products, Rubber, glass, paints, enamels and products, Residual Chemicals and Allied Products, Engineering goods like Iron & Steel, Manufacture of Metals, Machinery and Instruments, Transport equipment, Electronics Goods, Others, Textile and Textile Products like Cotton Yarn, Fabrics, Madeups etc., Natural Silk Yarn, Fabrics made ups etc., incl. silk waste, Man-made Yarn, Fabrics, made ups etc., Man-made Staple Fibre, Woolen Yarn, Fabrics, made ups etc., Readymade Garments, Jute & Jute Manufactures, Coir & Coir Manufactures, Carpets, Carpet Handmade, Carpet mill made, Silk Carpets, Gems and jewellery, Handicrafts (excluding handmade carpets), Other Manufactured Goods and other commodities not classified elsewhere.

Petroleum:

Petroleum products

Imports

1951-1971

Agriculture:

Dairy Products, Eggs and Honey, Fish and Fish preparation, Cereals and Cereals preparations, Fruits and vegetables, Coffee, Tea, Cocoa, and Spices, Alcoholic beverages, Tobacco manufactured, Hides, Skins and Fur skins undressed, Oilseeds, Oil nuts and Oil kernels, Crude rubber including synthetic reclaimed, Wood, Lumber and Cork, Pulp and Waste papers, Raw Wool and Wool Tops, Raw Jute, Cotton Raw other than Linters, Gums & Resins, Vegetable oil Non-essential.

Non-agriculture:

Fertilisers Crude and Manufactured. Sulphur, Raw Asbestos, Metalliferous ores and Metal scraps, Chemical Elements and compounds, Dyeing, Tanning & Colouring materials, Medical and Pharmaceutical Products, Essential oils, Perfume, Toilet materials, Explosives, Synthetic plastic material, Rubber manufactures, Art Silk yarn, Cotton twist & yarn and cotton fabrics, Iron & Steel, Non-Ferrous Metals, Machinery, Electrical Machinery Apparatus & Appliances, Transport Equipment, Professional, Scientific and Controlling instruments, Photographic & Optical goods and Clocks and Watches, Miscellaneous Manufactured Articles nes, Postal Packages.

Petroleum:

Minerals, Fuels, Lubricants and Related materials.

1971-1987

Agriculture:

Live animals and Food including Cereals and cereal preparations, Wheat, Rice and Others, Cashew nuts, raw, Spices and Others, Beverages and tobacco consisting of unmanufactured, Tobacco and Others, Crude rubber including synthetic and reclaimed, Cotton, Jute, Wool and other animal hair excluding wool tops, Man-made fibres and waste thereof, Animal and vegetable oils and fats.

Non-agriculture:

Chemicals like Chemical elements and compounds, Dyeing, tanning and colouring materials, Medicinal and pharmaceutical products, Fertilisers, manufactured, others, Manufactured goods like Pearls, precious and semi-precious stones, Paper, paper board and manufactures like Newsprint paper and Others, Textile yarn, fabrics, made-up articles and related products, Iron and steel, Non-ferrous metals, Manufactures of metal, n.e.s. Others, Machinery and transport equipment like Machinery, other than electric, Electrical machinery, apparatus and appliances, Transport equipment like Railway vehicles and others, Synthetic fibres suitable for spinning, metalliferrous ores and metal scrap, Crude fertilisers and crude minerals and others and miscellaneous manufactured articles.

Petroleum:

Mineral fuels, lubricants and related materials.

1987-2005

Agriculture:

Bulk consumption goods like Cereals and cereal preparations, Edible oils, Pulses, Sugar and Cashew nuts.

Non-agriculture:

Fertilisers of the type of Crude, Sulphur and unroasted iron pyrites and Manufactured Non-ferrous metals, Paper, paper boards, manufactures including news prints, Crude rubber, including synthetic and reclaimed, Pulp and waste paper, Metalliferrous ores, metal scrap, etc., Iron and steel. Capital goods like, Manufactures of metals, Machine tools, Machinery except electrical and electronic, Electrical machinery except electronic, Electronic goods, Computer goods, Transport equipment, Project goods, Mainly export related items, Pearls, precious and semi-precious stones, Organic and inorganic chemicals, Textile yarn, fabrics, made-ups, etc.

Other goods like Gold, Silver and Artificial resins and plastic materials, etc., Professional, scientific controlling instruments, photographic optical goods, Coal, coke and briquettes, etc., Medicinal and pharmaceutical products, Chemical materials and products, Non-metallic mineral manufactures and others.

Petroleum:

Petroleum, crude and products.

Invisibles:

Data for invisibles from 1951-2005 were taken from RBI handbook of statistics, and Business Beacon (CMIE). Invisibles exports denote receipts on account of non-factor services, investment income, private transfers and official transfers. Similarly invisible imports denote payments on account of non-factor services, investment income, private transfers and official transfers.

US Bank Interest Rates and Foreign Investments:

Data on US Federal Bank interest rates have been obtained from the website: *http://www.federalreserve.gov/datadownload/*. These data basically refer to the discount rate charged by the US FED bank which is probably the right counter part towards the RBI bank rate. The data have been converted into real terms by subtracting the GDP inflation rate. Data on foreign direct and portfolio investments are mainly from *Statistical Abstracts India*. US GDP data were collected from the website of the UN Statistical Office; visit *http://unstats.un.org/unsd/snaama/selectionbasicFast.asp*

All the data used in this study are given below in Tables A-3.1(a) to A-3.1(i).

Table A-3.1(a): Data

Year	GDP	AGDP	IGDP	SGDP	AGCF	IGCF	SGCF	APDFL	IPDFL	SPDFL
1952	144571	82278	21850	40443	4262	6531	9325	0.0682	0.0697	0.0751
1953	148487	84873	21932	41682	4100	4915	8091	0.0644	0.0657	0.0752
1954	157545	91409	23217	42919	3903	4607	8605	0.0659	0.0680	0.0775
1955	164187	94096	25100	44991	3992	5995	11270	0.0544	0.0662	0.0771
1956	168244	93283	27657	47304	4934	8349	12395	0.0532	0.0643	0.0776
1957	177969	98354	29992	49623	4849	12568	14413	0.0641	0.0699	0.0810
1958	175343	93936	29904	51503	5081	11992	16877	0.0658	0.0731	0.0841
1959	189026	103401	31920	53705	4820	7823	15952	0.0693	0.0744	0.0868
1960	192922	102360	34125	56437	3965	11784	16241	0.0703	0.0778	0.0895
1961	206882	109254	37834	59794	5258	15323	18509	0.0694	0.0834	0.0930
1962	212920	109346	40503	63071	5115	13918	18428	0.0718	0.0850	0.0935
1963	217197	107171	43306	66720	5625	16425	21089	0.0748	0.0878	0.0983
1964	228037	109678	47574	70785	6129	17487	21384	0.0860	0.0911	0.1021
1965	245546	119795	50808	74943	6559	19232	22756	0.0962	0.0952	0.1090
1966	236355	106567	52741	77047	7230	21708	22888	0.1079	0.1000	0.1158
1967	238996	105051	54499	79446	7216	25505	20201	0.1273	0.1081	0.1256
1968	259412	120673	56178	82561	7830	23166	20517	0.1387	0.1154	0.1355
1969	265829	120482	58999	86348	8450	21134	18762	0.1432	0.1194	0.1387
1970	282701	128226	63622	90853	8919	25264	20108	0.1471	0.1265	0.1424
1971	296909	137320	64258	95331	8587	25301	21412	0.1417	0.1357	0.1491
1972	299447	134742	65982	98723	9147	25779	23834	0.1475	0.1458	0.1578
1973	298073	127980	68418	101675	10077	25715	27382	0.1708	0.1551	0.1682
1974	311427	137197	69154	105076	10314	29272	27109	0.2099	0.1780	0.1869
1975	315199	135107	70295	109797	9567	35097	24694	0.2336	0.2195	0.2223
1976	344749	152522	74960	117267	11223	39099	25504	0.2051	0.2261	0.2355
1977	347887	143709	81505	122673	14165	34705	26526	0.2223	0.2361	0.2467
1978	373982	158132	87105	128745	13068	38517	27359	0.2392	0.2495	0.2595
1979	392917	161773	93714	137430	17979	46912	30686	0.2403	0.2605	0.2657
1980	372373	141107	90830	140436	17358	44451	31400	0.2851	0.3025	0.2928
1981	401128	159293	95082	146753	14233	37419	40534	0.3176	0.3354	0.3250
1982	425072	167723	102647	154702	14079	68959	42821	0.3391	0.3754	0.3661
1983	438079	166577	106418	165084	14529	61311	38621	0.3655	0.4109	0.3932
1984	471742	182498	115002	174242	14725	51652	39204	0.3985	0.4448	0.4290
1985	492077	185186	121641	185250	14948	67442	45673	0.4228	0.4792	0.4649
1986	513990	186570	127472	199948	14132	81463	49182	0.4510	0.5167	0.4978
1987	536257	185363	136224	214670	13708	79853	49972	0.4885	0.5428	0.5300
1988	556778	182899	145253	228626	14294	61823	46157	0.5509	0.5804	0.5727
1989	615098	211184	158649	245265	14762	82524	61005	0.5867	0.6347	0.6275
1990	656332	214315	175053	266964	13424	80849	65239	0.6387	0.6896	0.6758
1991	692871	223114	188601	281156	16416	81289	68372	0.7160	0.7488	0.7468
1992	701863	219660	187560	294643	14965	91728	66170	0.8455	0.8286	0.8416
1993	737791	232386	194994	310411	16141	92688	69419	0.8962	0.9228	0.9182
1994	781345	241967	205162	334216	15249	90735	75149	1.0000	1.0000	1.0000
1995	838031	254090	226051	357890	16785	117734	95360	1.0971	1.0995	1.0890
1996	899563	251892	252359	395312	17689	172568	94300	1.2033	1.1958	1.1849
1997	970083	276091	270218	423774	18326	145520	84785	1.3134	1.2625	1.2738
1998	1016594	269383	281788	465423	18294	148666	89591	1.4366	1.3433	1.3420
1999	1082748	286094	292347	504307	17470	139182	87045	1.5467	1.4488	1.4517
2000	1148368	286983	306336	555049	20024	144272	102988	1.6097	1.4872	1.5211
2001	1198592	286666	326391	585535	19578	124298	110977	1.6342	1.5512	1.5853
2002	1267833	305263	337480	625090	20458	114608	118164	1.7097	1.5909	1.6512
2003	1318321	289386	359216	669719	21867	133226	115732	1.7620	1.6662	1.7038

All the GDPs and GCFs are in Rs.crores at 1993-94 prices. PDFLs are sectoral GDP price deflators. 1952=>1951-52 and so on.

Table A-3.1 (b): Data

Year	Rainfall	RTB	RBD	RBD/RBD(t-1)	RBD/GDP(t-1)	RBR	PCSS	PCSS/NAGDP(t-1)
1952	87.47	-2985	57			NA	1939	
1953	85.39	-1376	533		0.0037	7.40	952	0.0153
1954	107.53	-591	519	0.9749	0.0035	0.92	1304	0.0205
1955	100.57	-993	1602	3.0852	0.0102	13.47	1897	0.0287
1956	130.22	-2666	2472	1.5434	0.0151	4.37	2175	0.0310
1957	149.27	-4054	3452	1.3965	0.0205	-9.29	2227	0.0297
1958	81.91	-5538	6864	1.9883	0.0386	0.28	1680	0.0211
1959	110.02	-4405	2395	0.3490	0.0137	0.21	1869	0.0230
1960	115.50	-4154	2420	1.0104	0.0128	1.18	2403	0.0281
1961	110.25	-6092	-1180	-0.4877	-0.0061	2.03	3571	0.0394
1962	121.01	-5338	1783	-1.5110	0.0086	1.52	3973	0.0407
1963	96.68	-5272	1418	0.7953	0.0067	-0.53	4079	0.0394
1964	94.03	-4670	1575	1.1104	0.0073	-4.32	4295	0.0390
1965	100.42	-5333	1341	0.8514	0.0059	-3.05	3904	0.0330
1966	71.76	-5548	3395	2.5318	0.0138	-2.77	3740	0.0297
1967	81.85	-7527	1512	0.4454	0.0064	-6.57	3475	0.0268
1968	104.25	-6100	2187	1.4462	0.0092	-2.39	3092	0.0231
1969	85.17	-4038	2389	1.0927	0.0092	2.12	3222	0.0232
1970	107.04	-1199	106	0.0445	0.0004	1.67	3902	0.0268
1971	107.54	-694	2935	27.5874	0.0104	4.25	4716	0.0305
1972	102.53	-1442	5215	1.7769	0.0176	0.56	5123	0.0321
1973	79.66	625	5142	0.9858	0.0172	-4.48	4866	0.0295
1974	113.97	-2215	2578	0.5015	0.0086	-10.81	5578	0.0328
1975	86.47	-5254	3316	1.2859	0.0106	-7.11	6484	0.0372
1976	112.36	-5560	1591	0.4799	0.0050	11.89	4920	0.0273
1977	104.71	290	572	0.3596	0.0017	2.54	5053	0.0263
1978	105.84	-2462	4087	7.1423	0.0117	2.84	5693	0.0279
1979	107.26	-4271	2484	0.6078	0.0066	6.82	6534	0.0303
1980	82.59	-9325	9085	3.6573	0.0231	-6.05	8240	0.0356
1981	106.12	-17990	10631	1.1702	0.0285	-2.05	7207	0.0312
1982	98.28	-16220	7042	0.6624	0.0176	-0.23	7156	0.0296
1983	84.20	-14187	6070	0.8620	0.0143	1.82	7701	0.0299
1984	109.43	-14392	5071	0.8353	0.0116	1.19	7728	0.0285
1985	87.03	-11910	11280	2.2245	0.0239	2.51	8927	0.0309
1986	103.38	-18049	7083	0.6280	0.0144	2.72	11176	0.0364
1987	91.29	-14731	17634	2.4895	0.0343	3.12	10284	0.0314
1988	87.51	-11576	9698	0.5500	0.0181	0.62	10452	0.0298
1989	109.81	-13008	8291	0.8550	0.0149	1.58	13791	0.0369
1990	95.26	-11493	15903	1.9180	0.0259	1.54	17749	0.0439
1991	99.51	-12933	15575	0.9794	0.0237	-0.50	20563	0.0465
1992	94.78	-4526	8437	0.5417	0.0122	-1.81	24191	0.0515
1993	96.01	-10615	13743	1.6289	0.0196	3.28	21883	0.0454
1994	105.08	-3429	12477	0.9079	0.0169	2.41	29866	0.0591
1995	117.27	-6668	-2097	-0.1681	-0.0027	2.57	32221	0.0597
1996	102.44	-13684	21214	-10.1151	0.0253	2.97	49067	0.0840
1997	106.50	-15682	10221	0.4818	0.0114	4.56	47658	0.0736
1998	112.93	-17606	45835	4.4845	0.0472	3.83	46426	0.0669
1999	115.48	-26138	-809	-0.0177	-0.0008	0.06	44056	0.0590
2000	103.01	-36783	-10718	13.2488	-0.0099	4.06	54966	0.0690
2001	89.49	-16974	1990	-0.1857	0.0017	3.51	54256	0.0630
2002	97.90	-21939	4964	2.4949	0.0041	2.62	48007	0.0526
2003	81.84	-24654	3317	0.6682	0.0026	2.79	55116	0.0573
MAX				13.2490	0.0472	4.56		0.0840
MIN				-10.1150	-0.0099	-1.81		0.0440
MEDIAN				0.7880	0.0117	2.71		0.0590

1952=>1951-52 and so on. MAX, MIN, MEDIAN denote the maximum, minimum and the median values between 1990 to 2003. RTB, RBD and PCSS are in Rs. Crores at 1993-94 prices. RBR is percentage.

Table A-3.1(c): Data

Year	WPF	WPF/WPF(t-1)	RM3	RM3/RM3(t-1)
1952	NA		30378	
1953	5.7198		31375	1.0328
1954	5.6201	0.9826	31725	1.0112
1955	5.5984	0.9961	38104	1.2010
1956	5.0328	0.8990	43430	1.1398
1957	5.6762	1.1278	41097	0.9463
1958	6.1294	1.0798	43698	1.0633
1959	6.2288	1.0162	46255	1.0585
1960	6.3842	1.0250	49735	1.0752
1961	6.4557	1.0112	50309	1.0115
1962	6.9001	1.0688	52549	1.0445
1963	7.0399	1.0203	53815	1.0241
1964	8.7358	1.2409	54709	1.0166
1965	8.7668	1.0036	55025	1.0058
1966	7.9366	0.9053	56432	1.0256
1967	8.4429	1.0638	55714	0.9873
1968	8.6721	1.0271	56250	1.0096
1969	8.8646	1.0222	60878	1.0823
1970	9.1281	1.0297	68368	1.1230
1971	9.3136	1.0203	77196	1.1291
1972	10.0684	1.0810	84331	1.0924
1973	10.2786	1.0209	90281	1.0706
1974	12.4931	1.2155	90344	1.0007
1975	18.0239	1.4427	86309	0.9553
1976	19.3050	1.0711	102199	1.1841
1977	20.1189	1.0422	118636	1.1608
1978	20.1747	1.0028	132371	1.1158
1979	20.7669	1.0294	157910	1.1929
1980	24.5676	1.1830	161602	1.0234
1981	34.0628	1.3865	171865	1.0635
1982	43.3332	1.2722	175423	1.0207
1983	44.6251	1.0298	189120	1.0781
1984	46.4850	1.0417	205495	1.0866
1985	46.5821	1.0021	227435	1.1068
1986	51.2182	1.0995	245915	1.0813
1987	52.8720	1.0323	272951	1.1099
1988	53.8410	1.0183	289452	1.0605
1989	54.6538	1.0151	314452	1.0864
1990	54.8775	1.0041	346058	1.1005
1991	70.2241	1.2797	360471	1.0416
1992	81.6713	1.1630	377746	1.0479
1993	91.9795	1.1262	398930	1.0561
1994	100.0000	1.0872	431084	1.0806
1995	108.1697	1.0817	482131	1.1184
1996	108.1645	1.0000	502212	1.0417
1997	124.5241	1.1512	542955	1.0811
1998	144.6225	1.1614	600628	1.1062
1999	148.1840	1.0246	664611	1.1065
2000	167.6212	1.1312	732738	1.1025
2001	207.1375	1.2357	827124	1.1288
2002	224.5036	1.0838	908514	1.0984
2003	240.1156	1.0695	1007543	1.1090
MAX		1.2797		1.1288
MIN		1.0000		1.0416
MEDIAN		1.1067		1.0995

MAX,MIN, MEDIAN denote the maximum, minimum and the median value between 1990 to 2003. RM3 is in Rs. Crores at 1993-94 prices.

WPF is fuel price index. 1952=>1951-52 and so on.

Table A-3.1(d): Data

Year	PFCE	PFCEgrt	HFS	HFSgrt	HPS	HPSgrt
1952	136787		199.65		8114.18	
1953	142307	4.04	1070.65	436.27	8401.63	3.54
1954	150862	6.01	2057.35	92.16	7432.53	-11.53
1955	155811	3.28	4533.94	120.38	7026.00	-5.47
1956	157301	0.96	6961.78	53.55	10012.63	42.51
1957	164259	4.42	4784.44	-31.28	12140.69	21.25
1958	161014	-1.98	4040.03	-15.56	9801.59	-19.27
1959	175796	9.18	4833.70	19.65	8732.70	-10.91
1960	177795	1.14	5625.14	16.37	11276.27	29.13
1961	187909	5.69	5794.26	3.01	10139.96	-10.08
1962	191112	1.70	6071.05	4.78	9832.86	-3.03
1963	193602	1.30	5916.29	-2.55	12259.41	24.68
1964	200804	3.72	8098.54	36.89	9537.32	-22.20
1965	212800	5.97	7166.59	-11.51	11653.24	22.19
1966	212988	0.09	9900.73	38.15	14130.70	21.26
1967	215756	1.30	7081.87	-28.47	19335.81	36.84
1968	227962	5.66	6524.13	-7.88	17686.82	-8.53
1969	233950	2.63	5834.37	-10.57	18743.37	5.97
1970	242640	3.71	6532.49	11.97	25028.19	33.53
1971	250880	3.40	9620.51	47.27	22896.95	-8.52
1972	255761	1.95	10359.13	7.68	24408.91	6.60
1973	257475	0.67	12846.63	24.01	21105.19	-13.53
1974	263793	2.45	18602.40	44.80	22521.67	6.71
1975	263594	-0.08	10507.84	-43.51	25255.99	12.14
1976	278563	5.68	17798.34	69.38	26461.28	4.77
1977	284118	1.99	20761.33	16.65	29554.52	11.69
1978	307285	8.15	23582.84	13.59	34252.13	15.89
1979	326066	6.11	26334.26	11.67	40964.84	19.60
1980	318753	-2.24	20895.31	-20.65	36454.26	-11.01
1981	347443	9.00	26531.10	26.97	34690.72	-4.84
1982	362552	4.35	26875.97	1.30	32458.59	-6.43
1983	366178	1.00	32919.56	22.49	27074.20	-16.59
1984	394599	7.76	31572.97	-4.09	35318.31	30.45
1985	405973	2.88	39504.48	25.12	37977.68	7.53
1986	422916	4.17	38182.57	-3.35	43782.88	15.29
1987	436262	3.16	44972.99	17.78	41889.48	-4.32
1988	451215	3.43	47256.70	5.08	56977.62	36.02
1989	479378	6.24	44175.97	-6.52	70651.01	24.00
1990	503167	4.96	56936.36	28.89	73357.37	3.83
1991	525641	4.47	67313.53	18.23	81710.54	11.39
1992	536980	2.16	73989.87	9.92	57945.88	-29.08
1993	550828	2.58	71636.58	-3.18	72008.09	24.27
1994	574772	4.35	94738.00	32.25	63572.00	-11.72
1995	601481	4.65	110328.90	16.46	71849.53	13.02
1996	638938	6.23	88608.47	-19.69	92549.45	28.81
1997	689566	7.92	110508.92	24.72	71449.61	-22.80
1998	707285	2.57	107335.78	-2.87	88968.10	24.52
1999	752440	6.38	122186.33	13.84	99225.49	11.53
2000	797653	6.01	134102.87	9.75	129485.51	30.50
2001	819637	2.76	140279.50	4.61	148324.50	14.55
2002	867139	5.80	154831.04	10.37	161182.48	8.67
2003	891419	2.80	148762.47	-3.92	187235.41	16.16

PFCE, HFS, HPS and the GDPs are in Rs.crores at 1993-94 prices. PDFLs are sectoral GDP price deflators. 1952=>1951-52 and so on.

Table A-3.1 (e): Data

Year	AGEXP	NONAGEXP	AGIMP	NONAGIMP	NETPETIMP	RINVEXP	RINVIMP
1951	3971	9886	5079	8662	1265	2051	1421
1952	4973	11437	11142	8965	1612	2545	1535
1953	5169	8277	6774	7768	1804	2855	1509
1954	4346	7703	4496	7437	1926	2754	1312
1955	6662	8283	5110	9358	2089	3283	1682
1956	6659	8516	4323	11525	1414	4136	1874
1957	6053	7584	3338	14071	1555	3810	1590
1958	4978	7227	4133	15924	2455	3439	1602
1959	5387	6786	5973	11521	1500	3367	1690
1960	5623	7415	5629	12185	1770	3287	1825
1961	5275	7922	7129	14263	1390	3300	2246
1962	5465	7793	5181	14545	1870	2898	2514
1963	5808	7476	5439	14063	1638	3357	2624
1964	5814	7756	5464	13667	1787	3541	2520
1965	5408	7457	5584	14595	1082	4073	2552
1966	4507	7223	6241	12969	990	3174	2502
1967	3485	5465	6791	7959	517	3759	3261
1968	3506	5532	5430	9142	565	3288	3325
1969	3435	6533	3982	9046	617	3533	3423
1970	2974	7018	3309	6934	978	3114	3561
1971	3169	7498	3009	7486	865	3475	3734
1972	3248	7359	2491	8338	1216	3628	3787
1973	3732	7930	1760	8242	1035	3091	3957
1974	4008	8849	3597	8679	2795	11693	3260
1975	5015	9591	4224	10618	5018	4349	2887
1976	6312	11872	6871	11490	5408	8251	3682
1977	6218	15603	5394	10238	5895	9412	4270
1978	6829	14814	5202	12773	6131	11131	4208
1979	6230	16234	3796	16375	6563	12538	4767
1980	6404	15487	3007	16876	11329	15008	5133
1981	5749	14844	3809	18550	16224	17469	5152
1982	6082	15111	4576	18843	13992	15834	5613
1983	5613	13931	3378	18676	11675	15665	6776
1984	5453	13976	4887	21162	7774	16371	7799
1985	5924	15997	4377	21409	8045	18213	9709
1986	5620	15471	3903	25849	9388	16220	8743
1987	5783	17410	3110	29780	5034	15946	9156
1988	5850	20624	2719	29351	5981	16350	11057
1989	5689	26369	3169	35636	6261	17756	14547
1990	7117	33283	1512	42026	8355	18706	17170
1991	8162	34716	1536	42368	13395	18163	18753
1992	9406	41849	1125	40247	14422	27938	22865
1993	9953	47483	2021	48646	17274	29631	24728
1994	12633	55871	1507	53547	16798	35501	26414
1995	12126	62228	3915	63339	15812	44629	28330
1996	17051	70817	3356	80799	19827	49822	34387
1997	19005	72349	3898	79424	26459	59359	31058
1998	18009	76173	4593	94580	21229	63070	36069
1999	17200	77229	7851	109190	17983	73482	47270
2000	15840	88053	7607	97064	35510	85679	48508
2001	17187	105651	4758	95624	39652	93077	64647
2002	17144	104024	6199	102493	34517	106668	63186
2003	18986	122894	7545	116311	42621	118546	70394
2004	19652	137590	8795	141418	44352	139327	67017
2005	20417	164406	8685	188299	58803	173908	98393

Rs Crores. The price deflator used is (AGDP+IGDP+SGDP) current prices / (AGDP+IGDP+SGDP) constant prices

Table A-3.1(f): Data

Year	FMMB	CLR	FLP	OT	ED	CO	MI	MD	TOT
1961	120966	25455	7943	12194	1707	292	9175	4145	181877
1962	121196	25917	8343	12587	1873	302	9166	4578	183962
1963	122909	26421	8596	12921	2134	336	9372	4985	187674
1964	126028	27825	9105	13513	2336	396	9439	5755	194397
1965	135510	29129	9176	14308	2505	450	9568	6585	207231
1966	135733	29234	9667	14585	2743	514	9822	7254	209552
1967	136435	30542	9545	15342	2951	593	9305	8179	212892
1968	147173	31120	9865	16252	3160	677	9822	8038	226107
1969	150309	32106	10277	17464	3524	781	9400	8345	232206
1970	155268	32199	10207	18712	3808	890	9697	8612	239393
1971	160042	33203	10347	20215	3912	1014	11100	8572	248405
1972	159782	34949	10674	21617	4101	1078	11972	8959	253132
1973	161681	35760	10643	21830	4296	1123	12163	9829	257325
1974	163204	37254	10784	22506	4329	1202	11776	10166	261221
1975	160043	38761	11070	22801	4759	1246	11953	10347	260980
1976	171747	40109	11171	24197	4876	1330	11622	10332	275384
1977	173135	43330	11211	25673	4932	1424	13260	10901	283866
1978	188345	44768	11888	26985	4951	1488	14591	11716	304732
1979	198787	46892	12334	29056	5049	1573	15042	12551	321284
1980	190383	47180	12218	29249	5498	1686	15190	15121	316525
1981	211651	51811	14073	30999	5619	1800	16550	14940	347443
1982	220469	53513	14452	33860	5551	1934	17501	15272	362552
1983	217081	56150	14698	36595	5655	2038	18357	15604	366178
1984	235853	59076	15279	41255	5619	2166	19415	15936	394599
1985	241104	60939	15805	44084	5711	2354	19708	16268	405973
1986	247533	64120	16291	47963	5294	2418	22682	16615	422916
1987	249092	66188	17075	54065	6440	2572	23878	16952	436262
1988	255017	68483	17715	57779	7075	2735	25101	17310	451215
1989	271069	72665	18438	62356	7525	2878	26750	17697	479378
1990	282019	74173	18940	68243	8486	3056	30151	18099	503167
1991	293000	77517	19477	73122	9581	3249	31223	18472	525641
1992	299285	77002	20121	76644	9581	3229	32239	18879	536980
1993	301327	79644	20719	80663	9646	3843	35775	19211	550828
1994	315243	81853	21385	85879	10092	4258	36519	19543	574772
1995	325436	82372	22494	94250	10244	4964	39951	21770	601481
1996	340124	85755	23333	103530	11101	5866	44997	24232	638938
1997	369285	89232	24379	112464	12020	6887	48421	26878	689566
1998	363253	93964	27396	118971	13526	7861	52501	29813	707285
1999	393468	91245	28495	125798	14605	9374	56376	33079	752440
2000	400587	98269	30284	134436	16303	11322	69370	37082	797653
2001	387447	100180	31529	150407	17518	16208	75135	41213	819637
2002	413672	101278	31892	158755	17192	19194	78948	45805	866736
2003	404034	107267	33765	169013	16914	26730	82765	50931	891419

All the commodity consumption expenditures are in Rs.crores at 1993-94 prices. Data are available from 1961-2003, 1961=>1960-61 and so on.

Table A-3.1(g): Data

Year	CRL	PUL	MIL	OF	CLR	FLP	CO	OT	TOT
1961	36676	8609	12369	63312	25455	7943	292	27221	181877
1962	38011	7917	13046	62222	25917	8343	302	28204	183962
1963	36096	7804	12913	66096	26421	8596	336	29412	187674
1964	38877	6818	13747	66586	27825	9105	396	31043	194397
1965	40986	8393	13237	72894	29129	9176	450	32966	207231
1966	38687	6723	12840	77483	29234	9667	514	34404	209552
1967	39299	5643	13407	78086	30542	9545	593	35777	212892
1968	44218	8181	13300	81474	31120	9865	677	37272	226107
1969	45871	7044	12896	84498	32106	10277	781	38733	232206
1970	47884	8037	12956	86391	32199	10207	890	40829	239393
1971	48384	7991	13881	89786	33203	10347	1014	43799	248405
1972	47641	7288	14598	90255	34949	10674	1078	46649	253132
1973	45394	7945	15429	92913	35760	10643	1123	48118	257325
1974	48300	6857	15309	92738	37254	10784	1202	48777	261221
1975	46934	7228	16430	89451	38761	11070	1246	49860	260980
1976	53606	8912	17431	91798	40109	11171	1330	51027	275384
1977	49308	9541	18922	95364	43330	11211	1424	54766	283866
1978	57653	10102	20651	99939	44768	11888	1488	58243	304732
1979	57694	9672	20731	110690	46892	12334	1573	61698	321284
1980	47373	8626	21812	112572	47180	12218	1686	65058	316525
1981	58280	9661	25312	118398	51811	14073	1800	68108	347443
1982	58410	10418	27174	124467	53513	14452	1934	72184	362552
1983	55572	10588	27955	122966	56150	14698	2038	76211	366178
1984	65445	11675	28859	129874	59076	15279	2166	82225	394599
1985	61420	10789	31258	137637	60939	15805	2354	85771	405973
1986	68004	12088	34979	132462	64120	16291	2418	92554	422916
1987	66774	10560	35656	136102	66188	17075	2572	101335	436262
1988	68380	9735	36237	140665	68483	17715	2735	107265	451215
1989	75424	12724	35323	147598	72665	18438	2878	114328	479378
1990	72672	11611	37972	159764	74173	18940	3056	124979	503167
1991	79454	12846	40698	160002	77517	19477	3249	132398	525641
1992	80874	10574	43771	164066	77002	20121	3229	137343	536980
1993	74262	11508	44222	171335	79644	20719	3843	145295	550828
1994	80267	11994	46594	176388	81853	21385	4258	152033	574772
1995	82525	12707	48790	181414	82372	22494	4964	166215	601481
1996	84123	11364	54491	190146	85755	23333	5866	183860	638938
1997	91119	13045	58634	206487	89232	24379	6887	199783	689566
1998	82564	11887	62189	206613	93964	27396	7861	214811	707285
1999	87535	13398	64371	228164	91245	28495	9374	229858	752440
2000	88637	11620	71406	228924	98269	30284	11322	257191	797653
2001	76194	9418	64528	237307	100180	31529	16208	284273	819637
2002	90739	11712	67166	244055	101278	31892	19194	300700	866736
2003	74246	9698	68067	252023	107267	33765	26730	319623	891419

All the commodity consumption expenditures are in Rs.crores at 1993-94 prices. Data are available from 1961-2003, 1961=>1960-1961 and so on.

Table A-3.1 (h): Data—Gross Availability and Gross Productions

Year	Gross availability ('000 tonne)					Gross Production ('000 tonne)				
	Rice	Wheat	Cereals	Other Cereals	Pulses	Rice	Wheat	Cereals	Other Cereals	Pulses
1951	22749	9529	50026	17748	9197	22058	6822	45814	16934	9197
1952	23118	8546	49788	18124	9123	22602	6343	46480	17535	9123
1953	24592	9491	54468	20385	9834	24301	7612	51950	20037	9834
1954	29367	9078	61836	23391	11120	29773	8102	61204	23329	11122
1955	27577	9404	60433	23452	11565	26544	9148	59091	23399	11648
1956	29479	10023	59621	20119	11688	28652	8869	57630	20109	11705
1957	30817	11740	63077	20520	12145	30215	9504	60306	20587	12151
1958	26932	11017	60009	22060	10099	26544	8001	56524	21979	10105
1959	31931	13321	68952	23700	13210	32016	9949	65586	23621	13217
1960	22161	13646	68977	33170	11859	31813	10327	65253	23113	11867
1961	35105	14105	73250	24040	12727	34600	10995	69592	23997	12734
1962	36244	15354	74681	23083	11700	35551	12063	70687	23073	11710
1963	34057	14664	73362	24641	11526	33376	10772	68789	24641	11541
1964	37608	16767	78121	23746	10073	37013	9849	70615	23753	10084
1965	40015	17966	83338	25357	12405	39324	12252	76954	25378	12413
1966	31472	18435	72602	22695	9919	30589	10394	62403	21420	9944
1967	30650	18036	74809	26123	8341	30438	11393	65884	24053	8347
1968	37514	20069	86602	29019	12086	37612	16540	82950	28798	12102
1969	39668	21592	86979	25719	10396	39761	18651	83595	25183	10418
1970	40479	22562	90273	27232	11859	40430	20093	87810	27287	11891
1971	41953	23729	96063	30381	11801	42225	23832	96604	30547	11818
1972	44119	29188	98277	24970	11087	43068	26410	94074	24596	11094
1973	39183	27874	91018	23961	9904	39245	24735	87119	23139	9907
1974	44325	26072	100216	29819	10009	44051	21778	94657	28828	10008
1975	38027	27616	91789	26146	10014	39579	24104	89812	26129	10014
1976	45936	27723	104164	30505	13045	48740	28846	107995	30409	13039
1977	42038	30310	101906	29558	11381	41917	29010	99806	28879	11361
1978	50226	33558	113836	30052	12190	52671	31749	114434	30014	11973
1979	52382	35554	118377	30441	12310	53773	35508	119719	30438	12183
1980	44273	35181	106426	26972	8705	42330	31830	101129	26969	8572
1981	53816	37122	119966	29028	10767	53631	36313	118962	29018	10627
1982	53618	37424	122039	30997	11507	53248	37452	121788	31088	11507
1983	48151	43056	119069	27862	11857	47116	42794	117662	27752	11857
1984	57589	43288	134788	33911	12893	60097	45476	139481	33908	12893
1985	56205	43310	130568	31053	11963	58336	44069	133576	31171	11963
1986	64263	47969	138599	26367	13964	63825	47052	137079	26202	13361
1987	63522	50520	140829	26787	11904	60557	44323	131711	26831	11707
1988	59290	50662	136312	26360	12054	56862	46169	129391	26360	10962
1989	69532	53178	154252	31542	14224	70489	54110	156073	31474	13849
1990	70215	46398	151272	34659	14131	73573	49849	158179	34757	12858
1991	74535	58547	165943	32861	14698	74291	55134	162125	32700	14260
1992	74435	56922	157176	25819	12356	74678	55689	156359	25992	12020
1993	70456	52155	158916	36305	13296	72868	57210	166669	36591	12820
1994	74269	58435	163949	31245	13880	80298	59840	170956	30818	13310
1995	83150	65344	178884	30390	14117	81157	65469	176976	30350	14038
1996	76100	68012	173077	28965	12792	76975	62097	168105	29033	12310
1997	81176	71134	186396	34086	14774	81737	69350	185192	34105	14460
1998	77794	62115	170293	30384	13316	82535	66345	179279	30399	12970
1999	80506	67635	179682	31541	15152	86077	71288	188700	31335	14907
2000	82060	67709	180247	30478	13379	89680	76370	196390	30340	13410
2001	75987	60584	167648	31078	11176	84980	69681	185739	31078	11070
2002	89411	65592	188372	33370	15441	93340	72770	199480	33370	13370
2003	74608	72811	173489	26070	12594	71820	65760	163650	26070	11130
2004						88530	72150	198280	37600	14910
2005						83130	68640	185230	33460	13130
2006						91040	69480	195190	34670	13110

Table A-3.1(i): Net Capital Inflow, Foreign Investments and Interest Rates

Data Year	At Current Prices					
	Gross Domestic Product (TGDP)	Gross Domestic Saving (GDS)	Net Capital Inflow (NCI)	Gross Capital Formation (GCFAEC)	Foreign Direct Investment in India & Abroad (FDI)	Foreign Portfolio Investment in India & Abroad (PI)
1999	1598127	374659	18362	393021	9956	-219
2000	1761838	468681	21988	490669	9079	13105
2001	1902999	490049	8130	498179	14924	11820
2002	2081474	532274	-18731	513543	22630	9290
2003	2254888	642298	-32010	610288	15594	4504
2004	2519785	776420	-49552	726868	10944	51898

Data Year	At 1993-94 Prices									
	Gross Domestic Product (TGDP)	GCF with all Adjustments (GCFAEC)	Adjustment for Type of Assets	GCF without Adjustments for Types of Assets (TCFIU = TGCF)	GCFAEC /TCFIU	GCF_PDFL	Real Net Capital Inflow (RNCI)	RNCI/ TGDP (%)	Real Foreign Direct Investment in India & Abroad (RFDI)	Real Foreign Portfolio Investment in India & Abroad (RPI)
1999	1082747	290971	47274	243697	1.19	1.3507	13594	1.26	7371	-162
2000	1148367	351624	84340	267284	1.32	1.3954	15757	1.37	6506	9391
2001	1198592	346682	84536	262146	1.32	1.437	5658	0.47	10386	8226
2002	1267945	336486	84822	251664	1.34	1.5262	-12273	-0.97	14828	6087
2003	1318362	395163	155209	239954	1.65	1.5444	-20727	-1.57	10097	2916
2004	1430548	449539	161595	287944	1.56	1.6169	-30646	-2.14	6768	32097

Year	RFDR	RBR	INTDIFF
1991	1.9540	-0.4996	2.4537
1992	0.9473	-1.8143	2.7616
1993	0.7025	3.2830	-2.5805
1994	1.4910	2.4086	-0.9177
1995	3.1708	2.5699	0.6008
1996	3.1163	2.9712	0.1450
1997	3.3296	4.5577	-1.2281
1998	3.8090	3.8255	-0.0166
1999	3.1751	0.0620	3.1122
2000	3.5501	4.0556	-0.5055
2001	0.9912	3.5139	-2.5227
2002	-0.5801	3.1041	-3.6841
2003	0.3761	2.0615	-2.4376
2004	-0.4970	3.0158	-3.5127

Data Rs. Crores.

GDS = Gross domestic savings;

AVSR is average savings rate = GDS/TGDP = 0.348.

TGCF = AGCF + IGCF + SGCF=TCFIU. TGDP = AGDP + IGDP + SGDP.

GCF adjustments are for types of assets and/or errors of omission and commission.

RNCI: NCI deflated by investment price deflator (GCF_PDFL).

RFDR = US Federal Bank real discount rate.

RBR = RBI's real bank rate.

INTDIFF = RFDR – RBR = Interest (%) differential.

Appendix A-3.2

In general, an optimal lag structure is to be obtained before a VEC is estimated. The number of cointegrating vectors (CIV) is in principle dependent on the lag structure of the model (see Banerjee *et al.*, 1993). For a given lag structure to determine the optimal number of cointegrating vectors in each sub-model, Johansen's trace test (JTT) and Saikkonen-Luetkepohl (2000) tests (SLT) have been used with the help of J-Multi software. The JTT requires a break point to be specified (specified as 1991 in our case) if there exists a shift in the cointegrating vector. Briefly, the results are as follows:

(a) Agriculture: JTT indicated that there exists one CIV between AGDP, AGCF and D(APDFL) with lag structure of 3 for a levels' VAR (i.e., VEC would have 2 lags). But, the SLT indicated non-existence of cointegration between these variables. When the model was estimated specifying one cointegrating vector, the results turned out quite satisfactory in terms of unit root test, residual auto-correlations and stability. So, the JTT result was conformed to. The test results of LR statistics are as follows:

Johansen's Trace Test						Saikkonen-Luetkepohl Test					
r0	LR	pval	90%	95%	99%	r0	LR	pval	90%	95%	99%
0	61.25	0.0080	51.46	54.50	60.49	0	17.26	0.5993	26.07	28.52	33.50
1	29.49	0.1641	31.54	34.10	39.25	1	6.95	0.6687	13.88	15.76	19.71
2	10.18	0.4182	15.64	17.84	22.47	2	1.25	0.7256	5.47	6.79	9.73

Included lags (levels): 3 and Trend and intercept included.

(b) Industry: JTT indicated that there exist two CIVs between D(IGDP) D(IGCF) and D(IPDFL) with lag structure of 2 for a levels' VAR (i.e., VEC would have 1 lag). SLT indicated that there exists one CIV with a lag structure of 2. The model was estimated in both ways. The one with two CIVs miserably failed in satisfying the residual auto-correlations and stability test. Besides, the loading coefficients (otherwise known as adjustment parameters) mostly turned out insignificant. On all these fronts, the model with only one CIV performed quite satisfactorily. Thus, the SLT was conformed to. The test results of LR statistics are as follows:

Johansen's Trace Test						Saikkonen-Luetkepohl Test					
r0	LR	pval	90%	95%	99%	r0	LR	pval	90%	95%	99%
0	69.19	0.0000	39.73	42.77	48.87	0	44.32	0.0002	26.07	28.52	33.50
1	27.87	0.0257	23.32	25.73	30.67	1	11.20	0.2406	13.88	15.76	19.71
2	3.72	0.7785	10.68	12.45	16.22	2	2.13	0.5094	5.47	6.79	9.73

Included lags (levels): 2 and Trend and intercept included.

(c) Services: Both the JTT and SLT indicated that there exists one CIV between D(SGDP), SGCF and D(SPDFL) with a lag structure of 3 for a levels' VAR (i.e., VEC would have 2 lags). The test results of LR statistics are as follows:

Johansen's Trace Test						Saikkonen-Luetkepohl Test					
r0	LR	pval	90%	95%	99%	r0	LR	pval	90%	95%	99%
0	73.80	0.0001	51.46	54.50	60.49	0	37.78	0.0021	26.07	28.52	33.50
1	32.43	0.0792	31.54	34.10	39.25	1	11.67	0.2081	13.88	15.76	19.71
2	7.31	0.6994	15.64	17.84	22.47	2	7.39	0.0361	5.47	6.79	9.73

Included lags (levels): 3 and Trend and intercept included.

(d) Households: Both the JTT and SLT indicated that there exists one CIV between D(PFCE), D(HFS) and D(HPS) with a lag structure of 3 for a levels' VAR (i.e., VEC would have 2 lags). The test results of LR statistics are as follows:

Johansen's Trace Test						Saikkonen-Luetkepohl Test					
r0	LR	pval	90%	95%	99%	r0	LR	pval	90%	95%	99%
0	42.04	0.0068	32.25	35.07	40.78	0	37.98	0.0004	21.76	24.16	29.11
1	13.42	0.3386	17.98	20.16	24.69	1	10.40	0.1029	10.47	12.26	16.10
2	1.57	0.8510	7.60	9.14	12.53	2	0.10	0.8021	2.98	4.13	6.93

Included lags (levels): 3 and Trend and intercept included.

Appendix A-3.3

Consider a traditional LES:

$$P_{it}\ X_{it} = P_{it}\ C_i + \beta_i\ [\ E_t - \Sigma\ (P_{jt}\ C_j)\ ]\ ; \qquad \Sigma\beta_i = 1. \tag{13}$$

where C_i (usually referred to as committed consumption) and β_i (marginal budget share) are parameters to be estimated, i and j=1, n commodity groups; P_{it} and X_{it} are price and consumption of i-th commodity and $E_t=\Sigma(P_{it}\ X_{it})$=total consumption expenditure over all commodities at current prices in time period t.

Here, we need to disaggregate the PFCE into different commodity groups. For estimating the LES (13) using the NAS data, the following three modifications/assumptions are made:

(a) In view of the data problems and the number of parameters to be estimated, the expenditure over all the committed consumptions put together is assumed to be a fixed fraction of the total expenditure; that means,

$$\Sigma\ (P_{jt}\ C_j) = \delta.E_t. \tag{14}$$

This implies, marginal budget $= [E_t - \Sigma\ (P_{jt}\ C_j)] = (1.-\ \delta)\ E_t$.

With this assumption, (13) becomes,

$$P_{it}\ X_{it} = P_{it}\ C_i + \beta_i.(1. - \delta)\ E_t \tag{15}$$

$$P_{it}\ X_{it} = P_{it}\ C_i + \gamma_i.E_t \tag{16}$$

where $$\gamma_i = \beta_i.(1. - \delta) \tag{17}$$

Summing over all the i=1 to n, (16) yields,

$$E_t = \delta.E_t + E_t.\ \Sigma\ (\gamma_i) \tag{18}$$

Obviously, $$\Sigma\ (\gamma_i) = (1.-\ \delta) \tag{19}$$

Substituting (19) in (17) leads to

$$\beta_i = \gamma_i\ /\ \Sigma\ (\gamma_i) \tag{20}$$

The assumption (14) facilitates matters: first (16) may be estimated (either single equation-wise or simultaneously) to obtain C_i and γ_i for i=1 to n; then the marginal budget shares β_i can be computed using (20). The entire LES thus obtained does not violate any of the conditions (Engel-aggregation, additivity and symmetry) required to be satisfied by a complete demand system.

(b) To reflect upon the changes in committed consumptions overtime, C_i are treated as time-varying; i.e., C_i becomes C_{it}. Denoting TR_t as a trend variable, it is assumed that

$$C_{it} = \alpha 1_i + \alpha 2_i.TR_t + \alpha 3_i.TR_t^2 + \alpha 4_i.X_{i,t-1} \tag{21}$$

and $$P_{it}\ X_{it} = P_{it}\ C_{it} + \beta_i\ [E_t - \Sigma(P_{jt}\ C_{jt})] \tag{22}$$

With the assumption that $\Sigma(P_{jt}\ C_{jt}) = \delta.E_t$.

we get $$P_{it}\ X_{it} = P_{it}\ C_{it} + \beta_i.(1. - \delta)\ E_t \tag{23}$$

Thus (16) is revised as,

$$P_{it}\ X_{it} = \alpha 1_i.P_{it} + \alpha 2_i.\ (P_{it}\ .TR_t\ ) + \alpha 3_i.\ (P_{it}\ .TR_t^2) + \alpha 4_i.(P_{it}\ X_{i,t-1}) + \gamma_i\ E_t \tag{24}$$

(c) In principle, one can estimate (24) and deduce the LES parameters using (20). However, there are no data available on commodity prices.* Therefore, we develop a commodity disaggregation system at constant prices data (in other words, a demand system accounting only for 'total expenditure' effects). Eqns. (22) and (24) at constant (1993-94) prices boil down respectively to

---

* Usually for estimation, the available commodity price-deflators data are used in place of prices.

$$P_{i\text{-}1993/94}\ X_{it} = P_{i\text{-}1993/94}\ C_{it} + \beta_i\ [PFCE_t - \Sigma(P_{j\text{-}1993/94}\ C_{jt})] \tag{25}$$

$$P_{i\text{-}1993/94}\ X_{it} = \alpha 1_i.\ P_{i\text{-}1993/94} + \alpha 2_i.(P_{i\text{-}1993/94}.TR_t\ ) + \alpha 3_i.(P_{i\text{-}1993/94}.TR_t^2) + \alpha 4_i.(P_{i\text{-}1993/94}\ X_{i,t-1}) + \gamma_i\ PFCE_t \tag{26}$$

where $PFCE_t = \Sigma(P_{i\text{-}1993/94}.X_{it})$ = total consumption expenditure over all commodities in time period t at 1993-94 prices. Let,

$Z_{it} = P_{i\text{-}1993/94}\ X_{it}$ = expenditure on i-th commodity at 1993-94 prices so that

$$PFCE_t = \Sigma(P_{i\text{-}1993/94}\ X_{it}\ ) = \Sigma(Z_{it}) \tag{27}$$

and $M_{it} = P_{i\text{-}1993/94}.C_{it}$ = committed expenditure on i-th commodity at 1993-94 prices.

(25) and (26) become

$$Z_{it} = M_{it} + \beta_i\ [\ PFCE_t - \Sigma(M_{jt})\ ] \tag{28}$$

$$Z_{it} = a1_i + a2_i.TR_t + a3_i.TR_t^2 + a4_i.Z_{i,t-1} + \gamma_i\ .PFCE_t \tag{29}$$

where

$$M_{it} = a1_i + a2_i.TR_t + a3_i.TR_t^2 + a4_i.Z_{i,t-1} \tag{30}$$

and $a1_i = \alpha 1_i.P_{i\text{-}1993/94}$, $a2_i = \alpha 2_i.P_{i\text{-}1993/94}$, $a3_i = \alpha 3_i.P_{i\text{-}1993/94}$, $a4_i = \alpha 4_i$; and $\beta_i = \gamma_i / \Sigma\ (\gamma_i)$.

The characteristic difference between (24) and (29) is that the former (with an additional assumption that $\Sigma(P_{jt}\ C_j) = \delta.E_t$) represents a complete LES demand system, whereas the latter (with an assumption that $\Sigma(M_{jt}) = \delta.PFCE_t$) is a mechanism to disaggregate PFCE, since it involves only fixed prices for all the years.

For disaggregating the PFCE into commodity groups two alternative groupings are made (n=8 in both the cases) as follows:

Group A:

(i)	(FMMB)	Food, beverages etc.
(ii)	(CLR)	Clothing etc.
(iii)	(FLP)	Fuel etc.
(iv)	(OT)	Transport, furnishings etc.
(v)	(ED)	Education
(vi)	(CO)	Communication
(vii)	(MI)	Miscellaneous
(viii)	(MD)	Medical expenditure

Table A-3.3(a) presents the corresponding LES estimated as Zellner's Seemingly Unrelated Equations System.*

Group B:

(i)	(CRL)	Cereals and bread
(ii)	(PUL)	Pulses
(iii)	(MIL)	Milk and milk products
(iv)	(OF)	All other foods
(v)	(CLR)	Clothing etc.
(vi)	(FLP)	Fuel etc.

* Estimation of the system of equations as in (28) would involve 39 (8x5-1) parameters to be estimated simultaneously with only 42 observations (1962-2003)!

(vii) (CO) Communication

(viii) (OT) All Others

Table A-3.3(b) presents the corresponding estimated LES.

(i), (ii), (iii) and (iv) in group B would add up to (i) in group A.

(iv), (v), (vii) and (viii) in group A would add up to (viii) in group B.

Table A-3.3(a): Estimation of LES-Type Commodity Disaggregation System—Group A

LES: $Z_{it} = M_{it} + \beta_i(PFCE_t - \Sigma M_{jt})$

Assume: $M_{it} = a1_i.T1_t + a2_i.T2_t + a3_i.T3_t + a4_i.Z_{i,t-1}$ and $\Sigma M_{jt} = \delta.PFCE_t$

Estimated equations at 1993-94 prices:

(i) For FMMB, CLR, FLP, OT, ED, and MI equations:

$$Z_{it} = a1_i.T1_t + a2_i.T2_t + a3_i.T3_t + a4_i.Z_{i,t-1} + \gamma_i\ PFCE_t$$

where $T1_t$ = 1. (constant), $T2_t = TR_t$ is a trend variable, i.e. TR_{1961} = 1. and so on; $T3_t = TR_t^2$.

(ii) For MD equation : Dependent variable is $D(Z_{MD,t}) = (Z_{MD,t} - Z_{MD,t-1})$ instead of $Z_{MD,t}$. $T1_t$, $T2_t$ and $T3_t$ are as above.

(iii) For CO equation : Dependent variable is $D(Z_{CO,t}) = (Z_{CO,t} - Z_{CO,t-1})$ instead of $Z_{CO,t}$. $T1_t = L93_t$, $T2_t = P01_t$ and $T3_t = P03_t$, where $L93_t$ is a level variable starting from year 1993, $P01_t$ and $P03_t$ are pulse variables at years 2001 and 2003 respectively.

LES representation implies $\beta_i = \gamma_i / \Sigma \gamma_i$

Commodity	a1	a2	a3	a4	γ	Rbar²	D-W	β
FMMB								
Coef	56369.4457	2399.666	0	0	0.301172	0.996349	1.037926	0.58268
t-statistics	22.31668	7.71560	0	0	16.37116			
CLR								
Coef	2954.4324	325.4383	0	0.725986	0.016731	0.997936	2.609175	0.032369
t-statistics	3.19889	2.99914	0	8.82472	2.85650			
FLP								
Coef	762.7328	-55.9046	0	0.416998	0.024494	0.998404	2.340621	0.047389
t-statistics	3.24119	-3.23955	0	4.52177	5.96931			
OT								
Coef	-13327.4123	-450.9510	0	0.70841	0.09979	0.999436	2.060402	0.193065
t-statistics	-5.51949	-4.29778	0	10.44333	5.28410			
ED								
Coef	-340.7158	0	0	0.805586	0.004856	0.994848	1.205431	0.009395
t-statistics	-1.74813	0	0	10.51161	3.07085			
CO (*)								
Coef	293.3892	3093.9929	4782.5042	1.1329583	0	0.989945	1.089500	0.000000
t-statistics	3.15594	17.65908	22.14119	12.03724	0			
MI								
Coef	-6983.8016	-381.4607	0	0.636424	0.062601	0.997326	1.699112	0.121115
t-statistics	-6.23904	-4.24863	0	9.00654	5.77684			
MD (*)								
Coef	0	-155.1570	2.4778122	1	0.007230	0.867600	1.050470	0.013987
t-statistics	0	-5.43786	5.52180		4.85876			

FMMB: Expenditure on food & beverages. CLR: Expenditure on clothing & footwear,

FLP: Expenditure on fuel, electricity, water & rent, OT: Expenditure on furniture, furnishings, transport etc. ,

ED: Expenditure on education, CO: Expenditure on communication. MI: Miscellaneous expenditure,

MD: Medical expenditure.

Table A-3.3(b): Estimation of LES-Type Commodity Disaggregation System—Group B

LES: $Z_{it} = M_{it} + \beta_i(PFCE_t - \Sigma M_{jt})$

Assume: $M_{it} = a1_i.T1_t + a2_i.T2_t + a3_i.T3_t + a4_i.P01_t + a5_i.P03_t + a6_i.L93_t + a7_i.Z_{i,t-1}$ and $\Sigma M_{jt} = \delta.PFCE_t$

Estimated equations at 1993-94 prices:

(i) For CRL, PUL, MIL, OF, CLR, FLP and OT equations: $Z_{it} = a1_i.T1_t + a2_i.T2_t + a3_i.T3_t + a4_i.P01_t + a5_i.P03_t + a6_i.L93_t + a7_i.Z_{i,t-1} + \gamma_i.PFCE_t$

where $T1_t = 1.$ (constant), $T2_t = TR_t$ is a trend variable, i.e. $TR_{1961} = 1.$ and so on; $T3_t = TR_t^2$.

(ii) For CO equation : Dependent variable is $D(Z_{CO,t}) = (Z_{CO,t} - Z_{CO,t-1})$ instead of $Z_{CO,t}$.

(iii) $L93_t$ is a level variable starting from year 1993, $P01_t$ and $P03_t$ are pulse variables at years 2001 and 2003 respectively.

LES representation implies $\beta_i = \gamma_i / \Sigma \gamma_i$

Commodity	a1	a2	a3	a4	a5	a6	a7	γ	Rbar²	D-W	β
CRL (*)											
Coef	32596.98585		25.78301	-16401.16990	-26331.82511	0	0.21138	0	0.972313	2.055223	0
t-statistics	7.49449		7.87786	-4.50720	-7.03672	NA	2.05533	NA			
PUL (*)											
Coef	5115.481975	126.348300		-2341.599765	-3415.856696	0	0.197127	0	0.880616	2.184945	0
t-statistics	6.37595	6.04467		-2.57363	-3.70034	NA	1.71791	NA			
MIL											
Coef	12553.27639	-219.45614	37.71087	0	0	0	0	0	0.993154	0.933684	0
t-statistics	11.79959	-2.02412	16.08140	NA	NA	NA	NA	NA			
OF											
Coef	24111.588174	783.832433	0	0	0	0		0.218679	0.998071	1.462118	0.590473
t-statistics	21.68095	5.71638	NA	NA	NA	NA		26.94285			
CLR											
Coef	3379.3367764	373.9130688	0	0	0	0	0.6799861	0.0192881	0.998016	2.471993	0.052081
t-statistics	3.82291	3.58407	NA	NA	NA	NA	8.77179	3.41666			
FLP											
Coef	631.3646095	-48.0076908	0	0	0	0	0.4872779	0.0217383	0.998461	2.396887	0.058697
t-statistics	2.64352	-2.73162	NA	NA	NA	NA	4.39647	5.17707			
CO (*)											
Coef	0	0	0	2971.5326047	4735.1357197	209.6682361	1.1425663	0	0.990214	0.929056	0
t-statistics	NA	NA	NA	16.02438	20.88655	2.22304	12.69337	NA			
OT											
Coef	-13534.51205	-564.40324	0	0	0	0	0.86467	0.11064	0.999493	1.668693	0.298748
t-statistics	-4.35271	-3.22456	NA	NA	NA	NA	15.80839	3.92934			

CRL: Expenditure on cereals & bread. PUL: Expenditure on clothing & footwear, MIL: Expenditure on milk & milk products,

OF: Expenditure on other foods. , CLR: Expenditure on clothing & footwear, FLP: Expenditure on furniture, furnishings, transport etc.,

CO: Expenditure on communication, OT: all other expenditure.

Appendix A-3.4

Diagnostics

Multicollinearity: We believe that most of the estimated coefficients, including short-run responses to the exogenous and predetermined variables, in the above models are as they ought to be. Canova and Pina (1999) attribute wrong and unexpected signs of short-run coefficients to misspecification in VAR models. Valadkhani (2004) discusses various arduous tasks in building macroeconometric models and says the VAR approach is difficult to implement when there are more than five variables due to over-parameterisation and resultant multicollinearity. The multicollinearity problem often could lead to unexpected and wrong signs. Therefore, in the above models multicollinearity was seen to be as low as possible. In fact the variance inflation factors (vif) of the explanatory variables are all less than 20 in each of the 4 models presented above.

Stationarity of the LREs: Table A-3.4(a) presents the unit root tests of the residuals of the above LREs. The tests show that the residual vectors are all I(0). Thus, the equations (31), (32), (33) and (34) indicate that the AGDP, AGCF and D(APDFL) are co-integrated in the agriculture; D(IGDP), D(IGCF) and D(IPDFL) in industry; D(SGDP), SGCF and D(SPDFL) in the services sector and D(PFCE), D(HFS) and D(HPS) in the households sector are co-integrated.

Autocorrelation: The estimated residuals of the models are free from first-order autocorrelation. Table A-3.4(b) shows results of the Breush-Godfrey LM test, useful for testing low order auto-correlations (see Luetkepohl and Kratzig(2004)).

Stability of the Coefficients: We have conducted tests based on recursive residuals, cusum and cusum-squares for testing the stability of the estimated parameters and the variance. The test results seem to be in general satisfactory. These results are usually presented in plots; and there are too many of them. See Figures 3.2.

Stability of the Models: According to Stock and Watson (2001), "Small VARs like our three-variables system have become a benchmark against which new forecasting systems are judged. But while useful as a benchmark, small VARs of two or three variables are often unstable and thus poor predictors of the future." This paper too estimates only small VECs/VARs. Thus, it is important that the stability issue is taken up seriously since the estimated coefficients will be used later for policy simulation results. For inference purposes, the estimated models must satisfy stability conditions. For stable VAR models, all the eigen values of the companion matrix should be strictly less than one; or equivalently all the roots of the reverse characteristic polynomial (RCP) should be strictly greater than one.* For stable VEC models with K endogenous variables and r co-integrating equations the companion matrix should have exactly (K-r) unit eigen values with the remaining eigen values being strictly (significantly) less than one. Equivalently, the RCP should have exactly (K-r) unit roots and the remaining roots strictly greater than one. This condition if satisfied indicates that the number of co-integrating equations in the VEC has been correctly specified. Table A-3.4(b) shows these details also. For each of the models, there are K=3 endogenous variables and r=1 CIV. The stability results show that (K-r)=2 unit roots with all the others being strictly greater than one. Thus, the estimated models are all stable. Therefore, the policy responses generated by using these models can be treated as reliable.

* Consider a VAR(p) model, $Y_t = c + A_1 Y_{t-1} + A_2 Y_{t-2} + \ldots\ldots + A_p Y_{t-p} + u_t$.

The reverse characteristic polynomial is defined as, det $(I_k - A_1 Z_1 - A_2 Z_2 - \ldots\ldots - A_p Z_p)$. The corresponding companion matrix is of the order kp x kp, where k=number of endogenous variables and p=number of lags. In the case of VEC (p-1) model, the coefficients of the corresponding levels VAR(p) model is first computed. Using the coefficients of the VAR(p) the companion matrix is computed. For further details refer to Luetkepohl Helmut (1991) and Reinsel C. Gregory (1993).

Table A-3.4(a): Stationarity Test for the CIVs

	ADF	SP		KPSS	
		Rho-test	Tau-test	Level Stationarity	Trend Stationarity
AGCIV	I(0)	I(0)	I(0)	I(0)	I(0)
INCIV	I(0)	I(0)	I(0)	I(0)	I(0)
SERCIV	I(0)	I(0)	I(0)	I(0)	I(0)
COCIV	I(0)	I(0)	I(0)	I(0)	I(0)

AGCIV= AGDP - 3.5491*AGCF -1311004.322*D(APDFL) + 57159.17*L91 – 9680.45*TR9

INCIV = D(IGDP) - 0.5851*D(IGCF) - 158848.3909*D(IPDFL) - 2149.3102*TR91

SRCIV = D(SGDP) - 0.51882*SGCF + 154343.4241*D(SPDFL)

COCIV = D(PFCE) - 3.0838*D(HFS) – 0.7632*D(HPS)

Note: ADF denotes the Augmented Dickey Fuller test, SP: Schimidt-Philips test, KPSS: Kwiatkowski Philips Schimidt and Shin test. SP has two test statistics: Tau-statistic and Rho statistic. KPSS tests are under two assumptions of stationarity: levels stationarity and trend stationarity.

Table A-3.4(b): Residual Auto-correlations and VEC Stability

AGRICULTURE :	LM-Statistic	p-value	df	lags
	13.2679	0.1509	9	1

Roots of reverse characteristic polynomial: 1.3858, 1.3858, 1.5844, 1.5844, 1.6631, 1.6631, 4.6800, 1.0000, 1.0000

INDUSTRY :	LM-Statistic	p-value	df	Lags
	13.7876	0.1301	9	1

Roots of reverse characteristic polynomial: 1.8997, 1.8997, 2.0219, 3.1522, 1.0000, 1.0000

SERVICES :	LM-Statistic	p-value	df	lags
	13.4913	0.1416	9	1

Roots of reverse characteristic polynomial: 1.1967, 1.1967, 1.4791, 1.5341, 1.5341, 2.7278, 2.7278, 1.0000, 1.0000

CONSUMPTION :	LM-Statistic	p-value	df	lags
	16.6217	0.0550	9	1

Roots of reverse characteristic polynomial: 1.0000, 1.1540, 1.1540, 1.2723, 1.2723, 4.8574, 4.8574, 1.3877, 1.0000

The LM-statistic is the Breush-Godfrey LM statistic to test for autocorrelation for a specified lag order (lags) and degrees of freedom (df).

Appendix A-3.5

Some Associated Computations:

CAGrowth Rates (Grt) of IPDFL to APDFL, and AGCF, AGDP, IGCF and IGDP: 2004-05 to 2011-12

RefRun /Scenario	IPDFL Grt	APDFL Grt	IPDFL Grt ÷ APDFL Grt	AGCF Grt	AGDP Grt	IGCF Grt	IGDP Grt
RefRun:	3.48	2.26	1.5398	4.95	2.58	20.14	10.74
S2:	4.79	2.49	1.9236	4.30	3.43	29.03	13.24
S3:	3.47	1.99	1.7437	4.33	2.23	19.85	10.65
S4:	3.98	1.99	2.0000	5.15	4.34	27.54	13.62
S5:	3.49	2.26	1.5442	4.93	2.59	20.24	10.75
S6:	3.47	2.26	1.5354	4.95	2.57	20.10	10.73
S7:	4.54	2.32	1.9569	6.13	3.70	31.17	15.29
S8:	3.88	1.77	2.1921	4.50	3.73	26.21	13.07
S9:	3.19	2.8	1.1393	5.75	2.00	14.34	8.89
S10:	3.50	2.25	1.5556	4.92	2.60	20.31	10.76
S11:	3.86	2.86	1.3497	4.09	3.30	17.52	10.09
S12:	3.73	2.32	1.6078	4.65	3.08	24.32	11.94
S13:	4.07	2.29	1.7773	4.55	2.48	15.99	10.00
S14:	4.28	2.32	1.8448	4.29	2.42	13.77	9.67
S15:	4.43	2.30	1.9261	5.06	2.47	10.31	9.24
S16:	4.46	2.51	1.7769	2.71	1.91	12.91	9.50
S17:	5.13	4.05	1.2667	7.45	2.87	8.77	11.98
S18:	5.61	3.21	1.7477	1.35	4.28	24.56	12.73
S19:	3.24	2.18	1.4862	4.11	0.87	15.35	9.05
S20:	3.23	2.18	1.4817	4.13	0.86	15.27	9.04
S21:	3.10	2.17	1.4286	4.33	0.50	12.18	8.40
S22:	3.91	2.15	1.8186	5.01	1.50	2.17	7.62
S23:	3.92	2.15	1.8233	5.00	1.51	2.34	7.63
S24:	3.91	2.06	1.8981	4.77	1.38	2.15	7.60
S25:	4.07	2.04	1.9951	4.54	1.78	7.65	8.25
S26:	4.16	2.05	2.0293	4.39	2.02	10.65	8.72

CAGR = Grt

CHAPTER 4

Global Economic Shocks and Indian Policy Response*

An Analysis Using a CGE Model

A. Ganesh Kumar and Manoj Panda

4.1 Introduction

The year 2008 has been a tumultuous one in the history of the world economy unparalleled in several decades. The first half of 2008 witnessed dramatic rise in the global prices of crude oil and petroleum products. From about US$90 a barrel toward the end of 2007, the price of crude oil reached unprecedented levels of close to US$150 a barrel by July 2008. During the second half of 2008, the major economies of the world, *viz.*, the USA and Europe, witnessed an unprecedented financial meltdown that began with sub-prime mortgage crisis in the USA. The effects of this financial meltdown soon began to be felt in the real side of these economies, and by the end of 2008 these economies were in the midst of a deep recession. The recession in these developed economies soon started cascading into a world-wide economic slowdown that has invoked comparisons with the Great Depression of the 1930s. Along side commodity prices too fell sharply; especially the price of crude oil and petroleum products came crashing down to below US$40 a barrel by the end of the year.

The fallout of these developments in the world economy is already being felt in India in several ways. Several export dependent sectors of the economy such as textiles, leather, IT and ITES sectors, etc., have seen a fall in their export orders and earnings. Foreign portfolio investment flows have more or less dried up/even reversed for a short while in the second half of 2008. Job losses in other countries are expected to result in a decline in foreign remittances by Indian workers living abroad. India being highly dependent on imported oil for its energy needs, the sharp changes in the world price of a critical input naturally can be expected to have significant impacts on several sectors of the economy.

These shocks emanating from the world economy have posed particular challenges to the Indian policymakers. India being highly dependent on imported oil, the sharp price rise witnessed in the first half of 2008 threatened to increase the cost of a critical input for several sectors of the economy and sections of the society. Given that the domestic price of several key petroleum products such as petrol, diesel, kerosene, LPG, etc., are administratively fixed by the government, the rise in import costs resulted in a

* This study is an outcome of the research sponsored by the Planning Commission, Government of India, New Delhi, under the Project titled "Modelling Work for Eleventh Plan and Beyond". The authors would like to thank the Deputy Chairman and Members of the Planning Commission, and other participants at the various meetings held at the Planning Commission, for their comments and suggestions. In particular, the suggestions by Kirit Parikh were extremely useful in designing the simulations carried out here. We have also benefited from discussions with Michiel Keyzer of the Centre for World Food Studies, Amsterdam. Usual disclaimers apply. The views expressed here are those of the authors and not of the IGIDR, CESS or the Planning Commission.

A. Ganesh Kumar, Indira Gandhi Institute of Development Research (IGIDR) and Manoj Panda, Centre for Economic and Social Studies (CESS).

serious imbalance in the finances of the oil sector. This imbalance between the costs and prices was partially bridged through government subsidies that were financed by special "oil bonds". In order to keep the subsidy burden somewhat under control, the government partially passed through the global price rise by increasing the domestic prices of petroleum products.

The world economic recession seen in the second half of 2008 and the consequent slow down in India's exports required a different set of policy response from the government. The Indian government has taken several counter-measures—both fiscal and monetary—to limit the adverse effects of the export slow down. These include a cut in indirect taxes, accelerating the implementation of several infrastructure projects, reducing interest rates, easing the liquidity available with the banks, etc.

What are the likely impacts of these events emanating from the rest of the world on the Indian economy and different sections of the society? What are the likely outcomes of the policy response of the Indian government to the different world economic shocks? This study aims to address these issues using a computable general equilibrium (CGE) model of the Indian economy. As will be elaborated later, the analytical framework of the CGE models allows us to study only "real" shocks arising from outside India and "fiscal" counter-measures, as opposed to "financial" shocks and "monetary" responses of the government.

The analysis is carried out in two parts. In the first part, we assess the impacts of global oil price rise on the Indian economy under some alternative policy options available to the government. Specifically, we look at the impacts of a 70 per cent rise in the world price of crude oil and a 50 per cent rise in the world price of petroleum products. The changes correspond roughly to the actual changes witnessed in the first half of 2008. We consider three alternative scenarios that represent different policy choices: (a) keeping the domestic prices of petroleum products unchanged despite the rise in global prices, (b) a 10 per cent rise in the domestic administered prices, and (c) switching over from the administered prices regime to a market price regime. We evaluate these policies from an efficiency angle in terms of their impact on key macroeconomic variables, and also on their distributional impacts.

In part two, we look at the impacts of: (a) fall in exports due to recession in the world economy, (b) a reduction in the foreign inflows into India, and (c) the fall in global oil prices. To counter the adverse effects of these changes coming from outside India, we look at three counter-measures, *viz.*, (i) a rise in government consumption, (ii) a cut in indirect taxes, and (iii) employment programmes, specifically the National Rural Employment Guarantee Scheme (NREGS), as a policy meant to protect the rural poor. We assess the potential of these policy responses to reduce the adverse impacts of the global recession on short-term growth and household welfare.

We begin with a description of the basic structure of the CGE model and the database used in this study.

4.2 The Basic CGE Model

The primary issues of concern here are shocks to the Indian economy coming from outside the economy, namely changes in world price of crude oil and petroleum products, fall in exports and reduction in foreign inflows. Oil being a critical input in the production of the economy, as a source of energy and as a vital raw material in the chemical industry, the cost structure of almost all sectors of the economy gets affected by a rise in its price. Fall in exports is likely to trigger a loss in output leading to a decline in demand for raw materials and unemployment of labour and capital. Similarly, reduction in foreign inflows implies a reduction in national savings and investment, and hence the level of activity in the economy as a whole. These first round impacts would have second round impacts on sectoral demands, output and prices, factor incomes, and hence household and government incomes, their consumption and savings. Thus, all these external shocks are expected to have economy-wide impacts through inter-sectoral and inter-agent linkages. Similarly, the policy responses of interest here, *viz.*, rise in administered price of petroleum products, rise in government consumption, cut in indirect taxes and employment programmes such as the NREGS, too would have sectoral, household and macro level impacts. Thus, it is important that the inter-sectoral and inter-agent linkages are carefully captured in the analytical framework while assessing the policy options. One such analytical framework that can capture such linkages is the CGE modelling framework.

In this study, we use a static CGE model that is built along the approach developed by Dervis, de Melo and Robinson (1982). A distinguishing feature of this approach is that it treats the domestically produced good and traded good in a particular sector as imperfect but close substitutes using the Armington specification. This avoids complete specialisation that perfect substitution may entail, and permits cross-hauling; i.e., the simultaneous imports and exports in the same sector as observed in reality. An important consequence of this specification is that domestic market prices do not change by the same order as the change in world price. The major features of our CGE model are mentioned here. Detailed description of the model structure along with the equations is given in Appendix A-4.1.

- The model is built around a modified Social Accounting Matrix (SAM) for the year 2003-04 prepared by Saluja and Yadav (2006). The data Appendix A-4.4 at the end discusses the SAM in greater detail.
- The model distinguishes 71 commodities/sectors, whose equilibrium output and prices are determined endogenously. Table 4.1 reports the sectoral classification.
- Sectoral outputs are specified as Constant Elasticity of Substitution (CES) production functions with labour and capital as factors that determine the sectoral value added. Intermediate inputs are considered through Leontief type input-output coefficients obtained from the input-output table embedded in the SAM.
- Sectoral demand for labour and capital depends upon factor prices and output price and are derived from profit maximising conditions.
- Given the static nature of the model, the supply of both capital and labour are assumed to be fixed in the short run.
- Capital is assumed to sector specific, and thus the returns to capital (profit rate) are sector specific. Labour is allowed to be mobile across sectors based on the ratio of wage rate to sectoral price.
- The model can solve for full employment level of wage and sectoral profit rates or allow for factor unemployment when factor prices are fixed. The equations for the basic model described in Appendix A-4.1 pertains to the full employment specification.
- The model distinguishes several types of prices, *viz.*, import price, export price, domestic market price and producer price. The wedge between these prices arise due to government's tariffs on imports, export subsidies, and indirect taxes/subsidies for domestic goods, and also due to the imperfect substitutability between domestic and traded goods mentioned earlier.
- The model distinguishes 10 household expenditure classes, five each in rural and urban areas (Table 4.1), which help us to capture the distributional impacts of policy alternatives.
- Household incomes depend on the factor income and initial endowment distribution. Households also receive transfers from the government and from abroad.
- Total consumption expenditure for households is determined by deducting direct taxes and savings from their income. Household commodity demands depend upon their consumption budget and commodity prices through a Linear Expenditure System (LES) demand system. The relevant price here is the so-called "composite" price, which is a weighted average of the market price of the domestically produced good and import price.
- The model considers several sources of government revenue such as direct taxes, tariff revenue, domestic indirect taxes, non-tax revenue and foreign inflows on government account. On the expenditure side, it distinguishes government consumption, transfers to households and subsidies for domestic goods and exports. The difference between government revenue and current expenditure is its savings.

- National savings are from three sources: private, government and foreign, the sum total of which determine aggregate investment in the economy. Sectoral composition of the demand for investment goods are determined by fixed proportions.

Table 4.1: Sectors and Household in the Model

Sectors

Agriculture (16)	Industry (39)		Services (16)
1. Paddy	17. Coal and lignite	37. Inorganic heavy chemicals	56. Electricity
2. Wheat	18. Crude petroleum, natural gas	38. Organic heavy chemicals	57. Gas
3. Other cereals	19. Iron ore	39. Fertilisers	58. Water supply
4. Pulses	20. Other Minerals	40. Pesticides	59. Railway transport services
5. Sugarcane	21. Sugar	41. Paints, varnishes and lacquers	60. Other transport services
6. Oilseeds	22. *Khandsari, boora*	42. Misc chemicals	61. Storage and warehousing
7. Jute	23. Edible & Vanaspati	43. Cement	62. Communication
8. Cotton	24. Misc food products	44. Iron & steel	63. Trade
9. Tea & coffee	25. Beverages & tabacco products	45. Non-ferrous basic metals	64. Hotels and restaurants
10. Rubber	26. Cotton textiles	46. Metal products	65. Banking
11. Tobacco	27. Wool synthetic, silk fiber textiles	47. Other non-electric machinery	66. Insurance
12. Other crops	28. Jute, hemp, mesta textiles	48. Electrical appliances	67. Ownership of dwellings
13. Milk and milk products	29. Textile products	49. Communication equipments	68. Education and research
14. Other livestock products	30. Furniture and wood products	50. Electronic equipments (incl. TV)	69. Medical and health
15. Forestry and logging	31. Paper, paper prods. & newsprint	51. Other electrical Machinery	70. Other services
16. Fishing	32. Printing and publishing	52. Rail equipments	71. Public administration
	33. Leather products	53. Other transport equipments	
	34. Rubber and plastic products	54. Misc manufacturing	
	35. Petroleum products	55. Construction	
	36. Coal tar products		

Households classes	Monthly per capita expenditure
1. Rural 1	Bottom 10%
2. Rural 2	10-30%
3. Rural 3	30-70%
4. Rural 4	70-90%
5. Rural 5	Top 10%
6. Urban 1	Bottom 10%
7. Urban 2	10-30%
8. Urban 3	30-70%
9. Urban 4	70-90%
10. Urban 5	Top 10%

- Domestic market prices clear the domestic market, while exchange rate clears the foreign exchange market given the level of foreign savings.
- As with any other CGE model, we determine only relative prices and all prices are relative to the given numeraire that can vary from one set of simulations to another. All real variables are invariant to the numeraire specification.
- Several parameters such as the input-output coefficients and tax rates used in the model are derived from the SAM for 2003-04, while the behavioural parameters such as consumption elasticities are taken from the literature.
- The model is solved numerically using the GAMS software.

For each of the two parts, some modifications to this basic structure has been made to meet the specific objectives. These modifications are described in the respective parts.

PART I—GLOBAL OIL PRICE RISE AND POLICY OPTIONS FOR INDIA

As mentioned earlier, we first examine the impacts of global oil price rise on the Indian economy under some alternative policy options available to the government. A key characteristic of the petroleum products sector in India is that the prices of the major petroleum products such as petrol, diesel, kerosene and LPG, are set administratively by the government. We evaluate the impacts of a 70 per cent rise in global crude oil prices and 50 per cent rise in global petroleum products prices under three alternative policy options: (a) When the domestic prices of petroleum products are administratively kept unchanged by the government, (b) when the government administratively raises the price of petroleum products by 10 per cent, and (c) when administered pricing mechanism is replaced with market determined pricing for petroleum products.

The basic CGE model described above assumes that all domestic prices are market determined. For the petroleum products sector, this specification is modified to introduce administered pricing mechanism. For this the relevant domestic price equation (Equation 5 in Appendix A-4.1) for the petroleum products sector is modified as follows to incorporate the implicit variable rate of tax/subsidy that supports the administered price mechanism:

$$\overline{PD} = PPR \cdot (1 + t + vt)$$

where, $\overline{PD}$ is the domestic price administratively fixed by the government, PPR is the (endogenous) producer's price, t is the explicit (fixed) indirect tax rate imposed on the sector, and vt is the variable tax/subsidy rate that supports the administered price mechanism. The net-revenue from both the explicit and implicit tax accrues to the government account. This modified version of the model is used in the simulations described below.

This set of simulations are carried out with the following specifications: (a) we fix the government consumption and transfers to households in real terms at the base level; (b) all foreign inflows (to households, government, factor account and foreign savings) are kept fixed in dollar terms at the base level, and the nominal exchange rate adjusts to clear the foreign exchange market; (c) there is full employment in all the factor markets with given factor supply; and (d) the wage rate acts as the numeraire and so all the prices are relative to the fixed wage rate.

4.3 Scenarios

BASE Scenario: The base scenario reflects the structure of the Indian economy as described in the SAM for 2003-04. Thus, in this scenario all the direct and indirect taxes, tariffs and subsidy rates correspond to the observed values implicit in the SAM. Further, the domestic price of petroleum products are administratively fixed by the government reflecting the prevalent domestic policy regime for this sector. The administered pricing mechanism is supported by a variable rate of tax/subsidy, which is determined endogenously. In the SAM, this sector is net-taxed and the BASE scenario replicates the SAM values. Domestic price of all other sectors including crude oil are market determined in the Base and all the policy scenarios.

Policy Scenario: As mentioned earlier, we study the impact of rise in international oil price on the Indian economy. Specifically, we look at the impacts of a 70 per cent rise in the world price of crude oil and a 50 per cent rise in the world price of petroleum products. The analysis is carried out under three alternative scenarios that represent different policy choices as described below. In all these three scenarios, the scale parameter of the production function for the crude oil sector has been re-calibrated to ensure that the output of this sector does not expand by more than 5 per cent in the simulations in order to incorporate constraints in domestic capacity expansion in the foreseeable future.

(1) *ADBL (Administered price for petroleum price kept unchanged at Base Level):* In this scenario the government administratively keeps the price of domestically produced petroleum products unchanged at the base level. Thus, this scenario captures the effect of policy inaction on the domestic price front in the face of rising global oil prices.

(2) *AD10 (Hike in administered price for petroleum products by 10 per cent):* In this scenario the administered price for petroleum products is raised by 10 per cent over base level to reduce the subsidy burden on the government.

(3) *NADPR (No administered prices):* In this scenario we consider the case of market clearing domestic pricing system for petroleum products. This scenario helps in assessing the implications of dismantling the administered price regime for petroleum products in the context of rising global price of crude oil and petroleum products.

4.4 Results

The impacts of the rise in global prices of crude oil and petroleum prices under the above mentioned three policy scenarios are discussed here. We focus on key variables for the crude oil and petroleum products sectors, macro aggregates, distribution of incomes across household, the government account and savings and investment balance. Tables 4.2 to 4.6 report the levels of the variables of interest in the base scenario and their percentage changes from their base values under each of the three scenarios. Detailed results at the sectoral level are reported in Appendix A-4.2. It must be stressed here that the present analysis captures only static (one-period) impacts and dynamic impacts are not captured here. The results are discussed for each of the policy scenario in turn.

4.4.1 ADBL—Administered Price Kept Unchanged at Base Level

The rise in global prices (in US Dollar) of crude oil and petroleum products by 70 per cent and 50 per cent, respectively, results in a 13.3 per cent rise in the index of world price of India's import basket (see Table 4.3). But due to the presence of import duties and the 7.3 per cent depreciation of the nominal exchange rate, the effective rise in price of imports/exports of these two commodities is larger by 82 per cent and 61 per cent, respectively (Table 4.2). In the case of crude oil there is full pass through of the world price rise because the domestic prices are market determined leading to price rise of a similar order after adjusting for domestic taxes. This 'exogenous' price shock results in a windfall gain for this sector reflected in the doubling of the price of value added in this sector. Surprisingly, imports and domestic output increase significantly by 8.5 per cent and 4.8 per cent, respectively, to meet additional demand in both domestic and export market.[1] Crude oil being an intermediate in the petroleum products sector, the growth in domestic demand is due to the 2.1 per cent expansion of output of the latter. What explains the expansion of output in the petroleum products sector in the face of rising global prices?

In petroleum products sector, the effective price of imports/exports rise by 61 per cent (Table 4.2) as stated above. But with the government keeping the domestic market price of domestically produced good unchanged at base level, the market price of the composite good rises by only 3.1 per cent reflecting the low share of imports in this sector.[2] With the substantial change in the relative price of imports and domestically produced good there is a shift in demand in favour of the domestically produced good within this sector. While imports fall by 37 per cent, demand for domestically produced goods rise by 2.5 per cent over an already large base. This increase in demand for domestically produced good is shown as a right-ward shift in the demand curve from D0 to D1 in Figure 4.1, which describes the changes in the domestic supply and domestic demand conditions arising out of increase in the relative price of imports under invariant administered price. The initial equilibrium is at point A, where at the administratively determined price P0 the quantity demanded/supplied is Q0. With the price remaining unchanged at P0, the new level of demand is Q1. With the cost of crude oil increasing one would expect the supply curve to shift left-wards from S0 to S1. The new supply curve shows that amount Q1 will be supplied only at

1. We also ran this simulation without imposing the output constraint for the crude oil sector mentioned earlier. The results showed that output of this sector rose by 29 per cent, which seemed unreasonable in the current situation in the country. Hence, we stick to the version with a 5 per cent constraint on crude oil output expansion.

2. As can be seen from Appendix Table A-4.2.4 this rise in composite price results in a decline in household demand for petroleum products by 1 per cent.

a higher price P1. The results show that producers' price for domestic sales rise by 69 per cent. But with domestic market price being administratively fixed quantity Q1 will be supplied only if the government provides subsidy to the producers. The results show that the government needs to provide a net-subsidy of about 35 per cent (as against a net-tax of 9.6 per cent in the base case) to induce producers to meet the additional demand. It is worth noting that the sector's characteristic changes from one that is taxed by Rs.134 billions in the base case to one that is subsidised by Rs. 851 billions (corresponding to the area of the rectangle P0-B-C-P1 in Figure 4.1) in this scenario. This administered price cum subsidy regime has two other implications for the producer. One, it allows producers a much higher (49%) net-price for factor payments. Two, producers find it more profitable to sell in the domestic market than in the export market and consequently exports fall by 1 per cent over base despite the rise in global prices.

Table 4.2: Impacts on Crude and Petroleum Products Sectors

	BASE (Levels)	ADBL	AD10	NADPR
		(% change over BASE)		
Crude petroleum, natural gas				
Price of imports (Rs. per unit)	1.0	82.3	83.7	87.8
Domestic market price of domestic good (Rs. per unit)	1.0	88.6	87.1	83.6
Market price of composite good (Rs. per unit)	1.0	83.6	84.4	86.9
Producer price for domestic sales (Rs. per unit)	1.3	88.6	87.1	83.6
Producer price for exports (Rs. per unit)	1.0	82.3	83.7	87.8
Producer average sales price (Rs. per unit)	1.3	88.6	87.1	83.6
Producer's net-/value added price (Rs. per unit)	1.1	100.4	98.5	93.6
Real output (Rs. billions)	242.0	4.8	4.1	2.2
Domestic demand for domestic good (Rs. billions)	240.1	4.8	4.1	2.2
Exports (volume)	2.0	2.3	2.7	3.9
Imports (volume)	900.3	8.5	6.1	-0.1
Net-indirect tax revenue (Rs. billions)*	-68.4	-135.3	-133.3	-128.4
Petroleum products				
Price of imports (Rs. per unit)	1.0	60.9	62.1	65.7
Domestic market price of domestic good (Rs. per unit)	1.0	0.0	10.0	43.0
Market price of composite good (Rs. per unit)	1.0	3.1	12.8	44.4
Producer price for domestic sales (Rs. per unit)	0.9	68.8	58.7	43.0
Producer price for exports (Rs. per unit)	1.0	60.9	62.1	65.7
Producer average sales price (Rs. per unit)	0.9	68.1	59.0	45.2
Producer's net-/value added price (Rs. per unit)	0.2	48.5	3.4	-70.4
Real output (Rs. billions)	1679.2	2.1	0.2	-5.0
Domestic demand for domestic good (Rs. billions)	1535.8	2.5	0.02	-6.0
Exports (volume)	144.6	-1.0	1.6	4.5
Imports (volume)	105.8	-36.6	-32.4	-19.0
Net-indirect tax rate*	0.096	-0.351	-0.240	0.096
Net-indirect tax revenue (Rs. billions)*	134.2	-850.5	-534.5	180.3

Note: * For these two variables alone levels are reported for all the scenarios (not percentage change over BASE); negative values indicate subsidy.

Table 4.3: Macro Aggregates

	BASE (Levels)	ADBL	AD10	NADPR
		(% change over BASE)		
Real GDP total (Rs. billions)	25248.1	-0.5	-0.4	-0.4
Real GDP agriculture (Rs. billions)	5715.5	0.4	0.3	-0.2
Real GDP non-agriculture (Rs. billions)	19532.6	-0.7	-0.6	-0.5
Real private consumption (Rs. billions)	18322.9	0.5	-0.3	-2.3
Real investments (Rs. billions)	6647.2	-14.3	-11.5	-5.1
Domestic price index	1.000	1.0	1.9	4.7
Index of world price of imports	0.903	13.3	13.3	13.3
Nominal exchange rate (Rs. / US $)	1.000	7.3	8.0	10.5
Real exchange rate (Rs. / US $)	0.903	20.2	20.1	19.5

Note: Real Exchange Rate = Nominal Exchange Rate × (World Price Index ÷ Domestic Price Index).

Table 4.4: Household Incomes and Prices

Household Class	Per Capita Real Income				Per Capita Nominal Income				Consumer Price Index			
	BASE	ADBL	AD10	NADPR	BASE	ADBL	AD10	NADPR	BASE	ADBL	AD10	NADPR
	(Rs. '000)	(% change over BASE)			(Rs. '000)	(% change over BASE)			(Levels)	(% change over BASE)		
Rural 1 : 0 to 10%	3.7	0.2	-0.3	-1.7	3.7	1.2	1.2	1.4	1.0	0.9	1.5	3.2
Rural 2: 10% to 30%	6.2	0.1	-0.6	-2.3	6.2	1.0	0.8	0.7	1.0	1.0	1.5	3.1
Rural 3: 30% to 70%	10.8	1.1	0.4	-1.3	10.8	2.0	1.9	1.9	1.0	0.9	1.5	3.2
Rural 4: 70% to 90%	30.6	1.6	0.3	-2.4	30.6	2.4	1.7	0.7	1.0	0.8	1.3	3.1
Rural 5: 90% to 100%	85.5	1.3	0.0	-2.9	85.5	2.2	1.5	0.6	1.0	0.9	1.6	3.7
Urban 1 : 0 to 10%	5.5	-0.1	-0.6	-1.9	5.5	0.8	0.7	0.8	1.0	1.0	1.4	2.7
Urban 2: 10% to 30%	10.5	-0.3	-0.9	-2.5	10.5	0.7	0.5	0.3	1.0	1.0	1.4	2.9
Urban 3: 30% to 70%	22.0	0.0	-0.6	-2.4	22.0	0.9	0.8	0.7	1.0	0.9	1.4	3.2
Urban 4: 70% to 90%	57.3	0.3	-0.6	-2.8	57.3	1.1	0.8	0.4	1.0	0.8	1.4	3.2
Urban 5: 90% to 100%	166.4	0.4	-0.6	-3.1	166.4	1.2	0.9	0.4	1.0	0.8	1.4	3.5

Table 4.5: Government Account (Rs. Billions, Nominal)

	BASE (Levels)	ADBL	AD10	NADPR
		(% change over BASE)		
Direct tax revenue	1245.1	1.4	1.1	0.7
Tariff revenue	556.5	8.1	9.3	12.5
Net-indirect tax revenue	1920.9	-58.7	-40.8	0.1
Non-tax revenue	824.4	2.9	1.6	-0.6
Foreign receipts	-24.8	7.3	8.0	10.5
Total revenue	4522.1	-23.1	-15.7	1.6
Government consumption	3279.3	0.6	0.9	1.8
Transfers to households	2430.5	3.1	4.0	6.8
Exports subsidy	15.6	14.6	15.5	18.2
Total expenditure	5725.4	1.7	2.3	4.0
Government dis-savings	-1203.4	94.9	69.7	13.0

Table 4.6: Savings-Investment Balance (Rs. Billions, Nominal)

	BASE (Levels)	ADBL	AD10	NADPR
		(% change over BASE)		
Private savings	8193.7	2.4	1.7	0.8
Government savings	-1203.4	94.9	69.7	13.0
Foreign savings	-343.1	7.3	8.0	10.5
Total savings	6647.2	-14.6	-10.9	-1.9
Total investment	6647.2	-14.6	-10.9	-1.9

Figure 4.1: Changes in Domestic Supply, Domestic Demand and Subsidies under Administered Pricing

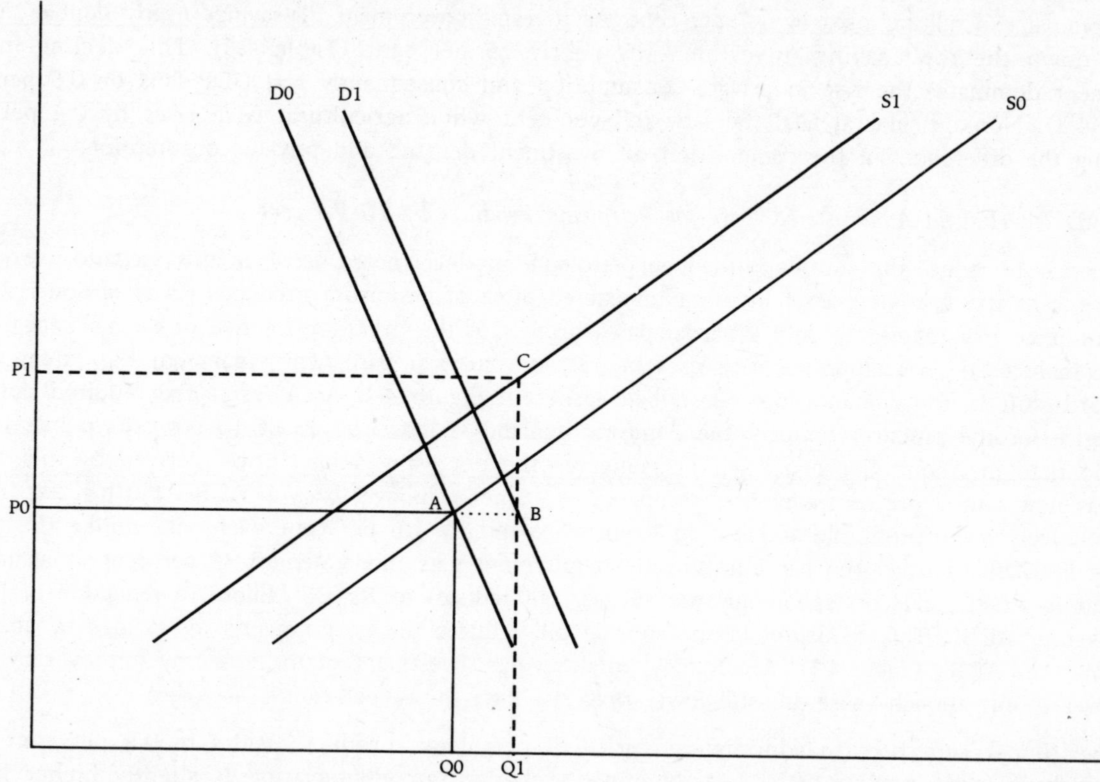

As seen earlier, with the administered price being unchanged at the base level, the composite market price of petroleum products rise by only 3.1 per cent. Consequently, the price shock to the economy in general is low. Overall domestic price index rises by 1 per cent (Table 4.3). Given that we have fixed the foreign inflows in dollar terms at the base level, nominal exchange rate (Rupee to Dollar) depreciates by 7.3 per cent to clear the foreign exchange market. The domestic price rise along with the depreciation of the nominal exchange and the 13.3 per cent rise in the world price results in a real exchange rate depreciation of 20.2 per cent over the base.

The price impacts in this scenario is not uniform across sectors (see Appendix Table A-4.2.1). The price rise is mostly in the intermediate commodities such as coal tar products, fertilisers, organic heavy chemicals, etc., that witness somewhat large price rise. Most consumer goods price show only moderate price rise, and some important consumption items such as paddy and textiles products even witness a decline in price due to changes in demand and supply conditions. Consequently, household specific consumer price indices show only moderate rise ranging between 0.8 per cent to 1 per cent across different household classes (Table 4.4). With nominal incomes rising by a higher percentage for all households except the bottom two urban classes, real incomes rise for all households with the exceptions noted above. The results also show that each of the rural households gain more than their urban counterparts, but within each rural and urban areas the upper classes generally gain more than the lower classes. Consequent upon the rise in household real incomes, aggregate private consumption rises by 0.5 per cent (Table 4.3).

The other side of the administered price regime is the huge rise in government subsidy for petroleum products noted earlier. Government's net-indirect tax revenue falls by 59 per cent (Table 4.5). The rise in world market price of crude oil and petroleum products increases the tariff base and results in a rise in tariff revenue by 8.1 per cent. Indeed direct tax collection also expands due to rise in nominal incomes seen earlier. Foreign receipts of the government in Rupee terms rise due to the exchange rate depreciation noted earlier. The rise in revenue from these sources, however, is inadequate to compensate the loss in net-indirect tax revenue, and thus total revenue of the government falls by 23 per cent over base. Although government's consumption expenditure and transfers to households are kept fixed in real terms, total nominal expenditure rises by 1.7 per cent. As a result government dis-savings nearly doubles, which brings down the total savings/investment by nearly 15 per cent (Table 4.6). This decline in real investment dominates the rise in private consumption and consequently real GDP falls by 0.5 per cent (Table 4.3). Non-agricultural GDP falls by 0.7 per cent while agricultural GDP rises by 0.4 per cent reflecting the differences in the composition of investment demand and private consumption.

4.4.2 AD10—Hike in Administered Price for Petroleum Products by 10 Per cent

In order to reduce the subsidy burden on petroleum products noted above in this scenario, we specify a 10 per cent rise over base level in the administered price of petroleum products. As is obvious, this 10 per cent price rise represents only a partial pass through of the import price rise of 62 per cent in this sector (Table 4.2). The composite price rises by 13 per cent over base, which dampens the extent of the rightward shift in the demand curve described earlier in Figure 4.1. As a result the required domestic sales price for the producer to meet the domestic demand is lower by about 10 per cent points in this scenario than in ADBL. Consequently, this squeezes the net-/value added price received by this sector, which is now only 3 per cent over base compared to 48 per cent over base in ADBL. Further, exports are now relatively more profitable and indeed exports expand by 1.6 per cent over base unlike the fall in exports in ADBL. Finally, the per unit subsidy requirement gets moderated to 24 per cent as against 35 per cent in ADBL, and correspondingly the subsidy bill reduces to Rs.535 billions, a reduction of Rs.316 billions over ADBL. This reduction in the subsidy bill reduces the government's dis-savings by about 25 per cent over ADBL (Table 4.5). Accordingly, total savings/investment of the economy improves by 3 per cent over ADBL, though these are still lower than the base by 11 per cent (Table 4.6).

The 10 per cent hike in administered price of petroleum product results in 0.9 per cent point additional rise over ADBL (Table 4.3). Nominal exchange rate depreciation is slightly higher in this scenario than ADBL, but real exchange rate appreciates a bit over ADBL due to the higher domestic price rise in AD10.

The near doubling of domestic price change naturally results in large rise in consumer prices in this scenario than under ADBL (Table 4.4). Further, the rise in consumer price is more than the rise in nominal income for all classes except the top three rural class resulting in loss in real income over base. Indeed for all the households there is a real income loss in this scenario compared to ADBL. Consequently, aggregate private consumption falls in this scenario by 0.3 per cent (Table 4.3) over base as against a 0.5 per cent rise in ADBL. Thus, there is clearly a short-term welfare loss for households in AD10 compared to ADBL.

The changes in the consumption and investment seen above results in a somewhat smaller GDP loss of 0.4 per cent in this scenario over the base. Similarly, the gain in agricultural GDP and loss in non-agricultural GDP are lower in AD10 than in ADBL.

4.4.3 NADPR—No Administered Prices

We now consider the case where administered pricing mechanism for petroleum products is dismantled, and the domestic price is completely market determined, representing a complete pass through of the rise in international price of this sector. All other sectors continue to face market determined prices. With market determined pricing system, the 50 per cent rise in world price of petroleum products results in a 43 per cent and 44 per cent rise in domestic market price and composite price of this sector, respectively (Table 4.2). Producer's domestic sales price rises by 43 per cent, while the export price rises more (66%) because of the depreciation of the nominal exchange rate, and consequently the average sales price realised by the producer (weighted average of the export price and domestic sale price) rises by 45 per cent. However, most of this rise in the average sales price is eaten away by the increase in input costs, including the international price of crude oil, and consequently the net-price of this sector falls by 70 per cent over base, as opposed to the rise noticed under administered pricing scenarios. Following the rise in both domestic and import prices, domestic demand for domestically produced petroleum products decline by 6 per cent, while import volumes decline by 19 per cent. Though export volumes rise by 4.5 per cent in response to the rise in export price it is insufficient to offset the contraction in domestic demand, and thus output of this sector falls by 5 per cent over base. It may be noted, that in this scenario this sector continues to be net-taxed at the base ad valorem rate yielding a much larger net-tax revenue due to the dominant effect of price rise.

Petroleum products being an important intermediate good for several sectors, the rise in its price has adverse effects on several sectors. From the detailed tables in Appendix A-4.4.2, it may be seen that sectors that are most affected are coal tar products, chemicals, fertilisers, construction and other transports services. Large rise in the price of these commodities are seen, which adversely affects their demand and hence output. It may be of interest to note that the price of other transport services rise by close to 9 per cent, which has a cascading effect on all other sectors.

As a result of these sectoral changes, there is a fall in real GDP of 0.4 per cent (Table 4.3), consisting of a 0.2 per cent decline in agricultural GDP and 0.5 per cent decline in non-agricultural GDP. Aggregate price index rise by 4.7 per cent resulting in a contraction of private consumption by 2.3 per cent, and investments by 5.1 per cent. Given our assumptions of fixed foreign inflows nominal exchange rate depreciates by 10.5 per cent, while real exchange depreciates by 19.5 per cent.

The changes in prices and output have adverse effects on the real incomes of all household classes (Table 4.4). Predictably, the urban households in each class suffer more loss than their rural counterpart. The richer classes in both rural and urban area suffer larger losses due to higher oil intensity of their consumption pattern.

The rise in world market price increases the tariff base and results in a rise in tariff revenue by 12.5 per cent over base (Table 4.5). Indeed direct tax collection and also domestic net-indirect tax collection expands marginally due to rise in nominal incomes (Table 4.4) and domestic prices in other sectors (see Appendix Tables A-4.2.1 and A-4.2.2). Foreign receipts of the government in Rupee terms rise due to the exchange rate depreciation. Non-tax revenue (profits from public sector enterprises) falls by 0.6 per cent due to a reduction in the price of capital. All these result in a rise in total revenue of the government by 1.6 per cent. On the other hand, government spends more on its own consumption, transfers to households and subsidy payments in nominal terms leading to a rise in total government expenditure by 4 per cent. Consequently, dis-savings by the government rises by 13 per cent, way below what was seen under administered pricing scenarios.

Turning to the savings-investment balance, private savings rise marginally by 0.8 per cent (Table 4.6) due to rise in nominal incomes. Overall savings and investments in the economy now decline by 1.9 per cent much lower than the decline seen in the earlier scenarios.

4.5 Conclusions

To summarise the above results, in the short-run, GDP falls by about half a percentage point over the base levels, due to the rise in international prices of crude oil by 70 per cent and of petroleum products by 50 per cent, irrespective of the pricing mechanism prevailing in the petroleum products sector. The rise in world prices results in a 1 per cent rise in aggregate domestic price index even when the government keeps the domestic price of petroleum products unchanged. The domestic price rises by 1.9 per cent following a 10 per cent hike in the administered price of petroleum products, and by as much as 4.7 per cent when the administered pricing mechanism is replaced with market determined pricing system. The rise in world prices results in depreciation of the nominal exchange rate by 7 per cent to 10 per cent under alternative pricing scenarios, with the depreciation being highest under free market situation. However, real exchange rate depreciation is about 20 per cent irrespective of the pricing regime. Domestic price rise by 84 per cent and 43 per cent for crude oil and petroleum products sector, respectively, when prices are not administratively controlled.

Under a market determined price regime, global oil price rise unambiguously hurts all households across both rural and urban areas. Urban households in each class suffer greater loss in real incomes than their counterparts in rural areas. Further, the loss for the richer classes in both rural and urban areas is more than that for the poorer classes. Administered pricing benefits or mutes the real income losses for most households. Users of petroleum products benefit from the administered price mechanism when the administered price is set below the free market price level. When the prices are left unchanged aggregate private consumption rises by 0.5 per cent in real terms, while a rise in price of petroleum products result in a decline in consumption.

When the administered prices do not respond adequately to the rise in global prices, the characteristic of the petroleum products sector changes from being net-taxed to being net-subsidised. Government's subsidy bill due to administered pricing works out to Rs.851 billions when the price of petroleum products is left unchanged at the base level, as against a tax revenue of Rs.134 billions in the base case. The subsidy bill reduces by Rs.316 billions following a 10 per cent hike in the administered price. In contrast under market determined prices, government get a larger tax revenue compared to the base. Under administered pricing, the subsidy provided to the petroleum products sector also benefits the producers in the form of higher net-/value-added price, which rise by nearly 50 per cent when the prices are not changed compared to a 70 per cent decline in the net-price under market determined pricing system. In other words, market determined prices forces the producers to absorb part of the global price rise.

The rise in government subsidy for petroleum products has adverse effects on the government's savings, and hence national savings and investment. Government's dis-savings nearly doubles when the administered price is kept unchanged, while a 10 per cent hike in the price reduces the government's dis-savings by 25 per cent. In contrast, government dis-savings rise by just 13 per cent under free market regime compared to base. The main cost of global oil price rise of the order considered here is in the form of a 5.1 per cent fall in real investments in the economy even when the pricing in the petroleum products sector is market determined. Real investments decline by a significantly larger amounts when the prices are administratively fixed and do not respond adequately to the change in the global price conditions. Real investments decline by 14.3 per cent under no change in administered price, compared to 11.5 per cent fall when administered prices are hiked by 10 per cent.

Since investments play a critical role in determining future growth of the economy, there is clear short-run *versus* long-run trade off of maintaining an administered price regime for petroleum products in a context of rising global oil prices. Consumers benefit at the cost of investments under administered pricing.

The main message that emerges from the above is that the global oil price rise will have adverse impacts on the Indian economy in the form of rising prices, loss in GDP and real investments. The current administered price regime that limits the price pass through does seem to help mute most of the short-run adverse effects on the households with only marginally more adverse impact on the short-run growth of the economy compared to free market situation. However, it puts severe pressure on the fiscal balance of the government, which significantly reduces the level of real investments in the economy that are critical for long-run growth. Choosing to retain administered price regime over market determined price regime essentially involves trading off fiscal balance and long-run growth for short-run benefits.

PART II—GLOBAL ECONOMIC RECESSION: IMPACTS AND COUNTER MEASURES

The recession in the global economy witnessed since the second half of 2008 has resulted in a slow down in India's export performance and in capital inflows into the country. In response to this reduction in aggregate demand, the government has taken several fiscal and monetary counter-measures. These include a cut in indirect taxes, accelerating the implementation of several infrastructure projects, reducing interest rates, easing the liquidity available with the banks, etc. This part analyses the likely impacts of the global recession on GDP and its distribution across household classes, and the effectiveness of some of the government's counter measures that aim to increase aggregate demand, *viz.*, a rise in government consumption and a cut in indirect taxes. Besides these two policy measures, we also study the impact of an expansion of the National Rural Employment Guarantee Scheme (NREGS), as a policy meant to protect the rural poor.

4.6 Extensions to the Basic CGE Model

Export demand: The primary shock of interest to us here is the autonomous fall in export demand reflecting the recessionary environment in the global economy. The basic CGE model described earlier captures only the supply of exports and assumes that the rest of the world would consume all that India can export. In the context of global recession, this assumption on export demand is obviously not valid, and the basic CGE has to be extended to incorporate an export demand function. Accordingly, following an export demand function is now incorporated into the CGE model:

$$E_i = \overline{EX_i} \cdot \left(\frac{PWEX_i}{PWE_i} \right)^{\varepsilon_i}$$

where, E_i is the sectoral export, which depends upon the ratio of an exogenously fixed reference export price (PWEX) and an endogenous actual export price (PWE), both in foreign currency. This equation along with the export supply function (Equations 22 and 23 in Appendix A-4.1) define a market for exportables, and this market solves for the export price (PWE) in foreign currency. This formulation allows us to shock the export demand by changing the base export levels $\overline{EX}$.

Labour market: The other important question that is of interest pertains to the distribution of income across households, and the role of NREGS in particular. The NREGS is basically an employment generation programme for the poor and guarantees to offer jobs to all those willing to undertake manual labour. As it is aimed at unskilled rural labour, it is essential to bring forth disaggregation of the labour market into the analysis. Accordingly, we first modify the SAM by distinguishing six types of labour based on the broad industry group in which they are employed. Thus, we have agricultural labour (sectors 1 to 16), mining labour (sectors 17 to 20), two types of manufacturing labour (Manufacturing 1 employed in labour-intensive manufacturing sectors 21 to 34, and Manufacturing 2 employed in capital-intensive manufacturing sectors 35 to 54), construction labour (sector 55) and services labour (sectors 56 to 71). Appendix A-4.4 describes the steps involved in modifying the SAM. In the model, we allow limited mobility of each of these labour types within the sub-sectors of these broad industry groups. However, on the production side, every sector is assumed to employ only one of the six types of labour. Thus, there are six labour markets with separate wage rates in each of them. Accordingly, the variables $LEMPL_h$ (labour employment for household h), L_i (labour demand in sector i), W (wage rate) and LUNEMP (labour unemployment) and the parameters $LENDWSH_h$ (share of household h in total labour supply) and $\overline{LENDOW_h}$ (labour endowment with household h) now have an additional subscript 'l' running over the six labour types. The labour employment equation 11 in Appendix A-4.4.1 is now written as,

$$LEMPL_{h,l} = LENDWSH_{i,l} \cdot \sum_i L_{i,l}$$

Similarly, the labour market equilibrium (Equation 38 in Appendix A-4.4.1) is rewritten as,

$$\sum_h \overline{LENDOW_{h,l}} = \sum_i L_{i,l} + LUNEMP_l$$

Factor unemployment: As already stated the basic version of the model permits two alternative closures. It can either solve for full employment level equilibrium factor price or allow for unemployment of factors when the factor prices are fixed. As we are interested in simulating the recessionary environment, we assume that the ensuing output loss would result in unemployment in all factor markets; i.e., all the six labour markets and the sectoral capital markets.

NREGS: As mentioned earlier, the NREGS is primarily targeted at the rural poor who are ready to undertake manual labour at the wage rate offered by the government. Thus, it is the unemployed labour in rural areas who are expected to offer themselves for employment under the programme. As per the current government norms, wage bill should constitute 60 per cent of the total expenditure under the programme. The non-wage component of expenditure under this programme would thus be two-thirds of the wage bill and this can generate demand for certain capital goods. These features of the NREGS are incorporated into the CGE model through the equations (a) to (e) below, while equations (f) and (g) below are modifications to equations 13 and 34 in Appendix A-4.4.1, respectively.

$$LSEGS = \sum_h EGSCLAS_h \left(\Sigma_l LENDWSH_{h,l} \cdot LUNEMP_l\right) \quad \text{(a)}$$

$$LDEGS = COVFAC \cdot LSEGS \quad \text{(b)}$$

$$WGBLEGS = WGREGS \cdot LDEGS \quad \text{(c)}$$

$$NWBLEGS = (2/3) \cdot WGBLEGS \quad \text{(d)}$$

$$ZEGS_i = (ZSH_i \cdot NWBLEGS)/PQ_i \quad \text{(e)}$$

$$\begin{aligned} YH_h = {} & \sum_l W_l LEMPL_{h,l} + \sum_i \pi_i KEMPL_{h,i} + \sum NFIW \cdot EXR + TRANS_h \cdot \overline{PQ} \\ & + REM_h \cdot EXR + EGSLABSH_h WGBLEGS \end{aligned} \quad \text{(f)}$$

$$GE = \sum_i G_i \cdot PQ_i + \sum_h TRANS_h \cdot \overline{PQ} + GS + WGBLEGS + NWBLEGS \quad \text{(g)}$$

Supply of labour to the programme (LSEGS) depends on the total amount of unemployed labour ($LUNEMP_l$) available with the eligible household classes (EGSCLAS=1 for the eligible classes, = 0 for others). It is assumed that the unemployed labour belonging to the bottom three rural classes (constituting 70 per cent of the rural population) are likely to offer themselves for employment under the NREGS. The employment created under the programme (LDEGS) depends upon the coverage factor (COVFAC), which can take any value between 0 and 1. Wage bill of the programme (WGBLEGS) then depends upon an exogenously fixed wage rate for the programme (WGREGS), and the non-wage bill of the programme (NWBLEGS) is two-thirds of the wage bill as is mandated under the programme. The non-wage bill generates demand for certain capital goods ($ZEGS_i$) based on fixed proportions (ZSH_i) and composite price (PQ_i). Equation (f) above is now the modified equation for household income incorporating both the labour type disaggregation and the NREGS income. Equation (g) above is the new equation for government expenditure.

4.7 Scenarios

BASE scenario: The Base scenario reflects the structure of the Indian economy as described in the SAM for 2003-04. Thus, in this scenario all the direct and indirect taxes, tariffs and subsidy rates correspond to the observed values implicit in the SAM. Domestic price of all sectors are market determined in the Base and in all the scenarios. Foreign inflows, and factor prices are fixed at the levels implicit in the SAM. The model solution of the Base scenario reproduces the SAM values of the exchange rate, sectoral prices, outputs and trade flows, generates full employment of all factors[3], household and government incomes, consumption and savings, national savings and investment and hence the GDP.

Scenarios: In all six scenarios are studied here, which can be clubbed into two broad sets. The first set of scenarios examines the impacts on the Indian economy of the shocks emanating from the rest of the world. These can be further sub-grouped into two categories, those that are expected to have a negative effect on India, and another that could potentially be positive for India. The second set of scenarios relates to some of the government fiscal initiatives on both expenditure and revenue side as counter-measures to the world economic shocks. Since CGE models are real models they are not suitable for analysing impact of monetary measures adopted by the government.

The six scenarios are described in Table 4.7. In all these scenarios, (i) different components of foreign inflows (and hence the total foreign inflows) are kept fixed as described in Table 4.7 and the exchange rate adjusts to clear the foreign exchange market, and (ii) factor prices are kept fixed at the base levels and unemployment of all factors are allowed.

Table 4.7: Scenarios

Number Description

Set 1: External shocks to Indian economy:

1a – World economic slow down:

(A) Aggregate exports decline by 10 per cent in Dollar value terms from the base levels, following the slowdown in the world economy. Foreign inflows are kept fixed at the base levels. This scenario will help quantify the pure effects of exports fall.

(B) (A) plus foreign inflows decline by 29 per cent comprising of 10 per cent decline in remittances to households (of Rs. 780 billion in Base) and 15 per cent decline in foreign savings (of Rs. 339 billion in Base). Decline in remittances may be expected following adverse income effect of Indians working abroad due to the global economic slowdown. Similarly, decline in foreign savings may be expected following a reduction in investible funds in the world as a whole.

1b – Fall in world oil price:

(C) (B) plus 10 per cent decline in world price of crude oil and petroleum products over base levels. This scenario is expected to reflect crude oil price of around US$40 a barrel currently prevailing. In the model price of domestic crude is administered, that of imported crude depends on the world price, and that of petroleum products is market determined. This is to reflect the fact that though in practice price of some petroleum products is administered, the government does from time to time passes on part of the world price to consumers.

Set 2 – Counter-measures

(D) (C) plus 5 per cent rise in government consumption of all goods and services in real terms as a direct counter measure to boost demand.

(E) (D) plus 25 per cent across the board cut in indirect tax rates from their base levels, except for petroleum products corresponding to the tax cuts announced by the government recently. This measure too is aimed at boosting demand via the price channel.

(F) (E) plus expansion of National Rural Employment Guarantee Scheme (NREGS) to protect the real incomes of the bottom three rural classes. It is assumed that all the unemployed in rural areas belonging to the bottom three rural classes (accounting for bottom 70 per cent of rural population) would seek employment under the NREGS. The simulation here assumes full coverage under the programme; i.e., (a) all those seeking employment under the programme are offered employment, and (b) employment under the programme is for as along as it is required, which could be more than the 100 days that the existing programme offers. The exogenously fixed wage rate for the NREGS is set at a lower level than the market wage rate (90 per cent of the average market wage rate over all labour types) so that NREGS does not act as a substitute for normal economic activity.

4.8 Results

The simulation results are discussed here. We focus on key macro aggregates, distribution of real incomes across households, the government account, and savings and investment balance. Tables 4.8 to 4.13 report the levels of the variables of interest in the base scenario and their percentage changes from their base values under each of the six scenarios. Detailed results at the sectoral level are reported in

3. Full employment in the BASE scenario is interpreted as the level of employment implicit in the SAM. To the extent that there are unutilised resources in the economy that are not captured in the SAM, the model too would not capture such unemployment in the solution to the BASE scenario.

Appendix A-4.4.3. It must be stressed here that the present analysis captures only static (one-period) impacts and dynamic impacts are not captured here. The results are discussed for each of the scenarios in turn.

4.8.1 Impacts of World Economic Slow Down

4.8.1.1 Scenario A—Exports Fall

As expected, a fall in exports adversely affects the final demand in the Indian economy leading to fall in output and income. If exports decline by 10 per cent in dollar terms, aggregate GDP loss turns out to be 3.3 per cent over the Base scenario (Table 4.8). The manufacturing sector is more adversely affected than agriculture or services since it accounts for most of India's exports. The loss in income results in a fall in private consumption by 3.1 per cent.[4] The across the board decline in income has strong impact on all three components of national savings—private, government and foreign (Table 4.9). As a result, real investment falls by 9.7 per cent, most of which is due to fall in nominal savings and a small part due to rise in prices (see below). Thus, effects of exports fall operate in a major way through the investment channel, apart from the direct channel. Total savings and investment fall by 1.3 percentage point of GDP (Table 4.10). Given that foreign inflows are fixed in dollar terms, the fall in exports results in exchange rate depreciation by 5.3 per cent in nominal terms and by 4.4 per cent in real terms. The depreciating currency and the downturn in the economy lead to fall in real imports by 9 per cent. The fall in GDP naturally affects all sources of government revenue (Table 4.11). While government consumption and transfers are fixed in real terms, the nominal expenditures on these items increase to price rise.

Table 4.8: Macro Aggregates

				I	II	III	IV
				- 10% fall in export value - 29% fall in foreign inflows - 10% fall in crude price	I plus Govt. real consumption increase by 5%	II plus indirect taxes cut by 25%	III plus full coverage NREG's
	Base (Levels)	(A) Exports fall	(B) = (A) + Inflows fall	(C) = (B) + Global oil price fall	(D) = (C) + Govt. cons rise	(E) = (D) + Indirect tax cut	(F) = (E) + NREGS
				(% change from BASE)			
Real GDP total (Rs.billions)	25189.2	-3.3	-5.1	-4.2	-3.5	-2.7	-2.2
Real GDP agriculture (Rs.billions)	5705.7	-2.5	-3.9	-3.2	-2.8	-1.8	-1.1
Real GDP industry (Rs.billions)	5768.5	-5.2	-8.0	-6.9	-7.2	-7.7	-6.8
Real GDP services (Rs.billions)	13715.0	-2.9	-4.3	-3.5	-2.2	-1.0	-0.8
Real private consumption (Rs.billions)	18320.8	-3.1	-4.6	-3.6	-2.9	-0.1	0.3
Real investments (Rs.billions)	6631.4	-9.7	-15.2	-12.9	-15.0	-19.1	-20.7
Real exports volume (base US$ value)	4353.0	-5.6	-5.8	-5.2	-5.1	-5.6	-5.0
Real imports volume (base US$ value)	4934.1	-9.0	-12.0	-10.3	-10.4	-10.2	-10.2
Aggregate price index	1.0	0.9	0.6	0.1	0.3	-0.5	0.1
Nominal exchange rate (Rs./US $)	1.0	5.3	5.5	5.1	5.1	5.2	5.1
Real exchange rate (Rs./US $)	0.9	4.4	4.9	3.1	3.2	2.8	3.5
				(% of Nominal GDP)			

4. Appendix Table A-4.2.1 to A-4.2.4 report sectoral output, private consumption, real imports and exports, respectively.

Why do prices rise in the face of a fall in exports? As mentioned above, the nominal exchange rate depreciates following fall in exports in order to meet the foreign exchange constraint. This raises the price of imports in rupee terms. Given the Leontief type raw materials requirement, the rise in price of imported raw materials, coupled with fixed factor prices, results in a rise in the unit cost of production, and hence domestic prices (Appendix Table A-4.3.5). Aggregate domestic price index rises by 0.9 per cent over Base scenario (Table 4.8). Given that both import price and domestic price increase in this scenario, the so-called composite price (which determines private consumption and investment in real terms) too rises (Appendix Table A-4.3.6). Hence, real investments fall by a larger proportion than fall in nominal investment as noted above.

Table 4.9: Savings-Investment Balance (Rs. Billions, Nominal)

	Base (Levels)	(A) Exports Fall	(B) = (A) + Inflows Fall	(C) = (B) + Global Oil Price Fall	(D) = (C) + Govt. Cons. Rise	(E) = (D) + Indirect Tax Cut	(F) = (E) + NREGS
		(% change from BASE)					
Private savings	8165.0	-3.7	-6.4	-5.5	-4.8	-4.1	-3.7
Government savings	-1209.0	18.2	27.2	22.1	32.9	72.5	93.1
Foreign savings	-339.3	5.3	21.4	20.9	20.9	21.0	20.9
Total savings	6616.6	-8.1	-14.0	-11.9	-13.5	-19.9	-23.0
Total investment	6616.6	-8.2	-14.0	-11.9	-13.5	-19.9	-23.0

Table 4.10: Key Macro Variables as a Percentage of Nominal GDP

	Base	(A) Exports Fall	(B) = (A) + Inflows Fall	(C) = (B) + Global Oil Price Fall	(D) = (C) + Govt. Cons. Rise	(E) = (D) + Indirect Tax Cut	(F) = (E) + NREGS
		(% change from BASE)					
Indirect tax revenue	8.5	8.5	8.4	8.4	8.4	6.1	6.4
Total revenue	18.8	18.8	18.6	18.6	18.6	16.3	16.6
Government consumption	13.0	13.5	13.8	13.6	14.2	14.0	14.0
Total expenditure	23.6	24.7	25.1	24.7	25.2	24.8	26.1
Trade deficit	2.1	2.2	1.6	1.6	1.6	1.7	1.6
Private savings	32.4	32.3	32.0	32.0	32.0	32.0	32.0
Government savings	-4.8	-5.9	-6.4	-6.1	-6.6	-8.5	-9.5
Foreign savings	-1.3	-1.5	-1.7	-1.7	-1.7	-1.7	-1.7
Total savings	26.3	25.0	23.9	24.2	23.7	21.8	20.8

Table 4.11: Government Account (Rs. Billions, Nominal)

	Base (Levels)	(A) Exports Fall	(B) = (A) + Inflows Fall	(C) = (B) + Global Oil Price Fall	(D) = (C) + Govt. Cons. Rise	(E) = (D) + Indirect Tax Cut	(F) = (E) + NREGS
		(% change from BASE)					
Direct tax revenue	1241.8	-2.8	-4.9	-4.2	-3.4	-2.5	-1.9
Tariff revenue	554.0	-4.4	-7.6	-7.5	-7.8	-7.9	-7.8
Indirect tax revenue	2150.5	-3.8	-6.9	-6.1	-5.4	-30.6	-26.8
Non-tax revenue	822.3	-3.3	-5.2	-4.4	-3.9	-3.0	-2.6
Foreign receipts	-24.5	5.3	5.5	5.1	5.1	5.2	5.1
Total revenue	4744.0	-3.6	-6.2	-5.5	-4.9	-16.0	-14.0
Government consumption	3275.5	0.6	0.4	0.2	5.2	4.7	5.1
Transfers to households	2424.0	1.3	1.1	0.4	0.2	-0.8	-1.0
Domestic subsidy	238.0	-0.3	-2.2	-4.2	-4.5	-4.9	-5.1
Exports subsidy	15.5	-5.3	-5.0	-5.3	-7.0	-8.8	-9.9
Total expenditure	5953.0	0.8	0.6	0.1	2.7	2.0	7.7
Government dis-savings	-1209.0	18.2	27.2	22.1	32.9	72.5	93.1

Table 4.12: Labour Market Results

	Labour Supply (millions)	Daily Wage Rate (Rs.)	Unemployment (% of Labour Supply)					
			(A) Exports Fall	(B) = (A) + Inflows Fall	(C) = (B) + Global Oil Price Fall	(D) = (C) + Govt. Cons. Rise	(E) = (D) + Indirect Tax Cut	(F) = (E) + NREGS
Agricultural	238.6	51.4	2.7	4.3	3.6	2.7	1.8	1.2
Mining & quarrying	2.2	342.2	2.3	3.9	7.1	6.9	6.7	6.5
Manufacturing-1	31.5	85.8	4.6	6.7	5.6	5.0	4.4	4.1
Manufacturing-2	16.4	176.5	5.4	7.9	6.6	6.1	5.7	5.3
Construction	22.7	217.7	8.6	13.8	11.7	11.4	11.1	10.9
Services	96.7	277.4	2.8	4.2	3.5	2.7	1.8	1.3
Total	408.1		3.3	5.1	4.3	3.5	2.7	2.2

As mentioned earlier, the base scenario is one of full employment of both labour and capital. The slow down of the domestic economy due to fall in exports results in an across the board unemployment of all labour types (Table 4.12) and all the sector specific capital (Appendix Table A-4.3.7). In particular, labour employed in the manufacturing sector suffers larger unemployment due to the higher export dependence of manufacturing sectors. Construction sector suffers the highest degree of unemployment of both labour and capital due to fall in investment demand. Given that this sector is non-tradeable, the entire burden of adjustment has to be borne by domestic producers. Consequent upon the unemployment of both factors of production, all households suffer loss in real incomes (Table 4.13). For each class, urban households suffer relatively larger income loss than their rural counterpart.

Table 4.13: Per Capita Real Income (Rs. '000)

	Base (Levels)	(A) Exports Fall	(B) = (A) + Inflows Fall	(C) = (B) + Global Oil Price Fall	(D) = (C) + Govt. Cons. Rise	(E) = (D) + Indirect Tax Cut	(F) = (E) + NREGS
		(% change from BASE)					
Rural 1 : 0 to 10%	288.1	-3.1	-4.4	-3.6	-3.2	-1.7	5.2
Rural 2: 10% to 30%	958.1	-3.6	-5.0	-4.0	-3.6	-1.8	4.3
Rural 3: 30% to 70%	3316.4	-2.6	-5.2	-4.3	-3.9	-2.3	2.1
Rural 4: 70% to 90%	4721.5	-3.5	-5.4	-4.4	-4.0	-1.9	-1.5
Rural 5: 90% to 100%	6591.3	-3.6	-5.2	-4.1	-3.7	-1.5	-1.1
Urban 1 : 0 to 10%	164.2	-3.6	-5.0	-4.0	-3.2	-1.5	-1.2
Urban 2: 10% to 30%	630.4	-3.9	-5.5	-4.3	-3.4	-1.5	-1.2
Urban 3: 30% to 70%	2640.6	-3.6	-5.7	-4.5	-3.6	-1.7	-1.3
Urban 4: 70% to 90%	3439.5	-3.8	-5.6	-4.4	-3.6	-1.5	-1.1
Urban 5: 90% to 100%	4994.1	-3.8	-5.4	-4.3	-3.5	-1.3	-1.0

4.8.1.2 Scenario B—Exports and Foreign Inflows Fall

Decline in capital flows along with exports fall discussed above has additional adverse effect on savings and investment. While foreign savings fall by about 16 per cent over and above that in scenario A, other sources of savings too fall moderately (Table 4.9). Total investment fall by 15 per cent in real terms. Consequently, GDP falls by 1.8 per cent over and above the 3.3 per cent fall in GDP in scenario A (Table 4.8). The combined effect on GDP, thus, turns out to be a fall of 5.1 per cent. At equilibrium, changes in exchange rate due to fall in foreign capital inflows is not substantial as it is accompanied by much larger fall in imports in this scenario compared to the previous scenario. Consequent upon the larger GDP loss in this scenario, private consumption falls further by an additional 1.5 percentage points over scenario A. Similarly, government's revenue loss is larger by 2.6 per cent over scenario A (Table 4.11), and dis-savings rise to 27 per cent from 18 per cent in scenario A. Unemployment rate of both labour (Table 4.12) and capital (Appendix Table A-4.3.7) rises further in this scenario compared to scenario A. Correspondingly, real income loss for all households turn out to be larger (Table 4.13).

4.9 Impacts of Oil Price Fall

While global economic slowdown *per se* has strong adverse effect on the Indian economy, the fall in global oil price provides some relief. Scenario C attempts to quantify these impacts. An average fall of 10 per cent in annual average global oil prices results in a fall in the composite price of petroleum products by 2.7 per cent over the base (6 per cent over scenario B). This neutralises the adverse GDP effect by 0.9 per cent. Consequently, GDP fall is only 4.2 per cent instead of 5.1 per cent in scenario B. All the components of final demand benefit from oil price fall and the adverse effects of world economic slowdown on each of them are smaller in Scenario C compared to those in scenario B. The aggregate domestic price index falls by 0.5 per cent due to the pass through of the fall in international price of crude oil and petroleum products.

The lower prices in this scenario compared to scenario B benefits both households and government. Fall in private consumption observed in scenario B is arrested by 1 percentage point (Table 4.8), while government's nominal expenditure is lower due to price fall. The higher GDP in this scenario helps all components of savings, especially that of government. As a result nominal and real investment are higher by about 2 per cent compared to scenario B (Tables 4.4 and 4.5). Changes in unemployment rates and household real incomes are as expected, and get moderated in this scenario (Tables 4.8 and 4.9).

We may note here that the results of this scenario reflect the combined effects of all the three external shocks studied here on the Indian economy. The next section explores the potential for government fiscal measures to counteract this drop in growth rate from its potential.

4.10 Impacts of Government Counter Measures

4.10.1 Scenario D—Government Consumption Rise

We first examine the potential for a rise in government real consumption as a counter measure to arrest the fall in growth due to the adverse world economic environment. In scenario D we increase government consumption expenditure by 5 per cent in real terms across all sectors. In a real CGE model such as the one used in this study with there being no scope for monetary expansion, the increase in government consumption has to be financed either by raising government revenue, and/or an increase in government dis-savings. In scenario D, we let government dis-savings to increase.

Government dis-savings increase by 10.8 per cent between scenario C and D (Table 4.9) following an expansion in government consumption. This has an adverse impact on real investment that falls by a further 2.1 per cent over scenario C (Table 4.8). The net effect of this expansionary fiscal policy is that it helps the economy to reduce the decline in GDP by about 0.7 per cent from -4.2 per cent in scenario C to -3.5 per cent in this scenario. The across the board increase in government real consumption benefits consumption goods sectors. However, sectors producing investment goods do suffer output losses (Appendix Table A-4.3.1) due to fall in real investment. As a result, while agricultural and services GDP rise, industrial GDP falls. The maximum increase is seen in the services sector reflecting the expansion in public administration. Consequent upon the increase in GDP in this scenario, private consumption is higher here compared to scenario C. This manifests in a reduction in the unemployment of all types of labour and improves capital utilisation in all the sectors (Appendix Table A-4.3.7). Overall labour unemployment is down by 0.8 per cent in this scenario with agricultural labour witnessing the biggest fall in unemployment (0.9 per cent).

Since the fiscal expansion is undertaken in a context where there are unemployed resources in the economy to start with, there is not much of an impact on the price level in the economy. Aggregate price index is up by only 0.2 per cent in scenario D over scenario C. Further, this fiscal expansion is met almost entirely by an increase in domestic output, while real imports is more or less the same as in scenario C. With real trade flows hardly changing between scenarios C and D, nominal exchange rate remains unchanged in this scenario. Real exchange rate shows a slight change reflecting the small changes in the domestic price level.

The rise in GDP in this scenario improves direct tax collection by 0.8 per cent and indirect tax collection by 0.7 per cent over scenario C (Table 4.11). As a result, government's total revenue is higher in this scenario by 0.6 per cent. But this is inadequate to offset the 2.6 per cent increase in government expenditure due to the 5 per cent increase in government consumption. As a result, government dis-savings is up 10.8 per cent as stated earlier.

Finally, with a decline in the unemployment rates of both labour and capital in this scenario, real incomes of all households improve compared to scenario C (Table 4.13). However, the gains for rural households is much less than that for the urban households reflecting the difference in the wage rates for agricultural labour compared to other labour types (Table 4.12). Indeed the order of gain for urban households is about twice that of rural households.

4.10.2 Scenario E—Indirect Tax Cut

Here we examine effects of a 2 percenatge point reduction in all indirect tax rates[5] (except for petroleum products). This corresponds to the announcement by Government of India of a 4 percentage

5. Thus, if indirect tax rate (t) was 10 per cent for a sector, it is reduced to 8 per cent in this experiment. Note that total indirect tax revenue stood at 8.5 per cent of GDP in the Base run.

reduction around middle of the financial year. The cut in indirect taxes reduces overall prices by 0.8 per cent in this scenario compared to the previous scenario (Table 4.8). Indeed the price level in this scenario is less than their base levels by 0.5 per cent. Consumers benefit substantially from this tax cut induced price fall by about 2.8 per cent over the base scenario. In fact, aggregate real private consumption is more or less back to the base level in this scenario. This expansion in demand benefits mainly the domestic producers as the domestically produced commodities become relatively cheaper in this scenario compared to imported commodities. This expansion in domestic demand helps neutralise the adverse effect on GDP by another 0.8 per cent. In contrast, real imports rise by a mere 0.2 per cent.

The cut in indirect taxes, however, is not costless. Government's indirect tax collection falls steeply by 25.2 per cent (Table 4.11) in this scenario compared to scenario D. As a result government revenue falls by 11.1 per cent resulting a sharp rise in government dis-savings by 39.6 per cent. Accordingly, national savings falls by 6.4 percentage points (Table 4.9) in this scenario, despite the 0.7 percentage point rise in private savings. This results in a fall in real investment by 4.1 percentage points in this scenario compared to the previous scenario (Table 4.8).

The expansion in domestic output, naturally, improves the utilisation of labour (Table 4.12) and capital resources (Appendix Table A-4.3.7) in the economy. Aggregate labour unemployment falls further by 0.7 percentage points in this scenario compared to scenario D. As a result, real income of all household classes improves further in this scenario. Though there is no discernible bias in favour of rural or urban households, the gains are higher for the richer classes in both rural and urban areas than their poorer counterparts.

4.10.3 Scenario F—NREGS

The scenarios thus far have shown that the world economic slow down would adversely affect all households, and that government counter-measures such as fiscal expansion and indirect tax cuts can bring some relief to the economy and all sections of the population. Nevertheless, real incomes of all households especially the poor remain below their base level in scenario E. While the richer classes may have a higher capacity to cope with the income loss, the poorer classes suffer enormously when pushed deeper into poverty. Thus, there could be a need for targeted programmes to bring additional relief to the poorer sections of the population. One such existing programme is the NREGS launched a few years ago by the government.

The NREGS is essentially a rural employment generation programme that guarantees up to 100-days of employment to all those willing to do manual work. This poverty reduction programme is expected to be self-targeted as it offers only manual job, which only the poor may be willing to undertake. In the context of this study, one can think of the unemployed people in the rural areas belonging to the bottom three classes offering themselves for employment under the NREGS. The programme is also likely to have macro level implications as the additional employment and income generated under the programme would have second round impacts in terms of household demand. Another channel through which macro level impacts may be felt is the additional fiscal strain that the programme is likely to cause. In scenario F, we examine these impacts of the NREGS and its potential to neutralise the loss in employment and incomes for the poor. As described in Table 4.7, in this scenario we consider "full coverage" under the NREGS meaning that (a) all those unemployed in the bottom three rural classes in the previous scenario are offered employment, and (b) employment under the programme is for as along as it is required, which could be more than the 100 days that the existing programme offers.

Table 4.14 presents key model outcomes pertaining to the size of the NREGS. It is seen that nearly 19 million additional jobs are created under the programme at a daily wage rate of Rs.87.30. The total cost of the programme works out to Rs.330.6 billions, or 1.4 per cent of the nominal GDP. Wage-bill constitutes 60 per cent of the total cost of the programme, and the non-wage bill generates demand for certain specific investment goods.[6]

6. The split of this demand is 60 per cent construction, 15 per cent transport equipment, 13 per cent other non-electrical machinery, 10 per cent other electrical machinery and 2 per cent communications equipment.

As might be expected, the NREGS benefits the bottom three rural classes, whose real incomes rise in this scenario exceeding their income levels in the base scenario (Table 4.13), thereby underlining the need for well designed targeted anti-poverty programmes. This spurs an expansion in the demand for various goods by these households, and aggregate private consumption is now 0.3 per cent higher than the base level (Table 4.8). This leads to an expansion of domestic output resulting in an increase in the GDP by another 0.5 percentage point over the previous scenario E. GDP in this scenario is just 2.2 per cent lower than the base. Thus, the three fiscal policy measures, *viz.*, expansion in government consumption, indirect tax cut and NREGS, together help neutralise the adverse impact of the global economic slow down on GDP by about 2 percentage points.

Table 4.14: NREGS Results

Variable	Value
Labour availability (millions)	18.9
Employment creation (millions)	18.9
Coverage factor (%)	100.0
Daily wage rate (Rs.)	87.3
Wage bill (Rs.billions)	198.3
Non-wage bill (Rs.billions	132.2
Total NREGS bill (Rs.billions)	330.6
Total NREGS bill (% of nominal GDP)	1.4

As with the other two fiscal policy measures considered earlier, the NREGS too puts the government budget under strain. Total government expenditure increases by 5.7 percentage points in this scenario compared to previous scenario E (Table 4.11), which results in an increase in government dis-savings despite the 2 percentage point increase in government total revenue (both direct and indirect tax) in this scenario due to buoyancy effect. Government dis-savings is up by 20.6 percentage points in this scenario to become almost double that in the base scenario. Naturally, total savings and investment in the economy are down in this scenario (Table 4.9) by another 3.1 percentage points over scenario E.

4.11 Conclusions

In this part, we have examined the likely impact of global economic slowdown on the Indian economy and the counter measures adopted by the government. The impact has been examined by carrying out several simulation exercises using a static CGE model developed for India based around a SAM for the year 2003-04. In particular, we have examined effects of three external developments: (a) a 10 per cent fall in Indian exports due to falling external demand, (b) a 29 per cent reduction in the foreign inflows into India comprising of 10 per cent fall in remittances and 15 per cent fall in foreign savings, and (c) a 10 per cent fall in global oil prices which is passed through to consumers. We have then attempted to analyse how much of the adverse impact on Indian economy could be offset by three government policies: a 5 per cent increase in government consumption, (b) 2 per cent cut in indirect tax rate, and (c) expansion of the rural employment guarantee scheme to ensure base level of living for the bottom 70 per cent of the rural population.

The results show that, the three external developments, exports fall alone results in a loss in GDP by about 3.3 per cent, while fall in capital inflows cause another 1.8 per cent loss in GDP. The fall in international crude prices mutes the GDP loss somewhat. Nevertheless the combined effect of the external shocks potentially could be a loss in GDP of about 4.2 per cent. About half of this combined effect could be offset by government counter measures examined here and overall adverse effect on GDP could be limited to fall by 2.2 per cent.

We have examined the above issues with the help of a static CGE model without growth dynamics. A question that arises at the end is: what would be the impact of the above external developments and counter policies on the growth rate for 2008-09 that could have been expected under normal circumstances? Assuming a growth rate of 9 per cent for 2008-09 as per the XIth Plan target under normal circumstances, the impact of three external shocks and the counter measures simulated is depicted in Figure 4.2. The external shocks together could reduce the growth rate to as low as 3.9 per cent, but the counter measures lift it up to 6.8 per cent.

Figure 4.2: Changes in Growth Rate across Scenarios

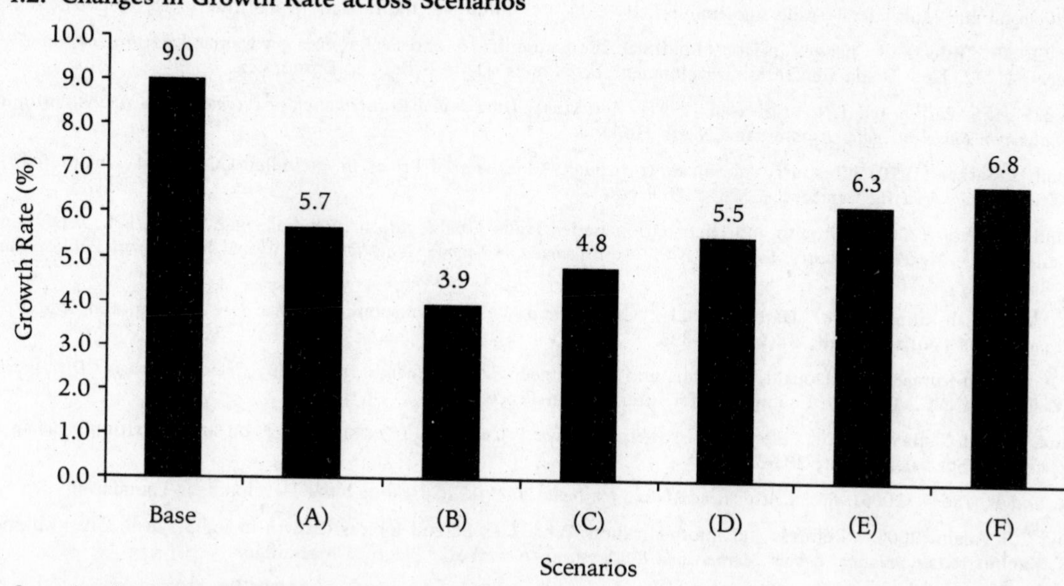

Note: Scenarios A to F are as defined in Table 4.7 above.

While the loss in growth could be arrested somewhat in the short-run through these countermeasures, it could be at the cost of long-term growth and fiscal erosion. The results show that all these global developments and the counter measures would lead to decline in real investment by 20.7 per cent and near doubling of government dis-savings.

Manufacturing sector suffers relatively more loss in output than agriculture or services sector in all the scenarios. In fact, two of the counter measures, *viz.*, rise in government consumption and reduction in indirect taxes actually hurt the manufacturing sector because of the fall in investment demand in these scenarios.

About 4.3 per cent of the total labour force could suffer unemployment following the three external shocks. Rising government consumption and cutting down indirect taxes could limit the unemployment to just 2.7 per cent. Expanding the NREGS to fully cover the bottom 70 per cent of the rural population could bring down the unemployment by an additional 0.5 per cent through its direct and indirect effects.

Real income losses for households following the external shocks range between 3.6 per cent and 4.5 per cent, with the urban households suffering slightly higher losses than their rural counterparts. An expanded NREGS can actually help in rising the real incomes of the bottom 70 per cent of the rural population over the base levels even under these recessionary conditions. And it would cost about Rs.331 billions or about 1.4 per cent of the nominal GDP.

Lastly, we might reiterate that CGE models are real models and consider only relative price movements. Since money market is absent in the model, we have not been able to directly examine the impact of several monetary measures adopted by Government of India to counter the external shocks.

References

Chadha R., S. Pohit, A.V. Deardorff and R.M. Stern (1998). *The Impact of Trade and Domestic Reforms in India: A CGE Modeling Approach.* Ann Arbor: The University of Michigan Press.

de Janvry, A. and K. Subbarao (1986). *Agricultural Price Policy and Income Distribution in India.* Delhi: Oxford University Press.

Dervis, K., J. de Melo and S. Robinson (1982). *General Equilibrium Models for Development Policy.* Cambridge: Cambridge University Press.

Ganesh-Kumar, A., G. Darbha and K.S. Parikh (1998). "Impacts of a Hike in the Administered Prices of Petroleum Products: Analysis using an Applied General Equilibrium Model for India", *Discussion Paper* No. 150. Mumbai: Indira Gandhi Institute of Development Research.

Ganesh-Kumar, A., M. Panda and M.E. Burfisher (2006). "Reforms in Indian Agro-processing and Agriculture Sectors in the Context of Unilateral and Multilateral Trade Agreements", *WP-2006-011.* Mumbai: Indira Gandhi Institute of Development Research.

Murty, K.N. (2000). "Effects of Changes in Household Size, Consumer Taste and Preferences on Demand Pattern in India", *Working Paper No.* 72. New Delhi: Centre for Development Economics, Delhi School of Economics.

Narayana, N.S.S., K.S. Parikh and T.N. Srinivasan (1991). *Agriculture, Growth and Redistribution of Income: Policy Analysis with a General Equilibrium Model of India.* Amsterdam: North Holland.

Panda, M. and H. Sarkar (1990). "Resource Mobilisation through Administered Prices in an Indian CGE", in L. Taylor (ed.), *Socially Relevant Policy Analysis.* Cambridge, MA: MIT Press.

Panda, M. and J. Quizon (2001). "Growth and Distribution under Trade Liberalization in India", in A. Guha, K.L. Krishna and A.K. Lahiri (eds.), *Trade and Industry: Essays by NIPFP-Ford Foundation Fellows.* New Delhi: National Institute of Public Finance and Policy.

Parikh, K.S., A. Ganesh-Kumar and G. Darbha (2003). "Growth and Welfare Consequences of a Rise in Minimum Support Prices", *Economic and Political Weekly,* 38(9): 891-895.

Polaski, S., A. Ganesh-Kumar, S. McDonald, M. Panda and S. Robinson (2008). *India's Trade Policy Choices: Managing Diverse Challenges.* Washington D.C.: Carnegie Endowment for International Peace.

Radhakrishna, R. and C. Ravi (1992). "Effects of Growth, Relative Prices and Preferences on Food and Nutrition", *Indian Economic Review* 27, Special Number: 303-323.

Saluja, M.R. and B. Yadav (2006). *Social Accounting Matrix for India 2003-04.* Gurgaon: India Development Foundation.

Sinha, A. and C.S. Adam (2006). "Reforms and Informalization: What Lies Behind Jobless Growth in India", in B. Guha-Khasnobis and R. Kanbur (eds.), *Informal Labour Markets and Development.* New York: Palgrave Macmillan.

Subramanian, S. (1993). *Agricultural Trade Liberalization and India.* Paris: Development Centre, OECD.

Storm, S. (1993). *Macro-economic Considerations in the Choice of Agricultural Policy.* London: Avebury.

Taylor, L. (1983). *Structuralist Macroeconomics.* New York: Basic Books.

Appendix A-4.1: Structure of the CGE Model

We have used here a CGE model for India which is broadly in the Dervis *et al.* (1982) tradition of trade focused models incorporating Armington type imperfect substitution formulation between domestically produced goods and foreign goods.[7] A distinctive feature of our model lies in its consideration of income distribution and expenditure pattern in some details. The equations of the model arranged in various blocks along with explanations. A glossary of all the variables, parameters, etc., appear at the end of this Appendix.

Price Block

1. $PM_i = PWM_i \cdot EXR \cdot (1+tm_i)$
2. $PE_i = PWE_i \cdot EXR \cdot (1+te_i)$
3. $PQ_i = (XD_i/Q_i) \cdot PD_i + (M_i/Q_i) \cdot PM_i$
4. $PS_i = (XD_i/X_i) \cdot PPR_i + (E_i/X_i) \cdot PE_i$
5. $PD_i = PPR_i \cdot (1+t_i)$ ·
6. $PN_i = PS_i - \sum_j a_{j,i} \cdot PQ_j$
7. $\bar{P} = \sum_i wx_i \cdot PD_i$

The first set of equations refers to different types of prices in the model. The first equation defines the price paid by consumers for imported good (PM) as exogenously given world price (PWM) times the exchange rate (EXR) inflated by the import tariff rate (tm). The second equation defines the price producers receive for exports on similar basis; the variable te here is export subsidy rate. The composite price (PQ) prevailing in the domestic market is a weighted sum of domestic price (PD) and import price (PM) with corresponding shares in total absorption (Q) as weights. Unit sales price (PS) received by producers is a weighted sum of domestic sales prices and export prices.

Producers' price (PPR) is derived from domestic price after netting out given indirect tax/subsidy rates. Net price (PN) received by the factors is defined as producer's unit sales price less sum of intermediate cost. We also make a provision for a variable tax (or subsidy) rate to incorporate administered petroleum price regime in India and consequent absorption of the difference between administered price and producers price by the government. Sectoral domestic market prices (PD) play the equilibrating role in bringing about supply and demand balance in each sector. The overall domestic price $(\bar{P})$ is a weighted sum of sectoral prices with output weights and changes in it indicates inflation in the domestic economy in relation to the wage rate, the numeraire in the model.

Production Block

8. $X_i = \alpha_i \left[d_i \cdot L_i^{-\rho_{ni}} + (1-d_i) \cdot K_i^{-\rho_{ni}} \right]^{-1/\rho_{ni}}$
9. $L_i = X_i \cdot \alpha_i^{\sigma_i - 1} \left[\frac{d_i \cdot PN_i}{W} \right]^{\sigma_i}$
10. $K_i = X_i \cdot \alpha_i^{\sigma_i - 1} \left[\frac{(1-d_i) \cdot PN_i}{\pi_i} \right]^{\sigma_i}$

---

7. Subramanian (1993), Panda and Quizon (2001) and Polaski *et al.* (2008) have developed CGE models for India with Armington assumptions. Taylor (1983), de Janvry and Subbarao (1986), Narayana *et al.* (1991), Panda and Sarkar (1990), Storm (1993), Chadha *et al.* (1998), Ganesh-Kumar *et al.* (1998), Parikh *et al.* (2003), Ganesh-Kumar *et al.* (2006), Sinha and Adam (2006) are some other CGE models for India.

Output (X) in a sector is specified through a constant elasticity of substitution (CES) production function with labour (L) and capital (K) as arguments. Given the static character of the model, capital stock is assumed to be sector specific, but labour is mobile across sectors. Demand for labour and capital are derived from the first order condition of profit maximisation. Apart from output level, factor demands in a sector depends on ratio of net price (PN) and respective factor price.

Factor Employment

11. $LEMPL_h = LENDWSH_h \cdot \sum_i L_i$

12. $KEMPL_{h,i} = KENDWSH_{h,i} \cdot K_i$

While sectoral demands for different factors determine the total employment in the economy, the distribution of employed factors across households are given in equations 11 and 12. Employment of labour of household h ($LEMPL_h$) is assumed to be in proportion to the share of household h in total supply of labour. A similar assumption is used to determine the employment of capital in sector i with household h ($KEMPL_{h,i}$).

Household Income and Expenditure

13. $$YH_h = W \cdot LEMPL_h + \sum_i \pi_i KEMPL_{h,i} + \sum NFIW_h \cdot EXR + TRANS_h \cdot \overline{PQ} + REM_h \cdot EXR$$

14. $CPI_h = \sum_i wc_{h,i} \cdot PQ_i$

15. $YHR_h = YH_h / CPI_h$

16. $S_h = \alpha_{sh} + \beta_{sh} \cdot YH_h \cdot (1 - td_h)$

17. $TC_h = YH_h \cdot (1 - td_h) - S_h$

18. $$CH_{i,h} = \left\{ \theta_{i,h} + \left(\frac{m_{i,h}}{PQ_i} \right) \cdot \left[\frac{TC_h}{POP_h} - \sum_j \theta_{j,h} \cdot PQ_j \right] \right\} \cdot POP_h$$

19. $C_i = \sum_h CH_{i,h}$

The next task is to allocate factor income determined above to households by income class. This step plays a crucial role in discussion of results relating to income distribution in various simulation experiments. As already stated, we consider 10 income classes with each of rural and urban population divided into 5 groups by size of per capita household expenditure. The link from factor income to rural and urban household class is established by considering initial endowment (factor income) in the SAM. This link is represented by the parameter sy_{hf}, the share of household h from factor income of category f. The total wage and non-wage income thus derived is distributed to households in proportion to their initial endowments (wage and non-wage income). To the total wage and non-wage income thus derived, transfer payments by government (TRANS) and remittances from abroad (REM) are added to obtain the total nominal income of the households (YH_h) in eqn.(12). In order to compute real incomes, consumer price index (CPI) is computed for each household class as a weighted average of the sectoral composite prices, the weights being share of various classes in base total consumption. Real income for each household class (YHR_h) is then determined by deflating class-wise nominal income by the class specific CPI.

Turning now to uses of income, different household classes save different proportions of their income after payment of income taxes in fixed proportions. Income net of taxes and savings determines the total private consumption expenditure of the households. Sectoral private consumption ($CH_{i,h}$) is modelled using the Linear Expenditure System (LES) with underlying StoneGeary type of loglinear utility functions. Sectoral demand is thus, a function of income and all the prices. The parameters of the LES are in per capita terms and are class specific so that consumption pattern differences across classes are captured adequately in demand estimates. The marginal budget share coefficients (m_{ih}) in the LES are computed from available Engel elasticities[8] and average propensity to consume implicit in the SAM. Committed consumption coefficients (θ_{ih}) are then calibrated to reproduce the consumption levels in the SAM. Finally, total sectoral consumption expenditure is derived by summing up of the class-wise consumption levels.

International Trade Block

20. $Q_i = \alpha_{qi}\left[d_{qi} \cdot M_i^{\rho qi} + (1-d_{qi}) \cdot XD_i^{\rho qi}\right]^{1/\rho qi}$

21. $\dfrac{M_i}{XD_i} = \left[\dfrac{d_{qi} \cdot PD_i}{(1-d_{qi}) \cdot PM_i}\right]^{\sigma qi}$

22. $X_i = \alpha_{xi}\left[d_{xi} \cdot E_i^{\rho xi} + (1-d_{xi}) \cdot XD_i^{\rho xi}\right]^{1/\rho xi}$

23. $\dfrac{E_i}{XD_i} = \left[\dfrac{(1-d_{xi}) \cdot PE_i}{d_{xi} \cdot PD_i}\right]^{\sigma xi}$

International trade specifications follow Armington assumption that goods produced by the same sector at home and abroad are close but not perfect substitutes. Domestic output and import (or export) in a sector are thus two different goods. The Armington formulation defines demand in terms of a composite commodity (Q) as a CES aggregation of the demand for domestically produced good (XD) and the level of imports (M). The ratio of imports to domestic demand is obtained as a function of ratio of domestic price (PD) and import price (PM) using the first order conditions. Similarly, total output produced (X) is specified as a Constant Elasticity of Transformation (CET) aggregate of exports (E) and domestic demand (XD). Ratio of domestic supply and exports depends on ratio of exports and domestic prices. Note that this formulation is based on small country assumption in so far as it assumes a horizontal export demand curve at given world prices.

Investment Block

24. $S_p = \sum_h S_h$

25. $TINV = S_p + S_g + S_f \cdot EXR$

26. $Z_i = wz_i \cdot (TINV/PQ_i)$

The model follows the neoclassical closure where total capital formation (TINV) is determined by total savings in the economy. Savings are from three sources: private savings (S_p), government savings (S_g) and foreign savings (S_f). Savings of 10 household classes are summed up to determine total private savings. Sectoral investment is determined from total investment by applying fixed base proportions (wz_i) on total investment and then deflating the nominal values by sectoral price. Since the model is a static one, it considers investment by origin only and not by destination.

---

8. Some recent studies in this context are Radhakrishna and Ravi (1992), Murty (2000).

Government Account

27. $GR_d = \sum_h td_h \cdot YH_h$

28. $GR_m = \sum_i tm_i \cdot PWM_i \cdot EXR \cdot M_i$

29. $GR_t = \sum_i t_i \cdot PPR_i \cdot XD_i \quad \text{if } t_i \geq 0$

30. $GR = GR_d + GR_m + GR_t + \sum_i \pi_i \cdot (K_i - \sum_h KEMPL_{h,i})$

31. $GS_d = \sum_i t_i \cdot PPR_i \cdot XD_i \quad \text{if } t_i < 0$

32. $GS_e == \sum_i te_i \cdot PWE_i \cdot EXR \cdot E_i$

33. $GS = GS_d + GS_e$

34. $GE = \sum_i G_i \cdot PQ_i + \sum_h TRANS_h \cdot \overline{PQ} + GS$

35. $S_g = GR - GE$

This block relates to government income and expenditure account and does not involve any behavioural relation. Direct taxes (GR_d) are obtained by using fixed tax rates (t_{dh}) on income of households. Import tariffs (GR_m) are computed by applying tariff rates (tm_i) on rupee value of sectoral imports and indirect tax revenue (GR_t) by applying indirect tax rates on producers' costs. Total government revenue (GR) is sum of direct tax, domestic indirect tax, import tariff and non-tax revenue (GNTR) which is mostly profit from public sector undertakings. On the expenditure side, domestic subsidy (GS_d) has the same base as domestic indirect tax, while export subsidies[9] (GS_e) are applied on rupee value of exports. Govern-ment total current expenditure (GE) consists of consumption expenditure (G) fixed exogenously, transfer payments (TRANS) and subsidies (GS). Of these G and TRANS are fixed in real terms and multiplied by corresponding prices to get nominal government expenditure. The difference between current revenue and current expenditure gives government savings (S_g).

Market Equilibrium Conditions

36. $Q_i = \sum_j a_{i,j} \cdot X_j + C_i + G_i + Z_i$

37. $\sum_i PWM_i \cdot M_i = \sum_i PWE_i \cdot E_i + \sum_h NFI_h + \sum_h REM_h + S_f$

38. $\sum_i \overline{LENDOW_h} = \sum_i L_i + LUNEMP$

39. $\sum_h \overline{KENDOW_{h,i}} + \overline{KENDOWG_i} = K_i + KUNEMP_i$

Lastly, this block of equations contains market equilibrium conditions for product market, foreign exchange market, labour market and sectoral capital market. The product market equilibrium condition is stated in terms of demand for composite commodity and its supply as defined in the trade block. Demand

9. The SAM by Saluja and Yadav (2006) show a small value of export subsidy (about 0.36 per cent of exports).

for composite commodity consists of intermediate demand, private consumption demand, government consumption demand and investment demand. In the product market, domestic prices play the equilibrating role to achieve demand and supply balances. The demand and supply balance for foreign exchange at world prices is obtained by variations in the exchange rate (EXR). Net foreign income (NFI), remittances (REM) and foreign savings (S_f) are given exogenously. The last two equations show the supply, demand and unemployment in the labour and capital markets. While factor supplies are fixed, demand is endogenous. The model provides for two types of factor market clearance. Depending upon whether factor prices are kept flexible or fixed, there would be full employment (LUNEMP and/or KUNEMP would be fixed at zero) or unemployment of factors (LUNEMP and/or KUNEMP would be non-negative). In this study, we fix the price of all factors and allow for unemployment of all factors.

In the base version of the model, the wage rate serves as a numeraire in the current version of the model. All prices determined by the model, including the exchange rate, are thus relative to the given wage rate. When numeraire changes by a given factor, all prices change by the same factor, but solution of the real variables remain unchanged. Alternative specification useful for certain other simulations could be to fix the exchange rate as numeraire and let S_f adjust to balance the foreign exchange market. Another alternative often used is to specify the overall domestic price as a numeraire so that inflation rate is kept exogenously.

Glossary

Endogenous Variables

EXR	=	Exchange rate.
PM_i	=	Price of imports in domestic currency.
PE_i	=	Price of exports in domestic currency.
PQ_i	=	Composite price paid by domestic users.
PS_i	=	Composite sales price received by producers.
PD_i	=	Domestic market price of domestic produce (inclusive of indirect tax/ subsidy).
PPR_i	=	Domesitc market price received by the producer (net of tax/subsidy).
PN_i	=	Net price received by factors of production.
$\overline{P}$	=	Overall price index
XD_i	=	Demand for domestically produced good.
Q_i	=	Composite demand commodity i.
M_i	=	Import demand.
X_i	=	Output level.
E_i	=	Export.
L_i	=	Labour demand in sector i.
K_i	=	Capital demand in sector i
W	=	Wage rate.
π_i	=	Sectoral profit rate (price of sectoral capital).
$LEMPL_h$	=	Employment of labour owned by household h.
$KEMPL_{h,i}$	=	Employment of sectoral capital i owned by household h.

YH_h = Income of household class h.

$\overline{PQ}$ = Index of composite price paid by domestic users.

CPI_h = Consumer price index for household class h.

YHR_h = Real income of household class h.

S_h = Savings of household class h.

TC_h = Total consumption expenditure of household class h.

$CH_{i,h}$ = Consumption on item i by household class h.

C_i = Consumption of item i by all households.

S_p = Private savings.

TINV = Total savings/investment in the economy.

S_g = Government savings.

Z_i = Investment demand by sector of origin.

GR_d = Government revenue from direct tax.

GR_m = Government revenue from import tariff.

GR_t = Government revenue from indirect taxes.

GR = Government revenue total.

GS_d = Government subsidies on domestic consumption.

GS_e = Government subsidies on exports.

GS = Government subsidy.

GE = Government expenditure total.

LUNEMP = Labour unemployment.

$KUNEMP_i$ = Unemployment of capital in sector i.

Exogenous Variables and Parameters

PWM_i = World price of imports in foreign currency.

PWE_i = World price of exports in foreign currency.

tm_i = Import tariff rate.

te_i = Export subsidy rate.

t_i = Indirect tax (or subsidy) rate.

$a_{i,j}$ = Input-output coefficient.

wx_i = Output weight in overall price index.

α_i = Scale parameter in CES production function.

d_i = Share parameter in CES production function.

σ_i = Elasticity of substitution in CES production function.

ρ_{ni} = $1-\frac{1}{\sigma_i}$; Exponent in the CES production function.

$LENDWSH_h$ = Share of household h in total labour endowment (supply).

$KENDWSH_{h,i}$	=	Share of household h in total endowment (supply) of sectoral capital i.
$NFIW_h$	=	Net factor income from abroad in foreign currency received by household h.
$TRANS_h$	=	Real transfers from government to household h.
REM_h	=	Remittances from abroad in foreign currency received by household h.
$wc_{h,i}$	=	Consumption weight of commodity i in consumption basket of household h.
α_{sh}	=	Constant term in savings function of household h.
β_{sh}	=	Marginal propensity to save by household h.
td_h	=	Direct tax rate applicable to household h.
θ_{ih}	=	Committed consumption of sector i by household h in the LES demand system.
m_{ih}	=	Marginal budget share of item i by household h in the LES demand system.
POP_h	=	Population in household class h.
α_{qi}	=	Scale parameter in Armington import function.
d_{qi}	=	Share parameter in Armington import function.
σ_{qi}	=	Elasticity of substitution in Armington import function.
ρ_{qi}	=	$1-\frac{1}{\sigma_{qi}}$; Exponent in the Armington import function.
α_{xi}	=	Scale parameter in CET export function.
d_{xi}	=	Share parameter in CET export function.
σ_{xi}	=	Elasticity of substitution in CET export function.
ρ_{xi}	=	$1-\frac{1}{\sigma_{xi}}$; Exponent in the CET export function.
S_f	=	Foreign savings.
wz_i	=	Weight of commodity i in investment demands
G_i	=	Government consumption
$\overline{LENDOW_h}$	=	Labour endowment with household h.
$\overline{KENDOW_{h,i}}$	=	Endowment of capital of sector i with household h.
$\overline{KENDOWG_i}$	=	Endowment of capital of sector i with Government.

Appendix A-4.2: Detailed Tables for Part I Simulations

Table A-4.2.1: Domestic Market Price (Rs. per unit)

Sector	BASE	ADBL	AD10	NADPR	Sector	BASE	ADBL	AD10	NADPR
	(Levels)	(% change over BASE)				(Levels)	(% change over BASE)		
Paddy	1.0	-0.1	0.4	2.0	Inorganic heavy chemicals	1.0	5.3	6.4	9.6
Wheat	1.0	1.6	1.9	3.0	Organic heavy chemicals	1.0	9.6	10.5	13.4
Other cereals	1.0	1.1	1.5	3.1	Fertilisers	1.0	10.6	13.1	21.1
Pulses	1.0	1.7	1.8	2.3	Pesticides	1.0	4.8	5.1	6.6
Sugarcane	1.0	1.1	1.0	0.9	Paints, varnishes and lacquers	1.0	2.6	3.8	7.3
Oilseeds	1.0	-0.2	0.2	1.3	Misc chemicals	1.0	2.7	3.6	6.4
Jute	1.0	7.6	7.2	6.5	Cement	1.0	-2.5	-0.6	4.7
Cotton	1.0	2.4	2.6	3.4	Iron & steel	1.0	-0.5	1.0	5.0
Tea & coffee	1.0	2.3	1.5	-0.3	Non-ferrous basic metals	1.0	2.4	3.7	7.2
Rubber	1.0	0.4	0.7	1.5	Metal products	1.0	-0.3	0.6	3.3
Tobacco	1.0	21.5	15.7	-4.3	Other non-electric machinery	1.0	-1.4	-0.1	3.3
Other crops	1.0	0.7	0.7	1.1	Electrical appliances	1.0	-2.8	-1.4	2.3
Milk and milk products	1.0	0.7	0.4	0.0	Communication equipments	1.0	-2.8	-1.4	2.1
Other livestock products	1.0	0.1	0.2	0.7	Electronic equipments (incl.TV)	1.0	-1.9	-0.4	3.3
Forestry and logging	1.0	1.0	1.0	1.1	Other electrical machinery	1.0	-1.8	-0.4	3.4
Fishing	1.0	-0.4	-0.3	0.3	Rail equipments	1.0	-1.9	-0.6	2.8
Coal and lignite	1.0	2.8	3.1	3.9	Other transport equipments	1.0	-1.3	-0.2	2.8
Crude petroleum, natural gas	1.0	88.6	87.1	83.6	Misc manufacturing	1.0	-0.3	0.6	3.0
Iron ore	1.0	1.5	3.0	7.2	Construction	1.0	0.1	1.0	3.5
Other Minerals	1.0	-1.4	0.2	4.5	Electricity	1.0	3.5	4.7	8.5
Sugar	1.0	0.3	0.4	0.7	Gas	1.0	-0.8	-0.6	0.1
Khandsari, boora	1.0	0.7	1.0	2.0	Water supply	1.0	0.5	0.7	1.3
Edible, oil & *vanaspati*	1.0	0.4	0.7	1.8	Railway transport services	1.0	0.0	0.6	2.6
Misc food products	1.0	0.6	0.9	2.0	Other transport services	1.0	0.5	2.4	8.7
Beverages & tobacco products	1.0	1.6	1.6	1.8	Storage and warehousing	1.0	0.8	1.3	2.8
Cotton textiles	1.0	1.7	1.9	2.8	Communication	1.0	0.7	0.5	0.1
Wool synthetic, silk fibre textiles	1.0	1.1	1.5	3.1	Trade	1.0	-1.4	-0.7	1.1
Jute, hemp, mesta textiles	1.0	2.6	2.7	3.3	Hotels and restaurants	1.0	0.0	0.1	0.8
Textile products	1.0	-2.1	-2.1	-1.9	Banking	1.0	0.1	0.1	0.1
Furniture and wood products	1.0	9.2	8.0	3.1	Insurance	1.0	0.0	0.1	0.7
Paper, paper prods. & newsprint	1.0	1.0	1.4	2.8	Ownership of dwellings	1.0	0.9	0.4	-0.5
Printing and publishing	1.0	1.5	1.8	2.7	Education and research	1.0	0.3	0.3	0.5
Leather products	1.0	-4.4	-4.5	-4.7	Medical and health	1.0	1.9	2.2	3.2
Rubber and plastic products	1.0	0.9	1.5	3.4	Other services	1.0	2.2	2.4	3.3
Petroleum products	1.0	0.0	10.0	43.0	Public administration	1.0	0.0	0.0	0.0
Coal tar products	1.0	15.4	16.3	18.9					

Table A-4.2.2: Composite Price Paid by Domestic Users (Rs. Per Unit)

Sector	BASE	ADBL	AD10	NADPR	Sector	BASE	ADBL	AD10	NADPR
	(Levels)	(% change over BASE)				(Levels)	(% change over BASE)		
Paddy	1.0	-0.1	0.4	2.0	Inorganic heavy chemicals	1.0	6.0	6.9	9.9
Wheat	1.0	1.6	1.9	3.0	Organic heavy chemicals	1.0	7.7	8.5	11.0
Other cereals	1.0	1.1	1.5	3.1	Fertilisers	1.0	10.4	12.8	20.4
Pulses	1.0	2.2	2.4	3.0	Pesticides	1.0	5.0	5.4	7.0
Sugarcane	1.0	1.1	1.0	0.9	Paints, varnishes and lacquers	1.0	3.2	4.4	7.7
Oilseeds	1.0	-0.2	0.2	1.3	Misc chemicals	1.0	3.5	4.4	7.2
Jute	1.0	7.6	7.3	6.8	Cement	1.0	1.4	2.9	7.0
Cotton	1.0	2.4	2.6	3.4	Iron & steel	1.0	0.1	1.5	5.4
Tea & coffee	1.0	2.3	1.5	-0.3	Non-ferrous basic metals	1.0	5.1	6.1	9.0
Rubber	1.0	0.5	0.8	1.6	Metal products	1.0	0.2	1.2	3.8
Tobacco	1.0	21.2	15.5	-4.1	Other non-electric machinery	1.0	2.2	3.3	6.3
Other crops	1.0	0.8	0.9	1.2	Electrical appliances	1.0	0.6	1.8	5.0
Milk and milk products	1.0	0.7	0.4	0.0	Communication equipments	1.0	4.1	5.1	7.9
Other livestock products	1.0	0.1	0.3	0.7	Electronic equipments (incl.TV)	1.0	0.8	2.1	5.4
Forestry and logging	1.0	1.6	1.6	2.0	Other electrical machinery	1.0	1.2	2.5	5.8
Fishing	1.0	-0.4	-0.2	0.3	Rail equipments	1.0	-1.5	-0.2	3.1
Coal and lignite	1.0	2.9	3.2	4.1	Other transport equipments	1.0	-0.8	0.3	3.3
Crude petroleum, natural gas	1.0	83.6	84.4	86.9	Misc manufacturing	1.0	3.7	4.5	6.9
Iron ore	1.0	2.4	3.8	7.7	Construction	1.0	0.1	1.0	3.5
Other Minerals	1.0	5.6	6.5	9.3	Electricity	1.0	3.5	4.7	8.5
Sugar	1.0	0.4	0.4	0.8	Gas	1.0	-0.8	-0.6	0.1
Khandsari, boora	1.0	0.7	1.0	2.0	Water supply	1.0	0.5	0.7	1.3
Edible, oil & *vanaspati*	1.0	2.4	2.8	4.3	Railway transport services	1.0	0.0	0.6	2.6
Misc food products	1.0	0.7	1.0	2.1	Other transport services	1.0	1.0	2.8	8.8
Beverages & tobacco products	1.0	1.6	1.7	1.9	Storage and warehousing	1.0	0.8	1.3	2.8
Cotton textiles	1.0	2.0	2.2	3.2	Communication	1.0	0.7	0.5	0.2
Wool synthetic, silk fibre textiles	1.0	1.6	2.1	3.8	Trade	1.0	-1.4	-0.7	1.1
Jute, hemp, mesta textiles	1.0	3.0	3.1	3.9	Hotels and restaurants	1.0	0.5	0.7	1.4
Textile products	1.0	-0.6	-0.6	0.0	Banking	1.0	0.1	0.1	0.1
Furniture and wood products	1.0	9.1	8.0	3.4	Insurance	1.0	0.6	0.8	1.5
Paper, paper prods. & newsprint	1.0	3.3	3.8	5.5	Ownership of dwellings	1.0	0.9	0.4	-0.5
Printing and publishing	1.0	3.0	3.4	4.7	Education and research	1.0	0.3	0.3	0.5
Leather products	1.0	-2.8	-2.8	-2.6	Medical and health	1.0	1.9	2.2	3.2
Rubber and plastic products	1.0	1.7	2.3	4.3	Other services	1.0	2.9	3.2	4.2
Petroleum products	1.0	3.1	12.8	44.4	Public administration	1.0	0.0	0.0	0.0
Coal tar products	1.0	12.4	13.2	15.7					

Table A-4.2.3: Real Output (Rs. Billions at Base Price)

Sector	BASE	ADBL	AD10	NADPR	Sector	BASE	ADBL	AD10	NADPR
	(Levels)	(% change over BASE)				(Levels)	(% change over BASE)		
Paddy	912.8	-1.0	-0.9	-0.7	Inorganic heavy chemicals	206.8	3.5	3.3	2.5
Wheat	598.2	0.9	0.5	-0.6	Organic heavy chemicals	158.8	-2.3	-2.5	-3.4
Other cereals	188.1	0.2	0.1	-0.2	Fertilisers	325.2	0.5	0.1	-1.0
Pulses	235.8	1.3	0.9	-0.1	Pesticides	57.6	3.0	2.7	2.2
Sugarcane	234.6	0.6	0.2	-0.7	Paints, varnishes and lacquers	120.2	-1.4	-0.6	1.0
Oilseeds	516.6	-0.3	-0.2	0.2	Misc chemicals	1092.9	1.1	1.0	0.8
Jute	13.9	8.7	8.0	6.6	Cement	501.4	4.2	4.6	5.5
Cotton	192.6	2.0	1.7	1.2	Iron & steel	1311.0	-2.9	-1.7	0.9
Tea & coffee	59.5	2.3	1.3	-1.2	Non-ferrous basic metals	379.0	0.7	1.4	2.9
Rubber	31.8	0.0	0.2	0.7	Metal products	437.7	-0.9	-0.5	0.2
Tobacco	19.2	18.0	13.8	-0.9	Other non-electric machinery	709.1	-5.3	-3.7	0.1
Other crops	1952.4	0.4	0.2	-0.3	Electrical appliances	89.7	2.2	2.9	4.3
Milk and milk products	1134.6	0.6	0.3	-0.3	Communication equipments	117.9	3.2	4.3	6.9
Other livestock products	717.6	-0.3	-0.3	-0.2	Electronic equipments (incl.TV)	221.1	-7.1	-5.7	-2.5
Forestry and logging	303.1	1.2	1.1	0.8	Other electrical machinery	367.1	-5.0	-3.6	-0.5
Fishing	318.4	1.0	1.0	0.9	Rail equipments	112.2	-8.2	-6.5	-2.8
Coal and lignite	330.4	1.8	1.7	1.5	Other transport equipments	766.9	-7.7	-6.2	-2.8
Crude petroleum, natural gas	242.0	4.8	4.1	2.2	Misc manufacturing	728.7	4.2	4.6	5.9
Iron ore	36.5	3.3	3.6	4.3	Construction	4165.7	-12.9	-10.3	-4.6
Other Minerals	98.3	-0.3	0.6	2.8	Electricity	1298.2	0.2	-0.1	-1.1
Sugar	200.0	-0.1	-0.3	-0.7	Gas	57.4	-3.6	-3.0	-1.3
Khandsari, boora	41.5	-1.7	-1.8	-2.3	Water supply	97.4	0.1	-0.1	-0.6
Edible, oil & *vanaspati*	437.6	1.3	0.9	0.1	Railway transport services	429.8	-1.0	-0.9	-0.7
Misc food products	1375.4	1.4	0.5	-1.6	Other transport services	3421.7	1.0	-0.4	-4.3
Beverages & tobacco products	581.3	-0.5	-1.0	-1.9	Storage and warehousing	25.4	-0.5	-0.2	0.5
Cotton textiles	512.7	5.5	4.4	1.7	Communication	592.8	0.1	-0.1	-0.6
Wool synthetic,silk fiber textiles	411.9	0.9	0.7	0.2	Trade	4574.8	-0.5	-0.2	0.5
Jute, hemp, mesta textiles	42.9	21.2	18.4	12.2	Hotels and restaurants	814.6	2.3	1.7	0.1
Textile products	577.0	9.3	8.8	7.9	Banking	1847.3	-0.1	-0.2	-0.3
Furniture and wood products	142.1	3.9	3.3	0.8	Insurance	388.8	0.0	-0.1	-0.2
Paper, paper prods. & newsprint	272.2	7.5	7.6	7.8	Ownership of dwellings	1269.4	0.2	0.1	-0.1
Printing and publishing	153.6	2.4	1.8	0.6	Education and research	1438.4	0.6	0.3	-0.4
Leather products	140.6	18.9	18.6	18.6	Medical and health	1033.0	0.2	-0.5	-2.2
Rubber and plastic products	449.8	-2.0	-1.4	-0.2	Other services	2856.9	0.3	0.1	-0.3
Petroleum products	1679.2	2.1	0.2	-5.0	Public administration	1568.2	0.0	0.0	0.0
Coal tar products	79.3	-0.5	0.4	2.7					

Table A-4.2.4: *Real Total Household Consumption (Rs. Billions at Base Price)*

Sector	BASE	ADBL	AD10	NADPR	Sector	BASE	ADBL	AD10	NADPR
	(Levels)	(% change over BASE)				(Levels)	(% change over BASE)		
Paddy	566.9	0.5	0.2	-0.5	Petroleum products	329.5	-1.0	-7.3	-21.6
Wheat	404.3	0.1	-0.2	-0.9	Coal tar products	0.5	-1.5	-1.6	-2.1
Other cereals	167.0	0.1	0.0	-0.2	Paints, varnishes and lacquers	6.7	-0.2	-0.4	-1.1
Pulses	176.2	0.0	-0.4	-1.2	Misc chemicals	240.1	-0.2	-0.4	-1.0
Sugarcane	72.4	0.4	0.1	-0.5	Cement	14.7	0.5	-1.6	-6.4
Oilseeds	76.6	0.9	0.4	-0.6	Metal products	87.1	1.7	0.1	-3.6
Tea & coffee	13.1	-0.1	-0.1	-0.1	Other non electric machinery	17.5	-0.4	-2.1	-6.2
Tobacco	1.1	-5.9	-4.6	1.5	Electrical appliances	9.0	1.4	-0.5	-4.8
Other crops	1087.1	0.4	0.1	-0.7	Communication equipments	6.7	-2.3	-3.9	-7.7
Milk and milk products	976.8	0.5	0.3	-0.2	Electronic equipments (incl.TV)	49.3	0.9	-1.1	-5.6
Other livestock products	380.0	0.8	0.4	-0.4	Other electrical machinery	11.8	0.8	-1.2	-5.6
Forestry and logging	216.9	0.3	0.0	-0.8	Other transport equipments	114.5	2.6	0.8	-3.6
Fishing	225.8	1.0	0.6	-0.3	Misc manufacturing	142.9	-1.5	-3.0	-6.5
Coal and lignite	7.4	-1.0	-1.4	-2.3	Electricity	173.7	-1.4	-2.9	-6.8
Sugar	139.4	2.0	1.1	-0.9	Gas	20.8	3.6	2.1	-1.1
Khandsari, boora	20.5	1.5	0.4	-2.2	Water supply	18.3	0.8	0.1	-1.5
Edible, oil & *vanaspati*	451.6	-0.1	-1.1	-3.4	Railway transport services	97.3	1.5	0.2	-2.8
Misc food products	1058.3	1.4	0.3	-2.2	Other transport services	1832.5	0.9	-1.4	-7.5
Beverages & tobacco products	494.0	0.6	-0.3	-2.1	Communication	300.7	0.6	0.2	-0.6
Cotton textiles	299.1	0.2	-0.8	-3.3	Trade	1903.3	0.0	0.0	0.0
Wool synthetic, silk fibre textiles	198.5	0.5	-0.8	-3.8	Hotels and restaurants	632.5	1.1	0.4	-1.4
Jute, hemp, mesta textiles	1.2	-0.8	-1.7	-3.9	Banking	590.3	1.4	0.8	-0.4
Textile products	300.0	3.7	2.4	-0.3	Insurance	191.8	1.0	0.3	-1.5
Furniture and wood products	25.8	-6.7	-6.6	-3.9	Ownership of dwellings	1269.4	0.2	0.1	-0.1
Paper, paper prods. & newsprint	36.5	-2.0	-3.2	-6.2	Education and research	807.8	1.1	0.5	-0.8
Printing and publishing	117.3	-1.0	-2.2	-4.9	Medical and health	819.2	0.3	-0.6	-2.8
Leather products	51.5	4.7	3.9	2.1	Other services	978.3	-0.7	-1.5	-3.4
Rubber and plastic products	91.4	0.1	-0.2	-0.7					

Table A-4.2.5: ***Import Volumes***

Sector	BASE	ADBL	AD10	NADPR	Sector	BASE	ADBL	AD10	NADPR
	(Levels)	(% change over BASE)				(Levels)	(% change over BASE)		
Paddy	0.003	-16.7	-17.1	-18.3	Printing and publishing	54.6	-7.5	-8.8	-12.0
Wheat	0.003	-11.5	-12.9	-16.1	Leather products	13.3	-7.4	-9.3	-13.8
Other cereals	0.0	-6.7	-7.2	-8.2	Rubber and plastic products	59.0	-12.8	-12.5	-12.0
Pulses	23.5	-5.0	-6.1	-9.0	Petroleum products	105.8	-36.6	-32.4	-19.0
Sugarcane	0.2	-6.3	-7.6	-10.9	Coal tar products	44.3	13.5	14.7	17.3
Oilseeds	0.018	-12.8	-13.3	-14.8	Inorganic heavy chemicals	68.5	-0.3	0.0	0.9
Jute	1.0	9.2	7.0	2.0	Organic heavy chemicals	193.0	2.6	2.6	2.6
Rubber	0.5	-7.8	-7.9	-9.1	Fertilisers	21.3	6.3	8.7	16.9
Tobacco	0.2	40.5	25.2	-19.4	Pesticides	5.1	-1.7	-2.7	-4.9
Other crops	36.3	-7.1	-8.0	-10.6	Paints, varnishes and lacquers	16.1	-9.6	-8.1	-4.6
Other livestock products	3.8	-8.3	-8.9	-10.7	Misc chemicals	208.1	-6.9	-6.7	-6.1
Forestry and logging	29.0	-6.0	-7.0	-9.6	Cement	112.7	-16.3	-13.5	-6.7
Fishing	0.8	-8.4	-9.1	-11.2	Iron & steel	107.4	-15.5	-13.3	-8.1
Coal and lignite	11.5	-3.3	-3.9	-5.7	Non-ferrous basic metals	417.3	-7.7	-6.2	-2.8
Crude petroleum, natural gas	900.3	8.5	6.1	-0.1	Metal products	31.3	-14.0	-13.3	-12.0
Iron ore	3.7	-5.5	-4.0	-0.5	Other non-electric machinery	461.8	-19.4	-17.1	-12.0
Other Minerals	363.1	-10.8	-8.8	-4.5	Electrical appliances	27.1	-17.5	-15.7	-11.8
Sugar	0.8	-11.7	-13.0	-16.2	Communication equipments	158.7	-16.5	-14.4	-9.8
Khandsari, boora	0.012	-12.2	-13.1	-15.3	Electronic equipments (incl.TV)	94.3	-21.3	-19.0	-13.9
Edible, oil & *vanaspati*	176.6	-6.7	-7.5	-9.5	Other electrical machinery	179.3	-19.7	-17.4	-12.2
Misc food products	11.1	-9.9	-11.4	-15.0	Rail equipments	4.8	-21.9	-19.6	-14.6
Beverages & tobacco products	4.1	-9.7	-11.3	-15.3	Other transport equipments	51.0	-21.2	-19.3	-15.2
Cotton textiles	25.9	-4.8	-6.8	-11.4	Misc manufacturing	457.4	-11.0	-10.3	-9.0
Wool synthetic, silk fibre textiles	39.6	-9.9	-10.5	-12.0	Other transport services	275.0	-7.2	-7.1	-6.3
Jute, hemp, mesta textiles	3.0	11.1	7.1	-1.7	Communication	2.8	-7.2	-8.4	-11.6
Textile products	61.7	-10.0	-11.9	-16.3	Hotels and restaurants	54.8	-6.6	-7.9	-11.1
Furniture and wood products	5.0	7.5	3.2	-11.3	Insurance	35.9	-8.4	-9.1	-11.1
Paper, paper prods. & newsprint	111.2	-4.9	-5.5	-7.0	Other services	385.4	-5.9	-6.7	-8.8

Table A-4.2.6: Export Volumes

Sector	BASE (Levels)	ADBL (% change over BASE)	AD10	NADPR	Sector	BASE (Levels)	ADBL (% change over BASE)	AD10	NADPR
Paddy	40.4	4.0	4.2	4.9	Printing and publishing	7.6	6.3	6.1	5.8
Wheat	26.3	4.7	4.6	4.3	Leather products	66.3	23.8	23.9	24.9
Other cereals	3.2	4.5	4.6	4.8	Rubber and plastic products	61.0	1.7	2.4	3.9
Pulses	2.4	5.2	5.2	5.5	Petroleum products	144.6	-1.0	1.6	4.5
Sugarcane	0.9	4.9	5.2	6.0	Inorganic heavy chemicals	72.0	4.4	4.1	2.8
Oilseeds	50.6	4.4	4.8	5.9	Organic heavy chemicals	115.9	-2.8	-3.1	-4.0
Jute	0.1	8.4	8.6	9.3	Fertilisers	0.4	-1.7	-3.1	-7.3
Cotton	5.0	5.4	5.5	6.0	Pesticides	15.3	4.2	4.2	4.1
Rubber	0.5	4.8	5.3	6.9	Paints, varnishes and lacquers	24.5	1.1	1.6	2.7
Tobacco	6.3	10.7	9.9	6.1	Misc chemicals	169.4	3.7	3.6	3.1
Other crops	59.1	4.9	5.2	6.1	Cement	343.2	6.4	6.6	6.8
Other livestock products	2.5	4.7	5.2	6.7	Iron & steel	80.0	2.2	2.8	4.3
Forestry and logging	13.5	5.5	5.8	7.1	Non-ferrous basic metals	56.8	3.6	3.9	4.8
Fishing	48.3	5.6	5.9	6.8	Metal products	75.8	3.4	3.7	4.2
Coal and lignite	1.7	4.9	5.2	6.0	Other non-electric machinery	101.6	-0.4	1.0	4.2
Crude petroleum, natural gas	2.0	2.3	2.7	3.9	Electrical appliances	41.0	5.7	6.2	7.1
Iron ore	18.9	5.2	5.3	5.4	Communication equipments	52.9	7.0	7.9	10.0
Other minerals	16.2	4.9	5.3	6.3	Electronic equipments (incl.TV)	14.7	-1.5	-0.5	1.9
Sugar	11.0	4.5	4.8	5.7	Other electrical machinery	43.2	0.3	1.3	3.7
Khandsari, boora	0.019	2.9	3.1	3.5	Rail equipments	1.1	-2.2	-0.8	2.3
Edible, oil & *vanaspati*	25.5	5.9	5.8	5.7	Other transport equipments	79.5	-2.7	-1.4	1.6
Misc food products	85.7	5.9	5.3	3.9	Misc manufacturing	349.4	7.0	7.4	8.6
Beverages & tobacco products	3.5	3.5	3.4	3.9	Railway transport services	22.6	3.8	4.0	4.4
Cotton textiles	80.9	9.0	8.1	6.2	Other transport services	404.8	5.1	3.0	-3.3
Wool synthetic, silk fibre textiles	48.7	4.7	4.7	4.6	Communication	4.7	4.7	5.2	6.6
Jute, hemp, mesta textiles	10.6	24.1	21.7	16.3	Trade	527.5	4.9	5.2	6.3
Textile products	258.5	13.1	12.9	12.8	Hotels and restaurants	100.9	6.8	6.6	6.0
Furniture and wood products	10.0	2.7	3.3	5.5	Insurance	20.2	4.8	5.2	6.3
Paper, paper prods. & newsprint	87.7	10.7	10.9	11.5	Other services	462.2	3.2	3.3	3.8

Appendix A-4.3: Detailed Tables for Part II Simulations

Table A-4.3.1: ***Real Output (Rs. Billions at Base Price)***

SECTOR	BASE	(% change over base)					
	(Levels)	A	B	C	D	E	F
Paddy	911.4	-2.6	-4.0	-3.3	-3.2	-3.3	-2.7
Wheat	597.7	-1.9	-2.8	-2.3	-1.7	-0.5	0.3
Other cereals	188.0	-0.6	-1.0	-0.8	-0.7	-0.4	0.0
Pulses	235.3	-1.5	-2.6	-2.0	-1.4	-0.1	0.9
Sugarcane	234.0	-3.6	-5.7	-4.7	-4.1	-1.9	-0.4
Oilseeds	514.8	-3.8	-6.0	-4.9	-4.7	-4.7	-3.8
Jute	13.8	-2.8	-3.5	-2.8	-2.2	-0.8	0.6
Cotton	192.0	-4.8	-6.8	-5.6	-5.2	-4.1	-3.0
Tea & coffee	59.4	-3.5	-5.4	-4.3	-3.3	0.1	1.6
Rubber	31.7	-3.9	-5.6	-4.5	-4.5	-4.0	-3.5
Tobacco	19.2	-2.4	-2.7	-2.2	0.2	9.0	12.1
Other crops	1949.2	-2.5	-3.9	-3.1	-2.7	-1.6	-1.0
Milk and milk products	1133.5	-1.9	-3.1	-2.5	-1.9	-0.4	0.0
Other livestock products	716.3	-2.8	-4.4	-3.6	-3.3	-2.8	-2.3
Forestry and logging	302.2	-2.1	-3.5	-2.9	-2.5	-1.4	0.0
Fishing	317.9	-2.8	-4.0	-3.4	-3.1	-2.3	-1.7
Coal and lignite	328.6	-3.4	-5.0	-3.8	-3.4	-2.6	-1.4
Crude petroleum, natural gas	238.9	1.3	0.4	-8.6	-7.7	-7.7	-6.3
Iron ore	36.3	-4.3	-5.4	-4.5	-4.6	-5.0	-3.9
Other minerals	97.0	-2.9	-5.8	-4.4	-5.2	-9.6	-8.8
Sugar	199.4	-4.8	-7.7	-6.3	-5.8	-3.6	-1.8
Khandsari, boora	41.4	-5.1	-8.2	-6.7	-6.2	-4.3	-3.1
Edible, oil & *vanaspati*	435.9	-3.1	-5.2	-4.1	-3.5	-2.6	-1.1
Misc food products	1372.7	-4.5	-6.9	-5.6	-4.6	-1.5	0.2
Beverages & tobacco products	580.2	-4.8	-7.7	-6.3	-5.5	-1.5	0.3
Cotton textiles	511.3	-4.0	-5.4	-4.4	-3.4	-0.5	1.3
Wool synthetic, silk fibre textiles	410.6	-5.0	-7.3	-6.0	-5.6	-3.5	-2.4
Jute, hemp, mesta textiles	42.7	-0.7	0.7	0.7	2.5	7.5	10.2
Textile products	575.1	-4.9	-6.1	-5.2	-4.9	-3.6	-2.8
Furniture and wood products	141.7	-3.8	-5.5	-4.4	-3.6	-0.9	1.0
Paper, paper prods. & newsprint	270.4	-2.9	-3.7	-2.9	-2.2	-1.7	-0.9
Printing and publishing	153.0	-2.8	-4.5	-3.5	-2.1	0.7	1.4
Leather products	140.2	-4.6	-5.2	-4.6	-4.1	-2.8	-2.1
Rubber and plastic products	447.7	-4.3	-6.5	-5.2	-5.4	-5.8	-5.5
Petroleum products	1676.3	-4.4	-6.1	-4.1	-3.6	-2.4	-1.9
Coal tar products	78.2	-0.8	-3.1	-1.2	-1.3	-1.4	1.8

SECTOR	BASE	(% change over base)					
	(Levels)	A	B	C	D	E	F
Inorganic heavy chemicals	205.3	-2.8	-3.4	-2.4	-2.1	-2.6	-1.5
Organic heavy chemicals	157.9	-3.9	-4.2	-3.0	-2.8	-3.6	-2.7
Fertilisers	324.2	-2.0	-3.2	-2.3	-1.8	-1.0	-0.2
Pesticides	57.4	-2.9	-3.7	-3.0	-2.6	-1.9	-0.9
Paints, varnishes and lacquers	119.6	-4.7	-7.0	-5.7	-5.9	-6.1	-4.9
Misc chemicals	1087.4	-2.6	-3.9	-2.9	-2.5	-2.1	-1.5
Cement	498.8	-4.9	-6.0	-5.1	-5.2	-6.2	-4.9
Iron & steel	1302.6	-5.0	-7.9	-6.4	-6.9	-7.9	-6.7
Non-ferrous basic metals	375.2	-3.3	-5.3	-3.9	-4.3	-6.8	-6.1
Metal products	435.8	-4.9	-7.2	-6.0	-6.0	-5.7	-4.8
Other non-electric machinery	704.0	-5.5	-9.0	-7.3	-8.2	-9.8	-8.8
Electrical appliances	89.3	-5.6	-7.1	-6.1	-6.3	-5.9	-5.6
Communication equipments	117.3	-5.3	-6.9	-5.8	-6.2	-6.6	-5.9
Electronic equipments (incl.TV)	220.1	-7.3	-11.4	-9.5	-10.7	-10.1	-11.3
Other electrical machinery	364.6	-6.0	-9.7	-7.9	-8.9	-10.4	-8.4
Rail equipments	111.8	-7.1	-11.4	-9.5	-10.6	-13.0	-13.8
Other transport equipments	764.4	-7.2	-10.9	-9.1	-10.0	-10.1	-8.3
Misc manufacturing	725.7	-4.5	-5.5	-4.7	-4.4	-5.0	-4.5
Construction	4151.9	-8.3	-13.3	-11.2	-12.7	-16.0	-15.4
Electricity	1294.4	-4.0	-5.8	-4.6	-4.1	-2.7	-1.9
Gas	57.2	-6.2	-10.0	-8.3	-8.0	-7.6	-8.5
Water supply	97.3	-1.7	-2.5	-2.0	1.2	2.1	2.3
Railway transport services	428.5	-4.5	-6.6	-5.4	-5.0	-4.3	-3.9
Other transport services	3414.4	-4.4	-6.3	-4.7	-4.1	-1.3	-0.6
Storage and warehousing	25.3	-2.9	-4.1	-3.5	-3.4	-3.6	-3.3
Communication	592.1	-3.3	-4.9	-3.9	-2.7	-0.7	-1.0
Trade	4565.6	-2.9	-4.2	-3.5	-3.5	-3.7	-3.4
Hotels and restaurants	813.1	-3.4	-5.0	-4.0	-3.1	-0.5	-0.1
Banking	1842.5	-3.8	-5.8	-4.8	-4.2	-3.1	-2.5
Insurance	387.6	-3.9	-6.1	-4.9	-4.5	-3.2	-2.6
Ownership of dwellings	1269.4	-3.0	-4.5	-3.7	-2.4	1.0	-0.1
Education and research	1437.7	-1.7	-2.7	-2.2	0.5	2.2	2.0
Medical and health	1032.9	-3.2	-4.6	-3.8	-2.1	1.2	1.2
Other services	2848.8	-3.7	-5.3	-4.3	-3.6	-2.0	-1.4
Public administration	1568.2				5.0	5.0	5.0

Note: Scenarios A through to F are as defined in Table 4.7 in the main text.

Table A-4.3.2: Real Total Household Consumption (Rs. Billions at Base Price)

SECTOR	BASE	(% change over base)						SECTOR	BASE	(% change over base)					
	(Levels)	A	B	C	D	E	F		(Levels)	A	B	C	D	E	F
Paddy	566.5	-1.1	-1.8	-1.4	-1.2	-0.5	0.3	Petroleum products	330.7	-4.7	-6.3	-1.7	-0.7	2.2	1.7
Wheat	404.1	-1.2	-2.0	-1.6	-1.2	-0.4	0.1	Coal tar products	0.5	-1.0	-1.4	-1.0	-0.8	-0.1	-0.3
Other cereals	166.9	-0.3	-0.5	-0.4	-0.3	-0.1	0.1	Paints, varnishes and lacquers	6.7	-1.0	-1.4	-1.1	-1.0	-0.2	0.0
Pulses	176.1	-1.8	-2.9	-2.4	-1.9	-0.8	0.0	Misc chemicals	240.2	-0.9	-1.3	-1.1	-0.9	-0.3	-0.1
Sugarcane	72.4	-1.6	-2.7	-2.2	-1.8	-0.8	0.0	Cement	14.8	-6.6	-8.3	-7.1	-6.0	-2.0	-0.5
Oilseeds	76.6	-1.7	-2.7	-2.2	-1.7	-0.7	0.1	Metal products	87.2	-5.0	-7.2	-6.0	-4.9	-0.2	1.0
Tea & coffee	13.1	-1.6	-2.6	-2.1	-1.6	-0.6	-0.2	Other non electric machinery	17.6	-6.3	-8.3	-7.1	-5.8	-0.3	-1.4
Tobacco	1.1	-1.9	-2.9	-2.5	-2.2	-1.8	-1.0	Electrical appliances	9.1	-6.3	-8.2	-7.1	-5.9	0.3	0.2
Other crops	1086.4	-1.7	-2.7	-2.2	-1.7	-0.6	-0.2	Communication equipments	6.8	-7.5	-9.5	-8.3	-7.0	-1.8	-3.3
Milk and milk products	976.1	-1.6	-2.6	-2.1	-1.6	-0.3	-0.1	Electronic equipments (incl.TV)	49.6	-6.1	-8.0	-6.8	-5.5	1.6	0.4
Other livestock products	379.6	-1.6	-2.7	-2.2	-1.8	-0.6	0.1	Other electrical machinery	11.9	-6.1	-8.2	-7.0	-5.9	-0.6	-0.6
Forestry and logging	216.7	-1.8	-2.9	-2.5	-2.1	-0.9	0.5	Other transport equipments	114.7	-4.9	-6.6	-5.4	-4.1	3.7	3.1
Fishing	225.6	-1.7	-2.7	-2.3	-1.8	-0.4	0.3	Misc manufacturing	143.8	-7.2	-9.5	-8.2	-7.2	-3.0	-3.2
Coal and lignite	7.4	-2.4	-3.5	-2.9	-2.0	0.1	-0.6	Electricity	173.8	-3.8	-5.7	-4.1	-3.0	0.6	0.5
Sugar	139.0	-4.2	-6.9	-5.7	-4.6	-0.9	1.6	Gas	20.8	-6.0	-9.3	-7.6	-5.3	0.8	-0.7
Khandsari, boora	20.4	-4.3	-7.0	-5.6	-4.5	-0.5	1.5	Water supply	18.3	-3.3	-5.0	-4.1	-2.9	0.5	-0.3
Edible, oil & *vanaspati*	452.0	-4.5	-6.7	-5.7	-4.8	-2.2	-0.7	Railway transport services	97.4	-3.8	-5.6	-4.4	-3.1	1.0	0.0
Misc food products	1056.5	-4.5	-7.1	-5.7	-4.6	-0.8	1.2	Other transport services	1833.5	-4.7	-6.9	-5.0	-4.0	1.4	2.0
Beverages & tobacco products	493.3	-4.6	-7.3	-6.0	-5.0	-0.1	1.9	Communication	300.8	-3.3	-4.8	-3.9	-2.7	0.6	-0.4
Cotton textiles	298.8	-4.9	-7.5	-6.1	-5.0	-1.6	0.2	Trade	1903.3						
Wool synthetic, silk fibre textiles	198.5	-5.3	-7.9	-6.5	-5.4	-0.5	1.4	Hotels and restaurants	632.3	-3.7	-5.5	-4.5	-3.5	-0.2	0.1
Jute, hemp, mesta textiles	1.2	-5.4	-8.3	-6.8	-5.9	-3.2	-1.5	Banking	589.6	-3.1	-5.0	-4.1	-3.1	-0.5	-0.2
Textile products	299.9	-6.0	-8.5	-7.2	-6.5	-3.1	-2.4	Insurance	191.8	-3.6	-5.4	-4.5	-3.5	-0.4	-0.1
Furniture and wood products	25.8	-4.8	-7.0	-5.8	-4.6	-1.5	-2.2	Ownership of dwellings	1269.4	-3.0	-4.5	-3.7	-2.4	1.0	-0.1
Paper, paper prods. & newsprint	36.8	-7.1	-9.1	-7.8	-6.3	-1.5	-3.4	Education and research	807.1	-3.1	-4.8	-4.0	-2.9	0.0	-0.2
Printing and publishing	117.7	-6.1	-8.6	-7.4	-6.2	-1.8	-1.4	Medical and health	819.2	-4.0	-5.8	-4.8	-3.9	0.3	0.3
Leather products	51.6	-5.6	-7.7	-6.6	-5.6	-2.1	-1.8	Other services	979.1	-4.2	-6.0	-4.9	-4.0	-0.5	0.0
Rubber and plastic products	91.5	-0.8	-1.2	-1.0	-0.8	-0.1	0.1								

Note: Scenarios A through to F are as defined in Table 4.7 in the main text.

Table A-4.3.3: *Import Volumes*

SECTOR	BASE	(% change over base)						SECTOR	BASE	(% change over base)					
	(Levels)	A	B	C	D	E	F		(Levels)	A	B	C	D	E	F
Paddy	0.003	-15.07	-17.5	-16.8	-17.0	-12.0	-13.4	Printing and publishing	55.4	-10.3	-12.9	-11.7	-10.4	-6.8	-7.4
Wheat	0.003	-14.23	-16.2	-15.8	-15.6	-9.5	-10.7	Leather products	13.5	-10.7	-13.2	-12.0	-10.9	-6.4	-7.0
Other cereals	0.02	-7.213	-8.1	-8.0	-8.0	-5.1	-5.8	Rubber and plastic products	59.8	-11.8	-15.3	-13.9	-14.4	-15.2	-16.2
Pulses	23.9	-8.133	-9.8	-9.1	-8.7	-4.8	-4.9	Petroleum products	106.3	-6.7	-8.8	-7.2	-6.8	-4.3	-4.3
Sugarcane	0.2	-10.31	-12.9	-11.7	-11.2	-6.4	-6.0	Coal tar products	44.5	-8.7	-11.6	-12.6	-12.9	-11.3	-9.5
Oilseeds	0.02	-13.23	-16.4	-15.0	-15.0	-11.1	-11.7	Inorganic heavy chemicals	68.8	-7.0	-9.0	-8.4	-8.2	-6.3	-6.0
Jute	1.0	-9.532	-10.8	-9.9	-9.4	-5.4	-5.1	Organic heavy chemicals	192.3	-4.0	-5.5	-4.7	-4.3	-3.4	-2.6
Rubber	0.5	-10.61	-12.8	-11.4	-11.5	-8.2	-8.7	Fertilisers	21.5	-8.4	-10.2	-13.2	-13.0	-10.4	-10.6
Tobacco	0.2	-7.218	-8.2	-7.3	-3.9	14.0	17.2	Pesticides	5.2	-8.1	-10.2	-9.6	-9.1	-7.8	-7.8
Other crops	36.9	-9.161	-11.1	-10.1	-9.8	-5.9	-6.4	Paints, varnishes and lacquers	16.2	-10.1	-13.9	-12.7	-13.2	-14.6	-14.0
Other livestock products	3.8	-9.494	-11.6	-10.5	-10.4	-7.8	-8.4	Misc chemicals	210.7	-9.3	-11.7	-11.2	-10.9	-9.9	-10.6
Forestry and logging	29.4	-8.83	-10.8	-9.8	-9.5	-6.6	-6.3	Cement	112.8	-9.0	-14.6	-12.7	-13.7	-13.5	-11.2
Fishing	0.8	-8.848	-10.9	-10.0	-9.8	-7.5	-8.0	Iron & steel	108.7	-13.1	-16.9	-15.5	-16.3	-17.1	-17.3
Coal and lignite	11.7	-9.707	-11.8	-10.5	-10.3	-7.7	-7.5	Non-ferrous basic metals	418.5	-9.1	-12.4	-10.9	-11.6	-12.9	-13.3
Crude petroleum, natural gas	900.3	-4.596	-6.0	-2.3	-1.5	1.0	1.6	Metal products	31.8	-12.5	-16.3	-14.8	-15.2	-15.7	-16.0
Iron ore	3.7	-8.598	-11.9	-10.4	-10.8	-9.6	-8.7	Other non-electric machinery	466.2	-13.1	-18.2	-16.3	-17.7	-22.1	-22.1
Other minerals	363.2	-8.925	-12.9	-11.1	-12.3	-14.8	-14.9	Electrical appliances	27.3	-12.2	-17.0	-15.1	-16.2	-20.5	-21.8
Sugar	0.8	-14.25	-18.0	-16.4	-16.0	-13.1	-12.8	Communication equipments	159.5	-11.2	-16.1	-14.1	-15.4	-18.9	-19.1
Khandsari, boora	0.01	-14.47	-18.1	-16.6	-16.4	-13.9	-14.2	Electronic equipments (incl.TV)	95.4	-14.3	-19.6	-17.6	-19.0	-24.4	-26.5
Edible, oil & *vanaspati*	178.5	-9.008	-11.8	-10.6	-10.1	-6.9	-6.4	Other electrical machinery	181.0	-13.4	-18.6	-16.5	-18.0	-22.1	-20.9
Misc food products	11.3	-13.44	-16.8	-15.4	-14.6	-10.2	-9.9	Rail equipments	4.9	-15.3	-20.1	-18.2	-19.5	-23.8	-25.6
Beverages & tobacco products	4.2	-13.49	-16.9	-15.5	-14.8	-12.1	-11.8	Other transport equipments	51.8	-15.2	-20.4	-18.4	-19.7	-25.3	-24.5
Cotton textiles	26.3	-12.28	-14.9	-13.9	-12.8	-7.3	-6.8	Misc manufacturing	460.3	-8.5	-11.8	-10.4	-9.9	-10.1	-11.0
Wool synthetic, silk fibre textiles	40.2	-12.79	-16.3	-14.9	-14.7	-13.5	-13.7	Other transport services	278.0	-9.6	-12.4	-11.8	-11.2	-10.2	-10.4
Jute, hemp, mesta textiles	3.0	-7.24	-6.2	-6.4	-4.0	6.5	8.4	Communication	2.8	-9.7	-11.8	-10.6	-9.6	-6.2	-7.5
Textile products	62.7	-12.14	-15.9	-14.3	-13.7	-10.4	-10.7	Hotels and restaurants	55.6	-9.4	-11.7	-10.6	-9.7	-6.1	-6.7
Furniture and wood products	5.1	-12.89	-15.4	-14.0	-13.4	-7.3	-6.9	Insurance	36.3	-10.3	-13.0	-11.6	-11.4	-8.9	-9.3
Paper, paper prods. & newsprint	112.0	-7.655	-10.0	-8.8	-7.9	-5.0	-5.2	Other services	389.5	-8.9	-11.4	-10.3	-9.6	-7.6	-8.0

Note: Scenarios A through to F are as defined in Table 4.7 in the main text.

Table A-4.3.4: *Export Volumes*

SECTOR	BASE	(% change over base)						SECTOR	BASE	(% change over base)					
	(Levels)	A	B	C	D	E	F		(Levels)	A	B	C	D	E	F
Paddy	40.3	-5.2	-5.4	-5.0	-4.9	-5.6	-5.0	Printing and publishing	7.6	-5.4	-5.7	-5.2	-5.0	-5.2	-4.6
Wheat	26.2	-5.1	-5.3	-4.8	-4.7	-5.3	-4.6	Leather products	66.1	-5.6	-5.7	-5.3	-5.2	-5.5	-4.9
Other cereals	3.2	-5.0	-5.1	-4.7	-4.6	-5.2	-4.6	Rubber and plastic products	60.8	-5.6	-5.9	-5.3	-5.3	-5.9	-5.3
Pulses	2.3	-5.1	-5.3	-4.8	-4.7	-5.2	-4.5	Petroleum products	144.4	-6.0	-6.3	-5.5	-5.4	-5.7	-5.2
Sugarcane	0.9	-5.3	-5.6	-5.1	-5.0	-5.5	-4.7	Inorganic heavy chemicals	71.8	-5.5	-5.6	-5.0	-4.9	-5.5	-4.9
Oilseeds	50.5	-5.3	-5.7	-5.2	-5.1	-5.8	-5.1	Organic heavy chemicals	115.7	-5.7	-5.8	-5.0	-5.0	-5.6	-4.9
Jute	0.1	-5.2	-5.3	-4.9	-4.8	-5.3	-4.6	Fertilisers	0.4	-5.5	-5.7	-4.8	-4.7	-5.1	-4.5
Cotton	5.0	-5.5	-5.8	-5.2	-5.1	-5.7	-5.0	Pesticides	15.2	-5.5	-5.7	-5.2	-5.0	-5.5	-4.8
Rubber	0.5	-5.3	-5.6	-5.1	-5.0	-5.7	-5.1	Paints, varnishes and lacquers	24.4	-5.9	-6.2	-5.6	-5.6	-6.1	-5.4
Tobacco	6.3	-5.1	-5.2	-4.8	-4.5	-4.3	-3.3	Misc chemicals	169.0	-5.4	-5.6	-5.0	-4.9	-5.4	-4.8
Other crops	58.9	-5.2	-5.4	-4.9	-4.8	-5.4	-4.8	Cement	342.4	-5.7	-5.9	-5.3	-5.3	-6.0	-5.3
Other livestock products	2.5	-5.2	-5.4	-5.0	-4.9	-5.6	-4.9	Iron & steel	79.8	-5.7	-6.0	-5.4	-5.4	-6.0	-5.4
Forestry and logging	13.4	-5.1	-5.3	-4.9	-4.8	-5.4	-4.7	Non-ferrous basic metals	56.7	-5.6	-5.9	-5.3	-5.3	-6.1	-5.5
Fishing	48.1	-5.2	-5.4	-5.0	-4.9	-5.5	-4.8	Metal products	75.6	-5.7	-6.0	-5.4	-5.4	-5.8	-5.2
Coal and lignite	1.7	-5.3	-5.6	-5.1	-5.0	-5.5	-4.8	Other non-electric machinery	101.4	-5.8	-6.2	-5.6	-5.7	-6.3	-5.7
Crude petroleum, natural gas	2.0	-4.7	-4.9	-7.8	-7.6	-8.3	-7.6	Electrical appliances	40.9	-5.8	-6.1	-5.5	-5.5	-5.9	-5.3
Iron ore	18.8	-5.4	-5.6	-5.1	-5.0	-5.8	-5.1	Communication equipments	52.8	-5.8	-6.0	-5.5	-5.5	-6.0	-5.3
Other minerals	16.1	-5.2	-5.6	-5.1	-5.1	-6.4	-5.7	Electronic equipments (incl.TV)	14.7	-6.1	-6.6	-6.0	-6.1	-6.4	-6.0
Sugar	10.9	-5.5	-5.9	-5.3	-5.2	-5.6	-4.9	Other electrical machinery	43.1	-5.9	-6.3	-5.7	-5.8	-6.5	-5.7
Khandsari, boora	0.02	-5.5	-6.0	-5.4	-5.3	-5.7	-5.0	Rail equipments	1.1	-5.9	-6.5	-5.8	-5.9	-6.7	-6.3
Edible, oil & *vanaspati*	25.4	-5.3	-5.6	-5.1	-5.0	-5.5	-4.8	Other transport equipments	79.3	-5.9	-6.4	-5.8	-5.9	-6.3	-5.5
Misc food products	85.5	-5.5	-5.8	-5.3	-5.1	-5.3	-4.5	Misc manufacturing	348.7	-5.8	-6.0	-5.5	-5.4	-5.9	-5.3
Beverages & tobacco products	3.5	-5.6	-6.0	-5.4	-5.3	-5.4	-4.6	Railway transport services	22.6	-5.5	-5.8	-5.2	-5.1	-5.6	-5.0
Cotton textiles	80.7	-5.5	-5.7	-5.1	-5.0	-5.2	-4.4	Other transport services	403.9	-5.6	-5.9	-5.1	-4.9	-5.2	-4.5
Wool synthetic, silk fibre textiles	48.6	-5.7	-6.0	-5.4	-5.3	-5.5	-4.9	Communication	4.7	-5.3	-5.5	-5.1	-4.9	-5.3	-4.8
Jute, hemp, mesta textiles	10.6	-5.1	-4.9	-4.5	-4.3	-4.3	-3.4	Trade	526.2	-5.2	-5.4	-5.0	-4.9	-5.7	-5.0
Textile products	257.9	-5.6	-5.8	-5.3	-5.2	-5.6	-4.9	Hotels and restaurants	100.6	-5.3	-5.6	-5.1	-4.9	-5.2	-4.6
Furniture and wood products	10.0	-5.4	-5.6	-5.1	-5.0	-5.3	-4.5	Insurance	20.1	-5.4	-5.7	-5.2	-5.1	-5.6	-4.9
Paper, paper prods. & newsprint	87.4	-5.5	-5.6	-5.1	-5.0	-5.5	-4.9	Other services	461.2	-5.5	-5.7	-5.2	-5.0	-5.4	-4.8

Note: Scenarios A through to F are as defined in Table 4.7 in the main text.

Table A-4.3.5: *Domestic Market Price (Rs. Per Unit)*

SECTOR	BASE	(% change over base)						SECTOR	BASE	(% change over base)					
	(Levels)	A	B	C	D	E	F		(Levels)	A	B	C	D	E	F
Paddy	1.0	0.4	0.2	-0.1	0.1	-0.2	0.0	Inorganic heavy chemicals	1.0	2.5	2.2	1.5	0.9	-1.4	0.3
Wheat	1.0	0.5	0.3	-0.1	0.2	-0.3	0.1	Organic heavy chemicals	1.0	3.7	3.5	2.6	1.3	-2.2	0.4
Other cereals	1.0	0.4	0.2	-0.2	0.2	-0.3	0.1	Fertilisers	1.0	2.1	2.0	-0.4	0.7	-1.2	0.2
Pulses	1.0	0.4	0.2	-0.1	0.1	-0.2	0.0	Pesticides	1.0	2.2	1.9	1.4	0.8	-1.3	0.3
Sugarcane	1.0	0.2	0.0	-0.2	0.1	-0.1	0.0	Paints, varnishes and lacquers	1.0	2.4	2.0	1.5	0.8	-1.4	0.3
Oilseeds	1.0	0.4	0.1	-0.1	0.1	-0.2	0.0	Misc chemicals	1.0	1.7	1.4	0.7	0.6	-1.0	0.2
Jute	1.0	0.2	0.0	-0.1	0.1	-0.1	0.0	Cement	1.0	2.4	1.1	1.0	0.8	-1.4	0.3
Cotton	1.0	0.4	0.2	-0.1	0.1	-0.2	0.0	Iron & steel	1.0	1.1	0.8	0.4	0.4	-0.6	0.1
Tea & coffee	1.0	0.1	-0.1	-0.1	0.0	-0.1	0.0	Non-ferrous basic metals	1.0	2.2	1.8	1.4	0.7	-1.2	0.2
Rubber	1.0	0.2	0.0	-0.1	0.1	-0.1	0.0	Metal products	1.0	1.3	0.8	0.5	0.5	-0.8	0.2
Tobacco	1.0	0.8	0.6	0.5	0.3	-0.5	0.1	Other non-electric machinery	1.0	1.3	0.8	0.5	0.5	-0.8	0.2
Other crops	1.0	0.3	0.0	-0.1	0.1	-0.1	0.0	Electrical appliances	1.0	1.8	0.8	0.7	0.6	-1.0	0.2
Milk and milk products	1.0	0.1	-0.1	-0.2	0.0	0.0	0.0	Communication equipments	1.0	2.0	1.0	0.9	0.7	-1.1	0.2
Other livestock products	1.0	0.2	0.0	-0.1	0.1	-0.1	0.0	Electronic equipments (incl.TV)	1.0	1.6	1.2	0.9	0.6	-0.9	0.2
Forestry and logging	1.0	0.2	0.0	-0.1	0.1	-0.1	0.0	Other electrical machinery	1.0	1.4	0.9	0.7	0.5	-0.8	0.2
Fishing	1.0	0.5	0.2	0.0	0.2	-0.3	0.1	Rail equipments	1.0	1.0	0.7	0.4	0.3	-0.6	0.1
Coal and lignite	1.0	0.5	0.3	0.1	0.2	-0.3	0.1	Other transport equipments	1.0	1.1	0.6	0.3	0.4	-0.6	0.1
Crude petroleum, natural gas	1.0	0.3	0.1	-0.1	0.1	-0.2	0.0	Misc manufacturing	1.0	2.7	2.1	1.9	0.9	-1.6	0.3
Iron ore	1.0	1.2	0.4	0.2	0.4	-0.7	0.1	Construction	1.0	1.1	0.9	0.5	0.4	-0.6	0.1
Other minerals	1.0	0.5	0.0	0.0	0.2	-0.3	0.1	Electricity	1.0	0.9	0.7	-0.2	0.3	-0.5	0.1
Sugar	1.0	0.4	0.1	-0.1	0.1	-0.2	0.0	Gas	1.0	0.1	-0.1	-0.1	0.0	-0.1	0.0
Khandsari, boora	1.0	0.4	0.2	-0.1	0.1	-0.2	0.0	Water supply	1.0	0.4	0.2	0.1	0.1	-0.2	0.0
Edible, oil & *vanaspati*	1.0	0.7	0.4	0.2	0.3	-0.4	0.1	Railway transport services	1.0	0.6	0.3	-0.1	0.2	-0.3	0.1
Misc food products	1.0	0.6	0.3	0.0	0.2	-0.4	0.1	Other transport services	1.0	1.2	0.9	-0.3	0.4	-0.7	0.1
Beverages & tobacco products	1.0	0.8	0.6	0.3	0.3	-0.5	0.1	Storage and warehousing	1.0	0.6	0.3	0.1	0.2	-0.3	0.1
Cotton textiles	1.0	0.9	0.5	0.2	0.3	-0.5	0.1	Communication	1.0	0.5	0.2	0.1	0.2	-0.3	0.1
Wool synthetic, silk fibre textiles	1.0	1.2	0.8	0.5	0.4	-0.7	0.1	Trade	1.0	0.5	0.2	0.0	0.2	-0.3	0.1
Jute, hemp, mesta textiles	1.0	1.4	1.4	1.0	0.5	-0.8	0.2	Hotels and restaurants	1.0	0.6	0.3	0.1	0.2	-0.4	0.1
Textile products	1.0	1.3	0.5	0.4	0.4	-0.7	0.1	Banking	1.0	0.2	0.0	0.0	0.1	-0.1	0.0
Furniture and wood products	1.0	0.6	0.3	0.2	0.2	-0.3	0.1	Insurance	1.0	0.4	0.2	0.0	0.1	-0.2	0.0
Paper, paper prods. & newsprint	1.0	2.3	1.9	1.6	0.8	-1.3	0.3	Ownership of dwellings	1.0	0.1	-0.1	-0.1	0.0	0.0	0.0
Printing and publishing	1.0	1.4	1.2	0.9	0.5	-0.8	0.2	Education and research	1.0	0.2	0.0	-0.1	0.1	-0.1	0.0
Leather products	1.0	1.7	1.1	1.0	0.6	-1.0	0.2	Medical and health	1.0	1.2	1.0	0.7	0.4	-0.7	0.1
Rubber and plastic products	1.0	1.3	0.9	0.6	0.5	-0.8	0.2	Other services	1.0	1.1	0.8	0.4	0.4	-0.7	0.1
Petroleum products	1.0	3.1	3.0	-2.9	1.1	-1.8	0.4	Public administration	1.0	0.0	-0.2	-0.2	0.0	0.0	0.0
Coal tar products	1.0	1.4	1.2	-0.6	0.5	-0.8	0.2								

Note: Scenarios A through to F are as defined in Table 4.7 in the main text.

Table A-4.3.6: ***Composite Price Paid by Domestic Users (Rs. Per Unit)***

SECTOR	BASE	(% change over base)						SECTOR	BASE	(% change over base)					
	(Levels)	A	B	C	D	E	F		(Levels)	A	B	C	D	E	F
Paddy	1.0	0.4	0.2	-0.1	0.1	-0.2	0.0	Inorganic heavy chemicals	1.0	3.4	3.3	2.7	1.2	-2.0	0.4
Wheat	1.0	0.5	0.3	-0.1	0.2	-0.3	0.1	Organic heavy chemicals	1.0	5.0	5.1	4.6	1.7	-2.9	0.6
Other cereals	1.0	0.4	0.2	-0.2	0.2	-0.3	0.1	Fertilisers	1.0	2.3	2.2	-0.1	0.8	-1.3	0.3
Pulses	1.0	0.8	0.7	0.4	0.3	-0.5	0.1	Pesticides	1.0	2.5	2.2	1.8	0.9	-1.4	0.3
Sugarcane	1.0	0.2	0.0	-0.2	0.1	-0.1	0.0	Paints, varnishes and lacquers	1.0	2.8	2.5	2.0	1.0	-1.6	0.3
Oilseeds	1.0	0.4	0.1	-0.1	0.1	-0.2	0.0	Misc chemicals	1.0	2.3	2.1	1.5	0.8	-1.3	0.3
Jute	1.0	0.6	0.4	0.2	0.2	-0.3	0.1	Cement	1.0	3.6	2.9	2.7	1.2	-2.0	0.4
Cotton	1.0	0.4	0.2	-0.1	0.1	-0.2	0.0	Iron & steel	1.0	1.5	1.1	0.7	0.5	-0.8	0.2
Tea & coffee	1.0	0.1	-0.1	-0.1	0.0	-0.1	0.0	Non-ferrous basic metals	1.0	3.9	3.9	3.5	1.3	-2.2	0.4
Rubber	1.0	0.3	0.1	0.0	0.1	-0.1	0.0	Metal products	1.0	1.6	1.2	0.9	0.6	-0.9	0.2
Tobacco	1.0	0.9	0.7	0.5	0.3	-0.5	0.1	Other non-electric machinery	1.0	3.0	2.8	2.5	1.0	-1.7	0.3
Other crops	1.0	0.4	0.1	0.0	0.1	-0.2	0.0	Electrical appliances	1.0	3.0	2.4	2.2	1.0	-1.7	0.3
Milk and milk products	1.0	0.1	-0.1	-0.2	0.0	0.0	0.0	Communication equipments	1.0	4.3	4.2	3.9	1.5	-2.5	0.5
Other livestock products	1.0	0.3	0.1	0.0	0.1	-0.2	0.0	Electronic equipments (incl.TV)	1.0	2.7	2.5	2.2	0.9	-1.6	0.3
Forestry and logging	1.0	0.7	0.5	0.4	0.2	-0.4	0.1	Other electrical machinery	1.0	2.8	2.5	2.2	1.0	-1.6	0.3
Fishing	1.0	0.5	0.2	0.0	0.2	-0.3	0.1	Rail equipments	1.0	1.2	0.9	0.6	0.4	-0.7	0.1
Coal and lignite	1.0	0.7	0.5	0.3	0.2	-0.4	0.1	Other transport equipments	1.0	1.4	0.9	0.6	0.5	-0.8	0.2
Crude petroleum, natural gas	1.0	4.2	4.4	-4.3	1.5	-2.4	0.5	Misc manufacturing	1.0	4.1	4.0	3.6	1.4	-2.4	0.5
Iron ore	1.0	1.9	1.3	1.0	0.6	-1.1	0.2	Construction	1.0	1.1	0.9	0.5	0.4	-0.6	0.1
Other minerals	1.0	4.4	4.5	4.2	1.5	-2.5	0.5	Electricity	1.0	0.9	0.7	-0.2	0.3	-0.5	0.1
Sugar	1.0	0.4	0.1	-0.1	0.1	-0.2	0.0	Gas	1.0	0.1	-0.1	-0.1	0.0	-0.1	0.0
Khandsari, boora	1.0	0.4	0.2	-0.1	0.1	-0.2	0.0	Water supply	1.0	0.4	0.2	0.1	0.1	-0.2	0.0
Edible, oil & *vanaspati*	1.0	2.1	1.9	1.6	0.7	-1.2	0.2	Railway transport services	1.0	0.6	0.3	-0.1	0.2	-0.3	0.1
Misc food products	1.0	0.7	0.4	0.1	0.2	-0.4	0.1	Other transport services	1.0	1.6	1.3	0.1	0.5	-0.9	0.2
Beverages & tobacco products	1.0	0.9	0.6	0.4	0.3	-0.5	0.1	Storage and warehousing	1.0	0.6	0.3	0.1	0.2	-0.3	0.1
Cotton textiles	1.0	1.1	0.8	0.5	0.4	-0.7	0.1	Communication	1.0	0.5	0.3	0.1	0.2	-0.3	0.1
Wool synthetic, silk fibre textiles	1.0	1.6	1.3	0.9	0.6	-0.9	0.2	Trade	1.0	0.5	0.2	0.0	0.2	-0.3	0.1
Jute, hemp, mesta textiles	1.0	1.8	1.7	1.3	0.6	-1.0	0.2	Hotels and restaurants	1.0	1.0	0.7	0.4	0.3	-0.6	0.1
Textile products	1.0	1.9	1.3	1.1	0.7	-1.1	0.2	Banking	1.0	0.2	0.0	0.0	0.1	-0.1	0.0
Furniture and wood products	1.0	0.8	0.5	0.3	0.3	-0.4	0.1	Insurance	1.0	0.8	0.6	0.4	0.3	-0.5	0.1
Paper, paper prods. & newsprint	1.0	3.4	3.2	2.9	1.2	-2.0	0.4	Ownership of dwellings	1.0	0.1	-0.1	-0.1	0.0	0.0	0.0
Printing and publishing	1.0	2.4	2.3	2.1	0.8	-1.4	0.3	Education and research	1.0	0.2	0.0	-0.1	0.1	-0.1	0.0
Leather products	1.0	2.2	1.8	1.6	0.8	-1.3	0.3	Medical and health	1.0	1.2	1.0	0.7	0.4	-0.7	0.1
Rubber and plastic products	1.0	1.8	1.5	1.2	0.6	-1.1	0.2	Other services	1.0	1.7	1.4	1.0	0.6	-1.0	0.2
Petroleum products	1.0	3.2	3.2	-2.7	1.1	-1.9	0.4	Public administration	1.0	0.0	-0.2	-0.2	0.0	0.0	0.0
Coal tar products	1.0	2.8	2.7	1.4	0.9	-1.6	0.3								

Note: Scenarios A through to F are as defined in Table 4.7 in the main text.

Table A-4.3.7: *Capital Supply and Unemployment*

SECTOR	BASE Capital Stock (Rs. billions)	Unemployed Capital(%)						SECTOR	BASE Capital Stock (Rs. billions)	Unemployed Capital(%)					
		A	B	C	D	E	F			A	B	C	D	E	F
Paddy	286.7	2.7	4.4	3.6	3.6	3.6	3.0	Inorganic heavy chemicals	42.7	3.5	4.3	3.3	3.1	3.5	2.4
Wheat	183.0	2.0	3.1	2.5	2.0	0.7	0.0	Organic heavy chemicals	37.3	4.5	4.9	3.7	3.5	4.3	3.4
Other cereals	58.2	0.7	1.2	1.0	0.9	0.6	0.2	Fertilisers	44.6	2.3	3.7	2.8	2.3	1.5	0.6
Pulses	75.3	1.7	3.1	2.4	1.8	0.6	-0.5	Pesticides	14.0	3.3	4.3	3.6	3.1	2.5	1.5
Sugarcane	87.2	3.8	6.1	5.1	4.5	2.3	0.8	Paints, varnishes and lacquers	16.2	5.2	7.6	6.3	6.6	6.8	5.5
Oilseeds	176.5	4.1	6.5	5.4	5.2	5.2	4.3	Misc chemicals	241.1	3.1	4.5	3.6	3.2	2.7	2.2
Jute	5.0	3.3	4.2	3.6	2.9	1.5	0.1	Cement	120.5	5.4	6.6	5.8	5.9	6.8	5.6
Cotton	66.6	5.1	7.3	6.1	5.7	4.5	3.5	Iron & steel	211.9	5.7	8.6	7.2	7.7	8.6	7.5
Tea & coffee	22.8	3.7	5.7	4.7	3.6	0.3	-1.3	Non-ferrous basic metals	62.0	4.3	6.5	5.1	5.5	7.9	7.3
Rubber	13.1	4.3	6.2	5.1	5.0	4.6	4.0	Metal products	49.7	5.3	7.8	6.5	6.6	6.2	5.4
Tobacco	8.1	2.4	2.9	2.4	0.0	-8.8	-11.9	Other non-electric machinery	89.8	6.2	9.8	8.1	9.0	10.7	9.7
Other crops	722.8	2.6	4.2	3.5	3.0	1.9	1.4	Electrical appliances	13.3	6.0	7.7	6.6	6.9	6.5	6.2
Milk and milk products	416.2	2.0	3.4	2.8	2.2	0.7	0.3	Communication equipments	11.3	5.8	7.5	6.5	6.9	7.3	6.6
Other livestock products	173.9	2.9	4.8	4.0	3.7	3.1	2.6	Electronic equipments (incl.TV)	22.2	7.7	12.0	10.0	11.2	10.7	11.9
Forestry and logging	124.5	2.4	4.0	3.4	3.0	1.9	0.4	Other electrical machinery	66.6	6.6	10.4	8.7	9.8	11.2	9.2
Fishing	103.7	3.0	4.4	3.7	3.4	2.6	2.0	Rail equipments	17.5	7.5	11.9	10.0	11.2	13.5	14.4
Coal and lignite	164.8	3.9	5.7	4.5	4.1	3.3	2.1	Other transport equipments	76.0	7.5	11.4	9.6	10.5	10.6	8.8
Crude petroleum, natural gas	186.9		1.1	9.9	9.1	9.1	7.7	Misc manufacturing	78.4	4.9	6.1	5.3	5.0	5.6	5.1
Iron ore	18.1	4.9	6.1	5.3	5.3	5.8	4.6	Construction	284.3	8.6	13.8	11.7	13.2	16.5	15.9
Other minerals	63.1	4.1	7.2	5.8	6.6	11.1	10.2	Electricity	58.9	4.2	6.3	5.1	4.5	3.1	2.4
Sugar	9.5	5.1	8.1	6.8	6.3	4.0	2.2	Gas	10.9	6.5	10.5	8.8	8.5	8.1	9.0
Khandsari, boora	1.5	5.3	8.6	7.1	6.6	4.8	3.5	Water supply	29.0	1.8	2.8	2.3	-0.9	-1.9	-2.0
Edible, oil & *vanaspati*	40.1	3.5	5.7	4.7	4.0	3.1	1.7	Railway transport services	81.4	4.8	7.1	5.9	5.5	4.8	4.4
Misc food products	99.5	4.7	7.3	6.0	5.0	1.8	0.1	Other transport services	496.3	4.6	6.7	5.1	4.5	1.7	1.0
Beverages & tobacco products	80.6	5.0	8.0	6.7	5.8	1.8	0.1	Storage and warehousing	6.8	3.1	4.5	3.8	3.8	4.0	3.7
Cotton textiles	67.1	4.2	5.9	4.9	3.8	0.9	-0.8	Communication	338.3	3.4	5.2	4.2	3.0	1.0	1.3
Wool synthetic, silk fibre textiles	57.2	5.3	7.8	6.5	6.1	4.0	2.9	Trade	2348.1	3.1	4.6	3.9	3.9	4.1	3.8
Jute, hemp, mesta textiles	3.9	1.1			0.0	0.0	0.0	Hotels and restaurants	99.3	3.6	5.3	4.4	3.5	0.9	0.4
Textile products	63.2	5.2	6.6	5.7	5.4	4.1	3.3	Banking	1021.5	4.1	6.3	5.2	4.7	3.5	2.9
Furniture and wood products	59.5	4.1	5.9	4.9	4.1	1.3	-0.6	Insurance	189.8	4.2	6.5	5.4	5.0	3.7	3.0
Paper, paper prods. & newsprint	28.4	3.5	4.5	3.7	3.1	2.6	1.7	Ownership of dwellings	988.4	3.0	4.7	3.9	2.6	-0.8	0.3
Printing and publishing	23.3	3.2	5.1	4.1	2.6	-0.1	-0.9	Education and research	267.0	1.8	3.0	2.5	-0.3	-2.0	-1.8
Leather products	10.8	4.9	5.7	5.0	4.5	3.2	2.5	Medical and health	88.8	3.2	4.8	4.0	2.3	-1.0	-1.1
Rubber and plastic products	49.4	4.7	7.1	5.8	6.0	6.4	6.1	Other services	587.2	4.0	5.8	4.7	4.1	2.4	1.8
Petroleum products	322.1	4.5	6.5	4.4	4.0	2.7	2.3	Public administration	152.3		0.2	0.2	0.2	0.2	0.2
Coal tar products	8.5	2.2	4.7	2.8	2.9	3.1	-0.3								

Note: Scenarios A through to F are as defined in Table 4.7 in the main text.

Appendix A-4.4: Social Accounting Matrix, 2003-04

As mentioned earlier, the underlying database for the CGE model is a modified version of the Social Accounting Matrix (SAM) for the year 2003-04 originally prepared by Saluja and Yadav (2006). The modifications pertain to (a) sectoral aggregation, (b) treatment of enterprise account, (c) breakdown of indirect taxes, and (d) disaggregation of labour and capital factors. Each of these modifications are briefly discussed here.

a) *Sectoral aggregation:* The original SAM of Saluja and Yadav (2006) contain 73 sectors. Problems with two sectors, *viz.*, animal services and other non-metallic mineral products, required them to be aggregated with other sectors to obtain a 71-sector SAM. Animal services sector was merged with other livestock sector due to the fact that the original SAM did not show any factor (labour or capital) incomes for animal services sector. Other non-metallic mineral products sector was aggregated with cement sector as the former showed large stock draw down and an exports figure that exceed gross output for that year implying a negative domestic demand from domestic production. Following these aggregations we work with a 71-sector SAM.

b) *Enterprise account:* The original SAM of Saluja and Yadav (2006) reports the income-expenditure accounts for private and public enterprises. In the CGE model used here the behaviour of enterprises are not explicitly modelled. Hence, we merge the private enterprise accounts with households, and public enterprise accounts with government accounts. In the original SAM the income of private enterprise is essentially from "capital factor", which is apportioned to the households. On the expenditure side, the original SAM has two entries for the private enterprise, *viz.*, (i) transfers (i.e., taxes) paid to the government, which is added to the government's income from "capital factor", and (ii) private corporate savings, which is apportioned to household and added to their savings. For public enterprise, the income and expenditure side has only one entry each (income from capital factor, and public enterprise savings), both of which are added to the government's account appropriately.

c) *Indirect taxes:* The original SAM of Saluja and Yadav (2006) reports only aggregate indirect tax collections from each sector. These have been broken down into import tariffs and domestic indirect taxes based on information on customs duty realisations from the *Economic Surveys* (various issues) and other available information on tariff rates, suitably calibrated to reflected the aggregate indirect tax collections reported in the original SAM.

d) *Factor disaggregations:* The final modification of the SAM pertains to the factor accounts. The original SAM reports only one aggregate labour and one aggregate capital factor. Income for both these factors come from the sectoral value added, and net factor income from abroad. The column entries in the SAM reflect the endowments of these two types of factors with households and the government.

As mentioned earlier, in the model we treat capital to be sector specific in the short run, implying a one-to-one mapping between the sectors and their payments to capital factor making the disaggregation of the capital row fairly obvious. To complete the disaggregation of the capital row, we assume that the net factor income accruing to capital goes to the capital used in the other services sector for want of more detailed information.[10] On the endowments side, we distribute each of the 71-sector specific capital to households and government in proportions reported in the original SAM. This assumption was necessitated due to absence of any information on the distribution of capital endowments across households and government in India.

Turning to labour, as mentioned earlier we distinguish labour into six types based on the broad industry of employment. We distinguish labour into agricultural labour, mining labour, two types of manufacturing labour (those employed in labour-intensive manufacturing and those employed in capital-intensive manufacturing), construction labour and services labour. The basis for this distinction of labour types is the data on the distribution of employment across industry groups from the National Sample

10. As per the original SAM, net foreign inflows to capital factor amounted to -0.9 per cent of the total earnings of capital in 2003-04.

Survey 61st Round survey on Employment and Unemployment Situation in India 2004-05 reported in Table A-4.4.1. It is seen that there is a clear difference in the employment pattern by industry types between rural and urban areas. This difference, along with the differences in the export dependence of different sectors, would mean that a shock to export demand is likely to have differential impact on rural and urban labour/households. The single labour in the original SAM is, therefore, disaggregated into the six types mentioned above.

Table A-4.4.1: Distribution of Workers in India by Industry of Employment, 2004-05

Industry of Employment	No. of Workers (millions)			Percentage Shares		
	Rural	Urban	Total	Rural	Urban	Total
Agriculture	230.8	7.9	238.6	72.6	8.7	58.5
Mining	1.6	0.7	2.2	0.5	0.7	0.5
Manufacturing-1	18.1	13.3	31.5	5.7	14.7	7.7
Manufacturing-2	7.6	8.9	16.4	2.4	9.8	4.0
Construction	15.4	7.3	22.7	4.9	8.0	5.6
Services	44.2	52.5	96.7	13.9	58.0	23.7
Total	317.7	90.5	408.1	100.0	100.0	100.0

Source: Authors calculations based on information in Statements 3.2 and 5.4 (Report 515-I), and Table 28 (Report 515-II), Employment and Unemployment Situation in India 2004-05 (61st Round), National Sample Survey Organisation.

We proceeded with labour disaggregation as follows: First, using the physical units of labour reported in Table A-4.4.1, and the value added accruing to these types of labour reported in the original SAM, we work out the implicit wage rate for each of these labour types.[11] The physical units of labour used in each sector and the sectoral payments made to each type of labour are then worked out. For simplicity, the net-foreign inflows accruing to labour factor are assumed to accrue to services labour, to complete the disaggregation of the labour row.[12] Turning to labour endowments across households, we assume that the distribution of labour by monthly expenditure classes reported in the NSS 61st Round Survey are applicable for each of the six labour types[13], and distribute the physical labour units reported in Table A-4.4.1 to complete the disaggregation of the labour column.

This modified SAM is reported in Table A-4.4.2.

11. These wage rates are used as the base wage rates in the simulations and are reported later along with the results on the labour market.

12. Net foreign inflows to labour factor amounted to -0.2 per cent of the total earnings of labour in 2003-04 in the original SAM.

13. Ideally, the distribution of each of these labour types across the expenditure classes should be worked out from the unit level data. Time constraints, however, did not permit us to process the unit level data and hence we had to resort to this assumption.

Table A-4.4.2: *Social Accounting Matrix (SAM), 2003-04 (Rs. Billions)*

	1	2	3	4	5	6	7	8	9	10	11	12	13	14	15
1) Paddy	84.7	0.8	0.0	0.9	0.0	0.0	0.0	0.0	0.0	0.0	0.0	11.1	0.0	5.1	0.0
2) Wheat	0.6	50.3	0.0	0.5	0.0	0.0	0.0	0.0	0.0	0.0	0.0	15.3	0.6	4.4	0.0
3) Other cereals	0.0	0.4	1.4	0.0	0.0	0.0	0.0	0.0	0.0	0.0	0.0	0.7	0.3	5.8	0.0
4) Pulses	0.5	5.0	0.0	14.3	0.0	0.0	0.0	0.0	0.0	0.0	0.0	7.8	7.0	8.9	0.0
5) Sugarcane	0.0	0.0	0.0	0.0	10.4	0.0	0.0	0.0	0.0	0.0	0.0	0.5	3.9	0.0	0.0
6) Oilseeds	0.0	0.0	0.0	0.0	0.0	16.4	0.0	0.0	0.0	0.0	0.0	0.5	0.0	0.0	0.0
7) Jute	0.0	0.0	0.0	0.0	0.0	0.0	0.0	0.0	0.0	0.0	0.0	0.0	0.0	0.0	0.0
8) Cotton	0.0	0.0	0.0	0.2	0.0	0.0	0.0	0.8	0.0	0.0	0.0	0.3	0.0	0.0	0.0
9) Tea & coffee	0.0	0.0	0.0	0.0	0.0	0.0	0.0	0.0	0.0	0.0	0.0	0.2	0.0	0.0	0.0
10) Rubber	0.0	0.0	0.0	0.0	0.0	0.0	0.0	0.0	0.0	0.0	0.0	0.0	0.0	0.0	0.0
11) Tobacco	0.0	0.0	0.0	0.0	0.0	0.0	0.0	0.0	0.0	0.0	0.0	0.0	0.0	0.0	0.0
12) Other crops	0.2	0.2	0.0	0.2	0.0	0.0	0.0	0.0	0.0	0.0	0.0	10.9	102.1	209.4	0.0
13) Milk and milk products	0.0	0.1	0.0	0.1	0.0	0.0	0.0	0.0	0.0	0.0	0.0	0.4	1.4	0.0	0.0
14) Other livestock products	19.3	11.7	17.2	13.5	3.0	30.9	1.1	7.4	3.6	0.0	0.2	70.6	0.0	0.1	0.0
15) Forestry and logging	0.0	0.0	0.0	0.0	0.0	0.0	0.0	0.0	0.0	0.0	0.0	0.0	0.4	0.0	1.2
16) Fishing	0.0	0.0	0.0	0.0	0.0	0.0	0.0	0.0	0.0	0.0	0.0	0.1	0.0	0.0	0.0
17) Coal and lignite	0.0	0.0	0.0	0.0	0.0	0.0	0.0	0.0	0.0	0.0	0.0	0.0	0.0	0.1	0.0
18) Crude petroleum, natural gas	0.0	0.0	0.0	0.0	0.0	0.0	0.0	0.0	0.0	0.0	0.0	0.0	0.0	0.0	0.0
19) Iron ore	0.0	0.0	0.0	0.0	0.0	0.0	0.0	0.0	0.0	0.0	0.0	0.0	0.0	0.0	0.0
20) Other minerals	0.0	0.0	0.0	0.0	0.0	0.0	0.0	0.0	0.0	0.0	0.0	0.0	0.0	0.0	0.0
21) Sugar	0.0	0.0	0.0	0.0	0.0	0.0	0.0	0.0	0.0	0.0	0.0	0.1	0.0	0.0	0.0
22) *Khandsari, boora*	0.0	0.0	0.0	0.0	0.0	0.0	0.0	0.0	0.0	0.0	0.0	0.0	0.0	0.0	0.0
23) Edible, oil & *vanaspati*	0.0	0.0	0.0	0.1	0.0	0.0	0.0	0.0	0.0	0.0	0.0	0.1	10.4	14.5	0.0
24) Misc food products	0.1	0.1	0.0	0.1	0.0	0.0	0.0	0.0	0.0	0.0	0.0	0.4	0.6	4.8	0.0
25) Beverages & tobacco products	0.0	0.0	0.0	0.0	0.0	0.0	0.0	0.0	0.0	0.0	0.0	0.1	0.0	0.0	0.0
26) Cotton textiles	0.0	0.0	0.0	0.0	0.0	0.0	0.0	0.0	0.0	0.0	0.0	0.0	4.8	0.2	0.0
27) Wool synthetic, silk fibre textiles	0.0	0.0	0.0	0.0	0.0	0.0	0.0	0.1	0.0	0.0	0.0	0.0	0.0	0.0	0.0
28) Jute, hemp, mesta textiles	2.0	1.1	0.0	0.2	0.0	0.0	0.0	0.0	0.0	0.0	0.0	1.1	0.0	0.0	0.0
29) Textile products	0.0	0.0	0.0	0.0	0.0	0.0	0.0	0.0	0.0	0.0	0.0	0.0	0.0	0.0	0.3
30) Furniture and wood products	0.0	0.0	0.0	0.0	0.0	0.0	0.0	0.0	0.0	0.0	0.0	0.0	0.0	0.0	0.0
31) Paper, paper prods. & newsprint	0.0	0.0	0.0	0.0	0.0	0.0	0.0	0.0	0.0	0.0	0.0	0.1	0.0	0.0	0.5
32) Printing and publishing	0.2	0.1	0.0	0.0	0.0	0.0	0.0	0.0	0.0	0.0	0.0	0.1	0.0	0.0	0.2

contd...

...contd...

	1	2	3	4	5	6	7	8	9	10	11	12	13	14	15
33) Leather products	0.0	0.0	0.0	0.0	0.0	0.0	0.0	0.0	0.0	0.0	0.0	0.0	0.0	0.1	0.0
34) Rubber and plastic products	0.0	0.0	0.0	0.0	0.0	0.0	0.0	0.0	0.0	0.0	0.0	0.1	0.0	0.0	0.6
35) Petroleum products	14.2	15.4	4.4	2.8	0.9	3.1	0.0	2.7	0.0	0.0	0.1	16.0	0.1	0.1	2.9
36) Coal tar products	0.0	0.0	0.0	0.0	0.0	0.0	0.0	0.0	0.0	0.0	0.0	0.0	0.0	0.0	0.0
37) Inorganic heavy chemicals	0.0	0.0	0.0	0.0	0.0	0.0	0.0	0.0	0.0	0.0	0.0	0.0	0.1	0.1	0.0
38) Organic heavy chemicals	0.0	0.0	0.0	0.0	0.0	0.0	0.0	0.0	0.0	0.0	0.0	0.0	0.1	0.1	0.0
39) Fertilisers	68.7	55.2	16.0	14.5	12.7	35.7	0.6	14.1	1.3	1.2	0.9	84.9	0.0	0.0	0.0
40) Pesticides	6.5	1.8	0.1	2.2	0.4	7.2	0.1	6.0	1.0	0.9	0.0	13.4	0.0	0.0	0.0
41) Paints, varnishes and lacquers	0.0	0.0	0.0	0.0	0.0	0.0	0.0	0.0	0.0	0.0	0.0	0.0	0.0	0.0	0.0
42) Misc chemicals	0.0	0.0	0.0	0.0	0.0	0.0	0.0	0.0	0.0	0.0	0.0	0.1	0.4	3.2	0.0
43) Cement	0.0	0.0	0.0	0.0	0.0	0.0	0.0	0.0	0.0	0.0	0.0	0.0	0.0	0.0	0.0
44) Iron & steel	0.0	0.0	0.0	0.0	0.0	0.0	0.0	0.0	0.0	0.0	0.0	0.0	0.2	0.2	0.0
45) Non-ferrous basic metals	0.0	0.0	0.0	0.0	0.0	0.0	0.0	0.0	0.0	0.0	0.0	0.0	0.0	0.4	0.0
46) Metal products	0.0	0.0	0.0	0.0	0.0	0.0	0.0	0.0	0.0	0.0	0.0	0.0	0.1	0.4	0.8
47) Other non-electric machinery	1.0	0.6	0.5	1.1	0.2	0.4	0.0	0.2	0.0	0.0	0.0	1.6	0.1	0.2	0.1
48) Electrical appliances	0.0	0.0	0.0	0.0	0.0	0.0	0.0	0.0	0.0	0.0	0.0	0.0	0.0	0.0	0.0
49) Communication equipments	0.0	0.0	0.0	0.0	0.0	0.0	0.0	0.0	0.0	0.0	0.0	0.0	0.0	0.0	0.0
50) Electronic equipments (incl.TV)	0.0	0.0	0.0	0.0	0.0	0.0	0.0	0.0	0.0	0.0	0.0	0.0	0.0	0.0	0.0
51) Other electrical machinery	0.0	0.0	0.0	0.0	0.0	0.0	0.0	0.0	0.0	0.0	0.0	0.0	0.0	0.0	0.1
52) Rail equipments	0.0	0.0	0.0	0.0	0.0	0.0	0.0	0.0	0.0	0.0	0.0	0.0	0.0	0.0	0.0
53) Other transport equipments	0.2	0.1	0.1	0.1	0.0	0.1	0.0	0.0	0.0	0.0	0.0	0.3	0.1	0.0	0.6
54) Misc manufacturing	0.0	0.0	0.0	0.0	0.0	0.0	0.0	0.0	0.0	0.0	0.0	0.0	0.0	0.0	0.8
55) Construction	3.6	3.9	2.4	2.5	1.1	1.9	0.1	1.5	0.4	0.0	0.1	3.1	0.1	0.6	7.3
56) Electricity	15.3	17.0	1.2	1.7	2.1	0.9	0.0	2.0	0.0	0.0	0.1	10.8	0.1	0.1	0.2
57) Gas	0.0	0.0	0.0	0.0	0.0	0.0	0.0	0.0	0.0	0.0	0.0	0.0	0.0	0.0	0.0
58) Water supply	0.0	0.0	0.0	0.0	0.0	0.0	0.0	0.0	0.0	0.0	0.0	0.0	0.0	0.0	0.0
59) Railway transport services	2.5	2.0	0.6	0.5	0.4	1.1	0.0	0.5	0.0	0.0	0.0	2.9	0.1	0.1	1.1
60) Other transport services	15.3	11.0	6.7	6.1	2.2	12.2	0.4	3.6	0.7	0.1	0.2	31.7	5.1	10.6	4.7
61) Storage and warehousing	0.0	0.0	0.0	0.0	0.0	0.0	0.0	0.0	0.0	0.0	0.0	0.0	0.0	0.0	0.0
62) Communication	0.2	0.2	0.0	0.0	0.0	0.0	0.0	0.0	0.0	0.0	0.0	0.2	0.0	0.0	0.4
63) Trade	28.4	19.8	4.3	5.4	4.8	10.4	0.2	4.6	0.8	0.4	0.2	28.3	20.8	39.3	1.0
64) Hotels and restaurants	0.0	0.0	0.0	0.0	0.0	0.0	0.0	0.0	0.0	0.0	0.0	0.0	0.0	0.0	0.8
65) Banking	10.5	6.5	2.3	2.7	2.9	6.0	0.2	2.1	0.7	0.4	0.2	12.1	2.8	1.6	0.3

contd...

...contd...

	1	2	3	4	5	6	7	8	9	10	11	12	13	14	15
66) Insurance	0.2	0.1	0.0	0.0	0.0	0.0	0.0	0.0	0.0	0.0	0.0	0.1	0.0	0.0	0.0
67) Ownership of dwellings	0.0	0.0	0.0	0.0	0.0	0.0	0.0	0.0	0.0	0.0	0.0	0.0	0.0	0.0	0.0
68) Education and research	0.0	0.0	0.0	0.0	0.0	0.0	0.0	0.0	0.0	0.0	0.0	0.0	0.0	0.0	0.0
69) Medical and health	0.0	0.0	0.0	0.0	0.0	0.0	0.0	0.0	0.0	0.0	0.0	0.0	0.0	0.0	2.1
70) Other services	0.0	0.0	0.0	0.0	0.0	0.0	0.0	0.0	0.0	0.0	0.0	0.2	0.1	0.1	1.5
71) Public administration	0.0	0.0	0.0	0.0	0.0	0.0	0.0	0.0	0.0	0.0	0.0	0.0	0.0	0.0	0.0
72) Factor labour agricultural	360.8	230.4	73.2	94.8	109.7	222.2	6.3	83.8	28.7	16.5	10.2	909.8	523.7	218.7	142.7
73) Factor labour mining															
74) Factor labour manufacturing1															
75) Factor labour manufacturing2															
76) Factor labour construction															
77) Factor labour services															
78) Factor capital paddy	286.7														
79) Factor capital wheat		183.0													
80) Factor capital other cereals			58.2												
81) Factor capital pulses				75.3											
82) Factor capital sugarcane					87.2										
83) Factor capital oilseeds						176.5									
84) Factor capital jute							5.0								
85) Factor capital cotton								66.6							
86) Factor capital tea & coffee									22.8						
87) Factor capital rubber										13.1					
88) Factor capital tobacco											8.1				
89) Factor capital other crops												722.8			
90) Factor capital milk and milk products													416.2		
91) Factor capital other livestock products														173.9	
92) Factor capital forestry and logging															124.5
.....															
Rows 93 to 159						— blank —									
.....															
160) Indirect tax	-9.1	-19.0	-0.5	-0.8	-3.5	-8.4	0.0	-3.6	-0.5	-0.8	-1.1	-1.3	32.5	14.4	9.3
161) Capital account															
162) ROW account	0.0	0.0	0.0	20.0	0.2	0.0	1.0	0.0	0.0	0.4	0.2	30.9	0.0	3.6	28.0
163) Total	912.8	598.2	188.1	259.4	234.8	516.6	14.9	192.6	59.5	32.3	19.4	1988.7	1134.6	721.4	332.1

contd...

...contd...

	16	17	18	19	20	21	22	23	24	25	26	27	28	29	30
1) Paddy	0.0	0.0	0.0	0.0	0.0	0.0	0.0	0.2	59.0	0.5	0.0	0.0	0.0	0.0	0.0
2) Wheat	0.0	0.0	0.0	0.0	0.0	0.0	0.0	0.3	76.2	1.1	0.0	0.0	0.0	0.0	0.0
3) Other cereals	0.0	0.0	0.0	0.0	0.0	0.0	0.0	0.0	8.9	0.3	0.0	0.0	0.0	0.0	0.0
4) Pulses	0.0	0.0	0.0	0.0	0.0	0.0	0.0	0.1	21.4	0.0	0.0	0.0	0.0	0.0	0.0
5) Sugarcane	0.0	0.0	0.0	0.0	0.1	124.4	21.3	0.0	0.2	7.2	0.0	0.0	0.0	0.0	0.0
6) Oilseeds	0.0	0.0	0.0	0.0	0.0	0.0	0.0	266.6	23.9	0.0	0.8	0.2	0.0	3.0	0.0
7) Jute	0.0	0.0	0.0	0.0	0.0	0.0	0.0	0.0	0.0	0.0	0.0	0.0	8.9	1.6	0.0
8) Cotton	0.0	0.0	0.0	0.0	0.0	0.0	0.0	1.4	0.0	0.0	113.1	14.3	0.0	16.7	0.0
9) Tea & coffee	0.0	0.0	0.0	0.0	0.0	0.0	0.0	0.1	48.2	0.0	0.0	0.0	0.0	0.0	0.0
10) Rubber	0.0	0.0	0.0	0.0	0.0	0.0	0.0	0.0	0.0	0.0	0.0	0.1	0.0	0.4	0.0
11) Tobacco	0.0	0.0	0.0	0.0	0.0	0.0	0.0	0.0	0.2	19.5	0.0	0.0	0.0	0.0	0.0
12) Other crops	0.1	0.0	0.0	0.0	0.0	0.1	4.5	1.0	137.5	31.2	0.9	1.9	0.0	0.3	0.2
13) Milk and milk products	0.0	0.0	0.0	0.0	0.0	0.0	0.0	0.3	115.7	0.1	0.0	0.0	0.0	0.0	0.0
14) Other livestock products	0.0	0.0	0.0	0.0	0.0	0.0	0.0	0.2	33.7	0.2	0.3	9.5	0.0	0.8	0.3
15) Forestry and logging	0.0	0.0	0.0	0.0	0.0	0.0	0.0	0.2	1.2	23.9	0.6	0.3	0.0	1.3	26.4
16) Fishing	4.0	0.0	0.0	0.0	0.0	0.0	0.0	0.0	17.2	0.0	0.0	0.0	0.0	0.0	0.0
17) Coal and lignite	0.0	0.9	0.0	0.0	0.0	0.0	0.0	1.9	5.0	2.4	2.0	1.5	0.2	0.6	0.2
18) Crude petroleum, natural gas	0.0	0.0	0.7	0.0	0.0	0.0	0.0	0.1	3.2	0.3	0.0	0.2	0.0	0.6	0.0
19) Iron ore	0.0	0.0	0.0	0.0	0.0	0.0	0.0	0.0	0.0	0.0	0.0	0.0	0.0	0.0	0.0
20) Other minerals	0.0	4.0	0.0	0.0	0.0	0.0	0.0	0.0	0.2	0.0	0.0	0.0	0.0	0.1	0.1
21) Sugar	0.0	0.0	0.0	0.0	0.0	0.0	0.0	0.0	12.8	5.1	0.0	0.0	0.0	0.0	0.0
22) *Khandsari, boora*	0.0	0.0	0.0	0.0	0.0	0.0	0.0	0.1	11.7	0.4	0.0	0.0	0.0	0.0	0.0
23) Edible, oil & *vanaspati*	0.0	0.0	0.0	0.0	0.0	0.0	0.0	27.3	8.5	0.0	0.1	0.0	0.0	0.0	0.0
24) Misc food products	1.1	0.0	0.0	0.0	0.0	0.0	0.1	0.7	109.4	7.7	1.0	0.3	0.1	0.3	0.0
25) Beverages & tobacco products	0.0	0.0	0.0	0.0	0.0	0.0	0.0	0.0	1.3	25.4	0.0	0.0	0.0	0.0	0.0
26) Cotton textiles	0.0	0.0	0.0	0.0	0.0	0.0	0.0	1.2	0.9	0.6	42.6	23.6	1.2	88.1	0.1
27) Wool synthetic, silk fibre textiles	0.0	0.0	0.0	0.0	0.0	0.0	0.0	0.0	0.0	0.0	2.6	60.4	0.1	51.1	0.2
28) Jute, hemp, mesta textiles	1.8	0.0	0.0	0.0	0.0	2.7	0.3	0.5	1.8	0.6	0.4	3.4	1.1	17.8	0.0
29) Textile products	6.7	0.0	0.0	0.0	0.0	0.2	0.0	0.4	0.9	0.4	0.6	1.8	0.1	10.2	0.3
30) Furniture and wood products	1.2	2.3	0.0	0.0	0.1	0.0	0.0	1.1	5.6	4.8	0.3	1.3	0.0	0.5	9.5
31) Paper, paper prods. & newsprint	0.0	0.4	0.0	0.0	0.0	0.2	0.0	2.3	9.0	24.7	1.7	2.4	0.1	2.7	1.2
32) Printing and publishing	0.0	0.2	0.0	0.0	0.1	0.0	0.0	0.0	0.4	0.0	0.2	0.0	0.0	0.2	0.0
33) Leather products	0.0	0.0	0.0	0.0	0.0	0.0	0.0	0.0	0.2	0.0	0.0	0.1	0.0	1.3	0.1

contd...

...*contd*...

	16	17	18	19	20	21	22	23	24	25	26	27	28	29	30
34) Rubber and plastic products	0.0	0.6	0.0	0.4	0.2	0.1	0.0	0.8	10.8	1.4	0.6	0.8	0.0	5.3	2.3
35) Petroleum products	7.4	4.0	4.7	2.0	1.8	0.8	0.8	2.6	19.3	4.3	3.7	3.5	0.4	2.8	1.1
36) Coal tar products	0.0	0.0	0.0	0.0	0.0	0.0	0.0	0.0	1.9	0.3	0.6	0.1	0.0	0.2	0.0
37) Inorganic heavy chemicals	0.0	0.0	0.0	0.0	0.1	0.7	0.3	1.5	4.1	0.5	2.8	3.0	0.1	2.3	0.2
38) Organic heavy chemicals	0.0	0.0	0.0	0.0	0.0	0.9	0.1	5.7	5.0	1.2	3.0	11.4	0.1	1.5	0.2
39) Fertilisers	0.0	0.0	0.0	0.0	0.0	0.0	0.0	0.1	1.6	0.0	0.0	0.0	0.0	0.0	0.0
40) Pesticides	0.0	0.0	0.0	0.0	0.0	0.0	0.0	0.0	0.2	0.0	0.0	0.0	0.0	0.0	0.0
41) Paints, varnishes and lacquers	0.0	0.0	0.0	0.0	0.0	0.0	0.0	0.1	0.4	0.1	6.8	3.5	0.1	3.9	0.4
42) Misc chemicals	1.0	7.9	2.9	1.1	3.0	0.0	0.0	13.7	18.5	10.5	12.9	39.9	0.7	22.7	1.6
43) Cement	0.0	0.0	2.4	0.0	0.0	0.0	0.0	0.1	2.6	11.6	0.2	0.3	0.0	0.3	0.3
44) Iron & steel	0.1	0.0	0.0	0.0	0.0	0.0	0.0	0.2	0.2	0.4	0.5	0.4	0.1	0.9	0.7
45) Non-ferrous basic metals	0.0	0.0	0.0	0.0	0.0	0.0	0.0	0.7	3.1	2.1	0.5	0.4	0.0	1.9	0.9
46) Metal products	1.2	2.7	2.3	1.1	0.2	0.6	0.3	1.1	2.6	8.0	1.3	0.6	0.2	1.8	0.8
47) Other non-electric machinery	0.0	14.1	6.8	0.2	1.1	0.2	0.1	0.5	2.6	7.9	2.2	3.0	0.9	3.3	0.5
48) Electrical appliances	0.0	0.0	0.0	0.0	0.0	0.0	0.0	0.0	0.4	0.3	0.5	0.2	0.0	0.4	0.2
49) Communication equipments	0.0	0.0	0.0	0.0	0.0	0.0	0.0	0.0	0.0	0.0	0.0	0.0	0.0	0.0	0.0
50) Electronic equipments (incl.TV)	0.0	0.0	0.0	0.0	0.0	0.0	0.0	0.0	0.1	0.0	0.0	0.0	0.0	0.0	0.0
51) Other electrical machinery	0.0	0.0	0.0	0.0	0.0	0.0	0.0	0.0	1.6	0.3	0.1	0.1	0.0	0.6	0.1
52) Rail equipments	0.0	0.0	0.0	0.0	0.0	0.0	0.0	0.0	0.0	0.0	0.0	0.0	0.0	0.0	0.0
53) Other transport equipments	5.8	2.2	0.0	0.0	0.1	0.0	0.0	0.0	0.2	0.0	0.0	0.0	0.0	0.0	0.0
54) Misc manufacturing	0.0	3.9	0.0	0.0	0.0	0.0	0.0	0.2	0.5	0.5	0.4	0.7	0.0	1.2	0.7
55) Construction	0.0	1.1	4.9	0.2	1.4	0.5	0.1	0.3	5.8	1.1	1.3	0.7	0.1	1.6	0.6
56) Electricity	0.2	14.7	1.9	1.5	2.6	1.6	0.5	11.1	5.5	5.3	47.4	18.8	2.6	11.6	4.8
57) Gas	0.0	0.0	0.0	0.0	0.0	0.1	0.0	0.0	0.0	0.0	0.0	0.0	0.0	0.0	0.0
58) Water supply	0.0	0.1	0.0	0.0	0.0	0.1	0.0	0.1	0.6	0.2	0.7	0.3	0.0	0.3	0.0
59) Railway transport services	0.2	1.7	0.4	0.4	0.4	0.1	0.0	1.2	5.4	2.4	1.0	0.9	0.1	0.8	0.3
60) Other transport services	2.6	10.9	2.2	0.9	1.3	2.2	0.8	12.1	78.6	20.1	40.7	24.5	5.5	30.9	4.3
61) Storage and warehousing	0.0	0.0	0.0	0.0	0.0	0.0	0.0	0.0	0.0	0.0	0.0	0.0	0.0	0.0	0.0
62) Communication	0.0	0.4	0.1	0.1	0.1	0.1	0.0	0.6	1.7	1.0	0.1	1.3	0.0	1.6	0.2
63) Trade	3.9	4.8	2.8	0.6	0.8	24.2	4.9	37.2	123.2	35.8	45.4	31.1	3.7	56.2	7.2
64) Hotels and restaurants	0.0	0.3	0.0	0.0	0.1	0.0	0.0	0.0	0.0	0.0	0.0	0.0	0.0	0.0	0.0
65) Banking	0.8	3.1	2.7	0.3	1.0	6.5	1.6	18.8	62.0	21.3	19.7	15.6	1.9	22.3	5.7
66) Insurance	0.5	0.1	0.0	0.0	0.1	0.8	0.0	1.1	5.3	1.6	1.8	1.8	0.2	1.0	0.2

contd...

...contd...

	16	17	18	19	20	21	22	23	24	25	26	27	28	29	30
67) Ownership of dwellings	0.0	0.0	0.0	0.0	0.0	0.0	0.0	0.0	0.0	0.0	0.0	0.0	0.0	0.0	0.0
68) Education and research	0.0	0.0	0.0	0.0	0.0	0.0	0.0	0.0	0.0	0.0	0.0	0.0	0.0	0.0	0.0
69) Medical and health	0.0	0.0	0.0	0.0	0.0	0.0	0.0	0.0	0.0	0.0	0.0	0.0	0.0	0.0	0.0
70) Other services	2.6	4.9	2.9	0.5	2.1	1.4	0.3	1.4	19.5	42.3	16.6	14.5	0.4	11.9	2.0
71) Public administration	0.0	0.0	0.0	0.0	0.0	0.0	0.0	0.0	0.0	0.0	0.0	0.0	0.0	0.0	0.0
72) Factor labour agricultura l	160.5														
73) Factor labour mining		75.7	85.8	8.3	29.0										
74) Factor labour manufacturing1						10.4	1.7	12.9	140.2	121.9	61.0	33.9	12.1	110.5	11.5
.....															
Rows 75 to 92 —— blank ——															
.....															
93) Factor capital fishing	103.7														
94) Factor capital coal and lignite		164.8													
95) Factor capital crude petroleum, natural gas			186.9												
96) Factor capital iron ore				18.1											
97) Factor capital other Minerals					63.1										
98) Factor capital sugar						9.5									
99) Factor capital *khandsari, boora*							1.5								
100) Factor capital edible, oil & *vanaspati*								40.1							
101) Factor capital misc food products									99.5						
102) Factor capital beverages & tobacco products										80.6					
103) Factor capital cotton textiles											67.1				
104) Factor capital wool synthetic, silk fibre textiles												57.2			
105) Factor capital jute, hemp, mesta textiles													3.9		
106) Factor capital textile products														63.2	
107) Factor capital furniture and wood products															59.5
.....															
Rows 108 to 159						—— blank ——									
.....															
160) Indirect tax	13.2	6.9	-3.5	0.9	10.6	11.6	2.3	21.1	40.8	43.4	9.9	27.3	-1.7	27.9	-2.5
161) Capital account															
162) ROW account	0.8	9.4	835.3	3.5	342.3	0.6	0.0	122.6	9.1	2.5	22.7	34.7	2.6	52.9	4.3
163) Total	319.3	342.0	1142.3	40.2	461.6	200.9	41.5	614.4	1386.6	585.4	538.6	451.7	46.0	639.3	147.1

contd...

...contd...

	31	32	33	34	35	36	37	38	39	40	41	42	43	44	45
1) Paddy	0.1	0.0	0.0	0.0	0.0	0.0	0.1	0.1	0.0	0.0	0.0	0.1	0.0	0.0	0.0
2) Wheat	0.1	0.0	0.0	0.0	0.0	0.0	0.1	0.1	0.0	0.0	0.0	0.1	0.0	0.0	0.0
3) Other cereals	0.0	0.0	0.0	0.0	0.0	0.0	0.0	0.0	0.0	0.0	0.0	0.0	0.0	0.0	0.0
4) Pulses	0.0	0.0	0.0	0.0	0.0	0.0	0.0	0.0	0.0	0.0	0.0	0.0	0.0	0.0	0.0
5) Sugarcane	0.0	0.0	0.0	0.0	0.0	0.0	0.9	0.0	0.0	0.0	0.0	0.0	0.0	0.0	0.0
6) Oilseeds	0.0	0.0	0.0	0.0	0.0	0.0	0.1	0.1	0.0	0.0	0.0	5.6	0.0	0.0	0.0
7) Jute	0.0	0.0	0.0	0.0	0.0	0.0	0.0	0.0	0.0	0.0	0.0	0.0	0.0	0.0	0.0
8) Cotton	0.0	0.0	0.0	0.0	0.0	0.0	0.0	0.0	0.0	0.0	0.0	0.0	0.0	0.0	0.0
9) Tea & coffee	0.0	0.0	0.0	0.0	0.0	0.0	0.1	0.1	0.0	0.0	0.0	0.0	0.0	0.0	0.0
10) Rubber	0.0	0.0	0.6	27.3	0.0	0.0	0.0	0.0	0.0	0.0	0.0	0.4	0.0	0.0	0.0
11) Tobacco	0.0	0.0	0.0	0.0	0.0	0.0	0.0	0.0	0.0	0.0	0.0	0.0	0.0	0.0	0.0
12) Other crops	4.9	0.0	0.0	0.5	0.2	0.0	3.7	3.0	0.0	0.0	0.4	72.4	0.5	0.0	0.0
13) Milk and milk products	0.0	0.0	0.0	0.0	0.0	0.0	0.1	0.1	0.0	0.0	0.0	0.2	0.0	0.0	0.0
14) Other livestock products	0.0	0.1	9.6	0.4	0.0	0.0	0.2	0.3	0.2	0.0	0.2	2.9	0.1	0.0	0.0
15) Forestry and logging	8.6	0.1	0.4	0.2	0.0	0.1	1.0	0.4	0.3	0.0	0.0	5.8	1.4	0.3	0.0
16) Fishing	0.0	0.0	0.0	0.0	0.0	0.0	0.0	0.0	0.0	0.0	0.0	0.0	0.1	0.0	0.0
17) Coal and lignite	13.0	0.1	0.1	1.1	0.2	22.6	5.8	2.7	4.0	0.1	0.9	13.2	36.0	63.0	8.5
18) Crude petroleum, natural gas	0.1	0.0	0.0	3.2	1062.7	15.0	3.8	15.6	30.4	0.1	1.2	11.6	0.0	1.9	1.1
19) Iron ore	0.0	0.0	0.0	0.0	0.0	0.0	0.0	0.0	0.0	0.0	0.0	0.0	0.0	21.6	0.4
20) Other minerals	0.2	0.0	0.0	0.4	0.0	0.1	3.6	0.9	12.2	0.1	0.3	1.5	64.9	12.3	39.1
21) Sugar	0.0	0.0	0.0	0.0	0.0	0.0	0.1	0.1	0.0	0.0	0.0	1.0	0.0	0.0	0.0
22) *Khandsari, boora*	0.0	0.0	0.0	0.0	0.0	0.0	0.1	0.5	0.0	0.0	0.0	0.1	0.0	0.0	0.0
23) Edible, oil & *vanaspati*	0.0	0.0	0.0	0.0	0.0	0.0	0.0	0.0	0.0	0.0	0.0	0.9	0.0	0.0	0.0
24) Misc food products	0.0	0.4	0.1	0.0	0.0	0.0	0.2	0.2	0.0	0.0	0.0	1.4	0.0	0.1	0.0
25) Beverages & tobacco products	0.0	0.0	0.0	0.0	0.0	0.0	0.0	0.0	0.0	0.0	0.2	0.4	0.0	0.0	0.0
26) Cotton textiles	0.5	0.1	0.2	2.2	0.0	0.0	0.3	0.3	0.0	0.0	0.1	5.8	0.2	0.0	1.4
27) Wool synthetic, silk fibre textiles	0.2	0.0	0.0	6.3	0.0	0.0	0.0	0.0	0.0	0.0	0.0	0.3	0.0	0.0	0.1
28) Jute, hemp, mesta textiles	1.5	0.1	0.1	0.3	0.0	0.0	1.0	0.3	1.7	0.0	0.1	1.9	7.5	0.3	0.1
29) Textile products	1.9	0.4	1.6	7.2	0.1	0.2	0.9	0.5	0.2	0.1	0.6	6.8	4.4	2.4	1.0
30) Furniture and wood products	5.9	0.6	0.6	1.1	0.8	0.1	0.5	0.5	0.1	0.1	0.2	4.4	2.2	1.7	0.7
31) Paper, paper prods. & newsprint	65.0	33.5	0.7	3.6	0.3	0.1	2.0	5.1	0.2	1.0	2.0	19.1	0.8	1.0	1.1
32) Printing and publishing	0.5	10.4	0.0	0.1	0.0	0.0	0.1	0.1	0.1	0.1	0.1	0.8	0.0	0.1	0.0
33) Leather products	0.0	0.0	32.0	1.4	0.0	0.0	0.0	0.0	0.0	0.0	0.0	0.0	0.0	0.0	0.0

contd...

...contd...

	31	32	33	34	35	36	37	38	39	40	41	42	43	44	45
34) Rubber and plastic products	0.4	0.3	1.9	16.2	0.1	0.0	2.1	1.4	3.8	0.5	1.4	8.4	5.6	1.0	0.4
35) Petroleum products	2.6	0.8	1.0	2.2	14.9	0.8	11.9	8.4	66.9	1.0	2.2	50.2	21.5	25.8	6.5
36) Coal tar products	0.0	0.0	0.0	0.2	0.0	0.9	3.1	0.4	0.4	0.0	1.1	0.6	3.7	55.1	10.4
37) Inorganic heavy chemicals	13.9	0.1	1.8	3.4	0.4	0.3	20.6	11.1	20.1	4.9	13.5	45.9	9.3	2.5	8.4
38) Organic heavy chemicals	5.0	0.2	2.5	6.3	0.3	0.1	15.3	23.3	6.9	4.0	23.6	58.3	5.4	6.0	0.9
39) Fertilisers	0.0	0.0	0.0	0.0	0.0	0.0	3.4	2.0	30.2	1.4	0.0	0.1	0.0	0.0	0.0
40) Pesticides	0.0	0.0	0.0	0.0	0.0	0.0	0.1	1.7	0.1	8.2	0.0	0.0	0.0	0.0	0.0
41) Paints, varnishes and lacquers	1.0	2.5	2.2	2.4	0.8	0.0	0.4	0.3	0.0	0.1	5.9	3.9	1.0	1.0	0.9
42) Misc chemicals	6.8	2.3	2.7	108.3	12.4	0.2	9.7	7.4	13.1	4.4	7.6	147.0	2.6	1.4	6.2
43) Cement	1.0	0.3	0.2	0.4	0.0	0.2	1.2	0.3	0.2	0.1	0.4	3.3	15.5	1.4	0.3
44) Iron & steel	0.3	0.2	0.1	2.0	0.0	0.1	0.7	0.3	0.2	0.0	0.5	0.9	3.4	370.8	32.8
45) Non-ferrous basic metals	1.5	2.0	0.4	3.8	0.2	0.5	3.7	0.5	0.6	0.1	1.4	3.9	1.8	18.9	87.2
46) Metal products	0.6	0.6	0.8	3.3	3.2	0.2	1.2	1.6	0.1	1.1	0.5	7.1	2.6	50.6	8.1
47) Other non-electric machinery	0.7	0.5	0.3	0.8	0.8	0.3	1.2	1.0	1.7	0.2	0.4	2.0	2.3	3.9	1.8
48) Electrical appliances	0.3	0.3	0.3	0.4	0.1	0.2	0.7	0.4	0.2	0.0	0.1	0.6	0.9	0.8	0.4
49) Communication equipments	0.0	0.0	0.0	0.1	0.0	0.0	0.0	0.0	0.0	0.0	0.0	0.0	0.0	0.0	0.0
50) Electronic equipments (incl.TV)	0.0	0.0	0.0	0.0	0.0	0.0	0.0	0.0	0.0	0.0	0.0	0.0	0.0	0.0	0.0
51) Other electrical machinery	0.1	0.0	0.4	0.2	0.0	0.0	0.1	0.0	0.0	0.0	0.0	0.2	0.1	0.9	0.1
52) Rail equipments	0.0	0.0	0.0	0.0	0.0	0.0	0.0	0.0	0.0	0.0	0.0	0.0	0.0	0.1	0.0
53) Other transport equipments	0.0	0.0	0.0	0.2	0.0	0.0	0.0	0.0	0.0	0.0	0.0	0.1	0.0	1.0	0.0
54) Misc manufacturing	0.7	0.9	0.4	0.6	0.2	0.1	1.0	0.6	5.1	0.0	0.2	3.4	4.6	1.8	1.9
55) Construction	0.6	0.3	0.4	0.9	1.0	0.4	0.7	0.4	0.7	0.1	0.3	2.6	1.7	1.8	0.9
56) Electricity	13.5	2.4	2.0	17.0	18.5	1.6	9.8	11.2	10.0	2.4	6.4	38.1	23.4	43.4	30.5
57) Gas	0.0	0.0	0.0	0.0	0.2	0.0	0.0	0.0	0.0	0.0	0.0	0.0	0.0	0.0	0.0
58) Water supply	0.7	0.1	0.0	0.2	0.9	0.1	0.4	0.3	0.8	0.1	0.2	2.1	0.2	0.9	0.2
59) Railway transport services	4.8	0.2	0.4	1.1	0.6	8.3	2.8	1.3	3.3	0.2	0.6	7.4	17.9	43.9	5.9
60) Other transport services	12.8	5.6	5.1	19.7	18.5	5.7	7.6	5.6	13.1	1.4	3.9	45.6	29.9	34.2	12.6
61) Storage and warehousing	0.0	0.0	0.0	0.0	0.0	0.0	0.0	0.0	0.0	0.0	0.0	0.0	0.0	0.0	0.0
62) Communication	1.0	0.6	0.3	1.2	0.4	0.1	1.4	1.0	0.4	0.1	0.4	21.7	1.1	1.7	2.1
63) Trade	19.0	5.9	19.0	32.5	34.4	9.2	13.6	9.9	22.0	3.5	8.3	73.9	35.2	116.8	26.0
64) Hotels and restaurants	0.0	0.0	0.0	0.0	0.0	0.0	0.0	0.0	0.0	0.0	0.0	0.0	0.0	0.0	0.0
65) Banking	10.4	5.1	5.5	16.8	34.2	3.2	8.7	7.0	13.1	2.2	4.9	39.0	19.9	50.3	18.2
66) Insurance	1.4	0.3	0.3	1.8	4.1	0.1	1.6	1.4	3.0	0.2	0.7	7.5	2.1	4.2	2.7

contd...

...*contd*...

		31	32	33	34	35	36	37	38	39	40	41	42	43	44	45
67)	Ownership of dwellings	0.0	0.0	0.0	0.0	0.0	0.0	0.0	0.0	0.0	0.0	0.0	0.0	0.0	0.0	0.0
68)	Education and research	0.0	0.0	0.0	0.0	0.0	0.0	0.0	0.0	0.0	0.0	0.0	0.0	0.0	0.0	0.0
69)	Medical and health	0.0	0.0	0.0	0.0	0.0	0.0	0.0	0.0	0.0	0.0	0.0	0.0	0.0	0.0	0.0
70)	Other services	0.6	2.7	5.6	8.7	1.1	5.0	1.8	0.9	1.3	0.3	0.8	8.6	5.2	28.8	1.7
71)	Public administration															
72)	Factor labour agricultural															
73)	Factor labour mining															
74)	Factor labour manufacturing 1	38.6	44.4	27.1	75.4											
75)	Factor labour manufacturing 2					12.5	3.0	16.0	12.3	17.4	3.8	6.9	75.4	56.0	85.7	21.4
.....																
	Rows 76 to 107						— blank —									
.....																
108)	Factor capital paper, paper prods. & newsprint	28.4														
109)	Factor capital printing and publishing		23.3													
110)	Factor capital leather products			10.8												
111)	Factor capital rubber and plastic products				49.4											
112)	Factor capital petroleum products					322.1										
113)	Factor capital coal tar products						8.5									
114)	Factor capital inorganic heavy chemicals							42.7								
115)	Factor capital organic heavy chemicals								37.3							
116)	Factor capital fertilisers									44.6						
117)	Factor capital pesticides										14.0					
118)	Factor capital paints, varnishes and lacquers											16.2				
119)	Factor capital misc chemicals												241.1			
120)	Factor capital cement													120.5		
121)	Factor capital iron & steel														211.9	
122)	Factor capital non-ferrous basic metals															62.0
.....																
	Rows 123 to 159						— blank —									
.....																
160)	Indirect tax	13.7	11.0	4.8	27.8	142.8	-4.4	8.2	9.2	-3.2	1.9	7.9	66.9	6.8	56.5	37.8
161)	Capital account															
162)	ROW account	100.2	49.2	11.6	50.6	97.2	40.7	58.8	165.6	20.9	5.0	13.8	178.6	96.2	90.6	354.6
163)	Total	383.4	208.2	153.9	508.8	1786.2	123.6	275.3	355.7	346.4	62.7	136.4	1301.3	614.5	1418.4	796.6

contd...

...contd...

	46	47	48	49	50	51	52	53	54	55	56	57	58	59	60
1) Paddy	0.0	0.0	0.0	0.0	0.0	0.0	0.0	0.0	0.0	0.0	0.0	0.0	0.0	0.0	0.0
2) Wheat	0.0	0.0	0.0	0.0	0.0	0.0	0.0	0.0	0.0	0.0	0.0	0.0	0.0	0.0	1.0
3) Other cereals	0.0	0.0	0.0	0.0	0.0	0.0	0.0	0.0	0.0	0.0	0.0	0.0	0.0	0.0	0.0
4) Pulses	0.0	0.0	0.0	0.0	0.0	0.0	0.0	0.0	0.0	0.0	0.0	0.0	0.0	0.0	4.7
5) Sugarcane	0.0	0.0	0.0	0.0	0.0	0.0	0.0	0.0	0.0	0.1	0.0	0.0	0.0	0.0	0.0
6) Oilseeds	0.0	0.0	0.0	0.0	0.0	0.0	0.0	0.0	0.0	0.1	0.0	0.0	0.0	0.0	0.0
7) Jute	0.0	0.0	0.0	0.0	0.0	0.0	0.0	0.0	0.0	0.0	0.0	0.0	0.0	0.0	0.0
8) Cotton	0.0	0.0	0.0	0.0	0.0	0.0	0.0	0.0	0.0	0.1	0.0	0.0	0.0	0.0	0.0
9) Tea & coffee	0.0	0.0	0.0	0.0	0.0	0.0	0.0	0.0	0.0	0.0	0.0	0.0	0.0	0.0	0.0
10) Rubber	0.0	0.0	0.0	0.0	0.0	0.0	0.0	0.0	0.3	1.3	0.0	0.0	0.0	0.0	0.0
11) Tobacco	0.0	0.0	0.0	0.0	0.0	0.0	0.0	0.0	0.0	0.0	0.0	0.0	0.0	0.0	0.0
12) Other crops	0.0	0.0	0.0	0.0	0.0	0.0	0.0	0.0	0.3	70.8	0.0	0.0	0.0	0.0	15.5
13) Milk and milk products	0.0	0.0	0.0	0.0	0.0	0.0	0.0	0.0	0.0	0.0	0.0	0.0	0.0	0.0	0.0
14) Other livestock products	0.0	0.0	0.0	0.0	0.0	0.0	0.0	0.0	4.2	2.3	0.0	6.9	0.0	0.0	0.0
15) Forestry and logging	0.2	0.1	0.0	0.0	0.0	0.1	0.0	0.2	1.2	14.3	0.0	0.0	0.0	0.0	0.0
16) Fishing	0.0	0.0	0.0	0.0	0.0	0.0	0.0	0.0	3.6	0.0	0.0	0.0	0.0	0.0	0.0
17) Coal and lignite	6.5	1.3	0.0	0.0	0.0	0.2	0.4	0.5	0.4	0.7	143.3	0.0	0.0	0.5	0.0
18) Crude petroleum, natural gas	0.7	1.0	0.3	0.3	0.0	1.0	0.0	0.0	3.8	0.4	33.4	0.0	0.0	0.0	0.0
19) Iron ore	1.7	0.0	0.0	0.0	0.0	0.0	0.0	0.0	0.0	0.2	0.0	0.0	0.0	0.0	0.0
20) Other minerals	5.6	0.2	0.0	0.0	0.5	0.2	0.0	0.0	5.2	160.2	0.0	0.1	0.0	0.0	0.0
21) Sugar	0.0	0.0	0.0	0.0	0.0	0.0	0.0	0.0	0.0	0.0	0.0	0.0	0.0	0.0	0.0
22) *Khandsari, boora*	0.0	0.0	0.0	0.0	0.0	0.0	0.0	0.0	0.0	0.0	0.0	0.0	0.0	0.0	0.0
23) Edible, oil & *vanaspati*	0.0	0.0	0.0	0.0	0.0	0.0	0.0	0.0	0.0	0.0	0.0	0.0	0.0	0.0	0.1
24) Misc food products	0.0	0.0	0.0	0.0	0.0	0.0	0.0	0.0	0.0	0.0	0.0	0.0	0.0	0.0	0.1
25) Beverages & tobacco products	0.0	0.0	0.0	0.0	0.0	0.0	0.0	0.0	0.0	0.0	0.0	0.0	0.0	0.0	0.0
26) Cotton textiles	0.3	0.2	0.0	0.1	0.5	0.1	0.0	0.0	0.7	0.2	0.0	0.0	0.0	0.0	1.4
27) Wool synthetic, silk fibre textiles	0.2	0.0	0.0	0.0	0.0	0.0	0.0	0.0	0.6	0.5	0.0	0.0	0.0	0.0	0.2
28) Jute, hemp, mesta textiles	0.1	0.1	0.0	0.0	0.0	0.0	0.0	0.1	0.8	6.0	0.0	0.0	0.0	0.0	0.0
29) Textile products	1.4	3.1	0.4	0.5	1.8	0.9	0.1	1.6	3.9	0.6	0.1	0.0	0.0	0.0	3.1
30) Furniture and wood products	0.8	5.2	0.5	1.1	2.0	2.5	1.3	3.0	7.0	94.6	0.4	0.0	0.0	0.2	1.0
31) Paper, paper prods. & newsprint	1.0	2.0	0.1	1.4	2.3	1.9	0.1	2.8	5.4	1.0	2.5	0.0	0.1	0.2	7.3
32) Printing and publishing	0.0	0.3	0.0	0.1	0.4	0.2	0.0	0.2	0.9	2.5	4.1	0.0	0.2	0.5	6.8
33) Leather products	0.1	0.2	0.0	0.0	0.2	0.1	0.0	0.2	0.5	0.1	0.0	0.0	0.0	0.0	0.3
34) Rubber and plastic products	1.2	6.4	0.9	2.4	8.7	5.8	0.4	20.3	9.1	1.2	0.2	0.0	0.0	0.0	102.1

contd...

...contd...

		46	47	48	49	50	51	52	53	54	55	56	57	58	59	60
35)	Petroleum products	6.3	9.9	2.0	1.4	2.2	4.4	0.8	11.3	4.9	53.1	98.9	0.1	0.2	11.4	572.0
36)	Coal tar products	5.6	1.5	0.0	0.0	0.0	0.1	0.0	1.4	0.8	120.1	0.0	0.0	0.0	1.8	0.0
37)	Inorganic heavy chemicals	2.6	3.6	0.9	1.2	1.5	3.1	1.5	3.3	2.6	0.4	0.0	0.0	0.1	0.0	0.0
38)	Organic heavy chemicals	1.4	3.2	0.8	1.2	0.9	2.4	0.4	2.3	23.6	0.5	0.0	0.0	0.1	0.0	0.0
39)	Fertilisers	0.0	0.0	0.0	0.0	0.0	0.0	0.0	0.0	0.1	0.8	0.0	0.0	0.1	0.0	0.0
40)	Pesticides	0.0	0.0	0.0	0.0	0.0	0.0	0.0	0.0	0.0	0.0	0.0	0.0	0.0	0.0	0.0
41)	Paints, varnishes and lacquers	1.4	2.0	0.4	0.2	0.4	1.6	0.7	7.3	2.1	61.5	0.0	0.3	0.0	0.0	5.0
42)	Misc chemicals	1.6	3.6	0.9	2.7	2.9	5.4	1.0	9.0	16.7	5.5	3.1	0.0	0.1	0.0	1.6
43)	Cement	1.1	1.5	1.4	1.5	0.4	2.6	0.1	1.7	1.2	341.4	0.0	0.2	0.0	0.0	2.6
44)	Iron & steel	108.9	157.5	10.3	22.1	27.0	51.9	32.4	101.1	84.2	305.5	0.0	0.0	0.2	0.0	0.1
45)	Non-ferrous basic metals	32.9	24.9	8.2	4.6	8.9	28.3	2.1	21.3	228.7	0.6	0.0	0.0	0.0	0.0	0.0
46)	Metal products	12.8	14.9	1.1	1.7	3.7	3.8	1.4	23.5	3.2	47.7	0.3	0.0	0.1	0.0	12.8
47)	Other non-electric machinery	2.3	75.5	1.2	0.2	0.4	2.5	0.5	11.1	1.4	3.6	17.7	0.0	0.2	0.5	27.5
48)	Electrical appliances	0.5	1.6	1.7	1.7	0.9	2.9	0.9	3.7	0.2	0.2	0.2	0.0	0.0	0.0	0.5
49)	Communication equipments	0.1	0.3	0.4	12.1	5.4	10.1	0.0	0.0	1.2	0.0	0.0	0.0	0.0	0.5	0.1
50)	Electronic equipments (incl.TV)	0.0	0.1	0.1	0.9	6.6	0.7	0.3	0.1	0.6	0.0	0.2	0.0	0.0	0.0	0.2
51)	Other electrical machinery	0.9	4.4	3.0	4.5	36.0	22.0	0.8	3.3	1.4	35.3	40.2	0.0	0.0	0.4	20.3
52)	Rail equipments	0.0	0.1	0.0	0.0	0.0	0.0	5.8	0.2	0.0	0.0	0.0	0.0	0.0	37.4	0.0
53)	Other transport equipments	1.1	0.6	0.0	0.0	0.0	0.5	0.0	56.5	1.2	1.2	1.2	0.0	0.0	0.0	42.8
54)	Misc manufacturing	1.4	2.5	6.3	1.7	1.3	6.9	0.2	9.1	7.5	7.1	7.8	0.0	0.1	0.2	19.7
55)	Construction	0.7	2.0	0.1	0.3	0.6	0.7	0.2	1.6	1.4	22.3	8.3	0.0	19.0	22.3	36.5
56)	Electricity	12.5	20.5	2.2	2.7	6.0	8.4	3.8	31.7	18.1	53.8	205.0	0.0	3.9	56.6	153.1
57)	Gas	0.0	0.0	0.0	0.0	0.0	0.0	0.0	0.0	0.0	0.0	10.5	0.0	0.0	0.0	0.0
58)	Water supply	0.2	0.3	0.0	0.0	0.2	0.2	0.1	1.9	0.4	5.6	1.6	0.0	3.2	0.0	3.5
59)	Railway transport services	6.0	3.9	0.3	0.6	1.2	1.4	0.9	3.5	2.8	42.8	51.1	0.0	0.3	0.8	14.7
60)	Other transport services	9.6	15.4	2.1	4.3	5.3	8.0	2.2	15.7	14.8	198.8	48.3	1.1	0.5	1.9	105.2
61)	Storage and warehousing	0.0	0.0	0.0	0.0	0.0	0.0	0.0	0.0	0.0	0.0	0.0	0.0	0.0	0.0	0.0
62)	Communication	1.1	3.1	0.2	2.1	4.6	2.4	0.1	1.4	5.1	17.3	6.1	0.0	0.8	1.0	41.8
63)	Trade	26.4	36.4	5.0	9.2	14.1	20.6	6.1	38.0	41.9	224.2	65.4	0.8	0.2	2.9	105.9
64)	Hotels and restaurants	0.0	0.0	0.0	0.0	0.0	0.0	0.1	0.0	0.0	0.4	2.6	0.0	0.2	0.7	62.1
65)	Banking	16.2	25.8	3.4	5.5	8.4	13.2	3.9	27.4	17.3	108.5	44.4	0.6	0.0	26.6	45.4
66)	Insurance	2.3	8.1	0.5	1.3	3.4	6.2	0.0	11.9	2.4	42.9	7.0	0.0	0.1	5.0	35.9
67)	Ownership of dwellings	0.0	0.0	0.0	0.0	0.0	0.0	0.0	0.0	0.0	0.0	0.0	0.0	0.0	0.0	0.0
68)	Education and research	0.0	0.0	0.0	0.0	0.0	0.0	0.0	0.0	0.0	0.0	0.0	0.0	0.0	0.8	0.0

contd...

...contd...

	46	47	48	49	50	51	52	53	54	55	56	57	58	59	60
69) Medical and health	0.0	0.0	0.0	0.0	0.0	0.0	0.0	0.0	0.0	0.0	0.0	0.0	0.0	4.0	0.0
70) Other services	16.6	31.9	2.5	0.5	1.7	10.8	0.5	67.3	9.8	81.8	30.8	0.0	5.4	15.1	290.7
71) Public administration															
72) Factor labour agricultural															
73) Factor labour mining															
74) Factor labour manufacturing 1															
75) Factor labour manufacturing 2	73.5	92.6	11.2	10.8	8.2	38.2	16.2	95.2	96.8						
76) Factor labour construction										1285.1					
77) Factor labour services											377.0	34.1	31.3	145.2	836.9
.....															
Rows 78 to 122						— blank —									
.....															
123) Factor capital metal products	49.7														
124) Factor capital other non-electric machinery		89.8													
125) Factor capital electrical appliances			13.3												
126) Factor capital communication equipments				11.3											
127) Factor capital electronic equipments (incl.TV)					22.2										
128) Factor capital other electrical machinery						66.6									
129) Factor capital rail equipments							17.5								
130) Factor capital other transport equipments								76.0							
131) Factor capital misc manufacturing									78.4						
132) Factor capital construction										284.3					
133) Factor capital electricity											58.9				
134) Factor capital gas												10.9			
135) Factor capital water supply													29.0		
136) Factor capital railway transport services														81.4	
137) Factor capital other transport services															496.3
.....															
Rows 138 to 159						— blank —									
.....															
160) Indirect tax	27.1	107.6	10.5	17.7	37.5	50.1	9.8	106.8	80.9	456.0	27.7	2.4	2.1	11.6	350.5
161) Capital account															
162) ROW account	26.5	406.6	25.1	146.9	87.3	157.8	4.4	46.3	386.7	0.0	0.0	0.0	0.0	0.0	275.0
163) Total	469.2	1171.7	117.6	276.9	315.8	546.7	117.1	820.0	1186.3	4165.6	1298.2	57.4	97.4	429.9	3702.6

contd...

...contd...

		61	62	63	64	65	66	67	68	69	70	71	72	73	74	75
1)	Paddy	0.0	0.0	0.5	33.9	0.0	0.0	0.0	0.4	0.5	5.1	0.0	0.0	0.0	0.0	0.0
2)	Wheat	0.0	0.0	0.3	18.5	0.0	0.0	0.0	0.5	0.6	4.5	0.0	0.0	0.0	0.0	0.0
3)	Other cereals	0.0	0.0	0.0	0.0	0.0	0.0	0.0	0.0	0.0	0.3	0.0	0.0	0.0	0.0	0.0
4)	Pulses	0.0	0.0	0.1	13.2	0.0	0.0	0.0	0.2	0.2	1.0	0.0	0.0	0.0	0.0	0.0
5)	Sugarcane	0.0	0.0	1.6	0.0	0.0	0.0	0.0	0.0	0.0	0.0	0.0	0.0	0.0	0.0	0.0
6)	Oilseeds	0.0	0.0	2.2	0.0	0.0	0.0	0.0	0.0	0.0	9.7	0.0	0.0	0.0	0.0	0.0
7)	Jute	0.0	0.0	0.1	0.0	0.0	0.0	0.0	0.0	0.0	0.5	0.0	0.0	0.0	0.0	0.0
8)	Cotton	0.0	0.0	1.1	0.0	0.0	0.0	0.0	0.0	0.0	12.7	0.0	0.0	0.0	0.0	0.0
9)	Tea & coffee	0.0	0.0	0.2	0.0	0.0	0.0	0.0	0.0	0.0	1.7	0.0	0.0	0.0	0.0	0.0
10)	Rubber	0.0	0.0	0.9	0.0	0.0	0.0	0.0	0.0	0.0	3.6	0.0	0.0	0.0	0.0	0.0
11)	Tobacco	0.0	0.0	0.2	0.0	0.0	0.0	0.0	0.0	0.0	2.1	0.0	0.0	0.0	0.0	0.0
12)	Other crops	0.0	0.0	2.8	143.7	0.0	0.0	0.0	2.8	0.6	17.2	0.0	0.0	0.0	0.0	0.0
13)	Milk and milk products	0.0	0.0	0.4	24.4	0.0	0.0	0.0	1.9	1.6	4.0	0.0	0.0	0.0	0.0	0.0
14)	Other livestock products	0.0	0.0	0.9	11.3	0.0	0.0	0.0	0.0	1.2	7.2	0.0	0.0	0.0	0.0	0.0
15)	Forestry and logging	0.0	0.0	1.2	5.0	0.0	0.0	0.0	0.0	0.0	6.1	0.0	0.0	0.0	0.0	0.0
16)	Fishing	0.0	0.0	0.1	2.5	0.0	0.0	0.0	0.0	0.0	0.8	0.0	0.0	0.0	0.0	0.0
17)	Coal and lignite	0.0	0.0	2.2	2.1	0.0	0.0	0.0	0.0	0.0	12.1	0.0	0.0	0.0	0.0	0.0
18)	Crude petroleum, natural gas	0.0	0.0	1.5	0.0	0.0	0.0	0.0	0.0	0.0	66.6	0.0	0.0	0.0	0.0	0.0
19)	Iron ore	0.0	0.0	0.4	0.0	0.0	0.0	0.0	0.0	0.0	0.8	0.0	0.0	0.0	0.0	0.0
20)	Other minerals	0.0	0.0	2.1	0.0	0.0	0.0	0.0	0.0	0.0	10.9	0.0	0.0	0.0	0.0	0.0
21)	Sugar	0.0	0.0	0.1	4.1	0.0	0.0	0.0	0.0	0.0	1.1	0.0	0.0	0.0	0.0	0.0
22)	*Khandsari, boora*	0.0	0.0	0.1	0.0	0.0	0.0	0.0	0.0	0.0	0.5	0.0	0.0	0.0	0.0	0.0
23)	Edible, oil & *vanaspati*	0.0	0.0	0.2	19.6	0.0	0.0	0.0	0.0	0.0	1.2	0.0	0.0	0.0	0.0	0.0
24)	Misc food products	0.0	0.0	0.5	69.0	0.0	0.0	0.0	0.0	0.0	5.0	0.0	0.0	0.0	0.0	0.0
25)	Beverages & tobacco products	0.0	0.0	0.3	17.2	0.0	0.2	0.0	0.0	0.0	2.8	0.0	0.0	0.0	0.0	0.0
26)	Cotton textiles	0.0	0.0	4.3	0.0	0.0	0.0	0.0	0.0	0.0	25.5	0.0	0.0	0.0	0.0	0.0
27)	Wool synthetic, silk fibre textiles	0.0	0.0	2.3	0.0	0.0	0.3	0.0	0.0	0.0	21.3	0.0	0.0	0.0	0.0	0.0
28)	Jute, hemp, mesta textiles	0.1	0.0	2.2	0.0	0.0	0.0	0.0	0.0	0.0	5.0	0.0	0.0	0.0	0.0	0.0
29)	Textile products	0.1	0.1	1.1	1.5	0.2	0.2	0.0	0.7	0.8	7.9	0.0	0.0	0.0	0.0	0.0
30)	Furniture and wood products	0.3	0.2	9.2	1.2	0.6	0.3	0.0	2.8	1.9	13.0	0.0	0.0	0.0	0.0	0.0
31)	Paper, paper prods. & newsprint	0.3	0.9	7.8	0.4	3.0	2.5	0.0	0.4	0.7	22.6	0.0	0.0	0.0	0.0	0.0
32)	Printing and publishing	0.0	4.0	1.9	0.0	5.8	6.1	0.0	6.2	3.4	6.6	0.0	0.0	0.0	0.0	0.0
33)	Leather products	0.0	0.0	1.4	0.0	0.0	0.0	0.0	0.0	0.0	3.9	0.0	0.0	0.0	0.0	0.0

contd...

...contd...

	61	62	63	64	65	66	67	68	69	70	71	72	73	74	75
34) Rubber and plastic products	0.1	0.4	3.4	0.0	0.2	0.5	0.0	0.0	0.1	11.6	0.0	0.0	0.0	0.0	0.0
35) Petroleum products	0.3	4.1	65.3	7.9	2.8	6.1	0.0	3.0	1.8	24.8	0.0	0.0	0.0	0.0	0.0
36) Coal tar products	0.0	0.0	1.3	0.0	0.0	0.0	0.0	0.0	0.0	4.5	0.0	0.0	0.0	0.0	0.0
37) Inorganic heavy chemicals	0.0	0.0	4.3	0.0	0.0	0.0	0.0	0.1	0.1	13.2	0.0	0.0	0.0	0.0	0.0
38) Organic heavy chemicals	0.0	0.0	4.0	0.0	0.0	0.0	0.0	3.3	2.1	14.9	0.0	0.0	0.0	0.0	0.0
39) Fertilisers	0.0	0.0	1.4	0.0	0.0	0.0	0.0	0.0	0.0	7.3	0.0	0.0	0.0	0.0	0.0
40) Pesticides	0.1	0.0	0.2	0.0	0.0	0.0	0.0	0.0	0.0	0.6	0.0	0.0	0.0	0.0	0.0
41) Paints, varnishes and lacquers	0.0	0.0	1.1	0.0	0.0	0.0	0.0	0.0	0.0	5.5	0.0	0.0	0.0	0.0	0.0
42) Misc chemicals	0.0	0.0	10.0	0.6	0.0	0.0	0.0	3.1	198.7	52.0	0.0	0.0	0.0	0.0	0.0
43) Cement	0.0	0.0	0.8	0.5	0.0	0.0	0.0	0.0	0.0	5.3	0.0	0.0	0.0	0.0	0.0
44) Iron & steel	0.0	0.0	16.9	0.0	0.0	0.0	0.0	0.0	0.0	88.7	0.0	0.0	0.0	0.0	0.0
45) Non-ferrous basic metals	0.0	0.0	7.6	0.0	0.0	0.0	0.0	0.0	0.0	36.7	0.0	0.0	0.0	0.0	0.0
46) Metal products	0.0	0.3	27.2	0.0	1.3	0.3	0.0	0.3	0.3	18.4	0.0	0.0	0.0	0.0	0.0
47) Other non-electric machinery	0.4	0.6	4.7	1.3	0.6	0.9	0.0	0.3	0.3	19.8	0.0	0.0	0.0	0.0	0.0
48) Electrical appliances	0.0	0.1	0.3	1.0	0.2	0.2	0.0	0.1	0.1	6.0	0.0	0.0	0.0	0.0	0.0
49) Communication equipments	0.0	26.7	0.3	0.0	0.0	0.0	0.0	0.0	0.0	13.2	0.0	0.0	0.0	0.0	0.0
50) Electronic equipments (incl.TV)	0.0	0.0	0.1	0.0	0.3	0.6	0.0	0.0	0.0	1.7	0.0	0.0	0.0	0.0	0.0
51) Other electrical machinery	0.0	1.4	1.0	0.0	0.2	0.1	0.0	0.0	0.0	10.2	0.0	0.0	0.0	0.0	0.0
52) Rail equipments	0.0	0.0	0.0	0.0	0.0	0.0	0.0	0.0	0.0	1.5	0.0	0.0	0.0	0.0	0.0
53) Other transport equipments	0.0	0.9	2.0	0.0	2.5	1.5	0.0	0.3	0.4	6.3	0.0	0.0	0.0	0.0	0.0
54) Misc manufacturing	0.2	0.4	35.5	1.5	5.8	2.7	0.0	3.5	1.8	163.6	0.0	0.0	0.0	0.0	0.0
55) Construction	0.4	22.2	9.2	8.0	24.4	1.8	85.7	13.0	4.1	25.5	0.0	0.0	0.0	0.0	0.0
56) Electricity	3.1	15.2	39.1	14.5	18.6	8.1	0.0	0.8	2.1	50.3	0.0	0.0	0.0	0.0	0.0
57) Gas	0.0	0.0	0.0	4.5	0.0	0.0	0.0	0.0	0.0	0.0	0.0	0.0	0.0	0.0	0.0
58) Water supply	0.0	0.1	0.2	0.7	0.2	0.1	0.0	0.0	0.0	1.0	0.0	0.0	0.0	0.0	0.0
59) Railway transport services	0.1	3.0	8.4	1.4	2.1	1.2	0.0	3.2	1.7	12.5	0.0	0.0	0.0	0.0	0.0
60) Other transport services	0.5	5.2	152.6	28.6	10.8	6.3	0.0	27.8	21.8	58.8	0.0	0.0	0.0	0.0	0.0
61) Storage and warehousing	0.0	0.0	25.0	0.0	0.0	0.0	0.0	0.0	0.0	0.0	0.0	0.0	0.0	0.0	0.0
62) Communication	0.3	4.1	18.6	1.6	32.9	19.3	0.0	5.2	1.8	19.5	0.0	0.0	0.0	0.0	0.0
63) Trade	0.3	6.5	30.9	59.2	3.3	2.9	0.0	3.8	49.0	110.2	0.0	0.0	0.0	0.0	0.0
64) Hotels and restaurants	0.1	2.2	2.2	0.1	18.0	6.1	0.0	16.9	5.1	3.1	0.0	0.0	0.0	0.0	0.0
65) Banking	0.4	2.6	156.5	0.3	92.3	19.4	0.0	27.1	6.5	89.6	0.0	0.0	0.0	0.0	0.0
66) Insurance	0.6	0.4	14.3	0.7	14.5	1.1	0.0	0.0	0.0	7.6	0.0	0.0	0.0	0.0	0.0

contd...

...contd...

	61	62	63	64	65	66	67	68	69	70	71	72	73	74	75
67) Ownership of dwellings	0.0	0.0	0.0	0.0	0.0	0.0	0.0	0.0	0.0	0.0	0.0	0.0	0.0	0.0	0.0
68) Education and research	0.0	0.0	0.0	0.0	0.0	0.0	0.0	5.5	0.0	0.0	0.0	0.0	0.0	0.0	0.0
69) Medical and health	0.0	0.4	0.0	0.0	0.0	0.0	0.0	0.0	0.0	0.0	0.0	0.0	0.0	0.0	0.0
70) Other services	2.2	29.0	182.1	18.4	135.4	19.3	0.0	39.1	357.2	88.3	0.0	0.0	0.0	0.0	0.0
71) Public administration	0.0	0.0	0.0	0.0	0.0	0.0	0.0	0.0	0.0	0.0	0.0	0.0	0.0	0.00.0	
72) Factor labour agricultural															
73) Factor labour mining															
74) Factor labour manufacturing 1															
75) Factor labour manufacturing 2															
76) Factor labour construction															
77) Factor labour services	8.2	107.6	1211.8	161.7	414.4	77.0	152.3	953.2	210.1	869.5	1383.1				
.....															
Rows 78 to 137						— blank —									
.....															
138) Factor capital storage and warehousing	6.8														
139) Factor capital communication		338.3													
140) Factor capital trade			2348.1												
141) Factor capital hotels and restaurants				99.3											
142) Factor capital banking					1021.5										
143) Factor capital insurance						189.8									
144) Factor capital ownership of dwellings							988.4								
145) Factor capital education and research								267.0							
146) Factor capital medical and health									88.8						
147) Factor capital other services										587.2					
148) Factor capital public administration											152.3				
149) Rural household 1												93.4	2.8	6.9	5.3
150) Rural household 2												337.0	9.9	25.1	19.1
151) Rural household 3												889.8	26.2	66.2	50.3
152) Rural household 4												620.8	18.3	46.2	35.1
153) Rural household 5												947.0	27.9	70.4	53.6
154) Urban household 1												4.6	1.7	7.4	9.0
155) Urban household 2												19.1	7.1	30.5	37.0
156) Urban household 3												78.4	29.3	125.5	152.1

contd...

...*contd*...

		61	62	63	64	65	66	67	68	69	70	71	72	73	74	75
157)	Urban household 4												87.6	32.8	140.3	170.0
158)	Urban household 5												114.1	42.7	182.8	221.5
159)	Government															
160)	Indirect tax	0.5	15.8	139.0	35.0	35.3	14.0	43.0	46.1	67.5	146.4	32.8				
161)	Capital account															
162)	ROW account	0.0	2.8	0.0	54.8	0.0	35.9	0.0	0.0	0.0	385.4	0.0				
163)	Total	25.4	595.6	4575.4	869.6	1847.3	424.8	1269.4	1438.4	1033.0	3244.0	1568.2	3191.9	198.8	701.4	753.0

		76	77	78	79	80	81	82	83	84	85	86	87	88	89	90
.....																
	Rows 1 to 148						— blank —									
.....																
149)	Rural household 1	17.0	48.1	1.2	0.8	0.2	0.3	0.4	0.7	0.0	0.3	0.1	0.1	0.0	3.0	1.7
150)	Rural household 2	61.3	173.4	5.0	3.2	1.0	1.3	1.5	3.0	0.1	1.1	0.4	0.2	0.1	12.5	7.2
151)	Rural household 3	161.8	457.8	21.4	13.7	4.3	5.6	6.5	13.2	0.4	5.0	1.7	1.0	0.6	54.0	31.1
152)	Rural household 4	112.9	319.4	69.9	44.7	14.2	18.4	21.3	43.1	1.2	16.2	5.6	3.2	2.0	176.4	101.6
153)	Rural household 5	172.2	487.2	93.6	59.7	19.0	24.6	28.4	57.6	1.6	21.7	7.4	4.3	2.6	235.9	135.9
154)	Urban household 1	11.5	82.9	0.6	0.4	0.1	0.2	0.2	0.4	0.0	0.1	0.0	0.0	0.0	1.5	0.9
155)	Urban household 2	47.7	342.2	2.6	1.6	0.5	0.7	0.8	1.6	0.0	0.6	0.2	0.1	0.1	6.5	3.7
156)	Urban household 3	196.1	1407.5	10.0	6.4	2.0	2.6	3.0	6.1	0.2	2.3	0.8	0.5	0.3	25.2	14.5
157)	Urban household 4	219.2	1573.5	23.0	14.7	4.7	6.1	7.0	14.2	0.4	5.4	1.8	1.1	0.7	58.1	33.5
158)	Urban household 5	285.5	2050.1	39.9	25.5	8.1	10.5	12.1	24.6	0.7	9.3	3.2	1.8	1.1	100.7	58.0
159)	Government	0.0	0.0	19.5	12.4	4.0	5.1	5.9	12.0	0.3	4.5	1.5	0.9	0.6	49.1	28.3
160)	Indirect tax															
161)	Capital account															
162)	ROW account															
163)	Total	1285.1	6942.1	286.7	183.0	58.2	75.3	87.2	176.5	5.0	66.6	22.8	13.1	8.1	722.8	416.2

contd...

...contd...

		91	92	93	94	95	96	97	98	99	100	101	102	103	104	105
.....																
	Rows 1 to 148						— blank —									
.....																
149)	Rural household 1	0.7	0.5	0.4	0.7	0.8	0.1	0.3	0.0	0.0	0.2	0.4	0.3	0.3	0.2	0.0
150)	Rural household 2	3.0	2.2	1.8	2.8	3.2	0.3	1.1	0.2	0.0	0.7	1.7	1.4	1.2	1.0	0.1
151)	Rural household 3	13.0	9.3	7.8	12.3	14.0	1.3	4.7	0.7	0.1	3.0	7.4	6.0	5.0	4.3	0.3
152)	Rural household 4	42.4	30.4	25.3	40.2	45.6	4.4	15.4	2.3	0.4	9.8	24.3	19.7	16.4	14.0	0.9
153)	Rural household 5	56.7	40.6	33.9	53.8	61.0	5.9	20.6	3.1	0.5	13.1	32.5	26.3	21.9	18.7	1.3
154)	Urban household 1	0.4	0.3	0.2	0.4	0.4	0.0	0.1	0.0	0.0	0.1	0.2	0.2	0.1	0.1	0.0
155)	Urban household 2	1.6	1.1	0.9	1.5	1.7	0.2	0.6	0.1	0.0	0.4	0.9	0.7	0.6	0.5	0.0
156)	Urban household 3	6.1	4.3	3.6	5.7	6.5	0.6	2.2	0.3	0.1	1.4	3.5	2.8	2.3	2.0	0.1
157)	Urban household 4	14.0	10.0	8.3	13.2	15.0	1.5	5.1	0.8	0.1	3.2	8.0	6.5	5.4	4.6	0.3
158)	Urban household 5	24.2	17.3	14.4	22.9	26.0	2.5	8.8	1.3	0.2	5.6	13.9	11.2	9.4	8.0	0.5
159)	Government	11.8	8.5	7.0	11.2	12.7	1.2	4.3	0.6	0.1	2.7	6.8	5.5	4.6	3.9	0.3
160)	Indirect tax															
161)	Capital account															
162)	ROW account															
163)	Total	173.9	124.5	103.7	164.8	186.9	18.1	63.1	9.5	1.5	40.1	99.5	80.6	67.1	57.2	3.9

		106	107	108	109	110	111	112	113	114	115	116	117	118	119	120
.....																
	Rows 1 to 148						— blank —									
.....																
149)	Rural household 1	0.3	0.2	0.1	0.1	0.0	0.2	1.3	0.0	0.2	0.2	0.2	0.1	0.1	1.0	0.5
150)	Rural household 2	1.1	1.0	0.5	0.4	0.2	0.9	5.6	0.1	0.7	0.6	0.8	0.2	0.3	4.2	2.1
151)	Rural household 3	4.7	4.4	2.1	1.7	0.8	3.7	24.1	0.6	3.2	2.8	3.3	1.0	1.2	18.0	9.0
152)	Rural household 4	15.4	14.5	6.9	5.7	2.6	12.0	78.6	2.1	10.4	9.1	10.9	3.4	4.0	58.8	29.4
153)	Rural household 5	20.6	19.4	9.3	7.6	3.5	16.1	105.1	2.8	14.0	12.2	14.6	4.6	5.3	78.7	39.3
154)	Urban household 1	0.1	0.1	0.1	0.1	0.0	0.1	0.7	0.0	0.1	0.1	0.1	0.0	0.0	0.5	0.3
155)	Urban household 2	0.6	0.5	0.3	0.2	0.1	0.4	2.9	0.1	0.4	0.3	0.4	0.1	0.1	2.2	1.1
156)	Urban household 3	2.2	2.1	1.0	0.8	0.4	1.7	11.2	0.3	1.5	1.3	1.6	0.5	0.6	8.4	4.2
157)	Urban household 4	5.1	4.8	2.3	1.9	0.9	4.0	25.9	0.7	3.4	3.0	3.6	1.1	1.3	19.4	9.7
158)	Urban household 5	8.8	8.3	4.0	3.3	1.5	6.9	44.9	1.2	6.0	5.2	6.2	1.9	2.3	33.6	16.8

contd...

...*contd*...

	106	107	108	109	110	111	112	113	114	115	116	117	118	119	120
159) Government	4.3	4.0	1.9	1.6	0.7	3.4	21.9	0.6	2.9	2.5	3.0	0.9	1.1	16.4	8.2
160) Indirect tax															
161) Capital account															
162) ROW account															
163) Total	63.2	59.5	28.4	23.3	10.8	49.4	322.1	8.5	42.7	37.3	44.6	14.0	16.2	241.1	120.5

	121	122	123	124	125	126	127	128	129	130	131	132	133	134	135
.....															
Rows 1 to 148							— blank —								
.....															
149) Rural household 1	0.9	0.3	0.2	0.4	0.1	0.0	0.1	0.3	0.1	0.3	0.3	1.2	0.2	0.0	0.1
150) Rural household 2	3.7	1.1	0.9	1.6	0.2	0.2	0.4	1.1	0.3	1.3	1.4	4.9	1.0	0.2	0.5
151) Rural household 3	15.8	4.6	3.7	6.7	1.0	0.8	1.7	5.0	1.3	5.7	5.9	21.2	4.4	0.8	2.2
152) Rural household 4	51.7	15.1	12.1	21.9	3.2	2.8	5.4	16.2	4.3	18.5	19.1	69.4	14.4	2.7	7.1
153) Rural household 5	69.2	20.2	16.2	29.3	4.3	3.7	7.2	21.7	5.7	24.8	25.6	92.8	19.2	3.5	9.5
154) Urban household 1	0.5	0.1	0.1	0.2	0.0	0.0	0.0	0.1	0.0	0.2	0.2	0.6	0.1	0.0	0.1
155) Urban household 2	1.9	0.6	0.4	0.8	0.1	0.1	0.2	0.6	0.2	0.7	0.7	2.5	0.5	0.1	0.3
156) Urban household 3	7.4	2.2	1.7	3.1	0.5	0.4	0.8	2.3	0.6	2.6	2.7	9.9	2.0	0.4	1.0
157) Urban household 4	17.0	5.0	4.0	7.2	1.1	0.9	1.8	5.4	1.4	6.1	6.3	22.9	4.7	0.9	2.3
158) Urban household 5	29.5	8.6	6.9	12.5	1.9	1.6	3.1	9.3	2.4	10.6	10.9	39.6	8.2	1.5	4.0
159) Government	14.4	4.2	3.4	6.1	0.9	0.8	1.5	4.5	1.2	5.2	5.3	19.3	4.0	0.7	2.0
160) Indirect tax															
161) Capital account															
162) ROW account															
163) Total	211.9	62.0	49.7	89.8	13.3	11.3	22.2	66.6	17.5	76.0	78.4	284.3	58.9	10.9	29.0

contd...

...contd...

	136	137	138	139	140	141	142	143	144	145	146	147	148	149	150
1) Paddy														35.3	81.2
2) Wheat														16.6	45.1
3) Other cereals														12.6	27.8
4) Pulses														6.2	17.5
5) Sugarcane														2.0	6.0
6) Oilseeds														2.6	7.1
7) Jute														0.0	0.0
8) Cotton														0.0	0.0
9) Tea & coffee														0.2	0.6
10) Rubber														0.0	0.0
11) Tobacco														0.0	0.1
12) Other crops														17.7	56.1
13) Milk and milk products														6.4	31.4
14) Other livestock products														8.1	26.5
15) Forestry and logging														13.1	30.9
16) Fishing														4.8	15.7
17) Coal and lignite														0.0	0.0
18) Crude petroleum, natural gas														0.0	0.0
19) Iron ore														0.0	0.0
20) Other minerals														0.0	0.0
21) Sugar														3.8	11.6
22) *Khandsari, boora*														0.6	1.7
23) Edible, oil & *vanaspati*														15.5	41.9
24) Misc food products														36.6	97.2
25) Beverages & tobacco products														15.0	44.2
26) Cotton textiles														10.3	28.1
27) Wool synthetic, silk fibre textiles														6.8	18.6
28) Jute, hemp, mesta textiles														0.0	0.1
29) Textile products														2.2	6.4
30) Furniture and wood products														0.0	0.0
31) Paper, paper prods. & newsprint														0.0	0.0
32) Printing and publishing														1.5	5.2
33) Leather products														0.1	1.0

contd...

...contd...

	136	137	138	139	140	141	142	143	144	145	146	147	148	149	150
34) Rubber and plastic products														2.7	7.6
35) Petroleum products														3.2	7.8
36) Coal tar products														0.0	0.0
37) Inorganic heavy chemicals														0.0	0.0
38) Organic heavy chemicals														0.0	0.0
39) Fertilisers														0.0	0.0
40) Pesticides														0.0	0.0
41) Paints, varnishes and lacquers														0.2	0.5
42) Misc chemicals														5.5	16.5
43) Cement														1.9	2.2
44) Iron & steel														0.0	0.0
45) Non-ferrous basic metals														0.0	0.0
46) Metal products														2.0	5.8
47) Other non-electric machinery														0.0	0.0
48) Electrical appliances														0.0	0.0
49) Communication equipments														0.0	0.0
50) Electronic equipments (incl.TV)														0.0	0.0
51) Other electrical machinery														0.1	0.4
52) Rail equipments														0.0	0.0
53) Other transport equipments														0.7	2.1
54) Misc manufacturing														1.0	3.7
55) Construction														0.0	0.0
56) Electricity														1.2	4.6
57) Gas														0.0	0.0
58) Water supply														0.0	0.0
59) Railway transport services														0.0	0.0
60) Other transport services														21.7	74.1
61) Storage and warehousing														0.0	0.0
62) Communication														0.0	0.0
63) Trade														24.7	75.6
64) Hotels and restaurants														8.2	25.1
65) Banking														7.6	23.4
66) Insurance														2.5	7.6

contd...

...contd...

	136	137	138	139	140	141	142	143	144	145	146	147	148	149	150
67) Ownership of dwellings														0.0	0.0
68) Education and research														2.7	11.5
69) Medical and health														2.4	14.2
70) Other services														15.7	50.4
71) Public administration														0.0	0.0
.....															
Rows 72 to 148						— blank —									
.....															
149) Rural household 1	0.3	2.1	0.0	1.4	9.8	0.4	4.3	0.8	4.1	1.1	0.4	2.0	0.6		
150) Rural household 2	1.4	8.6	0.1	5.8	40.6	1.7	17.6	3.3	17.1	4.6	1.5	8.1	2.6		
151) Rural household 3	6.1	37.1	0.5	25.3	175.4	7.4	76.3	14.2	73.8	19.9	6.6	35.1	11.4		
152) Rural household 4	19.9	121.1	1.7	82.6	572.9	24.2	249.2	46.3	241.2	65.1	21.7	114.6	37.2		
153) Rural household 5	26.6	162.0	2.2	110.4	766.4	32.4	333.4	61.9	322.6	87.1	29.0	153.3	49.7		
154) Urban household 1	0.2	1.1	0.0	0.7	5.0	0.2	2.2	0.4	2.1	0.6	0.2	1.0	0.3		
155) Urban household 2	0.7	4.4	0.1	3.0	21.0	0.9	9.1	1.7	8.8	2.4	0.8	4.2	1.4		
156) Urban household 3	2.8	17.3	0.2	11.8	81.7	3.5	35.6	6.6	34.4	9.3	3.1	16.4	5.3		
157) Urban household 4	6.5	39.9	0.5	27.2	188.8	8.0	82.1	15.3	79.5	21.5	7.1	37.8	12.2		
158) Urban household 5	11.3	69.1	1.0	47.1	327.1	13.8	142.3	26.4	137.7	37.2	12.4	65.4	21.2		
159) Government	5.5	33.7	0.5	23.0	159.4	6.7	69.3	12.9	67.1	18.1	6.0	39.9	10.3	2.0	3.6
160) Indirect tax															
161) Capital account														-35.8	20.1
162) ROW account															
163) Total	81.4	496.3	6.8	338.3	2348.1	99.3	1021.5	189.8	988.4	267.0	88.8	477.7	152.3	288.4	959.1

contd...

...contd...

	151	152	153	154	155	156	157	158	159	160	161	162	163
1) Paddy	175.4	92.6	48.2	9.8	24.0	53.8	30.8	15.7	2.6		99.8	40.4	912.8
2) Wheat	109.1	70.0	42.4	9.8	20.4	48.0	27.0	15.8	2.9		-10.4	26.3	598.2
3) Other cereals	63.2	32.3	13.6	2.3	4.4	7.6	2.3	0.8	0.0		-0.3	3.2	188.1
4) Pulses	47.0	31.2	20.3	2.9	7.7	21.1	13.8	8.3	0.8		-4.6	2.4	259.4
5) Sugarcane	18.7	14.3	10.5	1.1	3.0	8.3	5.3	3.2	0.0		-9.3	0.9	234.8
6) Oilseeds	19.4	13.3	8.8	1.2	3.4	9.9	6.7	4.3	0.0		59.9	50.6	516.6
7) Jute	0.0	0.0	0.0	0.0	0.0	0.0	0.0	0.0	0.0		3.6	0.1	14.9
8) Cotton	0.0	0.0	0.0	0.0	0.0	0.0	0.0	0.0	0.0		26.6	5.0	192.6
9) Tea & coffee	2.2	1.9	2.0	0.1	0.5	1.7	1.9	2.0	0.0		-4.2	0.0	59.5
10) Rubber	0.0	0.0	0.0	0.0	0.0	0.0	0.0	0.0	0.0		-3.2	0.5	32.3
11) Tobacco	0.3	0.2	0.1	0.0	0.0	0.1	0.1	0.1	0.0		-10.0	6.3	19.4
12) Other crops	182.6	149.1	140.6	22.4	62.7	189.5	143.6	122.8	2.9		0.0	59.1	1988.7
13) Milk and milk products	147.5	157.4	145.7	6.4	31.4	147.5	157.4	145.7	6.8		0.0	0.0	1134.6
14) Other livestock products	88.2	67.7	53.4	4.7	16.2	51.1	37.3	26.7	7.4		59.7	2.5	721.4
15) Forestry and logging	76.7	47.1	23.7	4.2	8.2	10.1	2.3	0.6	0.0		-0.8	13.5	332.1
16) Fishing	52.4	40.2	31.8	2.8	9.6	30.4	22.2	15.9	0.0		16.7	48.3	319.3
17) Coal and lignite	0.0	0.0	0.0	0.7	2.1	3.8	0.8	0.0	0.2		-23.7	1.7	342.0
18) Crude petroleum, natural gas	0.0	0.0	0.0	0.0	0.0	0.0	0.0	0.0	0.9		-121.1	2.0	1142.3
19) Iron ore	0.0	0.0	0.0	0.0	0.0	0.0	0.0	0.0	0.0		-3.8	18.9	40.2
20) Other minerals	0.0	0.0	0.0	0.0	0.0	0.0	0.0	0.0	0.0		120.2	16.2	461.6
21) Sugar	35.9	27.6	20.2	2.2	5.9	16.0	10.2	6.1	0.0		26.0	11.0	200.9
22) *Khandsari, boora*	5.3	4.1	3.0	0.3	0.9	2.4	1.5	0.9	0.0		7.6	0.0	41.5
23) Edible, oil & *vanaspati*	114.2	78.2	52.0	7.1	19.9	58.0	39.6	25.1	3.2		51.0	25.5	614.4
24) Misc food products	262.6	184.5	135.0	15.8	42.7	123.6	90.7	69.7	6.8		31.7	85.7	1386.6
25) Beverages & tobacco products	128.5	92.2	75.3	6.1	17.7	50.1	34.6	30.3	0.0		40.1	3.5	585.4
26) Cotton textiles	72.4	51.8	39.1	4.2	11.0	34.3	26.4	21.5	0.0		-49.2	80.9	538.6
27) Wool synthetic, silk fibre textiles	48.0	34.4	26.0	2.8	7.3	22.8	17.5	14.3	0.0		57.6	48.7	451.7
28) Jute, hemp, mesta textiles	0.3	0.2	0.2	0.0	0.0	0.1	0.1	0.1	0.0		-30.2	10.6	46.0
29) Textile products	17.8	230.3	11.6	1.0	2.9	9.9	8.8	8.9	0.5		0.0	258.5	639.3
30) Furniture and wood products	0.0	4.4	8.9	0.0	0.0	1.9	3.8	6.7	2.2		-86.6	10.0	147.1
31) Paper, paper prods. & newsprint	0.0	0.0	3.6	0.0	0.0	6.5	11.4	15.0	11.4		0.0	87.7	383.4
32) Printing and publishing	17.4	16.0	18.4	1.1	3.6	17.1	18.3	18.8	18.8		0.0	7.6	208.2
33) Leather products	7.8	8.0	11.0	0.4	1.5	7.3	7.1	7.3	0.0		-6.1	66.3	153.9

contd...

...contd...

		151	152	153	154	155	156	157	158	159	160	161	162	163
34)	Rubber and plastic products	21.0	14.3	10.8	1.2	3.1	8.9	16.6	5.1	2.1		111.6	61.0	508.8
35)	Petroleum products	23.8	28.1	48.2	2.6	10.1	50.3	55.8	99.5	29.5		49.0	144.6	1786.2
36)	Coal tar products	0.0	0.0	0.0	0.1	0.1	0.3	0.0	0.0	0.0		-92.9	0.0	123.6
37)	Inorganic heavy chemicals	0.0	0.0	0.0	0.0	0.0	0.0	0.0	0.0	0.1		-7.2	72.0	275.3
38)	Organic heavy chemicals	0.0	0.0	0.0	0.0	0.0	0.0	0.0	0.0	0.7		-9.8	115.9	355.7
39)	Fertilisers	0.0	0.0	0.0	0.0	0.0	0.0	0.0	0.0	0.0		-8.3	0.4	346.4
40)	Pesticides	0.0	0.0	0.0	0.0	0.0	0.0	0.0	0.0	0.0		-3.1	15.3	62.7
41)	Paints, varnishes and lacquers	1.4	1.2	1.2	0.1	0.2	0.8	0.6	0.6	0.0		-21.9	24.5	136.4
42)	Misc chemicals	50.4	43.4	41.9	2.6	8.1	27.0	21.8	23.0	24.0		77.0	169.4	1301.3
43)	Cement	2.4	0.0	3.3	0.0	0.0	0.0	1.8	3.2	0.0		-148.4	343.2	614.5
44)	Iron & steel	0.0	0.0	0.0	0.0	0.0	0.0	0.0	0.0	0.0		-84.6	80.0	1418.4
45)	Non-ferrous basic metals	0.0	0.0	0.0	0.0	0.0	0.0	0.0	0.0	0.0		198.4	56.8	796.6
46)	Metal products	18.1	15.0	13.4	1.0	3.1	10.9	9.4	8.4	1.3		22.0	75.8	469.2
47)	Other non-electric machinery	0.6	1.5	3.9	0.1	0.3	2.7	3.5	4.9	48.5		763.4	101.6	1171.7
48)	Electrical appliances	1.2	1.6	1.9	0.1	0.4	1.5	1.3	1.1	0.9		36.0	41.0	117.6
49)	Communication equipments	0.0	0.5	1.6	0.0	0.0	0.8	1.4	2.4	1.6		145.4	52.9	276.9
50)	Electronic equipments (incl. TV)	0.0	3.7	11.7	0.0	0.0	5.7	10.4	17.8	2.3		236.6	14.7	315.8
51)	Other electrical machinery	1.4	1.4	3.2	0.1	0.2	0.8	1.3	3.0	0.2		301.0	43.2	546.7
52)	Rail equipments	0.0	0.0	0.0	0.0	0.0	0.0	0.0	0.0	0.0		70.9	1.1	117.1
53)	Other transport equipments	6.6	8.1	29.1	0.3	0.9	5.5	11.9	49.3	7.6		487.9	79.5	820.0
54)	Misc manufacturing	15.2	19.5	36.0	0.9	3.3	16.0	18.6	28.6	132.8		243.6	349.4	1186.3
55)	Construction	0.0	0.0	0.0	0.0	0.0	0.0	0.0	0.0	154.1		3640.0	0.0	4165.6
56)	Electricity	19.1	19.7	19.2	2.0	7.4	29.2	26.6	44.8	24.3		-41.8	0.0	1298.2
57)	Gas	0.0	2.2	2.5	0.2	1.3	6.3	2.8	5.6	0.0		21.3	0.0	57.4
58)	Water supply	0.0	1.9	2.2	0.2	1.2	5.6	2.4	4.9	54.0		-4.3	0.0	97.4
59)	Railway transport services	0.0	8.4	12.8	0.0	1.3	18.6	22.0	34.2	10.4		9.5	22.6	429.9
60)	Other transport services	302.3	310.5	339.2	11.4	46.6	229.4	246.6	250.7	65.8		83.9	404.8	3702.6
61)	Storage and warehousing	0.0	0.0	0.0	0.0	0.0	0.0	0.0	0.0	0.3		0.0	0.0	25.4
62)	Communication	1.7	11.1	44.7	0.0	0.6	29.8	73.6	139.3	58.0		0.0	4.7	595.6
63)	Trade	253.3	252.6	334.5	12.4	41.8	207.2	276.8	424.4	41.7		259.7	527.5	4575.4
64)	Hotels and restaurants	84.2	83.9	111.2	4.1	13.9	68.9	92.0	141.0	15.0		0.0	100.9	869.6
65)	Banking	78.6	78.3	103.7	3.8	13.0	64.3	85.9	131.6	43.1		0.0	0.0	1847.3
66)	Insurance	25.5	25.5	33.7	1.2	4.2	20.9	27.9	42.8	0.0		0.0	20.2	424.8

contd...

...contd...

	151	152	153	154	155	156	157	158	159	160	161	162	163
67) Ownership of dwellings	3.3	8.7	23.7	30.4	93.0	341.3	333.9	435.1	0.0		0.0	0.0	1269.4
68) Education and research	62.4	81.9	129.7	3.9	20.0	124.7	163.5	207.5	624.3		0.0	0.0	1438.4
69) Medical and health	66.0	131.0	279.1	1.8	7.9	77.1	98.8	140.9	207.4		0.0	0.0	1033.0
70) Other services	161.6	133.7	149.1	8.9	29.1	109.3	121.1	199.4	93.8		75.1	462.2	3244.0
71) Public administration	0.0	0.0	0.0	0.0	0.0	0.0	0.0	0.0	1568.2		0.0	0.0	1568.2
72) Factor labour agricultural												0.0	3191.9
73) Factor labour mining												0.0	198.8
74) Factor labour manufacturing 1												0.0	701.4
75) Factor labour manufacturing 2												0.0	753.0
76) Factor labour construction												0.0	1285.1
77) Factor labour services												-31.3	6942.1
78) Factor capital paddy												0.0	286.7
79) Factor capital wheat												0.0	183.0
80) Factor capital other cereals												0.0	58.2
81) Factor capital pulses												0.0	75.3
82) Factor capital sugarcane												0.0	87.2
83) Factor capital oilseeds												0.0	176.5
84) Factor capital jute												0.0	5.0
85) Factor capital cotton												0.0	66.6
86) Factor capital tea & coffee												0.0	22.8
87) Factor capital rubber												0.0	13.1
88) Factor capital tobacco												0.0	8.1
89) Factor capital other crops												0.0	722.8
90) Factor capital milk and milk products												0.0	416.2
91) Factor capital other livestock products												0.0	173.9
92) Factor capital forestry and logging												0.0	124.5
93) Factor capital fishing												0.0	103.7
94) Factor capital coal and lignite												0.0	164.8
95) Factor capital crude petroleum, natural gas												0.0	186.9
96) Factor capital iron ore												0.0	18.1
97) Factor capital other Minerals												0.0	63.1
98) Factor capital sugar												0.0	9.5
99) Factor capital *khandsari, boora*												0.0	1.5

contd...

contd...

		151	152	153	154	155	156	157	158	159	160	161	162	163	
100)	Factor capital edible, oil & *vanaspati*												0.0	40.1	
101)	Factor capital misc food products												0.0	99.5	
102)	Factor capital beverages & tobaco prod.												0.0	80.6	
103)	Factor capital cotton textiles												0.0	67.1	
104)	Factor capital wool syn, silk fibre textiles													0.0	57.2
105)	Factor capital jute, hemp, mesta textiles													0.0	3.9
106)	Factor capital textile products												0.0	63.2	
107)	Factor capital furniture and wood prod.												0.0	59.5	
108)	Factor capital paper, paper prods. &												0.0	28.4	
109)	Factor capital printing and publishing												0.0	23.3	
110)	Factor capital leather products												0.0	10.8	
111)	Factor capital rubber and plastic prod.												0.0	49.4	
112)	Factor capital petroleum products												0.0	322.1	
113)	Factor capital coal tar products												0.0	8.5	
114)	Factor capital inorganic heavy chemicals													0.0	42.7
115)	Factor capital organic heavy chemicals												0.0	37.3	
116)	Factor capital fertilisers												0.0	44.6	
117)	Factor capital pesticides												0.0	14.0	
118)	Factor capital paints, varnishes												0.0	16.2	
119)	Factor capital misc chemicals												0.0	241.1	
120)	Factor capital cement												0.0	120.5	
121)	Factor capital iron & steel												0.0	211.9	
122)	Factor capital non-ferrous basic mtals												0.0	62.0	
123)	Factor capital metal products												0.0	49.7	
124)	Factor capital other non-electric mch.												0.0	89.8	
125)	Factor capital electrical appliances												0.0	13.3	
126)	Factor capital communication eqipment													0.0	11.3
127)	Factor capital electronic eqipment												0.0	22.2	
128)	Factor capital other electrical mach.												0.0	66.6	
129)	Factor capital rail equipments												0.0	17.5	
130)	Factor capital other transport eqipment												0.0	76.0	
131)	Factor capital misc manufacturing												0.0	78.4	
132)	Factor capital construction												0.0	284.3	

contd...

...contd...

		151	152	153	154	155	156	157	158	159	160	161	162	163
133)	Factor capital electricity												0.0	58.9
134)	Factor capital gas												0.0	10.9
135)	Factor capital water supply												0.0	29.0
136)	Factor capital railway transport services												0.0	81.4
137)	Factor capital other transport services												0.0	496.3
138)	Factor capital storage & warehousing												0.0	6.8
139)	Factor capital communication												0.0	338.3
140)	Factor capital trade												0.0	2348.1
141)	Factor capital hotels and restaurants												0.0	99.3
142)	Factor capital banking												0.0	1021.5
143)	Factor capital insurance												0.0	189.8
144)	Factor capital ownership of dwellings												0.0	988.4
145)	Factor capital education and research												0.0	267.0
146)	Factor capital medical and health												0.0	88.8
147)	Factor capital other services												-109.5	477.7
148)	Factor capital public administration												0.0	152.3
149)	Rural household 1									64.7			0.0	288.4
150)	Rural household 2									125.7			0.0	959.1
151)	Rural household 3									328.9			444.0	3323.6
152)	Rural household 4									412.5			227.1	4726.7
153)	Rural household 5									800.9			112.4	6597.0
154)	Urban household 1									21.2			0.0	164.1
155)	Urban household 2									39.0			0.0	630.2
156)	Urban household 3									81.9			151.0	2640.5
157)	Urban household 4									172.7			75.9	3438.9
158)	Urban household 5									383.1			37.7	4993.1
159)	Government	172.8	107.4	35.5	0.0	0.0	206.9	496.9	220.0		2461.6		-24.8	4506.3
160)	Indirect tax												-15.7	2461.6
161)	Capital account	257.9	1882.5	3824.7	-34.7	11.9	37.1	492.5	1737.5	-1203.5			-343.1	6647.0
162)	ROW account													4902.7
163)	Total	3323.5	4726.6	6596.9	164.1	630.2	2640.6	3439.0	4993.2	4506.3	2461.6	6647.0	4902.7	

CHAPTER 5

Shocks, Meltdowns, Policy Responses and Feasibility of High Growth in the Indian Economy

A Macroeconometric Approach

Sabyasachi Kar and Basanta K. Pradhan

5.1 Introduction

The 11th Plan for the Indian economy, like other plans in the past, has set specific targets for growth rates for this period. In this paper, we analyse the feasibility of these targets, based on some simulations of growth rates and associated macroeconomic variables for this period. These simulations are based on a structural macroeconometric model known as the DPC-IEG model that has emerged from an ongoing modelling and forecasting exercise at the Development Planning Centre (DPC) of the Institute of Economic Growth (IEG). The objective of this exercise is to help the Planning Commission with periodic assessments of the macro behaviour of the economy and provide forecasts of the same. In 2000-01, B.B. Bhattacharya and Sabyasachi Kar initiated the construction of the current version of this model. It began with a critical review of the existing models in India and abroad. It was felt that an eclectic version incorporating all major macroeconomic schools of thought was necessary to characterise the different aspects of the economy. To begin with, a series of working papers were prepared on different aspects of modelling and forecasting. The overall model and forecasts were presented in various seminars and conferences and submitted to the Planning Commission as an input into the Plan formulations. After establishing that the model robustly simulated the Indian economy, the focus shifted to medium and long run growth as well as policy analysis.

The DPC-IEG model is based on a detailed characterisation of the Indian economy. It has been tried and tested for its power of explaining the Indian economic performance over the last few years. Till recently, there had been no long-standing models of the Indian economy that could be used repeatedly for projections and policy analysis, with regular updating. Along the lines of such efforts in industrialised countries, there was a need for such a model that could be revised periodically, taking into account changing economic realities, revisions in data and new theoretical developments. This was the motivation behind the construction of the DPC-IEG model. The strength of this model is that it combines a number of characteristics, which gives it an edge over many other models in the literature. These characteristics are:

Sabyasachi Kar and Basanta K. Pradhan, Institute of Economic Growth (IEG).

- This model is based on a continuous macroeconometric exercise that "learns from experience" rather than a one-time modelling exercise. This is a characteristic that this model shares with a few other similar models for India.
- A significant time series data belonging to the post-reform period allows this model to analyse the post-reform changes in the economy.
- The post-reform data (generated during a period of significantly less state intervention than before) also makes it possible to accommodate various theories about different parts of the economy that are based on the assumption of a market-oriented economy.
- The theoretical model has adopted a significantly market-oriented structure (even though the 70s and the early 80s adopted significant state interventions) enabling it to give better forecasts for the future when recent market orientations are expected to continue.

The final version of the model is the result of several experiments carried out during the last few years of the model building process. In the early stages, the exercise continuously tested the robustness of the model—by comparing the short-run forecasts with the observed data—and making suitable changes to the model. As a result, the final version of the model is significantly different from the earlier versions that were presented at various seminars during the development of the model.

The rest of the paper is planned as follows. The next section describes the recent performance of the Indian economy. This is followed by a section describing the model and a section on the baserun and alternative simulations. The paper ends with very brief concluding remarks.

5.2 The High Growth and the Current Slow Down in the Indian Economy

In recent years, the Indian economy has achieved a high growth trajectory and has become one of the largest and fastest growing economies in the world. A close review of the performance of the economy shows three most important features of our growth story. First, agricultural growth has been subject to large variation over decades. Second, growth of manufacturing production in terms of decadal averages is roughly constant at around 5.6-5.9 per cent during 1951-2000, except for the 1970s and growth acceleration in the Tenth Five Year Plan. Third, the continuing and consistent acceleration in growth in service sector (from the late 1990s and onward) really accounts for the high growth pick up in the recent years (Mohan, 2008). The sector-wise performance of the Indian economy for the period 2002-03 to 2007-2008 has been analysed below.

Agriculture

The experience of Indian economy shows that Indian agriculture is largely rain dependent. It experienced one of the worst droughts in 2002-03 which led to an absolute decline in agricultural activity. The resultant growth rate in agricultural sector was -3.2 per cent in 2002-03. The performance of agriculture in 2003-04 was typical of a normal monsoon year. It recorded an impressive growth of 9.1 per cent in 2003-04 with oil seed production scaling a new peak. The growth in this sector decelerated sharply to 1.1 per cent during 2004-05. This was essentially the outcome of the uneven and deficient South-West monsoon. Real GDP growth originating from agriculture and allied activities registered a growth of 3.9 per cent in the year 2005-06, led by improvement in the production of food grains. This is entirely on account of recovery in the production of rice to 91.0 mt in 2005-06 from 83.1 mt in 2004-05. Due to uneven rainfall, growth again decelerated to 2.7 per cent in 2006-07. Although the overall food grains production rose by 3.6 per cent in 2006-07, the production of major crops still did not reach the previous peak attained during 2001-02. In 2007-08, growth in agriculture and allied activities recovered to 4.5 per cent which was higher than the average of 4.0 per cent targeted for the Eleventh Plan (2007-2012) (*RBI Annual Reports*, 2002-2008).

The average growth in agriculture during the Tenth Five Year Plan (2002-2007) and for the period 2001-2008 was 2.5 and 2.9 per cent respectively. The above analysis shows that weather conditions continue to remain a key influence on agricultural production in India, and has undergone wide fluctuations from year to year.

Industry

Industrial performance in India is dominated by the behaviour of manufacturing sector. In 2002-03, it was the distinct improvement in manufacturing which led to a growth of 5.7 per cent in industrial sector. The expansion of industrial performance (6.8 per cent growth) in 2003-04 was enabled by a rebound in rural demand, rising exports, increased consumer durables fuelled by low interest rate and reduction in excise duties on a host of intermediate inputs. Growth in industry rose to 8.3 per cent in 2004-05 with favourable domestic climate, improvement in world output and liberalised foreign direct investment. In 2005-06, growth in industrial activities (7.6 per cent) was driven by sustained expansion in domestic as well as export demand. Industry-wise manufacturing growth was led mainly by basic chemicals, basic metal and alloy industries, machinery and transport equipment industries. An impressive feature during 2005-06 was the double digit growth in both capital and consumer goods. According to the CSO's revised estimates, real GDP growth originating from industrial sector increased to 11.0 per cent in 2006-07. The upsurge in the industrial growth entered the fifth year of expansion with strong investment and consumption demand. The industrial upturn which started in April 2002 and peaked by the end of March 2006-07 moderated during 2007-08. The growth of industrial sector for year 2007-08 was 8.1 per cent with manufacturing growth (8.8 per cent) lower than that in the preceding three years due to a marked slow down in the consumer goods sector (*RBI Annual Reports, 2002-2008*).

The experience of Indian industrial sector shows that industrial growth is driven by the manufacturing activity, which in turn depends on domestic and eternal demand. The average industrial growth during the Tenth Plan period and for the period 2001-2008 was 8.0 and 7 per cent respectively.

Services

The service sector is the principal driver of the Indian economy for the last several years. The near trend growth in services was enabled by a pick up in activity in construction, insurance, real estate and business services. The service sector continued to be the mainstay of expansion during 2002-03 and 2003-2004 with a growth of 7.1 and 8.5 per cent respectively. The growth of 8.6 per cent in service sector in 2004-05 was led mainly by trade, hotel, transport and communication. The strong growth in the trade sector was on account of surge in exports and imports during the year. According to CSO's revised estimate, service sector recorded a growth of 10.3 and 11.0 per cent during 2005-06 and 2006-07 respectively. "The most visible dimension of the sustained growth in the service sector during this period has been the contribution of the software sector including ITES (Information Technology Enabled Services) and BPO (Business Process Outsourcing) segments. The high growth components of service sector such as IT and BPO provided a stable anchor to the economy in face of risks emanating from high oil prices" (*RBI Annual Report, 2006-07*). The service sector continued to record double digit growth for the third successive year with some moderation (from 11.0% in 2006-07 to 10.7% in 2007-08). Construction activity moderated to 9.8 per cent after posting double digit growth for the preceding four years, reflecting rise in input costs and slow down in real estate. Financial sector also witnessed some deceleration (*RBI Annual Reports, 2002-2008*).

The growth in service sector in recent years is led by hotels, transport, finance, insurance and communication. This is fuelled partly by domestic demand from the other sectors and partly by the external demand for services exports. The average growth in service sector during the Tenth Five Year Plan was 9.7 per cent.

External Sector

Significant gains were posted in the external sector during the period 2002-2008, indicating the growing resilience of the economy against external and internal shocks. The run of current account surplus that began in 2001-02 was extended to 2003-04—a steady rise from 0.2 to 1.4 per cent of GDP.

The foreign exchange reserve rose to US$113 billion by end-march 2004. India's balance of payment recorded current account deficit in 2004-05. The massive increase in merchandise imports driven by the surge in international crude oil prices led to a substantial trade deficit of 5.5 per cent of GDP during this period. With capital flows remaining in excess of current account deficit, the balance of payments continued to record an overall surplus during 2005-06. As a result, India's foreign exchange reserves increased to US$151.6 billion at end of March 2006. With significantly higher capital inflows than the current account deficit during the year 2007-08, India's foreign exchange reserves in this year increased to US$309.7 billion at end-March 2008 as compared with US $199.2 billion at end-March 2007. The trade deficit as a percentage of GDP widened from 2.1 per cent in 2002-03 to 7.7 per cent in 2006-07 due to higher growth of imports (from US$10.7 billion in 2002-03 to US$64.9 billion in 2006-07). The growth of merchandise exports and imports accelerated to 25.8 per cent and 29.0 per cent respectively during 2007-2008, thus widening the trade deficit further to 7.7 per cent in 2007-08. The merchandise exports recorded an average growth of 20.3 per cent during the period 2001-2008, a remarkable improvement over 8.6 per cent growth during the previous decade. Net capital flows to India remained buoyant with net FDI inflows to India increasing sharply from US$7.7 billion in 2005-06 to US$19.4 billion during 2006-07. This higher volume of capital inflows could be attributed to the strengthening of macroeconomic fundamentals, greater investor confidence and ample global liquidity (*RBI Annual Reports, 2002-2008*).

The High Growth

The sustained high growth since 2003-04 has been supported by steady upward trend in domestic savings and investment rates. The gross domestic saving rate as a per cent of GDP at market prices increased from 24.2 per cent in 2002-03 to 34.8 per cent in 2006-07 due to improvement in public sector saving and private corporate saving. Similarly gross domestic investment rate rose from 25.2 per cent to 35.9 per cent during this period (*RBI Annual Reports, 2002-2008*). The average saving and investment rate at 31.4 per cent of GDP each during the Tenth Plan was high in any of Five Year Plan period. Inflation based on WPI was below 5.0 per cent during the Tenth Five Year Plan. During 2006-07, inflation firmed up from 4.0 per cent on April 1, 2006 to 5.9 per cent on March 31, 2007 with an intra high of 6.7 per cent on January 27, 2007. Both demand and supply side factors added to inflationary pressure.

The Indian economy performed reasonably well in 2002-03 during a period of generalised uncertainty and high international crude prices. The strong performance in the year 2003-04 was due to the resurgence of agricultural production, buoyant external demand and continued industrial recovery. Indian economy recorded a growth of 4.3 and 8.2 per cent during 2002-03 and 2003-04 respectively. The GDP growth moderated to 6.9 per cent in 2004-05 due to low agricultural sector growth of 1.1 per cent and volatile international crude oil prices. In an environment of macroeconomic and financial stability, real GDP accelerated to 8.4 per cent in 2005-06 on the back of buoyant manufacturing and service sector supported by the recovery in agricultural sector. The GDP growth in 2006-07 and 2007-08 was 9.4 and 9.0 per cent respectively. This growth acceleration was due to manufacturing and service sector activities. Though growth moderated marginally in 2007-08, it is still a high growth performance in an environment of deteriorating global economic condition with rising inflation and growth deceleration in major advanced economies. The average growth during the last six years (2002-2008) was 7.7 per cent.

The Slowdown

The sub-prime crisis that started in US housing mortgage market in 2007 has turned into a global financial crisis and now a global economic meltdown following the collapse of the leading US investment banks such as Bear Stearns and Lehman Brothers in August-September 2008. The impact of this financial crisis on Indian economy is already significant and expected to worsen in the foreseeable future. In the globalising world, expectedly, India has got integrated with the global macroeconomic behaviour to a fair degree. Though domestic consumption and investment continue to be the key drivers of our growth, India's integration into the world economy through trade and financial activities has increased over the years. Going by the common measure of globalisation, India's two way trade (merchandise exports plus imports), as proportion of GDP grew from 21.2 per cent in 1997-98 to 34.7 per cent in 2007-08 (Subbarao, 2008a).

There is evidence of a slowdown in the economic activity in India following the global economic meltdown. The real GDP growth has moderated in the first half of 2008-09. Both industry and service sector growth has declined. The decline in industrial activity is mainly due to turn down of manufacturing and infrastructure sectors. "The service sector which has been our growth engine for the last five years is slowing down mainly due to decline in trade, hotels, transport and communication sectors" (Subbarao, 2008a). Index of Industrial Production dipped to 1.3 per cent in August 2008 due to decline in both domestic demand and slow down in exports. For the first time in seven years, exports have declined in absolute terms in October 2008. The demand for bank credit is decreasing despite comfortable liquidity in the system. The foreign exchange reserves declined sharply to US$274 billions by October 2008. This could be due to outflow of short-term foreign capital and widening of trade deficit. On the positive side, headline inflation as measured by the wholesale price index has fallen sharply. The falling commodity prices including the international crude oil prices have been the key drivers behind the disinflation.

5.3 A Description of the DPC-IEG Model

The Indian economy, like other large developing economies, is heterogeneous in terms of production, investment and price behaviour. Hence, we have divided the economy into three parts, i.e., the agricultural sector, the industrial sector and the tertiary sector (which includes the rest of the economy and is the aggregate of the services sectors including public administration), and for each sector we have an output, private investment and price function (GDP Deflator). To incorporate dynamic behaviour and to distinguish between the short and long-run effects, we have incorporated lagged dependent variables in the estimation of these functions. In the case of output, this would represent the generalised distributed lag behaviour between output and capital. In the case of investment this would represent the discrepancy between the desired and actual investment behaviour. In the case of prices, the lagged dependent variable will incorporate the adaptive expectations in price formation.

In this paper, it may be noted that in interpreting the implication of each equation, we draw conclusions mainly on the basis of statistical significance, i.e., in terms of the t-statistics. In the model presented below, figures in parenthesis are standard errors. Number of *s on the right side of regressors indicate the level of significance of the coefficients (i.e., * denotes 10%, ** denotes 5% and *** denotes 1% level of significance). Also, DW is the Durbin-Watson statistics while Dh gives the Durbin's h statistic.

Output

We postulate that agricultural output (XA) is constrained by supply side factors like capital stock in agriculture (KA) and rainfall (RF). The agricultural output function has an irregular dummy DUMXA (representing the extreme drought effect of 1979) and a structural dummy D80S (to take care of the secular fall in agricultural growth since the eighties).

$$XA = EXP(-8.16 + 1.43*LOG(KA)^{***} + 0.27*LOG(RF)^{***} - 0.12*D80S^{***} - 0.14*DUMXA^{***} + 0.10*LOG(XA(-1)))$$

$$(1.31) \quad (0.24) \quad (0.05) \quad (0.03) \quad (0.03) \quad (0.14)$$

$$R^2 = 0.99 \qquad Dh = -1.06$$

The results indicate that capital stock in agriculture and rainfall affects agricultural output significantly. The relatively low value of the lagged dependent variable shows that capital formation in agriculture does not have a strong long-run impact on output in this sector.

Industrial sector output (XI) and tertiary sector output (XT) are postulated to be functions of the productive capacity in these sectors and the capacity utilisation rates. The productive capacity is determined by the capital stock (KI and KT) while large pools of unemployed labour ensure that there are no labour constraints in these sectors. Consistent with some recent theoretical and empirical studies on India, we postulate that output and capacity utilisation in industry and the tertiary sector are sensitive to changes in demand. In industrial output function, domestic and external demands are represented by the autonomous expenditure[1] (RAE), which is the sum of government expenditure and exports of goods and

1. The variable "autonomous expenditure" is autonomous in the sense that it is exogenous to the determination of industrial sector output. However, it is an endogenous variable in the whole model as it is determined within the model.

services. Industry also depends on agricultural demand. Moreover, industrial output is negatively related to industrial price (PI), again reflecting the demand-constrained nature of this sector. The industrial output function has two structural dummies, DPLIB (representing the partial liberalisation of the economy in the mid-eighties) and D95 (representing the peak effect of liberalisation in 1995 following large deregulation of the economy in 1994). In the tertiary sector, the demand constraints are captured by the commodity output (XCOM), i.e., the sum of the output in the other two sectors. The tertiary output function has two dummies DPLIB (partial liberalisation) and DUMPAY (representing the impact of large hikes in the salaries and wages of public administration that inflate the value added in the tertiary sector).

$$XI = EXP(-2.57 + 0.08*LOG(KI) + 0.34*LOG(XA)^{***} + 0.18*LOG(RAE)^{***} - 0.06*LOG(PI) + 0.02*DPLIB$$

(0.83) (0.09) (0.07) (0.05) (0.04) (0.01)

$$+ 0.6*LOG(XI(-1))^{***} + 0.04*D95^{**})$$

(0.06) (0.01)

$R^2 = 0.99$ Dh = -1.32

$$XT = EXP(-5.06 + 0.67*LOG(KT)^{***} + 0.13*LOG(XCOM)^{**} + 0.01*DUMPAY^{*} + 0.02*DPLIB^{**} + 0.52*LOG(XT(-1))^{***})$$

(1.02) (0.17) (0.05) (0.006) (0.008) (0.09)

$R^2 = 0.99$ Dh = -1.54

The results indicate that demand side factors like agricultural output and autonomous expenditure are the crucial determinants of industrial output. Capital stock has a small impact on current periods output but the lagged dependent variable seems to indicate that capital has a strong long-term impact on industrial output. The output in the tertiary sector is largely determined by capital stock, which has an impact on current as well as future services output. The demand factor, i.e., the output from the commodity producing sectors also affects the output in this sector.

Capital Stock and Investments

The capital stock in each of the three sectors is the sum of past capital stock in that sector (adjusted for depreciation) and private and public investments in that sector. The private investment functions are postulated to be a synthesis of a flexible accelerator theory and a Keynesian investment function (represented by interest rate). It may be noted that due to institutional constraints, non-agriculturists cannot invest in agriculture. Hence, the agricultural investment function is based on agricultural output whenever the same in industry and tertiary sectors are dependent on aggregate GDP. The nature of government expenditures also plays a crucial role in investments. We have postulated that public investment (IGA, IGI and IGT) plays a positive role by crowding in private investments, reflecting the fact that the Indian economy is still constrained by physical infrastructure, etc. On the other hand, other government expenditure (ORGE)—including government consumption and transfers—loosely representing the fiscal profligacy of the government, crowd out private investment by using up scarce resources. Agricultural investments (IPA) have a structural dummy D80S (representing a secular fall since the eighties). The industrial and tertiary sector investment functions (IPI and IPT) have an irregular dummy D95 (peak liberalisation effect).

$$IPA = -4714.17 + 0.05*XA^{***} + 0.44*IGA^{**} - 2700.76*D80S^{***} + 0.28*IPA(-1)^{**}$$

(1704.33) (0.01) (0.2) (706.1) (0.13)

$R^2 = 0.9$ Dh = -1.81

$$IPI = -25029.76 + 0.20*XGDP^{***} + 0.71*IGI^{**} - 0.56*ORGE^{***} - 649.003*RPLR - 939.56*IFR + 41506.12*D95^{***}$$

(10074.05) (0.04) (0.3) (0.13) (696.28) (791.82) (7846.02)

$$+ 0.22*IPI(-1)^{*}$$

(0.11)

$R^2 = 0.96$ Dh = -0.91

IPT = -33116.9 + 0.08*XGDP** + 0.71*IGT – 663.11*RPLR – 2920.68*DFEMRPLR* + 0.45*IPT(-1)**

(12348.49) (0.04) (1.1) (590.26) (1628.1) (0.19)

$R^2 = 0.86$ DW = 2.07 (Dh not computable)

The results indicate that the accelerator plays a strong role in determining private investment in all three sectors. Further, public investment crowds-in investment in the agricultural and the industrial sector, but not in the tertiary sector. Similarly, other government-expenditures crowd-out investment only in the industrial sector. The real interest rates (RPLR) have no impact on private investment in agriculture and a weak impact on industrial and tertiary sector investment. In the industrial sector, this is partly due to the fact that investors are worried of inflationary tendencies (IFR).

As far as public investment is concerned, it is assumed that the government exogenously determines their nominal values in all three sectors.

Aggregate Demand

The demand side of the economy is largely determined by private consumption, while the other components are government consumption and investment, private investment and net exports. Private consumption (RCP) is postulated to be a function of private disposable income (RPDI). The private consumption function has a lagged dependent variable representing long-run adjustments of consumption to income and a structural dummy DWTO (representing the effect of higher consumption of imported goods following the opening up of trade under WTO agreement).

RCP = EXP(2.89 + 0.65*LOG(RPDI)*** + 0.03*DWTO*** + 0.11*LOG(RCP(-1)))

(0.33) (0.06) (0.01) (0.08)

$R^2 = 0.99$ Dh = 1.74

The results show that, like in many other developing economies, private consumption is largely determined by private disposable income. The low significance of the lagged dependent variable indicates that income does not have strong long-run effect on consumption.

Private disposable income is equal to nominal output at factor cost (YGDP) plus government transfers minus taxes. The nominal output at factor cost is estimated to have a unitary elasticity with nominal output at market prices (GDPMP).

YGDP = EXP(-0.08 + 0.99*LOG(GDPMP)***) + [AR(1)=0.66***]

(0.03) (0.002) (0.12)

$R^2 = 0.99$ DW = 2.05

Prices

The aggregate GDP deflator is assumed to be a weighted average of the sectoral deflators—the weights being the share of the sectors in real output in the base year (1993). Agricultural prices (PA) are determined by both demand and supply factors. Agricultural output determines the supply in this sector while private disposable income (PDI) determines demand for agricultural output. The agricultural price function has an outlier dummy DUMPA (that takes care of the unusually high agricultural prices in 1973 and 1974 as a result of severe drought conditions in those years).

PA = EXP(4.002 – 0.71*LOG(XA)*** + 0.59*LOG(PDI)*** + 0.12*DUMPA*** + 0.31*LOG(PA(-1)**))

(1.71) (0.15) (0.08) (0.02) (0.14)

$R^2 = 0.99$ Dh = 1.29

The industrial sector is assumed to have mark up pricing and hence cost factors determine industrial prices (PI). The cost factors include agricultural prices, tariff rates (TRF) and import prices of oil (PMO) and non-oil commodities (PMN) separately.

PI = EXP(-0.20 + 0.37*LOG(PA)*** + 0.05*LOG(PMO)*** + 0.01*LOG(PMN) + 0.53*LOG(PI(-1)***)

(0.06) (0.05) (0.009) (0.014) (0.05)

+ 0.06*LOG(TRF)***)

(0.013)

$R^2 = 0.99$ Dh = 0.61

The tertiary sector prices (PT) are assumed to adjust to agricultural and industrial prices.

PT =EXP(0.11 + 0.16*LOG(PA)*** + 0.42*LOG(PI)*** + 0.39*LOG(PT(-1)***))

(0.01) (0.02) (0.04) (0.04)

$R^2 = 0.99$ Dh = 0.61

The results indicate that both the demand and the supply factors are equally important in the determination of agricultural prices. Industrial prices are found to be strongly affected by agricultural prices, tariff rates and import prices of oil, but the import price of non-oil commodities has no impact on them. The tertiary sector prices are strongly affected by prices in the other two sectors.

Monetary and Fiscal Sector

The monetary sector in this model defines the Prime Lending Rate (PLR) to be the representative rate for the financial sector and the economy. We assume that the monetary policy stance determines the prime lending rate of commercial banks.

In the fiscal sector, government expenditure is equal to government consumption, investments and transfers, all of which are assumed to be exogenous variables. The revenue side consists of tax and non-tax revenue, of which the latter is assumed to be exogenous. Tax revenue (TAX) is estimated as a function of nominal output (GDPMP). The tax function has two dummies DLIB (representing the effects of lowering of domestic tax rates as a part of the liberalisation process) and DWTO (representing effects of lowering customs duties following India joining the WTO).

TAX = EXP(-2.95 + 1.08*LOG(GDPMP)*** – 0.104*DLIB*** – 0.11*DWTO)***

(0.18) (0.01) (0.02) (0.02)

$R^2 = 0.99$ DW = 1.906

The difference between the revenue earned and the expenditure gives the gross fiscal deficit.

External Sector

In the external sector, the current account balance is the sum of net exports and remittances etc. Exports (EGS) are postulated to be a function of the volume of world trade (WT)—which is captured in our model by world imports—and the depreciation in the real exchange rate. The export function has three structural change dummies—D80S (representing the beginning of export promotion policies since the eighties), DFEM (representing the effect of trade and exchange rate deregulation in 1993) and DWTO (representing the positive effect on exports of joining the WTO). It also has an irregular dummy DUMEGS.

EGS = EXP(-6.62 + 1.02*LOG(WT)*** + 0.34*LOG(REXR)** + 0.09*D80S + 0.12*DFEM* + 0.14*DWTO**

(1.13) (0.05) (0.14) (0.05) (0.06) (0.05)

+ 0.23*DUMEGS***)

(0.05)

$R^2 = 0.99$ DW = 1.49

The results show that world trade is the most important determinant of exports although the depreciation in real exchange rate is also found to boost exports.

Imports are divided into two parts—oil imports and non-oil imports. It may be noted that oil imports were extremely volatile before 1985 due to the two oil shocks as well as the discovery and extraction of large volumes of oil since the beginning of the eighties. Hence, we have estimated the oil import function post-1985. We postulate that oil imports (MGSO) are strongly related to commodity production (the tertiary sector is much less oil-intensive), import price of oil (PMO), domestic prices (PGDP) and exchange rate (EXR)(the last three determining the relative price of oil). It also has an irregular dummy DUMMGSO.

MGSO = EXP(-3.26 + 0.43*LOG(XCOM)* + 1.005*LOG(PMO)*** + 0.55*LOG(PGDP)** - 0.69*LOG(EXR)***

(2.09) (0.21) (0.02) (0.2) (0.1)

+ 0.05*DUMMGSO)***

(0.01)

$R^2 = 0.99$ DW = 1.85

The non-oil imports (MGSN) are postulated to be a function of output, price of non-oil imports (PMN), domestic prices, exchange rate and tariff rates. The non-oil import function also has two structural dummies D95 (peak liberalisation effect) and DWTO (effect of joining WTO).

MGSN = EXP(-10.22 + 1.37*LOG(XGDP)*** + 0.09*LOG(PMN)** + 1.36*LOG(PGDP)*** – 1.34*LOG(EXR)***

(2.29) (0.2) (0.03) (0.1) (0.06)

– 0.18*LOG(TRF)*** + 0.18*D95*** + 0.05*DWTO)

(0.03) (0.05) (0.04)

$R^2 = 0.99$ DW = 1.66

The results show that oil imports are largely determined by factors that affect its relative price i.e., import price of oil, domestic prices and the exchange rate. Non-oil imports are also strongly affected by these three variables as well as the level of output and tariff rates.

The foreign exchange reserves are equal to the sum of past reserves, the current account balance and the capital account balance. The capital account balance is assumed to be an exogenous variable. The exchange rate (EXR) is hypothesised to be a function of the foreign exchange reserve (FER) as well as prices in the economy. We also postulate that the exchange rate adjusts to its past values. There is a dummy in the exchange rate equation DEV91 (representing a large devaluation undertaken in 1991).

EXR = EXP(0.39 - 0.07*LOG(FER)*** + 0.27*LOG(PGDP)*** + 0.19*DEV91*** + 0.69*LOG(EXR(-1))***)

(0.1) (0.01) (0.04) (0.04) (0.06)

$R^2 = 0.99$ Dh = -1.17

The results indicate that the exchange rate is strongly influenced by the size of the foreign exchange reserve (FER), as well as prices in the economy. The exchange rate is also found to stıongly adjust to past values.

5.4 Feasibility of the 11th Plan Growth Targets

The 11th Plan growth targets set by the Planning Commission are given in Table 5.1. This includes targets for aggregate and sectoral growth rates, investment rates and the fiscal and external sector balances as a ratio to GDP. We analyse the feasibility of these target rates based on forecasts for the 11th Plan period, based on the DPC-IEG model described in the earlier section. Past versions of the model have been presented and validated in Bhattacharya and Kar (2006).

Table 5.1: 11th Plan Targets for Growth Rates and Other Macroeconomic Variables

Variables	Targeted Values (%)
GDP Growth Rate	9.0
Agricultural Growth Rate	4.1
Industrial Growth Rate	10.5
Services Growth Rate	9.9
Total Investment Rate	35.1
Public Investment Rate	10.2
Private Investment Rate	24.9
Revenue Deficit Ratio	0.2
Fiscal Deficit Ratio	6.0
Current Account Balance Ratio	-2.8

Base Run: Business-as-Usual

We start with the base run forecasts. This is the business-as-usual scenario and the significant assumptions made are:

- Rainfall is assumed to be normal during the 11th Plan period
- Import price of oil calibrated on the assumption that international prices of oil are equal to US $67 in 2006, goes up to $80 in 2007, rises further to $90 in 2008 and falls to $60 thereafter.
- Based on past trends, import price of non-oil products are assumed to be 500, 550, 600, 650 and 700 for the five years of the plan period
- Based on past trends and FRBM constraints, public investment in agriculture is assumed to be 0.4 per cent of nominal GDP for the period
- Based on past trends and FRBM constraints, public investment in industry is assumed to be 2.2 per cent of nominal GDP for the period
- Based on past trends and FRBM constraints, public investment in tertiary sector is assumed to be 3.4 per cent of nominal GDP for the period
- Based on past trends the monetary policy is assumed to maintain PLR at 14 per cent for the plan period.
- Based on past trends, total exports are assumed to grow at 21 per cent per annum for the period
- Based on past trends, net external capital flows are assumed to grow at a rate of 2.9 per cent per annum for the period
- Based on past trends, public consumption growth rate is assumed to be equal to 4.3 per cent for the period

In the fiscal sector, we assume that the annual fiscal and revenue deficit targets according to the FRBM Act will be achieved. These targets for each of the five years of the 11th Plan period are specified in Table 5.2.

Table 5.2: FRBM Targets for the 11th Plan Period

Years	Fiscal Deficit	Revenue Deficit
2007-08	7.53	1.53
2008-09	6.00	0.00
2009-10	6.00	0.00
2010-11	6.00	0.00
2011-12	6.00	0.00

The forecasts corresponding to the above assumptions are presented in Table 5.3.

Table 5.3: Base Run

Variables	2007-08	2008-09	2009-10	2010-11	2011-12	Average
Aggregate Growth Rate	8.53	7.17	8.10	8.86	9.41	8.41
Agricultural Growth Rate	4.58	2.73	3.03	3.26	3.45	3.41
Industrial Growth Rate	8.77	8.98	9.22	9.59	10.18	9.35
Tertiary Growth Rate	9.80	7.74	9.14	10.16	10.69	9.50
Inflation Rate	5.30	5.46	8.04	8.01	6.48	6.66
Total Investment Ratio	29.86	33.71	35.16	38.26	41.41	35.68
Public Investment Ratio	6.00	6.00	6.00	6.00	6.00	6.00
Private Investment Ratio	23.86	27.71	29.16	32.26	35.41	29.68
Govt. Expenditure Ratio	26.35	24.89	25.09	25.22	25.32	25.37
Tax Revenue Ratio	15.11	15.18	15.38	15.51	15.61	15.36
Gross Revenue Deficit Ratio	1.53	0.00	0.00	0.00	0.00	0.31
Gross Fiscal Deficit Ratio	7.53	6.00	6.00	6.00	6.00	6.31
Current A/c Balance Ratio	2.27	-0.97	-0.75	-3.78	-5.02	-1.65
Export Growth Rate	21.00	21.00	21.00	21.00	21.00	21.00
Import Growth Rate	13.24	34.24	22.88	30.22	25.32	25.18

Note: Growth and inflation rates are in percentage terms. Investment ratios and other ratios are as percentages of GDP at current market prices.

It is clear from the above table that according to the DPC-IEG model, if past trends continue, the aggregate growth rates will be lower than the 11th Plan targets. The aggregate growth rates are lower due to the agricultural, industrial and services growth rates all falling below the plan targets. The total investment rate will be slightly higher than the plan targets, mainly due to a significantly higher private investment rate. The public investment rate will be much lower than the target. Compared to the 11th Plan targets, the base run predicts that a higher investment rate will result in lower growth rates. This implies that the adverse impact of demand side factors will lead to lower capacity utilisation than is envisaged in the Plan. In the fiscal sector, strong assumptions made about government spending based on the FRBM Act and past trends in tax buoyancy leads to very reasonable government expenditure ratio and tax ratio. The resultant revenue deficit ratios and fiscal deficit ratios are very close to the 11th Plan targets. Finally in the external sector, the rate of growth of imports is higher than that of exports, leading to a current account deficit.

Alternative Scenario 1: Feasibility of 4 Per cent Growth in Agriculture

Next, we simulate a scenario where the agricultural growth rate is higher than the base run, in order to achieve the 11th Plan growth targets in that sector. In order to increase the agricultural growth rate from the base run rate of 3.41 per cent, the public investment rate in agriculture is assumed to increase from 0.4 per cent of nominal GDP to 0.5 per cent of nominal GDP. Other assumptions are similar to that in the base run. The forecasts corresponding to the above assumptions are presented in Table 5.4.

The results from the table indicate that, compared to the base run, if public investment in agriculture is increased by 0.1 per cent of GDP then it will be possible to achieve the agricultural growth targets. This also leads to higher industrial and services growth, resulting in a higher GDP growth rate that is closer to the 11th Plan targets. The higher growth rates are based on higher investment rates that result from an increase in both public and private investment rates. The revenue deficit remains the same as a result of unchanged revenue expenditures but the fiscal deficit is slightly larger due to the additional public investment in agriculture. The higher growth rate also leads to a higher current account deficit due to an associated rise in imports, particularly non-oil imports.

Table 5.4: Alternative Scenario 1 (4 Per cent Agricultural Growth)

Variables	2007-08	2008-09	2009-10	2010-11	2011-12	Average
Aggregate Growth Rate	8.68	7.42	8.44	9.28	9.91	8.75
Agricultural Growth Rate	5.02	3.41	3.87	4.21	4.45	4.19
Industrial Growth Rate	8.91	9.29	9.69	10.20	10.90	9.80
Tertiary Growth Rate	9.85	7.82	9.27	10.35	10.98	9.66
Inflation Rate	5.24	5.21	7.62	7.49	5.93	6.30
Total Investment Ratio	29.97	33.85	35.36	38.57	41.90	35.93
Public Investment Ratio	6.10	6.10	6.10	6.10	6.10	6.10
Private Investment Ratio	23.87	27.75	29.26	32.47	35.80	29.83
Govt. Expenditure Ratio	26.46	24.99	25.19	25.31	25.40	25.47
Tax Revenue Ratio	15.12	15.18	15.38	15.50	15.59	15.35
Gross Revenue Deficit Ratio	1.53	0.00	0.00	0.00	0.00	0.31
Gross Fiscal Deficit Ratio	7.63	6.10	6.10	6.10	6.10	6.41
Current A/c Balance Ratio	2.22	-1.05	-0.86	-3.96	-5.34	-1.80
Export Growth Rate	21.00	21.00	21.00	21.00	21.00	21.00
Import Growth Rate	13.36	34.32	22.94	30.30	25.45	25.28

Note: Growth rates are in percentage terms. Investment ratios and other ratios are as percentages of GDP at current market prices.

Alternative Scenario 2: Feasibility of 9 Per cent GDP Growth

In the last scenario, we find that even though the agricultural growth rate is in excess of 4 per cent, the GDP growth rate falls short of the 11th Plan target. In this scenario, we simulate a 9 per cent GDP growth scenario. In order to increase the aggregate growth rate from the base run rate of 8.41 per cent, the public investment rate in agriculture is again assumed to increase from 0.4 per cent of nominal GDP to 0.5 per cent of nominal GDP. Moreover, public investment rate in industry is assumed to increase from 2.2 per cent of nominal GDP to 2.3 per cent of nominal GDP and the public investment rate in the tertiary sector is assumed to increase from 3.4 per cent of nominal GDP to 3.5 per cent of nominal GDP. Other assumptions are similar to that in the base run. The forecasts corresponding to these assumptions are presented in Table 5.5.

Table 5.5: Alternative Scenario 2 (9 Per cent GDP Growth)

Variables	2007-08	2008-09	2009-10	2010-11	2011-12	Average
Aggregate Growth Rate	8.86	7.66	8.70	9.56	10.20	9.00
Agricultural Growth Rate	5.04	3.44	3.91	4.24	4.49	4.22
Industrial Growth Rate	8.93	9.36	9.81	10.37	11.10	9.91
Tertiary Growth Rate	10.16	8.21	9.67	10.75	11.38	10.03
Inflation Rate	5.59	5.34	7.65	7.49	5.96	6.41
Total Investment Ratio	30.31	34.24	35.85	39.19	42.66	36.45
Public Investment Ratio	6.30	6.30	6.30	6.30	6.30	6.30
Private Investment Ratio	24.01	27.94	29.55	32.89	36.36	30.15
Govt. Expenditure Ratio	26.67	25.21	25.40	25.53	25.62	25.69
Tax Revenue Ratio	15.13	15.20	15.39	15.52	15.61	15.37
Gross Revenue Deficit Ratio	1.53	0.00	0.00	0.00	0.00	0.31
Gross Fiscal Deficit Ratio	7.83	6.30	6.30	6.30	6.30	6.61
Current A/c Balance Ratio	2.05	-1.33	-1.25	-4.43	-5.87	-2.17
Export Growth Rate	21.00	21.00	21.00	21.00	21.00	21.00
Import Growth Rate	13.85	34.62	23.11	30.30	25.35	25.45

Note: Growth rates are in percentage terms. Investment rates and other ratios are as percentages of GDP at current market prices.

The results from the table indicate that, compared to the base run, if public investment in agriculture, industry and services are all increased by 0.1 per cent of GDP, then it will be possible to achieve the GDP growth target. This increased GDP growth will be due to increases in all the three sectoral growth rates. In fact, the sectoral growth rates will also be very close to those targeted in the 11th Plan. The increase in public investment in this scenario will crowd in more private investment as well. This results in a total investment rate that is somewhat higher than the total investment rate envisaged in the 11th Plan. The fiscal deficit ratio goes up further due the public investment in the industrial and services sectors and the current account balance deteriorates even more due to sharper increases in mainly non-oil imports.

Alternative Scenario 3: Impact of Oil-Price Shock

A potential threat to the 11th Plan targets is the increasing trends in international petroleum prices. In this scenario, we analyse the impact of an oil-price shock on the economy. Apart from the impact of the oil price rise, other assumptions about the economy are similar to that in the base run. Thus, the impact of the shock can be gauged by comparing the forecasts of this scenario with that from the base run. Here, the import price of oil is calibrated on the assumption that international prices of oil are equal to US$67 in 2006-07, goes up to $80 in 2007-08, $120 in 2008-09, $130 in 2009-10, $140 in 2010-2011 and $150 in 2011-12. Exports are again assumed to grow at 21 per cent, while import growth reflects the oil-price rise in this scenario. The forecasts corresponding to the above assumptions are presented in Table 5.6.

Table 5.6: Alternative Scenario 3 (Oil Shock)

Variables	2007-08	2008-09	2009-10	2010-11	2011-12	Average
Aggregate Growth Rate	8.53	6.77	7.26	8.06	8.81	7.89
Agricultural Growth Rate	4.58	2.61	2.71	2.83	2.97	3.14
Industrial Growth Rate	8.77	9.05	8.99	8.99	9.38	9.04
Tertiary Growth Rate	9.80	7.01	7.82	9.16	10.19	8.80
Inflation Rate	5.30	3.85	7.34	10.37	10.67	7.50
Total Investment Ratio	29.86	35.55	40.07	44.24	47.79	39.50
Public Investment Ratio	6.00	6.00	6.00	6.00	6.00	6.00
Private Investment Ratio	23.86	29.55	34.07	38.24	41.79	33.50
Govt. Expenditure Ratio	26.35	24.78	24.87	25.02	25.18	25.24
Tax Revenue Ratio	15.11	15.07	15.16	15.31	15.47	15.22
Gross Revenue Deficit Ratio	1.53	0.00	0.00	0.00	0.00	0.31
Gross Fiscal Deficit Ratio	7.53	6.00	6.00	6.00	6.00	6.31
Current A/c Balance Ratio	2.27	-4.20	-8.11	-11.45	-11.60	-6.62
Export Growth Rate	21.00	21.00	21.00	21.00	21.00	21.00
Import Growth Rate	13.24	42.68	29.39	26.76	21.39	26.69

Note: Growth rates are in percentage terms. Investment rates and other ratios are as percentages of GDP at current market prices.

The results indicate that an oil-price shock of the given magnitude will adversely impact the GDP growth rate bringing it down by nearly half a percentage point. This adverse impact will be borne by all the sectors, but the services sector is affected more than the other two sectors. Interestingly, the investment ratio goes up due to a sharper fall in the GDP than in total investments. The deficits in the fiscal sector remain unaffected as the assumptions about the variables in this sector remain unchanged from the previous scenario. However, the current account balance worsens significantly due to increases in the value of oil imports.

Alternative Scenario 4: Impact of World Trade Shock

Another potential threat to the 11th Plan targets is the fall in world trade following the recession in the advanced economies. This would directly impact the Indian economy by bringing down growth of exports. In this scenario, we analyse the impact of a world trade shock on the economy. Apart from the impact on exports growth, the fall in world trade is also expected to affect commodity prices in general, and this is manifested in terms of a fall in the import price of non-oil imports. Exports growth is assumed to be 21 per cent in 2007-08, falls to 10 per cent in 2008-09 and 2009-10, and rises again to 15 per cent in the last two years of the plan. Import price of non-oil products are assumed to be 500, 400, 400, 450 and 450 for the five years of the plan period, which is much lower than those in the base run. Other assumptions about the economy are similar to that in the base run and the impact of the shock can be gauged by comparing the forecasts of this scenario with that from the base run. The forecasts corresponding to the above assumptions are presented in Table 5.7.

Table 5.7: Alternative Scenario 4 (World Trade Shock)

Variables	2007-08	2008-09	2009-10	2010-11	2011-12	Average
Aggregate Growth Rate	8.53	6.55	6.95	7.60	8.10	7.55
Agricultural Growth Rate	4.58	2.65	2.83	2.98	3.10	3.23
Industrial Growth Rate	8.77	8.56	8.65	9.14	9.67	8.96
Tertiary Growth Rate	9.80	6.83	7.40	8.23	8.73	8.20
Inflation Rate	5.30	2.63	4.35	5.35	4.24	4.37
Total Investment Ratio	29.86	34.11	36.19	39.66	42.79	36.52
Public Investment Ratio	6.00	6.00	6.00	6.00	6.00	6.00
Private Investment Ratio	23.86	28.11	30.19	33.66	36.79	30.52
Govt. Expenditure Ratio	26.35	24.79	24.90	24.98	25.03	25.21
Tax Revenue Ratio	15.11	15.08	15.19	15.27	15.32	15.19
Gross Revenue Deficit Ratio	1.53	0.00	0.00	0.00	0.00	0.31
Gross Fiscal Deficit Ratio	7.53	6.00	6.00	6.00	6.00	6.31
Current A/c Balance Ratio	2.27	-2.24	-3.09	-6.53	-7.47	-3.41
Export Growth Rate	21.00	10.00	10.00	15.00	15.00	14.20
Import Growth Rate	13.24	26.91	15.69	25.40	19.85	20.22

Note: Growth rates are in percentage terms. Investment ratios and other ratios are as percentages of GDP at current market prices.

The results indicate that a world trade shock of the given magnitude will adversely impact the GDP growth rate bringing it down by nearly one percentage point. This adverse impact will be borne by all the sectors, but the services sector is affected more than the other two sectors. The investment ratio goes up due to a sharper fall in the GDP than in total investments. The deficits in the fiscal sector remain unaffected as the assumptions about the variables in this sector remain unchanged from the previous scenario. However, the current account balance worsens significantly due to a drastic fall in the growth rate of exports.

Alternative Scenario 5: Impact of Economic Meltdown

The economic meltdown that has been experienced globally will have very significant impact on the Indian economy. This would directly impact the Indian economy by bringing down growth of exports. Additionally, it will impact private investments significantly due to a combination of a squeeze in the domestic and international financial markets and business uncertainty among investors. In this scenario, we analyse the impact of global meltdown on the Indian economy. Exports growth is assumed to be 21 per cent in 2007-08, falls to 10 per cent in 2008-09 and 2009-10, and rises again to 15 per cent in the last two years of the plan. Import price of non-oil products are assumed to be 500, 400, 400, 450 and 450 for the five years of the plan period. In order to capture the impact of financial market squeeze and business uncertainty, the private investment function in industry is assumed to shift below its long-run specification during the meltdown. More specifically, we assume that it falls to 80 per cent of its long-run specification in 2008-09, to 60 per cent in 2009-10, up to 90 per cent in 2010-11 and goes back to its long-run specification in 2011-12. Other assumptions about the economy are similar to that in the base run and the impact of the meltdown can be gauged by comparing the forecasts of this scenario with that from the base run. The forecasts corresponding to the above assumptions are presented in Table 5.8.

Table 5.8: Alternative Scenario 5 (Meltdown)

Variables	2007-08	2008-09	2009-10	2010-11	2011-12	Average
Aggregate Growth Rate	8.53	5.67	4.89	6.43	7.55	6.62
Agricultural Growth Rate	4.58	2.52	2.49	2.73	2.95	3.05
Industrial Growth Rate	8.77	7.84	6.56	7.34	8.62	7.83
Tertiary Growth Rate	9.80	5.63	4.81	7.13	8.38	7.15
Inflation Rate	5.30	-0.51	0.01	8.06	6.43	3.86
Total Investment Ratio	29.86	31.00	28.96	37.04	40.98	33.57
Public Investment Ratio	6.00	6.00	6.00	6.00	6.00	6.00
Private Investment Ratio	23.86	25.00	22.96	31.04	34.98	27.57
Govt. Expenditure Ratio	26.35	24.64	24.58	24.88	24.99	25.09
Tax Revenue Ratio	15.11	14.93	14.87	15.17	15.28	15.07
Gross Revenue Deficit Ratio	1.53	0.00	0.00	0.00	0.00	0.31
Gross Fiscal Deficit Ratio	7.53	6.00	6.00	6.00	6.00	6.31
Current A/c Balance Ratio	2.27	-0.76	1.22	-3.78	-6.23	-1.46
Export Growth Rate	21.00	10.00	10.00	15.00	15.00	14.20
Import Growth Rate	13.24	22.63	10.16	30.14	23.82	19.43

Note: Growth rates are in percentage terms. Investment ratios and other ratios are as percentages of GDP at current market prices.

The results indicate that a global meltdown of the given magnitude will adversely impact the GDP growth rate very significantly, bringing it down by nearly two percentage points. This adverse impact will be borne by all the sectors, but the industrial and services sector is affected more than the agricultural sector. The fall in private investment brings down the total investment ratio. The deficits in the fiscal sector remain unaffected as the assumptions about the variables in this sector remain unchanged from the previous scenario. The current account balance improves compared to the base run due to a relatively lower import growth as a result of the lower GDP growth rate.

Alternative Scenario 6: Economic Meltdown + Monetary Policy Stimulus

Following the global meltdown, policy makers across the world have started adopting counter-shock policies. The Indian government has also come up with their strategy to counter this meltdown. One important aspect of that strategy is to have an expansionary monetary policy. In this scenario, we analyse the impact of a combination of global meltdown and monetary policy stimulus on the Indian economy. As in the meltdown scenario, exports growth is assumed to be 21 per cent in 2007-08, falls to 10 per cent in 2008-09 and 2009-10, and rises again to 15 per cent in the last two years of the plan. Import price of non-oil products are assumed to be 500, 400, 400, 450 and 450 for the five years of the plan period. The private investment function in industry is assumed to fall to 80 per cent of its long-run specification in 2008-09, to 60 per cent in 2009-10, up to 90 per cent in 2010-11 and goes back to its long-run specification in 2011-12. In order to capture the monetary policy stimulus, we assume that the Prime Lending Rate (PLR) is brought down from 14 per cent in 2007-08, to 12 per cent in 2008-09, 11 per cent in 2009-10 and 10 per cent thereafter. Other assumptions about the economy are similar to that in the base run. The forecasts corresponding to the above assumptions are presented in Table 5.9.

Table 5.9: Alternative Scenario 6 (Meltdown + Monetary Policy Stimulus)

Variables	2007-08	2008-09	2009-10	2010-11	2011-12	Average
Aggregate Growth Rate	8.53	6.02	5.52	7.31	8.54	7.19
Agricultural Growth Rate	4.58	2.55	2.54	2.79	3.02	3.09
Industrial Growth Rate	8.77	7.82	6.60	7.52	8.99	7.94
Tertiary Growth Rate	9.80	6.28	5.93	8.60	9.95	8.11
Inflation Rate	5.30	0.11	0.43	8.30	6.52	4.13
Total Investment Ratio	29.86	31.72	30.27	38.73	43.18	34.75
Public Investment Ratio	6.00	6.00	6.00	6.00	6.00	6.00
Private Investment Ratio	23.86	25.72	24.27	32.73	37.18	28.75
Govt. Expenditure Ratio	26.35	24.67	24.62	24.92	25.03	25.12
Tax Revenue Ratio	15.11	14.96	14.91	15.21	15.32	15.10
Gross Revenue Deficit Ratio	1.53	0.00	0.00	0.00	0.00	0.31
Gross Fiscal Deficit Ratio	7.53	6.00	6.00	6.00	6.00	6.31
Current A/c Balance Ratio	2.27	-1.15	0.24	-5.07	-7.94	-2.33
Export Growth Rate	21.00	10.00	10.00	15.00	15.00	14.20
Import Growth Rate	13.24	23.66	11.08	30.94	24.08	20.00

Note: Growth rates are in percentage terms. Investment ratios and other ratios are as percentages of GDP at current market prices.

The results indicate that a monetary stimulus of the given magnitude will mitigate the impact of the meltdown to a certain extent, bringing up the growth rate by more than half a percentage point. This impact will be borne by all the sectors, but mostly by the services sector. The fall in interest rates will increase the private investment ratio and the total investment ratio. The deficits in the fiscal sector remain unaffected as the assumptions about the variables in this sector remain unchanged from the previous scenario. The current account balance worsens compared to the meltdown scenario due to relatively higher import growth as a result of the higher GDP growth rate.

Alternative Scenario 7: Economic Meltdown + Monetary and Fiscal Policy Stimulus

Together with an expansionary monetary policy, the Indian government is attempting to regenerate growth by adopting expansionary fiscal measures. In this scenario, we analyse the impact of a combination of global meltdown and monetary and fiscal stimulus on the Indian economy. As in the meltdown scenario, exports growth is assumed to be 21 per cent in 2007-08, falls to 10 per cent in 2008-09 and 2009-10, and rises again to 15 per cent in the last two years of the plan. Import price of non-oil products are assumed to be 500, 400, 400, 450 and 450 for the five years of the plan period. The private investment function in industry is assumed to fall to 80 per cent of its long-run specification in 2008-09, to 60 per cent in 2009-10, up to 90 per cent in 2010-11 and goes back to its long-run specification in 2011-12. We assume that the Prime Lending Rate (PLR) is brought down from 14 per cent in 2007-08, to 12 per cent in 2008-09, 11 per cent in 2009-10 and 10 per cent thereafter. The expansionary fiscal policy is assumed to increase public investment by 1 per cent in 2008-09 and thereafter. This means that from 2008-09 onwards, public investment in agriculture is assumed to be 0.6 per cent of nominal GDP, public investment in industry is assumed to be 2.6 per cent of nominal GDP and public investment in tertiary sector is assumed to be 3.8 per cent of nominal GDP. Other assumptions about the economy are similar to that in the base run. The forecasts corresponding to the above assumptions are presented in Table 5.10.

Table 5.10: Alternative Scenario 7 (Meltdown + Monetary and Fiscal Policy Stimulus)

Variables	2007-08	2008-09	2009-10	2010-11	2011-12	Average
Aggregate Growth Rate	8.53	6.89	6.72	8.80	10.30	8.25
Agricultural Growth Rate	4.58	3.38	3.80	4.40	4.83	4.20
Industrial Growth Rate	8.77	8.12	7.34	8.75	10.65	8.73
Tertiary Growth Rate	9.80	7.44	7.35	10.20	11.72	9.30
Inflation Rate	5.30	1.33	0.30	7.68	5.80	4.08
Total Investment Ratio	29.86	33.30	32.18	41.01	46.17	36.51
Public Investment Ratio	6.00	7.00	7.00	7.00	7.00	6.80
Private Investment Ratio	23.86	26.30	25.18	34.01	39.17	29.71
Govt. Expenditure Ratio	26.35	25.74	25.68	25.97	26.08	25.96
Tax Revenue Ratio	15.11	15.03	14.97	15.26	15.37	15.15
Gross Revenue Deficit Ratio	1.53	0.00	0.00	0.00	0.00	0.31
Gross Fiscal Deficit Ratio	7.53	7.00	7.00	7.00	7.00	7.11
Current A/c Balance Ratio	2.27	-1.95	-1.22	-6.73	-9.98	-3.52
Export Growth Rate	21.00	10.00	10.00	15.00	15.00	14.2
Import Growth Rate	13.24	25.93	11.93	31.38	24.06	20.72

Note: Growth rates are in percentage terms. Investment ratios and other ratios are as percentages of GDP at current market prices.

The results indicate that the combination of a fiscal and monetary stimulus of the given magnitude will mitigate the impact of the meltdown significantly, bringing up the growth rate by more than one and a half percentage points compared to the meltdown scenario. This impact will be borne more equally by all the sectors, but again more by the services sector. The fall in interest rates will increase the private investment ratio while the fiscal policy will increase the public investment ratio, both increasing the total investment ratio. The fiscal deficit ratio goes up further due the increased public investment in the agricultural, industrial and services sectors. The current account balance worsens further compared to the meltdown scenario due to relatively higher import growth as a result of the higher GDP growth rate.

5.5 Conclusion

This paper analyses the feasibility of the 11th Plan growth targets. This is done by studying the forecasts for the 11th Plan period made by the DPC-IEG model corresponding to assumptions for the base run and alternative scenarios. We find that if past trends continue, the growth in the agricultural sector will fall below the 11th Plan targets. The targeted agricultural growth rates can be achieved by reasonable increases in public investments in that sector, although this alone will not be sufficient to achieve the GDP growth targets. Thus, a more balance increase in public investments in all the three sectors will be necessary to attain 9 per cent growth in the economy.

The results also indicate that the rising oil prices and falling world trade can prove to be an impediment in achieving these growth rates. Moreover, the global meltdown is going to have a very significant impact on these growth rates. In such a scenario, fiscal and monetary policies will be necessary to ensure that the economy continues on a high growth path. However, they are not sufficient as the current account balances also worsens significantly. Thus, other complimentary policies targeting the external sector are required to ensure that high growth rates do not lead to a balance of payments crisis.

References

Ahluwalia, I.J. (1979). *Behaviour of Prices and Outputs in India: A Macroeconomic Approach*. New Delhi: Macmillan.

Ahluwalia, I.J. and C. Rangarajan (1986). *Agriculture and Industry: A Study of Linkages, the Indian Experience*. VIII World Economic Congress of International Economic Association, December.

Balakrishnan, P. (1991). *Pricing and Inflation in India*. New Delhi: Oxford University Press.

Bhattacharya, B.B. (1984). *Public Expenditure, Inflation and Growth: A Macro-Econometric Analysis For India*. Delhi: Oxford University Press.

Bhattacharya, B.B., R.B. Barman and A.K. Nag (1994). "Stabilisation Policy Options: A Macroeconometric Analysis", *Development Research Group Studies* No. 8. Bombay: Reserve Bank of India.

Bhattacharya, B.B. and S. Kar (2002a). "A Macro-Econometric Model of the Indian Economy: Some Theoretical Aspects", *Discussion Paper No. 48/2002*. Institute of Economic Growth. Delhi, March.

———. (2002b). "A Macro-Econometric Model of the Indian Economy: Some Empirical Results", *Discussion paper No. 49/2002*. Delhi: Institute of Economic Growth, March.

———. (2002c). "Short and Medium Run Growth and Stability: A Macro-Econometric Analysis and Forecasts for India", *Working Paper* No. E/224/2002. Delhi: Institute of Economic Growth.

Bhattacharya, B.B. and S. Kar (2006), *Macroeconomic Reforms, Growth and Stability*. Delhi: Oxford University Press.

Chakrabarty, T.K. (1987). "Macroeconomic Model of the Indian Economy", *RBI Occasional Papers* 8(3).

Diebold, Francis, (1998). "The Past, Present and Future of Macroeconomic Forecasting", *Journal of Economic Perspectives* 12(2).

Fair, R.C. (1994). *Testing Macroeconometric Models*. Cambridge Mass: Harvard University Press.

Kannan, R. (1985). "An Econometric Model of Foreign trade Sector (1956/57-1979/80)", *Reserve Bank of India Occasional Papers* 6(1), June.

Klein, L.R. (1984). *Econometric Model, Planning and Developing Countries*. Silver Jubilee Lecture. Institute of Economic Growth. Delhi.

———. (1986). "Economic Policy Formulation: Theory and Implementation (Applied Econometrics in the Public Sector)", Ch. 35 in Z. Griliches and M.D Intrilligator (eds.), *Handbook of Econometrics*, Vol. III. Amsterdam: North Holland.

Kohli, Atul (2006). "Politics of Growth in India, 1980-2005 (Part-I & Part-II), *Economic and Political Weakly*.

Krishna, K.L., K. Krishnamurty, V. Pandit and P.D. Sharma (1991). "Macroeconometric Modeling in India: A Selective Review of Recent Research", in *Econometric Modeling and Forecasting in Asia, Development Papers* No. 9. Bangkok: United Nations (ESCAP).

Krishnamurty, K. and V. Pandit (1985). *Macroeconometric Modeling of the Indian Economy*. Delhi: Hindustan Publishing.

Krishnamurty, K., Pandit, V. and P.D. Sharma (1989). "Parameters of Growth in a Developing Mixed Economy: The Indian Experience", *Journal of Quantitative Economics* 5(2).

Mammen, T. (1999). *India's Economic Prospects: A Macroeconomic and Econometric Analysis*. Singapore: World Scientific Publishing.

Mohan, Rakesh (2008). "The Growth Record of the Indian Economy, 1950-2008: A Story of Sustained Savings and Investment", Keynote Address at the Conference on *Growth and Macroeconomic Issues and Challenges in India*. Organised by Institute of Economic Growth, Delhi on February 14.

Pandit, V. (1985). "Macroeconomic Adjustments in a Developing Economy: A Medium Term Model of outputs and Prices in India", in Krishnamurty and Pandit (eds.), *Macro-econometric Modelling of the Indian Economy*. Delhi: Hindustan Publishing Corporation.

———. (1995). "Macroeconomic Character of the Indian Economy", in P. Patnaik (ed.), *Themes in Economics: Macroeconomics*. New Delhi: Oxford University Press.

———. and B.B. Bhattacharya (1987). "Resource Mobilisation Growth and Inflation: A Trade-off Analysis for India", in M. Datta (ed.), *Asia Pacific Economics: Promises and Challenges*. New York: Jai Press.

Pradhan, B.K., D.K. Ratha, and A. Sharma (1990). "Complementarity between Public and Private Investment in India", *Journal of Development Economics* 33(1).

Rangarajan C. and R.R. Arif (1990). "Money Output and Prices, A Macroeconometric Model", *Economic and Political Weekly* 25(16).

RBI Annual Reports (2002-03 to 2007-08).

RBI Monthly Bulletin (August. 2008-December 2008).

Subbarao, D. (2008a). India's Statement at the International Monetary and Financial Committee Meeting, at the International Monetary Fund, Washington DC, on October 11, 2008.

———. (2008b). India's Speech at the Bankers' Club, Kolkata on December 10, 2008.

Appendix A-5.1: The DPC-IEG Macro-econometric Model

GDP at Factor Cost

1. XGDP = XA + XI + XT
2. GR = 100* (XGDP – XGDP(-1))/ XGDP(-1)
3. XA = EXP(-8.16+ 1.43*LOG(KA)*** + 0.27*LOG(RF)*** – 0.12*D80S*** – 0.14*DUMXA*** + 0.10*LOG(XA(-1)))

   (1.31) (0.24) (0.05) (0.03) (0.03) (0.14)

   R^2 = 0.99 Dh = -1.06
4. XAG = 100*(XA-XA(-1))/XA(-1)
5. XI = EXP(-2.57 + 0.08*LOG(KI) + 0.34*LOG(XA)*** + 0.18*LOG(RAE)*** – 0.06*LOG(PI) + 0.02*DPLIB

   (0.83) (0.09) (0.07) (0.05) (0.04) (0.01)

   + 0.6*LOG(XI(-1))*** + 0.04*D95**)

   (0.06) (0.01)

   R^2 = 0.99 Dh = -1.32
6. XIG = 100*(XI-XI(-1))/XI(-1)
7. XT = EXP(-5.06 + 0.67*LOG(KT)*** + 0.13*LOG(XCOM)** + 0.01*DUMPAY* + 0.02*DPLIB** + 0.52*LOG(XT(-1))***)

   (1.02) (0.17) (0.05) (0.006) (0.008) (0.09)

   R^2 = 0.99 Dh = -1.54
8. XTG = 100*(XT-XT(-1))/XT(-1)
9. XCOM = XA + XI
10. RAE = 100*(GE + EGSR)/PGDP

Capital Stock

11. K = KA + KI + KT
12. KA = KA(-1) *(1-DKAR) + IGA + IPA
13. KI = KI(-1) * (1-DKIR) + IGI + IPI
14. KT = KT(-1) * (1-DKTR) + IGT + IPT

Private Investment

15. IP = IPA + IPI + IPT
16. IPN = IP * PGDP*.01+EIPN
17. IPA = -4714.17 + 0.05*XA*** + 0.44*IGA** – 2700.76*D80S*** + 0.28*IPA(-1)**

    (1704.33) (0.01) (0.2) (706.1) (0.13)

    R^2 = 0.9 Dh = -1.81
18. IPI = -25029.76 + 0.20*XGDP*** + 0.71*IGI** – 0.56*ORGE*** – 649.003*RPLR – 939.56*IFR + 41506.12*D95***

    (10074.05) (0.04) (0.3) (0.13) (696.28) (791.82) (7846.03)

    + 0.22*IPI(-1)*

    (0.11)

    R^2 = 0.96 Dh = -0.91

19. IPT = -33116.9 + 0.08*XGDP** + 0.71*IGT – 663.11*RPLR – 2920.68*DFEMRPLR* + 0.45*IPT(-1)**

(12348.49) (0.04) (1.1) (590.26) (1628.1) (0.19)

R^2 = 0.86 DW = 2.07 (Dh not computable)

20. RPLR = PLR - IFR

Public Investment

21. IGA= 100*IGAN/PGDP

22. IGI = 100*IGIN/PGDP

23. IGT = 100*IGTN/PGDP

24. IG = IGA + IGI + IGT

25. IGN = IGAN + IGIN + IGTN + EIGN

Total Investment

26. INV = IGN + IPN

27. INVR = 100*INV/GDPMP

Aggregate Demand

28. GDPMP = CP + GC + IGN + IPN + EGSR - MGSR + RESGDP

29. CP = RCP * PGDP*.01

30. RCP = EXP(2.89 + 0.65*LOG(RPDI)*** + 0.03*DWTO*** + 0.11*LOG(RCP(-1)))

(0.33) (0.06) (0.01) (0.08)

R^2 = 0.99 Dh = 1.74

31. PDI = YGDP -TAX + GTR + OPDI

32. RPDI = PDI*100/PGDP

33. YGDP = EXP(-0.08 + 0.99*LOG(GDPMP)***) + [AR(1)=0.66***]

(0.03) (0.002) (0.12)

R^2 = 0.99 DW = 2.05

Price

34. PGDP = 0.309*PA + 0.26*PI + 0.42*PT

35. IFR = 100*(PGDP - PGDP(-1))/PGDP(-1)

36. PA = EXP(4.002 – 0.71*LOG(XA)*** + 0.59*LOG(PDI)*** + 0.12*DUMPA*** + 0.31*LOG(PA(-1)**))

(1.71) (0.15) (0.08) (0.02) (0.14)

R^2 = 0.99 Dh = 1.29

37. PI = EXP(-0.20 + 0.37*LOG(PA)*** + 0.05*LOG(PMO)*** + 0.01*LOG(PMN) + 0.53*LOG(PI(-1)***)

(0.06) (0.05) (0.009) (0.014) (0.06)

+ 0.06*LOG(TRF)***)

(0.013)

R^2 = 0.99 Dh = 0.61

38. PT = EXP (0.11 + 0.16*LOG(PA)*** + 0.42*LOG(PI)*** + 0.39*LOG(PT(-1)***))

(0.01) (0.02) (0.04) (0.04)

$R^2 = 0.99$ Dh = 0.61

Money and Interest

39. M3 = RM3*PGDP/100

40. RM3 = EXP(-9.801 + 1.68*LOG(XGDP)*** + 0.008*RPLR*** – 0.01*DFEMRPLR*** + 0.19*DUMM3***

(0.5) (0.03) (0.002) (0.004) (0.03)

– 0.07*DWTO*)

(0.03)

$R^2 = 0.99$ DW = 1.52

41. PLR = 0.49 + 1.65e-05*M3*** – 7.2e-05*M0*** + 0.43*CRR*** + 1.13*BR***

(1.42) (3.9e-06) (1.7e-05) (0.09) (0.21)

$R^2 = 0.88$ DW = 2.45

42. M3G = 100*(M3 - M3(-1))/ M3(-1)

43. M0 = FERR + GSRBI - NNML

44. FERR = FER * EXR/10

45. GSRBI = GSRBI(-1) + MGFD

Fiscal Sector

46. GE = GC + IGN + GTR

47. RGE = GE *100/PGDP

48. ORGE = RGE - IG

49. GFD = GE - TAX - NTAX

50. GFDR = 100*GFD/GDPMP

51. TAX = EXP(-2.95 + 1.08*LOG(GDPMP)*** – 0.104*DLIB*** – 0.11*DWTO)***

(0.18) (0.01) (0.02) (0.02)

$R^2 = 0.99$ DW = 1.906

External Transactions

52. FER = FER (-1) + CAB + KAB + RESFER

53. CAB = EGS - MGS + REM

54. CABR = 100*(CAB*EXR*0.1)/GDPMP

55. EGS = EXP(-6.62 + 1.02*LOG(WT)*** + 0.34*LOG(REXR)** + 0.09*D80S + 0.12*DFEM* + 0.14*DWTO**

(1.13) (0.05) (0.14) (0.05) (0.06) (0.05)

+ 0.23*DUMEGS***)

(0.05)

$R^2 = 0.99$ DW = 1.49

56. EGSR = EGS*EXR/10

57. MGS = MGSO + MGSN

58. MGSO = EXP(-3.26 + 0.43*LOG(XCOM)* + 1.005*LOG(PMO)*** + 0.55*LOG(PGDP)** – 0.69*LOG(EXR)***

(2.09) (0.21) (0.02) (0.2) (0.1)

+ 0.05*DUMMGSO)***

(0.01)

$R^2 = 0.99$ DW = 1.85

59. MGSN = EXP(-10.22 + 1.37*LOG(XGDP)*** + 0.09*LOG(PMN)** + 1.36*LOG(PGDP)*** – 1.34*LOG(EXR)***

(2.29) (0.2) (0.03) (0.1) (0.06)

– 0.18*LOG(TRF)*** + 0.18*D95*** + 0.05*DWTO)

(0.03) (0.05) (0.04)

$R^2 = 0.99$ DW = 1.66

60. MGSR = MGS*EXR/10

61. PM = 0.2788*PMO + 0.7212*PMN

62. EXR = EXP(0.39 – 0.07*LOG(FER)*** + 0.27*LOG(PGDP)*** + 0.19*DEV91*** + 0.69*LOG(EXR(-1))***)

(0.1) (0.01) (0.04) (0.04) (0.06)

$R^2 = 0.99$ Dh = -1.17

63. REXR = 100*EXR/PGDP

Appendix A-5.2: List of Variables

Exogenous Variables

BR Bank rate set by central bank; **CRR** Cash Reserve Ratio set by central bank; **D80S** Dummy for structural changes since the eighties; **D95** Dummy for peak liberalisation effect; **DEV91** Dummy for large devaluation in 1991; **DFEM** Dummy for financial and external market liberalisation in 1993; **DFEMRPLR** Slope dummy for effect of DFEM on RPLR; **DKAR** Depreciation rate of agricultural capital stock; **DKIR** Depreciation rate of industrial capital stock; **DKTR** Depreciation rate of tertiary sector capital stock; **DLIB** Dummy for liberalisation in 1991; **DPLIB** Dummy for partial liberalisation in mid-eighties; **DUMEGS** Outlier dummy for exports; **DUMM3** Outlier dummy for money demand; **DUMMGSO** Outlier dummy for oil imports; **DUMPA** Outlier dummy for agricultural prices; **DUMPAY** Dummy for pay hike in public administration; **DUMXA** Outlier dummy for agricultural output; **DWTO** Dummy for effect of joining WTO; **EIGN** Errors and omissions in IGN; **EIPN** Errors and omissions in IPN; **EOINV** Errors and omissions in INV; **GC** Government consumption; **GTR** Government transfer payments; **IGAN** Nominal public investment in agriculture; **IGIN** Nominal public investment in industry; **IGTN** Nominal public investment in tertiary sector; **KAB** Capital account balance; **MGFD** Monetised gross fiscal deficit; **NNML** Net non-monetary liabilities; **NTAX** Non-tax revenues; **PMN** Import price of non-oil products; **PMO** Import price of oil; **REM** Remittances etc.; **RESFER** Errors and omissions in BOP account; **RESGDP** Errors in 'GDP at market prices' identity; **RF** Rainfall index; **TRF** Average tariff rate

Endogenous Variables

CAB Current account balance; **CABR** Current account balance ratio; **CP** Nominal personal consumption expenditure; **EGS** Export of goods and services in dollars; **EGSR** Export of goods and services in rupees; **EXR** Exchange rate; **FER** Foreign exchange reserves in dollars; **FERR** Foreign exchange reserves in rupees; **GDPMP** Nominal GDP at market price; **GE** Government expenditure; **GFD** Nominal gross fiscal deficit; **GFDR** Gross fiscal deficit ratio; **GR** GDP growth; **GSRBI** Central bank credit to government; **IFR** Inflation rate based on GDP deflator; **IG** Real public investment; **IGA** Real public investment in agriculture; **IGI** Real public investment in industry; **IGN** Nominal public investment; **IGT** Real public investment in tertiary sector; **INV** Total nominal investment; **INVR** Total real investment; **IP** Real private investment; **IPA** Real private investment in agriculture; **IPI** Real private investment in industry; **IPN** Nominal private investment; **IPT** Real private investment in tertiary sector; **K** Capital stock; **KA** Capital stock in agriculture; **KI** Capital stock in industry; **KT** Capital stock in tertiary sector; **M0** Nominal reserve money; **M3** Nominal money demand; **M3G** Nominal money demand growth rate; **MGS** Nominal Imports of goods and services in dollars; **MGSN** Nominal Imports of non-oil goods and services in dollars; **MGSO** Nominal Imports of oil in dollars; **MGSR** Nominal Imports of goods and services in rupees; **ORGE** Other real government expenditure (other than public investments); **PA** Agricultural deflator; **PDI** Nominal private disposable income; **PGDP** GDP deflator; **PI** Industrial deflator; **PLR** Interest rate (Prime lending rate); **PM** Import price; **PT** Tertiary sector deflator; **RAE** Real autonomous expenditure; **RCP** Real personal consumption expenditure; **REXR** Real exchange rate; **RGE** Real government expenditure; **RM3** Real money demand; **RPDI** Real private disposable income; **RPLR** Real interest rate; **TAX** Tax revenues; **XA** Real agricultural output; **XAG** Growth in agricultural output; **XCOM** Real commodity output; **XGDP** Real GDP; **XI** Real industrial output; **XIG** Growth in industrial output; **XT** Real tertiary sector output; **XTG** Growth in tertiary output; **YGDP** Nominal GDP at factor cost.

CHAPTER 6

Impact of External Economic Environment

An Assessment Using a Macroeconometric Model

Shashanka Bhide and Purna Chandra Parida*

6.1 Introduction

The evolution of macroeconometric models (MEMs) has a long history since II World War, and it has been used for two important purposes, forecasting and policy analysis. A more general definition of MEMs is that it is built up by a set of behavioural equations, as well as institutional and definitional relationships, representing the structure and operations of an economy, in principle based upon the behaviour of individual economic agents. The literature on macroeconometric model suggests that it is classified into five important categories (Challen and Hagger, 1983). These are the Keynes-Klein (KK) model, the Phillips-Bergstrom (PB) model, the Walras-Johansen (WJ) model, the Walras-Leontief (WL) model and the Muth-Sargent (MS) model. These approaches go beyond the traditional specification of the macroeconometric models and include the other strand of modelling, the applied general equilibrium models (AGE) or computable general equilibrium models (CGE) and dynamic stochastic general equilibrium (DSGE) models. Favero (2007) provides a review of the DSGE approach to macroeconometric models.

The KK model has extensively been used by economists for developing countries to explain the macroeconomic fluctuations due to demand side factors during the short to medium term. This model is mainly used for analysing the macroeconomic instability of an economy related to output and employment. Notwithstanding its extensive application, the model it is recognised that the approach does not incorporate adequately the importance of supply side factors and the role of money market, relative prices and expectations. The PB model is also a demand-oriented model, but it captures the dynamics of the economy in an intrinsic way as it is based on difference equations using theories of both Keynesian and neoclassical. The WJ approach leads to a multi-sector model in which each sector is interlinked with the other sectors via its purchases and sales to the other sectors. Although this model has similar approach like Input-Output model, it is different from the latter as it is highly non-linear and uses logarithmic differentiation. The WL model applies an Input-Output analytical framework into the Walarasian general equilibrium system, enabling analysts to obtain sectoral output, value added, employment given the values of sectoral and aggregate final demand components. The MS model is based on the theory of rational expectations and has similar empirical properties like KK model, where both are dynamic, non-linear, stochastic and discrete.

* The work reported here has evolved over the years based on the work by D.K. Joshi, Ila Patnaik, Rachna Sharma and D.K. Pant. The model is currently being re-estimated with the new data. The authors wish to acknowledge with comments we received from Prof. Kirit Parikh on the earlier drafts of this paper. The authors are solely responsible for any errors in the paper.

Shashanka Bhide and Purna Chandra Parida, National Council of Applied Economic Research (NCAER).

But, the constant change of macroeconomic theories over the last three decades has created additional difficulties for the model builders to stick to a specific kind of macro models from the above. Klein (2004) points out that models dealing with policy issues need to be diverse rather than parsimonious in their structure. Moreover, non-availability of reliable data and unquantifiable phenomena pose serious difficulties as such models can never be properly interpreted. Thus, there is a need to depart from pure and prototype textbook models and incorporate details of the economies into the models.

Evolution of Macro Modelling in India

Macroeconometric modelling in India has one of the longest histories particularly amongst developing countries and has had a policy focus. These models have been concerned with the level of economic activity, price behaviour, fiscal and monetary policies, intersectional linkages, investment, saving and consumption, resource mobilisation and public sector capital formation, trade flows and balance of payments. The first MEM for a developing country was constructed by Narasimham (1956) for India under the supervision of Tinbergen. The earliest models for developing countries were mainly small versions of the KK model capturing the demand side of the economy. Since the early 1950s there were a number of MEMs developed by research organisations and individuals. According to Marwah (1991) about 80 different models were built for the Indian economy since the 1950s. Krishnamurthy (1992) refers to 40 econometric macro models built for India since the early fifties. Comprehensive reviews of MEMs for India are provided by Desai (1972), Marwah (1985), Jadhav (1990) and Krishna, Krishnamurthy, Pandit and Sharma (1991).

Most of the models on Indian economy have a Keynesian flavour as components of effective demand are carefully modelled on Keynesian lines. The supply side often responds to demand signals. In some models supply constraints are explicitly modelled. The models incorporate on Keynesian lines, consumption function and a private investment behaviour on the lines of accelerator hypothesis. Inventories are modelled differently by various modellers. Bhattacharya (1984) has treated inventory investment as a residual. On the other hand Pani (1977) and Ahluwalia (1979) try to explicitly model capacity utilisation to reconcile supply to demand which is sought to be influenced by imports, raw material availability and public investment which represent different capacity constraints.

The Planning Commission of India has also been using a macroeconomic model in which an I-O model is embedded for analysing alternative growth targets for the economy. This approach has been followed over the years, since the early 1950s, with several extensions and modifications. These models were used to specify the investment levels of various sectors of the economy to achieve a certain target of output, employment and poverty reduction etc. A thorough review of planning models is given in Dahiya (1982). During the eighties, National Council of Applied Economic Research (NCAER) with support from Ministry of Finance built a macroeconomic model of CGE variety. Different versions of CGE models have been reported in Sarkar and Subbarao (1981), Panda and Sarkar (1990, 1991), Sarkar and Panda (1989) and Bhide and Pohit (1993). Other institutions like RBI, and IEG-DSE, IGIDR have developed macroeconometric or economy-wide models for forecasting and policy analysis for the short and medium term.

The NCAER Macroeconometric Model for India

A macroeconometric model was developed by NCAER team to provide a medium-term perspective on the economy. The model is essentially a structural model of the economy. It captures both the demand and supply characteristics of major sectors but output is determined from the supply side. It has the major blocks of the income-expenditure accounting of the national income. The model has been used in the past for both forecasting and analysis of alternative scenarios with respect to petroleum sector prices and medium-term growth perspectives. In this paper, we provide a brief description of the model and present some applications of the model. The applications are obtained for the five year period of the Eleventh Five Year Plan.

6.2 Model Structure Specification and Estimated Equations

The macroeconometric model of the Indian economy developed and maintained at NCAER is a system of equations describing the production, demand and pricing of major sectors of the economy inter-linked with each other mainly through the impact of relative prices operating under a common fiscal, monetary and trade environment. The model has a relatively strong supply side specification of output on which the expenditure side fluctuations have a secondary influence. The specification, thus, follows an eclectic approach in which the economy is viewed in terms of a set of equations each describing a particular relationship between different economic variables. The relationships include those derived from economic theory as well as statistical relationships which are estimated to provide links between variables.

The model was developed to provide medium-term assessment of the Indian economy with respect to the major macroeconomic variables such as output, prices, investment and trade and fiscal balances. The dynamic nature of the model emerges from the capital formation process and lagged impact between variables in some relationships. The model provides a time-path for selected variables over the period for which alternative simulations are carried out.

The present model can be viewed as a set of equations describing (a) output of various production sectors, (b) demand for output in terms of consumption and investment demand, (c) prices, (d) international trade, (e) fiscal balance, (f) monetary linkages and (g) national income identities.

The model incorporates explicitly the impact of some of the sources of improvement in productivity. The model reflects the impact of (a) infrastructure development, (b) growing strength of linkages between agriculture and industry, and (c) rising FDI on the productivity of various sectors. Rather than assuming a fixed total factor productivity growth in different sectors, these three channels represent a set of specific sources of improvement in productivity.

The output is determined by both supply and demand side influences, although there are sectoral level differences in this specification. Output is determined at the level of broad sectors, *viz.*, (a) agriculture and allied sector, (b) manufacturing, mining and quarrying and construction, (c) electricity, gas and water supply, (d) transport, storage and communication, (e) financial, banking and insurance, and business services, and (f) other services. The output of the sectors is aggregated to provide estimates of overall output such as GDP and GNP.

The model assumes that labour is not a constraining factor of production. Therefore, output is determined by capital stock and demand. The utilisation of capital would be determined by demand conditions in the case of non-agricultural sectors and by other factors such as rainfall in the case of agriculture.

Prices are estimated at the sectoral level, which are then aggregated to provide overall inflation measures.

The model has endogenously determined interest rate and an exogenously specified exchange rate. The interest rate is sensitive to the gap between supply and demand for money and the fiscal deficit of the Central government relative to its borrowing from the market. Thus, excessive fiscal deficit will have an impact on interest rate which will in turn affect subsequent interest payments and sustainability of the fiscal position. Higher interest rate may also affect production depending on its impact on investment.

The model has been estimated by OLS wherever the autocorrelation problem was not severe. In case the autocorrelation problem existed, as per the Durbin-Watson statistic, the equation was estimated after adjusting for autocorrelation. In a few cases, equations have also been estimated in the error correction modelling framework using a two stage procedure. Data used for estimation is mainly for the period 1970-1971 to 2000-01. The model is solved as a system of equations using the software package Eviews.

6.2.1 Agricultural Output

In the case of agriculture and allied sectors, there is further disaggregation in terms of crop categories, *viz.*, rice, wheat, other food grains and non-food grains. Although production of all the allied sectors is not strictly related to the production of crop sector, in some ways agricultural production is 'land-based' and depends on the utilisation of land. With this in view output of non-crop sectors is linked to the production of crop sectors. The basic relationships are defined below.

The crop output is defined based on crop area and crop yield per area. The total gross cropped area is first determined based on the gross irrigated area and rain fall during the monsoon season. This specification reflects the emergence of higher cropping intensity as the main source of growth in gross cropped area now. This in turn is mainly influenced by availability of irrigation. The gross cropped area is then allocated among three categories of crops Rice, wheat, other food grains and non-food grain crops based on irrigated area under these respective crops, expected price of the crop relative to other crops and rainfall during the monsoon season. The gross irrigated area is specified as an exogenous variable.

The irrigated area under each crop is related to the gross cropped area under all crops. We allow the allocation of gross cropped area to the individual crop groups to be determined by the past trend.

Crop yield is estimated as a function of the extent of irrigation in the total area under the crop, price of inputs relative to the expected crop price and rainfall during the monsoon season.

Common form of the estimated equations is specified below for crop area, irrigated area and crop yield.

Crop Area Equations

Gross cropped area

1) $\text{Log (A)} = 3.828142 + 0.227503^{*}\text{Log (AI)} + 0.065578^{*}\text{Log (RAIN)} - 0.031871^{*}\text{D87}$

(30.15) (4.09) (3.03)

$R^2 = 0.97$ DW=1.84 OLS

Area under specific crops

2) $\text{Log (ARICE)} = 2.168976 + 0.093225^{*}\text{Log (RAIN)} + 0.314848^{*}\text{Log (AIRICE)} - 0.001793^{*}\text{Log (WPIRICE}_{-1}/\text{WPIOTFOOD}_{-1})$

(6.34) (26.53) (2.78)

$R^2 = 0.98$ DW=1.87 OLS

3) $\text{Log (AWHEAT)} = -1.498187 + 0.534375^{*}\text{Log (AWHEAT}_{-1}) + 0.460161^{*}\text{Log (A)} + 0.087163^{*}\text{Log (RAIN)}$

(5.08) (1.83) (2.71)

$- 0.075113^{*}\text{Log (WPIWHEAT}_{-1}/\text{WPIOTFOOD}_{-1}) - 0.111380^{*}\text{D7374}$

(2.45) (4.78)

$R^2 = 0.95$ Dh=0.70 OLS

4) $\text{Log (ANFG)} = 0.096335 + 0.508326^{*}\text{Log (AINFG)} + 0.479582^{*}\text{Log (A)} - 0.045779^{*}\text{Log (WPINFG}_{-1}/\text{WPIFG}_{-1})$

(9.23) (3.04) (1.91)

$+ 0.791592^{*}\text{AR (1)}$

(8.66)

$R^2 = 0.99$ DW=2.30 OLS

5) Area under food grains other than rice and wheat

$\text{AOTFD} = \text{A} - (\text{ARICE} + \text{AWHEAT} + \text{ANFG})$

Irrigated Area under Crops

Area under rice, wheat and non-food grains is determined based on crop specific equations such as,

Area under a crop (Rice)

$\text{Ln AI\_R} = \text{a0} + \text{a1 Ln AI}$

More specifically, the estimated equations for the major crop groups are,

6) $\text{Log (AIRICE)} = -0.218870 + 0.774575^*\text{Log (AI)} + 0.513873^*\text{AR (1)}$

(15.77) (3.05)

$R^2 = 0.98$ DW=2.24 OLS

7) $\text{Log (AIWHEAT)} = -1.001649 + 0.956271^*\text{Log (AI)} + 0.647921^*\text{AR (1)}$

(7.74) (4.59)

$R^2 = 0.97$ DW=2.44 OLS

8) $\text{Log (AINFG)} = -3.521433 + 1.544203^*\text{Log (AI)} + 0.536056^*\text{AR (1)}$

(23.98) (3.24)

$R^2 = 0.99$ DW=1.87 OLS

9) AIOTFOOD = AI – AIRICE – AIWHEAT – AINFG

Crop Yields

Crop yield per hectare of crop area is determined from an equation that incorporates the impact of monsoon rainfall besides extent of irrigation and expected relative prices. Crop yields in the case of rice, wheat, other food grains and non-food grains are estimated using following generic type of specification

Crop yield per hectare (Rice)

$\text{Ln YLD\_R} = a0 + a1 \text{ Ln RAIN} + a2 \text{ Ln (AI\_R/ A\_R)} + a3 \text{ Ln (WPI\_INP/ WPI\_R)}$

The estimated equations are,

10) $\text{Log (YRICE)} = 5.854149 + 0.425927^*\text{Log (RAIN)} + 1.746604^*\text{Log (AIRICE/ARICE)} - 0.048366^*\text{Log (WPIINPUT/WPIRICE}_{-1})$

(4.07) (14.78) (3.32)

$R^2 = 0.92$ DW=1.35 OLS

11) $\text{Log (YWHEAT)} = 8.124768 + 1.951787^*\text{Log (AIWHEAT/AWHEAT)} - 0.030573^*\text{Log (WPIINPUT/WPIWHEAT}_{-1})$

(14.45) (2.24)

$+ 0.229052^*\text{AR (1)}$

(1.43)

$R^2 = 0.96$ DW=2.08 OLS

12) $\text{Log (YOTFOOD)} = 6.262459 - 0.189006^*\text{Log (WPIINPUT/WPIOTFOOD}_{-1}) + 0.016520^*\text{T}$

(2.68) (13.15)

$R^2 = 0.86$ DW=1.89 OLS

13) $\text{Log (YNFGI)} = 4.381039 + 0.817479^*\text{Log (AINFG/ANFG)} + 0.206117^*\text{Log (RAIN)}$

(7.03) (4.81)

$- 0.099536^*\text{ Log (WPIINPUT/WPINFG}_{-1}) + 0.644859^*\text{AR (1)}$

(3.03) (4.10)

$R^2 = 0.95$ DW=2.12 OLS

Crop Output

Output is determined as a product of area and yield. Crop output is aggregated to food grains and non-food grains. The specification is,

14) QRICE = (ARICE * YRICE)

15) QWHEAT = (AWHEAT * YWHEAT)

16) QOTFOOD = (AOTFOOD * YOTFOOD)

17) QFG = QRICE + QWHEAT + QOTFOOD

In the case of non-food grains the output is estimated through a link equation rather than as a definitional identity

18) Log (QNFGI) = -3.578296 + 0.542402*Log (ANFG) + 1.324427*Log (YNFGI) + 0.416755*AR (1)

(7.23) (14.92) (2.29)

$R^2 = 0.99$ DW=1.78 OLS

The gross output is transformed into value added using a link equation. In this equation we also incorporate the potential for improvements in varieties and higher value added composition of crop output by including capital stock per hectare of crop area as an independent variable.

One way to specify the total value added from agriculture and allied sectors is,

Ln (RVAAG/ A) = a0 + a1 Ln {(RK + RK)/2} + a2 Ln QFG + a3 Ln QNFG

However, this does not capture some of the sources of improvement in productivity that may be achieved by changes in crop mix within the broad aggregates and some value addition at the farm level that may occur because of the stronger links between agriculture and agro-based industry.

Modification of the Standard Specification

We further modify this equation to incorporate the effects of stronger links between agriculture and industry which enables production of higher value addition at the farm level either by some primary processing activity such as grading of the produce or in fact in the choice of crop varieties for which there is greater demand by the agro processing industry. The modified estimated equation is

19) LOG (RVAAG/A) = -5.2506 + 0.6585 * LOG (($RKAGR_{-1}$+RKAGR)/2*A) + 0.2289 * LOG (QNFGI/QFGI)

(5.49) (2.58)

+ 0.1401 * LOG (SHAREALLIED) + 0.0641 * LOG (SHAREAGRO) – 0.1237 * D79

(0.70) (0.43) (3.32)

$R^2 = 0.98$ DW = 1.41 OLS

The modification not only captures the impact of changes in the composition of output at a broader level such as between food grain and non-food grain crops but it also captures the changing composition of agricultural output between crop and non-crop sectors and the impact of changing share of agricultural produce that is processed by the industry.

The capital formation and capital stock in agriculture are linked to each other through the standard linear specification in which capital stock at the beginning of each year is updated taking into account capital stock at the beginning of the previous year, depreciation of this capital stock and capital formation during the previous period

20) RKAGR = $RKAGR_{-1}$ + RGCFAGR – RCFCAGR

21) RCFCAGR = (DRATAGR * $RKAGR_{-1}$)/100

22) RGCFAGR = RGCFPAGR + RGCFGAGR

6.2.2 Non-Agricultural Output

In the case of non-agricultural output five main sub-sectors are identified. The sub-sectors are (1) mining, quarrying and manufacturing, (2) Construction, (3) Electricity, gas and water supply, (4) Transport, storage and communication, and (5) Other services.

The specification of production or output equations reflects the impact of both supply side 'production capacity' and the 'demand pressures'. On the supply side, the capital stock in the respective sectors influences output. The demand pressure is captured by the real value of 'compensation to employees'. The general form of output equation adopted in each sub-sector that reflects the impact of capital stock and demand pressures is described by the case of mining, quarrying and manufacturing as follows

Mining and Manufacturing

$$\text{Ln RVAMQM} = a0 + a1 \text{ Ln } \{(\text{RKMQM}_{-1} + \text{RKMQM})/2\} + a2 \text{ Ln } (\text{CETOT}/\text{PALL})$$

However, this specification does not reflect the impact of various sources of productivity growth.

Modification of the Standard Specification

The specification of output in the standard specification does not capture the potential improvements in productivity that may come about through improvements in complementary inputs such as infrastructure. Although some of the non-agricultural sectors themselves constitute infrastructure industries, the impact of development of one infrastructure sector such as electricity on the other infrastructure sector such as communication can be significant. A second source of improvement in productivity can be the impact of growing integration of the economy with the international markets. This integration is likely to influence adoption of technology and practices which would improve value addition per unit of capital. Foreign direct investment is the most direct influence globalisation may have on productivity. Taking into account these potential sources of improvement in productivity, the output equations for non-agricultural sectors have been modified and estimated as follows:

23) Log (RVAMQM) = – 1.255705 + 0.131015 * Log ((RKMQM$_{-1}$+RKMQM)/2) + 0.006544 * Log (RFDIMQM)

(1.14) (2.49)

+ 0.330444 * Log (CETOT_T*100/PALL) + 0.573557 * Log ((RKEGW$_{-1}$ + RKEGW + RKTSC$_{-1}$ + RKTSC)/2)

(2.43) (5.49)

0.085218 * D89956

(4.74)

$R^2 = 0.99$ DW = 1.94

24) LOG (RVACON) = 1.9289 + 0.3994 * LOG ((RKCON$_{-1}$+RKCON)/2)

(3.20)

+ 0.3861* LOG ((RKEGW$_{-1}$+RKEGW +RKTSC$_{-1}$+RKTSC)/2) + 0.1483 * D77 – 0.1060 * D8456

(2.78) (2.60) (3.13)

$R^2 = 0.98$ DW = 1.44

25) LOG (RVAEGW) = – 4.7895 + 0.6752 * LOG ((RKEGW$_{-1}$+RKEGW)/2) + 0.5162 * LOG (CETOT_T*100/PALL)

(16.48) (8.49)

+ 0.0051 * LOG (RFDIEGW) + 0.0767 * D912

(1.60) (4.47)

$R^2 = 0.99$ DW = 1.19

26) LOG (RVATSC) = – 5.2268 + 0.6991 * LOG ((RKTSC$_{-1}$+RKTSC)/2) + 0.0052 * LOG (RFDITSC)

(5.28) (1.58)

+ 0.6206 * LOG (CETOT_T*100/PALL) + 0.0628 * D8012

(6.65) (4.43)

$R^2 = 0.99$ DW = 1.87

27) $LOG (RVASER) = -5.9133 + 0.5831 * LOG ((RKSER_{-1}+RKSER)/2) + 0.5453 * LOG (CETOT\_T*100/PALL)$

(3.44) (6.56)

$+ 0.0031 * LOG (RFDISER) + 0.2986 * LOG ((RKEGW_{-1}+RKEGW+RKTSC_{-1}+RKTSC)/2)$

(2.18) (5.74)

$- 0.0330 * D834$

(3.73)

$R^2 = 0.99$ DW = 1.42

A summary of the modification of the standard specification for different sectors is given in Table 6.1.

Table 6.1: Incorporation of the Effect FDI and Infrastructure Growth on the Production of Non-Agricultural Sectors

Sector	FDI Variable	Infrastructure Variable (Capital stock in)
Mining, quarrying and manufacturing	FDI in the sector	EGW, TSC
Construction		EGW, TSC
Electricity, gas and water supply (EGW)	FDI in the sector	
Transport, storage and communication (TSC)	FDI in the sector	
Other services	FDI in the sector	EGW, TSC

The modification allows one to incorporate two important sources of productivity growth in the non-agricultural sectors. In the standard specification, improvement in infrastructure has no direct impact on the production of the other sectors of the economy.

The capital stock is updated for each year based on the standard linear specification taking into account the depreciation and fixed capital formation.

6.2.3 Aggregation of Output and National Income Identities

The output from each of the production sectors is aggregated to the overall economy level output by first transforming gross output to value added wherever relevant. Value added or sectoral GDP is then aggregated to the overall GDP as follows

28) GDPFC_R = RVAAG + RVAMQM + RVACON + RVAEGW + RVATSC + RVAOSER

Nominal GDP is defined at the sectoral by multiplying real GDP with a price index relevant for each sector. The overall GDP at factor cost in current prices is an aggregation of the nominal GDP at the sectoral level.

29) GDPFC = RVAAG* PAG + RVAMQM* PMQM + RVACON* PCON + RVAEGW* PEGW + RVATSC* PTSC + RVAOSER* PSER

Gross national product at market price is defined as the sum of consumption and investment expenditures including international trade transactions.

30) GNPMP = CP + GTCEP_T + GCFGTOT + XTOT – MTOT + NETINV + DISC

31) GDPMP = GNPMP – NFIAB

The values of GDP aggregates in constant prices are defined by deflating the nominal values by their respective price deflators.

Private Income (Real)

The relationship between real private income and real GNP ast market prices has been estimated using a two-stage model

32) Real Private Income

First Stage Equation

Log (RPVTINCOME) = -0.6164 + 1.0356 * Log (RGNPMP)

(160.57)

$R^2 = 0.99$ DW= 0.48 OLS

Second Stage Equation

Δ(Log (RPVTINCOME) = -0.239 * RES_RPVTINCOME$_{-1}$ + 1.0437 * Δ(Log (RGNPMP))

(1.84) (28.85)

$R^2 = 0.90$

Compensation to Employees (Nominal)

33) Log (CETOT_T) =126.1607 + 0.2652 * Log (WRATE_T) + 0.3502 * Log (GNPMP) + 0.9996 * AR (1)

(3.09) (3.24) (18.05)

$R^2 = 0.99$ DW= 2.35 OLS

Personal Disposable Income (Real)

Again, we adopt a two-stage procedure to estimate the relationship between private income and disposable income

34) Real Personal Disposable Income

First Stage Equation

Log (RPDI) = 0.2043 + 0.9809 * Log (RPVTINCOME)

(357.19)

$R^2 = 0.99$ DW= 0.79 OLS

Second Stage Equation

ΔLog (RPDI) = -0.3947 * RES_RPDI$_{-1}$ + 0.9996 *Δ(Log (RPVTINCOME))

(2.72) (56.72)

$R^2 = 0.97$

6.2.4 Fiscal Block

We have incorporated fiscal accounts of the Central government as well as Centre plus States and Union Territories. However, these accounts are not integrated to account for the transfers from Centre to States endogenously. This is a major limitation of the specification that would require further development of the model in the future.

We have identified the main components of revenue and expenditures of the budget and they have been linked to overall economic activity, prices and some policy variables.

a. Total Government (Centre, States and Union Territories)

Expenditure

The expenditure of the 'Total Government budget', inclusive of the Centre, States and Union

Territories is defined as a sum of expenditure on current account and on capital account. The current expenditures are wage bill, budgetary subsidies, interest payment and others.

35) GTCEX_T = GWBILL_T + SUB_T + INTPAY_T + GOCEX_T

The wage rate is estimated based on an implicit relationship with the consumer price index

36) Log (WRATE_T) = 0.3061 + 0.8092 * Log (WRATE_T$_{-1}$) + 0.3214 * Log (CPIIW)

(15.66) (4.17)

$R^2 = 0.99$ Dh= 1.62 OLS

37) GWBILL_T = WRTAE_T * EMPPUB_T

38) INTPAY_T = (IRATEDOM_T * DLIB_T$_{-1}$ + IRATEEXT * ELIB_T$_{-1}$)

The capital expenditure of the government is specified in terms of investment in different sectors of the economy. In current prices (nominal value) the total gross capital formation in the government sector is the sum of capital formation in the government sector across the production sectors.

39) GCFGTOT_N = GCFGAG_N + GCFGCON_N + GCFGMQM_N + GCFGEGW_N + GCFGTSC_N + GCFGOSER_N

All the government investment variables are specified exogenously to the model.

Revenue

Non-tax revenue is specified as a function of GDP from non-agricultural sectors. Although agriculture also is a source of some of the non-tax revenue for the states such as market fees, we have adopted a simpler specification here and the estimation is in two-stages.

40) Non-Tax Revenue

First Stage Equation

Log (NTREV_T) = -3.0929 + 1.0356 * Log (GDPNAG)

(55.71)

$R^2 = 0.99$ DW= 0.74 OLS

Second Stage Equation

Δ(Log (NTREV_T)) = -0.3847 * RES_NTREV_T$_{-1}$ + 1.0775 * Δ(Log (GDPNAG))

(2.63) (7.71)

$R^2 = 0.28$

The tax revenues are specified as a function of the tax rate and the tax base, essentially the GDP from non-agricultural sectors. The rates are the collection rates relative to the specified base. The estimation procedure uses a two-stage approach

41) Direct Tax

First Stage Equation

DTAX_T = -12517.95 + 2622.2740*DTRATE_T + 0.0478 * GDPNAG

(5.14) (79.71)

$R^2 = 0.99$ DW= 1.37 OLS

Second Stage Equation

Δ(DTAX_T) = -0.6672 * RES_DTAX_T$_{-1}$ + 3449.2180*Δ(DTRATE_T) + 0.0464 * Δ(GDPNAG)

(3.26) (4.49) (12.45)

$R^2 = 0.85$

42) Indirect Tax

First Stage Equation

INDTAX_T = -30031.71 + 2675.7620 * INDTRATE_T + 0.1215 * GNPFC

(6.83) (105.58)

R^2 = 0.99 DW= 0.60 OLS

Second Stage Equation

Δ(INDTAX_T) = -0.3100 * RES_INDTAX_T$_{-1}$ + 2733.1960 * Δ(INDTRATE_T) + 0.119260*(GNPFC)

(2.15) (3.23) (21.17)

R^2 = 0.87

Total tax revenue

43) TREV_T = DTAX_T + INDTAX_T

Accounting Relationships

Total revenue of the government,

44) TOTREV_T = TREV_T + NTREV_T

Receipts on the capital account include recovery of loans and revenues from disinvestment of public sector assets

45) CAPRCPT_T = RECLOAN_T + DISINV_T

Fiscal deficit is the difference between all expenditures of the government (current and capital) and the revenues on revenue and capital account

46) FDEF_T = GTCEX_T + GCFGTOT – TREV_T – CAPRCPT_T

The revenue deficit is the balance of accounts on the current expenditures and revenues and the primary deficit is fiscal deficit plus interest payments.

47) PDEF_T = FDEF_T – INTPAY_T

48) RDEF_T = GTCEX_T – TREV_T

The deficits give rise to liabilities which may arise through financing in the domestic financial market or in external market

49) DLIB_T = DLIB_T$_{-1}$ + CAPRD_T

50) ELIB_T = ELIB_T$_{-1}$ + CAPRE_T

b. Central Government Accounts

The specification of accounts for the Central government follows the same approach as in the case of 'total government sector'.

Expenditures

51) REXP_C = GWBILL_C + SUB_C + INTPAY_C + GOCEX_C

52) INTPAY_C = (IRATEDOM_C * DLIB_C$_{-1}$ + IRATEEXT * ELIB_C$_{-1}$)

The wage rate of the Central government employees is again estimated based on its relationship with the consumer price index

53) Log (WRATE_C) = 0.7073 + 0.6784*Log (WRATE_C$_{-1}$) + 0.5157*Log (CPIIW)

(8.18) (4.11)

R^2 = 0.99 Dh= 1.82 OLS

54) GWBILL_C = WRATE_C * EMPUB_C

We do not specify capital expenditures of the Centre in terms of government investment across individual sectors. The total capital expenditure of the Centre is fixed exogenously.

Revenues

55) Direct Tax (Central Government)

First Stage Equation

DTAX_C = -9751.2160 + 3343.2920*DTRATE_C + 0.0307*GDPNAG

(4.62) (47.12)

$R^2 = 0.99$ DW= 0.51 OLS

Second Stage Equation

Δ(DTAX_C) = -0.2253*RES_DTAX_C$_{-1}$ + 3421.3260 * Δ(DTRATE_C) + 0.03262 * Δ(GDPNAG)

(1.60) (4.96) (11.69)

$R^2 = 0.84$

56) INDTAX_C = -25254.60 + 4688.5970 * INDTRATE_C + 0.0498 * GNPFC

(6.24) (43.73)

$R^2 = 0.99$ DW= 0.56 OLS

57) Non-Tax Revenue (Central Government)

First Stage Equation

Log (NTREV_C) = -3.3679 + 1.0106 * Log (GDPNAG)

(89.23)

$R^2 = 0.99$ DW= 1.86 OLS

Second Stage Equation

Δ(Log (NTREV_C)) = -0.9465*RES_NTREV_C$_{-1}$ + 0.9687*Δ(Log (GDPNAG))

(5.06) (8.89)

$R^2 = 0.44$

Total tax revenue of the Centre

58) TREV_C = DTAX_C + INDTAX_C

Accounting Relationships

Total revenues on current account,

59) TOTREV_C = TREV_C + NTREV_C

Revenues on capital account

60) CAPRCPT_C = RECLOAN_C + DISINV_C

Deficits (fiscal, revenue and primary) and liabilities (domestic and external)

61) FDEF_C = REXP_C + CEXP_C – TREV_C – CAPRCPT_C

62) PDEF_C = FDEF_C – INTPAY_C

63) RDEF_C = GTCEX_C – TREV_C

64) DLIB_C = DLIB_C$_{-1}$ + CAPRD_C

65) ELIB_C = ELIB_C$_{-1}$ + CAPRE_C

6.2.5 Price Block

Prices need to be distinguished at different levels. In the present model, we have essentially two sets of prices. One is the set of commodity prices and the other is the GDP deflators. The commodity prices are defined in terms of whole sale price indices. The GDP deflators are defined for both commodity sectors and service sectors. In the case of commodity prices, there are three categories the agricultural prices, manufactured product prices and the price index for fuel, power, light and lubricants (FPLL). The price of FPLL is assumed to be exogenous and in the other sectors, price variables are estimated as described below.

Agricultural Prices

In the case of agricultural sectors, the production was estimated primarily from the supply side. The previous year's prices are taken as an indicator of expected demand side pressures and the resources are allocated accordingly. Therefore, the prices in these sectors would have to bring the markets to clear. The demand side is also influenced by the government operations in food grains. The government purchases food grain, mainly rice and wheat, and distributes the grain through public distribution system.

Taking into account these demand side factors, the general form of the price equation has been tailored for each case

WPI for rice

66) $\text{Log (WPIRICE)} = -1.6355 - 0.2929{*}\text{Log ((QRICE-GPR+ SFR}_{-1}\text{)/POPLN)} + 0.1484{*}\text{Log ((GDR+GDW)/POPLN)}$

(2.00) (2.35)

$+ 1.0012{*}\text{Log (PPR)}$

(48.37)

$R^2 = 0.99$ DW= 1.74 OLS

WPI for wheat

67) $\text{Log (WPIWHEAT)} = -1.7045 - 0.2645{*}\text{Log (QWHEAT/POPLN)} + 0.1866{*}\text{Log ((GDR+GDW)/POPLN)}$

(2.88) (2.79)

$+ 1.0911{*}\text{Log (PPW)} - 0.1167 * \text{D89929798}$

(26.22) (3.45)

$R^2 = 0.99$ DW= 1.77 OLS

WPI for other food grains

68) $\text{Log (WPIOTFOOD)} = -0.9409 - 0.4995{*}\text{Log (QOTFOOD/POPLN)} + 0.8919{*}\text{Log (WPIOTFOOD}_{-1}\text{)}$

(1.99) (17.68)

$R^2 = 0.98$ Dh= -0.12 OLS

WPI for non-food grains

69) $\text{Log (WPINFG)} = 0.0359 - 0.0283{*}\text{Log (QNFGI/POPLN)} + 0.9943{*}\text{Log (WPINFG}_{-1}\text{)} + 0.1336{*}\ \text{D739194}$

(3.17) (35.04) (3.52)

$R^2 = 0.99$ Dh= -1.25 OLS

Overall WPI for food grains

70) WPIFG = (2.44907 * WPIRICE + 1.38408 * WPIWHEAT + 1.17634 * WPIOTFOOD)/5.00949

Overall WPI for agriculture

71) WPIAGR = (5.00949 * WPIFG + 16.53108 * WPINFG)/21.54057

The price index for food grain is defined as a weighted average of the price indices for rice, wheat and other food grains. The price index of for agricultural sector as a whole is defined as a weighted average of the price indices for food grain and non-food grains. The weights for aggregation are based on the weights of the wholesale price index.

Non-Agricultural Commodity Prices

Manufacturing sector

72) $\text{Log (WPIMQM)} = -0.3662 + 0.1850^*\text{Log (UVIIMP)} + 0.0592^*\text{Log (M3}^* \text{ 100/PGNPMP)}$

(5.93) (2.35)

$+ 0.6857^*\text{Log (WPIMQM}_{-1}) + 0.0770^*\text{D945} - 0.1289^*\text{D75678}$

(10.83) (3.87) (8.46)

$R^2 = 0.99$ Dh= 1.81 OLS

The agricultural prices, manufacturing sector prices and the wholesale price index for fuel, power, light and lubricants is aggregated to obtain overall wholesale price index using the same weights as in the wholesale price index.

73) $\text{WPI} = (21.54057 * \text{WPIAGR} + 14.23319 * \text{WPIENERGY} + 64.23319 * \text{WPIMQM}) /100$

GDP Deflators and Overall Price Indices

The basic approach here is to define link equation between the commodity prices and the respective GDP deflators. The general form used is illustrated below for agricultural sector

$\text{Ln PAG} = \text{a0} + \text{a1 PAG}_{-1} + \text{a2 WPIAGR}$

The deflators are defined in the case of

(1) Agriculture, (2) Mining, quarrying and manufacturing, (3) Electricity, gas and water supply, (4) Construction, (5) Transport, storage and communication, and (6) Other services.

The estimated equations are presented below.

Agriculture

74) $\text{Log (PAG)} = -0.2594 + 0.1270^*\text{Log (PAG}_{-1}) + 0.9263^*\text{Log (WPIAGR)}$

(2.03) (7.14)

$R^2 = 0.99$ Dh= 1.07 OLS

Construction

75) $\text{Log (PCON)} = -0.1097 + 0.8164^*\text{Log (PCON}_{-1}) + 0.2251^*\text{Log (WPI)}$

(15.23) (3.36)

$R^2 = 0.99$ Dh= 0.98 OLS

Manufacturing

76) $\text{Log (PMQM)} = -0.0365 + 0.3616^*\text{Log (PMQM}_{-1}) + 0.6539^*\text{Log (WPIMQM)}$

(4.96) (8.49)

$R^2 = 0.99$ Dh= 1.14 OLS

Electricity, gas and water supply

77) $\text{Log (PEGW)} = -0.1680 + 0.5995^*\text{Log (PEGW}_{-1}) + 0.4462^*\text{Log (WPI)}$

(6.38) (4.17)

$R^2 = 0.99$ Dh= 0.85 OLS

Transport, storage and communication

78) $Log (PTSC) = -0.087735 + 0.8497*Log (PTSC_{-1}) + 0.1849*Log (WPI) - 0.0935*D9901$

(13.13) (2.49) (4.03)

$R^2 = 0.99$ Dh= 0.84 OLS

79) $Log (PSER) = 0.0319 + 0.4851*Log (PSER_{-1}) + 0.5169*Log (WPI) + 0.030015*D91$

(12.57) (13.12) (2.43)

$R^2 = 0.99$ Dh= 1.71 OLS

The overall GDP deflator

80) PALL = GDPFC/RVATOT

Note that the GDPFC itself is calculated as the sum-product of real GDP at the sectoral level and their respective deflator values.

Consumer price index for agricultural labour

81) $Log (CPIAGL) = 1.0240 + 0.5210*Log (WPIAGR) + 0.4019*Log (WPIMQM) + 0.626861*AR (1)$

(2.63) (2.78) (3.95)

$R^2 = 0.99$ DW= 1.85 OLS

Consumer price index for industrial workers

82) $Log (CPIIW) = 0.8794 + 0.6440*Log (WPIAGR) + 0.1956*Log (WPIMQM) + 0.1775* Log (WPIENERGY)$

(7.33) (2.65) (2.96)

$+ 0.7340*AR (1)$

(5.92)

$R^2 = 0.99$ DW= 1.77 OLS

Deflators for Capital Formation

The deflators are differentiated for public and private sector capital formation as these two components of capital formation are estimated separately. The equation used for estimation of the price index of capital formation links the wholesale price index either at the sectoral level or at the overall level with the price index of capital formation. For an illustration, we consider the price deflator for gross capital formation in agriculture by the government sector

$$Ln\ PGCFGAG = a0 + a1\ Ln\ PGCFGAG_{-1} + a2\ Ln\ WPI$$

In the other sectors, the WPI may be replaced by WPI for the respective sector, overall WPI or the GDP deflator for the sector.

The estimated equations are

83) $Log (PGCFGAG) = -0.1707 + 0.7432*Log (PGCFGAG_{-1}) + 0.3092*Log (WPIAGR)$

(11.29) (3.88)

$R^2 = 0.99$ Dh= 1.29 OLS

84) $Log (PGCFGCON) = -0.3342 + 0.2357*Log (PGCFGCON_{-1}) + 0.8496*Log (WPI)$

(2.34) (4.19)

$R^2 = 0.97$ Dh= -1.20 OLS

85) Log (PGCFGMQMF) = -0.2342 + 0.4471*Log (PGCFGMQMF$_{-1}$) + 0.6132*Log (WPIMQM) + 0.0569*D91

(6.99) (8.41) (2.40)

R^2 = 0.99 Dh= 1.42 OLS

86) Log (PGCFGEGW) = 0.1217 + 0.9724*Log (PGCFGEGW$_{-1}$) + 0.0175*Log (PEGW)

(9.12) (2.17)

R^2 = 0.99 Dh= 1.82 OLS

87) Log (PGCFGTSC) = 0.0510 + 0.8655*Log (PGCFGTSC$_{-1}$) + 0.1383*Log (WPI)

(8.47) (2.18)

R^2 = 0.99 Dh= 1.57 OLS

88) Log (PGCFGSER) = -0.3831 + 0.3179*Log (PGCFGSER$_{-1}$) + 0.7730*Log (WPI)

(2.22) (4.69)

R^2 = 0.98 Dh= -0.03 OLS

The same formulation has been used in the case of capital formation by the private sector at the aggregate level.

Ln PGCFPTOT = a0 + a1 Ln PGCFPTOT$_{-1}$ + a2 Ln PALL

The estimated equation is

89) Log (PGCFPTOT) = 0.0579 + 0.8027*Log (PGCFPTOT$_{-1}$) + 0.1957*Log (PALL)

(6.63) (2.42)

R^2 = 0.99 Dh= 0.98 OLS

Overall Price Deflators

The deflators for consumption expenditures, GNP and GDP at market prices are linked to one of the aggregate price indices such as WPI or GDP deflator. These are link equations estimated to enable conversion of real variables into nominal and vice versa.

Price index for GNP at factor cost

90) Log (PGNPFC) = -0.0325 + 0.5418*Log (PGNPFC$_{-1}$) + 0.4739*Log (WPI) – 0.0856*D75 +0.0596*D73

(7.85) (6.49) (4.34) (3.05)

R^2 = 0.99 Dh= 1.92 OLS

Price index for GNP at market price

91) Log (PGNPMP) = -0.0961 + 0.4170*Log (PGNPMP$_{-1}$) + 0.6107*Log (WPI) + 0.0621*D73

(4.91) (6.81) (2.70)

R^2 = 0.99 Dh= 1.63 OLS

Price index for GDP at market price

92) Log (PGDPMP) = -0.0432 + 0.4983*Log (PGDPMP$_{-1}$) + 0.5188*Log (WPI) – 0.0748*D75 + 0.0465*D7391

(7.52) (7.38) (4.32) (3.82)

R^2 = 0.99 Dh= 1.64 OLS

6.2.6 Private Consumption Expenditure and Private Investment

Private final consumption expenditure on each of the various sectors is estimated as a function of its own lagged value, real personal disposable income and its price relative to the overall price level. As an illustration, we present the equation for real private consumption expenditure on food and food products

$$\text{Ln REXPFOOD} = a0 + a1 \text{ Ln REXPFOOD}_{-1} + a2 \text{ Ln RPDI} + a3 \text{ Ln (WPIAGR/WPI)}$$

The estimated equations are presented below.

93) $\text{Log (REXPFOOD)} = 3.7439 + 0.2751{*}\text{Log (REXPFOOD}_{-1}) + 0.4928{*}\text{Log (RPDI)} - 0.2585{*}\text{Log (WPIAGR*100/WPI)}$

(2.02) (5.44) (2.18)

$R^2 = 0.99$ Dh= 0.81 OLS

94) $\text{Log (REXPMQM)} = -0.0365 + 0.7902 * \text{Log (REXPMQM}_{-1}) + 0.1742{*}\text{Log (RPDI)}$

(7.87) (1.99)

$R^2 = 0.99$ Dh= -0.53 OLS

95) $\text{Log (REXPEGW)} = 1.2987 + 0.8212{*}\text{Log (REXPEGW}_{-1}) + 0.0393{*}\text{Log (RPDI)} + 0.042170{*}\text{Log (WPIENERGY)}$

(9.10) (1.93) (1.98)

$R^2 = 0.99$ Dh= -0.46 OLS

96) $\text{Log (REXPTSC)} = 5.9905 + 0.2077{*}\text{Log (RPDI)} + 0.1926{*}\text{Log (PTSC)} + 0.0588{*}T + 0.7813{*}\text{AR (1)}$

(2.51) (2.91) (4.56) (6.73)

$R^2 = 0.99$ DW= 1.77 OLS

97) $\text{Log (REXPSER)} = -0.7754 + 0.9208{*}\text{Log (REXPSER}_{-1}) + 0.1288{*}\text{Log (RPDI)}$

(9.03) (2.16)

$R^2 = 0.99$ Dh= 0.19 OLS

The total final consumption expenditure is the sum of expenditures at the sectoral level,

$$\text{CP} = (\text{REXPFOOD} + \text{REXPMQM} + \text{REXPEGW} + \text{REXPTSC} + \text{REXPOSER}){*}\ \text{PEXPTOT}$$

The overall consumption expenditure deflator is estimated as

98) $\text{Log (PEXPTOT)} = 0.0072 + 0.5814{*}\text{Log (PEXPOTOT}_{-1}) + 0.4282{*}\text{Log (WPI)} + 0.0900{*}\text{D7374}$

(9.63) (7.07) (5.84)

$R^2 = 0.99$ Dh= 1.75 OLS

Private Investment or Capital Formation

There is significant difference in the manner in which construction by using industries has been specified in model and therefore, we describe each case separately.

In the case of agriculture, both price and non-price factors have been found to be important determinants of private investment. The price factors include variables such as lagged relative prices and cost of capital. The non-price factors include government investment in agriculture or infrastructure and credit. Even when the government investment in agriculture takes place, the constraining factor on private investment is availability of finances, either own funds or credit. In the present case, we have estimated real capital formation in agriculture as a function of income (value added) and institutional credit to agriculture

99) $\text{Log (RGCFPAGR)} = -1.2767 + 0.6884{*}\text{Log (RVAAG)} + 0.2482{*}\text{Log (INSCRAG*100/WPI)}$

(2.05) (2.57)

$- 0.5689{*}\text{D81456} + 0.3863{*}\text{D9900}$

(5.40) (2.73)

$R^2 = 0.86$ DW= 1.46 OLS

Private gross capital formation in construction

100) RGCFPCON = -226.8373 – 16.1716*RRINT + 0.0706*RVACON$_{-1}$ – 0.18751*RGCFGCON + 2556.193466 * D95780

(2.01) (6.25) (2.58) (8.01)

– 1245.855818 * D9199

(3.48)

R^2 = 0.94 DW= 1.83 OLS

In the case of mining, quarrying and manufacturing, the estimated equation incorporates the effect of public sector investment in the sector and also the cost of capital reflected by the real interest rate. The specification is,

101) RGCFPMQMF = -10656.57 – 0.7342*RGCFGMQMF – 340.2507*RRINT + 0.634369*RVAMQM

(2.18) (2.33) (24.06)

+ 27924.33*D9599

(5.21)

R^2 = 0.98 DW= 1.11 OLS

Private gross capital formation in electricity, gas and water supply

102) RGCFPEGW = -874.5064 – 76.5161*RRINT + 0.3975*RVAEGW$_{-1}$ – 2885.068*DRGCFPEGW

(1.98) (9.43) (4.39)

R^2 = 0.86 DW= 1.43 OLS

Private gross capital formation in transportation, storage and communication

103) RGCFPTSC = -1194.186 – 46.6711*RRINT + 0.3087*RVATSC$_{-1}$ – 4909.452*D82692378

(2.71) (16.5) (5.85)

R^2 = 0.93 DW= 1.14 OLS

Private gross capital formation in other services

104) RGCFPSER = -3993.582 – 99.9131*RRINT + 0.1570*RVASER$_{-1}$ + 9358.0950*D9094

(2.52) (21.78) (3.36)

R^2 = 0.96 DW= 1.82 OLS

The results point to 'crowding out' effect of public investment in manufacturing on private investment in manufacturing. A similar equation has been estimated for private investment in construction also where a negative relationship between public investment and private investment has been found to hold.

In the other sectors, besides real interest rate, the lagged value of GDP from the respective sectors was found to be a significant independent variable in the equation for private investment. In other words, access to finance for investment is a crucial variable in the non-agricultural sectors also. The access to capital is reflected by its own earnings whether for use directly for investment or by leveraging it to borrow capital.

Total private investment is the sum of private investment in specific sectors,

(105) RGCFPTOT = RGCFPAGR + RGCFPCON + RGCFPMQM + RGCFPEGW + RGCFPTSC + RGCFPSER

The nominal value of private investment is calculated by multiplying the real value of private investment by the price deflator.

106) GCFPTOT = RGCFTOT* PGCFPTOT

6.2.7 Monetary Block

Demand for Money

Demand for money is specified as holing of high powered money to meet the transactions requirements as well as some choice between holding money and other financial assets

107) Log (RMD) = -1.9269 + 0.7587*Log (RMD_{-1}) + 0.3845*Log (RGNPMP) – 0.0579*Log (SI) – 0.1319*D7374

(13.06) (4.36) (2.60) (5.94)

$R^2 = 0.99$ Dh= 0.09 OLS

Supply of Money

Reserve money is defined as a sum of stock at the end of the previous year and net accruals from supply of RBI credit to government, net foreign exchange reserves and non-monetary liabilities of the RBI.

108) RM = RM_{-1} + Δ RBCCG + Δ RBNFA + Δ RBOTH

RBI credit to government is seen as a residual after the Central government exhausts its borrowing options from the market, both domestic and external.

109) RBCCG = $RBCCG_{-1}$ + FDEF_C – CAPRD_C – CAPRE_C

The net foreign exchange position of the RBI is a function of previous year's closing position, balance from external account transactions and net capital inflow on balance of payments.

110) RBNFA = $RBNFA_{-1}$ + CAB + KINF

The supply of money to the economy is a function of reserve money and inflation rate. The specification reflects the monetary policy decisions to influence money supply in relation to inflation rate.

111) M3 = -183.6506 + 1.0581*$M3_{-1}$ – 93.8440*INFL + 0.328*RM – 21913.99 * D95 + 23307.42*D979800

(80.00) (2.69) (6.81) (5.07) (8.41)

$R^2 = 0.99$ Dh= -1.73 OLS

The supply of money in real terms is simply the nominal money supply deflated by an aggregate price level.

112) RMS = M3/PGNPMP

We have selected a key benchmark rate which is the IDBI minimum lending rate which has been extended using the PLR of the major commercial banks. This bench markrate is modelled as a function of a short-term lending rate, such as the 91-day treasury bill rate. In other words, the longer-term interest rate is affected by the movements in the short-term rate. The short-term rate is a function of another policy rate, *viz.*, the bank rate, and the gap between money supply and demand at a given level of short-term rate. In other words, demand for money and short-term interest rate are determined simultaneously. This also implies much larger level of interaction of the monetary and real variables in the model as demand for money is also influenced by real interest rate which in turn is a function of the short-term rate.

113) Log (IDBIPLR) = 0.3076 +0.6312*Log ($IDBIPLR_{-1}$) + 0.2987*Log (SI) + 0.1846*D809199 – 0.1696*D9701

(9.47) (4.27) (7.20) (5.56)

$R^2 = 0.97$ Dh= -0.37 OLS

114) Log (SI) = 0.3551 + 0.8189*Log (BRATE) + 1.0546*(Log RMD – Log RMS) – 0.3013*D734789

(8.73) (2.56) (6.94)

$R^2 = 0.84$ DW= 1.87 OLS

RRINT = IDBIPLR – INFL

The interest rate on domestic borrowing by the government, Central or total government, is linked to the short-term interest rate.

115) LOG (IRATEDOM_C) = -0.0040 + 0.7596*LOG (IRATEDOM_C$_{-1}$) + 0.2336*LOG (SI)

(18.33) (3.67)

R^2 = 0.97 Dh= 0.07 OLS

116) LOG (IRATEDOM_T) = 0.0502 + 0.7998*LOG (IRATEDOM_T$_{-1}$) + 0.1788*LOG (SI) + 0.2553*D78 – 0.2890*D80

(15.69) (2.11) (3.95) (4.88)

R^2 = 0.95 Dh= -0.04 OLS

The interest rate on external borrowing is a function of the rate in the international financial market, in the present case interest rate on 3-month US dollar deposits is taken as the international benchmark rate.

117) LOG (IRATEEXT) = 0.0138 + 0.9634*LOG (IRATEEXT$_{-1}$) + 0.0165*LOG (LIBOR) – 0.1952*D7692 + 0.4802*D01

(9.10) (2.28) (2.88) (4.70)

R^2 = 0.86 Dh= 0.16 OLS

6.2.8 Trade

The external trade is modelled at an aggregate level. The merchandise trade has been estimated as total exports and total imports. Net invisibles inflow on current account is specified exogenously.

The unit values of merchandise trade are linked essentially to domestic prices and exchange rate. In the case of exports the domestic prices influence production costs and, therefore, would also have an impact on the price at which the exports may take place. In the case of imports, the specification essentially captures the interdependence of domestic prices and the international prices. The rise in domestic prices may itself be related to the international price conditions. As domestic prices rise, therefore, the import prices may also rise and when domestic prices decline, import prices also decline in tandem. This relationship may also imply that India's imports are in areas where its entry into the market, which may happen when internal price rise is high. As domestic prices rise, in such cases, international prices may also increase. The exchange rate also reflects a similar competitive effect as rupee depreciates with respect to the other currencies, the price of imports increases. As rupee appreciates, the import prices decrease.

Exports

Merchandise exports are linked to global demand, reflected in the estimated world GDP, UVI of exports and exchange rate. World income is expected to be related to exports positively and the other two variables, *viz.*, UVI of exports and the nominal effective exchange rate are expected to be related to exports inversely. As UVIs rise, demand for exports would decrease. Similarly, an appreciating rupee would make India's exports more expensive and therefore, would imply a negative impact on exports.

Merchandise Exports

Ln RXTOTAL = a0 + a1 Ln RWINC + a2 Ln (UVIEXP/WPI) + a3 Ln NEER

118) Real Exports

First Stage Equation

Log (RXTOTAL) = 14.3648 + 1.0275*Log (RWINC) – 0.9230*Log (UVIEXP*100/WPI) – 0.9717*Log (NEER)

(5.19) (3.98) (6.50)

R^2 = 0.98 DW= 1.04 OLS

Second Stage Equation

$$\Delta(\text{Log (RXTOTAL)}) = -0.5799{*}\text{RES\_RXTOTAL}_{-1} + 1.8536{*}\Delta(\text{Log (RWINC)}) - 0.4941{*}\Delta(\text{Log (UVIEXP*100/WPI)})$$

(3.58) (4.80) (2.56)

$$- 0.2595{*}\Delta(\text{Log (NEER)})$$

(1.38)

$R^2 = 0.48$ DW = 1.83

Unit Vale Index of Exports (UVIEXP)

The unit value of exports would be influenced by domestic price conditions directly and by the exchange rate of the rupee.

119) Unit Value Index for Exports

First Stage Equation

$$\text{Log (UVIEXP)} = 3.4398 - 0.3874{*}\text{Log (NEER)} + 0.8832{*}\text{Log (WPI)}$$

(3.72) (12.03)

$R^2 = 0.99$ DW= 0.79 OLS

Second Stage Equation

$$\Delta(\text{Log (UVIEXP)}) = -0.4257{*}\text{RES\_UVIEXP}_{-1} - 0.5031{*}\Delta\ (\text{Log (NEER)}) + 0.749321{*}\Delta\ (\text{Log (WPI)})$$

(2.18) (2.51) (4.35)

$R^2 = 0.20$

The two variables, real exports and UVI of exports give the nominal value of exports,

120) XTOTAL = RXTOTAL * UVIEXP

Merchandise Imports

Total imports are related to real income or output of the economy in terms of demand for goods both for final consumption as well as for intermediate production requirements. The UVI of imports have an adverse impact on imports as higher UVI would make imports expensive. The exchange rate, similarly affects imports by making them either cheaper, when appreciating, or more expensive when depreciating.

121) $\text{Log (RMTOTAL)} = -2.9179 + 1.4716{*}\text{Log (RVATOT)} - 1.0574{*}\text{Log (UVIIMP*100/WPI)} - 0.1917{*}\text{Log (NEER)}$

(13.79) (8.26) (2.03)

$$- 0.1320 * \text{D7791} + 0.1923 * \text{D798012}$$

(3.07) (5.63)

$R^2 = 0.99$ DW= 1.88 OLS

UVI for Imports (in Rupee Value)

The UVI for imports may not be completely insulated by the price conditions of internal markets. Higher domestic prices may imply that international prices are also on the rise. The exchange rate influences import prices directly, appreciating rupee makes imports cheaper and a depreciating rupee makes imports costlier.

122) Unit Value Index for Imports

First Stage Equation

$$\text{Log (UVIIMP)} = 3.8626 + 0.6890{*}\text{Log (WPI)} - 0.3310{*}\text{Log (NEER)}$$

(8.45) (2.86)

$R^2 = 0.98$ DW= 1.20 OLS

Second Stage Equation

$$\Delta(\text{Log (UVIIMP)}) = -0.6051{*}\text{RES\_UVIIMP}_{-1} + 0.8063 * \Delta(\text{Log (WPI)}) - 0.2491 * \Delta(\text{Log (NEER)})$$

$$(3.13) \qquad (3.67) \qquad (1.06)$$

$$R^2 = 0.38$$

Nominal value of imports are calculated from real value of imports and the UVI of imports as,

123) MTOTAL = RMTOTAL * UVIIMP

Current account balance is defined from trade balance and net invisibles inflow on current account as,

124) CAB = XTOTAL – MTOTAL + NETINV

6.3 Applications of the Model

The model presented in the previous section provides a basic framework to analyse some issues within an economy-wide structure. In other words, as many of the inter-linkages of the economy are captured in the model, the structure allows us to examine the impact of some alternative scenarios on the economy under the assumption that the basic structure remains unchanged. We present in this section two main applications of the model. Both the applications relate to an analysis of the external shocks to the economy during the Eleventh Five Year Plan (EFYP) period of 2007-08 to 2011-12. In the first application, we examine the implications of the alternative petroleum crude oil prices to growth and inflation during the Eleventh Five Year Plan period of the economy. In the second application, we examine the impact of the current slowdown in the global economic activity. In both the applications, the main concern is to assess the robustness of the high growth scenario that has been adopted in the EFYP.

6.3.1 Base Run Scenario

For a reference point of both the applications, we first develop a base run scenario of the main macroeconomic indicators for the EFYP period. The base run scenario has been obtained under a number of assumptions on the exogenous variables. Values of the key exogenous variables are summarised in Table 6.2 for the periods of 2002-03 to 2006-07 and 2007-08 to 20011-12. The two periods provide a comparison between the scenario for periods covered by the Tenth Five Year Plan (TFYP) and the EFYP.

The exogenous variables relate to both external and domestic economic conditions. For the EFYP the variables are generally held at the same levels as the actual. We have specified some variables as exogenous variables for this specific application of the model keeping in view the main focus which is to assess the overall growth implications over the next five year period. For example, we have assumed that the monetary variables would be essentially exogenous. The M3 growth is fixed at 14 per cent per year and interest rates are kept at a fixed level. On the external front, the global growth, capital inflows, net invisible inflows on current account and the exchange rate are held at pre-determined levels. The international crude oil price is fixed exogenously, at roughly the same level as in the base year for the EFYP.

The results of one scenario developed from the model are summarised in Table 6.3.

The results provide an estimate of annual average growth rate of 9 per cent per year for the EFYP period. It does not coincide with the sectoral distribution of growth rates provided in the EFYP because of the likely differences in a number of parameters of the model. The model results point to the overall sustainability of the strategy in terms of fiscal balance, which for the Central government has been projected at 2.1 per cent of GDP.

Table 6.2: Exogenous Variables for the Model—The Xth and XI FYP Periods

Variable	Unit	Averages for 2002-2006	Averages for 2007-2011
Agriculture related			
Gross irrigated area	%yoy	1.66	1.32
GCFGAG (Public investment agriculture)	%yoy	12.00	12.22
WPIINPUT (Input price index)	%yoy	8.14	5.00
PPW (Procurement price-rice)	%yoy	5.02	6.00
PPR (Procurement price-wheat)	%yoy	4.99	6.00
INSCRAG (Institutional credit-agriculture)	%yoy	17.00	18.00
Global parameters			
RWINC (Real world output)	%yoy	4.87	4.82
LIBOR (interest rate)	%	4.06	4.55
NEER (Nominal Effective Exchange Rate)	%yoy	-1.09	-1.00
FDI	%yoy	13.92	15.26
NETINV (Net invisible inflows, US$)	%yoy	29.40	30.00
Capital inflow (US$)	%yoy	18.00	18.00
Crude oil price (US$)	%yoy	42.42	1.01
Monetary variables			
BRATE	%	6.22	6.30
M3	%yoy	14.00	14.00
Fiscal parameters			
Public investment (total)	%yoy	17.70	15.45
Public investment infrastructure	%yoy	12.77	13.58
Central government subsidies	%yoy	9.60	10.00
Budgetary support to public investment-infrastructure	%	20.00	20.00
Budgetary support to public investment-other	%	20.00	20.00
Other Parameters			
WPI fuel, power, light and lubricants	%yoy	7.47	4.20

In the case of external current account balance the projected deficit of 2.7 per cent is above the conventional norm of 2-3 per cent, pointing to the need for maintaining positive investment climate which would ensure that net positive capital flows would permit financing of the need for foreign saving. Another major deviation in the results of the present model from the macroeconomic conditions specified by the EFYP is the share of investment in GDP. The model estimates the ratio at 29.8 per cent whereas the EFYP estimates the requirement at 35 per cent. One explanation for the difference is the productivity impact of spending on infrastructure, impact of growing agriculture-industry linkages and foreign direct investment which has been incorporated in the present model.

Although we have provided only the averages for the five year period in this section, year-wise estimates of the main macro variables are available from the model.

Table 6.3: Results of the Base Run for the Tenth and Eleventh Five Year Plan Periods

Variables	Average for	
	2002-2006	2007-2011
% Change YOY		
Real GDP		
- Agriculture	2.4	2.4
- Industry	7.7	9.2
- Services	9.0	10.9
Total	7.3	9.0
Exports ($-term)	21.3	17.1
Imports ($-term)	27.4	16.6
Inflation (WPI)	5.7	5.4
As Percentage of GDPMP		
Fiscal deficit centre	3.6	2.1
Current account balance	-1.8	-2.7
GCF	27.7	29.8
GCF_Infra	6.2	6.7
PFCE	63.9	57.2
% YOY		
M3	14.0	14.0
Net invisibles	29.4	30.0
RGCF	7.4	9.3
RGCF_Infra	7.68	9.47
% Share in GCF		
GCF_Infra	22.7	22.4
Share in GCF_Infra		
Public sector	47.3	39.5
Domestic private sector	49.1	57.1
FDI	3.7	3.4
Total private sector	52.7	60.5

Note: Infrastructure is taken here as comprising of only two sectors (1) electricity, gas and water supply and (2) transport, storage and communications.

6.3.2 Alternative Petroleum Crude Oil Prices and Impact on the Macro Economy

The petroleum sector is critical to the economy as it supplies a variety of intermediate inputs to the industry and fuel for transportation, power generation, irrigation and domestic uses. The petroleum sector is also an important consideration in economic policy because of the fact that nearly two-thirds of the consumption of petroleum in the economy is imported. The extreme fluctuation in crude oil prices in the international markets experienced during 2007 and 2008 makes it imperative to understand the implications of such shocks to the economy.

In this section, we provide an estimate of the impact of the high crude oil prices on the course of the key macroeconomic variables during the EFYP period. The impact is assessed with reference to the base run scenario presented earlier. The basic model described in the previous sections required some modifications to account for the interactions between the 'pass through mechanism' of the international prices of crude oil to the domestic prices, consumption and fiscal balances.

The key relationships relating to the transmission of oil price shocks are as follows. The direction of the impact on the dependent variable for each independent variable is indicated by the sign (+ or -)

1. Excise duty collection from petroleum products production = f (collection rate +, energy price +, consumption +)
2. Custom duty collection from crude oil imports = f (custom duty rate +, crude price +, imports +)

3. Price of manufactured products = f (UVIIMP +, M3/PGNPMP +, WPIENERGY +)
4. Wholesale price index = f (WPIAGR +, WPIMQM +, WPIENERGY +)
5. Real personal final consumption expenditure on electricity, gas and water = f (RPDI +, WPIENERGY +)
6. Crude oil consumption = f (Real GDP +, WPI +)
7. Crude oil imports = Crude oil consumption + Crude oil exports – Crude oil production

Where WPIENERGY is the wholesale price index of fuel, power, light and lubricants, WPIAGR and WPIMQM are the wholesale price indices of agriculture and mining, quarrying and manufacturing. The other abbreviations are self-explanatory and the details are also provided in the list of variables in Annexure A-6.1. In the above specification, crude oil refers to consumption, production, exports or imports of crude oil equivalent of all petroleum products.

WPIENERGY responds to international crude oil price changes depending on the pass through mechanism of these changes. The impact on fiscal balances is captured through the impact of price changes and tax rate changes on tax revenues and as we will indicate on the method of financing of the gaps emerging from the pass through mechanisms.

The key relationships relating to the transmission of oil price shocks incorporate the effect of price rise on fiscal position as well as on overall prices. In the analysis presented below, we also consider the alternative strategies in terms of absorbing the impact through fiscal measures or decrease in public investment in manufacturing—primarily in the oil sector as generation of surpluses there becomes infeasible.

The Transmission and Adjustment Mechanisms

The crude oil prices in the international markets get transmitted to the domestic prices in a phased manner. The present transmission mechanism is that domestic prices of four major fuels, petrol, diesel (HSD), LPG and kerosene do not adjust to the price shocks immediately or proportionately. In the WPI for fuels, power and lubricants (WPIENERGY), these four items account for about 38 per cent of the weight. The other items in the WPIENERGY can be expected to follow the crude price changes proportionately with some lag. Although the power sector prices may not change immediately the adjustment is likely to take place with some lag.

Within this framework two alternative cases of the pass through of international oil price change can be considered.

1. Where the price change is passed on proportionately to domestic prices (WPIENERGY).
2. Where the pass through is to only 62 per cent of WPIENERGY.

Price of petroleum crude was at $82 per barrel during 2007-08. In the base run scenario of the model, the crude oil price is retained at this level for the remaining four years of EFYP period. The alternatives considered here are US$ 100, $150 and $200 per barrel in the last four years of EFYP period. The prices are increased to these new levels in 2008-09 and then maintained at this level.

When the crude price increases from $82 to $100 per barrel, 'full pass through' would mean an increase by 22 per cent in WPIENERGY in that year and when the pass through is to only items other than the four fuels mentioned above the increase in WPIENERGY is 13.2 per cent again in the year in which the crude price increase takes place.

The other issue is what happens to the difference between international crude price change and the sticky prices of some sub-sectors? We estimate that for an increase in crude price by $1 per barrel, the increased cost is US$700 million. The oil companies should be able to recover at least 50 per cent of the increased cost of imports through higher prices of non-price administered petro-products. Thus, if 50 per cent of this increased cost is recovered by the oil sector, then the remaining $350 million would have to be offset by other measures. We have considered three alternatives

1. Where the difference is offset by instruments such as oil bonds which will be redeemed in the long term with little immediate outgo to the government. It is difficult to estimate the revenue outgo of this strategy and the impact presented here may be an underestimate of the fiscal impact.
2. The difference is fully absorbed in the fiscal deficit of the Centre. For instance, when the international crude price increases by $18 per barrel the deficit to be met by revenue offsets is Rs 28,350 crore.
3. The gap in sales revenue and import cost is borne entirely by the petroleum sector leading to a decline in investments to the tune of Rs. 28,350 crore per year when the international crude price rises to $100 per barrel from $82 per barrel.
4. The price rise even under partial pass through of higher international prices will mean reduced profit margins for sectors consuming petroleum products. Therefore, we should expect some cut back on investments by these sectors also unless these petroleum consuming sectors are able to raise efficiency. Although the impact on the profits of the petroleum consuming sectors cannot be computed accurately, the impact may be the higher fuel/intermediate inputs cost that is transferred by the oil companies to these sectors, amounting to Rs. 28,350 crore in the case when crude price goes from $82 to $100 per barrel.

The above four scenarios are examined under three alternative international crude prices $100 per barrel, $150 per barrel and $200 per barrel.

The model does not capture the efficiency improvements that may occur because of higher cost of petro products. It also does not capture the shifts from one type of fuel to another and the impact of such shifts to the consumption of petroleum products. To this extent the adverse impact of higher oil prices on growth may be over-estimated.

Alternative Scenarios

The summary of findings of the analysis are presented in Table 6.4. Details are provided in Tables 6.5-6.7.

We first note that analysis of the alternative scenarios provide a range of results. Under the base run scenario, the real GDP growth over the medium-term of five years is an average of 9.0 per cent per year. The annual inflation rate, on WPI basis, is 5.4 per cent per year.

Table 6.4: A Summary of the Impact of International Crude Price Increase on Growth and Inflation Average Annual Growth during the Eleventh Five Year Plan (%)

Scenario/Variable	Crude oil at $100/barrel	Crude oil at $150/barrel	Crude oil at $200/barrel
GDP at Factor Cost (Constant prices)			
I. Base run with crude price at $82/barrel		9.0	
II. Partial pass through with oil bonds	8.9	8.6	8.4
III. Partial pass through with fiscal offsets	8.9	8.6	8.4
IV. Partial pass through with oil companies decreasing investment	8.9	8.0	7.8
V. Full price pass through without cut back on private investment	8.8	8.4	8.1
VI. Full pass through with private investment decline	8.5	7.1	5.8
Inflation (WPI-based)			
I. Base run with crude price at $82/barrel in 2008-09		5.4	
II. Partial pass through with oil bonds	6.3	8.6	10.7
III. Partial pass through with fiscal offsets	6.3	8.6	10.7
IV. Partial pass through with oil companies decreasing investment	6.3	8.6	10.7
V. Full price pass through without cut back on private investment	6.8	10.6	14.1
VI. Full pass through with private investment decline	6.8	10.6	14.1

Note: The amount of revenue gap of the oil companies to be borne by the government is estimated at Rs. 28,350 crore when the crude price rises from $82 to $100, Rs. 107,100 crore when the crude price rises to $150 per barrel and Rs. 185,850 crore when the crude price rises to $200 per barrel. The investment by non-petro sectors is assumed to decline by an equivalent amount under the last scenario of full pass through and decline in private investment.

When the international crude increases to $100 per barrel and it is maintained at that level over the next three years, the average growth rate of real GDP ranges from 8.9 per cent to 8.5 per cent per year and the inflation rate rises between 6.3 per cent to 6.8 per cent per year.

Thus, there is a reduction in GDP growth and rise in inflation rate as a consequence of the external shock of higher crude oil prices. If the international crude price increase is fully passed on to the consumers, and the investment of non-petroleum producing sectors were to reduce by the increase in their costs, then the loss in GDP growth and rise in inflation rate are the greatest among the alternatives considered.

At higher crude price, the drop in GDP growth and rise in inflation rate is larger. The real GDP growth drops by as much as 3.2 percentage points per year and inflation rate rises by 8.7 percentage points in the extreme case of $200 per barrel over the base run scenario.

At $150 per barrel, the overall inflation rate reaches double digit level under full pass through scenario and the growth rate drops by 0.6 percentage points when the non-petro sectors somehow absorb the price rise through increase in their own prices or through greater efficiency. Thus, for an increase of about $68 per barrel in crude price, the growth rate drops by 0.6 percentage points. When the price rises by $118 per barrel growth rate drops by 0.6 percentage points under the optimistic scenario and by 3.2 percentage points when the investment by petroleum consuming sectors drops by an amount which has to be absorbed by them in terms of higher cost of petroleum costs. For every $10 per barrel increase, the growth rate drops by 0.1 to 0.3 percentage points. The inflation rate as pointed out earlier would rise to double digit levels under the full pass through scenario when the international crude price reaches $150 per barrel and stays at that level.

The inflation rate estimated here is based on an active monetary policy stance that will try and rein in inflation by a slower growth of money supply.

The intermediate scenarios do imply that the loss of growth and rise in inflation rates may be lower than the extreme case. However, it should be noted that the fiscal costs of intermediate situations are high. The fiscal deficit rises relative to the base run and the debt to GDP ratio will also increase. Details are in Table 6.5-6.7.

Table 6.5: Impact of Alternative Strategies to meet International Crude Price Increase Scenarios under Crude Oil Price at $100 Per Barrel

Variables	Base Run with Crude Price at $82/barrel	Partial Pass through with Oil Bonds	Partial Pass through with Fiscal Offsets	Partial Pass through with Oil Companies Decreasing Investment	Full price Pass Through	Full Pass through with Private Investment Decline
Average annual percentage change during the Eleventh Five Year Plan						
Real GDP	9.0	8.9	8.9	8.7	8.8	8.5
Export	19.9	20.3	20.3	20.3	20.6	20.6
Import	19.3	19.0	19.0	18.6	18.8	18.0
Inflation	5.4	6.3	6.3	6.3	6.8	6.8
Average percentage of GDP at market prices						
Current account balance	-2.7	-2.8	-2.8	-2.6	-2.5	-2.1
Fiscal deficit (Centre)	2.1	1.9	2.2	1.9	1.7	1.8
Total investment (GCF+FDI)	29.5	29.1	29.1	28.8	28.8	28.1
Debt(Centre)	41.1	39.9	40.6	39.9	39.2	39.5

Table 6.6: Impact of Alternative Strategies to meet International Crude Price Increase Average Annual Percentage Change during the Eleventh Five Year Plan for Scenarios under Crude Oil Price at $150 Per Barrel

Variables	Base Run with Crude Price at $82/barrel	Partial Pass through with Oil Bonds	Partial Pass through with Fiscal Offsets	Partial Pass through with Oil Companies Decreasing Investment	Full Price Pass Through	Full Pass through with Private Investment Decline
Average annual percentage change during the Eleventh Five Year Plan						
Real GDP	9.0	8.6	8.6	8.0	8.4	7.1
Export	19.9	21.4	21.4	21.4	22.2	22.2
Import	19.3	18.2	18.2	16.8	17.6	14.6
Inflation	5.4	8.6	8.6	8.6	10.6	10.6
Average percentage of GDP at market prices						
Current Account Balance	-2.7	-1.8	-1.8	-1.0	-1.1	0.4
Fiscal Deficit (Centre)	2.1	1.3	2.4	1.2	0.8	1.1
Total Investment (GCF+FDI)	29.5	28.0	28.0	27.1	27.2	24.7
Debt(Centre)	41.1	37.0	39.3	37.1	34.9	36.2

Table 6.7: Impact of Alternative Strategies to meet International Crude Price Increase Average Annual Percentage Change During the Eleventh Five Year Plan for Scenarios under Crude Oil Price at $200 Per Barrel

Variables	Base Run with Crude Price at $82/barrel	Partial Pass through with Oil Bonds	Partial Pass through with Fiscal Offsets	Partial Pass through with Oil Companies Decreasing Investment	Full Price Pass Through	Full Pass through with Private Investment Decline
Average annual percentage change during the Eleventh Five Year Plan						
Real GDP	9.0	8.4	8.4	7.8	8.1	5.8
Export	19.9	22.3	22.3	22.3	23.5	23.5
Import	19.3	17.5	17.5	16.1	16.6	11.3
Inflation	5.4	10.7	10.7	10.7	14.1	14.1
Average percentage of GDP at market prices						
Current Account Balance	-2.7	-1.0	-1.0	-0.3	-0.1	2.2
Fiscal Deficit (Centre)	2.1	0.8	2.6	0.5	0.1	0.5
Total Investment (GCF+FDI)	29.5	27.2	27.2	26.0	26.0	21.8
Debt(Centre)	41.1	34.7	38.5	34.7	31.7	33.9

6.3.3 Impact of the Current Slowdown in Global Economic Activity

The current global financial crisis and the economic slowdown have a number of implications to the Indian economy and the likely policy responses to this new external economic environment. How serious are the implications of this new scenario to the overall economic growth rates envisaged in the EFYP? In this section we present an application of the econometric model described previously to the analysis of the alternative scenarios relating to this issue.

The main manifestation of the global slowdown of economic activity is the deceleration in growth rates of output across the countries. Although this approach assumes certain slowdown of activity in India as well, it would be useful to consider the channels by which the global slowdown would influence Indian economy. One major channel is through the trade linkages. Export markets would contract and India's exports would be adversely affected. There would also be a decline in the prices, especially in the commodity markets. As we have already considered the impact of changes in crude oil prices in the previous section, we do not repeat this exercise. The elasticity of exports to changing global output simulates the impact of the slowdown of global output through the trade linkage. In the case of net invisibles, the impact is more difficult to measure. In all our simulations, we have assumed that the growth of net invisibles would be 20 per cent per year, a figure which is nearly half the rate at which net invisibles were rising in the previous three years. The second channel by which the global slowdown would be affected is through their impact on investment and consumption spending. The impact is essentially through capital markets and investment climate. In 2008, there has been a net outflow of capital, in excess of $10 billion, through the sale of equity and bonds by the FIIs. The stock prices have nearly halved, reflecting this withdrawal of capital and the need for re-assessing the prospects of any new investments.

The past data on private investment and private final consumption expenditure do show that these variables exhibit considerable variations over the years. As it is difficult to estimate the impact of the prevailing scenario on investment and consumption expenditure, we have taken an indicative shock to these variables in 2008-09 and 2009-10. These are exogenous shocks to investment and consumption expenditure. We assume that the current slowdown in global economic activity would give way to recovery by 2010-11.

The base run of the model does not capture the fiscal push to the economy contained in the 2008-09 budget. In the Central government budget for 2008-09, there were some measures that implied higher expenditures implementation of the Sixth Pay Commission recommendations and a farm loan waver scheme. In both the cases, the actual outgo was not estimated. We estimate that the outgo on account of these measures in 2008-09 would be of the order of Rs. 20,000 crore.

As a consequence of the present economic crisis there has been a fiscal stimulus package announced by the Central government which provides for additional spending to the tune of Rs. 20,000 crore in the current year and a tax relief of the order of Rs. 10,000 crore. There are several other measures which liberalise credit flow to the firms and individuals to borrow for investment.

With these considerations, we have carried out four alternative simulations of the macroeconometric model. The simulations are summarised in Table 6.8.

Table 6.8: Key to Alternative Simulations of the Global Slowdown in Economic Activity

Scenarios	WGDP	Private GCF	PFCE	2008-09 Budget Parameters	Fiscal Stimulus (December 2008 announcement)
	% YOY	% YOY	% YOY		
Base run					
2008-09	5.00	0.00	0.00	NI	NI
2009-10	5.00	0.00	0.00	NI	NI
Simulation 1					
2008-09	3.70	-4.50	-1.50	NI	NI
2009-10	2.20	-2.25	-0.75	NI	NI
Simulation 2					
2008-09	3.70	-4.50	-1.50	YES	YES
2009-10	2.20	-2.25	-0.75	YES	NI
Simulation 3					
2008-09	3.70	-9.00	-3.00	NI	NI
2009-10	2.20	-4.50	-1.50	NI	NI
Simulation 4					
2008-09	3.70	-9.00	-3.00	YES	YES
2009-10	2.20	-4.50	-1.50	YES	NI

Note: 1. The world GDP (WGDP) growth rates are obtained from the November 2008 update of the *World Economic Outlook* of International Monetary Fund.

2. The impact on private gross capital formation (GCF) and private final consumption expenditure (PFCE) is expressed for these variables in real terms. These changes are introduced in the respective equations as exogenous decrease.
3. The 2008-09 budget parameters refer to the additional expenditure of Rs. 20,000 crore for additional pay to government employees and the farm loan waiver related expenditure.
4. The fiscal stimulus refers to the net outgo of Rs. 20,000 crore as additional expenditure and tax relief of Rs 10,000 crore due to measures announced in December 2008.
5. NI= Not incorporated.

The simulations essentially capture the impact of the current economic crisis on growth trajectory of the economy over the medium-term. A summary of the results of simulations is presented in Table 6.9 and the year-wise results are presented in Tables 6.10-6.13.

Table 6.9: Summary of the Results of Alternative Simulations Relating to Slowdown in Economic Activity

Variables	Base run	Simulation 1	Simulation 2	Simulation 3	Simulation 4
% change YOY					
Real GDP					
- Agriculture	2.7	2.7	2.7	2.7	2.7
- Industry	9.1	8.4	8.5	8.0	8.1
- Services	10.8	9.8	9.9	9.4	9.6
Total	9.0	8.3	8.3	7.9	8.0
Exports (US$)	21.9	18.9	18.9	18.9	18.9
Imports (US$)	23.3	22.6	22.8	21.9	22.1
Inflation (WPI)	5.4	5.8	5.8	5.8	5.8
As % of GDPMP					
Fiscal deficit (Centre)	2.1	2.2	2.9	2.4	3.0
Current account balance	-2.7	-4.6	-4.7	-3.9	-3.9
Private consumption	57.2	59.8	59.1	60.0	59.2

The summary results show that the current external shock of global economic slowdown may reduce the average growth rate for the Indian economy by about one percentage point from the base run growth rate of nine per cent per year. The impact is significant for both fiscal balance and external current account balance.

The year-wise results presented in Table 6.10-6.14 show that the impact of the slowdown is sharper in 2008-09 and 2009-10 than in the subsequent years. The fiscal measures to minimise the output losses have an impact in the short run as they are also at present focused on only the short-term.

Table 6.10: The Macroeconomic Scenario During the Eleventh Five Year Plan Period Base Run

Variables	2007-08	2008-09	2009-10	2010-11	2011-12	2007-2011 Average
% Change YOY						
Real GDP						
- Agriculture	3.4	2.3	2.7	2.6	2.4	2.7
- Industry	9.6	9.7	9.2	8.8	8.5	9.1
- Services	10.5	10.8	10.6	10.8	11.2	10.8
Total	9.0	8.8	8.9	8.9	9.1	9.0
Exports (US$)	34.7	18.2	20.2	18.8	17.7	21.9
Imports (US$)	34.4	24.2	19.2	19.2	19.6	23.3
Inflation (WPI)	4.7	6.7	5.1	5.2	5.2	5.4
As % of GDPMP						
Fiscal deficit (Centre)	3.1	2.3	2.0	1.7	1.5	2.1
Current account balance	-2.0	-3.6	-3.1	-2.5	-2.3	-2.7
Private consumption	61.5	60.0	55.2	54.8	54.5	57.2

Table 6.11: The Macroeconomic Scenario during the Eleventh Five Year Plan Period

Variables	Simulation 1					
	2007-08	2008-09	2009-10	2010-11	2011-12	2007-2011 Average
% Change YOY						
Real GDP						
- Agriculture	3.4	2.3	2.7	2.6	2.4	2.7
- Industry	9.5	8.1	7.8	8.4	8.4	8.4
- Services	10.3	8.7	9.1	10.2	10.6	9.8
Total	8.8	7.4	7.7	8.5	8.8	8.3
Exports (US$)	35.3	14.8	10.8	16.5	17.1	18.9
Imports (US$)	38.8	16.4	17.9	19.7	20.1	22.6
Inflation (WPI)	4.9	7.2	5.7	5.7	5.7	5.8
As % of GDPMP						
Fiscal deficit (Centre)	3.1	2.5	2.2	1.8	1.6	2.2
Current account balance	-2.9	-3.9	-4.9	-5.2	-6.2	-4.6
Private consumption	64.4	62.9	57.5	57.6	56.7	59.8

Table 6.12: The Macroeconomic Scenario during the Eleventh Five Year Plan Period

Variables	Simulation 2					
	2007-08	2008-09	2009-10	2010-11	2011-12	2007-2011 (Average)
% Change YOY						
Real GDP						
- Agriculture	3.4	2.3	2.7	2.6	2.4	2.7
- Industry	9.5	8.4	7.8	8.5	8.4	8.5
- Services	10.3	9.2	9.2	10.3	10.7	9.9
Total	8.8	7.8	7.7	8.6	8.8	8.3
Exports (US$)	35.3	14.8	10.8	16.5	17.1	18.9
Imports (US$)	38.8	17.1	17.9	19.8	20.2	22.8
Inflation (WPI)	4.9	7.2	5.7	5.7	5.7	5.8
As % of GDPMP						
Fiscal deficit (Centre)	3.1	4.0	3.0	2.3	2.1	2.9
Current account balance	-2.9	-4.0	-5.0	-5.2	-6.2	-4.7
Private consumption	63.3	62.1	56.9	57.0	56.2	59.1

Table 6.13: The Macroeconomic Scenario during the Eleventh Five Year Plan Period

Variables	Simulation 3					
	2007-08	2008-09	2009-10	2010-11	2011-12	2007-2011 Average
% Change YOY						
Real GDP						
- Agriculture	3.4	2.3	2.7	2.6	2.4	2.7
- Industry	9.5	6.9	6.6	8.4	8.7	8.0
- Services	10.3	7.4	8.3	10.4	10.8	9.4
Total	8.8	6.4	6.9	8.6	8.9	7.9
Exports (US$)	35.3	14.8	10.8	16.5	17.1	18.9
Imports (US$)	38.8	14.1	16.1	19.8	20.6	21.9
Inflation (WPI)	4.9	7.2	5.7	5.7	5.7	5.8
As % of GDPMP						
Fiscal deficit (Centre)	3.1	2.6	2.4	1.9	1.7	2.4
Current account balance	-2.9	-3.5	-3.9	-4.1	-5.1	-3.9
Private consumption	65.8	63.4	57.1	57.2	56.4	60.0

Table 6.14: The Macroeconomic Scenario during the Eleventh Five Year Plan Period

Variables	Simulation 4					
	2007-08	2008-09	2009-10	2010-11	2011-12	2007-2011 Average
% Change YOY						
Real GDP						
- Agriculture	3.4	2.3	2.7	2.6	2.4	2.7
- Industry	9.5	7.2	6.6	8.4	8.7	8.1
- Services	10.3	7.8	8.4	10.4	10.9	9.6
Total	8.8	6.7	6.9	8.6	9.0	8.0
Exports (US$)	35.3	14.8	10.8	16.5	17.1	18.9
Imports (US$)	38.8	14.8	16.1	19.9	20.7	22.1
Inflation (WPI)	4.9	7.2	5.7	5.7	5.7	5.8
As % of GDPMP						
Fiscal deficit (Centre)	3.1	4.3	3.2	2.5	2.2	3.0
Current account balance	-2.9	-3.5	-3.9	-4.1	-5.2	-3.9
Private consumption	64.7	62.5	56.5	56.6	55.9	59.2

6.4. Concluding Remarks

In this paper we have presented a medium-term macroeconometric model for India and its applications to provide an analysis of implications of selected alternative scenarios that may be considered as 'external shocks' to the economy. The analysis has been carried out taking the EFYP as the reference period. The model has evolved and maintained at NCAER in the last 10 years. Although it follows a traditional approach to macroeconomic modelling and takes the structure of the model parameters as given for various applications, it provides useful estimates of the impact of various alternatives as a benchmark for other assessments.

Analysis of the impact of the alternative petroleum crude oil prices presented in this paper shows that costs of oil price increase to growth can be substantial. Increase of every $10 per barrel would imply a reduction the rate of growth of GDP by 0.1 to 0.3 percentage points per year depending on the extent of 'pass through' of international prices to domestic prices and the manner in which the higher prices are accommodated either in government budget or by the firms.

The analysis of the impact of current global economic crisis shows that the growth costs can be significant. The model results point to a reduction of one percentage point in the annual growth rate of the economy during the EFYP.

In both the cases, policy measures to bring the economy back to higher growth path are indicated. However, direct fiscal interventions do increase fiscal deficit. Higher international oil prices increase current account deficit. Improvements in productivity growth would be the key to maintaining higher economic growth in the face of adverse shocks to the economy.

References

Ahluwalia, I.J. (1979). *Behaviour of Prices and Outputs in India.* New Delhi: Macmillan.

Bhattacharya, B.B. (1984). *Public Expenditure, Inflation and Growth: A Macroeconomic Analysis for India.* Oxford University Press, New Delhi.

Bhide, S. and S. Pohit (1993). "Forecasting and Policy Analysis through a CGE Model for India", *Margin* 25(2).

Challen, D.W. and A.J. Hagger (1983). *Macroeconometric Systems Construction, Validation and Applications.* London: Macmillan.

Desai, M.J. (1972). "Macro-econometric Models for India-A Survey", *Sankhya*, Series B, 3(2): 169-206.

Dahiya, S.B. (ed.) (1982). *Development Planning Models*, Vols. 1 and 2. New Delhi: Inter-India publishers.

Favero, Carlo A. (2007). "Model Evaluation in Macroeconometrics from Early Empirical Macroeconomic Models to DSGE Models", IGIER *Working Paper* no. 327, September. Italy.

Jadhav, N. (1990). "Monetary Modelling of Indian Economy A Survey", *Reserve Bank of India Occasional Papers* 11(2).

Klein, L.R. (2004). "Economic Stabilization Policy Pitfalls of Parsimonious Modelling", in V. Pandit and K Krishnamurthy (eds.), *Economic Policy Modelling for India.* Oxford University Press.

Krishna, K.L., K. Krishnamurthy, V.N. Pandit and P.D. Sharma (1991). "Macroeconometric Modelling in India A Selective Review of Research", *Development Paper* No. 9, ESCAP, U.N. New York.

Narasimham, N.V.A. (1956). *A Short-Term Planning Model for India*, Amsterdam North-Holland.

Marwah, K. (1991). "Macroeconometric Modelling of South-East Asia: The Case of India" in R.G. Bodkin, L.R. Klein and K. Marwah (eds.), *A History of Macroeconometric Model-Building.* UK: Edward Elgar.

———. (1985). "The Indian Trade Structure and the Optimality of Indo-U.S. Bilateral Trade Flows", *Journal of Quantitative Economics* 1: 91-123.

Panda, M.K. and H. Sarkar (1991). "Analysis of Fiscal Squeeze through a Structuralist CGE Model", *Margin* 23(3).

———. (1990). "Resource mobilisation through Administered Prices in an Indian CGE. in L. Taylor (ed.), *Socially Relevant Policy Analysis, Structuralist Computable General Equilibrium Models for the Developing World.* Cambridge MA: The MIT Press.

Pani, P.K. (1977). *A Macroeconomic Model of India.* Delhi: Macmillan.

Sarkar, H. and M.K. Panda (1989). "A Short Term Structural Macroeconomic Model for India Applications to Policy Analysis in Econometric Modelling and Forecasting in Asia", *Development Paper* No. 9, ESCAP, UN, New York.

Sarkar, H. and S.V. Subbarao (1981). "A Short-Term Macro Forecasting Model for India Structure and Uses", *India Economic Review* 16.

Appendix 1: List of Variables

We provide here the lists of exogenous and endogenous variables in the model.

The variables are listed in alphabetical order, along with the units of the variables.

Sl No.	Variables	Description	Types
1.	A	Gross Cropped Area (Million Hectares)	Endogenous
2.	AI	Gross Irrigated Area (Million hectares)	Exogenous
3.	AINFG	Gross Irrigated Area under Non-Food grain (Million Hectares)	Endogenous
4.	AIOTFOOD	Gross Irrigated Area under Pulses and Coarse Cereals (Million Hectares)	Endogenous
5.	AIRICE	Gross Irrigated Area under Rice (Million Hectares)	Endogenous
6.	AIWHEAT	Gross Irrigated Area under Wheat (Million Hectares)	Endogenous
7.	ANFG	Gross Cropped Area under Non-Food grain (Million Hectares)	Endogenous
8.	AOTFOOD	Gross Cropped Area under Pulses and Coarse Cereals (Million Hectares)	Endogenous
9.	ARICE	Gross Cropped Area under Rice (Million Hectares)	Endogenous
10.	AWHEAT	Gross Cropped Area under Wheat (Million Hectares)	Endogenous
11.	BRATE	Bank Rate (Percentage)	Exogenous
12.	CAB	Current Account Balance (Rs crore)	Endogenous
13.	CAPRCPT_C	Capital Receipts – Centre (Rs crore)	Endogenous
14.	CAPRCPT_T	Capital Receipts – All India (Rs crore)	Endogenous
15.	CAPRD_C	Domestic Borrowings – Centre (Rs crore)	Exogenous
16.	CAPRD_T	Domestic Borrowings – All India (Rs crore)	Exogenous
17.	CAPRE_C	External Borrowings – Centre (Rs crore)	Exogenous
18.	CAPRE_T	External Borrowings – All India (Rs crore)	Exogenous
19.	CETOT_T	Compensation to Employees in the Economy (Rs crore)	Endogenous
20.	CEXP_C	Capital Expenditure – Center (Rs. crore)	Exogenous
21.	CP	Private Final Consumption Expenditure (Rs Crore)	Endogenous
22.	CPIAGL	Consumer Price Index of Agricultural Labourers (Index, 1986-87=100)	Endogenous
23.	CPIIW	Consumer Price Index of Industrial Workers (Index, 1982=100)	Endogenous
24.	DISC	Statistical Discrepancies (Rs. crore)	Exogenous
25.	DISINV_C	Disinvestment Receipts – Centre (Rs crore)	Exogenous
26.	DISINV_T	Disinvestment Receipts – All India (Rs crore)	Exogenous
27.	DLIB_C	Domestic Liabilities – Centre (Rs crore)	Endogenous
28.	DLIB_T	Domestic Liabilities – All India (Rs crore)	Endogenous
29.	DRATAGR	Depreciation Rate of Gross Capital Formation – Agriculture (Per cent)	Exogenous
30.	DRATCON	Depreciation Rate of Gross Capital Formation – Construction (Per cent)	Exogenous
31.	DRATEGW	Depreciation Rate of Gross Capital Formation – Electricity, Gas and Water Supply (per cent)	Exogenous
32.	DRATMQM	Depreciation Rate of Gross Capital Formation – Mining, Quarrying and Manufacturing (Per cent)	Exogenous
33.	DRATSER	Depreciation Rate of Gross Capital Formation – Services (Per cent)	Exogenous
34.	DRATTSC	Depreciation Rate of Gross Capital Formation – Transport, Storage and Communication (Per cent)	Exogenous
35.	DTAX_C	Domestic Tax Collection – Centre (Rs crore)	Endogenous
36.	DTAX_T	Domestic Tax Collection – All India (Rs crore)	Endogenous
37.	DTRATE_C	Direct Tax Collection Rate – Centre (Per cent)	Exogenous
38.	DTRATE_T	Direct Tax Collection Rate – All India (Per cent)	Exogenous
39.	ELIB_C	External Liabilities – Centre (Rs crore)	Endogenous

contd...

...contd...

Sl No.	Variables	Description	Types
40.	ELIB_T	External Liabilities – All India (Rs crore)	Endogenous
41.	EMPUB_C	Employment in Public Sector – Central (crore)	Exogenous
42.	EMPUB_T	Employment in Public Sector – All India (crore)	Exogenous
43.	FDEF_C	Fiscal Deficit – Centre (Rs crore)	Endogenous
44.	FDEF_T	Fiscal Deficit – All India (Rs crore)	Endogenous
45.	GCFGAG	Gross Capital Formation – Agriculture (Rs crore)	Exogenous
46.	GCFGCON	Gross Capital Formation – Construction (Rs crore)	Exogenous
47.	GCFGEGW	Gross Capital Formation – Electricity, Gas and Water Supply (Rs crore)	Exogenous
48.	GCFGMQMF	Gross Capital Formation – Mining, Quarrying and Manufacturing (Rs crore)	Exogenous
49.	GCFGSER	Gross Capital Formation – Services (Rs crore)	Exogenous
50.	GCFGTOT	Gross Capital Formation – Public Sector (Rs crore)	Endogenous
51.	GCFGTSC	Gross Capital Formation – Transport, Storage and Communication (Rs crore)	Exogenous
52.	GCFPTOT	Gross Capital Formation – Private Sector (Rs crore)	Endogenous
53.	GDPAG	Gross Domestic Product at Factor Cost – Agriculture (Rs crore)	Endogenous
54.	GDPCON	Gross Domestic Product at Factor Cost – Construction (Rs crore)	Endogenous
55.	GDPEGW	Gross Domestic Product at Factor Cost – Electricity, Gas and Water Supply (Rs crore)	Endogenous
56.	GDPFC	Gross Domestic Product at Factor Cost – Total (Rs crore)	Endogenous
57.	GDPMP	Gross Domestic Product at Market Price – Total (Rs crore)	Endogenous
58.	GDPMQM	Gross Domestic Product at Factor Cost – Mining, Quarrying and Manufacturing (Rs crore)	Endogenous
59.	GDPNAG	Gross Domestic Product at Factor Cost – Non-Agriculture (Rs crore)	Endogenous
60.	GDPSER	Gross Domestic Product at Factor Cost – Services (Rs Crore)	Endogenous
61.	GDPTSC	Gross Domestic Product at Factor Cost – Transport, Storage and Communication (Rs crore)	Endogenous
62.	GDR	Public Distribution of Rice (Million Tonne)	Exogenous
63.	GDW	Public Distribution of Wheat (Million Tonne)	Exogenous
64.	GNPFC	Gross National Product at Factor Cost (Rs crore)	Endogenous
65.	GNPMP	Gross National Product at Market Price (Rs crore)	Endogenous
66.	GOCEX_C	Government Current Expenditure excluding Wage Bill, Interest Payment and Subsidies – Centre (Rs crore)	Exogenous
67.	GOCEX_T	Government Current Expenditure excluding Wage Bill, Interest Payment and Subsidies – All India (Rs crore)	Exogenous
68.	GPR	Procurement of Rice (Million Tonne)	Exogenous
69.	GPW	Procurement of Rice (Million Tonne)	Exogenous
70.	GTCEX_T	Government Current Expenditure – All India (Rs crore)	Endogenous
71.	GWBILL_C	Government Wage Bill – Centre (Rs crore)	Endogenous
72.	GWBILL_T	Government Wage Bill – All India (Rs crore)	Endogenous
73.	IDBIPLR	IDBI's Prime Lending Rate (Per cent)	Endogenous
74.	INDTAX_C	Indirect Tax Collection – Centre (Rs crore)	Endogenous
75.	INDTAX_T	Indirect Tax Collection – All India (Rs crore)	Endogenous
76.	INDTRATE_C	Indirect Tax Rate – Centre (Per cent)	Exogenous
77.	INDTRATE_T	Indirect Tax Rate – All India (Per cent)	Exogenous
78.	INFL	Inflation Rate (Per cent)	Endogenous
79.	INSCRAG	Institutional Credit for Agriculture (Rs crore)	Exogenous
80.	INTPAY_C	Interest Payment – Centre (Rs crore)	Endogenous
81.	INTPAY_T	Interest Payment – All India (Rs crore)	Endogenous

contd...

...contd...

Sl No.	Variables	Description	Types
82.	IRATEDOM_C	Interest Rate on Domestic Debt – Centre (Per cent)	Endogenous
83.	IRATEDOM_T	Interest Rate on Domestic Debt – All India (Per cent)	Endogenous
84.	IRATEEXT	Interest Rate on External Debt (Per cent)	Endogenous
85.	KINFL	Net Capital Inflows in External Account (Rs crore)	Exogenous
86.	M3	Money Supply (Rs crore)	Endogenous
87.	MTOTAL	Total Imports (Rs crore)	Endogenous
88.	NEER	Nominal Effective Exchange Rate (Index, 1985=100)	Exogenous
89.	NETINV	Net Invisible Receipts (Rs crore)	Exogenous
90.	NFIAB	Net Factor Income from Abroad (Rs crore)	Exogenous
91.	NTREV_C	Non-tax Revenue – Centre (Rs crore)	Endogenous
92.	NTREV_T	Non-tax Revenue – All India (Rs crore)	Endogenous
93.	PAG	Implicit Price Deflator for Gross Domestic Product from Agriculture (Index, 1993-94=100)	Endogenous
94.	PALL	Implicit Price Deflator for over all Gross Domestic Product at Factor Cost (Index, 1993-94=100)	Endogenous
95.	PCON	Implicit Price Deflator for Gross Domestic Product from Construction (Index, 1993-94=100)	Endogenous
96.	PDEF_C	Primary deficit – Centre (Rs crore)	Endogenous
97.	PDEF_T	Primary deficit – All India (Rs crore)	Endogenous
98.	PEGW	Implicit Price Deflator for Gross Domestic Product from Electricity, Gas and Water Supply (Index, 1993-94=100)	Endogenous
99.	PEXPTOT	Implicit Price Deflator for over all Private Final Consumption Expenditure (Index, 1993-94=100)	Endogenous
100.	PGCFGAG	Implicit Price Deflator for Public Investment in Agriculture (Index, 1993-94=100)	Endogenous
101.	PGCFGCON	Implicit Price Deflator for Public Investment in Construction (Index, 1993-94=100)	Endogenous
102.	PGCFGEGW	Implicit Price Deflator for Public Investment in Electricity, Gas and Water Supply (Index, 1993-94=100)	Endogenous
103.	PGCFGMQMF	Implicit Price Deflator for Public Investment in Mining, Quarrying and Manufacturing (Index, 1993-94=100)	Endogenous
104.	PGCFGSER	Implicit Price Deflator for Public Investment in Services (Index, 1993-94=100)	Endogenous
105.	PGCFGTSC	Implicit Price Deflator for Public Investment in Transport, Storage and Communication (Index, 1993-94=100)	Endogenous
106.	PGCFPTOT	Implicit Price Deflator for Overall Private Investment (Index, 1993-94=100)	Endogenous
107.	PGDPMP	Implicit Price Deflator for Gross Domestic Product at Market Price (Index, 1993-94=100)	Endogenous
108.	PGNPFC	Implicit Price Deflator for Gross National Product at Factor Cost (Index, 1993-94=100)	Endogenous
109.	PGNPMP	Implicit Price Deflator for Gross National Product at Market Price (Index, 1993-94=100)	Endogenous
110.	PMQM	Implicit Price Deflator for Gross Domestic Product from Mining, Quarrying and Manufacturing (Index, 1993-94=100)	Endogenous
111.	POPLN	Mid-Year Population (Million)	Exogenous
112.	PPR	Procurement Price of Rice (Rs/Qtl.)	Exogenous
113.	PPW	Procurement Price of Wheat (Rs/Qtl.)	Exogenous
114.	PSER	Implicit Price Deflator for Gross Domestic Product from Services (Index, 1993-94=100)	Endogenous
115.	PTSC	Implicit Price Deflator for Gross Domestic Product from Transport, Storage and Communication (Index, 1993-94=100)	Endogenous
116.	QFG	Production of Food grain (Million Tonne)	Endogenous

contd...

...contd...

Sl No.	Variables	Description	Types
117.	QNFGI	Production of Non-Food grain (Index, Triennium Ending 1981-82=100)	Endogenous
118.	QOTFOOD	Production of Pulses and Coarse Cereals (Million Tonne)	Endogenous
119.	QRICE	Production of Rice (Million Tonne)	Endogenous
120.	QWHEAT	Production of Wheat (Million Tonne)	Endogenous
121.	RAIN	Rainfall during Monsoon Period (mm)	Exogenous
122.	RBCCG	Net RBI Credit to Central Government (Rs crore)	Endogenous
123.	RBNFA	Foreign Exchange Assets of RBI (Rs crore)	Endogenous
124.	RCFCAGR	Real Consumption of Fixed Capital in Agriculture (Rs crore)	Endogenous
125.	RCFCCON	Real Consumption of Fixed Capital in Construction (Rs crore)	Endogenous
126.	RCFCEGW	Real Consumption of Fixed Capital in Electricity, Gas and Water Supply (Rs crore)	Endogenous
127.	RCFCMQM	Real Consumption of Fixed Capital in Mining, Quarrying and Manufacturing (Rs crore)	Endogenous
128.	RCFCSER	Real Consumption of Fixed Capital in Services (Rs crore)	Endogenous
129.	RCFCTSC	Real Consumption of Fixed Capital in Transport, Storage and Communication (Rs crore)	Endogenous
130.	RDEF_C	Revenue Deficit – Centre (Rs crore)	Endogenous
131.	RDEF_T	Revenue Deficit – All India (Rs crore)	Endogenous
132.	RECLOAN_C	Recovery of Loans – Centre (Rs crore)	Exogenous
133.	RECLOAN_T	Recovery of Loans – All India (Rs crore)	Exogenous
134.	REXP_C	Revenue Expenditure – Centre (Rs crore)	Endogenous
135.	REXPEGW	Real Private Final Consumption Expenditure on Electricity, Gas and Water Supply (Rs crore)	Endogenous
136.	REXPFOOD	Real Private Final Consumption Expenditure on Food (Rs crore)	Endogenous
137.	REXPMQM	Real Private Final Consumption Expenditure on Mining, Quarrying and Manufacturing (Rs crore)	Endogenous
138.	REXPSER	Real Private Final Consumption Expenditure on Services (Rs crore)	Endogenous
139.	REXPTSC	Real Private Final Consumption Expenditure on Transport, Storage and Communication (Rs crore)	Endogenous
140.	RGCFAGR	Real Gross Capital Formation in Agriculture (Rs. crore)	Endogenous
141.	RGCFCON	Real Gross Capital Formation in Construction (Rs crore)	Endogenous
142.	RGCFEGW	Real Gross Capital Formation in Electricity, Gas and Water Supply (Rs crore)	Endogenous
143.	RGCFGAGR	Real Gross Capital Formation in Agriculture - Public (Rs crore)	Endogenous
144.	RGCFGCON	Real Gross Capital Formation in Construction – Public (Rs crore)	Endogenous
145.	RGCFGEGW	Real Gross Capital Formation in Electricity, Gas and Water Supply – Public (Rs crore)	Endogenous
146.	RGCFGMQMF	Real Gross Capital Formation in Mining, Quarrying and Manufacturing – Public (Rs crore)	Endogenous
147.	RGCFGSER	Real Gross Capital Formation in Services– Public (Rs crore)	Endogenous
148.	RGCFGTSC	Real Gross Capital Formation in Transport, Storage and Communication – Public (Rs crore)	Endogenous
149.	RGCFMQMF	Real Gross Capital Formation in Mining, Quarrying and Manufacturing (Rs crore)	Endogenous
150.	RGCFPAGR	Real Gross Capital Formation in Agriculture- Private (Rs crore)	Endogenous
151.	RGCFPCON	Real Gross Capital Formation in Construction - Private (Rs crore)	Endogenous
152.	RGCFPEGW	Real Gross Capital Formation in Electricity, Gas and Water Supply- Private (Rs crore)	Endogenous
153.	RGCFPMQMF	Real Gross Capital Formation in Mining, Quarrying and Manufacturing - Private (Rs crore)	Endogenous
154.	RGCFPSER	Real Gross Capital Formation in Services- Private (Rs crore)	Endogenous
155.	RGCFPTOT	Real Gross Capital Formation – Overall - Private (Rs crore)	Endogenous
156.	RGCFPTSC	Real Gross Capital Formation in Transport, Storage and Communication - Private (Rs crore)	Endogenous

contd...

...contd...

Sl No.	Variables	Description	Types
157.	RGCFSER	Real Gross Capital Formation in Services .(Rs crore)	Endogenous
158.	RGCFTSC	Real Gross Capital Formation in Transport, Storage and Communication (Rs crore)	Endogenous
159.	RGDPMP	Real Gross Domestic Product at Market Prices (Rs crore)	Endogenous
160.	RGNPFC	Real Gross National Product at Factor Cost (Rs crore)	Endogenous
161.	RGNPMP	Real Gross National Product at Market Cost (Rs crore)	Endogenous
162.	RKAGR	Real Capital Stock in Agriculture (Rs crore)	Endogenous
163.	RKCON	Real Capital Stock in Construction (Rs crore)	Endogenous
164.	RKEGW	Real Capital Stock in Electricity, Gas and Water Supply (Rs crore)	Endogenous
165.	RKMQM	Real Capital Stock in Mining, Quarrying and Manufacturing (Rs crore)	Endogenous
166.	RKSER	Real Capital Stock in Services (Rs crore)	Endogenous
167.	RKTSC	Real Capital Stock in Transport, Storage and Communication (Rs crore)	Endogenous
168.	RM	Reserve Money (Rs crore)	Endogenous
169.	RMD	Real Money Demand (Rs crore)	Endogenous
170.	RMS	Real Money Stock (Rs. crore)	Endogenous
171.	RMTOTAL	Real Imports (Rs crore)	Endogenous
172.	RPDI	Real Personal Disposable Income (Rs crore)	Endogenous
173.	RPVTINCOME	Real Private Income (Rs crore)	Endogenous
174.	RRINT	Real Rate of Interest (Per cent)	Endogenous
175.	RVAAG	Real Value Added at Factor cost in Agriculture (Rs crore)	Endogenous
176.	RVACON	Real Value Added at Factor cost in Construction (Rs crore)	Endogenous
177.	RVAEGW	Real Value Added at Factor cost in Electricity, Gas and Water Supply (Rs crore)	Endogenous
178.	RVAMQM	Real Value Added at Factor cost in Mining, Quarrying and Manufacturing (Rs crore)	Endogenous
179.	RVANAGR	Real Value Added at Factor cost in Non-Agriculture (Rs crore)	Endogenous
180.	RVASER	Real Value Added at Factor cost in Services (Rs crore)	Endogenous
181.	RVATOT	Real Value Added at Factor cost - Total (Rs crore)	Endogenous
182.	RVATSC	Real Value Added at Factor cost in Transport, Storage and Communication (Rs crore)	Endogenous
183.	RWINC	World Income (Index, 1995-96=100)	Exogenous
184.	RXTOTAL	Real Exports (Rs crore)	Endogenous
185.	SFR	Stock of Rice (Million Tonne)	Exogenous
186.	SI	Short–term Rate of Interest (1-3 years deposit rates of 5 major public sector banks, Per cent)	Endogenous
187.	SUB_C	Subsidies – Centre (Rs crore)	Exogenous
188.	SUB_T	Subsidies – All India (Rs crore)	Exogenous
189.	T	Time Trend (for 1970-71 and so on)	Exogenous
190.	TOTREV_C	Total Revenue – Centre (Rs crore)	Endogenous
191.	TOTREV_T	Total Revenue – All India (Rs crore)	Endogenous
192.	TREV_C	Tax Revenue – Centre (Rs crore)	Endogenous
193.	TREV_T	Tax Revenue – All India (Rs crore)	Endogenous
194.	UVIEXP	Unit Value Index for Exports (Index, 1978-79=100)	Endogenous
195.	UVIIMP	Unit Value Index for Imports (Index, 1978-79=100)	Endogenous
196.	WPI	Wholesale Price Index – All Commodities (Index, 1993-94=100)	Endogenous
197.	WPIAGR	Wholesale Price Index – Agricultural Commodities (Index, 1993-94=100)	Endogenous
198.	WPIENERGY	Wholesale Price Index of Fuel, Power, Light and Lubricants (Index, 1993-94=100)	Exogenous
199.	WPIFG	Wholesale Price Index – Food grain (Index, 1993-94=100)	Endogenous
200.	WPIINPUT	Wholesale Price Index of Inputs for Agriculture (Index, 1993-94=100)	Exogenous

contd...

...contd...

Sl No.	Variables	Description	Types
201.	WPIMQM	Wholesale Price Index – Mining, Quarrying and Manufacturing (Index, 1993-94=100)	Endogenous
202.	WPINFG	Wholesale Price Index – Non-Food grain (Index, 1993-94=100)	Endogenous
203.	WPIOTFOOD	Wholesale Price Index – Pulses and Coarse Cereals (Index, 1993-94=100)	Endogenous
204.	WPIRICE	Wholesale Price Index – Rice (Index, 1993-94=100)	Endogenous
205.	WPIWHEAT	Wholesale Price Index – Wheat (Index, 1993-94=100)	Endogenous
206.	WRATE_C	Public Sector Wage Rate – Centre (Rs)	Endogenous
207.	WRATE_T	Public Sector Wage Rate – All India (Rs)	Endogenous
208.	XTOTAL	Total Exports (Rs crore)	Endogenous
209.	YNFGI	Yield Rate of Non-Food grain (Index, Triennium Ending 1981-82=100)	Endogenous
210.	YOTFOOD	Yield Rate of Pulses and Coarse Cereals (Kg/Hectare)	Endogenous
211.	YRICE	Yield Rate of Rice (Kg/Hectare)	Endogenous
212.	YWHEAT	Yield Rate of Wheat (Kg/Hectare)	Endogenous

Appendix

Mathematical Models used in Indian Five Year Plans

Kirit S. Parikh, K.L. Datta and Arvinder S. Sachdeva

The Planning Commission has been using mathematical models from the early days of planning. A brief description of these models is given here.

The First Five Year Plan (1951-1956)

There is no officially recorded model that was used to formulate the First Five Year Plan. The technical work behind the target setting was inspired by the Harrod-Domar model.

The Harrod-Domar model is a highly simplified version of economic reality that production requires capital and to augment capital investment are needed, which calls for savings. It assumes production of a homogenous product. Such an assumption ignores the commodity composition of the total product. This, in turn, presumes absence of structural change in the economy, even as the total product increases as a result of economic growth. The relative prices of the commodities constituting the national product remain unchanged. The system assumes absence of foreign trade. The national product is either consumed or invested. The percentage of income saved defined as savings rate remain constant in the model frame. The model treats capital as the only factor of production. Capital goods are assumed to have infinite life span without any depreciation. There is one period time lag between investment and creation of productive capacity. The technological relationship in the model remains fixed.[1]

The savings function in the model is assumed to be linear and it goes through the origin, as given below.

$$S_t = sY_t \quad (1)$$

where, S_t = savings in time period t.

Y_t = income in time period t.

s = proportion of income saved, i.e., savings propensity.

Thus, it is assumed that marginal propensity to save is equal to average propensity to save. Investment incurred at time period t, leads to an increment of income at period t+1.

$$\Delta Y_t = \beta I_t \quad (2)$$

where $\Delta Y_t = Y_{t+1} - Y_t$

β = incremental output-capital ratio

The system is in equilibrium when $I_t = S_t$ (3)

From (2) $I_t = \Delta Y_t/\beta$

Since $I_t = S_t$, $\Delta Y_t/\beta = S_t$ (4)

Substituting the value of S_t from (1) in (4),

$$\Delta Y_t/\beta = sY_t$$

or,

$$\Delta Y_t/Y_t = s\beta \quad (5)$$

1. The discussion in this section has largely been drawn upon Bhagwati Jagdish N. and Sukhamoy Chakravarty (1972). *Contributions to Indian Economic Analysis: A Survey*. Bombay: Lalvani Publishing House. pp. 5–8.

Kirit S. Parikh, K.L. Datta and Arvinder S. Sachdeva, Planning Commission.

This implies that the proportional rate of growth of income is equal to the savings ratio multiplied by the inverse of the incremental capital-output ratio, which is also the equilibrium growth rate as shown below.

From (5): $Y_{t+1} = Y_t\,(1 + s\beta)$, which is a first order difference equation. Its solution yields

$$Y_t = Y_0\,(1 + s\beta)^t$$

In the First Plan, this model was applied to determine the equilibrium rate of growth from the system, given the savings ratio and incremental capital-output ratio (ICOR). It stressed investment for capital accumulation and argued that production required capital and that capital can be accumulated through investment. The faster one accumulates, the higher the growth rate will be. The model is used to provide answers to questions such as: Given a certain ICOR, the savings rate required to realise a particular rate of growth. The answer is: The required savings rate is equal to the rate of growth multiplied by the incremental capital-output ratio (ICOR). However, application of the model in planning for the economy is beset with problems. Its underlying assumptions that there are no structural deficiencies in transforming savings into investment and that too in the desired form i.e., in sectors misses out on an important element of development. Also, model ignores the fundamental choice problem of planning over time, which requires a weighing of present *versus* future gains, by assuming a constant marginal propensity to save for the economy.

It should, however, be noted that the model was not given an explicit analytical form, but was implicit in the numerical figures which constituted the perspective plan for developing the Indian economy. It should also be pointed out that the Harrod-Domar model in original was not used in the first plan. It was modified, though marginally. The modification in the model was by way of the distinction between the average and the marginal propensities to save. The capital-output ratio was assumed to be the same on the margin as on the average. The model was developed for a closed economy, though the model could have been extended to deal with an open economy, with one part of investment being financed by import surplus.[2]

Harrod-Domar model is a very orthodox tool in itself. Such models are useful in indicating the basic macroeconomic features. The main and most important job that this model does is to indicate the problem of increasing per capita income in an underdeveloped economy. It is highly aggregative in nature which prevents it from being used as a tool in detailed quantitative policy making. It also conceals many structural aspects of the problem of a steady rate of growth. Considering the simplicity of the model in answering broad policy issues in the Indian economy in the early 1950, when data availability was a major constraint, the application of Harrod-Domar model was widely considered as an appropriate decision.

The Second Five Year Plan (1956-1961)

The macroeconomic framework of the Second Five Year Plan was a model of growth generated by capital accumulation based on domestic savings and foreign capital. The model developed by P.C. Mahalanobis, addressed the problem of converting savings into investment goods and distinguished two sectors, consumer goods and capital goods. This came to be known as the two-sector model. This two sector model was later on elaborated into a four sector model with consumer goods sector split into factory produced, small and household industry produced and services. The four sector model developed by Mahalanobis guided India's planning strategies in the Second Five Year Plan.[3] This was a marked change from the first plan as it emphasised the physical aspect of investment.

2. This is demonstrated by Bhagwati and Chakravarty *op. cit.* They have also noted that unlike the usual Harrod-Domar model, the rate of growth here rises from period to period. Thus, an economy which decides to save more on the margin than on the average, can hope to do better and better over time in terms of its rate of growth.

3. The model related work at this time was carried out by Mahalanobis and his team at the Indian Statistical Institute, Calcutta. The two sector model was published in Mahalanobis, P.C. (1953). "Some Observations on the Process of Growth of National Income", *Sankhya*: 307-12, September. The four sector model was publishing in Mahalanobis, P.C. (1955). "The Approach to Operational Research to Planning in India", *Sankhya*: 3-130, December. In drafting this section use have been made of Chakravarty S. (1957). "The Mahalanobis Model of Development Planning", *Arthaniti*: 57-69, November.

The Structure of the Two Sector Model

In the two-sector model, the economy is divided into two sectors as:

(a) Consumer goods sector

(b) Investment goods or capital goods sector

Each sector is assumed to be vertically integrated. The sectors producing raw materials for consumption goods are aggregated with the sectors producing consumption goods. Similar is the case in the investment goods sector. But, investment in any period of time (I_t) is decomposed into two components, as:

(a) the investment used in the investment goods sector ($\lambda_k I_t$), that is investment used to augment productive capacity, and

(b) the investment used in the consumption goods sector ($\lambda_c I_t$).

Thus, $I_t = \lambda_k I_t + \lambda_c I_t$;

$\lambda_k + \lambda_c = 1$

I_t = total investment.

λ_k = proportion of investment going to capital goods sector;

λ_c = proportion of investment going to consumption goods sector;

Let,

β_k = capital coefficient in capital goods sector

β_c = capital coefficient in consumer goods sector

It implies,

$$\beta_c = \Delta C_t / \lambda_c I_t$$

$$\Delta C_t = \beta_c \lambda_c I_t \qquad (1)$$

C_t = total consumption

In a similar way,

$$\Delta I_t = \beta_k \lambda_k I_t \qquad (2)$$

(1) and (2) are production relations. These relate input with output, in incremental sense.

$$Y_t = C_t + I_t$$

$$\Delta Y_t = \Delta C_t + \Delta I_t \qquad (3)$$

Y_t = Income

$$I_t = (1+ \beta_k \lambda_k)^t I_0 \qquad (4)$$

In this equation, I_0 is the initial level of investment to start with. Therefore, I_0 is historically fixed. b_k is a constant and l_k is a parameter and thus is fixed. The equation (4) can also be written as

$$I_t - I_0 = I_0[(1+ \beta_k \lambda_k)^t -1] \qquad (5)$$

Similarly,

$$C_t - C_0 = [\beta_c\lambda_c I_0 \{(1+\beta_k\lambda_k)^t -1\}]/\beta_k\lambda_k \qquad (6)$$

In (6) C_0 is initial consumption and therefore, is a datum and I_0 is historically fixed. Therefore, $\beta_c\lambda_c/\beta_k\lambda_k$ and $(1+\beta_k\lambda_k)$ do not change over time. Using the equations (3), (5) and (6), the model can be reduced to:

$$Y_t = Y_0 + I_0\{(1+\beta_k\lambda_k)^t-1\}\{1+(\beta_c\lambda_c/\beta_k\lambda_k)\} \qquad (7)$$

The model in (7) is solved for Y_t, λ_c, λ_k. Since $\lambda_k + \lambda_c = 1$, there is one degree of freedom. Mahalanobis closed this gap by choosing the income path.

The time path of income in Mahalanobis model depends on the policy variables, that is the l's in addition to the savings rate and the capital coefficient or the output-capital ratios on which Harrod-Domar model depends. In Mahalanobis model, the overall capital coefficient i.e., ICOR is a weighted average of sectoral ICORs, the weights being proportional to the investment in the two sectors, i.e., the investment goods and consumption goods sector. Since the weights change depending on the l's, aggregate ICOR also change over time.

If the incremental output-capital ratio in the consumer and capital goods sectors in the model are technologically fixed then income growth depends on the initial proportion of investment to income and the proportion of investment allocated to the investment goods sector. The model is described by five elements *viz.*, the initial proportion of investment to income, the output-capital ratios of the investment goods and consumption goods sectors, and the proportion of investment in the investment goods and the consumption goods sectors. Among these, (a) the output-capital ratios of the investment goods and the consumption goods sectors are technologically fixed, (b) the proportion of investment in the consumption goods sector is determined as soon as the proportion of investment in the capital goods sector is known. If the constant ratio at which the initial investment has been allocated is known then the only policy instrument that the planner can play with is the proportion of current investment in capital goods or investment goods sector. With one instrument, only one target can be attained. Once λ_k or λ_c is decided, the pattern of output and consumption are determined.

The relative rates of growth of consumption and output changes overtime. The asymptotic rate of growth of the system is given by the proportion of capital goods output devoted to further production of capital goods and the incremental output-capital ratio of the capital goods sector. A higher value of the investment devoted to the capital goods sector always has a favourable effect on the asymptotic growth rate of the system, irrespective of whether it is consumption or output. If a high value of the proportion of investment going to the capital goods sector is chosen, then in the beginning the system grows at a somewhat slow rate, while it gains acceleration with passage of time. If the output-capital ratio of the consumption goods sector is greater than that of the capital goods sector, then a higher value of the proportion of investment devoted to the capital goods sector imply a lower immediate increment in consumption. Thus, there is implicit in the choice of the proportion of investment devoted to the capital goods sector, a choice of alternative streams of consumption.

Mahalanobis assumes that one-third of the total investment would be devoted to the capital goods sector. Thus, Mahalanobis does not address himself to this choice problem. He points out that a specification of the horizon over which planning is done is essential if any meaningful answer is to be given to the choice of the proportion of investment going to the capital goods sector. One can first build up capacity to make capital goods and after some years use it to expand consumption goods production. How long one waits for this depends on the planning horizon.

The model operates under a closed economy assumption along with total non-shiftability of capital from the consumption goods to capital goods sector, i.e., capital equipment once installed in any specific producing sector of the economy may not be shifted to other sectors.

The Structure of the Four Sector Model

Mahalanobis extended the Two-Sector Model to a Four-Sector Model by keeping the capital goods sector unchanged but splitting up the consumer goods sector into three different sectors as:

(a) factory production of consumer goods,

(b) production of consumer goods including agricultural products by small and household industries and

(c) service sectors such as health, education etc.

In the four-sector model, the time path for income remains the same except that the output-capital ratio or the technological coefficient of the consumer goods sector is a weighted average of the output-capital ratios of the three different consumer goods sectors, as mentioned above. Also, a new variable, *viz.*, employment and a new set of parameters, *viz.*, output-labour ratios are introduced in the model. The output-labour ratios are assumed to be independent of the productivity coefficients.

The problem Mahalanobis sets is how to determine the investment allocation between investment goods sectors and the three consumption goods sectors with the following constraints.

(a) Total investment to allocate is Rs. 56 billion.

(b) Total increment in income is Rs. 29 billion

(c) Total new employment to be created is 11 million.

(d) From the consideration of long term growth one-third of the total investment is devoted to the capital goods sector.

The resultant growth of national income becomes 25 per cent during the five years of the Second Plan. Mahalanobis assumes that for each sector, there is a constant incremental output-capital ratio and constant incremental output-labour ratios.

Policy Use of the Model

The four-sector model was introduced for solving certain problems of policy. Basically, with two targets in mind, *viz.*, (a) postulated rate of growth of income over a certain definite period of time, and (b) increase in employment over the same period, the instruments used in the model are the proportion in which the investments are distributed between different sectors of the economy. Therefore, the instruments are: the proportion of investment going to the capital goods sector and the three consumption goods sector, i.e., λ_{c1}, λ_{c2}, λ_{c3} and λ_k; with $\lambda_{c1}+\lambda_{c2}+\lambda_{c3}+\lambda_k=1$

The data given are:

(a) Four output-capital ratios (β_k, β_{c1}, β_{c2}, β_{c3}), one each for the four sectors ($\beta=I/\Delta Y$).

(b) Four output-labour ratios (θ_k, θ_{c1}, θ_{c2}, θ_{c3}), one each for the four sectors ($\theta=\Delta Y/\Delta N$).

(c) One value for the aggregate investment (I).

The targets as already mentioned above, are:

(a) Increase in income during the Plan period (ΔY).

(b) Increase in employment during the Plan period (ΔN)

On theoretical plane, the model was criticised for the reason that the sectoral values of income are not used as separate targets. All the four sectors in the model had independent output-capital and output-labour ratios. Mahalanobis assumes a given total investment. The problem is to allocate the total investment between the sectors in such a way that specified increase in income and employment are reached. The policy variables are the share of investment in each sector. The model is determined if and only if one of the three independent investment shares is exogenously determined. Since there are two objectives, *viz.*, increase in income and increase in employment, with the share of investment in the capital goods sector given a pre-assigned value, the system is solved to allocate investment among the three remaining sectors.

In the model, investment is a single homogenous good, foreign trade is not considered, and savings come only from the industrial sector. Developing countries, however, do not have this tendency, as the first stages of saving usually come from the agricultural sector. The model also does not consider taxation, an important potential source of savings.

Mahalanobis appears to have used the model merely to provide the rationale for a shift in industrial investments towards building up a capital goods base.

Individual economists and mathematical model builders have commented upon several areas of the model. The important ones may be summed up as:

(a) Haldane[4] showed though simulation exercises that over a 10- to 15-year period, given certain reasonable data, the assumption of one-third of the total investment devoted to the capital goods sector is, in fact, the appropriate choice in maximizing inter-temporal growth.

(b) Komiya[5] points out that Mahalanobis solution is inefficient in that it is situated in the interior of the feasibility locus between incremental output and incremental employment. Thus, it is possible to generate greater employment and/or output by merely reallocating the given investment among the three sectors, although such a solution will not assign a positive fraction of investment to every sector.

(c) Tsuru[6] points out that identification of investment with the output of a sector defined as basic investment goods is a mistake. Investment could take various physical forms and not only that of production of new durable equipment. Thus, increase in inventories of all kinds of goods may constitute investment though such increase obviously does not correspond to the output of one specific sector.

These limitations largely prompted the necessity for developing more extensive multi-sectoral and multi-period model for an efficient resolution of the choice problem facing the Indian economy. Such models were constructed in the 1960s during the period of the Third Five Year Plan.

Planning in the 1960s

The Third Five Year Plan covers the period 1961-1966. It commenced on 1st April 1961. The targets set in the Third Plan had to be revised due to large change in the sectoral allocation eventuated by the border conflict with China in October 1962. Though the war was brief, lasting only a few days, it triggered a significant change in the planning and development strategy and the policies towards economic development. The problem was accentuated by another war with Pakistan in September 1965. The economic woes were compounded by the three successive years of drought, which began within the period of the Third Five Year Plan. These put a brake on the process of planning in the country and the Fourth Five Year Plan was launched after a gap of three years of the conclusion of the Third Plan period. The Fourth Five Year Plan covered the period 1969-1974. The models used in the Plan formulation during the period 1961-1974 are discussed in this section.

The Third Five Year Plan (1961-1966)

Plan models which provide guideline regarding the phasing of investment can be divided into two categories, *viz.*, consistency models and optimisation models. From this categorisation, the models used in the Third Plan model can be described as an inter-temporally consistent planning model. These models attempted multi-sectoral balances to achieve consistency and marked a shift to examination of consistency at the inter-sectoral level. Alan Manne, Ashok Rudra, Sukhamoy Chakravarty, Richard Eckaus, Louis Lefebar, Kirit Parikh and others attempted to construct plan models for India around the 1960s. But, there is no mention of any explicit mathematical model in the official plan document. The only conceivable planning model that may hold the variables in a formal way is that formulated by Chakravarty.[7] However, a few models were worked out for the Third Plan though perhaps not officially recognised. Jan Sandee constructed a simple linear programming model during his visit to Indian Statistical Institute (ISI), Calcutta, during 1957-58. Sandee prepared this model in the context of the Third Plan. The Perspective Planning Division of the Planning Commission at this time conducted several exercises on the Third Plan. This was done by Pitambar Pant in association with I.M.D. Little and known as Pant-Little exercise.

4. Haldane, J. B. S. (1955) "Maximisation of National Income", *Sankhya* 16, December.
5. Komiya, R. (1959). "A Note on Professor Mahalanobis' Model of Indian Economic Planning", *Review of Economics and Statistics* 41: 29-35, February.
6. Tsuru, S. (1957). "Some Theoretical Doubts on Indian Plan Frame," *The Economic Weekly* IX, January.
7. Chakravarty, S. (1964). "The Mathematical Framework of the Third Five Year Plan" in P. N. Rosenstein-Rodan (ed.), *Capital Formation and Economic Development*. London: George Allen and Unwin Ltd. pp.11-22.

These two models are briefly mentioned in the context of the Third Plan, despite the fact that the plan was subjected to considerable mid-course correction for the reasons of warfare and natural catastrophes mentioned above, rendering their efficacy in application.

During the period of the Third Plan, Manne-Rudra constructed a terminal year model for the Indian economy, without specifying in a complete way the path that the economy was to follow from a given initial point to the terminal year configuration. It is a static multi-sector consistency model.

The other category of models dealt with optimisation over time. The most important of all optimisation models constructed for the Indian economy was the one build by Chakravarty, Eckaus, Lefeber and Parikh. It is a dynamic multi-sectoral model and came to be known as CELP model.

Sandee's Model

The model is used to maximise aggregate consumption in the terminal year as an excess of consumption over the base year subject to maintaining inter-sectoral consistency conditions and feasibility conditions on the side of balance of payments. It is a straightforward static linear programming exercise involving a 13-sector terminal year linear optimisation model with 1960 as the base year and 1970 as the terminal year.[8] The objective function was aggregate household consumption in 1970. The main plank of the statistical scaffolding of Sandee's model was provided by a 36 sector inter-industry table, which was constructed then by the Indian Statistical Institute, Calcutta.

Terminal year investment problem is tackled by a straight line growth path for investment in each sector. The variables used in the model are defined in terms of increments between base and terminal year level. The model is characterised by three features:

(a) Sector is identified with commodities.

(b) Capacity is not distinguished from production.

(c) Non-competitive imports are not recognised.

Leontief type production function is established in all sectors excepting agriculture. In agriculture, a linear production function is used. The input-output coefficients for the remaining sectors are calculated by considering the 36-sector input-output table developed by Indian Statistical Institute, Calcutta. The model does not address the crucial choice centred on whether "more investment at present or in future". There are also problems of correcting the input-output coefficients for changes due to technology and product composition between base and terminal year. The adjustments made in this regard were sometimes arbitrary, mostly due to insufficient data base.

Pant-Little Exercise

In this model, total investment and net foreign aid are treated as exogenous variable. The initial values are: income in the base year and savings in the base year of the plan. The parameters are: (i) income elasticity of demand for agricultural production; (ii) global capital-output ratio; (iii) proportion of investment expenditure undertaken by the Government; (iv) proportion in which the existing tax revenue is earned from current consumption; (v) proportion in which the existing tax revenue is earned from current agricultural income; (vi) proportion in which the existing tax revenue is earned from current non-agricultural income.

The Derivation of the Model: Investment is equal to savings plus foreign income. Increase in income is determined from the aggregate investment and the global capital-output ratio. The system is determined once the annual increment in savings, the capital-output ratio and the aggregate investment are determined. Using the elasticities in agriculture and non-agriculture, the model was used to estimate the production in these two areas separately.[9]

---

8. Sandee, Jan (1960). "A Demonstration Planning Model for India", *Indian Statistical Series* No. 7. Calcutta: Statistical Publishing Society and Asia Publishing House.

9. This frame was structured by Chakravarty in "The Mathematical Framework of the Third Five Year Plan", *op.cit.*

Observations: While the model covered a period of five years, it did not track year-to-year changes. The model thus provides the initial and final year values. The model consists of definitional equations, behaviour equations, technological equations and institutional equations. The model had 15 unknowns and 13 equations. Thus, there are two degrees of freedom. Therefore, two variables are set from outside and the remaining are estimated endogenously. This yields a number of policy constellations from which a choice can be made. The two open ends in the model are filled up by investment and net foreign aid.

Manne-Rudra Model

Alan S. Manne and Ashok Rudra developed a consistency model for the Fourth Five Year Plan.[10] Projection for sectoral investment and output levels are made to set the Plan targets. The core model consists of a 30-sector terminal year consistency model, which is a conventional Leontief inter-industry model with a few embellishments for the indigenous treatment for capital formation. The base and terminal year of the model is 1960 and 1970 respectively. The important findings of the model are as follows.

There is an almost block-angular structure of current account transaction taking place within two virtually independent complexes, one based upon agriculture and the other upon mining, metals and machinery and forestry products. Agriculture is the predominant source of consumption goods and mining, metals, machinery etc., are the source of investment goods. A third and a smaller complex produced item is described as universal intermediaries i.e., fuel, power, transport and chemical items that are virtually consumed within all sectors of the economy. The production targets in physical units are derived for 12 sectors in the model. The current input is based on inter-industry table for the year 1960 as prepared in the Indian Statistical Institute, Calcutta.

In case of capital formation, two categories of construction and three categories of equipments are taken. Thus, in all five categories of capital goods are assumed. The model has two variants. In the first variant, the flow of a commodity into fixed capital formation is treated as exogenous. In the second variant, the current flow of capital goods of each of these five sectors is related to expansion of capacities in different sectors.

Household consumption in the model is treated as exogenous, being of the nature of a target. Individual demand is estimated by Engel elasticities. The distribution of per capita consumption is assumed to be log-normal. Government consumption is treated as exogenous in the model. The model has a foreign trade sector. In all, three categories of imports are considered. Thus, foreign trade is treated in three ways/versions. The model is used to project upto 1975-76.

Manne-Rudra model is a terminal year model for the Indian economy. They do not specify in a complete way the path the economy is to follow from a given initial point to the terminal configuration. Thus, this model may be said to give a perspective rather than a plan. However, the construction of a terminal configuration is an essential ingredient in any finite horizon planning model so that the Manne-Rudra model does provide some guidelines for the planner, even though it does not specify a complete time phased course of action.

CELP Model

Chakravarty and Eckaus outlined the logic of an inter-temporally consistent multi-sectoral planning model and pointed out the basic difficulties. The planning model first developed by Chakravarty, Eckaus, Lefeber and Parikh and later extended by Eckaus and Parikh[11], known as the CELP model, is the most detailed of all the models then developed in the context of Indian planning. Within the limitation of a linear programming model, CELP enjoys sufficient flexibility to handle important questions relating to planning. The model maximises the present discounted value of private consumption including a steady

10. Manne, A. S. and Ashok Rudra (1965). "A Consistency Model of India's Fourth Plan", *Sankhya*, Series B, Vol.27: 57-144. February.

11. Eckaus, R. S. and Kirit S. Parikh (1968). *Planning for Growth : Multisectoral, Interregional Model Applied to India*. Cambridge Mass, USA: MIT Press.

state growth of post-terminal consumption subject to commodity balance, capacity constraint, capacity creation gestation lags, post-terminal requirements and balance of payments.

CELP is a finite horizon, linear optimisation model, which maximises discounted flow of private consumption and involving explicit inter-sectoral and inter-temporal relationships, which satisfies boundary conditions relating to the initial year as well as to the terminal year of the plan based on a steady state growth path of the economy in the post-terminal period. The model provides an inter-temporally optimal path of development which brought the economy from the initial situation to the desired terminal situation. It also distinguishes between investment starts, investment in execution and completed investment. Foreign trade problems are introduced in the model. Export demand levels are assumed to be exogenous. Imports are divided into two categories: competitive imports and non-competitive imports. Non-competitive imports are related to sectoral production levels by fixed proportions. Competitive imports within import ceilings are determined by sectoral demand balances. The model brings out the post-plan feature into focus in terms of investment in the terminal year. In a word, it was the most detailed of all the models developed until then in the context of Indian Planning.

The Fourth Five Year Plan (1969-1974)

The mathematical model used in the Fourth Five Year Plan brings out two new features in the Plan model. These are:

(a) the recognition of the need for sectoral balances over intervening years as a check on overall consistency of plan targets, and

(b) the introduction of explicit treatment of foreign trade.

While these were treated by the CELP model, the Fourth Plan approach treats them at a more disaggregated level through material balances, though sacrificing the rigors and consistency of a formal model. The formal quantitative plan model is worked out in a macro structure based on highly simplified assumptions and under very broad and distinctly identifiable objectives. The macro frame is subsequently fitted into the sectoral and disaggregated framework and ultimately translated into specific micro level plan decisions. The model consists of: (a) allocation of resources in an inter-industry consistency model, and (b) material balances for specific commodities for intervening years.

(a) Inter-Industry Consistency Model

This model has 77 sectors and is formulated exclusively for deriving a consistent set of gross output targets for 1970-71 (which is the terminal year of the plan), within the boundary conditions set by the macro-model. For this purpose, an exercise is attempted on the lines of Leontief's static inter-industry model. The entire final demand *viz.*, private and public consumption, net capital formation, replacement investment, stock changes and exports less imports is treated as exogenous. The macro dimensions of these variables are projected based on time trends and modified as per feedback from line ministries. The vector conversion of the scalar values are computed in this inter-industry model.

On the basis of targeted growth in per capita private consumption and population growth, the aggregate consumption expenditure in the terminal year is computed. The expenditure elasticities are estimated for major expenditure groups. The sectoral consumption in the terminal year is projected for each item, using the growth in per capita total consumption, the sectoral expenditure elasticities obtained separately for rural and urban areas utilising the National Sample Survey data on household consumer expenditure relating to the 10th Round covering the period December 1955 to May 1956[12] and per capita consumption in the base period.

(b) The Material Balances

Specific material balances for certain commodities covering large number of sectors both in physical and monetary terms are worked out for the terminal and intermediate years of the plan to obtain some

12. This round was selected in preference to more recent period data as it contained a very detailed information as compared to its later rounds.

inter-temporal consistency. The material balances precisely enumerates for the consuming sector, targets of production in the consuming sector, consumption norms, the requirement in each consuming sector and the total requirement aggregated over all the sectors. In many cases, the total requirement is further multiplied by the unit price of the specific commodity to give a value figure for that production sector. But, these individual sectors were not integrated with the 77-sector inter-industry flow matrix.

The parameters and variables of the model are summarised below.

Exogenous Variables

(i) Sectoral growth in terms of value-added in the plan period. The economy is divided into four sectors; via, agriculture, mining and manufacturing, small-scale industries and services sectors.

(ii) Value added of the four sectors (agriculture, mining and manufacturing, small-scale industries and services) in the base period.

(iii) Rate of growth of value added of the four sectors (agriculture, mining and manufacturing, small-scale industries and services) in the plan period.

(iv) Foreign aid in the terminal year.

(v) Export in the terminal year.

(vi) Capital formation.

Initial Conditions

(i) Urban population at the base period.

(ii) Rural population at the base period.

(iii) Per capita consumption in the rural sector.

(iv) Per capita consumption in the urban sector.

(v) Indirect tax at the base period.

Parameters

(i) Current flow co-efficient matrix, known as A-matrix. This is a 27-sector matrix.

(ii) Investment/income ratios for four sectors (agriculture, mining and manufacturing, small-scale industries and services).

(iii) Expenditure elasticity for rural and urban sectors for different commodities.

(iv) Rate of growth of rural and urban population.

(v) Rate of growth of indirect tax.

(vi) Proportion of public consumption to domestic expenditure.

(vii) Rate of growth of public consumption.

(viii) Proportion of capital goods imports to total imports for each sector.

(ix) Proportion of other imports to total imports of each sector.

(x) Sectoral share of public consumption

(xi) Proportion of capital goods imports to total gross domestic output in the base year.

(xii) Sectoral share of exports.

(xiii) Fraction of capital formation made in a year to the total Plan period.

(xiv) Sectoral share of capital.

(xv) Share of private consumption in the rural areas to total private consumption.

(xvi) Intermediate import coefficient vector.

Endogenous Variable

(i) National income.

(ii) Gross Domestic Expenditure.

(iii) Capital formation over the Plan period.

(iv) Sectoral capital formation.

(v) Public Expenditure.

(vi) Public Consumption.

(vii) Total private consumption.

(viii) Consumption vector in the rural and urban areas.

(ix) Per capita expenditure in the rural and urban areas.

(x) Total import.

(xi) Intermediate imports, capital-goods imports, other-goods imports and sectoral share of other goods import.

(xii) Gross output.

The Fifth Five Year Plan (1974-1979)

Removal of poverty and attainment of self-reliance are the two major objectives of the Fifth Plan. It may be recalled that the Fifth Plan was prepared at the background of *Garibi Hatao* (remove poverty) slogan coined by Smt. Indira Gandhi, the then Prime Minister at the time of 1971 Parliamentary elections. It is at this background that the strategy of poverty removal was incorporated in the mathematical model.

The object of poverty removal is sought to be attained by providing a minimum level of consumption for the people living below the poverty line. The poverty line is defined in terms of a minimum desirable consumption standard and quantified as per capita monthly consumption of Rs. 40.60 at 1972-73 prices.

The professed goal of poverty removal demanded that the strategy must seek not only the overall rate of economic growth of 5.5 per cent per year in the Plan, which is considered higher in comparison to the prevailing trend growth rate, but also reduced inequality in the distribution of per capita income (consumption).

Self-reliance was defined in terms of elimination of special forms of external assistance. It sought to reach a situation in which by 1980-81 the country's foreign exchange receipts from exports, invisibles and private capital transactions becomes adequate to meet import requirements and interest obligations on foreign debt.

The Fifth Plan model articulated by Sukhamoy Chakravarty consists of three parts. These are: (a) macroeconomic model (b) a static terminal year input-output model, and (c) consumption model.

(a) *Macroeconomic Model:* The macro model considers the macroeconomic balance amongst income and expenditure comprising aggregate gross domestic product (GDP), public and private consumption, savings and investment and net inflow from the rest of the world. The various macroeconomic aggregates are worked out through the macro model for a number of alternative growth rates in GDP, to be appropriate for consideration of financial resources and domestic production supply possibilities.

The macroeconomic model provides projections for: (a) income measured by GDP at factor cost, which is consistent with the desired growth rate of the plan, and (b) total investment. Aggregate imports in the terminal year of the Plan obtained from the input-output model are used to derive domestic savings required to achieve the desired level of investment. Consumption in the model is endogenous, though not strictly on a closed loop basis. Export in the model is exogenously determined.

(b) *Input-Output Model:* This is similar to the Fourth Plan model. The static terminal year input-output model uses the 66-sector input-output transaction matrix generated jointly by the Central Statistical Organisation (CSO) and the Perspective Planning Division of the Planning Commission for the year 1965-1966 calibrated for the terminal year 1978-79 for some anticipated technical changes. The final demand of the product of each sector is determined separately in respect of private consumption, public consumption, gross fixed investment, changes in stocks and export. The sectoral imports are determined in the model through an import coefficient matrix to give the total supply along with the estimated domestic production level to meet the total demand of products of each sector. The model provides sectoral targets for the terminal year that are thus mutually consistent. This, however, does not ensure that given the gestation lag these targets can be attained from the base year over the five years of the plan.

Deliveries of different sectors to public consumption, exports and to gross fixed investments are estimated exogenously in the model such that their total agree with the macro aggregates obtained in the macro model. The gross fixed investment by delivering sector is estimated by using the sectoral composition of the base year. The public consumption vector for the terminal year is generated by using the base year sectoral composition. The export vector for the terminal year is estimated by a detailed study on the export growth of various commodities and the export promotion possibilities in light of situations prevailing in the major importing countries and potential markets. Sectoral changes in stocks are obtained as fixed proportions of the increase in output levels of the different sectors.

(c) *Consumption Model:* This was the innovation of the fifth plan model. The sectoral consumption vector used in the input-output model is estimated separately in the rural and urban areas based on the consumption vectors of 27 different expenditure classes obtained from the NSS data. The following two sets of alternatives are generated:

(i) The log-normal consumption distribution in rural and urban areas remains unchanged during the Plan period so that the inequality in consumption expenditure in the terminal year of the Plan (1978-79) is assumed to remain the same as in the base year (1973-74). This produces the average monthly private consumption for the poorest 30 per cent of the population as Rs. 26.33 in the rural areas and Rs. 28.44 in the urban areas.

(ii) In the second variant, the log-normal consumption distribution parameters and growth rates of rural and urban consumption expenditures are changed to reduce inequality to give the monthly per capita consumption expenditure of the poorest 30 per cent of the population in the rural and urban areas is estimated as Rs.36.64 and Rs.39.64 respectively. In order to meet the objective of narrowing down the per capita consumption differential between the rural and urban areas, the urban-rural differential in per capita consumption is adopted as 1.28 in the base year of the plan (1973-74) and 1.26 in the terminal year (1978-79) as against the observed value of 1.356 in 1968-69.[13]

Minimum Needs Programme (MNP): It may be noted that there was no explicit policy instrument in the model through which income inequality was to be reduced. The growth strategy in the Fifth Five Year Plan (1974-1979) contained certain programmes of basic services and social consumption, code named Minimum Needs Programme (MNP). It emphasised social consumption programmes with a network of basic services and facilities of social consumption of nationally accepted norms. The components of the programme are: (a) elementary education, (b) rural health services, (c) rural water supply, (d) rural roads, (e) rural electrification, (f) rural sanitation, (g) housing assistance to rural landless labourers, (h) environmental improvement of urban slums, and (i) provision for raising the nutritional level of rural poor. The target group of these programmes is the bottom 30 per cent of the population who are the poorest of the poor (because the incidence of poverty in 1973-74 was around 55 per cent) and the aim is to maximise their consumption.

The Sixth Plan Model

The Fifth Plan was to be concluded in 1978-79, to be precise on 31st March 1979. There was a change

13. This is estimated as the ratio of per capita consumption in the urban areas to that in rural areas, as obtained from the National Sample Survey data on consumer expenditure of the 24th Round (July 1968 to June 1869).

in Government in March 1977. The new Government on attaining office prematurely terminated the Fifth Plan by one year and framed a Sixth Plan for the period 1978-1983. In India, the five year plans do not get statutory approval unless endorsed by the National Development Council (NDC), which is the highest policy making body in the country consisting of the Chief Ministers of all the states and union territories, with the Prime Minister as its Chairman. The Sixth Plan 1978-1983 could not be placed before the NDC for consideration. There was a further change in the Government in January 1980.[14] This Government on attaining office decided to prepare a new Sixth Plan covering the period 1980-1985, which was actually implemented.

Using the Fifth Plan model as the basic structure, the mathematical framework of the Sixth Plan 1978-1983 presents several noteworthy improvements. The Sixth Plan 1980-1985 carries forward the changes over the mathematical models used in the Sixth Plan 1978-1983. Because of this, the Sixth Plan 1978-1983 is discussed first. Then the Sixth Plan 1980-1985, is discussed.

Sixth Plan: 1978-1983

The basic structure of the Sixth Plan 1978-1983 is more or less similar to the Fifth Plan. The quantitative framework of the Sixth Plan (1978-1983) is built around the growth rate of 4.7 per cent per year for the period 1978 to 1983. A long term perspective of development up to 15 years was drawn with an annual rate of growth of 5.5 per cent in 1983-1988 and 6.0 per cent in 1988-1993. This was considered feasible for removal of poverty and unemployment by 1992-1993, the post-terminal year of the plan.

As compared to the Fifth Plan, the important changes introduced in the Sixth Plan 1978-1983 model[15] are:

(a) Input-output model is extended to 89 sectors at 1978-79 prices.

(b) The level of living of the poor is attempted to be elevated to a minimum level, defined in terms of poverty line.

(c) The consumption estimates of the households are derived through a consumption model, which is more broad-based as compared to the Fifth Plan.

(d) Employment generation as a result of likely growth strategy is estimated through sectoral employment coefficients.

While the basic structure of the macroeconomic and input-output models is similar to those considered for the Fifth Plan formulation, the consumption sub-model introduced is different. Also the input-output model used in the Sixth Plan 1978-1983 is more disaggregative, using 89 sectors (15 in agriculture, 53 in industry and 11 in services), as against 66 sectors (5 in agriculture, 56 in industry and 5 in services) considered in the Fifth Plan.

Consumption Model: The sectoral private consumption used in the input-output model is estimated through a two-stage nested behaviouristic consumption model. This model comprises a Linear Expenditure System (LES), which is a complete demand system is derived from the additive utility functions for broad groups of commodities (13 sectors) and a set of best-fitting Engel curves for items of consumption within each LES commodity group. This two-stage procedure resulted in a consumption vector compatible with 89 sectors of the input-output model. The aggregate private consumption given in the macro model is used in this model.

In the first stage, the parameters of the LES are estimated form the time series of cross section data obtained from the 17th through 28th Round of National Sample Survey (excluding 18th, 26th and 27th

14. The frequency of the change in government under normal circumstances is quinquennial. In 1979, the government reduced to minority, necessititating fresh election, which was held in January 1980.

15. The Technical Note for Sixth Plan 1978-1983 was not published by the Planning Commission. However, the model algebra was published in Alagh Y. K. and K.C. Majumder (1980). "Input-output Model used for 1978-83 Plan" in A. Ghosal (ed.), *Cybernetics of Planning*. New Delhi: South-Asian Publication.

Rounds) on household consumption expenditure, separately for rural and urban areas, and also, within each area, separately for population below and above the poverty line.

The poverty line was quantified by a Task Force[16] considering the average calorie norm and the age-sex-activity distribution of the population. The Task Force defines the poverty line as per capita consumption expenditure level, which meets the average per capita daily calorie requirement of 2400 kcal in the rural areas and 2100 kcal in the urban areas along with a minimum of non-food expenditure such as, clothing, shelter, transport, education, health care, etc. The average calorie requirement is calculated from the age-sex-activity distribution of the population (as projected for 1982-83) and the associated calorie norm recommended by the Nutrition Expert Group (1968) of the Indian Council of Medical Research (ICMR). Using the 28th Round (1973-74) NSS data relating to household consumption both in quantitative and value terms, the monetary equivalent of the calorie norm mentioned above are quantified. The monetary equivalent of the calorie norms were treated as the poverty line. The monetary equivalent of the calorie norm (i.e., the poverty line) is estimated as the mid-point of the expenditure class in the (1973-74) consumer expenditure data, in which the calorie needs are satisfied. Thus, by implication, the expenditure on non-food items included in the poverty line is the actual expenditure in this expenditure class. On this basis, the poverty cut-off point turns out to be consumption expenditure of Rs. 49.09 per capita per month in the rural areas and Rs. 56.64 per capita per month in the urban areas, both at 1973-1974 prices.

In the second stage, the consumer demand functions for poor and non-poor group of population within rural and urban areas are estimated in the form of Engel equations using household consumption expenditure of the 28th Round of the NSS (1973-74) for disaggregated commodity levels (71 items of consumption aggregated to 56 commodity groups in the input-output classification).

The private consumption vectors of each of these four groups of population (for people below and above the poverty line in rural and urban areas) are added to obtain the private consumption for the entire population, which is used as the final demand vector in the input-output model.

Normative Demand: The monthly per capita consumption of different commodities and services corresponding to this poverty line are considered to be normative demand. However, it was observed that if private consumption based on these normative demands is provided for all population below the poverty line, and the remainder is apportioned to those above the poverty line by the corresponding demand function, then an infeasible situation is reached resulting from the constraint of domestic production of food grains. In order to counter such a situation, consumer demand is projected on the assumption that the consumption deficiency (i.e., the difference between the actual/observed consumption and the normative consumption) of households below the poverty line is made upto the extent of 75 per cent of the poverty level. The balance of the total monthly per capita consumption is considered to be available to the people above the poverty line. This decision leans on the findings of the studies that the average calorie standards assumed for defining the poverty line is high considering the variations in calorie requirements across regions and age, sex and occupation groups, and hence 75 per cent of the poverty line may be considered sufficient to provide normal calorie requirements in most areas.

Estimation of Gross Fixed Investment, Public Consumption and Export

The gross fixed investment by delivering sector is estimated by using sectoral composition of the base year. However, the sectoral proportions in construction are increased for the terminal year on the basis of the increased construction activity arising from the need to meet the demand of Minimum Needs Programmed (MNP), which were earlier introduced in the Fifth Plan and strengthened in the Sixth Plan. This resulted in the reduction of proportion of other sectors mostly on pro-rata basis.

16. The Planning Commission, in July 1977, constituted the *Task Force on Projections of Minimum Needs and Effective Consumption Demand* under the chairmanship of Dr Y.K.Alagh. The Task Force was set up to outline the methodology of forecasting the national and regional structure and pattern of consumption levels and standards (in the Sixth Plan, 1978-1983 and in the subsequent perspective plan) taking into consideration the basic minimum needs of the poor and the effective consumption demand of the non-poor. In order to compute the minimum desirable normative consumption for the poor, the Task Force formulated this quantitative index of poverty. For details see: *Report of the Task Force on Projections of Minimum Needs and Effective Consumption Demand*. New Delhi: Perspective Planning Division, Planning Commission, Government of India, January 1979.

The public consumption vector for the terminal year is generated by using the base year sectoral composition. The impact of MNP on education and health is taken into consideration in adjusting the sectoral proportion for future.

The export vector for the terminal year is estimated by a detailed study on the export growth of various commodities, and export promotion possibilities in the light of the situations prevailing in the major importing countries and potential markets.

Employment Model

Employment in the Sixth Plan is conceptualised in terms of "Standard Person Year" (SPY), which is defined as a person working for 273 days in a year, eight hours per day. The estimates of employment are obtained in terms of equivalent full time standard person year. A set of employment coefficient, indicating the employment generation per each unit of output produced, is estimated for different sectors. This is used to quantify the likely employment generation.

Commodity Balance

The input-output model estimates sectoral output in the terminal year of the Plan. A sector may comprise more than one commodity. The commodity-wise demand and supply within each input-output sector is obtained through material balance studies. Special econometric studies are also carried out in case of some specific commodities. The production targets of the commodities within a sector are set in such a way that their aggregate growth rate is the same as that of the input-output model comprising these commodities.

The material balances are prepared for key products such as coal, electricity, petroleum products, steel, heavy machinery and petro-chemicals, sugar, cloth, cotton, jute, non-ferrous metal.

The Model Result

A number of exercises are carried out with alternative growth rates of gross domestic product (GDP) between the base and the terminal year of the plan, i.e, for the period 1977-78 to 1982-83, and also for the perspective period (1982-83 to 1992-93). The scenario which gives the feasible sectoral growth profile and meets the primary objective of the Plan corresponds to a GDP growth rate of 4.7 per cent per year and mean monthly per capita consumption of 75 per cent of the poverty line for the people below the poverty line.

It has already been mentioned that the Sixth Plan 1978-1983 was withdrawn as a result of change of Government in 1980 and a fresh Sixth Plan was formulated for the period 1980-1985 and implemented during this five year period. Since the Sixth Plan 1980-1985 was actually implemented, it is known and is described here as the Sixth Plan.

Sixth Plan: 1980-1985

The Sixth Plan 1980-1985 adopted the model structure of the Sixth Plan 1978-1983 and introduced a few changes in order to accommodate the new objectives and targets. An important change in the existing model structure was effected by way of endogenisation of investment.

Absence of a capital-flow matrix forced the investment estimate in the earlier plans to be one for the entire five year plan period and that too, at the aggregate level. The investment vector by sources under the circumstances used to be derived using the aggregate investment and allocating them to different sources, using parameters, determined outside the model. As a result, the impact of possible alternative investment allocations on sectoral growth profile can not be explored. Besides, investment in the terminal year of the plan was estimated from the total investment of the entire five year of the plan, on the assumption of exponential growth. Thus, the relationship between the level of activities in the five year plan period and that of the perspective plan can not be distinguished. To fill up this gap, a 14-sector investment planning sub-model is developed and integrated with the existing input-output model in the Sixth Plan, 1980-1985.

The Model Description

The Sixth Plan model consisted of a core model with several blocks and several sub-models solved in an iterative manner. The core model blocks comprised: (a) input-output, (b) investment, (c) private consumption and poverty, (d) financial resources, (e) import, (f) employment, and (g) perspective planning.

The input-output block is based on the Leontief System as in the earlier 1978-1983 Sixth Plan. The input-output table used in 1978-1983 plan is used after updating the coefficients to 1979-80 prices, which is set as the base year of the Plan. The new element in this model is endogenisation of investment. Investment need for a desired level of output is estimated in the investment block. Investment by destination is converted into investment by sources with the help of a capital-coefficient matrix. Private consumption and poverty block is structured on the lines of consumption model of the Sixth Plan 1978-1983, with the difference that instead of satisfying 75 per cent of the poverty level of consumption for all the poor population, the income/consumption of the poor are so increased with a mix of income growth and reduction of inequality that people living below the poverty line in the terminal year of the plan (1984-85) is restricted to 30 per cent of the total population. The financial resource block provides the estimates of domestic savings generation in the economy. In the import block, sectoral imports are estimated on the basis of an import-coefficient matrix. Employment block estimates employment generation on the basis of output in non-agriculture sector and land allocation made in the agriculture sub-model. In the perspective plan block it is checked that the requirement of output in the post-terminal year of the plan is consistent with the long term objectives of the economy and match the growth potentials that is developed within the Sixth Plan period. These blocks are inter-dependent, though the degree of inter-dependence differs between the blocks.

Sub-Models

A family or sub-models are formulated in order to accommodate the highly complex non-linear relations, covering various aspects of economic activities, with varying levels of disaggregation and conceptual differences. These sub-models are ultimately geared to the core model. The sub-models are: (a) agriculture, (b) exports, (c) demography, (d) autonomous investment and public consumption, and (e) long-term objectives with both cardinal and ordinal values.

The agriculture sub-model gives the estimate of capacity output in agriculture. The export sub-model estimates sectoral exports. The demographic sub-model provides estimates of population growth in urban and rural areas and the estimates of labour force. The sub-models on autonomous investment and public consumption and long term objectives appear in the model as targets. The values of variables from all these five sub-models enter into the core model as exogenous variables. These five sub-models are recursive to the core model.

The material balancing system as in the earlier Plans remains a part of the model in order to disaggregate the macro and sectoral dimensions into their detail physical units and to check overall consistency.

Constraints

The model equations represent a class of constraints. The constraints are: (a) demand, (b) financial resources, (c) supply/capacity in activity sectors, (d) demand supply balance, (e) foreign exchange, (f) land and natural resources, (g) manpower, (h) welfare programme, (i) public sector financing, (j) fiscal, (k) private sector investment financing, and (l) long range perspective plan.

These constraints, when expressed as a system of equations, represent a typical case of a non-linear problem. But a large number of endogenous variables is treated as fixed from outside the model and the system is uniquely solved by assigning alternative values to the key policy variables until the system is reduced to a state with just one degree of freedom.

The Model Result

The Sixth Plan was formulated against a perspective covering a period of 15 years from 1980-81 to 1994-95. The strategy was set in such a way that the percentage of population living below the poverty line reduces to 30 per cent in the terminal year of the Plan (1984-85) and to less than 10 per cent by the post-terminal year (1994-95).

The model results also show increase in employment by 34 million standard person years in the Sixth Plan. This increase in employment during the plan period is almost equal to the increase in labour force during the corresponding period, which meant that if all the new jobs are created on a full-time basis, then the total jobs created in the Sixth Plan can accommodate the entire increase in the labour force.

The required growth rate was 5.2 per cent per year in the Sixth Plan (1980-1985) and 5.5 per cent per year in the subsequent ten-year period (1985-1995).

The projected rates of sectoral output growth are translated in terms of physical targets for important commodities to facilitate formulation of necessary investment projects and production programmes. The physical targets for key commodities are also cross checked with the material balances.[17]

The Seventh Five Year Plan (1985-1990)

The structure of the model used in the Seventh Plan (1985-1990)[18] remains exactly the same as in the Sixth Plan. The only addition is a poverty sub-model, incorporated to find out the impact of the anti-poverty programmes. However, a noticeable change is that the input-output sectors in the model are reduced from 89 in the Sixth Plan to 50 in the Seventh Plan.

The investment programmes and policy initiatives for the Seventh Plan is related to the goals set for 2000 A.D. The growth rate in the plan is framed against the perspective of 15 years (1985-2000). Three factors namely, food production, employment and productivity are outlined as the immediate objectives in order to achieve the goals set in the light of the development perspectives traced upto 2000 A.D. The growth rate in the Plan (1985-1990) is targeted as 5 per cent per annum.

The development strategy and the pattern of growth emerging from it is expected to create an employment potential of 40 million standard person years and to bring down the incidence of poverty from 36.9 per cent in 1984-85 to 25.8 per cent in 1989-90, which is the terminal year of the plan, i.e., by more than 2 per cent point every year during the plan period. This decline is the combined result of contemplated growth pattern and implementation of re-distributive programmes. The results show that 45 per cent of the poverty reduction in the rural areas originates from redistribution and 55 per cent from growth process. In the urban areas the reduction of poverty due to growth is estimated as 84 per cent and the remaining 16 per cent from re-distribution. The consumption sub-model used in the Sixth Plan is modified by adding a poverty block to assess the impact of the income generation out of the redistributive programmes on the incidence of poverty. The aim is to find out the effect of income growth in reducing poverty and also the effectiveness of the redistributive measures adopted in the plan in ultimately benefiting the poor. This requires estimation of the interrelationship between growth, plan programmes and poverty alleviation, completely integrated with the aggregated model structure. This is carried out in the poverty block of the consumption sub-model.

17. The model algebra of the Sixth Plan, 1980-1985 may be found in: *A Technical Note on the Sixth Plan of India 1980-85*. New Delhi: Perspective Planning Division, Planning Commission, Government of India. July 1981.

18. *A Technical Note on the Seventh Plan of India 1985-90*. New Delhi: Perspective Planning Division, Planning Commission, Government of India. June, 1986.

Poverty Block

The Sixth Plan initiated a large number of income generating programmes earmarked for certain target groups who are from the weaker sections of the society. Both asset generation and wage employment programmes were developed for this purpose. Integrated Rural Development Programme (IRDP) is the asset generation programme and National Rural Employment Programme (NREP) and Rural Landless Employment Guarantee Programme (RLEGP) are the two employment generation programmes. The generation and distribution of income out of these programmes are supposed to benefit a certain targeted sub-set of the society. Hence, they need a special treatment in the overall planning model. Accordingly, the planning model used in the sixth plan is adapted, by dividing all variables relating to the generation of income, employment and consumption into two separate Blocks.[19] The first block includes those variables which relate to all activities of the economy, excluding those arising from the implementation of the major poverty alleviation programmes such as, IRDP, NREP and RLEGP. The second block includes all variables relating exclusively to these poverty alleviation programmes. The distributional effects of all activities belonging to the first block are estimated in the light of past observations regarding the pattern of household consumption distribution over time. In the second block of the model, the distributional impacts are estimated by identifying the beneficiaries (belonging to certain target groups) of these redistributive programmes and assessing the net improvement in their initial level of income and consumption as a result of the implementation of these programmes. Their initial levels of consumption are assumed to be dependent on the general activities covered in the first block of the model.

It may, however, be emphasised that any water-tight separation of the two blocks is impossible. In fact, they are interrelated with the overall model frame with the help of an inter-industry transaction matrix. Besides, some part of the income generation from the programmes earmarked for target groups, might accrue to the non-target groups of the society because of leakages. This may happen partly because of the poor implementation and partly because of the very nature of these programmes when they cover many administrative and other material costs which might generate income in the first block of the model. This income effect, however, is picked up in the income and distributional estimates of the model. Besides, when more than one redistributive programmes overlap by covering the same group of beneficiary households, a further correction is needed to remove double counting.

The Analytical Gaps

Despite several improvements in the mathematical model structure in the Sixth Plan, the major analytical gaps that remained are:

(a) The treatment of household consumption is still not strictly on a "closed-loop' basis.

(b) The income distribution and the production structure of the economy are not explicitly functionally related, and

(c) The model is run only for terminal year knowing fully well that the feasibility of a production target and that of a demand-supply balance in the market can be tested only when it is examined as a flow over time.

The Eighth Five Year Plan (1992-1997)

The model structure used in the Eeighth Plan is not only similar to those used in the Seventh Plan, but also to the Fifth and Sixth Plans. The model integrates macroeconomic parameters with consistency requirements at a disaggregated level of inter-sectoral relationships. As in the Sixth and Seventh Plans, investment and import, the two variables determining the growth rate and, consumption, determining the levels of living are determined endogenously in the Eighth Plan. The model system in the Eighth Plan comprises a core model and a set of sub-models.[20] The core model consists of: (a) macroeconomic model,

19. For the model algebra see: Gupta S.P. and K.L. Datta, (1984). "Poverty Calculation in the Sixth Plan", *Economic and Political Weekly*, April.

20. For details see: *A Technical Note to the Eighth Plan of India:1992-97*. New Delhi: Perspective Planning Division, Planning Commission, Government of India, May, 1995. The model algebra of the Eighth Plan may be found in "Mathematical Scaffolding of Eighth Five Year Plan", pp. 15 to 22.

(b) input-output model, and (c) investment model. The sub-models are developed for agriculture, financial resources, consumption, industry and trade.

The input-coefficient matrix in the base year of the Plan (1991-92) is a calibrated version of the input-output transaction matrix generated jointly by the Central Statistical Organisation (CSO) and the Perspective Planning Division of the Planning Commission, relate to the year 1983-84 are aggregated to 60 sectors.

The Sub-models

Among the sub-models important changes are in the agricultural and financial resources sub-models.

(a) *Agricultural Sub-model:* The feasibility of levels and growth of production of important agricultural commodities is checked in the agricultural sub-model on the basis of detailed requirements and use of inputs. The impact of application of certain critical inputs such as land (type of land use), water and some of the input constraints (for example, fertiliser) and other infrastructure both in terms of quality and quantity on agricultural production and productivity in the long and medium term cannot be appropriately captured in the input-output model.

In the context of regional development, locational aspects of agricultural growth in terms of crops and input-intensity are also not possible to be quantified under the input-output frame. The parameters relating to cropping intensity, area under irrigation and rain-fed crops as well as area under high yielding and traditional variety of seeds by major crops at regional level are measured in the agricultural sub-model in conjunction with the input-output model. The sub-model determines crop output at detailed regional level treating area allocation under different crops and between different seed varieties as exogenous. The supply is determined at regional level using land, water, seed and fertiliser as explanatory variables. The models specification is not uniform for all the regions. The supply of food grains is estimated from this model. The demand for food grains is estimated from the consumption sub-model, using consumer demand function and Linear Expenditure System as well as input-output model. The determinants of supply and parameters affecting supply are estimated separately for each major state. The feasibility of demand for food grains is tested with its supply estimated from the regional models.

The Plan objectives of growth and diversification of agriculture, self-sufficiency in food and generation of surpluses for exports are also assessed through the parameters estimated in the agriculture sub-model. Besides, several features of the agricultural plan such as development of rain fed areas and agricultural planning in terms of homogenous agro-climatic regions are captured in the agricultural sub-model.

(b) *Financial Resources Sub-model:* The assessment of investible resources is taken up in detail in the Financial Resources sub-model. The Financial Resources sub-model estimates the availability of resources in order to finance the investment needs estimated in the input-output and investment model, which is necessary to generate the desired growth rate. The sub-model assesses the level of domestic savings sectorally as well as in terms of its composition using econometric estimation procedure. The gross domestic savings in the economy is composed of the savings of the public sector and savings of the private sector. Specifically, the savings in the public sector comprise budgetary savings of the Government and savings of the public sector enterprises. Within the private sector, the savings are estimated separately for household sector, private corporate and private co-operative sectors. The household sector comprises individuals, non-government and non-corporate private enterprises engaged in various economic activities as well as non-profit institutions such as charities and trusts. The gross savings of the households are made up of additions to financial assets net of financial liabilities and additions to physical assets including depreciation. Therefore, household savings takes the form of financial and physical assets. The savings of the households in the form of physical assets relate to gross capital formation in terms of productive assets, such as machinery and equipment, construction of residential and non-residential building. The financial assets of the household sector consist of currency, deposits with the commercial banks and co-operative institutions and non-banking companies, investment in shares and debentures, mutual funds, pension funds, etc. These estimates are consistent with the macro aggregates of the Plan.

The estimate of resource in the financial resources sub-model is procedurally recursive to the input-output cum investment model due to the simultaneity between savings and income.

The Eighth Plan model like earlier models is basically a production and investment model. The social objectives of the plan get integrated into the model only through their additional consumption requirements or through their additional investment requirements both of which are components of the final demand in the model system. The plan documents mention that appropriate policies would be designed to attain the plan targets. It is not obvious that feasible policies were available that could attain the targets.[21]

Planning in a Market Economy: Ninth and Tenth Plan Models

The Five Year Plans in India have traditionally been used to set out the dimensions of economic development and growth in the country and postulate the macroeconomic features, such as aggregate resources, savings, investment, the GDP growth and other broader economic and social requirements. Thus, the Five Year Plans lays out a programme of investment and activities to steer the country's economy in the desired direction.

The planning models in India prior to the initiation of economic reforms were used to set the sectoral investment in order to attain a particular sectoral rate of growth. The formulation of the Five Year Plan in the pre-reform days can be summarised as: The Planning Commission estimates the size of national resources. The balance of payments situation is assessed from a detailed calculation of exports and imports. The incremental capital-output ratio (ICOR) is quantified. The material and social requirements are worked out at sectoral level. The material requirements are related to targeted growth rates and are worked out from the input-output based consistency-cum-investment model. The social requirements are assessed more in a normative manner keeping in view the resource constraint. The overall growth rate is set matching the demand and supply of resources. The sectoral targets of growth are made consistent with the aggregate growth rate.

The Five Year Plan is implemented through Annual Plans, which contains in somewhat detail, the resource allocation pattern between Centre and States and also for different sectoral activities in the Government. The allocation of budgetary resources is a part of the annual budget of the Central government. Sanction of Government expenditure is made also through the annual budget. The annual allocation of Government resources and expenditure is made keeping the Five Year Plans in view.

The economic reforms and liberalisation policies, particularly those relating to the deregulation of industry, liberalisation of trade, elimination of protective tariff barriers, privatisation of financial institutions and public enterprises, streamlining of state sector, privatisation of social programme and rationalising the tax system, initiated in the early 1990s (during the Eighth Plan period) allowed a greater play for market and replaced the different agents of the Government as dominant decision makers. As a consequence, the Government relinquished much of its control on the investment pattern and there was a change in the nature of instruments that the Government employed to guide economic matters. The Plans came to be formulated and implemented in an environment in which market played a dominant role. The role of the public-private partnership is promoted and the public sector is also exposed to market forces and made more autonomous. Trade with the rest of the world exposed the economy to greater competition and global economic trends and compulsions mattered more than before. State intervention in the areas governing production and distribution gave way to reliance on market mechanism. The role of Government became generally confined to the creation of suitable environment for growth and development rather than directly taking part in production and trade. In sum, the instruments of policy became market determined with the economic reform and could not be used in the manner in which they used to be employed earlier in the pre-reform era. This changed the manner and method of planning. As several variables are no longer controlled by the Government and their values are determined in the market

21. For example, Narayana and Parikh, "Will the farmers fulfill the planners expectations?", *Economic and Political Weekly*, show that the relative price required to induce farmers to produce food grains as per the Eighth Plan targets were unrealistic.

place, the planning strategy had to change and so also the manner and method of the formulation of the mathematical models that go behind the estimation of the range of parameters and variables associated with the plan. In order to capture the hitherto controlled and regulated variables, which under the openness of the market became dependent on it, several new models are added to the existing input-output-cum-investment planning model.

Ninth Plan and its Perspective

The growth prospects for the future need to be based on a careful assessment of the resources which could be mobilised and the imperatives of meeting certain minimum social needs and aspirations. Care also has to be taken to ensure that the growth process is sustainable both in terms of external indebtedness of the country and the fiscal viability of the Government not only in the current Plan period but in the future as well.

Keeping these factors in mind, the likely macroeconomic performance of the economy, during the Ninth Five Year Plan, was projected on the basis of a model that was developed specifically for this purpose. In calculating the parameters of the model for the Ninth Plan period, a number of specific assumptions were made. First, it was assumed that the trend towards improvement in total domestic savings, as well as in public savings, witnessed in the last few years prior to the Plan would continue during the Ninth Plan. The improvement in Government savings would have to arise essentially from combined improvement in taxes net of subsidies, with public consumption expenditure more or less maintaining its share of GDP. Total public investment, which includes investment by the Centre, the States and all public sector enterprises, was determined with a view to achieving a pre-determined fiscal deficit target of 4.0 per cent for the Centre during the Plan period. In view of the emphasis that was being placed on investment in infrastructure, the ICOR was expected to rise during the Ninth Plan in the base-line scenario from the levels prevailing in the Eighth Plan. This was done to ensure that the growth rate of the economy would not suffer in the post-Plan period due to infrastructural bottlenecks which could arise from the shortfalls in pipe-line investment that occurred during the Eighth Plan period.

The Model

The model for Ninth Plan was developed with the specific purpose of examining the implications of different target growth rates for the economy. The main target variables contained in the model were: (a) the rate of growth on GDP; (b) the current account deficit as a percentage of GDP; (c) the unemployment rate; (d) government borrowings as a percentage of GDP.

The model started with an exogenously specified target growth rate of GDP at factor cost. This was broken up into 18 sectoral growth rates on the basis of sectoral consistency ratios. The investment requirements for attaining the target growth rate are computed on the basis of the sector specific incremental capital-output ratios (ICOR) of the 18 NAS sectors.

$$Iit = (Yit+1 - Yit) * vi \quad (1)$$

and $$It = \Sigma\ Iit \quad (2)$$

where vi = incremental capital-output ratio of sector i

Iit = investment in sector i in the year t

Yit = value added in sector i in the year t

These sectoral ICORs were assumed to remain constant over the Plan period.

Sectoral employment (Usual Principal Status) was computed by using sectoral employment elasticities which are then aggregated to give total additional employment generated.

$$Empl\_i = Empl\_i * (Yt-Yt-1) \quad (3)$$

$$Empl = Empl\_i \quad (4)$$

Additions to employment are then compared with the increase in labour force (15+ Years) including the back log of unemployed in order to derive the unemployment rates.

$$\text{Urate} = (\text{Backlog} + (\Delta\text{Lab. force} - \Delta\text{Empl}))/\ \text{Lab. Force} \quad (5)$$

Aggregate and sectoral private investment [It (Pvt), Iti (Pvt)] are estimated on the basis of investment demand functions which are primarily explained by the accelerator principle and the credit availability to the private sector.

$$\text{It (Pvt.)} = a + b^*\text{It-1 (Pvt.)} + c^*(\text{Yt} - \text{Yt-1}) + d^*\text{Credit} \quad (6)$$

Sectoral private investment behaviour could not be estimated for sectors which were earlier either reserved for public investment such as rail transport, banking & insurance and public administration; or those that did not display any systematic and stable behavioural pattern in the past such as hotels and resturants, trade and mining & quarrying.

Public investment [It(Pub)] was assumed to bridge the gap between the required investment as given by equation (2) and investment forthcoming from the private sector as derived from equation (6). It was therefore, a residual.

$$\text{It (Pub)} = \text{It} - \text{It (Pvt.)} \quad (7)$$

GDP at market prices (GDPmp) was estimated as a function of GDP at factor cost (GDPfc).

$$\text{GDPmp} = a + b * \text{GDPfc} \quad (8)$$

Since the difference between the two estimates of GDP is the estimated behaviour of net indirect taxes (NIT) (i.e., indirect taxes less subsidies), this formulation implicitly assumed that the trend behaviour of net indirect taxes would continue.

$$\text{NIT} = \text{GDPmp} - \text{GDPfc} \quad (9)$$

Net factor incomes from abroad (NFI) and other current transfers (OCT) were independently estimated and added to GDP at market prices to obtain the national disposable income (NDI).

$$\text{NFI} = a + b * \text{GDPmp} \quad (10)$$

$$\text{OCT} = a + b * \text{GDPmp} \quad (11)$$

$$\text{NDI} = \text{GDPmp} + \text{NFI} + \text{OCT} \quad (12)$$

Private disposable income (PDI) was estimated as a function of national disposable income, and the difference between the two gives an estimate of direct taxes and other current revenues of the Government (DT).

$$\text{PDI} = a + b * \text{NDI} \quad (13)$$

$$\text{DT} = \text{NDI} - \text{PDI} \quad (14)$$

Private savings (including corporate savings) [S(Pvt)] and private consumption [C(Pvt)] were separately estimated as functions of private disposable income.

$$\text{S(Pvt)} = a + b^*\text{PDI} \quad (15)$$

$$\text{C(Pvt)} = a + b^*\text{PDI} \quad (16)$$

Public consumption [C(Pub)], was projected independently.

$$\text{C(Pub)} = a + b * \text{GDPmp} \quad (17)$$

Total consumption, that is the sum of private and public consumption as derived in equations (16) and (17), was deducted from national disposable income to yield total gross domestic savings (S).

$$\text{S} = \text{NDI} - [\text{C(Pvt)} + \text{C(Pub)}] \quad (18)$$

revenue deficit and plan outlay target. For this purpose upper limit of primary deficit has been calculated as under.

$$P_{st} = \frac{b_{t-1}}{(1+g_t)} * (g_t - i_t) \qquad (3)$$

where,

P_{st} = upper limit of Primary Deficit to GDP ratio in time period t.

i_t = Interest Rate charged on government debt in time period t

g_t = Rate of growth of nominal GDP in time period t

b_{t-1} = Debt/GDP in time period t-1

Primary deficit limit is separately estimated for the Centre and the States and then reconciled with the projected primary deficit with a view to assess the extent of fiscal correction required during the plan period.

Concluding Observations

The brief review of the Planning Models in India shows how they have evolved to address changing concerns and scope of planning. In the era of planned economy that the country followed till the Seventh Five Year Plan, the focus of most quantitative works in the formulation if Five Year Plans in the country was based on the premise that Government (state) is the dominant agent in the decision making process as the private sector is either too small to commit large investment and the markets could not be relied upon for making decisions that were fully beneficial. However, as the economy began its 'tryst' with liberalisation and globalisation regime in 1991, that was soon followed by the beginning of the Eighth Five Year Plan from 1st April 1992, the focus of economic modelling also shifted from detailed disaggregated planning to indicative planning and relinquishing on the part of government much of the control in detailed investment decision making. Although the Eighth Five Year Plan model was essentially the same, as were the plan models from Fifth to the Seventh Plans, it was being increasingly felt that focus of planning as well as quantitative framework of the Five Year Plans would have to undergo a change.

A beginning was made in the Ninth Five Year Plan to move away from deterministic to indicative planning and the practice has continued since then. The Tenth and the Eleventh Plan models were also set in the mould that of Ninth Plan (of course with appropriate modifications); while the earlier plans, particularly from Fourth (or is it Fifth) to Eighth Plan, were essentially optimisation models and disaggregated, the subsequent plan models were consistency types and certainly more aggregative.